Europe and the Making of England, 1

A wide-ranging and original re-interpretation of En
tity during the vital century (1660–1760) in which the country emerged as the leading world power and developed its peculiarly free political culture. Disputing the insular and xenophobic image of the English in the period, and denying that this was an age of secularisation, Tony Claydon demonstrates instead the people's active participation in a 'Protestant international' and their deep attachment to a European 'Christendom'. He shows how these outward-looking identities shaped key developments by generating a profound sense of duty to God's foreign faithful. The English built a world-beating state by intervening abroad to defend Christendom and the reformation, and their politics were forged as they debated different understandings of these international entities. England may have diverged from continental norms in this period but this book shows that it did so because of its intense religious engagement with that continent.

TONY CLAYDON is Senior Lecturer in History at the School of History and Welsh History, University of Wales, Bangor. His previous publications include *William III and the Godly Revolution* (1996) and, as co-editor, *Protestantism and National Identity: Britain and Ireland, 1650–1850* (1998).

Cambridge Studies in Early Modern British History

Series editors

This is a series of monographs and studies covering many aspects of the history of the British Isles between the late fifteenth century and the early eighteenth century. It includes the work of established scholars and pioneering work by a new generation of scholars. It includes both reviews and revisions of major topics and books which open up new historical terrain or which reveal startling new perspectives on familiar subjects. All the volumes set detailed research into our broader perspectives, and the books are intended for the use of students as well as of their teachers.

For a list of titles in the series, see end of book.

EUROPE AND THE MAKING OF ENGLAND, 1660–1760

TONY CLAYDON

University of Wales, Bangor

CAMBRIDGE UNIVERSITY PRESS
Cambridge, New York, Melbourne, Madrid, Cape Town, Singapore, São Paulo

Cambridge University Press
The Edinburgh Building, Cambridge CB2 8RU, UK

Published in the United States of America by Cambridge University Press, New York

www.cambridge.org
Information on this title: www.cambridge.org/9780521615204

First published 2007

Printed in the United Kingdom at the University Press, Cambridge

A catalogue record for this publication is available from the British Library

ISBN 978-0-521-85004-9 hardback
ISBN 978-0-521-61520-4 paperback

CONTENTS

ILLUSTRATIONS

ACKNOWLEDGEMENTS

As this work sprang from an idea I had about fifteen years ago, I have incurred many debts whilst researching and writing it. However, I hope that I thanked colleagues, librarians, students and friends for their help as they gave it, and that they will forgive me not repeating it here. Institutions, however, are impersonal, so can be recognised only in print for their generosity. I am grateful to the University of Wales, Bangor for its supportive working environment, and for regular periods of leave whilst writing this work. I was honoured to be a visiting scholar in the history department of Brown University in 2004: this permitted steady progress in one of America's finest schools. I spent a similarly rewarding period at the Huntington Library in San Marino, California in 2001. I was grateful for a research fellowship from that body, as are the many other recipients of its support. In 2003–4, a research fellowship from the Leverhulme Trust provided funds to replace my teaching, and allowed me to believe the book might be finished. The trust's understanding of the needs of scholarship is exemplary, and many more people than me are indebted to it. Finally, the Arts and Humanities Research Council provided resources for a sabbatical to finish this work. I thank the council, and applaud its commitment to study-leave as a major stream of its research funding. I am grateful to Blenheim Palace for permission to reproduce the detail of the Blenheim Tapestry on the cover of this book. This work is dedicated to my husband.

NOTES ON STYLE

Dates before 1752 are give old style (i.e. according to the Julian calendar standard in England until that year), but the year is assumed to have begun on 1 January, not Lady Day, as some contemporaries held. Place of publication is London unless otherwise stated. I eschew a bibliography which would merely reproduce information in references.

ABBREVIATIONS USED IN REFERENCES

BIHR	*Bulletin of the Institute of Historical Research*
BL	*British Library*
CJ	*Commons Journals*
Cobbett	William Cobbett, ed., *The parliamentary history of England* (36 vols., 1808–1820)
EHR	*English Historical Review*
HLQ	*Huntington Library Quarterly*
HJ	*Historical Journal*
JBS	*Journal of British Studies*
JEH	*Journal of Ecclesiastical History*
JMH	*Journal of Modern History*
LJ	*Lords Journals*
ODNB	Colin Matthew and Brian Harrison, eds., *The Oxford dictionary of national biography* (Oxford, 60 vols., 2004)

INTRODUCTION

A funny thing happened to William Bromley on his way to the speakership of the Commons in 1705. As a stern Tory, whose party had just retained their majority in a general election, Bromley could have expected a good run at the chairmanship of the house. Yet strangely, as he began to work for support amongst his fellow MPs, his campaign was torpedoed from a quite unexpected direction. Nearly two decades earlier, Bromley had toured Europe and had published an account of his travels.[1] Now the work reappeared without his permission, this time accompanied by a spoof table of contents drawing attention to the youthful absurdities of the volume.[2] Bromley's reputation sank in general hilarity, and his Whig rival, John Smith, carried the election.[3]

It is not entirely clear who engineered this debacle. John Oldmixon, writing long after the event, attributed Bromley's downfall to Robert Harley, the secretary of state. Oldmixon claimed the minister had invited groups of leading statesmen to evenings at his house and had then distributed the republished volume as after-dinner entertainment, exclaiming 'have you not seen Mr Bromley's *Travels*?'[4] The story is plausible. Harley was a master manipulator of public opinion, and was determined to block Bromley's elevation because he feared a rabidly Tory speaker would undermine his mixed and moderate administration.[5] Bromley himself suspected Harley. A note in his handwriting on one copy of the offending work accused 'one of the ministry' of being 'very conversant in this sort of calumny'.[6] Yet whatever

1 Bromley toured in 1688–9 to produce [William Bromley], *Remarks in the grande tour* (1692).

2 [William Bromley], *Remarks made in travels through France and Italy* (1693), exactly reproduced the 1692 work despite the title change. A 'table of principal matters' was added in 1705.

3 For more on the contest, W. A. Speck, 'The choice of speaker in 1705', *BIHR*, 37 (1964), 20–46.

4 John Oldmixon, *The history of England during the reigns of King William and Queen Mary* (1735), p. 345.

5 For Harley's propaganda activities, J. A. Downie, *Robert Harley and the press* (Cambridge, 1979).

6 David Hayton, Evelyn Cruikshanks and Stuart Handley, eds., *The House of Commons, 1690–1715* (3 vols., Cambridge, 2002), III:348.

the pleasure of guessing who was behind Bromley's embarrassment, the precise manner of his humiliation is far more interesting. Reading the table of contents – and exploring how it helped to frustrate a career – reveals much about the fundamental assumptions of the English Augustan age.

For the most part, the spoof contents took aim at the almost unrelieved banality of Bromley's prose. By the time the young man had toured Europe, a tradition of travel writing had emerged, in which authors not only noted the places they visited, but also commentated on the historical, scientific, geographic or political significance of what they had seen.[7] In capable hands, this tradition could produce valuable works of reference. In Bromley's case, unfortunately, it resulted in a straining for profundity: a catalogue of tautology and failed analysis which the new contents page exposed ruthlessly. Thus Bromley was trying to write good travel literature when describing the geographical situation of his landing point on the continent. He had so little of importance to say, however, that 'the table of principal matters' which was attached to the satirical edition could reduce his thoughts to 'Boulogne, the first City on the French shore, lies on the Coast.' Similarly, his attempt to describe the difficulties of travelling in winter became 'A deep Snow in January, and the Weather cold'; whilst comments upon town construction in Europe were summarised as 'Pavements of . . . broad Stones, convenient for walking on' or 'A Door shut up, and clos'd to the Middle with Brick, not pass'd through since'. By the time Bromley had arrived in Italy, this style of ridicule had got into its stride. Observations on architecture became 'The English Jesuits Colledge at Rome may be made larger than tis, by uniting other Buildings to it', whilst the author's stab at natural history in the Alps came out as 'Carponi, a fish in the Lake di Garda, by the similitude of the Fish and Name, the Author much questions if they are not the same with our Carps.' Towards the end of the table, the jokes got pithier, ranging from the magnificently tautologous – 'Parmesan ham . . . from Parma'; on through the blindingly obvious – 'Travelling by Night not proper to take a View of the adjacent Countries'; to the gratuitously cruel – 'The Author visits a Mad House.'[8]

By themselves, such comments may not have destroyed Bromley's reputation. His own sense that his 'trifling' observations should be excused because he was 'very young' when he wrote them, may well have been shared by many who chuckled over the work in Harley's drawing room.[9] What really did the damage was the spoof's suggestion that the author condoned Roman Catholicism. In the instances above, humour stemmed from a condensation of Bromley's prose into a summary so bare that it revealed the emptiness

[7] See below, ch. 1. [8] Quotes from [Bromley], *Remarks made* (1705 edn), table.
[9] Hayton, *House of Commons*, III:348.

of the original. At other points in the work, this same satirical compression removed qualifications in the author's descriptions of Roman worship, and so made him appear sympathetic to a faith which most Englishmen viewed as a wicked perversion of Christianity. The satirist's treatment of miracles was typical. Again and again, the process of summary removed any sense that Bromley was merely reporting superstitious traditions, and left him apparently repeating miraculous stories as true. For example, the table of principal matters omitted the words 'they say' from Bromley's account of Catholic folklore in the Spanish Netherlands. Consequently it advertised 'A Side Chappel in the great Church at Aix, into which if any Woman enters she is immediately struck Blind'. Again, all sense that Bromley was simply relaying popular beliefs and noting public monuments disappeared in the satirist's 'Divers miracles wrought by St Nicholas' Arm, as the Author was assur'd, and which were afterward confirm'd . . . by a Description on the Wall'. At its worst, such condensation actually put Roman Catholic words in Bromley's mouth (as in its treatment of what was obviously a guide's spiel: 'The Shelves of a Library supported by the Statues of Arch Hereticks, viz. Luther, Calvin, Cranmer &c.'); or simply twisted the meaning of the author's original prose to suggest complicity in papal claims. In one passage of Bromley's original *Remarks*, he had commented with surprise on the Pope's tolerance of other faiths: 'In the evening I was admitted to the Honour of Kissing the Pope's Slipper; who, though he knew me to be a Protestant, gave me his Blessing and said nothing of Religion.'[10] In the table of contents, however, Bromley's folly in reporting this meeting in such friendly terms was magnified by a summary which suggested it was the writer, rather the pontiff, who ignored the inappropriateness of a Protestant's participation in a popish ceremony. 'The author kiss'd the Pope's Slipper, and had his Blessing, . . . but not a word of Religion'. When the satirist added to this subterfuge by highlighting a section which suggested Bromley might have sympathies with the exiled dynasty of Catholic Stuarts, the demolition was complete.[11] The candidate for the speakership stood revealed as a fellow traveller as well as a banal one. He was in league with a sinful faith, whose troops in the armies of Louis XIV were even then endangering all Protestant nations.

There are perhaps two important things to note about this story and its implications for contemporary attitudes. First, it reveals the continuing purchase of religious commitment in England in the early eighteenth century. In contrast to a tradition of scholarship which has argued that English society became rapidly more secularised and religiously indifferent after the civil

10 [Bromley], *Remarks made* (1693 edn), p. 149.

11 Bromley referred to William III as prince of Orange, not king of England – the satirist accused him of questioning of the monarch's legitimacy.

war, Bromley's humiliation suggests that the defence of England's faith was still a very live issue fifty years after that conflict.[12] When the man's enemies wanted to ruin his chances of becoming speaker, they insinuated that he was a closet Catholic, presumably believing that there was still no other charge which could be more damaging to his reputation. Second, the republication of Bromley's work reveals the strong European dimension of popular English thought in the period. In contrast to interpretations which have suggested pre-modern England was insular and xenophobic – or that with the rise of national sentiment, it was becoming even more so – the 1705 incident suggests that people were actually closely interested their European neighbours.[13] After all, the satire launched at Bromley was only possible because he had taken a tour on the continent and had published an account of it which he thought people would like to read. The satire was also only possible because Bromley had tried to write in a tradition of travel literature which had been established by authors making the journey before him, and which had already become dominant enough to influence the young tourist. Finally, it is probable that the satire was aimed at an audience who had themselves visited places Bromley described. Jokes about the suffocating obviousness of what Bromley reported, and about the author's credulousness in the face of tawdry superstition, would have been funniest to those who had seen what he had seen. Therefore, alongside a fiercely Protestant England there was a cosmopolitan one: the English were familiar with, and fascinated by, their neighbours.

This book sets out to explore the obvious paradox contained in the attitudes revealed by the shaming of William Bromley. For the crucial period between the restoration in 1660 and the accession of George III a century later, it aims to explain how the English to adhered to a vehement Protestantism, yet remained closely connected to a continent on which Catholicism predominated. Examining this apparent contradiction is vital – not only because the paradox clouds England's attitudes to the outside world at precisely the moment when she emerged as the world's premier power – but also because scholarship has deepened the problem. Traditional narratives, as mentioned above, saw the English becoming less interested in religious conflict in the century after 1660. One result of this, it was assumed,

[12] For explicit statements of this tradition: Christopher Hill, *Some intellectual consequences of the English revolution* (1980); Steven C. A. Pincus, *Protestantism and patriotism: ideology and the making of English foreign policy, 1650–1668* (Cambridge, 1996); J. G. A. Pocock, *The Machiavellian moment* (Princeton, NJ, 1975), last sections; C. J. Somerville, *The secularization of early modern England* (Oxford, 1992).

[13] For English xenophobia: Paul Langford, *Englishness identified: manners and character, 1650–1850* (Oxford, 2000), pp. 199–225, and works in n. 15 below. Linda Colley, *Britons: forging the nation 1707–1837* (New Haven, CT, 1992), chs. 1–2, suggested 'Britishness' meant alienation from a benighted continent.

was that the population fell in love with Europe as an enlightened tolerance ended bigoted shunning of alien faiths. Established accounts, therefore, could explain the cosmopolitanism of late Stuart and Georgian England, but only at the expense of ignoring its continuing loyalty to the Protestant cause.[14] Some more recent scholars, most notably Linda Colley, have tried to reverse this trend by reasserting the importance of religious rivalries in post-civil war society.[15] They have argued that the English saw themselves primarily as a Protestant people: a nation chosen by God to uphold the true religion and to crush the anti-Christian distortions of his faith which were embodied in the church of Rome. The problem here is the opposite intellectual trap. Whilst arguing strongly that anti-Catholicism survived, this reading of the past suggests this staunch Protestantism set the English apart from other Europeans. Anti-popery made the Catholic-dominated continent alien, whilst the notion that the English were a chosen people gave them a sense of isolating uniqueness. Looking at these interpretations together, there is a clear and urgent problem. We have religiously committed Englands on offer, and cosmopolitan ones: but there are few accounts of that simultaneous anti-popery and engagement with the continent which destroyed Bromley in 1705.

The chapters which follow try to supply this deficiency. As they do so, they uncover a complex story, in which attitudes to religion and to foreigners interacted in different ways, were constantly renegotiated, and affected a range of political and cultural disputes. On examination, it appears it has not only been historians who have had difficulty reconciling a deep attachment to an English faith and a sense that England was part of a wider continent. Contemporaries wrestled with the tension between these attitudes, and tried to resolve it in an inventive variety of action and argument. For example, the first chapter illustrates the ambiguities by continuing where the Bromley story left off. It explores English travel writing, and finds authors struggling to describe a continent which they knew would be of interest to readers, but whose prevailing cultural force – the Roman Catholic church – had to be condemned. In this struggle, travellers divided Europe into reformed

14 Almost all histories of the enlightenment assume a connection between cosmopolitanism and shunning religious conflict. For a concise guide: Dorinda Outram, *The enlightenment* (Cambridge, 1995); though Roy Porter, *The englightenment* (Houndmills, 2001), suggests pride in enlightenment could lead to British patriotism.

15 Colley, *Britons*, passim; Linda Colley, 'Britishness and otherness: an argument', *JBS*, 31 (1992), 309–29. Also, Colin Haydon, 'I love my king and country, but a Roman Catholic I hate', in Tony Claydon and Ian McBride, eds., *Protestantism and national identity: Britain and Ireland, 1660–1850* (Cambridge, 1998), pp. 33–52; Kathleen Wilson, *The sense of the people: politics, culture and imperialism in England 1715–1785* (Cambridge, 1995), pp. 169–74; though Jonathan Scott, *England's troubles* (Cambridge, 2000), asserts strong continentalism in English anti-popery.

and unreformed regions. They denigrated the latter and expressed solidarity with the former, but they also saw things which linked their contrasted mental entities. Especially, they recognised a common Christian civilisation which provided familiar points of reference even at the darkest heart of the Catholic world. Chapter 2 similarly illustrates a continual remodelling of identities, this time within works of history. Surveying ways in which English authors wrote about their nation's past, it demonstrates a sense that the country had been radically separated from its neighbours by the sixteenth-century reformation; but also a sense of participation in a broad renewal which had also gripped Germany, France, the Netherlands and Switzerland. At yet another level, elements of the nation's story – particularly the medieval heritage of its church – drove historians to identify with communities larger than Protestantism. They were forced to acknowledge that England had once been part of a culture which had included the lands still dominated by popery, and that in some important senses, she still was.

The remaining chapters build on such ambiguities, and examine how ideas about faith and geography fuelled debates about England's role in the world, and about her domestic settlement. Chapter 3 looks at foreign policy. It admits it can be hard to see this driven by religious or cosmopolitan identities because England allied with people of a variety of faiths to pursue what looked like material national interests. Yet the chapter also examines public justifications of foreign relations, and in these the picture changes. The English often discussed their external interventions as attempts to defend the European reformation in complex situations where it was unwise to alienate all Roman Catholics. They also showed considerable concern for Christianity as a whole. They supported campaigns to protect the faith from Islam in the Balkans and Mediterranean, and took vigorous action against its enemies from within. Thus policies which can certainly be read as political moves against rival nations must also be understood as attempts to uphold Protestantism or an international Christian order. The fourth chapter goes on cataloguing clashing identities. Concentrating on the battles between Whigs and Tories which dominated English history from the 1670s to the 1720s, it shows these driven by different readings of England's participation in communities of faith which spanned Europe. So, party debates over the constitution were shaped by disagreement about how best to serve England's obligations to believers abroad. Must the English assert popular rights against bad rulers if they were to protect the faithful of the continent, or would such ideas destabilise the nation and ensure it failed in this duty? Ecclesiastical arguments between Whigs and Tories had a similarly foreign focus. Should the English identify more with the international reformation charted by the historians in the second chapter, or with the broader

Christian church which those scholars had also outlined? In all these discussions, widely shared – but often also contradictory – assumptions led protagonists to startlingly different conclusions. Individuals were forcing diverse pieces of their worldview to create responses to ambiguities and dilemmas; this could lead to hopeless inconsistencies, bitter disagreements and sudden shifts of position.

Much of what follows, therefore, may seem to deepen rather than dispel the confusions of English faith and cosmopolitanism. Yet there are broad lessons which emerge from the late Stuart and Georgian material which can begin to simplify what was going on in English minds. Most importantly, it becomes clear that a religious confession cannot ultimately be a force for insularity, however frequently Protestantism might appear to have isolated England from her neighbours. Contemporary commentators may have implied that upholding the Protestant faith made the English a unique people, and modern historians may analyse the construction of a foreign Catholic 'other' which forged English identity in rejection of the alien abroad, but in fact religious commitment tends to introduce wider perspectives than this. As Israel's God made clear in the later books of the Old Testament, deities who confine their attentions to one country are diminished deities.[16] Religions usually have missions to the whole of mankind. They claim to have branches across the world and to recruit for a universal struggle against the ungodly, so their adherents cannot base a narrow nationalism on their faith.[17] Late Stuart and early Georgian Protestantism was no exception. As will be demonstrated, it had a supranational vision, which saw the English as only a part of a European community of the reformed. If the English were in any way special or chosen, this election merely meant they had a peculiar duty to protect this widely dispersed community. For them, Protestantism and cosmopolitanism were not contradictory, but flowed straight from each other.

The second lesson also reconciles religion and Europe, but does so in a context even broader than the protestant international. It is that the concept of 'Christendom', an identity encompassing all followers of Jesus of whatever denomination, survived in England into the Georgian era. Even through the bitterest wars of religion, and even amongst those most committed to the Protestant cause, there remained a belief that all Christians were united and that the continent on which they lived shared a common destiny. Traditional interpretations would doubt this. The Protestant reformation is usually held

[16] For instance Isaiah 49:6 made it clear the Messiah would be a light to the Gentiles, not simply a saviour of the Jews.

[17] Historians of the Tudor and early Stuart church have recognised the internationalism of English Protestantism: Patrick Collinson, *The birthpangs of Protestant England* (Basingstoke, 1988), ch. 1.

to have destroyed the medieval vision of a single western church, and replaced it by bitter rivalries.[18] It is this interpretation which demands a weakening of religious affiliation before cosmopolitanism could re-emerge. Europe had to be integrated through a *secular* enlightenment, the argument implies, because after the sixteenth century faith could only divide. However, whilst it is true some people sought to unite Europeans by attacking religious enthusiasm, this was not the only type of cosmopolitanism. Those most deeply committed to their own confessions, including English Protestants, retained a vision of a single Christendom. As we shall repeatedly see, they tried to defend it against infidel enemies from outside, they believed it enshrined a moral order of international relations which must be upheld, and they even felt the pull of a transnational church which had somehow survived the schisms of the sixteenth century.

A third lesson is simply how powerful the two religious internationalisms were. As the following chapters show, concepts of a Protestant international, and of a united Christendom, emerged repeatedly in the century after the civil war. They shaped the possibilities of thought, formed vital parts of English identity, and frequently determined the grounds of debate. Indeed, they provide material for a profound challenge to existing interpretations of English history. The period between 1660 and 1760 has long been recognised as crucial to England's development. This was when the country emerged from international impotence to become the world's strongest power; and when she secured her peculiarly free, pluralistic and stable politics. Yet existing accounts of these achievements have centred on internal processes. To explain progress, scholars have analysed England's constitutional settlements; her social, economic and cultural development; and the bureaucratic organisation of her 'fiscal-military' state.[19] By contrast, prominent discussion of Christians overseas suggests that those involved in remodelling the country did not always focus on such domestic matters. Frequently, they were driven by their profound sense of belonging to a transnational reformation, or to a Europe-wide – even worldwide – faith. Put simply, the English often felt their strongest duties were to their coreligionists abroad. It was these duties which led them to support the wars which built England's international strength; and these which led them to reject internal settlements which might hobble the country's godly obligations.

[18] A recent statement is Edwin Jones, *The English nation: the great myth* (Sutton, 1998), which asserts: 'The reformation was the greatest revolution in English history. It meant that England was suddenly separated from the Europe of Western Christendom', p. 15. General accounts of the reformation also assume a sundering: e.g. Euan Cameron, *Early modern Europe* (Oxford, 1999) – which sees the 'harmony of the Christian world . . . in fragments' by 1550, p. 100.

[19] See below, chs. 3–4.

Fourthly, whilst it is clear we must go beyond England to explain the English, we must also choose the right international context in which to study their history. In the last decades of the twentieth century, scholars urged each other to avoid considering England in isolation, but the wider picture many adopted was still pretty local. A style of 'new British history' demanded that the English past be understood as a constant interaction with Scots, Welsh and Irish, and for a while the field came to be dominated by studies of 'anglo-celtic' entanglements.[20] The chapters which follow obey some of this interpretation's strictures by considering the importance of such themes as the 1707 union with Scotland. Yet even as the new 'British' interpretation gained momentum, doubts crept in. Some commentators objected that the narrative of full, reciprocal interaction between the 'British' nations was too complex to tell; or that many who had tried to tell it had actually fallen back on an 'enriched English' history, which only attempted to understand the other countries in so far as they had affected their larger neighbour.[21] This work accepts such criticism by making no bones about its English bias. This is a study of England, not Britain; and it sacrifices many of the fascinating complexities of 'anglo-celtic' interaction in order to tell a focused story. It also, however, challenges the assumptions behind the new British history. Concentration on England can be defended both because the 'British' nations remained very different cultures throughout our period (so including Scotland or Ireland would confuse an already complex story of multiple identities), and because England remained the dominant core of the British state created in 1707. Beyond this, the fact that the English cared so much about an extremely wide-ranging Protestantism, and about an even broader Christendom, suggests relations with immediate neighbours were not always their most pressing anxiety. As we shall see, the English *were* concerned about the fate of the Scots and Irish; but they were at least as concerned about the reformation's survival in France, Holland, Switzerland, Germany and Austria; about Christianity's struggle with infidels at the borders of the faith; and about dangerous apostates in the very heart of the

[20] The original call for 'British history' was made in J. G. A. Pocock, 'British history: a plea for a new subject', *JMH*, 47 (1975), 601–28. Glenn Burgess, ed., *The new British history* (1999), usefully analyses the historiography for the Stuart age. For a flavour of the scholarship: Steven G. Ellis and Sarah Barber, eds., *Conquest and union: fashioning a British state 1685–1725* (Harlow, 1995); Brendan Bradshaw and Peter Roberts, eds., *British consciousness and identity: the making of Britain, 1533–1707* (Cambridge, 1998); S. J. Connolly, ed., *Kingdoms united? Great Britain and Ireland since 1500* (Dublin, 1999).

[21] For criticisms: Nicholas Canny, 'Irish, Scottish and Welsh responses to centralisation, 1530–c1640', in Alexander Grant and Keith J. Stringer, eds., *Uniting the kingdom? The making of British history* (1995), pp. 147–69; Tony Claydon, 'Problems with the British problem', *Parliamentary History*, 16 (1997), 221–7; Tony Claydon, 'British history in the post-revolutionary world', in Burgess, *New British history*, pp. 115–37.

faithful's territory. The new British history, therefore, has helped set England in a wider context, but the evidence suggests this context was not wide enough, and in what follows we will deliberately play it down to stress a continental alternative.

This geographic lesson has another aspect. Although some scholars concentrated on the three kingdoms at the expense of Europe, some others ranged way beyond these. A long tradition of imperial history charted interactions with peoples around the globe, and this has recently been joined by an 'Atlantic' history, stressing the particular interdependence of Britain, Ireland and their settlements in North America and the Caribbean.[22] Again, much admirable work has been done in these spheres: but again it risks demoting continental Europe in English perceptions. First, we will see that England's inhabitants were relatively ignorant of far-flung places in the late Stuart and early Hanoverian periods. Few went to Africa or Asia; these regions had relatively little impact on the consciousness of those who stayed at home; and although the American colonies were being settled, they were of surprisingly little concern to people of the metropolis before the crisis of the 1760s.[23] The Ottoman Turks have been claimed as a possible exception to this neglect of non-Europeans, but the claim dissolves on examination. English comment on the Turks peaked in the 1680s when they were at the gates of Vienna, but as they were driven from the heart of Europe in the next decades, interest faded. Second, we should note that even the transnational religious identities we will examine rarely directed eyes across the great oceans. Almost all the world's Protestants lived in north-west Europe, and the English tended to worry about reformed Christians elsewhere primarily as colonial extensions

[22] The fruits of imperial scholarship were summarised in Nicholas P. Canny, ed., *The Oxford history of the British empire*, vol. 1, *The origins* (Oxford, 1998); and Peter Marshall, ed., *The Oxford history of the British empire*, vol. 2, *The eighteenth century* (Oxford, 1998). For examples of Atlantic history: Bernard Bailyn and Philip D. Morgan, eds., *Strangers within the realm: cultural margins of the first British empire* (Williamsburg, 1991); David Armitage and Michael J. Braddick, eds., *The British Atlantic world* (2002); David Armitage, ed., *Greater Britain, 1516–1775* (2004).

[23] For lack of travel, see below, pp. 63–6. Arguing for a lack of interest in America is difficult when there are real examples of engagement. See the missionary activity mentioned below, p. 355, or the interchange of people across the ocean (Gillian Wagner, *Thomas Coram, gent., 1668–1751* (Woodbridge, 2004), takes a figure whose American links are often forgotten). However, the point is the *relative* lack of interest. This is demonstrated, for example, by the European focus of English discussion of 1689 (see below, ch. 4) even though American colonies also experienced political turmoil: Richard R. Johnson, 'The revolution of 1688–9 in the American colonies', in Jonathan I. Israel, ed., *The Anglo-Dutch moment* (Cambridge, 1991), pp. 215–40. Similarly, English politicians were happy to give away American gains to secure European allies at the 1748 Peace of Aix-la-Chapelle; and many readings of the 1760s crisis stress the ignorance in England of American circumstances: e.g. I. R. Christie, *Crisis of empire* (1966); P. D. G.Thomas, *British politics and the Stamp Act crisis* (1975).

of European wars.[24] Of course Christians generally were more widespread than their reformed variant. Beyond the lands occupied by Protestants and Roman Catholics (which will be the core of this study) there were the Orthodox of the near east and Russia; the African churches of Ethiopia and southern Sudan; and groups of the faithful in the Caucausus and elsewhere. Many of these communities were respected and ancient, and were sometimes mentioned in English ecclesiological discussions.[25] However, the existence of such Christians was usually marginal to the public discourse on which we shall focus. For example, few non-westerners featured in debates on foreign policy because these people were not major powers. The exception was Russia, but her influence was only becoming clear towards the end of our period, and her spheres of control were only starting to impinge upon English interests.[26] In discussion of domestic issues, tensions within Protestantism and the threat of Rome were familiar and hotly discussed. In comparison, Orthodoxy and other theologies were too little known to have much purchase.[27] For the English, therefore, 'Christendom' meant largely Christianity in western and central Europe. For all these reasons we will discuss Africa, the Orient, the Levant, Russia or the Americas when they became relevant to contemporary perceptions, but this did not happen nearly as often as Italy, Germany, the Netherlands, France or Spain came to the front of people's minds.

The final lesson is implicit in the other four. It is simply that English identity was – and almost certainly remains – far more fluid, open and multi-layered than is often believed. Commentators on modern culture often assume a fixed and narrow Englishness. They lament a bigoted English insularity, which accounts for everything from reluctance to learn languages to scepticism about the pan-European project.[28] Historians, meanwhile, have noted an

[24] In our period, concern for the American colonies was concentrated at times when European wars spread over the Atlantic. Thus there was far more in the 1740s than in the 1720s: see Kathleen Wilson, *The sense of the people: politics, culture and imperialism in England, 1715–1785* (Oxford, 1995); Robert Harris, *A patriot press: national politics and the London press in the 1740s* (Oxford, 1993).

[25] There was sympathy for Greek Christians under the Turk, and interest in their evasion of Rome's clutches. See (among figures who will feature elsewhere in this book): Paul Rycaut, *The present state of the Greek and Armenian churches* (1679); Bishop Henry Compton's care for the Greeks in his diocese – Edward Carpenter, *The Protestant bishop* (1965), ch. 19; or Edward Stephens' work for reconciliation between English and Greek churches – Geoff Kemp, 'Stephens, Edward', *ODNB*, LII:461–2.

[26] For Russia's increasing impact and cultural prominence: e.g. A. Rothstein, *Peter the Great and Marlborough* (1986); Anthony Cross, *Anglo-Russian relations in the eighteenth century* (1977).

[27] Interestingly, the preface to Rycaut's *Present state* assumed readers would need guiding through unfamiliar material, and stressed the lessons the eastern churches had for the more familiar Romanists and reformed.

[28] Press comment is joined by scholarly analysis: Robin Cohen, *Frontiers of identity: the British and the others* (Harlow, 1994); and the introduction and conclusion of Colley's *Britons*.

abiding English xenophobia; and they have charted the rise of a nationalism (albeit dating it to very different periods), which set up the national interest as its highest ideal, and was based on rejection of a series of alien, foreign 'others'.[29] Yet in the vital period when England emerged as the major, and as a peculiarly liberal, power, there was no such unreflecting introspection. Certainly, the people we shall meet were aware of their Englishness. They appealed to English law and history, to the rights of Englishmen, to England's trading interests, even to England's extraordinary covenant with God. But whilst English people *were* English, they were just as clearly Protestants and Christians. These broader (though sometimes contradictory) identities exploded any constricting nationality, and ensured England was endlessly tossed between different levels of self-understanding. This was especially true as neither Protestantism nor Christianity were themselves fixed bodies. They could be envisioned as encompassing different people (for instance, the English disagreed bitterly whether all followers of the reformation were equal brethren), and they could be understood in different senses (Christendom was by turns a geographical, a moral, a military and an ecclesiological construct). As William Bromley discovered, such ideological turbulence could be uncomfortable. Yet it opened people to a vast range of experience; and it explained much of the astonishing dynamism of English society in the century after the civil war.

[29] For attempts to date English nationalism: Leah Greenfeld, *Nationalism: five roads to modernity* (Cambridge, MA, 1992), and Jones, *English nation*, argue for Henry VIII's reign; Steven Pincus, '"To protect English liberties": the English nationalist revolution of 1688–9', in Tony Claydon and Ian McBride, eds., *Protestantism and national identity: Britain and Ireland, 1660–1850* (Cambridge, 1998) – the late seventeenth century; and Gerald Newman, *The rise of English nationalism, 1740–1830* (1987) – the mid-Georgian period. Other scholars plump for the middle ages, or the nineteenth century.

1

Space: travel books and English confessional geography

THE BIRTH OF THE TRAVEL GUIDE

In July 1650, tragedy struck a small party of English people travelling through Italy. The group was headed by the Yorkshire Catholic Thomas Wetenhall, a gentleman who had decided to leave England for a while to avoid the anti-popish prejudices of the new republican government. Accompanying him were his wife, Lady Catherine; his brother John; two of the household servants; and the group's guide, Richard Lassels, another Yorkshire Catholic who had been ordained priest at Douai in 1631. At first the trip had gone well. Although the situation at home was hair-raising, the tourists had enjoyed their time abroad. They had arrived in Rome in time for Christmas 1649, and in the next few months they had had an audience with the pope, had participated in the jubilee celebrations to mark the half-century, and had viewed the classical remains of the ancient imperial capital. In late spring they had toured other parts of the Italian peninsula, but in midsummer their return to Yorkshire was halted by a catastrophe. As they got back to Padua, the pregnant Lady Catherine caught a fever, and gave birth to a stillborn child. On 6 July she died, having never recovered from the complications of her miscarriage. Her family were devastated. Thomas' deep mourning prevented any rapid return home, and he took until early 1651 to get as far as Paris. Only then did he part with his guide to cross the Channel.

The deaths of Lady Catherine and her baby were heartbreaking for the Wetenhalls. Yet they were also a significant moment in the English awareness of Europe. The family's guide, Richard Lassels, was to mark the death of his patron by writing a manuscript account of her journey, which he presented to Thomas in Paris as a memorial of his wife.[1] As he did this, he produced

[1] Richard Lassels, 'Voyage of Lady Catherine Whetenhall' (1650, imperfect copy surviving as BL Add. MS 4217); and Edward Chaney, *The grand tour and the great rebellion* (Geneva, 1985).

the first draft of what would become a standard guide to travelling in Italy. Over the next years, Lassels revised and supplemented his memorial, turning it into a comprehensive account of how to tour the peninsula. In the 1650s, he took further notes on Italy as he guided other English exiles from Cromwell's regime, added these to the Wetenhall manuscript, and so left his friend Simon Wilson a pretty full reference work when he died in 1668. Wilson revised this again and then published it in Paris in 1670 as *A voyage of Italy*. The work was an instant and a lasting success. The Paris edition was shipped to London and sold there in large numbers, and within months the work had been reissued by the English book trade.[2] Further editions followed in 1686, 1697, 1698 and 1705, and by the end of the Stuart age it had become the authority on the Italian section of the 'grand tour'. Later writers tried to update or correct Lassels, but they acknowledged their debts to Lady Catherine's guide even as they did so. Authors as diverse as John Ray, William Acton and Joseph Addison praised Lassels' coverage, and went as far as recommending that readers consult the *Voyage* for more detailed accounts of some of the things they described.[3] Even our old friend William Bromley tripped over Lassels' dominance. Describing several Italian cities, he admitted the *Voyage* had described almost everything and so allowed his merciless persecutor to pounce again: 'The Author observes that Mr. Lassels . . . has superceded the Endeavours of all coming after him, p. 106 . . . Little remains to others, p. 224.'[4]

The canonisation of Lassels' *Voyage* is a useful starting point for a study of what might be called 'English confessional geography'. Because the book provided a detailed description of a large part of Europe, and because it was so popular, it allows us to examine how late Stuart people viewed the European continent and its religious landscape. The success of the *Voyage* can tell us something of how the English understood the territorial divisions between the different branches of the Christian faith; it can suggest how far their attitudes to different confessional areas diverged; and may say much about where, how defined and how significant they believed the boundaries between these areas to be. Moreover, the book suggests something startling about this confessional geography. Whereas earlier generations of Englishmen had held a strongly Protestant worldview, which drew hard lines between a virtuous reformed Europe and its evil popish antithesis,

[2] Richard Lassels, *The voyage of Italy* ([Paris], 1670; citations below are to this edition unless otherwise stated). For details of the publication history: Chaney, *Grand tour*, p. 140.

[3] Joseph Addison, *Remarks on several parts of Italy* (1705), preface; William Acton, *A new journal of Italy* (1691), p. 21; John Ray, *Observations topographical, moral and physiological made in a journey* (1673), p. 376.

[4] [William Bromley], *Remarks made in travels through France and Italy* (1705 edn), 'table of principal matters'.

the acceptance of Lassels implies this militantly confessional understanding was fading after 1660.

Most obviously, when people purchased the *Voyage*, they demonstrated they were willing to be guided round Italy by a Roman Catholic priest. They also endorsed a volume which took readers into the non-Protestant continent without turning it into a monstrous circus of anti-Christian popery. As we might expect, Lassels did not present Italy as a diabolical 'other' to be rejected by a godly English audience. Rather, it could be a place of beauty and instruction, even for reformed Christians. In Lassels' descriptions, many features of the Catholic continent which had traditionally been derided were instead justified and re-presented in a far more positive light. For example, the Catholic churches covered by the *Voyage* were not pagan temples festooned with the icons of an idolatrous faith. Rather they were impressive and appropriate settings for an approach to God, and even the greatest temple of Catholicism, St Peter's in Rome, received approval. For many, St Peter's had been the great symbol of popish vainglory. Indeed, there was a sense in which protest about the cost of its building in the early sixteenth century had sparked the Protestant reformation against ecclesiastical corruption. For Lassels, by contrast, St Peter's was a masterpiece, whose scale and richness brought worshippers closer to God. The basilica was the 'Queen of Churches'; its altar was the noblest in the world; and the vaults supporting its dome seemed to 'walke into heaven'.[5]

Elsewhere, Lassels excused other marks of Italian religion. The often-criticised wealth of the clergy was essential for their social role. Rituals which might have been condemned for their impolite excess demonstrated the piety of the people. Religious images which might spark fears of idolatry were aids to meditation on the mercies of Christ.[6] If Lassels recognised that all was not absolutely well with Italian religion – he questioned dubious traditions, and protested against superstition in worship – he balanced rebuke with comments on the virtues of many of the Catholics he encountered. Thus the description of Rome, the place which for many Englishmen had been the source of all corruptions of faith, opened with an exhaustive list of the charities the town supported.[7] In this city the poor and the sick were cared for in the many hospitals attached to monasteries, whilst other foundations helped people with lawsuits, preached popular sermons, taught impecunious children, buried the dead and treated pilgrims so well they found Rome 'as Adam found Paradise'.[8] Just occasionally, Lassels even supplemented his praise of Catholics with jokes at Protestants' expense. Shown a hundred-year-old cheese by the Calvinist mayor of a small town in Grisons,

[5] Lassels, *Voyage* (Paris edn), pt 2, pp. 32, 34.
[6] E.g. the description of Loretto, ibid., pp. 326–40. [7] Ibid., pp. 6–20 [8] Ibid., p. 7.

he reflected on the new-fangled artifice of his host's faith in comparison to the ancient certainties of his own. 'A venerable *Cheese* indeed!' he quipped, 'and well nigh as old as his *Religion*.'[9]

Given such content, the popularity of the *Voyage* implies a shift occurred in English confessional geography around the middle of the seventeenth century. No longer interested in knee-jerk condemnations of popery, audiences seemed prepared for a more balanced treatment of the subject. If we wanted to take the argument further, we could suggest the circumstances in which the *Voyage* was produced explain the shift. Lassels, after all, had gained most of his experience of Italy by guiding Englishmen who had fled from the civil wars and republican regimes of the 1640s and 1650s. He had thus succoured refugees from disturbances which had been fuelled by fears of popery, and had written as his countrymen were realising overzealous Protestantism might dissolve all bonds of obedience and cohesion.[10] If the English were looking for a less dangerous reaction to the Catholic faith, the writer may have provided a usefully moderate description of its foreign strongholds. Lassels may also have reflected a shift of mood on the continent he visited. Europeans had fought each other over religion for a century after Luther's break with Rome, but by the time Lassels travelled a peace of exhaustion had begun to settle. Only months before the Wetenhalls set out for Italy, the Thirty Years War in Germany had been ended by treaties which recognised the rights of different faiths to exist in different areas, and from this point practical accommodations began to emerge.[11] The bitterest clashes between reformation and counter-reformation may thus have been played out: Lassels' *Voyage* may have been one of the earliest indicators of the new mood.

Such an interpretation of Lassels' success, and of a shift in attitudes, has considerable strengths. It certainly coheres with a raft of scholarly theories which have argued that the excesses of the early and mid-seventeenth century led to much less religious certainty: a greater nervousness about intolerant, crusading, or millenarian protestantism.[12] Yet it would be well to pause before swallowing the argument whole. The most obvious reason

[9] Ibid., pt 1, p. 58.

[10] For anti-Catholic origins of the civil war: Robert Clifton, 'Fear of popery', in Conrad Russell, ed., *The origins of the English civil war* (1973); William M. Lamont, *Godly rule: religion and politics 1603–1660* (1969).

[11] E.g. Diarmaid MacCulloch, *Reformation: Europe's house divided, 1490–1700* (2003), ch. 11, ends his narrative of events in 1648 because confessional struggle was supposedly exhausted. For the different mood of eighteenth-century religion: Jeremy Black, 'Confessional state or elect nation?' in Tony Claydon and Ian McBride, eds., *Protestantism and national identity: Britian and Ireland, 1660–1850* (Cambridge, 1998), pp. 53–74.

[12] E.g. Lamont, *Godly rule*; Christopher Hill, *Some intellectual consequences of the English revolution* (Madison, 1980); Alan Houston and Steven Pincus, eds., *A nation transformed: England after the restoration* (Cambridge, 2001).

for Lassels' popularity was not, after all, his calmer description of Catholicism. It was, quite simply, that he had had written a practical guidebook to Italy. He had produced a work which was clear, easy to use and reliable, and which supplanted everything else for these reasons. In other words, the *Voyage* was sensational, not because it gave the first systematic description of a non-threatening Catholicism, but because it gave the first systematic description of anything foreign at all. There had been travel books before Lassels, but these had not been much help to real travellers. With the honourable exception of John Raymond's 1648 *Itinerary* (which had provided a city-by-city approach), they had merely mused vaguely on the benefits of touring; had mixed fact and fantasy; had hopped around the continent on unrepeatable itinerancies or described foreign places merely to satirise or comment on human nature.[13] Whilst some of these earlier writers had given some good advice on precautions to take before crossing the Channel, or provided useful summaries of national customs and constitutions, no one had really done what Lassels did.[14] No one had told people exactly where to go and what to see; no one had been as comprehensive in coverage; and no one had brought such a wealth of scholarship and personal experience to their writing.

If it was these features of the *Voyage* which made it so attractive, we might start to doubt whether it really pointed to a less Protestant geography in the later Stuart age. If Lassels was welcomed for his practical approach rather than for expressing a new zeitgeist, it is possible his audience saw his Catholicism as a blemish in a work whose usability, rather than its opinions, made it irresistible. In fact, there is strong evidence that this was so. From the start, there was a battle for the genre Lassels had invented. The English recognised that the *Voyage* was the first, and perhaps would always be the best, guide to Italy, but they also sensed that guidebooks needed rescuing from the popery which had infected them at birth. So many of the tours published after 1670 corrected Lassels, restoring the idolatrous continent which he had expunged. In 1686, for example, Gilbert Burnet produced his recent travels, and denounced the persecution, irrationality and blasphemy of the popish territories.[15] This work soon became even more successful than the *Voyage*, going through nine editions in its first fours years; and a further six by 1752. William Acton, to take another instance, published his

[13] Andrew Hadfield, *Literature, travel and colonial writing in the English renaissance, 1545–1625* (Oxford, 1998), ch. 1. For an example of such writing still published after 1660: *Poor Robin's guide to France* (1666). Michael G. Brennan, *The origin of the grand tour* (2004), notes there were few accounts of travel before the 1640s, p. 31. Raymond's full title was John Raymond, *An itinerary contayning a voyage made through Italy* (1648).

[14] [James Howell], *Instructions for forraine travell* (1642), offered good generalised advice.

[15] Gilbert Burnet, *Some letters containing an account of what seemed most remarkable* (1686).

Italian travels in 1691 and commented dryly on Lassels' overly credulous description of popish Europe. This included Rimini, a town which had been badly damaged by an earthquake in the intervening years: 'The chappel of *St Antony*, which *Lassel* . . . doth say, proved miraculously the real prescence in the Sacrament, was likewise . . . shaken down with the rest' so that the historical painting 'which should have informed us concerning the Miracle, fell with the Chappel Walls'.[16] Even the publication history of the *Voyage* revealed efforts to purge the book's sympathy to popery. In an atypical burst of partisanship, the Paris edition of Lassels' work castigated Geneva as a powerhouse of a dangerous Protestantism. It had stated that the town, 'like a good *sinke* at the bottom of the streets, is built at the bottom of the *Savoye*, *France* and *Germany*, and therefore fit to receive into it the corruption of the Apostates of the Roman Church'.[17] By the time the work was published in London, however, there was more pandering to reformed sensibilities. The second edition bowdlerised the passage into the meaningless (if still vaguely scatological) 'Geneva is built at the bottom of the Savoye, France and Germany'.[18]

In the end, therefore, the lesson of Lassels is that we must look more deeply into the success of his *Voyage* before interpreting English confessional geography in the century after the civil war. Certainly the English were prepared to endorse a text which dealt calmly with continental Catholicism, but they seemed uneasy about its lack of Protestant zeal. In their writing and patronage of other guides, they yearned for volumes which confirmed the Roman faith was an alien perversion of godliness, and drew starker contrasts between reformed and unreformed Europe. What follows, therefore, is an account of a culture making a slow and uneven transition. The more vehement anti-popery of the early modern era may have gone, but many of its assumptions, images and strands of thought remained.

TOURS THROUGH A DIVIDED EUROPE

As has been suggested, the genre Lassels had developed proved fertile. Within three years of his *Voyage* appearing, the Cambridge naturalist John Ray had produced his own travel guide. Acknowledging Lassels' influence, Ray wrote up his botanical observations in Europe as an itinerary, adding descriptions of cities, monuments and landscapes as well as foreign flora, and extending Lassels' geographic range to include France, Germany and the Netherlands. In the succeeding decades, many followed this example. By 1760, at least thirty extensive tours of the continent had been published, along with a

[16] Acton, *New journal*, p. 59. [17] Lassels, *Voyage*, pt 1, p. 46.
[18] Lassels, *Voyage* (Paris – to be sold in London, 1670), pt 1, p. 46.

host of works which charted shorter journeys abroad. Several of the more comprehensive guides were reissued in collections of travellers' accounts (such as John Harris' 1705 *Navigantium*), and some proved as enduringly popular as Lassels or Burnet.[19] Ray, for example, was reprinted in 1738; whilst Edward Brown's travels (also first published in 1673) appeared again in 1677, 1685 and 1687.[20] Later, Maximilian Misson's *New voyage to Italy* had editions in 1699, 1714 and 1739 as well as its original in 1695; Charles Thompson's *Travels* would come out in 1744, 1745 and 1752; and Joseph Addison's tour of Europe would reflect the fame of its author with editions in 1705, 1718, 1726, 1733, 1745, 1753, 1755 and on into George III's reign.[21] The rush of travel guides was such that John Northleigh, adding to the corpus in 1702, claimed he had at first laid aside thoughts of writing up his journey since 'almost every one [was] putting his Pilgrimage into the Press'.[22]

These works were not only numerous, they provided a variety of types of guide. Though almost all were structured as city-to-city itineraries, their precise contents and interests were different. It is true that many traced a fairly standard route through the continent. They took their readers down through the central swathe of Europe, leading them through France – or sometimes through the Netherlands and Germany – to Italy, and then returned on the other side of the Rhine. Yet even in these standard works, the exact places visited were never quite the same, and some guides had a far greater range. Ray's book set a pattern ignoring Spain – there was 'nothing there which might answer [tourists'] trouble and expense' – but William Bromley's 1702 *Travels* (maturer than his earlier efforts) was more comprehensive.[23] It covered the Iberian peninsula, and ranged as far as Prussia, Poland and Scandinavia. Other guides crossed the continent on their way to more exotic locations, so found themselves in the deepest Balkans or Russia.[24] The thematic focus of the works also diverged. If Lassels worried he over-concentrated on religious ceremony, and if Ray had been obsessed by plants and feats of engineering, the eyes of other travellers were attracted elsewhere.[25] Acton confessed to filling his pages with classical antiquities; Thomas Frankz (travels published 1735) was most interested in trade; whilst John Clenche (writing 1675) gave

19 John Harris, *Navigantium atque itinerantium bibliotheca* (2 vols., 1705).

20 Edward Brown, *A brief account of some travels* (first published 1673; citations below are from the 1685 edn).

21 [François] Maximilian Misson, *A new voyage to Italy* (2 vols., 1695); Charles Thompson, *The travels of the late Charles Thompson* (1744); Addison, *Remarks*.

22 John Northleigh, *Topographical descriptions* (1702), epistle.

23 Ray, *Observations*, preface; William Bromley, *Several years travels through Portugal, Spain* (1702).

24 E.g. Brown, *Brief account*; Alexander Drummond, *Travels through different cities of Germany, Italy* (1754).

25 Lassels expressed his worry at *Voyage*, pt 1, p. 2.

blow-by-blow descriptions of every church he saw and Alexander Drummond (1754) treated readers to a wide collection of random curiosities.[26] As a result, the English had been supplied with a thick description of neighbouring lands by the time Thomas Nugent's magisterial *Grand tour* (1749) provided an exhaustive compendium for travellers.[27] Added to this wealth of material were a series of works which concentrated on describing the politics, culture and geography of single states.[28] The corpus of travel literature thus provides rich evidence to map English perceptions of Europe in the century after the civil war.

Before launching into this analysis, however, there are concerns which need to be addressed. The first is whether such a diversity of texts could lead to any coherent conclusions. The works were written over many decades, and their authors differed in itinerary, interests and religious sympathies. It might, therefore, be illegitimate to distil a single 'English' attitude, or even spectrum of attitudes, from such variety. In what follows, therefore, there must be great sensitivity to divergences of prejudice among the travellers, and to changes of approach over the century. Yet for all this, it may be that the travel guides are a more unified source than at first appears. To a surprising extent, the works were a collaborative enterprise, in which authors consciously contributed to a *shared* stock of fact and opinion.

The most obvious examples of co-operation between writers were the frequently acknowledged debts to earlier commentators. As authors took their readers round Europe, they pointed them to other texts, with writers such as Nugent thanking extensive lists of earlier sources for providing information about places they had not visited.[29] They also recommended other authors to fill in gaps in details; they shaped their own accounts to correct or supplement what others had said; or – like Joseph Shaw – they hoped to summarise other works so that tourists could carry fewer volumes in their travel luggage.[30] In extreme cases, writers accepted they had been so reliant on other works that they were not sole authors. Charles Thompson's popular travels had been compiled from the deceased author's manuscript notes, but his anonymous editor said he had filled up 'chasms' with 'the writings of other Travellers, which I had so interwoven with Mr Thompson's, that I imagine they will

[26] Acton, *New journal*, epistle; Thomas Frankz, *A tour through France, Flanders and Germany* (1735); [John Clenche], *A tour in France and Italy* (1676); Drummond, *Travels*.

[27] Thomas Nugent, *The grand tour* (4 vols., 1749) – this edition is, however, rare: future citations will be from the 1756 edition.

[28] William Temple, *Observations upon the united provinces of the Netherlands* (1673) – new editions in 1676, 1680, 1690, 1693 and later – provided a model.

[29] Nugent, *Grand tour*, p. vi.

[30] Joseph Shaw, *Letters to a nobleman from a gentleman travelling* (1709), pp. xvii–xviii. For examples of correction and supplementation: Addison, *Remarks*, preface; John Breval, *Remarks on several parts of Europe* (2 vols., 1726), preface.

not easily be distinguish'd'.[31] In the 1720s, Edward Wright had started to purge the borrowings in his guide because he had become ashamed of them, but then friends had persuaded him the passages were useful in producing a comprehensive picture of Europe.[32] Again, Philippe de Blainville's travels purported to be translations of an original manuscript by a Frenchman. Yet the writings had been so adapted by editors, and so much other material had been incorporated, that it is difficult to get to the words of an original author.[33] Such debts accounted for a considerable, in fact often tedious, similarity between the guides.

As for possible changes over the century, these were smoothed by the collaboration between authors and by the enduring popularity of many older guides. If each text depended on earlier ones for its full meaning, and if works written years before were still being produced as useful and interesting contributions to the genre, then observations first made in distant decades were given later currency. Change was also minimised by some pretty blatant plagiarism. Certain accounts were so full, or gained such authority, that they were simply cribbed by those authors who had not been to certain areas, or who could not see past earlier accounts to their own interpretation. Temple's *Observations* on the Netherlands were the clearest case in point. Its 1670s account of Holland was still shaping comment decades later. Some subsequent authors referred readers to the venerable Temple rather than wasting ink on the Low Countries; whilst others simply copied his analysis, failing to acknowledge either their source or the possibility that Dutch society might have altered since Temple looked at it.[34] As a result, the Dutch were condemned for aping the fashions of Louis XIV's court, long after that king and his fashionable courtiers had died.[35] English travel literature was thus an unexpectedly homogenous product. Written semi-collaboratively over the years, its view of abroad could remain curiously frozen.

A second set of fears about travel literature as a key to English confessional geography concerns the connection between the guides and their readers. Put most simply, we might be afraid that the attitudes revealed in these works actually found little echo in their audience, or that that audience was not wide enough to tell us much about the English as a whole. Discussing these fears takes us to extremely knotty problems about the relationship between 'print culture' and a less easily recoverable 'popular culture', but we need to enter this bear-pit if we are to assess the true significance of the travellers' accounts.

[31] Thompson, *Travels*, preface.
[32] Edward Wright, *Some observations made in travelling* (2 vols., 1730), I:vi.
[33] Philippe de Blainville, *Travels through Holland, Germany* (3 vols., 1743–5), I:preface.
[34] Burnet, *Some letters*, p. 298; [William Carr], *An accurate description of the United Netherlands* (1691), preface.
[35] E.g. Nugent, *Grand tour*, I:42.

The easiest place to start would be the impact of the published works on their direct users. Here, the key evidence is the writings of those who toured Europe under our commentators' guidance. Following the encouragement of our authors to travel, English people did so, and by the early eighteenth century there was a recognised 'grand tour' of the continent, undertaken by many as a finishing touch to their education.[36] A good number of these people produced personal records of their journey: either keeping diaries of the trip, or forced to write letters home to parents or patrons who were paying for the whole experience, the tourists recorded their own impressions. Comparing these to the published accounts can tell us something about the volumes' impact, and generally the comparison brings good news. Ordinary travellers do seem to have shared many of the interests and judgements of the guides. They kept close to the recommended routes, they visited the places thought most remarkable in their books, and they parroted many of the comments on the beauty, richness, rareness or morality of what they saw. Thus Jeremy Black, in his excellent modern surveys of the grand tour, can quote manuscript and published accounts almost interchangeably to illustrate English experiences and attitudes: whilst John Evelyn, as a specific example, only wrote in his diary what he could add to the authoritative guides he consulted.[37]

Reflecting *why* there should be such parallels between published and more ordinary travellers, we recognise the hold guides had over audiences. Travellers went to the same places and looked at the same things as their books because they were using these volumes to tell them what was worth seeing. The authors were thus shaping their readers' experiences, and influenced them further by telling them what to think of what they saw. Some writers acknowledged this explicitly, warning that people should follow their guides, or risk a too highly personalised and incoherent experience. Alexander Drummond, for example, criticised those who ignored the works of other travellers, suggesting that 'those things which made the deepest impression upon their own imagination' were unlikely to be those which would be of more general interest or instruction.[38] Beyond this shaping of the tour as it occurred, the guides also controlled memories of it after it had happened. Just as a modern tourist's photographs can *become* the holiday when they recall it later, continued possession of the guidebook – with its authoritative descriptions of what was witnessed – must have moulded what earlier

[36] E.g. Christopher Hibbert, *The grand tour* (1987); Edward Chaney, *The evolution of the grand tour* (1998); and works by Black, next footnote.

[37] Jeremy Black, *The British and the grand tour* (1987); Jeremy Black, *The British abroad: the grand tour in the eighteenth century* (1992); Brennan, *Origin*, p. 33. The Black volumes include useful bibliographies of the most accessible manuscript records.

[38] Drummond, *Travels*, p. 1.

readers thought they had seen. This was a process as good as acknowledged by one guide to Paris. Those who had not been to France would find the work valuable; but 'others who have had the satisfaction of seeing what is here mentioned, will not find it unpleasant to refresh their memory with the descriptions given in this book'.[39]

A less easily bridgeable gulf between travel literature and popular attitudes is the social status of writers and readers. Of course, authors were leisured men with time and resources to tour and to write; and the price of most of the large guides restricted the potential audience. We are, therefore, looking at an elite genre, composed by and appealing to a narrow class of people, who may have been atypical of the English as a whole. Proper discussion of this objection is important, but it might take longer than analyis of the guides themselves. It would involve entering debates about the precise differences between elite and mass culture; whether a society steeped in print could be influenced by literature even if it was expensive; and whether elite writings actually reflected widely held prejudices. Rather than take these lengthy diversions, therefore, it may be best merely to note warnings about the social representativeness of the writing at this stage, and provide evidence later that its vision of Europe had wider purchase. As the argument of this book unfolds, the attitudes we are about to explore will be found in many different types of work, absorbed by a very popular and diverse readership.[40] This will be the best proof that the guides were reflecting something real and deep-seated in English views of abroad.

So if travel literature gives us insight into English perceptions of Europe after the civil war, what does it tell us? The first and most important thing is that the English still saw the continent as profoundly divided along religious lines. If not all writers were as rude about Catholic countries as Burnet had been – and if many openly welcomed the new spirit of religious accommodation which seemed to advance in Europe after 1648 – almost all retained a keen sense of religious distinctions. In the guides there was a discrete *Protestant* Europe (sometimes subdivided into Lutheran and Calvinist realms); and there was a very different and separate Catholic Europe. Writers saw it as a crucial task to define the characteristics and boundaries of each.

This sense of division was most clear in the careful rhetorical mapping of the two continents. Although there were no actual, diagrammatic maps of the divisions (in fact, the sparcity of cartography of any kind was a remarkable feature of the travel genre), the writers' prose carefully assigned each square mile of land to one faith or the other. Countries, cantons, cities – even

[39] Germain Brice, *A new description of Paris* (1687), epistle.

[40] E.g. the use of images of Catholic Europe during the exclusion crisis, or anti-Dutch stereotypes during conflict. See below, pp. 132–52, 229–30.

individual streets, fields or buildings – belonged in a Protestant block or to the rival popish one; and the exact territory of each had to be painstakingly described. Good examples of this mapping can be drawn from Nugent's *Grand tour*. Coming at the end of our period, and summarising the finds of many other writers, Nugent exemplified all the authors' obsession with delineating confessional boundaries. Despite a dry and factual tone, which betrayed few signs of particular religious sympathies, the author assumed his readers would want to understand exactly how rival faiths had carved up the continent, and that they would be interested in this from the broadest to the most detailed level. Taking an eagle's perspective, the *Grand tour* used religion to explain the broad structure of Europe. For example, it opened its account of Germany with a section on the country's 'divisions'. It stated that the most received division of the region was into the political circles of the Holy Roman Empire (Lower Saxony, Swabia and so on) – but then went on to say another 'very natural' way to describe the whole area was by its ecclesiastical government.[41] What followed was a list of the medieval dioceses of Germany and Switzerland, and then a categorisation of these by their modern religion. Although most dioceses had remained Catholic, Nugent explained, 'there are two archiepiscopal and thirteen episcopal sees that have been secularised . . . in favour of protestants [he then listed these]. We may add *Osnabruck*, which the catholics and Lutherans possess alternately. The Calvinists are in possession of Geneva and Lausanne.'[42] A little later, Nugent was careful to counter the idea that Germany should be assigned to Protestant Europe. Although the reformation had started in the country, great swathes of it had not been converted, and its credentials as a mainstay of Protestantism were weakening. The greatest part of the country, it was explained, still adhered to the Roman communion, and that church had 'been greatly gaining ground within this century, by the change which some of the greatest protestant princes, such as the duke of Neuberg, the elector of Saxony, the duke of Wurtemburg, have made of their religion'.[43]

Such writing provided an overall picture of the religious fissuring of the continent. Nugent, however, did not stop there. As he moved from overall survey, to place-by-place description, he supplemented the broad view with larger-scale mapping of individual towns. Along with many others, he gave a prominent place to the religion of all the major urban settlements, and so ensured each town was instantly assigned to one confessional block or another. Hamburg, therefore, was categorised as a Lutheran city, as were Nuremburg and Frankfurt; whilst Heidelberg was Calvinist and Metz and Erfurt predominantly Catholic. Where places were not overtly labelled, Nugent's information on their political masters, or his stress on

[41] Nugent, *Grand tour*, II:11 [42] Ibid., II:12. [43] Ibid., II:53.

clearly confessional features such as convents, assigned them pretty clearly. Augsburg was odd because it did not fit neatly into a spiritual block, but Nugent explained this was the result of a peculiar historical decision. When the imperial Diet had met there in 1555 to negotiate a religious peace, it had come to a near-unique settlement for its host which had allowed full liberty for both faiths.[44] Focusing still more tightly, Nugent assigned particular precincts or even streets and buildings to confessional rivals. He was careful to note anomalous enclaves, or close juxtapositions, of faith; and paid particular attention when a city contained different confessions, or when the territories of a rival religion began just outside town walls. Describing Cleve, for example, the *Grand tour* noted how the ground held by the dominant religion was intimately intermixed with the territory of its rivals: 'As the town is subject to the king of *Prussia*, the government is protestant, but the *Roman* catholics have most of the churches here as well as in the rest of duchy, by virtue of an agreement made with the elector *Palatine*.'[45] In all this, Nugent followed a century of careful religious cataloguing. Many other writers had placed jurisdictions, towns and buildings in one confessional block or other: to fly back to the beginning of our period, Lassels' description of one mixed area shows how sensitive travellers could be to detailed divisions.

> Sometimes in one days Journey I passed into a *Papal Canton*, and by and by into a *Protestant Canton* again, for here Papist and Protestant Villages are mingl'd together, and make the County look like the back side of a pair of Tables – chequer'd white and black. In one Village you have a Cross set up, to signifie that it is Papal, belonging to the Canton of *Friburg*; by and by, is another Village with the picture of a Bear in it, to signifie that it belongs to the Canton of *Berne*, and is Protestant.[46]

Such close attention to confessional territory suggests the English remained highly sensitive to the religious division of Europe well into the eighteenth century. Certainly in some accounts old animosities had drained away. Although some writers condemned popish Europe, others merely delineated it, and many praised examples of peaceful coexistence between faiths. Yet for all this, the writers went on mapping. They continued to believe they must make clear where Protestant Europe stopped and Catholic Europe began, and even those who noted religious tolerance showed it required meticulous observance of boundaries when populations lived side by side. Thus, there were places where Protestants and Catholics cohabited, but this cohabitation only worked because of intricate division of territory. Maximilion Misson chronicled the phenomenon particularly closely (perhaps because his history as an exiled French Protestant interested him in the conditions necessary for

[44] Ibid., II:335. [45] Ibid., I:201. [46] Lassels, *Voyage*, pt 1, p. 51.

toleration), so his 1695 travels explained that mixed populations were possible because of a strict spatial division of worship. Almost all towns had an official faith and so belonged squarely in a confessional block, but minorities could be accepted if they withdrew from the general run of the city to extremely precise places for religious service. Thus at Nuremburg, Roman Catholics could live in the Lutheran town. However, they were few in number and had 'but half a church' where they were suffered to worship.[47] At Worms, the Catholics dominated: but Lutherans had the use of one church and a pulpit in the Dominican convent, and the Calvinists could worship in a church in Newhawsel 'in the Palatinate, about half a League from the City'.[48] At Cologne and at Metz, Protestants were safe in devoutly Catholic cities, but, like the Calvinists of Worms, had to leave the walls to praise God.[49] Other writers may not have had Misson's personal interest in religious accommodations, but they nevertheless detailed how confessions spatially separated themselves on Sundays. For instance, de Blainville corrected Misson's particulars, but still noted the division of denominations. Misson had said Cologne's Lutherans could only worship on the nearby 'Lands of the Duke of *Newbourg*'.[50] The later writer agreed some worshipped there, but also pointed out they had a designated church within the city itself.[51]

Sometimes, writers admitted, different confessions did use exactly the same space. Yet even in these examples the sense of different Europes, separated by confession, remained keen. Often, for instance, readers were told of rigid rules governing *when* the different confessions might move into shared places. In these cases temporal divisions replaced strictly spatial ones: or one might say that the spatial division remained clear, but that it moved at particular moments as different communities occupied particular spaces, temporarily shifting the exact boundaries of Protestant and Catholic Europe. Thus the half-church in Nuremburg in which Catholics might worship was only available once the Lutherans had finished their service in the rest of the building.[52] Similarly, the 'Protestant' pulpit in Worms was actually only Protestant on alternate Sundays (the Dominican friars preached from it every other week); whilst in Spire, Edward Brown reported that 'the *Romanists*, the *Lutherans* and *Calvinists* preach[ed] . . . at several hours' in the cathedral.[53] This last practice of staggered worship was reported by travellers in many places to allow multiple use of church buildings. Burnet noted that in the mixed Appenzel and Glaris the papists and the Protestants alternated their times of service: one Sunday mass would precede a sermon, the next week it would be the other way round.[54]

[47] Misson, *New voyage*, I:76. [48] Ibid., I:56. [49] Ibid., I:35, 49. [50] Ibid., I:35.
[51] De Blainville, *Travels*, I:86. [52] Ibid., I:216. [53] Brown, *Brief account*, p. 122.
[54] Burnet, *Some letters*, p. 27.

Perhaps even more precise than this temporal division were the changes in behaviour noted when confessions did have to use one another's space. When people could not avoid trespassing on the territory of another religion, travel writers stressed that people showed a marked respect for the sensibilities of the territory they had invaded, and praised folk for keeping the peace by modesty when on alien ground. Joseph Addison, for example, described in detail the religious divisions in St Gall in Switzerland and showed how restraint by Catholics on Protestant land avoided disturbance. In the canton, jurisdiction was divided between a Calvinist town government and the Romish abbot of the monastery, but harmony was maintained in ways which might have lessons for divided communities today. The religions knew not to insult each other with triumphal displays and so toned down religious observance when on their rivals' soil. In particular, priests knew not to hold crucifixes aloft in religious processions, except when they were on the abbot's estates.[55] Burnet was so pleased by this Swiss sensitivity that he hinted that God had intervened to preserve it. In one valley of Grisons, he reported that Catholics had traditionally shown respect by lowering the cross and ceasing singing when on Protestant ground. However, on an occasion in the early 1680s when tension had flared, providence had reimposed the old order. Local papists had tried to drive a passage through a reformed village whilst still celebrating their procession, but when they had been blocked by the inhabitants and had called for reinforcements, a minor miracle occurred. Although two thousand Catholics arrived to intimidate the Protestants, a thick mist fell and scared them into retreating when they mistook a wood for 'a vast body of men' ranged against them.[56] Bloody battle was avoided, and the old accommodation survived.

Other writers were less sure that God would police delicate territorial sensitivity, but they described the phenomenon just the same. Peter Heylyn, for example, saw how the communities of Rouen had very different uses for the bell which accompanied the host through the town. Whilst Catholics heard it as a call to prayer, Protestants used it as a warning not to go onto the streets.[57] Misson similarly recorded the people of several German cities avoiding clashes. In Duisberg, Catholics had the right to carry the Host in public but desisted as they did not want to disturb 'the peaceable manner of living which they and the Protestants enjoy together'. In Frankfurt, the Catholics avoided processions into the Protestant streets beyond their church. In Mannheim, the church of Concord – which was used by Calvinists, Lutherans *and* Romanists – illustrated how respectful behaviour could combine with temporal division to make sharing space possible. All three

[55] Addison, *Remarks*, pp. 491–3. [56] Burnet, *Some letters*, pp. 73–4.
[57] Peter Heylyn, *The voyage of France* (1673), p. 15.

confessions worshipped in the building on Sunday; but the services took place one after the other using a rota to decide who started first, and the Catholics – knowing that the sight of an altar offended the other two religions – pulled a curtain over it once they had finished mass.[58]

In all these examples, writers portrayed religious mingling but did not blur the separation of Protestant and Catholic territory. Indeed, as writers explained the precise arrangements which made mixed living possible they mapped divisions ever more intricately. They showed boundaries running along town walls, down streets, and even through the body of individual churches. They showed how these borders could shift by yards at particular moments to give one group use of a pulpit or a chapel; and they charted the acute sense of the territorial division in the local populations. For these English writers, religious peace might be welcome after the turmoil of the sixteenth century, but Europe remained fundamentally divided.

THE POPISH CONTINENT

If we accept that travel writers visited separated continents, the next stage is to ask what their perceptions of each of these continents were. Here it is harder to generalise, as attitudes and descriptions varied considerably. Whilst some guides wished to perpetuate a view of popery as an evil empire, others took a more moderate line, trying to understand the Catholic way of life or at least simply reporting it. Again, whilst descriptions of Protestant countries were usually sympathetic, there were critics of the avarice (in Holland), the autocracy (in Denmark), the overzealous iconoclasm (in Huguenot France), or the hostility to English interests (almost everywhere) which could be found in parts of the reformed world.[59] Probably there was a fading of bigotry over the century after the civil war. Mid-Georgian travellers could be more inclined than their predecessors to privilege observed facts over editorial opinions.[60] Yet whilst this trend was real, it was not clear-cut. Rabidly anti-popish travels were still produced in the high eighteenth century (including some salaciously scurrilous attacks), and one of the most benign views of Catholicism – Lassels' – was the earliest work in the corpus.[61] All periods, therefore, saw a spectrum of presentations of the rival Europes. Beneath this diversity, however, there were some standard features. One of the most

[58] Misson, *New voyage*, I:32, 50, 60–1.

[59] E.g. Ellis Veryard, *An account of divers choice remarks . . . taken in a journey through the Low Countries* (1701), pp. 22–3; Bromley, *Several years travels*, p. 260; Heylyn, *Voyage*, p. 210.

[60] Jeremy Black has detected a softening of attitude: Black, *British abroad*, pp. 248–9.

[61] For one late attack on popery: *A trip to the jubilee by a gentleman that was at the late grand one in Rome* (1750).

important relates to the Catholic realm. Although not all writers were overtly hostile to the forms of life found in Italy, France, Spain and large parts of Germany, almost all presented these regions as strange and alien. They were more peculiar, more different from England, than the Netherlands, northern Germany or Scandinavia.

The extraordinary nature of Catholic Europe was, of course, most obvious in the passages which *were* hostile to it. These offered an analysis of popery which denigrated the territory it controlled as visions of perversity. Significantly, this analysis leant on reformation-era dissections of Rome. The first generations of English Protestants had defended their faith with an account of what they dressed as the destructive progress of Catholicism, and their account had solidified into a standard model of popish corruption which would heavily influence the later travel guides. At the core of this analysis was the insistence that popery was an anti-religion. Rather than fixing its eyes on God, Catholicism had been driven by the avarice of its priests. They had wanted a faith which would deliver the riches and authority of their flock into their hands, and had consequently set about subverting the gospel. Their first target had been scripture. Knowing that Christ's message of humility and modesty would undermine their ambitions, the clergy had ensured ordinary folk would have little access to it. They had hidden the bible in Latin (a language which few understood), and then they had obscured the word of God in a mass of later doctrine which they had themselves invented. Once scripture had been neutralised, clerics redesigned Christianity to suit their ends. They had insisted they took precedence over all lay authority; they had used the temporal power this brought to persecute critics; and they had encouraged beliefs and practices which enriched them. Most perniciously, Protestants claimed Christians had been told gifts to the clergy brought spiritual benefits. If the faithful paid for masses, built monasteries or gave offerings at sacred sites, they would gain the grace which could shorten their sufferings in an invented post-death purgatory. In case anyone should uncover the deception (and this might be possible through biblical study, use of reason, or direct prayer to God), priests had devised a welter of distractions. Worship had been designed to dazzle men out of their senses. Elaborate ritual, artistic splendour and appeal to powerful emotions swept everyone into believing priestly lies. Similarly, attention to the one true God was diverted to a host of false sub-deities. Priests claimed there was a divine essence in the bread and wine consecrated during mass; whilst saints, relics and images were said to have supernatural and semi-autonomous powers.[62]

[62] Most anti-Catholic polemic was founded on this picture. For modern analysis: Peter Lake, 'Anti-popery: the structure of a prejudice', in Richard Cust and Anne Hughes, eds., *Conflict in early Stuart England* (Harlow, 1989), pp. 72–106.

Perhaps the best example of a guide influenced by this sixteenth-century analysis was Gilbert Burnet. A Protestant Scot, who had become an anglican clergyman on moving to London and starting a career at the royal court, he had fought the Rome-leaning factions which surrounded Charles II, and had been forced into exile in the reign of the Catholic James II.[63] He might therefore be seen still waging reformation-era battles, and this helps explain why his *Some letters concerning . . . Switzerland* (written during his reluctant continental sojourn in the mid-1680s) catalogued the standard popish evils outlined by reformation writers. So although Burnet's description raced through a France the author felt was familiar to Englishmen, it paused long enough to comment on the relative poverty of the people compared to the riches of Catholic churches.[64] Once in Switzerland, the account slowed because the country was less well known, but also because it allowed Burnet to paint the horror of popery clearly. Consisting, as it did, of an alliance of Catholic and Protestant cantons, the Swiss confederation gave ample opportunity to contrast the perversions of the former with the sanity of the latter. Thus whilst Geneva and Zurich were praised for their just government and honest charitable foundations, the Catholic cantons were scenes of extreme bigotry.[65] In papist regions, for example, it was a capital offence to be converted from the Roman religion, though converts from Protestantism in reformed states only lost their property.[66] Religious services also distinguished the two faiths. Whilst Protestants listened soberly to sermons, papists worshipped with all the overcharged emotion and superstition one would expect. In Fribourg and Soloturn the excesses were extraordinary. Burnet explained that the religious images in both towns were 'extreme gross' and that long before they came to church, the locals 'kneel down in the streets when Masse is saying'.[67] Elsewhere, Burnet commented on the ridiculous miracle stories which sprang up in almost every Catholic village, and stressed the intolerant paranoia which papists encouraged against their unbelieving neighbours. Yet it was in Berne that his prejudice overflowed. Breaking into an otherwise matter-of-fact overview of the city, Burnet lovingly related a ten-page story from the town's pre-reformation days which painted its medieval faith in the blackest colours.

The events of the story, Burnet claimed, had occurred around 1500. The background was the intense rivalry between the Franciscans and Dominicans, and particularly the latter's resentment that the former were cashing in on devotion to the Virgin Mary by arguing she had been born without

[63] T. E. S. Clarke and H. C. Foxcroft, *A life of Gilbert Burnet* (Cambridge, 1907), is so comprehensive that Burnet has not received the recent attention he deserves, but Martin Greig, 'Burnet, Gilbert', in *ODNB*, VIII:908–23, is illuminating.

[64] Burnet, *Some letters*, p. 4. [65] Ibid., pp. 7–12, 46–50. [66] Ibid., p. 26.

[67] Ibid., pp. 43–4.

original sin. Dominicans had long rejected this notion of an 'immaculate conception', and when a Franciscan preacher had denounced them as heretics for this, they decided to act. The instrument of their plan was to be an impressionable lay brother by the name of Jetzer. Knowing that this young friar was pious and credulous, one of the leaders of the Dominican convent resolved to play upon his acute concern for salvation. Accordingly, his superior burst into his cell to impersonate a soul in purgatory. He dressed 'in a strange figure'; he had a pyrotechnic box near his mouth which made seem he was breathing fire; and he took some dogs along to play his tormentors. Once Jetzer had been terrified by this vision, he was told to lie prostrate in a chapel as mass was said. When the young friar followed the instructions, the leaders of the plot knew they had him in their power and staged more spectaculars to mould him into a passive tool of the conspiracy. Several appeared as devils. One dressed as 'a Nun in Glorie, and told the poor Friar that she was St Barbara, for whom he had a particular devotion'. Finally, the head of the house visited as the Blessed Virgin Mary accompanied by angels which were actually plaster statues attached by cords to fly about the impostor's head. In her interview with Jetzer, the fake Mary told him she was born in original sin as the Dominicans asserted, and ordered him to spread this word. Jetzer noted that the virgin had a voice that 'resembled the Prior's', but at first thought little of this and organised special services to relay Mary's message. To ensure he was believed, the plotters stirred Jetzer into a religious mania. They injured him with the five wounds of Christ and slipped him poisons to produce severe convulsions. As he recovered from these, a conspirator spoke down a tube to a hole behind a statue of Mary above the high altar. This told the congregation she was weeping to see the Franciscans spreading lies about her: the performances drew crowds to the Dominican convent, and outdid Franciscan efforts to retain popular devotion. Eventually, the pretence became too gross even for Jetzer. Investigating similarities between his visions and senior colleagues, he was undeceived. At first, the prior and the others persuaded him to keep up the performance to preserve his reputation, but Jetzer was angry and dangerous (he had nearly killed one friar who appeared to him as the Queen of Heaven) and the plotters decided they must silence him. They tried to poison him with a tainted eucharist, but when that failed, they beat him with chains, telling him he would suffer worse torments than that if he ever revealed their secrets. In the end, Jetzer told all to the city magistrates. The bishop investigated the affair, and ejected the friars who had carried it on.[68]

There were several reasons for Burnet to expand on this story at such length. He himself said that the tale explained the hole in the wall behind the

[68] Ibid., pp. 31–42.

statue of the virgin; that he wished to report his own research of the story in the city archives; and that the events might even account for the reformation in the town. The melodrama had occurred only a few years before Luther's message arrived, so it was 'very probable . . . that it contributed not a little to the preparing of the Spirits of the People'.[69] Yet Burnet also concentrated on Jetzer's story because it perfectly illustrated his worldview, proving almost every part of the reformation-era analysis of popery. Thus the tale's basic dynamic was clerical aggrandisement. Rather than trying to lead their flocks to God, friars had tried to outdo each other in capturing the devotion of the laity. They had done this by leading people from the bible: Franciscans promoting devotion to a Virgin whom they claimed (unscripturally) was born without sin; Dominicans responding with ghostly messages from a fictitious purgatory. Throughout, invented sub-deities and emotional assaults abounded, and when these failed to convince, the church had resorted to bullying. Given all this, the story was impossible for Burnet to resist. It confirmed every accusation he had ever believed against Rome and became emblematic of the whole religion in his book. As the author commented, this 'was certainly one of the blackest and yet the best Carried on Cheat that has been ever known', but most other miracles of the Roman church were likely to have been 'of the same nature, but more successfully finished'.[70]

Burnet may have been an extreme case of anti-popish fervour, but he was not alone. A good proportion of the travel writers repeated the standard Protestant charges even if they did not put the case so systematically. Many, for example, made the economic arguments against the Roman church. In their works, southern Europe was shaped by the avarice of the clergy, and this gave it a very different appearance and character from England. Most notable was the grinding poverty of popish societies. Some of those who travelled through France, many who visited Italy and almost all who went to Spain were shocked by the lot of ordinary people. Guides commented on the meagre diet, the mean housing and the ragged clothes of locals, and they were especially disgusted by the huge armies of beggars whom they met in on the roads.[71] Other writers noted the endless decay of trade in Catholic cities, and there was widespread regret at the wasted lives of the idle unemployed. William Bromley's remarks on the Iberian peninsula were perhaps the most horrified. He had been surprised by the 'great Indications of Poverty' he had seen in the French realm, but things were yet worse over the Pyrenees.[72] The poor there 'do certainly fare as bad as any People whatsoever', he told his

[69] Ibid., p. 30. [70] Ibid., pp. 41–2.

[71] Addison, *Remarks*, p. 14; [William Bromley], *Remarks made in travels through France and Italy* (1693 edn; citations below are to this edition), pp. 73–4; Wright, *Some observations*, I:124.

[72] [Bromley], *Remarks made*, p. 12.

readers. 'Hundreds of Families during the course of their Lives never taste Meat', and there was 'nothing of good Husbandry or Industry encouraged'.[73] In fact, the situation was so terrible that Bromley could not recommend going to Spain at all. There were so few provisions that the tourist himself might become short of food, and the standard of accommodation was dangerously low.[74] The result was a sort of anti-guide. Bromley thought Spain so poor that he discouraged the discovery of foreign places which his own preface recommended.[75]

The writers who chronicled such dearth had little doubt about its causes. Although they admitted that absolutist governments in southern Europe played some role, they were adamant that most blame lay with corrupted faith. It was the doleful effects of rapacious Catholicism which produced the pervasive poverty: writers stressed economic hardship was *not* the result of climate or geography. Many parts of Catholic Europe were poor despite fruitful soil and favourable weather, and there were prosperous Protestants living close to papists who made a good living from local resources. Thus William Carr noted that unreformed Cologne was needy, even though it was among the most fertile plains of Germany. The 'priest-ridden' population was so wretched 'that Canvas Cloathes, Wooden Shoes and Straw to sleep . . . were the greatest worldly Happiness that most of them can attain to'.[76] Other writers concurred. John Ray noted that reformed Zurich was the envy of the contiguous Swiss papists, whilst Joseph Shaw drew contrasts between the Dutch and the Spanish Netherlands, noting that the Romanists in Flanders had squandered trading opportunities which were exploited in provinces immediately north and which had turned Amsterdam and Rotterdam into thriving ports.[77] To clinch the argument, some showed cities became poor only when they became popish. Towns in southern Flanders, for example, had ejected their Protestant populations in the earlier seventeenth century, and had immediately lost out to the more dynamic centres of Holland.[78] Similarly Strasbourg had done well until French conquest brought it into the Catholic world, and the countryside around Rome – described in classical texts as fruitful and beautiful – had now been depopulated by the avarice of the pontiffs, and turned into a noxious wasteland.[79]

If writers chronicled the hardship suffered by ordinary Catholics, they were even more keen to show where their money had gone – namely into

[73] Bromley, *Several years travels*, p. 30. [74] Ibid., p. 62.
[75] Also, *A trip to Spain, or a true description of the comical humours, ridiculous customs and foolish laws* (1705).
[76] [Carr], *Accurate description*, pp. 83, 85.
[77] Ray, *Observations*, p. 102; Shaw, *Letters*, pp. 71–2.
[78] Northleigh, *Topographical descriptions*, pp. 196–7.
[79] [Carr], *Accurate description*, pp. 95–6. For the campagna, see Addison, *Remarks*, pp. 179–84; [Stephen Whatley], *A short account of a late journey to Tuscany, Rome* (1741), pp. 16–20.

the coffers of the priests. Usually they did this by contrasting the mean lives of laymen with the luxury of the clerical estate. In many accounts, it was economic inequality between church and society which really marked southern Europe, not just general poverty. Joseph Addison's account of Italy is typical. Its opening sections juxtaposed passages on the suffering of ordinary Italians with descriptions of the vast ecclesiastical wealth, and tacitly invited the reader to make the connection. Thus there were beggars on the roads outside Milan, but in the city's churches 'it would be endless to count up the Riches of Silver, Gold, and Precious Stones'.[80] Other writers agreed there were unacceptable inequalities of wealth; and some were more explicit about how these had come about. At the heart of the process was that clerical deception which was central to the old model of Catholic corruption. Priests had falsely claimed they could give spiritual advantage to people who paid them for their services, so Sacheverell Stephens, describing how Parisians made gifts to the clergy to finance masses for dead, protested how 'easily are people in popish countries deluded of their money'.[81] Others noted how tales of miracles were used to rake in cash at pilgrimage sites: money donated was thought to grease the wheels of divine favour, and make it more likely that people's business would be blessed, or their diseases cured.[82] All over the Catholic continent, folk in the most desperate circumstances would worsen their lot further by giving what little they had to avaricious priests in vain hopes of supernatural relief. Overall, many writers agreed with Francis Willoughby's first item on his list of reasons for the poverty of Spain. For him the most important explanation for dearth was simply 'A bad Religion'.[83]

Clerical greed was one feature of the Catholic continent. For our writers, gross superstition, idolatry and hysteria were others. In their accounts, as in so much earlier writing, Catholic worship was not centred on God, but rather involved abasement before man-made idols. Some of the easiest targets were the wonder-working relics and images. Writers sometimes denounced these angrily as blasphemous fakes, but more often they used humour to mock what Addison called the 'bungling tricks' of the clergy.[84] Humour lightened the guides' prose, and allowed them to avoid the intolerant tone of earlier Protestants without abandoning their basic case. As Edward Wright explained, he included some amusing superstitions as examples to illustrate

[80] Addison, *Remarks*, p. 32. The author of *A supplement to Dr Burnet's letters* (1687) thought those under the pope's temporal authority 'the most miserable on earth', p. 16.

[81] Sacheverell Stephens, *Miscellaneous remarks made on the spot* (1754), pp. 19–20.

[82] The attacks on superstition over the next few pages all had a financial element.

[83] Francis Willoughby, *A relation of a voyage made through a great part of Spain* (1673), p. 493.

[84] Addison, *Remarks*, p. 196. See also William Lucas, *A five weeks tour to Paris* (2nd edn, 1753), p. 33 – religious remains at St Denis were 'most pleasing to Children, or very young People'.

the general farce of popular Catholicism: 'they are laughed at indeed by Men of Sense, even there, but as they have their Effect upon the weaker Minds in subjugating them still more to the Power of the Priests'.[85] Following such encouragement, many writers made merry with Catholic traditions. A favoured tactic was to jest about the lameness of the frauds perpetrated. Anyone with any sense could see through the priests' tricks: it was a sad reflection on the faithful that they, alone, could not. William Bromley went down this line describing the body of St Antony at Padua. The tongue of this holy man was supposed to be incorruptible, and was paraded through the streets in a crystal case to celebrate its supernatural preservation. Bromley, however, commented, 'I could not look upon it of any great Authority; for I observed it was black and withered, and cannot but believe those who have the Art of embalming Bodies, may preserve any one's Tongue to appear as well.'[86] The rest of St Antony was left rather more peacefully in its tomb, but ridiculous subterfuge affected it too.

> The Fryars take care to keep this Sepulchre perfum'd, and the common People are made to believe that to be the Odour of Sanctity . . . but this fallacy is easily detected, for his Stone in the Morning smells very strong, in the Afternoon grows more languid, till by the People kissing it, and rubbing their Beads upon it, the Perfume is spent and gone.[87]

The saint had reputedly performed many other wonders besides body embalming and air freshening, but for Bromley he would work his greatest miracle 'if he could convert those of his Order, and reduce them to a more sober, regular way of Living'.[88]

Another route to humour was to pile up miracle stories to the point of absurdity. Misson, for example, repeated with a straight face the huge number of traditions surrounding the bones St Ursula at Cologne, but by the time readers get to the tale of a corpse that floated out of the soil, and to a patch of ground which would only support virgins, they are quietly laughing with the author.[89] John Clenche used a similar technique at St Peter's in Rome, though here the guide's attitude burst out in more overtly dry comment.

> The most considerable Reliques are the Spear that Wounded Christ's Side, the Handkerchief He wiped his Face with; a piece of the Holy Cross, some of the Hay that lay on in the Manger; the great Pincers or Plyers, with which they took the Primitive Saints in pieces; the Head of Thomas Becket of Canterbury, with as many Arms, Leggs, Ribbs &c as would Re-build him at the Resurrection.[90]

For John Northleigh, meanwhile, the excess was quite literal. He complained that in the chapel of St Louis in Paris, priests displayed all the relics of the

[85] Wright, *Some observations*, I:ix. [86] [Bromley], *Remarks made*, p. 79.
[87] Bromley, *Several years travels*, p. 207. [88] Ibid., p. 208.
[89] Misson, *New voyage*, I:37–9. [90] [Clenche], *Tour in France*, p. 45.

passion (spear, sword, sponge, vinegar and the whole robe), even though the spear was also supposed to be in Rome, and in spite of scripture's assurance that the robe had been divided. Meanwhile at Liège, more of Christ's teeth were worshipped than any person, even the Messiah, could reasonably have had.[91]

This treatment of miracle stories could be humorous because they tended to take in only the ignorant, and had few serious consequences beyond the wasted time and cash. However, other attacks on Catholic superstition were not so indulgent. For many writers, popish Europe was marked not only by absurdity, but by a sustained attempt to rob men of their reason – even of their humanity – which could not be forgiven. At its least vile, the process involved luxurious theatricality. The Catholic church made use of sumptuous sights and sounds to excite men out of questioning priests, and in particular used art, rituals and plays to whip up pro-Catholic emotion. Popish Europe thus became an endless scene of festival and pageantry, as glorious religious services spilled out of churches onto streets, and swept all bystanders into the excitement. At Florence, for instance, Stephen Whatley reported such 'fopperies' taking up most of the population's lives. He began to describe the endless religious processions in the town, with their cloying clothing, images and enactments, but then abandoned the full catalogue because 'the frequency of such things became quite tiresome'.[92] Elsewhere, protests were entered at the inappropriate dressing up of worship, so that it became more of a glorious charade than sober religious service. John Northleigh, for instance, protested that the annual procession in Bruges to celebrate a miraculous bleeding host was 'over-acting it, and as it were, crucifying out Saviour afresh'.[93] Similarly, Alexander Drummond denounced the overblown plays staged by the church in Innsbruck. Spiritually they were outrageous, but he had to admit they worked 'politically' since 'all this mummery is calculated for inspiring the people with awe and veneration for the church: and in this point they never fail to succeed, let their expedients be never so ridiculous, or opposite to common sense'.[94]

Even more disturbing than this dazzling of men away from reason was the appeal to the grossest emotions. Several writers observed that priests could excite individuals to mania, and crowds to baying frenzies, by producing bloody spectacles of physical pain. In writing which most dramatically distanced Catholic Europe from English norms, guides stood amazed as clergy convinced men to suffer torments for piety's sake, and drove bystanders to encourage this through hysteria at the sight of suffering. The ever-critical

[91] Northleigh, *Topographical descriptions*, pp. 50, 158.
[92] [Whatley], *Short account*, p. 84. [93] Northleigh, *Topographical descriptions*, p. 140.
[94] Drummond, *Travels*, p. 15.

Sacheverell Stephens reported one Florentine procession in bloodcurdling vein. According to the author, the ceremony involved a man impersonating St John the Baptist, who rode on top of a 'large machine' which tossed him about as he moved through the streets. The crowd paid such noisy devotions to the spectacle that Stephens believed 'they took him for the real saint', but more shockingly still did nothing as the participant was horribly injured. The actors were often 'so dreadfully bruised, that they never recover, and so die martyrs to ignorance, superstition and folly'.[95] Writers also noted monks half-starved by their ascetic exercises in France, and processions of flagellants in Italy, and mused on what perversion of sense could lead men to such extreme behaviour.[96] Stephens was again horrified, and observed that clerics 'have introduced superstition, idolatry and darkness, deprived mankind of the light of their understandings, and have the matchless effortery to make their abominable system pass under the denomination of Christianity'.[97] In such passages, popish Europe mirrored hell. Here was a wholly alien society – beyond full comprehension, let alone ordinary standards of decency.

Yet despite such confirmation of the traditional picture of Catholic Europe, we cannot simply claim an older confessional geography had survived. Readers may have noticed – if they had not already been warned – that the quotations used above were selective. A few particularly angry writers (Burnet, Stephens, Addison) kept surfacing; many other examples were garnered from particularly ripe passages in travels whose overall tone was less judgemental. Yet although some writings were not so angry, examining them alters things less than we might imagine. Even in 'moderate' commentary, guides confirmed that Protestant and popish Europe were separate entities and described the two continents in different ways. The pope's kingdoms were an exotic contrast to the Protestant world, even for those not openly averse to their strangeness. Once we have outlined the chief difference in description, it may seem that the old reformation model of Catholic degeneration was still operating covertly. It shaped perceptions even when it did not burst through into condemnation.

The universally agreed divergence between northern and southern Europe was in their physical appearance. Virtually without exception, writers described continents contrasted by the sheer visibility of religion in the Catholic world. In papist countries, writers noted a faith which dominated the visual field with its buildings, artworks, ceremonies and symbols; whilst Protestantism seemed to play only a bit part in its own realm. This divergence

95 Stephens, *Miscellaneous remarks*, pp. 124–6.

96 E.g. Martin Lister, *A journey to Paris in the year 1698* (1699), pp. 18–20 – this attack came in a work satirised for its excessive praise of France: William King, *A journey to London in the year 1698 after the ingenious method of that made by Doctor Martin Lyster* (1699).

97 Stephens, *Miscellaneous remarks*, p. 212.

was evident in all writers, whether or not they called overt attention to it, and whether or not they thought it a sign of deeper evils.

The treatment of ecclesiastical buildings was the most obvious illustration of this fundamental point. In Protestant towns, travel writers would certainly note the chief church. They would describe its features and any unusual treasures it contained, and might well mention other churches, especially as part of their project to map the precise standing of denominations across the continent. However, such passages of religious architecture would not dominate description. Churches held their own among other public edifices but, as we shall see, they tended to do no more than that.[98] In Catholic towns, by dramatic contrast, religious establishments drowned all else out. Writers emphasized the huge number of cathedrals, chapels, monasteries, convents and religious charities, and so left the impression of communities huddling round their great ecclesiastical establishments.[99] John Northleigh's account of Paris spoke openly what many other writers tacitly implied. In the great French city, churches had covered the ground so thickly that everything else disappeared into their shadows. 'In these portions', the writer explained of the capital's core, 'they count 40 Parish Churches, 42 Abbies and Monasteries, 40 Nunneries, 24 Hospitals; 48 Colleges, besides about 17 small Churches or Chapels.' The concentration left little room for much else: 'Charity and Religion engrosses the best part of the town, even to compose it.'[100]

Northleigh, admittedly, was one of the more hostile witnesses of popish Europe, but his point that papist regions were crawling with churches was made across the spectrum of opinion. Take, for instance, Thomas Nugent at Rome. As we saw, Nugent aimed for a cool objective tone, but in the old imperial capital he gave a far greater prominence to ecclesiastical buildings than in his accounts of northern cities. He noted that there reckoned 'over three hundred fine churches' in Rome, and admitted that (even though he opened his section on the city with them) he could not detail them all unless he gave over his whole guide to this one subject.[101] Similarly John Ray restricted attacks on the Catholic religion to its greater excesses, but his powers of description wilted under the sheer number of religious houses in Italy. Summing up the country just before he left it, he called this number 'vast and incredible', and estimated it at between eight and ten thousand for the peninsula as a whole.[102] Edward Brown was another tolerant traveller, whose publication did little more than note the religion prevailing in the places he

[98] See below, pp. 52–3.

[99] E.g. [Laurence Echard], *Flanders or the Spanish Netherlands most accurately described* (1691), pp. 10–11, noted fifty religious houses in both Ghent and Bruges.

[100] Northleigh, *Topographical descriptions*, p. 5 (second pagination). Note also Lister, *Journey*, p. 7.

[101] Nugent, *Grand tour*, III:234. [102] Ray, *Observations*, p. 409.

visited. Yet on arriving at Cologne he was startled by the sudden prominence of ecclesiastical buildings, and – comparing the place to the headquarters of its religion – he suggested this was a defining mark of Catholicism. 'Most of the City are of the *Roman* Church', he observed, 'and the whole Town is so full of Convents, Churches, Churchmen and Relics, that it is not undeservedly styled the *Rome* of *Germany*.'[103] Many others agreed describing Catholicism meant describing a vast number of churches, and some succumbed to a kind of rhetorical strain injury. 'Churches for ever', de Blainville exclaimed, imagining the reader's despair at wading through his account of Naples.[104] 'The Churches are some of them very fine', sighed Wright at Bologna, 'but, after having said so much of those at *Rome* and *Naples, &c* I shall forebear enlarging upon those of that City.'[105] Fatigue caught up with Bromley even before he wrote up his observations. Abandoning church-hopping in Padua, he confessed, 'I had seen so many in Travelling thro' *Italy* that I was heartily weary of running into their Churches, when what I saw was only a Repetition of the same things over and over.'[106]

It was not only the sheer numbers of churches which dominated the Catholic scene. Some of these buildings were huge and prominently placed, so they constructed a total visual environment in which the eye could not escape religious architecture, and this too was stressed across the spectrum of opinion. At Rome, for instance, everyone from the anti-popish Burnet to the priest Lassels expressed astonishment at St Peter's. This largest church in the world was described as enveloping and overwhelming any worshipper who entered its caverns.[107] Catholic buildings filled and controlled vistas elsewhere. At Naples, most of John Clenche's account was taken up with the huge Carthusian convent, which brooded over all its inhabitants from its hilltop location.[108] At Milan, Burnet was impressed out of his usual snideness once he had paced the enormous Duomo and surveyed the 'royal' dimensions of the nearby hospital.[109] Outside Italy, writers reflected on the imposing presence of such great churches as Cologne's cathedral, or Notre Dame in Paris: and travellers sometimes described truly astonishing constructions, which constituted entire architectural landscapes.[110] At Bologna several were amazed at a portico, or covered walkway, which linked the town to an outlying shrine. According to Edward Wright, this ran 'three miles in length . . . from one of the City Gates along a Flat of a Mile and a half and

103 Brown, *Brief account*, p. 115. 104 De Blainville, *Travels*, III:304.
105 Wright, *Some observations*, II:435. 106 Bromley, *Several years travels*, p. 210.
107 Burnet, *Some letters*, p. 225; Lassels, *Voyage*, pt 2, pp. 26–46. See also David Jefferies, *A journal from London to Rome by way of Paris* (1755), p. 67.
108 [Clenche], *Tour in France*, p. 95. 109 Burnet, *Some letters*, pp. 105–8.
110 E.g. *A view of Paris and places adjoining* (1701), p. 3; Abel Boyer, *The draught of the most remarkable fortified towns in Europe* (1701), p. 22 – this was a catalogue of fortifications, but described the towns contained within, so came close to the travel guides.

from there for a Mile and a half more up an Ascent to a little Church on the top of a Hill, where is lodg'd a Picture of the *Blessed Virgin*'.[111] By this means, what had started life as an unimpressive chapel, hidden away in the mountains, had become a major landmark.

The Bologna portico had been built to stage processions from the city to the image of the virgin. This brings us to another aspect of Catholicism's dominance of its realm, namely its use of ceremony to extend its presence beyond buildings. We have stressed Catholic ritual already: those hostile to popery accused it of employing religious performance to induce hysteria, or invade Protestant territory. Here, however, we must note a feature of processions on which all agreed. Catholic ritual was visually commanding: it operated on a large scale, involved ranks of participants, and was marked by colour, drama and spectacle. It therefore filled the streets, captivated the attention of bystanders, and suspended all non-religious business. Curiously, some of the most vivid examples came from uses of livestock in ceremony. As Stephen Whatley related, one mass blessing of animals in Padua involved 'a thousands Horses, Mules and Asses' being driven through the city on the festival of St Antony to be sprinkled with holy water. If this did not disrupt urban life enough, it was accompanied by a 'masquerade procession', captivating the whole the population of the town.[112] In Ghent, the anonymous author of *A trip to the jubilee* explained that the citizens re-enacted the Holy Family's flight into Egypt on St Joseph's day. A young woman and baby were seated on an ass, and were paraded through the packed streets by a Capuchin friar, who blessed the assembled multitude as he impersonated the saint. The ritual ended in church (the first time the author had seen an ass in such a place, apart from the usual Catholic devotees) where townsmen massed to kiss the virgin's garment. Interestingly, the author of the *Trip* claimed this domination of urban space was policed by coercion as well as spectacle. He thought the event 'so preposterously comical' that he had to laugh, but his lack of restraint earned 'three knocks on the Pate' from people who forced him to kneel as the ass went by.[113]

Most of the evidence so far deployed to illustrate the visibility of Catholicism has been drawn from towns. Yet writers were also keen to emphasise faith in the countryside. By and large, comment on spaces between urban centres was very sparse for northern Europe. Our travellers toured before romanticism taught people to appreciate landscape, so cities remained the focus of attention, and any rural comment centred on agricultural productiveness, or the efficiency of local transport. In Catholic Europe too, cities were central, but here there was more description of the roads between

[111] Wright, *Some observations*, II:446–7. [112] [Whatley], *Short account*, preface.
[113] *Trip to the jubilee*, p. 24.

as writers noticed how remarkable the local religion made them appear. Catholic highways had signs and symbols of faith at frequent intervals along them. There were endless crucifixes and local shrines marking the route, and this was often the clearest signal that one had crossed onto Catholic territory. William Bromley noticed the change at the very start of his tour. On the way south from Calais, 'Crosses and crucifixes are so plentiful everywhere . . . that from them alone an *Englishman* will be satisfied he is out of his own Countrey.'[114] John Northleigh commented that 'in all these Countries on the Roads as you go along, are Crosses and Crucifixes, with little Chappels, some cut out in hollow Trees', and Stephen Whatley agreed, observing that roadside crucifixes and statues of saints became more frequent the nearer one got to Rome.[115] Elsewhere John Clenche noted the statue of Mary guiding travellers through a rut-cut road south of Naples; Edward Wright described the passes of the Tyrol marked by pictures of St George and St Martin; and Francis Willoughby observed that the grinding poverty of Spain did not choke off the ornamentation of the countryside. Spaniards, he noted, could not afford the elaborate little shrines and statues of France or Italy; but their fields were nevertheless littered with pathetic wooden crosses set up in piles of stones.[116]

Lifting their eyes above the immediate roadside, travellers noted how dominating symbols of Catholicism were placed on prominent sites. Monasteries and churches were sited on hilltops, and those not so elevated commanded the view with the sheer size of their buildings.[117] Many tracts of countryside were 'crowded with churches', and the large urban cathedrals and convents had domes, spires or towers so that they could be seen miles before one arrived.[118] Up in the mountains, highland roads were marked by crosses to guide the route, and church-run hostels were provided to shelter those venturing above the snowline. Lassels noted the Catholic paraphernalia at the top of the Mount Cenis pass, which turned the whole trip across the Alps into a lesson in charity and piety: 'We came to the top of hill, and a little after to the *Posthouse*, and the little *Hospital* upon the plain: Thence passing by the *Chappel*, of the *Transis* (that is, of those who are found dead in the snow, and are buryed here) we came to the *Great Cross* and *Tavern*.'[119] Elsewhere, religious art was used to control the view. At Seefeld in Germany, Alexander Drummond noted 'a famous crucifix of stone, in the hollow of a very high perpendicular rock'. It was inaccessible to any but those who dangled

[114] [Bromley], *Remarks made*, p. 4.
[115] Northleigh, *Topographical descriptions*, p. 150; [Whatley], *Short account*, p. 21
[116] [Clenche], *Tour in France*, p. 96; Wright, *Some observations*, II:495; Willoughby, *Relation of a voyage*, p. 496.
[117] E.g. the dominant placing of the huge church outside Turin: Jefferies, *Journal*, p. 33.
[118] Drummond, *Travels*, p. 7. [119] Lassels, *Voyage*, pt 1, p. 70.

over the cliff on a rope, but it had nevertheless been placed to inspire (and, local innkeepers insisted, to work miracles for) those below. Near Genoa, the same writer noted a huge statue of the virgin, set high and highly visible on a mountain. Locals held that the statue protected their flocks from sheep-rustlers, though Drummond observed they also relied on teams of watchmen housed in huts scattered among the slopes.[120]

Taken together, this stress on the visual dominance of religion in Catholic regions amounted to a wholesale sacralisation of the landscape. For English writers, the towns and countryside of the south were not spiritually neutral spaces (as their descriptions of Protestant Europe tended to leave them), but rather were huge theatres of Catholicism. Buildings, squares, fields and mountains: all were filled with religious meaning. At the very least, they became arenas in which the popish faith was to be practised. Streets in the Catholic continent were never simply streets, and meadows never simply meadows. Rather, they were stages for the next elaborate procession or ritual. More dramatically, the landscape itself carried spiritual messages. Shaped and ornamented by the church, territory was redesigned to inspire the faithful and to remind them of their confessional loyalties. Moreover, this sacralised landscape was exceptionally fertile. It not only provided the people with an inescapable memorial of their faith, but new monuments were springing up constantly, and invested territory with ever deeper spiritual meanings.

Alexander Drummond noticed the process as he described how the merest suggestion of divine action resulted in prominent commemoration. Some years before he toured Genoa, a boy had fallen from the town walls. Fortunately, he had not been killed, as the depth of his drop risked, but the local population had not rested content with his deliverance. They had taken it for a miracle, and turned the story into landmark. By the time Drummond arrived, a statue of Mary had been set on the walls (for she was held to have saved the boy), and the writer was sure the story would not stop there. 'A great many oblations have already been offered to her on this account, and it is not at all impossible that a church should be built out of the growing fund.'[121] Taking this sort of process back in time, other commentators accounted for the current visibility of Catholicism by its constant itch to commemorate. John Clenche, for example, showed how many of the churches of Rome were founded on the sites of miracles or New Testament stories. The church of St Agnes was supposed to be on the very spot where that lady had been saved from her potential ravishers by divine intervention, whilst the 'Chappel Domine quo vadis' was built exactly where Jesus had stood to greet St Peter.[122] Meanwhile in Provence, Andrew Balfour reported that

[120] Drummond, *Travels*, pp. 12–13, 28. [121] Ibid., p. 32.
[122] [Clenche], *Tour in France*, pp. 57, 47.

the supposed retreat of St Mary Magdalene was now covered in shrines to cater for the pilgrims who flocked there.[123] Perhaps the most striking stories came from John Northleigh and the anonymous author of *A succinct description of France*. Explaining the location of Turin's huge Duomo, Northleigh related how an 'impious fellow' had once stolen a silver monstrance from a city church, and had made his getaway on a donkey. The beast, however, 'sensible that it carried a God [the consecrated host]', refused to go far, and when he stopped the host escaped its container and mounted to heaven. To mark this event, the townspeople had 'immediately built this Church of Marble'.[124] Meanwhile near Paris, the *Succinct description* told how a cathedral had been erected where the martyred St Denis had ended a three-mile walk carrying his own head, and that at each place where he had rested, a stone had gone up 'to perpetuate this ridiculous story'.[125] In such accounts, Catholic Europe was more than sacralised. It became almost magical: new monuments to the faith sprang spontaneously out of the soil and crowded the scene with further reminders of its confessional allegiance.

Considering such a vision of Catholic Europe, the reader might wonder if the old Protestant analysis of popery was reasserting itself in simple physical description. Even if the sort of account we have been surveying was presented as objective reporting of what Catholic Europe looked like, much of it gelled well with the old criticisms of the sensual overload and vainglory of popery. For contemporary audiences, steeped in Protestant propaganda, the leap from appearance to condemnation would be small. The visual dominance of the church, and its ability to sacralise landscapes, were obvious metaphors for its corrupt usurpation of worldly power. After all, the church could only dominate the country because it had amassed the wealth necessary to build its huge edifices and stage its rich ceremonies. Also, as it had created its visual environment, the church had constructed the imposing, reason-quelling monuments which the old Protestant analysis would predict. Some authors advanced such arguments explicitly. The editors of de Blainville, for example, excused their endless catalogue of churches in Naples by claiming it illustrated how an uncontrolled clergy engrossed wealth and imposed on the 'credulous multitude'.[126] To stretch this suggestion further, even basic stress on the visibility of Roman religion might tell against it. According to a well-rehearsed Protestant argument, the true church was something 'invisible'. It was a mystical union of those who had received Christ's salvation, and its actual membership was known only by God. Counterposed to this was a

[123] Andrew Balfour, *Letters writ to a friend . . . containing excellent direction for travelling* (1700), pp. 52–3.
[124] Northleigh, *Topographical descriptions*, pp. 158–9 (second pagination).
[125] Eugenius Philo-patriae, *A succinct description of France* (1700), p. 19.
[126] De Blainville, *Travels*, III:304.

'visible' church. This was the concrete human institution of clergy, buildings and congregations, and although it dominated the worldly realm (as the popish establishment did in travellers' accounts), it was either wholly false, or bore so accidental a correspondence with the truly faithful that it came close to being so. Whether or not any readers made a conscious connection between the physical and the theological 'visibility' of the Catholic church, virtually all of our travellers provided material to support a subconscious one. English audiences had been trained to see antichrist in proud, rich and glorious institutions. Even those writers who were not overtly critical of the Roman ecclesia fed this prejudice with their account of its visual and spatial hegemony.

For almost everyone, then, Catholic Europe was alien. The influence of the old Protestant analysis of popery created a world which was strikingly different, if not perverted. The church was inescapably visible, landscapes were sacred, the soil had a magical capacity to generate new monuments to the faith, and towns and fields were full of religious ceremony. Often, of course, this spectacle led to bitter criticisms of the corruptions of priests. Yet even when it did not, it rendered the south strange. There was something highly charged, almost unworldly, about it. All accounts agreed that a separate, spiritual dimension seemed closer in Catholic Europe, and appeared ready to break through into the everyday. To conclude this section, perhaps it would be fairest to quote Richard Lassels one more time. This author had great sympathy with the popish realm, but often Catholicism's alien, magical, strange quality haunted even his prose. Nowhere was it closer than at La Sainte Beaumme, that wild area of Provence where Mary Magdalene was supposed to have spent her final years. She had led 'a most penitential life' in its mountains, but for Lassels her influence had sunk into the land itself. The countryside was thus no longer simply countryside, but had become sacred text. In the silences and monuments of its deserts, the landscape became a call to piety, whose otherworldliness was enough 'to make any man that considereth it well, melt into some penance too'.[127]

A COMMON PROTESTANT WORLD?

If, then, authors' descriptions of Catholic Europe were still dominated by an old Protestant analysis of its evils, what of perceptions of the Protestant continent? Here it is rather harder to generalise. Without the controlling account of degeneracy which affected almost all English writing on popery, accounts of northern Europe could diverge more thoroughly. Moreover,

[127] Lassels, *Voyage*, pt 1, pp. 42–3.

Protestant Europe was more internally fractured than its Catholic counterpart. Whilst the church of Rome had prided itself on its solidarity during the sixteenth century (in an age of great uncertainty it had remained united under papal authority), its critics had been unable to match this success. Within years of Luther's emergence, his followers divided, and these divisions survived for our travellers to comment upon.

The first and most technical disagreement between Protestants concerned the nature of the Lord's Supper. Whilst Luther had insisted some sort of miracle occurred when priests prayed over the bread and wine, and that in some sense they became the actual body and blood of Christ, Protestants in Switzerland and southern Germany had their doubts. Conferences had been held to resolve the dispute, but these had failed and more differences had emerged, so that Protestants were sundered by the end of the sixteenth century. In Scandinavia, and most of Germany, a 'Lutheran' or 'evangelical' brand of the faith prevailed. Along with its miraculous eucharist, this concentrated on the individual's experience of salvation, and was relatively relaxed about ritual and precise structures of church government. By contrast the Swiss, the Dutch, and the Huguenots of France, had endorsed 'Calvinist' or 'reformed' beliefs. These rejected any real presence of Christ in the sacrament; placed as much stress on the moral community as the individual; and claimed the bible insisted on precise forms of worship and ecclesiastical structure. By the time our travellers visited, these strands had coalesced into separate confessions.[128] In places where adherents mingled, their rivalries could be as bitter as those between Protestants and Catholics, and English commentators noticed the distance between them.

At its simplest level, awareness of division emerged in authors' religious mapping. When travellers assigned the continent to popish or Protestant blocks, they usually subdivided the latter entity into Calvinist and Lutheran realms, and the charting of this subdivision could be as careful as that of the basic frontiers of the reformation. Thus cities were often categorised as 'reformed' or 'evangelical' rather than simply Protestant; and there was as much coverage of Calvinist or Lutheran minorities living among the other confession as there was of the intricate divisions of Catholic and non-Catholic Europe. At Nuremburg, for instance, several writers noted how a haughty Lutheran magistracy made life even more difficult for their fellow Protestants than their papist rivals. They rejected attempts at reconciliation; and although they allowed Catholics to gather in one church in the town, they had forced Calvinists to walk over half a league on Sundays before pressure from 'reformed' princes persuaded them to permit a chapel just outside the

[128] Reformation historiography concentrates on 'confessionalisation': Euan Cameron, *The European reformation* (Oxford, 1991), ch. 20, for an introduction.

walls.[129] What gave extra edge to such mapping was the different attitude to worship among the two types of Protestants. Whilst Calvinists had believed the bible frowned on religious art and ceremony as idolatrous, Lutherans had shared the Catholic sense that images and ritual were acceptable so long as there was no confusion between beautifying the worship of God and worshipping the means of beautification. As a result, the 'reformed' had purged their territory of highly visible religion, but 'evangelicals' left their landscape more sacralised. Thus Edward Brown could note how 'handsome' and 'richly-set off' Lutheran churches were across Germany, and John Northleigh reported that Catholics sometimes wandered into Lutheran churches without realising they were in a Protestant building.[130] Similarly John Ray, although noting that Nuremburg was an extreme case, suggested its evangelicals may have been closer to popery than was entirely healthy: they 'seemed to us in the Ornaments of their Churches, and the manner of their Worship more to symbolize with the *Roman Catholics* than any other People of that Profession'.[131] In such writing, our 'two-continent' model of English description was replaced by *three* Europes. Like some of the towns, or even individual churches, Christendom was finely divided between Roman, 'evangelical' *and* 'reformed'.

Even if there had been no schism between Lutherans and Calvinists, it is probable that travellers' accounts of Protestant Europe would have been diverse. Catholic Europe had internal differences which were important to many commentators, but the fact that most descriptions were influenced by the old Protestant analysis of popish evil meant there was a certain smoothing of the accounts. Everywhere priests were supposed to use deception and sensuality to engross wealth and power, and attention was drawn to the effects of this. For the liberated north, however, there was no such master narrative, and accounts ranged more widely. Freed from recounting the doleful effects of priestcraft, writers could concentrate upon *varieties* of climate, soil, economy, custom, architectural style, degrees of religious toleration or quirks of political systems. There was also more room for disagreement about the salient features of particular societies. Without a corrupt church as the mainspring of human interaction, travellers could take different views about what truly made a community function, and whether it was worthy of emulation. In fact, Protestant lands became flexible projections of writers' attitudes. Their descriptions were distorted to support a variety of arguments about ideal cultures, societies or politics: the main restraint was less the realities of conditions abroad than the tendency to rely on other writers.

[129] E.g. Misson, *New voyage*, I:76; de Blainville, *Travels*, I:216.
[130] Brown, *Brief account*, p. 173; Northleigh, *Topographical descriptions*, p. 129.
[131] Ray, *Observations*, p. 111.

To illustrate this, it is useful to contrast Holland and Spain. These were both countries with which England had had extensive dealings as rivals, trading partners or allies, and one might therefore expect English descriptions to be rich and subtle. In fact, however, only Protestant Holland really got this treatment. As we have seen, English travellers in Spain came to a uniform (and uniformly depressing) view of the country. Even though English relations with the Habsburg realm had been complex (Spain had been England's great enemy in the Tudor era, had been transformed into an ally by William III's reign, and then became a battlefield in England's early eighteenth-century struggle with France), little ambiguity surfaced in accounts of the country. Almost everyone reported the country's grinding poverty; they ascribed this to the superstitious bigotry of the people; and then they got out as quickly as they could.[132] In Holland, by contrast, there was no army of priests to blame for sucking the culture's lifeblood. As a result, guides were far more varied. Travellers noted a diversity of Dutch characteristics, and they ranged their opinions along a spectrum of attitudes created by Holland's shifting relations with England. Through the seventeenth century, reversals of international alliances had produced two very different views of the Netherlands in English political discourse; our writers found their guides refracted around these contrasting poles.

The first view of Holland had been highly positive. It had stressed the common interest and natural sympathy which existed between the English and Dutch, and so held up the foreign nation as worthy of emulation and support. This view was rooted in shared Protestantism, and gained strength when England and Holland found themselves united, first against Spain, and then against France. The positive image was truly cemented, however, by its great proponent, Sir William Temple. Sir William had been an envoy from Charles II's court to various parts of the Low Countries in the 1660s, and although he had initially worked to cement an *anti*-Dutch alliance, he had become concerned that the region was threatened with French invasion and this had led him to work closely with, and gain an affection for, the people of the Netherlands. Sent as England's ambassador to The Hague in 1668, he negotiated a treaty with the Dutch, and continued to promote this alliance even as it became clear he was being undermined by the court in London. Temple was recalled in 1670, since his diplomactic stance now clashed with the king's wish to team up with the French, but this did not stop him attempting to unite the Protestant powers of Europe.[133] He retired to cultivate fruit in his garden at Sheen, and spent his spare time writing *Observations upon*

[132] Bromley, *Several years travels*, pp. 66–72; Willoughby, *Relation of a voyage*; *A trip to Spain* (1705).
[133] See below, p. 156.

the United Provinces of the Netherlands (1672). An instant classic, the work was a manifesto for a closer understanding of the Dutch.

Temple's *Observations* set out to explain the power and riches of the nation to which he had been ambassador. Despite an objective tone which left room for less admirable aspects of the Provinces, this explanation turned rapidly into a hymn of praise. If a few causes of Dutch greatness were due to geographical luck rather than character (the country had had access to seas for commercial adventures, and was able to defend its great towns by flooding its fields), Temple thought the essential foundation of strength was the virtue of the people. He rejected the idea that the nation was particularly favoured, pointing out that the climate, soil and mineral deposits were relatively poor. Rather, Holland was powerful because massive immigration had boosted her human resources, and this inflow was due to her political system and the popular attitudes underpinning it. Effectively, the Dutch had established a virtuous circle, in which liberty, industry, prosperity and power had reinforced one another. This had begun with the struggle for independence in the sixteenth century. Although they had been lovers of personal and national freedom since at least Roman times, the people of the Netherlands had become truly attached to these ideals during their battle against Spanish tyranny. Liberty had become a symbol of their fight, and the rejection of the Habsburg kings had allowed them to found a government based around representative assemblies and laws protecting private rights. The religious circumstances of the revolt had further widened freedoms. Attacking a power which supported the persecuting Catholic church and finding people of many different denominations on their side, the Dutch had adopted a policy of spiritual toleration. The result was not only to make the Provinces attractive to migrants, but to encourage people to enrich themselves once they arrived. People came to escape persecution and found they were extraordinarily free to make money. They were not barred from economic activity by petty discriminations; the law protected their property once they had accumulated it; and government was run in their interests rather than that of any parasitic court. Consequently, trade came to shape the whole culture. A commercial society encouraged traits such as honesty, frugality and hard work; and these in turn fed back to support the characteristics which had bred them. Springing from all these processes was a rich and internationally powerful society; and one in which a strong public spirit supported impressive charity, commercial infrastructure and public works.[134]

Temple's analysis of Dutch greatness was to prove hugely influential. The *Observations* themselves produced a description of the Provinces which

[134] Temple, *Observations*, passim.

centred on admirable public institutions, prosperity, freedom, frugality and the neatness and convenience of cities. They were kept current by numerous later editions; and as noted earlier, many other writers referred to them when penning their own descriptions of the Low Countries. As a result, guides such as William Carr, Joseph Shaw, Thomas Nugent and Edward Brown portrayed a wealthy and virtuous Holland. Readers were asked to admire the great monuments of Dutch commercial enterprise: banks, docks, company headquarters and fine merchants' houses became the defining marks of the Netherlands' townscapes, and there was much comment on the hard work, sound business sense and public spirit which had built these edifices. Certainly the people had faults, but these were alien imports. Long commerce with the French had introduced luxury and sapped the original strengths of the society, so folk were now less willing to forgo instant gratification for longer-term reward. Despite such recent blemishes, however, Temple established the Dutch as the most admirable of people. His followers agreed they had harnessed their intense industry and love of liberty to build a great nation.[135]

Against all this praise, however, was a completely contradictory image of Holland. Some Englishmen (and at some moments, a great majority of them) concentrated not on shared faith and liberty, but on the rivalries of the two realms. In the seventeenth century, both countries had emerged as major trading powers. This had led to a series of clashes between them, culminated in three full-scale wars between 1652 and 1674.[136] As can be imagined, these disputes bred highly unflattering pictures of the Dutch in English political polemic, and this spilled over into travellers' accounts. We shall say far more about this anti-Dutch ideology later, but for now its key elements were the astonishing avarice and ambition of Hollanders. According to this analysis, the Provinces had become great, not by virtue and hard work, but by an insatiable lust for power and riches which had emerged in the very birth of the nation. If Spain had been wrong to rule tyrannously, Hollanders had gone too far in establishing a republic as they fought off Madrid. Their refusal to accept the natural system of monarchy showed a determination to act in their own interests, and released a popular pride and greed which had fuelled their efforts to monopolise global trade. So the Dutch had poured resources into their navy in order to beat off potential rivals, and had tutored themselves in the black arts of commercial deception. Back home, such policies corrupted morals. Placing personal gain above all other considerations, they became

[135] Brown, *Brief account*, pp. 92–105; [Carr], *Accurate description*, pp. 4–79; Shaw, *Letters*, pp. 1–51. See also *A late voyage to Holland* (1691).

[136] See below, pp. 133–4.

cruel and mendacious. Allowing no controls on their behaviour, they became wilful, insubordinate and frequently drunk.[137]

As an account of the Dutch, this negative analysis proved as enduring and influential as the more appreciative view. Even Temple occasionally fell under its sway. He admitted, for instance, that Dutch commercial classes were obsessed with making money, and criticised their lack of political discipline; and images dark enough to cast shadows in his prose blackened other accounts more profoundly.[138] So Ellis Veryard described some of the usual Dutch virtues in his physical description of Holland, but when commenting on the people's character, he was far less complimentary. For him, decades of devotion to enrichment had destroyed men's more admirable qualities, so although 'industrious' and 'thrifty', they had become 'churlish' and more 'crafty than wise'. In religion, they certainly permitted adherence to many denominations, but Veryard suspected this stemmed from an indifference to Christianity rather than any deep commitment to toleration.[139] Still more negative was the author of *A trip to the jubilee*. Earlier, we saw this scurrilous guide mocking the excesses of Catholic Europe, but it treated Protestants little more kindly. In particular, the *Trip* warned tourists not to enter the Provinces if they were short of money. The standard Dutch vice of avarice ensured they had no sympathy for anyone down on their luck and would fear such persons might become a burden. If poor, the satirist exclaimed, 'I should much rather chuse to ship off for the Region of the *Canibals*, being sure to meet with as much *Charity* among those *Barbarians*, as amongst a self-loving People, who have raised their own Welfare out of the Spoils and Miseries of their Neighbours.'[140] Patrick Barclay's account curdled blood further. Although his *Universal traveller* was primarily concerned with European expansion beyond the continent, he reflected bitterly on the Dutch expansion into the South Seas. Here the notorious 'Amboyna massacre' of 1623 (when Dutch East India merchants had murdered an entire English trading community) was merely one incident in a catalogue of vicious cruelties against both natives and rival tradesmen.[141]

Of course, in arguing that English attitudes to a Protestant state varied widely, it is important to remember the divergences in descriptions of Catholic Europe. Not all popish countries suffered the near universal condemnation endured by Spain, and not all writers were overtly critical of

[137] For more on the political tension and anti-Dutch polemic, see below, pp. 132–52.

[138] Temple, *Observations*, pp. 140, 238–40.

[139] Veryard, *Account*, p. 23.

[140] *Trip to the jubilee*, p. 9.

[141] Patrick Barclay, *The universal traveller* (1735), bk 2, ch. 2. For more vitriol disguised as travel writing: *A trip to Holland* (1699) – this abridged Owen Felltham, *A brief character of the Low Countries* (1652), which appeared under various titles at moments of tension with the Dutch, including 1662, 1672 and 1697.

Rome. Nevertheless, a fundamental point stands. Descriptions of Holland opposed each other not just on outward appearances or superficial comment, but fundamentally: on their accounts of the driving forces of Dutch society. Whilst a common awareness of priestcraft lurked behind an admittedly diverse spectrum of attitudes to the Catholic south, radically different analyses stood behind the contrasting pictures of the Provinces. The Dutch miracle had either been achieved by liberty and industry; or alternatively by avarice, licentiousness and cruelty. The lack of a religious master-narrative had allowed authors to project profoundly different images of their subjects, and to point to very, very different lessons for visitors. There is, indeed, a sense in which the real Holland disappeared in these disagreements. The Netherlands were represented not for their own sakes, but as ammunition in England's domestic debates about the benefits of republicanism, religious toleration or commerce.[142]

This fundamental diversity in accounts of Protestant Europe was reflected in descriptions of other countries. Denmark was a case in point. Being off the standard circuit of the grand tour, this Scandinavian realm was missed by many writers. For some decades, the only useful description was that by Guy Miege, written in 1683 to mark the wedding of the Princess Anne to Prince George of Denmark and based on a short trip he had made as secretary to a diplomatic mission two decades earlier.[143] Although providing a brief physical account of many Danish towns, Miege gave little opinion beyond observing the country was very flat. However, in the late 1690s the northern realm suddenly became prominent in English domestic debate. The political pamphleteer, Robert Molesworth, thrust Denmark into the spotlight with an *Account* of the country which included a controversial analysis of its 1665 conversion from constitutional to absolute monarchy. Redeploying material related in a neutral tone by Miege, this led to an extensive account of the growing corruption of Danish society, and the dangers posed by the new regime.[144] Yet, as many contemporaries suspected, Molesworth was only marginally interested in Denmark itself. He had used his account to express concern about England's political culture, and especially to code his disappointment that the 1688 revolution had not curbed the English monarchy's powers. His opponents, who wished to defend the revolutionary settlement, engaged with the author and, accordingly, the nature and character of

[142] For more on the flexibility of the Dutch image: Steven Pincus, *Protestantism and patriotism* (Cambridge, 1996); Tony Claydon, 'Holland, Hanover and the fluidity of facts', in Joseph Canning and Hermann Wellenreuther, eds., *Britain and Germany compared* (Göttingen, 2001), pp. 85–98.

[143] [Guy Miege], *The present state of Denmark* (1683). [Guy Miege], *A relation of three embassies* (1669), described the mission.

[144] Robert Molesworth, *An account of Denmark as it was in the year 1692* (1694).

Denmark was contested in the press.[145] As with the Netherlands, the country's faith allowed this. Although Molesworth chose to analyse this particular kingdom because its slide to arbitrary government had been fairly recent, the absence of popery helped him to establish his argument. The writer wished to highlight the dangers of absolutism in England; had he chosen a country like France as his warning, his appeal would have been blunted by the perception that priest-ridden countries were always liable to a popular ignorance which permitted governmental tyranny, and that their example was therefore probably irrelevant for the English. Once again, a Protestant country, without the dominant image of clerical corruption, had provided a clearer screen on which to project domestic prejudices.

Yet despite all these divergences in guides to Protestant Europe, there was still a strong sense amongst the travel writers that it was essentially united. Areas which had escaped Rome's control had common features, and there were bonds which held them together and to England. To use the language of historians of the twentieth century, a strong sense of a 'Protestant international' survived into our period. For all their frequent disagreements about how to describe the northern continent, most of our guides wrote as if non-Catholic Christians had a shared identity, which demanded sympathy and support for those in other lands.

The most obvious similarity between Protestant areas was the lack of that sense-stunning ecclesiastical visibility which so marked southern Europe. In the reformed continent, people were not constantly reminded of the duties of their faith by a sacralised landscape. This shared absence was most marked in surveys of urban areas. Whilst the rhetorical townscape of popery was dominated by endless cathedrals, chapels and convents, the north was described in secular terms. Of course, the chief church in a Protestant city was usually mentioned, but this rarely led on to accounts of further religious foundations or to ecclesiastical decoration and ceremony as it might have done in descriptions of the south. Rather, the church had to jostle with town halls, fortifications, libraries, hospitals and even engineering marvels. Joseph Shaw's prose is typical here. In the passage introducing Rotterdam, ecclesiastical building was mentioned only because one church provided common prayer services for Englishmen: the true genius of the place was its patriotic hard work which had produced 'the Grandeur and haughty Magnificence in their Admiralty, *East India* House, Dock or Yard for Ships, stupendous Graffs, or Canals, Bridges and other Publick Ornaments'.[146] Similarly at Leiden, Shaw described the markets and the central mall, the townhouse, the hospital,

[145] John Crull, *Denmark vindicated* (1694); William King, *Animadversions on a pretended account of Denmark* (1694); T. R., *The commonwealth's man unmasqu'd* (1694).
[146] Shaw, *Letters*, pp. 18–19.

the bedlam, the almshouses and the magazine, and raced through only two churches before going on to praise the library and university. At Amsterdam a further two churches were mentioned, but the true glories of the city were the admiralty, the exchange, the Latin school and the fine houses along the canals.[147] To prove this was a specifically Protestant description, rather than a general bias in Shaw's writing, one only has to look to Antwerp. Once back in Catholic Europe, ecclesiastical visibility recovered. 'Images and Crucifix's adorn every Street,' Shaw told his readers, 'and nothing can be seen more Rich, Glorious and Surprising than their Churches.'[148] The contrast was as clear in many other writers. Thomas Frankz concentrated on streets and houses when describing the cities of Protestant Germany – though he had been bowled over by the number of churches in Cologne, and his comment on the Spanish Netherlands was that 'their Churches are numerous, magnificent and exceedingly richly adorned'.[149] Similarly, Edward Brown – who had called Cologne the Rome of Germany for its ecclesiastical structures – introduced Protestant Holland in wholly secular terms. For him, Amsterdam was justly famous for its trade, shipping, hospitals, houses of correction, 'fair streets and pleasant habitations'; and the country as a whole for its inns, learned men, industry, justice and 'their extraordinary neatness in their Buildings and Houses'.[150]

What tied Protestant Europe together more tightly than this shared secular townscape was the history which underpinned it. Some writers identified the religious changes of the sixteenth century as the moment when Holland, Germany and Switzerland were desacralised, and so linked the distinctive appearance of these places with their common participation in the European reformation. Thus de Blainville explained that the first act of the Protestants of Zurich was the removal of images from churches.[151] At Geneva, Bromley reported that the town still displayed the most excessive forms of ecclesiastical art to show 'the absurdity' of the faith they had rejected.[152] For Veryard, the progress of the reformation in Holland was marked by a wholesale purging of religious sumptuousness, characterised by the iconoclasm on the walls of Haarlem in 1572. In that year, the newly converted Protestants of the town had been surrounded by Catholic forces, but rather than surrender, they had showed their defiance by burning 'an infinity of Crosses, Images and Pictures, in sight of their Enemy'.[153]

147 Ibid., pp. 26, 36. 148 Ibid., p. 59. 149 Frankz, *Tour*, p. 9.

150 Brown, *Brief account*, pp. 97–102. *A description of the cityhouse of Amsterdam* (1738) opened by noting the Romans devoted most attention to religious temples and secular capitals. The ensuing description of a spectacular centre of political government demonstrated which dominated Holland.

151 De Blainville, *Travels*, I:331. 152 [Bromley], *Remarks made*, p. 363.

153 Veryard, *Account*, pp. 6–7.

And just as the Protestant reformation had destroyed the old visibility of the church, it had made the new secular landscapes possible. Wealth which had been tied up in convents and chapels was now available for the good of the whole populace, and the results were the great public institutions and lay prosperity which became the chief features of Protestant cities. John Breval, for example, explained that Haarlem had suffered much damage in its siege but had been able to rebuild from funds previously purloined by 'lazy Lubbers' (the clergy).[154] Thirty years earlier, Burnet had praised the sober architecture in post-reformation Zurich, stating the city fathers had redirected the church's funds from pointlessly sumptuous almshouses to convenient dwellings for the destitute.[155]

A sense of the past forged even stronger bonds between parts of Protestant Europe as travel writers described monuments of the later struggles of the reformation. In the guides, the non-Catholic continent had not been shaped only by its initial rejection of Rome. That rejection had initiated a long battle for the survival of the reformed faith as popish forces had attempted to recapture their lost territory, and this in turn had created landmarks which reminded readers of the mutual dependence of Protestants. Indeed, travel literature may have promoted such feelings of solidarity more effectively than histories or other accounts of the events, since, by concentrating on particular sites where Catholics had attacked their enemies, it could ignore the often complex context of these battles. In reality, the European conflicts which had stemmed from the reformation had rarely divided the continent on strictly confessional lines. Protestants in danger were often part of broad alliances which included Catholic states, and a full historical narrative would have to acknowledge this.[156] At an individual location, by contrast, travel writers might dwell on religion without analysing the overall balance of continental politics, so their stories of local resistance, survival or loss could stand as less ambiguous tales of Protestant heroism.

Perhaps the most obvious examples came in descriptions of the main frontier. Although the struggle between the reformation and its enemies had been waged all over Europe, much of it had been concentrated along that ancient division between the Latin and Germanic worlds. From the Alps in the south, to Flanders in the north, there had been zones of conflict in which broadly Catholic Frenchmen, Italians and Spaniards had faced broadly Protestant Swiss, Germans and Dutch, and all along this frontier the contest had militarised the landscape (in the imagination of its observers, if not always on the physical ground). There were battlefields to visit, fortifications to admire, tales of heroism to relate, and the border consequently meant more than a

[154] Breval, *Remarks*, I:40. [155] Burnet, *Some letters*, p. 49. [156] See below, p. 155.

change in descriptive tone. It was itself a feature, standing witness to Protestant survival.

At one end of this fortified territory was Geneva. As we shall see later, the English image of this city was contested because it was the birthplace of John Calvin's controversial brand of Protestantism.[157] Yet for many travel writers, fine theological disputes mattered less than the city's long struggle for its faith. For them, Geneva was the epitome of the embattled frontier. The town had had to fight for its beliefs from the moment it rebelled against the Catholic duke of Savoy: the duke's family had waged a decades-long battle to regain control in alliance with France and the Catholic Swiss cantons. The city had therefore been on constant guard against Rome, and many found it easy to portray it as a bulwark against its united forces. This vision of Geneva was already well established when Lassels invented the guidebook, and may even have explained his snide remarks about the city. For example, John Raymond's 1648 account observed the city had been raised to glory by the reformation. Calvin had chosen it as the ideal location from which to spread his word through France, Switzerland and Germany, and its citizens' effort against popish foes had made them Protestant heroes. Raymond drove home the point in his physical descriptions. He noted public inscriptions celebrating the city's escape from anti-Christianism, and had been shown a point on the walls where Savoy's men had been repulsed when they had tried to scale them.[158] Later writers continued in similar vein. William Bromley noted how the citizens remembered victories over the Catholics for years afterwards with preaching and prayers, and reaffirmed Raymond's vision of a courageous Protestant bastion. 'The Walls are strong', he confirmed, and their guards 'always on Duty, because of the constant danger apprehended from *France* and *Savoy*'.[159] The author of the *Trip to the jubilee* put aside his mockery on arriving in this city to recognise its citizens' dedication to their faith. Agreeing with Bromley that Genevans displayed the absurd relics of popery to fire their zeal, he tempered disgust at the townsmen's poverty with acknowledgement that they would give what little they had to its defence. 'Every Citizen,' the author claimed, 'will lay down his Life and Means to maintain their Cause.'[160]

Geneva, then, became a symbol of Protestant perseverance, but it was not the only one. Not far to the west of the city was the source of the Rhine. In its upper reaches, this great river curled north through Switzerland, Alsace and Swabia: and on its way it traced a broad zone of conflict. As our guides criss-crossed this country, they noted monuments to Protestant struggles, and commented how frequently the great contest between the two Europes had

[157] See below, p. 94. [158] Raymond, *Itinerary*, pp. 255–9.
[159] [Bromley], *Remarks made*, p. 363. [160] *Trip to the jubilee*, p. 30.

returned to these same territories. Near the Rhine and its tributaries, readers learned where the reformed Swiss cantons had repeated defended their faith against their popish rivals; they heard where godly cities had been besieged by the forces of the counter-reformation; they were warned that the land had been ruined in endless warfare; and they saw where great battles had been fought to thwart Catholic domination of the continent. In particular, the role of Strasbourg was advertised. Like Geneva, this place had stood as an outward bastion of the true faith. Until its capture by Louis XIV in 1682, it had defended German Protestants from popish advance, benefiting from its strategic position just on the French side of the Rhine. Accordingly, those who visited before France's occupation saw this city very much as they did Calvin's. John Ray described the town's fortifications and presented it as a great bulwark against the counter-reformation. 'It lies', he stated, 'as a Block in the *Frenchmen's* way', and he called it a 'rampart' of their opponents' cause.[161] Guides who came after Louis' occupation could not be as confident of the city's strengths, but nevertheless preserved Strasbourg's importance in Protestant defence as they lamented its fall.[162]

Flowing north from Strasbourg, the Rhine ran through the religious patchwork of the Palatinate and Westphalia, before spilling out into the Netherlands. Here, of course, it entered the most emotive and intense battlefield. For nearly two hundred years, the Low Countries had been the crucible of Europe's religious dispute. Catholic kings of Spain had tried to crush the revolt of the Protestant Dutch until the 1640s, the independent Netherlands had then resisted an expansionist Catholic France, and all this activity had defined an area of constant warfare. Guides therefore described an embattled landscape. Towns here were introduced by their parts in the great conflict as much as by their geographical situation or physical appearance; and writers noted the high-water marks of enemy advance.[163] Sometimes, this was literally a high-water mark. The Dutch had been forced to breach their dykes and flood their fields to stop foreign armies on occasion, and the most graphic example was at Gorcham. In Edward Brown's account, this town's watergate became the great marker of Dutch resistance. Brown described the 'handsome' gate with its inscription boasting that it had been unconquered in war, and then noted the building had delivered on its bravado in 1672. 'When *Louis* the Fourteenth, king of *France* came down with so powerful an Army into the *Low Countries*,' Brown reported, 'this Watergate [was] the Limit to his Conquests this way.'[164] Other writers observed the roles of other walled

[161] Ray, *Observations*, p. 95.
[162] Esp. Misson, *New voyage*, II:272–3; also Boyer, *Draught*, p. 26.
[163] E.g. John Macky, *A journey through the Austrian Netherlands* (1725), preface, explained the book detailed lands which had been battlefields in recent decades.
[164] Brown, *Brief account*, p. 103.

cities in the wars, and similarly observed how their stubbornness was remembered by their people. Whilst several guides spoke of the heroics of Leiden, Naarden and Haarlem, Ellis Veryard noted how the struggles of the whole country were remembered in its capital.[165] At The Hague the great hall was filled, somewhat ingloriously, with the shops of artisans. Above this, however, all was honour. The room was 'hung round with Armour, Trumpets, and Standards, taken from the *Spaniards* in the *Low Countrey* Wars'.[166]

This concentration on the frontier struggle obviously reinforced the sense of a divided Europe. As significantly, it strengthened the bonds between the various parts of the reformed continent as travel guides remembered the battles were rarely just the concern of local Protestants. Not only had those on the front line defended Protestant hinterlands (as Geneva protected the Swiss, and Strasbourg the Germans), they had also received help from the whole Protestant world. Troops, money and messages of support had all poured from distant lands to the points of conflict, and the guides noted how vital such encouragement had been.[167] Crucially, this co-operation integrated England into this single Protestant entity. Writing for an English audience, guides were especially proud of the role their country had played as the chief support for the reformation, and they constantly singled out and commented upon English aid. Thus Addison and Burnet claimed that the Genevans saw England, along with Holland, as their greatest ally.[168] Although the English and Dutch had in fact sent little material help, the writers reported the city recognised the northern nations at the strongest pillars of Protestantism, and believed their own cause was inextricably linked with them. Elsewhere, the English had played a more concrete role. Elizabeth I had sent aid to the Protestant Huguenots of France in the sixteenth century, and guides such as John Northleigh commented on this.[169] In the early eighteenth century, England's armies under Marlborough and George II had defended Germany against the French, and travel writers praised this glory when visiting battlefields.[170] Above all, England had preserved Dutch independence. Guides noted towns whose liberty had been secured by Elizabeth's troops; and they described the regiments of English soldiers defending the Netherlands in the wars after 1689. Those whose politics leant that way built this co-operation into a manifesto for Protestant collaboration. They

[165] For such other writers: Breval, *Remarks*, I:29, 40, 44; de Blainville, *Travels*, I:50; Northleigh, *Topographical descriptions*, pp. 30–45, 50.
[166] Veryard, *Account*, p. 10.
[167] E.g. Protestant Strasbourg had allied with the Protestant Swiss – Boyer, *Draught*, p. 29; Geneva had received money and men from Dutch and French Protestants over the years – *The present state of Geneva* (1681), pp. 4, 55.
[168] Addison, *Remarks*, pp. 507–8; Burnet, *Some letters*, pp. 258–60.
[169] Northleigh, *Topographical descriptions*, p. 76.
[170] Stephens, *Miscellaneous remarks*, pp. 372, 378.

ascribed the liberty of all Europe to the Anglo-Dutch alliance, and stressed in particular the friendliness of the Dutch towards English visitors which it engendered.[171] One rather moving story told by Edward Wright summarised this fellow feeling. In Rotterdam, he met a woman who had given lodgings to an English youth who had subsequently died in her house. In response she had erected a memorial to the man and Wright thought this showed 'in how sacred a manner *Holland* observes the League between the *English* and the *Dutch;* which they endeavour to ratify not less by private good Offices than by their confederate Arms'.[172]

Military conflict, then, drew Protestant Europe together. Even though unequivocally religious wars were rare, the fact that Protestants in particular places had been endangered and that other Protestants had helped them was seen as confirmation of an underlying solidarity. The travel guides were even clearer about cohesion when describing Catholic persecution. From the early seventeenth century, there had been waves of legal and physical attack on reformed communites within Roman Europe, but whilst this had eliminated many heterodox enclaves, our writers suggested it had also drawn the reformation together. Most obviously this had happened through exile. When people were persecuted, they had often fled to other Protestant lands, and though this had been traumatic, it had bolstered the sense that the reformed were one community by mixing together folk from different places. Thus our guides were keen to record numbers, dwelling places and social roles of refugees in towns which had welcomed them. Bromley, for instance, estimated that 6,000 of Geneva's 40,000 inhabitants were displaced Huguenots.[173] Dutch cities were similarly recorded as destinations for refugees from all over the continent; and several German states had taken pity on the suffering. At Marburg in Hesse, for example, Sacheverell Stephens reported that the local ruler had built an entire town to house fleeing French Protestants.[174] Others told how some of Strasbourg's population had emigrated to Hamburg after the French had captured the city; how many Protestants from Cologne had gone to the same place; and how Frankfurt, Hanau and Berne had all opened their gates to the desperate.[175] In such writing, the physical dispersal of the reformation collapsed. When Nugent described the churches built for French and German Protestants in Amsterdam, or Misson spoke of communites of German, French and even Italian Protestants in Geneva, they created cosmopolitan microcosms of the whole reformed movement.[176]

[171] E.g. *Late voyage to Holland*, p. 23. [172] Wright, *Some observations*, II:508.
[173] [Bromley], *Remarks made*, p. 365. [174] Stephens, *Miscellaneous remarks*, p. 379.
[175] Nugent, *Grand tour*, I:70; Burnet, *Some letters*, p. 57; [Carr], *Accurate description*, pp. 83, 89, 95–6; Wright, *Some observations*, p. 57.
[176] Nugent, *Grand tour*, I:71; Misson, *New voyage*, II:262.

Apart from re-emphasising the cruelty of Catholicism, and stressing the physical togetherness of Protestants which exile created, accounts of migration further unified the reformation by emphasising inter-Protestant charity. As they described the movements of population in such tragic circumstances, many guides highlighted the welcome which refugees had received and noted that locals thought it was their duty to help coreligionists in distress. Misson, for example, noted that the Vaudois of the Savoyard valleys, who had been harried by the popish duke and brought to Geneva 'in a manner half dead', were 'receiv'd by the Inhabitants with all imaginable marks of Compassion and Charity'. French refugees were 'also kindly treated'.[177] Similarly, William Carr reported the generosity of Amsterdamers to waves of migrants. 'I ought not', he stated, 'to omit telling you of their great Charity to the distressed French Protestants', and then set this in context by revealing 'this is no other than they formerly did to the Poor distressed Protestants of *Ireland* and *Piemont*'.[178] Gilbert Burnet charted an even more organised relief effort in which the cantons of Switzerland had clubbed together to help Huguenots expelled from France. The city of Berne had opened a sanctuary for exiles, but this had been supported by funds from Zurich and 'other neighbouring protestant States', taken to a central place for more efficient relief.[179] In all this, sympathy for refugees created loyalties and identities which transcended locality. The guides suggested links of faith allowed strangers to be treated as if they were fellow citizens. When Burnet reported of Switzerland that it had 'been animated with such a Spirit of charitie and compassion, that every Mans house and purse has been opened to the Refugees', he was confirming that the Swiss felt part of a far wider Protestant Europe.[180]

Vitally, this sense that refugees created a common Protestant world included England. Just as the country's participation in war had bound her into the European reformation, her history of receiving refugees, and of needing sanctuaries for her own Protestants, tied her into this united entity. Recent examples concerned English relief of others' distress. Most writers who talked about the persecutions in France at least mentioned that many Huguenots had found refuge in England, whilst both John Northleigh and Thomas Nugent noted that weavers from Habsburg Flanders had enriched London's economy as intolerance had increased.[181] Perhaps more significantly, travel writers also commented on places to which English communities had escaped over the centuries. England, after all, had not escaped Catholic persecutions. In the 1550s Mary I had launched her bloody attack on the reformed church; Henry VIII and Charles I had imposed elements of

[177] Misson, *New voyage*, II:261. [178] [Carr], *Accurate description*, pp. 26–7.
[179] Burnet, *Some letters*, p. 57. [180] Ibid., p. 58.
[181] Northleigh, *Topographical descriptions*, pp. 196–7; Nugent, *Grand tour*, II:64.

worship which more committed Protestants thought popish; and from 1685 to 1688 England was once more ruled by a Catholic king. These events produced exiles, and although we shall later see these were controversial among historians and pamphleteers, the main attitude in the travel literature was simple gratitude to European Protestants for providing refuge.[182] So, many writers commented on English communities in Holland who had fled difficulties at home, whilst Joseph Shaw suggested an almost continuous traffic across the North Sea. 'The Dutch', he observed, 'are of the same Religion with ourselves' and their 'Provinces have ever been a safe and kind Azilum for all Great and Good *Englishmen*'.[183] Similarly, several guides mentioned the role of German and Swiss cities during the reign of Mary Tudor, whilst Burnet, with his acute sense of pan-Protestantism, suggested the 1550s sojourn of English reformers in Geneva had forged an enduring bond between the Swiss and his adopted countrymen. He had spent a slice of his own exile in the city and welcomed the lasting sympathy for England which his predecessors seemed to have planted there. The magistrates, Burnet reported, offered him a church in which to hold English services, and had told him they were glad to do this since the corporation had once provided the same facility for the Marian refugees.[184]

Persecution, then, combined with warfare to produce a Protestant international which included England. When added to the desacralised landscape of northern Europe, which made it seem less corrupted and so less alien than the south, there is a case for claiming that a strongly confessional geography challenged our guides' very sense of Englishness. When in Protestant parts of the continent, many writers felt the pull of a Protestant identity. This gave them a sense of close connection to the local inhabitants, and confused any simple or narrow nationality. Sometimes, in fact, they hardly felt they were abroad. Stories quoted above testified to the warmth of the welcome Englishmen could receive as fellow Protestants, and for some, such as Joseph Shaw in Holland, this could wipe away more national barriers. Shaw, who travelled to the Netherlands in Queen Anne's reign, was a keenly patriotic writer. He admitted to homesickness; he reported the problems of not being able to speak Dutch or of understanding indigenous culture; and he frequently expressed his envy that Holland was so much more prosperous than his native land.[185] Yet he soon overcame these nationalistic attitudes when the locals were so welcoming. Shaw found the Dutch were 'very civil, affable and obliging to Strangers', and this was especially true when they met Englishmen. At least during the war of Spanish succession, when the Provinces allied

[182] See below, p. 93. [183] Shaw, *Letters*, preface, p. xix.

[184] Burnet, *Some letters*, p. 258.

[185] Shaw, *Letters*, pp. 1–13, 26, 35. See also *Late voyage to Holland*, p. 23.

with England, the Dutch were 'kind and loving to the *English*, whom they look on as a sort of Countrymen'.[186] At its most extreme, the sense that England was part of a wider Protestant whole could distort the whole travel genre. The books we have been studying claimed to introduce Englishmen to an unfamiliar continent. Yet contact with at least some parts of Protestant Europe had been so close that the writers did not think they were unfamiliar, and edited them out of their guides. Addison, for instance, thought Geneva too well known to merit attention, and several writers refused to waste ink on the Netherlands.[187] Although William Carr thought it useful to provide information on the Provinces because so many Englishmen were going, Drummond, Wright, Bromley and Breval took the opposite line that there was little point detailing such well-trodden territory.[188] As Misson put it, the English had a thousand opportunities to go to the fellow Protestant state, so he would cut short his coverage; or as Northleigh suggested, England's involvement in Holland's wars meant actual travel had superseded travel literature.[189] In such instances, the division between England and the continent was lost. The Netherlands were overseas, but they were so closely integrated into the audience's experience that a true travel guide (whose point was to describe *foreign* places) should exclude these lands. In these passages, as in so many others in the travel literature, the reformed continent stood as an integrated whole: the boundaries of England were blurred by its involvement in this transnational body.

PROTESTANT ENGLAND, CHRISTIAN ENGLAND

Having crossed and recrossed the continent with our band of travellers, it is time to present some conclusions. The most important is that a confessional view of Europe survived strongly in the century after the English civil war. Writers continued to describe a continent fundamentally divided between religions and presented the Catholic realm in ways still influenced by the earliest reformation polemicists. Explicitly or tacitly, they suggested that southern Europe bore the marks of an engrossing clergy who used spectacle, invention and coercion to keep all in thrall. Whilst the lack of this underlying priestcraft allowed accounts of Protestant lands to diverge, its very absence provided points of similarity between them, whilst the reformed continent was drawn further together by the memorials of its long struggle to survive. The result was a well-developed sense of a 'Protestant international'. England

[186] Shaw, *Letters*, p. 43. [187] Addison, *Remarks*, p. 470.

[188] [Carr], *Accurate description*, preface; Drummond, *Travels*, p. 3; Wright, *Some observations*, p. 506; Bromley, *Several years*, p. 274; Breval, *Remarks*, I:1 – though Breval provided some Dutch history which he thought even frequent visitors might not know.

[189] Misson, *New voyage*, I:1–2; Northleigh, *Topographical descriptions*, p. 1.

did not stand alone, but participated in a wider reformation, whose adherents felt warmly towards Englishmen, and to whom they had pressing duties. As the rest of this book will argue, this sense of the English as Protestants was one of the most important and powerful emotions in the late Stuart and early Hanoverian eras, and prevented any narrow national identity. Yet before we go on to explore this, a considerable qualification is in order. We have to remember that not all guides were overtly hostile to Catholicism. They might map divisions and describe Catholic areas differently, but they could still be complimentary about the civility, beauty or sophistication of the south, and for many, the corruptions of priestcraft have to be teased out of the prose. We must, therefore, avoid overstating polarisation in travellers' view of the continent and try to analyse the roots of this moderation.

One source of tolerance was the hope that the reformation might spread further. Although some appreciative comments on Catholicism sprang from confessional indifference, much emerged from Protestant sentiment itself. In several of the guides, the popish realms were praised for starting to reform themselves. Writers asserted that papists had been inspired by the example of Protestantism and had begun to purge the worst excesses of their superstition. The best example is perhaps Joseph Addison. In his extract on Naples, he explained that there were degrees of Catholic corruption, and that large parts of the continent had begun to rescue themselves from the worst excesses. 'I must confess,' he told his audience,

> tho' I have liv'd above an Year in a *Roman* Catholick Country, I was surpriz'd to see many Ceremonies and Superstitions in *Naples*, that are not so much as thought of in *France*. But as it is certain there has been a kind of Secret Reformations made, tho' not publickly own'd in the *Roman* Catholick Church, since the spreading of the Protestant Religion, so we find the several Nations are recover'd out of their Ignorance, in proportion as they have converse more or less with those of the Reform'd Churches.[190]

Addison went on to explain that this was why France, which had wrestled with its own Protestants, was so much more enlightened than Spain or Italy. Other writers did not lay out the theory in such richness, but were certainly influenced by it. Charles Thompson, in Rome, declared that the Catholic church had improved once it had heard Luther's message: its clergy were now more learned, less debauched and less haughty than they had been.[191] John Northleigh detected a growing dissatisfaction with the unreformed church in Paris, and compared this to the public mood in England under Henry VIII.[192] Elsewhere, several praised Venice for getting the inquisition and

190 Addison, *Remarks*, pp. 197–8. 191 Thompson, *Travels*, p. 164.
192 Northleigh, *Topographical descriptions*, p. 104. Others praised the learning and civility of French clergy: e.g. *A new description of Paris* (1725), pp. 35–6, 38–9, 50.

more ridiculous superstitions under control; and there was a general sense that France had been moderated by contact with their Protestant neighbours, and the desire of its kings to evade papal diktat.[193] In such passages, there was an intense belief that the reformation might eventually have relevance for *all* Europe. Over time, it might roll across the south, abolish the division between the two continents, and integrate England (which already belonged to the continental reformed movement) into an even wider whole.

And even without this utopia, the English had affinities with Catholics. These stemmed from the relative familiarity of Spain, Italy, France and Austria compared with the rest of the world. Although popish countries seemed strange to our guides, they were not as strange as the realms beyond western Europe. It was not that nothing was known about Asia, Africa or the Americas. Travellers to these distant parts had published their tales: indeed as early as the 1650s, Peter Heylyn had produced his *Cosmographie*, a work which provided a respectable guide to distant parts, and which remained the standard description of them for decades.[194] Later explorers filled in details. In 1668 Paul Rycaut gave an intimate portrait of the Ottoman empire, John Chardin described Persia in 1686 and in 1697 William Dampier told of his voyages in the Pacific and the Far East.[195] What was significant about these guides, however, was their emphasis on the exotic. Accounts of Catholic lands might stress the alien nature of that faith, but they never assumed the great chasms of culture evident in guides to the world beyond the local continent. People who went to Asia, Africa and native America painted radically unfamiliar realms: the societies they visited were thought so peculiar that they would need describing from the bottom up, and in these descriptions the utterly strange was paraded for the amazement of readers. John Chardin, for example, told his audience to expect things 'wholly new and unknown to us in Europe' and places so different they might be called 'Another World'.[196] Similarly, Rycaut stressed his comprehensive account of the Ottomans would be useful since they were so unlike Englishmen that they were easily misunderstood or underestimated.[197] Audiences were thus treated to the most sensational features of places beyond Europe; and it is telling that well into

193 For Venice: Burnet, *Some letters*, p. 145; Misson, *New voyage*, I:176; John Gailhard, *The present state of the princes and republics of Italy* (1668), p. 106; John Gailhard, *The present state of the republick of Venice* (1669). Gailhard's early works set later attitudes, as did a general acknowledgement among Europeans that Venice had escaped full papal control: see *The city and republic of Venice* (1699), pt II, pp. 52–71; and Bruce Radford, *Venice and the grand tour* (New Haven, CT, 1996), p. 52.

194 Peter Heylyn, *Cosmographie in four books* (1652) – further editions 1657, 1665, 1666 (two), 1669, 1670, 1674 (two), 1677, 1682.

195 Paul Rycaut, *The present state of the Ottoman empire* (1668); Jean Chardin, *The travels of Sir John Chardin into Persia* (1686); William Dampier, *A new voyage round the world* (1697).

196 Chardin, *Travels*, preface.

197 Rycaut, *Present state*, dedication and epistle.

the Stuart age the fabulous, myth-ridden and fifteenth-century *Voyages and travels of Sir John Mandeville* remained a popular source of (mis)information on the Levant and Asia.[198]

We have to be a little cautious here. The distant world became slowly more familiar to English readers in the eighteenth century, and reaction was not always hostile. For instance, China and Islamic lands were admired for their ancient civilisations, whilst Europeans sometimes allied with powers outside their continent.[199] Similarly Linda Colley – studying English people made captive by Barbary pirates and native Americans in our period – found exposure to a different culture leading some to an unexpected sympathy.[200] Yet for all this, guides still stressed the strange. Travellers emphasised the exotic even as they admired aspects of extra-European cultures or stressed friendly relations with distant rulers; whilst – for me, at least – the praise in Colley's captivity narratives seemed to spring from heartening astonishment that people could bridge very real gulfs between them, or from a desire to criticise English society as radically as possible. Moreover, there was a noticeably different purpose behind accounts of more distant lands. Whilst those who visited France, Italy or Austria frequently wrote to help the people who would flock after them, guides to the world beyond Europe had little expectation their readers would follow. The comprehensive sight-by-sight account therefore never developed, and descriptions of Muslim, African or oriental lands remained daring tales of first contact, or anthropological comparisons, which could not guide an actual trip. The different style of travel literature thus made exotic regions still more exotic: they could not be covered in the same way as Protestant and Catholic realms.

Of course there were very concrete reasons for the gulf between western Europe and the rest of the world. Distant lands were harder to visit, so were less familiar by definition. Yet examining Heylyn's *Cosmographie* an ideological fissure emerges: and it is one which points to English identities wider than Protestantism. Heylyn opened his work with a general chapter covering the biblical history of the world and outlining the scientific principles of geography. After this, however, he got down to describing the different parts of the globe, and he introduced diversity by concentrating upon religion. He pointed out that if one divided the world into thirty equal areas, nineteen of them were inhabited by 'infidels'. These were men who worshipped no

[198] Editions in 1657, 1670, 1677, 1696.

[199] For admiration, see P. J. Marshall and Glyndwr Williams, *The great map of mankind: British perceptions of the world in the age of the enlightenment* (1982), ch. 1. For the extra-European alliances of European powers, see below, ch. 3. For the Ottoman empire as an increasingly 'normal' European power: Daniel Goffman, *The Ottoman empire and early modern Europe* (Cambridge, 2002).

[200] Linda Colley, *Captives: Britain, empire and the world, 1600–1850* (2002), esp. pp. 99–134, 186–98.

deity at all, or – perhaps worse – bowed before gods created by the people themselves. Of the remaining eleven-thirtieths, six were controlled by men who believed in a universal being but who, like Jews and Muslims, had not received the gospel. Followers of Jesus dominated the remaining five parts, but two of these were lost to the Greek faith, which later passages made clear had strange doctrines, and was more or less limited to barbaric Russia.[201] This left only a tenth of the globe for Protestants and Romanist to share between them. What is noticeable about this passage is its clear evocation of a Christian, and more particularly western Christian, community. The key division of the world was into its different faiths. Protestants and Catholics were huddled together in one corner: the differences between them were petty set against the bizarre beliefs which prevailed elsewhere.

It has to be admitted that Heylyn was a special case. As we shall see, his position in English ecclesiastical politics demanded he stress the similarities between the Roman church and his Protestant one. Nevertheless, he delineated an entity many contemporaries took seriously, and which they still labelled 'Christendom'. Although they knew this had been divided at the reformation, and although they were hazy about its precise limits, people felt tied to an embracing Christianity, and this book will explore many examples of this sentiment. In the travel literature, the wider community was evident in the divide between western Europe and elsewhere. Boundaries between the familiar and the exotic mapped closely divisions between Christian and un-Christian – except along the hazy eastern frontier where Russia's primitive popular beliefs and rituals contrasted with its official Christianity. Aside from this confusion, the distinctions were neat. Italy, Spain, France and Austria were more familiar because of their religion. This might be attacked for lost purity; but writers recognised Christian cultural forms; they applauded attempts to cool confessional strife because Christians should live peacefully together; and even those most hostile to popery applied a common set of standards, criticising Catholics for not living up to the ideals of the faith. By contrast, Africa, the orient and native America were odd because their beliefs were odd. Here there were no familiar rituals or ecclesiastical buildings to reassure readers they were somewhere approachable; instead, alien faiths produced incomprehensible and frightening ways of life. Thus Rycaut spent reams of paper detailing Islam because the Ottoman's peculiar society was so shaped by it.[202] Dampier made much less effort to comprehend other creeds, but he nevertheless stressed that the outlandish poverty, perversion

201 Heylyn, *Cosmographie* (1666 edn), pp. 31–2; pp. 511–12 described an unlearned Russia 'destitute of human affections', whose church differed 'much both from the Romish and Reformed'; whilst p. 575 pointed out few Christians were left in the old heartlands of orthodoxy.

202 Rycaut, *Present state*, p. 97, explains Ottoman civil law was based on Mahomet's teaching.

or barbarity of the East Indies was accompanied by its characteristic infidelity.[203] Chardin, who was by origin a French Protestant, was grateful for a Catholic travelling companion in Persia. In the east, Christians were such an isolated minority that they must 'keep good Correspondence one with another, notwithstanding their disagreements in Opinions'.[204]

In the end, therefore, travellers confirmed England's international Protestant identity, but also confused it. Travel writing proved the English were a part of the reformation, but this both led to, and was overlain by, a wider sense of a united Christian community. It led to it because Protestant guides hoped Catholics would be converted very soon. It was overlain by it because even if papists were never enlightened, their societies were already more familiar than Muslim, Buddhist, Hindu, or even eastern Orthodox, ones. As this book unfolds, we will repeatedly see this embracing Christianity cutting across both reformation solidarity and any narrow sense of English nationality. Most obviously in histories of England – to which we will now turn – we will see unions of Christians rather wider than Protestantism providing a third alternative to English understandings of their place in the world.

[203] Dampier, *New voyage* – note his description of the savages of New Holland, pp. 464–6.
[204] Chardin, *Travels*, p. 2.

2

Time: English confessional chronology

A HISTORY OF THE REFORMATION

When Gilbert Burnet travelled through Europe in the mid-1680s, and circulated his highly Protestant guide to his tour, it was not his first major publication. He had been active in many polemical campaigns over the preceding fifteen years, and had published much on the moral, political and ecclesiastical affairs of the day. His writings included a series of works on the dangers of popery; works debating the status of the church of England; and a fantastically popular account of the author's ministrations to the dying libertine, the earl of Rochester.[1] Among this material, however, one work made his reputation. In 1679 Burnet published the first volume of his *History of the reformation*, taking the story of the nation's break with Rome down to the death of Henry VIII.[2] Although the author had not gained unalloyed support during its writing (a quarrel with the earl of Lauderdale barred access to the crucial Cotton Library), on its publication it met widespread acclaim. It sold well, it was read and discussed in the highest circles (Rochester had called Burnet to his deathbed after reading the work), and it even gained the official approval of parliament.[3] Once established as the nation's favorite historian, obstacles to Burnet's scholarship dissolved. A second part of the work, covering the reigns of Edward VI and Mary Tudor, was rushed to the press and appeared later in 1681.[4]

There were, and have subsequently been, many ways to read Burnet's history. At one level it was a formidable piece of scholarship. Although writers

[1] E.g. Gilbert Burnet, *The mystery of iniquity unveiled* (1673); Gilbert Burnet, *A vindication of the ordinations of the church of England* (1677); Gilbert Burnet, *Some passages of the life and death of the right honourable John, earl of Rochester* (1680) – four further editions by 1700.

[2] Gilbert Burnet, *The history of the reformation . . . first part* (1679).

[3] Burnet, *Some passages*, preface; *LJ*, VIII:729. The *History*'s second edition was 1681 – remarkably soon given its expense – and was translated as Gilbert Burnet, *Histoire de la réformation* (1683).

[4] Gilbert Burnet, *The history of the reformation . . . second part* (1681).

had already outlined England's reformation, Burnet was the first to be quite so comprehensive, and he was the first to write with close reference to the original documents. His work remained a standard account of the sixteenth century until at least the Victorian era.[5] At a very different level, the history was a propagandist work, intervening in the debates of its day. Produced in the middle of the exclusion crisis (in which parliament tried to remove the Catholic heir presumptive – the future James II – from the succession to the throne), Burnet's book included much kindling for the exclusionist fire. It ridiculed the pretensions of the popish church; it upheld the power of parliament over religious policy; and it lambasted clerical interventions in politics just as the church of England was emerging as James' great defender.[6] In fact, so enthusiastic was Burnet in the cause that he undermined a good deal of his scholarly achievement. As critics have never ceased to insist, he could be a slapdash researcher. Whilst he certainly consulted and reproduced his sources, he far too often used them out of context, quoted them highly selectively, or downplayed those which did not fit his Protestant and parliamentary vision.[7]

Burnet was therefore a complex writer. At least partly an erudite academic, and as clearly a partisan politician, he has won champions and enraged detractors in almost equal measure. What must interest us here, however, is a level between detached scholarship and squalid polemic. As Burnet used extensive research to make a political argument, the historian fashioned an impressive and influential interpretation of the reformation itself. Far more than a simple narrative of the sixteenth century, his work provided a magisterial account of the fundamental causes, the essential nature and the ultimate significance of the nation's break with Rome, and it shaped England's conception of her spiritual past for many decades. Burnet's history, therefore, makes the best starting point for exploring English 'confessional chronology'. Through its pages, we can begin to see how the English people of the late Stuart and early Georgian eras understood the origins and later development of their peculiar version of the Protestant faith – and in particular, we can ask if they saw the story as a purely domestic tale, or one integrated into European movements. In the eyes of those who lived after the civil war,

[5] E.g. Gilbert Burnet, *The history of the reformation*, ed. Nicholas Pocock (6 vols., Oxford, 1865).

[6] Andrew Starkie, 'Gilbert Burnet's *Reformation* and the semantics of popery', in Jason McElligott, ed., *Fear, exclusion and revolution: Roger Morrice and his worlds* (Aldershot, 2006), pp. 138–53.

[7] For early criticism, Simon Lowth, *Of the subject of church power* (1685), epistle; [Henry Wharton], *A specimen of some errors and defects in the 'History of the reformation'* (1693). Andrew Starkie, 'Contested histories of the church: Gilbert Burnet and Jeremy Collier', *HLQ*, 68 (2005), 335–51, shows the third volume (1715) was even more controversial.

had England's faith isolated her from the continent, or had it instead tied her ever closer to her neighbours across the Channel?

Given that Burnet's travel writing had such a strong international dimension, the immediate answer to this question is puzzling. At least in the first volume of his *History*, the author appears to have played down his pan-European vision, and replaced it with a stress on the separateness and autonomy of England. As Burnet's account of the sixteenth century unfolded, it became the story of England's heroic recovery of control over her own faith and affairs. The key moment had been Henry VIII's decision to destroy the authority of the universal church over his realm, and it was this radical separation from the continent which needed explaining. Thus the *History* began with the illegitimate pretensions of the old European church. Of all the crimes which could be counted against medieval Catholicism, it was the pope's ambitious claim to judicial authority over the whole world which was painted the blackest, and Burnet charted how it had bulldozed the legitimate power of English rulers during the reigns of weak and vacillating princes. Similarly, the historian devoted much space to the excesses of clerical power in the early years of Henry's rule. He traced the king's growing anger at the clergy's evasions of royal will (evasions founded on the church's ubiquitous jurisdiction), and of course he presented Rome's resistance to the king's divorce from Catherine of Aragon as another enraging example of papal usurpation.[8] Once into the story of the early 1530s, Henry's decision to defy the universal church dominated the narrative. Burnet detailed the political calculations which led to the elimination of Rome's authority; he related the arguments used to justify this; and he clearly intended that the sixteenth-century polemic would convince seventeenth-century readers. After Henry had established England's independence, this achievement remained at the centre of the story, and even rendered his other faults forgivable. Throughout his *History*, Burnet had admitted the Tudor king had serious vices. In youth, he had been lazy and lustful. In old age, he had been tyrannical and suspicious. All his life he had adhered to irrational, erroneous and ridiculous elements of the excluded Catholic faith. Yet on English resistance to foreign ecclesiastical authority, perhaps on this issue alone, Henry had been right. This one true conviction excused all else: indeed it illustrated how God's providence could bring good out of the most unpromising material.[9]

In all this, there was little sign of any transnational perspective. Henry was shown dividing England from a European jurisdiction, and the principles which he (and ultimately, Burnet) upheld were profoundly separatist. As the historian told his tale, he illustrated two maxims which had guided

[8] Burnet, *History . . . reformation* (Pocock edn), I:38–48 for royal anti-clericalism.
[9] Ibid., I:11–12, 17, 31–2.

the king and which justified England's break from the continental church. The first was that earthly rulers must have entire and autonomous control over their people. The bible, human reason and the English constitution all agreed that a king's prime responsibility was to uphold law and justice, but they also asserted he could not do this if foreign powers interfered in his realm. This axiom was so fundamental that Burnet began the whole work with it. The opening lines of the dedication to Charles II praised the king's predecessor for his 'great step' in regaining royal freedom: Henry had restored 'to your ancestors the rights of the crown, and an entire dominion over all their subjects; of which they had been disseized by the craft and violence of an unjust pretender'.[10] The second separatist principle was that national churches must have absolute control over religion within their territories. Although Burnet made clear that some truths had been promulgated to all mankind in the New Testament, and that reform must always refer to these universal ideals, he just as firmly maintained that each local province of the church had autonomy to decide how these truths should be explained in doctrinal statements and made manifest in worship. This meant that the church of England had always been a 'complete body within itself'. When it reformed without consulting the wider church, it had merely exercised its inherent rights.[11] To underline both this assertion and the theory of royal autonomy, the pictorial frontispiece of the *History* depicted English authorities triumphing over outside claims. In the centre of the image superstition is demolished as true religion is built up, but at the sides Henry tramples a triple tiara labelled the 'Pope's supremacy', whilst Thomas Cranmer, the first protestant archbishop of Canterbury, treads papal decrees into the dust.[12]

Burnet's history writing therefore seems in a state of tension with his travel guides. Touring contemporary Europe, Burnet saw a Protestant international, which bound England closely into a European body. Yet when he examined England's reformation, he homed in on national rights and rejoiced in English separation. Faced with this, it is tempting to accuse Burnet of politically motivated inconsistency. When exiled by James II's Catholic court, as he was when he wrote his travels, he stressed his fellow feeling with other persecuted Europeans. A few years earlier, however, when he had hoped to use his *History* to influence Charles II's regime to accept exclusion, he had flattered the king with talk of his absolute national sovereignty, and had accordingly emphasised the kingdom's autonomy from the continent. Yet, whilst there is some justice in this charge, it is not quite the whole story. At points, even in the highly separatist first volume of Burnet's work, there were

[10] Ibid., I:1 [11] Ibid., I:13. [12] Figure 1.

Fig. 1. Frontispiece of Gilbert Burnet, *The history of the reformation of the church of England* (1681)

hints of something else. Beneath the political narrative of Henry's break with Rome the author seemed aware of another set of processes which, whilst less obvious both at the time and in Burnet's prose, may have had greater long term importance.

This undercurrent broke the surface once the *History* had finished detailing the legal separation from the Catholic church in the 1530s. At this moment, Burnet told his readers that he would proceed to the 'third part' of Henry's reign (he had divided the era into the periods before, during and after the break), but that before he went on he was 'to stop a little' to 'give an account of the progress of the reformation in the years I have passed through'.[13] For readers who might have thought they had already ploughed through a substantial history of the reformation, this statement would have come as a jolt. Suddenly, it became clear that the legal separation from Rome which so far had dominated the *History* was not, in fact, the reformation at all. Instead, it had been a vastly important – but nevertheless different – development. As Burnet was to make clear as his recap unfolded, the true reformation was the progress of Protestant belief among the ordinary population. Henry's attack on the papacy might initially have been more dramatic than this spread of true faith, but it was not that spiritual revolution, and indeed could run counter to it, since the king retained many Roman beliefs about doctrine and worship and persecuted some Protestant 'heretics'. Once we understand the distinction between the true reformation and Henry's church policy, we must look again at Burnet's supposed inconsistency. His account of the legal break cut across the internationalism of his travel writing; but what about his relation of the reformation?

Here, all the missing continentalism flooded back. Burnet equated the true reformation with the spread of Luther's European doctrine. Although the Lollards (the remnants of medieval English protest against Catholic superstition) had certainly helped to prepare the ground, it was the arrival and growth of *European* ideas which had woken the natives to their religious errors. People had come to question idolatry, purgatory and transubstantiation because news of similar questioning reached them from Saxony, Swabia and Switzerland. Protestant books had been smuggled in from the continent in bales of hay; presses in the Low Countries had supplied the English appetite for the new ideas; and many of the Englishmen who had urged their countrymen forward, men such as Simon Fish or William Tyndale, had only been able to operate by fleeing overseas. The true reformation was thus an international movement which had forged strong links between the English and Europeans. In fact, when Henry's authorities had battled to suppress Lutheran teaching – as they had done sporadically through his reign – the

[13] Burnet, *History . . . reformation* (Pocock edn), I:261.

contrast between an internationalist reformation and the monarch who had isolated his realm became stark. Searching imported goods for heretical literature, or prosecuting men who had adopted too radical a faith through foreign contact, the Henrician regime appeared rigidly, but now sinfully, nationalistic.[14]

The European dimension of Burnet's *History* became even clearer in its second volume. This work, covering the reigns of Edward VI and Mary Tudor, closed the gap between royal action and international reformation. Under Edward, this was because the government itself backed reform of doctrine and worship. The history of royal supremacy and popular reformation thus converged, and the internationalism of the latter was no longer hidden by the insularity of the former. As a result, Burnet's narrative became heavily continental. The history of England was interspersed with accounts of the reformation in Germany, France, the Low Countries and Scotland; and European influence on English policy was stressed. Continental reformers such as Martin Bucer in Strasbourg, or John Calvin in Geneva, were shown writing to English rulers – whilst communities of foreign Protestants were portrayed setting up shop in London and swaying English opinion by their example.[15] Under Mary, the distinction between a separatist supremacy and a European reformation collapsed for a very different reason. This Catholic queen worked to reverse England's ecclesiastical autonomy, so the torch of religious progress passed solely to the individual Protestants who suffered her wrath. Whilst the meat of their story was to be the persecution of those who stayed in England, Burnet acknowledged the role played by Europeans in taking in those who fled and in preserving the English reformation. As he would later observe during his own exile, Protestant cities such as Frankfurt, Strasbourg and Geneva had provided refuge, and even people who did not flee were comforted by books and greetings from such places.[16]

Ultimately, therefore, there was no contradiction between Burnet's *History* and his travels. The separatism of the first volume was an optical illusion, caused by the need to narrate Henry's destruction of papal authority, even though this was not the reformation itself. When that reformation emerged, it was an international venture – and this made sense of another section of Burnet's dedication to Charles II. After praising the great Tudor monarch for regaining national independence, the historian outlined work still to do. This included an end to factional division within the Protestant church, and a moral renewal to match the reform in worship, but it would also entail 'a closer correspondence with the reformed churches abroad'.[17] Burnet thus

[14] Ibid., I:261–3. Also I:401–16 – Burnet regretting Henry's cooling to German Lutherans.
[15] Ibid., II:167, 266–9. [16] Ibid., II:403, 443, 453, 600.
[17] Burnet, *History of the reformation . . . first part*, epistle.

asserted that English spiritual progress had always had a European dimension, and that the reformation could not be complete until this was acknowledged. The point was to be put even more strongly in 1715 when the much delayed third volume of the *History* appeared. Its dedication, to George I, was a panegyrical hymn to the unity of a continental reformation. This international movement had had its internal differences, but the monarch's duty was now to be its 'Head and Chief Strength'. He must 'by a Wise and Noble Conduct, form all these Churches into One Body; so that tho' they cannot agree to the same Opinions and Rituals with us in all Points, yet they may join in One Happy Confederacy, for the Support of the Whole, and of every Particular Branch of that Sacred Union'.[18]

ENGLISH PROTESTANTISM AND ITS EUROPEAN PAST

Burnet's great work was released on an England hungry for history. A nation which based its legal system on precedent, its constitution on prescription and its pride on old military victories had always taken the past seriously; and in the century after the civil war, interest was deepened by the need to explain that disaster.[19] Scholars pored over the records of the early Stuart decades and apportioned blame for the bloody conflict between traitorous parliamentarians and an over-authoritarian king.[20] Meanwhile, a burgeoning print industry relayed the results of historical study to a wide audience and fed a rather different appetite for romantic, instructive or inspiring tales from the past. Consequently, the English were soaked in accounts of their nation's development. Perhaps most dramatically, the second most familiar book of the period was a work of history. After the bible (itself a sort of history), John Foxe's account the sufferings of English martyrs through the ages was the most commonly owned, and probably the most commonly consulted, volume in the land. Old copies of Foxe's *Acts and monuments* were passed down through families; it was one of the great 'chained works' in most parish churches; and new editions (of at least of substantial extracts) appeared in 1676, 1677, 1684, 1702, 1732, 1741, 1746 and 1747.[21] Other interpretations of the past were encountered elsewhere. Each week, the entire population was required to attend a religious service. Once there, they would listen to sermons whose preachers drew frequent analogies between the

[18] Gilbert Burnet, *The history of the reformation . . . third part* (1715), epistle.
[19] For multiple uses, Pauline Kewes, 'History and its uses', *HLQ*, 68 (2005), 1–31.
[20] R. C. Richardson, *The debate on the English revolution revisited* (1988), chs. 1–2.
[21] For Foxe's persistence, Linda Colley, *Britons: forging the nation 1707–1837* (New Haven, CT, 1992), pp. 25–8; Eirwen Nicholson, 'Eighteenth century Foxe', in David Loades, ed., *John Foxe and the English reformation* (Aldershot, 1997), pp. 143–77.

unfolding story of the Jews and that of England.[22] Rather differently, the cheap book trade was dominated by easy-to-swallow history. Almanacs laid out the great pattern of the past as comprehensive time-lines; early periodicals included historical articles; and ballads popularised instructive incidents from the lives of kings or summarised whole periods with their memorable jingles.[23] There was even a popular audience for more comprehensive treatments of the nation's past. One of the great publishing successes of the age was John Lockman's *New history of England*. First appearing in 1729, and selling six London editions by 1741, this consisted of a dialogue in which the nation's story was sliced into digestible chunks by successive queries, and by their short, easy-to-understand replies.[24]

Underpinning this varied market for the past were key works of scholarship. Cheap literature may have included much trivia and cod fable, but it was influenced by a catalogue of higher-brow writings produced in a golden age of English historiography.[25] In the century after the civil war, scholars discovered new sources, reinterpreted old ones, and developed new genres of historical work, so the whole approach to the past became more professional and comprehensive. One trend was the first serious interest in the earliest sources of national history. Writers such as Edward Stillingfleet (investigating the first centuries of the English church), Robert Brady (examining the origins of parliament) or William Wake (investigating whether clerics had always had the right to meet to advise the king) broke new ground in reading medieval sources – even if their conclusions were frequently encased in political controversy.[26] The sixteenth century was also opened up. Burnet complained that the reformation had had few authoritative chroniclers, but his work, along with that of Peter Heylyn and John Strype, supplied this deficiency.[27] Burnet went on to advance contemporary history. His account of his own times, published posthumously from 1724, gave first-hand

22 Tony Claydon, 'The sermon, the public sphere and the political culture of late seventeenth century England', in Lori Anne Ferrell and Peter McCullough, eds., *The English sermon revised* (Manchester, 2000), pp. 208–34.

23 Almanacs included Richard Saunders, *1667: Apollo anglicanus* (1667); George Rose, *A new almanack* (1686); *Rider's British Merlin* (1696). Helen Berry found 5 per cent of questions answered by John Dunton's *Athenian Mercury* (a 1690s periodical) were on historical topics: Helen Berry, *Gender, society and print culture in late Stuart England* (Aldershot, 2003), p. 44; Henry Care's *Weekly Pacquet of Advice from Rome* (5 vols., 1678–83) serialised reformation history. Ballad examples: *An excellent new song . . . giving you a full and true account of the transactions from King James I to King James II* (1685); *Warning piece to England . . . being the fall of Queen Eleanor, wife to Edward the first* (1693); *A new ballad of King John* (1740).

24 [John Lockman], *A new history of England by question and answer* (1729).

25 For sensational wonders, William E. Burns, *An age of wonders: prodigies, politics and providence in England, 1657–1727* (Manchester, 2002), pp. 130–5.

26 Edward Stillingfleet, *Origenes britannicae* (1685); Robert Brady, *A full and clear answer* (1681); William Wake, *The authority of Christian princes* (1697).

27 See below, pp. 83–5, 90–9.

evidence of late Stuart politics; while earlier, the earl of Clarendon's *History of the rebellion* had read the outbreak the civil war from a similarly personal and posthumous vantage point.[28] By the eighteenth century, multi-volumed histories of England were becoming popular. Luminaries such as Laurence Echard, Paul de Rapin Thoyras and John Oldmixon displaced each other as the definitive account, so that by the time David Hume cast the whole genre back into the melting pot with his sociological and atheistic version of the English past, the nation's whole history had been extensively explored.[29]

Admittedly, many of these substantive works were dry, and all were expensive.[30] Yet they were not wholly divorced from a wider market, and their findings filtered into popular perceptions by a variety of routes. The works themselves could become available by being abridged, serialised, lent or sold second hand. For example, Rapin's *History of England* was serialised as it was translated from its original French, and it went through six editions between 1725 and 1763 despite running to fifteen volumes in its first version, and twenty-one in later reprintings. This *History* was also plundered shamelessly. Its authorised publishers had to advertise furiously to kill rival versions, whilst John Lockman admitted he was cannibalising Rapin in his own guide to the past.[31] Similarly Burnet's *History of the reformation* was abridged and it also became very popular, though it is doubtful many readers had as much faith in it as the lawyer Dudley Ryder who read it to the ladies in his guest house as part of his technique of seduction.[32] Other serious scholars also participated in the wider press, and repeated their historical conclusions there. Echard, Heylyn, Burnet and Stillingfleet were all clerics, and drew on their academic studies in the inexpensive sermons they had printed through their careers.[33] Oldmixon was a substantial poet, playwright and pamphleteer who (along with Burnet, Stillingfleet and many others) waded into the political controversies of his day.[34] Even historians who avoided the

[28] Gilbert Burnet, *Bishop Burnet's history of his own time*, vol. 1 (1724); Edward Hyde, earl of Clarendon, *The history of the rebellion* (3 vols., Oxford, 1702–4).

[29] For Echard, Rapin and Oldmixon, see below, pp. 83, 118–20, 88. David Hume's complete history appeared as *The history of England from the invasion of Julius Caesar* (1762), but had been published in parts from 1754.

[30] D. R. Woolf, *Reading history in early modern England* (Cambridge, 2003), ch. 5, prices large works from many shillings to several pounds.

[31] Woolf, *Reading history*, p. 279; Lockman's full title advertised the work '*extracted from the most celebrated English historians, particularly M. Rapin de Thoyras*'.

[32] Gilbert Burnet, *The abridgment of the history of the reformation* (1682) – three further editions by 1684; Woolf, *Reading history*, p. 124.

[33] One example: Gilbert Burnet, *A sermon preached before the queen at Whitehall on 16 July, 1690* (1690), provided an internationalist reading of England's past based on his academic history.

[34] For Burnet and Stillingfleet, see below *passim*, but esp. 284–340. Oldmixon contributed to party battles under Anne: [John Oldmixon], *Remarks upon a false, scandalous and seditious libel* (1711); [John Oldmixon], *The Dutch barrier ours* (1712); [John Oldmixon], *A detection of the sophistry and falsities in a pamphlet* (1714).

mass market could influence popular perceptions when their findings were used in contemporary debate. As we shall see, readings of the sixteenth century became central to the religious divisions of the late Stuart era; whilst the frequent constitutional disputes of the period were fuelled by rival interpretations of ancient English government.[35]

Of course, we cannot know exactly how history was read. Daniel Woolf's attempts to reconstruct audience response to Stuart and Georgian scholarship warn us not to assume contemporaries absorbed the same messages we might today. Woolf records people editing and digesting history for peculiar purposes, especially abstracting events which they thought had lessons for their own lives; squirrelling away facts of particular interest to their family, lands, county or trade; or attempting to establish timeless principles of political behaviour from particular incidents. Staccato, chronicle-like histories facilitated such magpie approaches, and should make us wary of thinking readers gained *any* overall sense of the past from their perusal. Despite this, however, Woolf suggests people became more prepared to see the broad sweep of history as the Stuart era progressed. He argues that readers gradually accepted the past could not be sliced into discrete incidents for direct application to the present, but that events had to be understood in a changing chronological context and that history unfolded as an integrated whole. To accommodate this growing awareness, accounts with a grander narrative (such as Clarendon's or Burnet's) displaced unconnected lists of events, and this new style of writing allowed a larger, identity-forming picture of events.[36] Coupled with the active demand for accounts of the past, and the close links between elite and popular markets, these grander narratives justify study of the most substantial histories of England written after 1660. In them, we might hope to recover the English confessional chronology, and establish the typicality of Burnet's vision.

However, on examining these writings, we instantly hit a problem. When we looked at travel literature, we noticed considerable borrowings between writers, and an underlying unity of method and assumption, which allowed us to treat the texts as one corpus. By contrast, although historians did cite one another's discoveries, the differences between them were very wide indeed. In the end, the past was too political to allow scholarly consensus. Disputes in this period (as in almost every other) reached back in time to defend positions, so historians took stances in contemporary controversies and were polarised by their commitments in these. In particular, our aspect of history was hotly contested. The nature of English Protestantism was a

[35] See below pp. 78–101, 223–53; J. G. A. Pocock, *The ancient constitution and the feudal law* (Bath, 1974); Justin Champion, *The pillars of priestcraft shaken: the church of England and its enemies, 1660–1713* (Cambridge, 1992); Starkie, 'Contested histories'.

[36] Woolf, *Reading history*, ch. 2; Daniel R. Woolf, 'From histories to the historical', *HLQ*, 68 (2005), 33–70.

central public issue from the 1660 restoration through to the Georgian period, and writing on England's religious past was swept into the maelstrom.[37] Whether the nation's recovery of the true faith should be understood in a domestic or in a European context – and which continental context to understand it in – were questions driven by the keenest arguments of the day.

Gilbert Burnet, once again, provides a good place to begin the illustration. A few moments ago, we saw him stress that the reformation was a European movement, in which the English had participated fully. He had plenty of documents to back this reading, but his personal beliefs also promoted this international emphasis. Burnet, after all, was an eminently political beast. He contributed to national debates from the heart of court circles from the late 1660s, and this meant taking a stance, not only in the controversy over exclusion, but on the equally crucial question of how to treat dissident Protestants. We shall examine why this was such a divisive issue after the restoration in a later chapter, but for now we need just enough background to explain why Burnet's position drew him to emphasise continental contacts in his *History*.

From its origins in the 1520s, there had been disputes within English Protestantism. Even under Henry VIII and Edward VI there had been intense discussion about whether to rest satisfied with the break with Rome or to introduce more thoroughgoing change to match the more advanced models of reformation in Germany and Switzerland. Under Elizabeth, this dispute continued because the queen imposed a mixed settlement which admitted continental doctrine, but preserved many features of the medieval English church such as a fixed liturgy, ceremony and episcopal government. For many of her subjects, these were corrupt remnants of popery, and controversy about them festered until it overthrew Charles I. That king's opponents had been substantially motivated by desire for a more Protestant settlement, and they had abolished ceremony and episcopacy when victorious. The problem, of course, had been what to do when the Stuarts returned. Charles II (probably no Protestant at all) could not see that the disputed areas much mattered, but his supporters were intransigent. Those most enthusiastic for royal restoration favoured the mixed church of the pre-war era, and insisted on a full return of bishops and ceremonial liturgy. In 1662 they ejected all ministers who could accept the form of the established church which they reimposed, and from then on the key debate in England was how to treat these 'dissenters' or 'nonconformists'.[38]

[37] Good survey: John Spurr, 'A special kindness for dead bishops: the church, history and testimony in seventeenth century protestantism', *HLQ*, 68 (2005), 313–34.

[38] For fuller treatment, see below, ch. 4.

In this dispute, Burnet was passionate in his moderation. He agreed with most of his clerical colleagues that dissenters were proud and wilful men who had let trivial scruples drive them from a perfectly good church.[39] They had been wrong not to conform in 1662, and even when they were granted legal toleration in 1689, he continued to insist they had a duty to come back to the establishment. As he explained in his 1692 *Discourse of the pastoral care*, the law might no longer oblige men to worship in the church of England, but the gospel, with its message of Christian unity, certainly still did so.[40] On the other hand, Burnet could not agree that dissenters should suffer persecution. Wilful schism was bad, but punishing sincere Christians for their beliefs was worse. Intolerance contravened Christ's message of charity; it involved using earthly censures in a wholly spiritual cause; and – most horrifically – it mirrored the bloodthirsty zeal Burnet attributed to papists. He therefore sought ways to move beyond the raft of discriminatory laws passed against dissenters in the 1660s, and explained that efforts to win over nonconformists must be limited to loving approaches, peaceful persuasion and attempts to demonstrate the holiness in the established church.[41]

Understanding Burnet's position in the debate over nonconformity, we can see the strong Protestant internationalism of his *History* as a vindication of his late Stuart views. Partly a piece of objective scholarship, partly an intervention in the exclusion crisis and partly an interpretation of Tudor Protestantism, the work was yet further an answer to critics in contemporary church debates who cast their eyes abroad as they attacked Burnet's conformity or his moderation. As we shall see later, restoration nonconformists defended their separation from the church of England because it had failed to follow foreign Christians in eradicating popery.[42] As we shall also see, rigid supporters of the establishment defended their institution by making it part of a universal European body which must retain its medieval heritage.[43] Burnet's foreign engagement was his balanced response to both these arguments. Through his *History* he tried to demonstrate that England had a common cause with European Protestants, but that this did not demand slavish adherence to their practices. Dissenters were therefore wrong to cite

[39] Burnet's harshest condemnation was of those who rejected the restored episcopal church in Scotland: Gilbert Burnet, *A modest and free conference betwixt a conformist and a nonconformist* (1669); Gilbert Burnet, *A vindication of the authority, constitution and laws of the church and state of Scotland* (1673).

[40] Gilbert Burnet, *The discourse of the pastoral care* (1692), p. 203.

[41] Ibid. Burnet supported schemes of 'comprehension' to moderate offensive features of establishments to allow dissenters in.

[42] See below, pp. 85–8. For early appeals to foreign Protestants, see Richard Baxter's controversy with the newly restored bishops in 1660: Matthew Sylvester, ed., *Reliquiae Baxterianae* (1696), pp. 248–58.

[43] See below, pp. 95–102.

continental example against the English church, but the bitter enemies of nonconformists were also wrong to anathematise the dissenting position, as this was frequently shared by Protestant churches abroad.

So Burnet's key point in his *History* was that England had *not* deviated from the mainstream of the reformation as nonconformists alleged – or as their bitterest rivals hoped – it had. Its retention of bishops and ceremony might have been unusual, but neither Tudor Englishmen, nor their contemporaries in other countries, had felt this disqualified them from the international godly movement. In fact, in the years when the church was most definitively shaped, it had been the very centre of European Protestantism. Under Edward VI (from 1547 to 1553), England had moved cautiously towards her moderate settlement, but far from rejecting this as lukewarm, foreign Protestants had praised it. As Burnet demonstrated, circumstances had forced the faithful throughout the continent to accept English reform and even look upon it as their brightest hope. In the 1540s Emperor Charles V had launched a highly effective campaign against the reformation in Germany. Burnet covered this in detail, both to show that it attracted continental Protestants towards England (it was now the only place their beliefs were advancing), and to hint England's progress vindicated her gradual approach to change. As Burnet pointedly put it, 'as they were carrying on the reformation here, it was declining apace in Germany'.[44] If one wanted an explanation for disaster abroad, it was primarily that some foreigners had been so keen to purge out popery that they had divided Protestants by disputing the process of salvation and the nature of communion. Valuing unity, the English had been wise to leave their doctrinal statements moderate, conservative and vague.[45]

Burnet thus emphasised that foreign Protestants had not disowned the moderate English church. It had been their refuge, and in fact they had helped design it. As Edward's ministers planned the new ecclesiastical structures, Burnet proved foreigners were closely consulted. Some, like Calvin in Geneva, wrote to England with advice. Others, such as Martin Bucer from Strasbourg and the Italian Peter Martyr, were forced into exile by the decline of the European reformation, but then found a new lease of life in England, shaping Protestantism there. Bucer, in particular, was shown as a chief architect of the church of England. He wrote long letters to King Edward, setting out a spiritual agenda which Burnet thought Edward would have implemented had he not died. Burnet suggested that Bucer's criticisms of existing structures were almost always addressed; and he presented Thomas Cranmer, the archbishop of Canterbury and the guiding light of English reform, as a man of 'singular modesty and distrust of himself' who would not promote a religious position till he had spoken with his friend from

[44] Burnet, *History . . . reformation* (Pocock edn), II:108. [45] Ibid., II:155.

Strasbourg.[46] Calvin may have had less direct influence, but Burnet stressed his approach to England was constructive and enthusiastic. Whilst certainly urging some greater Protestant zeal, he praised many aspects of the English settlement (such as a set form of prayers which expressed the 'consent of all the churches'), and attacked those who wished to break with the establishment to pursue a more thoroughgoing reformation.[47] For Calvin, such dissenters had no grounds for departing from a broadly godly communion. Peter Martyr, too, denounced those who refused to wear the clerical vestments ordered by Edward's church. He claimed such people caused unnecessary division and so slowed the reformation; and Burnet set this opinion down at length to show the foreigner had not 'cherished' the more zealous Protestants.[48]

By stressing the foreign churches' participation in the English reformation, Burnet blunted the dissenting contention that England had strayed from the continental path. Yet he also admitted enough of the nonconformist's case to counter intolerance of them. Foreign churchmen may have welcomed the English establishment, but Burnet admitted they had also had valid criticisms. By implication, the dissenters, who continued these criticisms in the modern age, had the authority of the wider European reformation, and should not be harshly treated. Thus Burnet emphasised that Bucer, Peter Martyr and Calvin had pushed for more reform of ceremony. Although they had urged clerics to wear the English vestments, they had done so to preserve unity in an otherwise valid church, and not because they thought dressing up the best solution. In fact, all three suggested elaborate garb should be abandoned because it was too closely associated with popish superstition. Similarly, the European reformers demanded attention to moral reform. The English must do more to train ministers so that they could be better teachers of holiness in their parishes, and they should be far more active in imposing 'discipline' by excluding the vicious from communion.[49] For Burnet, this was an area where the church of England had never been sufficiently reformed. He returned constantly to this theme throughout his career, and by putting the case in the mouths of European reformers he recruited them for his cause.[50] At the same time he suggested the dissenters might have *some* legitimate reason for disappointment with the church of England. They were not simply troublemakers; they should at least be listened to as spokesmen of a broader Protestant point of view.

In sum, then, Burnet's stress on the continental reformation stemmed from his contemporary position in ecclesiastical debates. In the foreign churches of

[46] Ibid., II:265. [47] Ibid., II:67. [48] Ibid., II:267.

[49] For Calvin on this topic see ibid., II:167; for Bucer, II:269–71.

[50] E.g. Burnet's concern in the preface to the *History of the reformation . . . third part*, or Burnet, *Discourse of the pastoral care*, ch. 8.

the sixteenth century he had found people who had praised and constructed the anglican church (so were a case against nonconformity), but who had had valid criticisms of her lack of zeal (and so legitimated parts of the nonconformists' case). Given this, Burnet's Eurocentrism might be thought the particular stance of a peculiar politician. His unusually moderate approach was vindicated by close attention to the European context of the English reformation, but one might wonder if others who held more polarised views would find this context useful. In fact, though, divisions between historians rarely led them away from international analysis. Although they were driven in different directions by their ecclesiastical convictions, almost all chose to stress European dimensions of English reform. Burnet's interpretation dominated those stressing the Protestant moderation of the church of England, but dissenting historians continued to parade foreign churches as an embarrassment to the English church, whilst those most willing to persecute nonconformity also included continental analysis in their histories. Although glorying in the unique achievement of the English church, this last group was drawn to Europe to trace the roots of the nonconformist heresy which had endangered their domestic paradise, and they developed their own internationalism to draw its sting. As we survey English accounts of the reformation, therefore, the consensus of the travel writers may be lost. It will, however, be replaced by a rich variety of engagements with Europe.

If we start examination of the range of opinion with the moderates, it would be hard to understate Burnet's dominance. As we shall examine later, quite a number of restoration churchmen had doubts about persecuting dissent, and their position became stronger in the late 1680s when the political cost of Protestant division became clear.[51] For members of the establishment seeking sympathetic accommodation, Burnet's *History* was ideal. It defended the church whilst keeping it open to a wider reformation, and for many it became a key text. Some scholars simply quoted it. As late as 1756, Ferdinando Warner – a writer whose political and ecclesiological position shared much with Burnet – produced a church history of England which admitted it would simply paraphrase the late Stuart historian for the sixteenth century.[52] Paul de Rapin Thoyras was similarly dependent. This writer was an exiled French Protestant, whose family traditions and refuge in England in the 1690s gave him sympathy for both the English church and its dissenting critics. His *History of England* – easily the most consulted in the decades after it began to appear in translation (1725) – reflected this stance by drawing its Tudor church narrative from Burnet, and by recommending readers to

[51] See below, pp. 300–3.

[52] Ferdinando Warner, *The ecclesiastical history of England* (2 vols., 1756–7), I: preface.

consult that author for more detail.[53] Again, the writings of Laurence Echard revealed Burnet's influence. In 1707, Echard produced a monstrously old-fashioned (though surprisingly successful) chronicle of English history whose year-by-year coverage piled up the facts but left little space for analysis.[54] Dimly aware of this, the author asserted that the reformation 'carry'd on by contin'd Steps and Progressions' in the Tudor age, and then told readers to consult Burnet if they wanted a closer (or, he might have added, a remotely coherent) treatment.[55]

If Burnet's own scholarship sustained a moderate reading of the reformation, he was ably assisted by the other great student of the sixteenth century in our period. John Strype was the retiring, but highly erudite, church of England minister at Leyton, just to the east of London. Family connections with dissenters had given him some sympathy with their cause, and when he began to produce his massive studies of the founders of English Protestantism after the 1688 revolution, this drove him to a Burnetine reading of the sixteenth century. It is true his prose did not always help interpretation. It was built around lengthy transcriptions of documents, which were placed in somewhat whimsical order and which drove Gordon Goodwin, the author of Strype's entry in the 1898 *Dictionary of national biography*, to exclaim that his 'lack of literary style, unskilful selection of materials, and unmethodological arrangement, render his books tiresome to the last degree'.[56] Despite this handicap, however, the historian gained influence from the sheer quantity of the facts he uncovered. His dense and learned scholarship provided a major boost to a moderate churchmanship which stressed the establishment's shared heritage with reformed Christians abroad.

Thomas Cranmer was Strype's first project.[57] This divine, the chief spiritual adviser to both Henry VIII and Edward VI, could be said to be the father of English Protestantism. Yet in Strype's biography, published in 1694, it was clear his religious journey was driven from abroad. Cranmer had first been exposed to the reformation during a visit to Germany in the 1520s. There he had met the Protestant thinker Ossiander, from whom he had picked up a wife (the theologian's niece) as well as enduring religious proclivities.[58] In fact, Strype suggested this trip had formed the man. It had not only effected Cranmer's conversion, but had left him with a lifelong fascination with German religious reform which would keep him ever open to foreign

53 Paul de Rapin Thoyras, *The history of England*, trans. Nicholas Tindal (15 vols., 1725–31), VII:349.
54 Laurence Echard, *The history of England* (5 vols., 1707). Seven editions by 1729.
55 Ibid., I:725–6.
56 Sidney Lee, ed., *The dictionary of national biography*, vol. 55 (1898), p. 68.
57 John Strype, *Memorials of the most reverend father in God, Thomas Cranmer* (1694).
58 Ibid., pp. 10–11, 285.

thought. So in the vital years when Cranmer had led the construction of Edward's church, his household became a species of international theological workshop. Sheltering those fleeing from Catholic persecution on the continent, the archbishop had entertained Martin Bucer and Paul Fagius from Strasbourg, Peter Martyr and Bernadino Ochino from Tuscany, and Pierre Alexander from northern France. These men had contributed greatly to the Edwardian settlement, bringing a European flavour to it as they reviewed his new liturgies that they 'might be the more exact, and perhaps agreeable to the Doctrine and Practice of Foreign Churches'.[59] Expanding Burnet's coverage, Strype also provided blow-by-blow accounts of the interventions Bucer and Martyr had made to denounce opponents of royal decisions on ecclesiastical affairs, and so further underlined foreign approval of the emerging English establishment.[60]

As Strype moved on to studies of Elizabeth's archbishops, his purpose in defending the church by placing it at the centre of the international reformation became still clearer. In the preface to his biography of Matthew Parker (published in 1711), Strype said he wished to inspire modern clerics with their predecessor's zeal against both papists and nonconformists, and to this end he reminded them of the esteem their church had been held in abroad. For 'learned protestants' from other lands, Strype insisted, the English church had been 'the Top of the Reformation'. It was 'honoured by our Friends, feared by our Enemies, and contemned by none but ourselves at home'.[61] The bulk of the biography underlined these themes. Parker corresponded with many representatives of the foreign churches as he constructed the Elizabethan version; he offered asylum to Protestants persecuted abroad; and he cited European opinions in defence of the structures he established. In particular, Strype tried to draw John Calvin's sting. Traditionally, Calvin had been seen as a stern critic of the Elizabethan church, but Strype used his letters to Parker to suggest he had been encouraged by the English settlement, and that his position had been maliciously misrepresented in later decades. Although doubtful about some details of the emerging church, Calvin would have enjoyed a respectful dialogue with Parker had the former not died before this could develop and so allowed papal agents to insinuate he had been hostile to English forms.[62]

Edmund Grindal offered more of a challenge for Strype.[63] Parker's successor as archbishop of Canterbury had also had close European contacts (many picked up during his exile under Mary), but these seemed to have made him rather *too* enthusiastic for foreign models. The real problem emerged in the

[59] Ibid., pp. 194–8, 210. [60] Ibid., pp. 212–14.
[61] John Strype, *The life and acts of Matthew Parker* (1711), p. vi. [62] Ibid., pp. 70–1.
[63] John Strype, *The history of the life and acts of the most reverend father in God, Edmund Grindal* (1710).

1560s when Grindal had encouraged 'prophesyings' among the clergy. These were meetings of local ministers to discuss preaching practice and pastoral care; but since they occurred without supervision by bishops, critics thought them stalking horses for a Genevan-style church which might do without episcopal oversight. The queen was concerned, and when Grindal refused to suppress the meetings she suspended him from his duties. Strype therefore had his work cut out if he wanted to use this archbishop's career to defend the European credentials of Elizabeth's foundation. He rose to the challenge, however, by presenting the dispute as an unfortunate misunderstanding by the monarch. The queen, Strype insisted, had been mistaken in thinking that the meetings would threaten episcopacy; and, unusually, he portrayed the whole controversy as a minor domestic matter, with little reference to foreign Protestants.[64] By contrast, the many more positive aspects of Grindal's work were soaked in the European context. Grindal joined with continental Protestants in stating core doctrines. He worked for their relief and shelter from Catholic persecution. Like Parker and Cranmer before him, he cited their opinions as he disciplined radical separatists.[65] In sum: Strype's works might have been ungainly, but they provided the archival backing for Burnet's cause. He set the church of England firmly within the Protestant international, arguing both that it was wholly legitimate, and that it should have sympathy for those who preferred other models of the faith.

The writers we have been examining so far defended the English church by placing it at the centre of a European reformation. Yet, of course, there were those from a dissenting tradition who wished to attack the institution. For the puritans of the sixteenth century, the church had never done enough to rid itself of popery. Their heirs in the Stuart age were hounded out of the establishment in 1662, and in response they constructed a historical case for their nonconformity which suggested a very different relationship between England and the Europeans. This account of the past emerged in fragmentary form as dissenters argued their position in the decades after Charles II's restoration. As we shall see, a vigorous press campaign lambasted the ceremony and government of the church of England, and as part of this writers such as Richard Baxter and Henry Hickman covered the reformation to construct a nonconformist chronology. This saw an early English Protestantism fired by the radicalism of the continent, but betrayed as popishly affected clerics trapped it in a hierarchical and ceremonial institution.[66] Yet for all the energy of the interpretation, a systematic account waited until 1732. Then Daniel Neal, a London presbyterian minister, began his sweeping *History*

[64] Ibid., bk II, chs. 8–9. [65] E.g. ibid., bk II, pp. 74, 75, 112–13, and passim.

[66] Henry Hickman, *Historia quinq-articularis-exarticulate* (1673); for Baxter, see below, pp. 303–11.

of the puritans.[67] In this, Neal redirected Burnet's vision, radically shifting emphasis from the support the foreign churches had given England towards their frequent censures of her establishment. As he performed this manoeuvre, Neal placed the English *outside* the European movement. Though the writer retained Burnet's sense that English faith should be weighed against continental standards, Neal diverged sharply by finding it wanting in that balance.

Parallels between Burnet's and Neal's reading were obvious in their accounts of the three reigns before Elizabeth's. For both historians, Henry VIII's reformation had barely been worth the name. Although the king had done valuable work destroying the pope's authority, the official religious settlement had followed his idiosyncratic (and largely Catholic) whims, and the only real progress had come as Englishmen had been moved by ideas from abroad.[68] Under Edward – Burnet and Neal still agreed – the establishment had itself begun to move in the right direction, but again influence from Europe was crucial. Advice from Bucer, Calvin and Martyr had also been central: and Neal merely added Huldrych Zwingli, Johannes Oecolampadius, Heinrich Bullinger, Wolfgang Capito and others to the common list.[69] Mary's persecutions brought similar consensus. Both Burnet and Neal noted that exiles encountered advanced Protestant opinions in Frankfurt and Geneva (with Neal adding Emden, Strasbourg and Zurich), and both traced the puritan tradition in the Elizabethan church to this experience.[70]

Thus far then, Burnet and Neal had travelled together – with the latter providing an even richer international dimension. Where they parted was in assessing the nature of the foreign influence. Burnet read European engagement as endorsement, which just occasionally tumbled over into unhelpful zealotry. Neal, however, saw it as repeated rebuke. For him, foreigners had intervened primarily to chastise the English church for not living up to their more reformed models, and for betraying the international reformation to boot. The division was best illustrated in Burnet's and Neal's account of the 'vestarian' controversy. This dispute (over whether the crown had the right to insist that ministers wear ornate surplices whilst officiating in worship) rumbled through Edward's and Elizabeth's reigns, and occasioned the first clear split between a 'puritan' and 'conformist' party in the church. In Burnet's version, foreign churches had doubts about surplices, but they had advised English ministers to comply.[71] Neal, by contrast, stressed the doubts. In his

[67] See also Neal's political defence of nonconformity: Daniel Neal, *A letter to the reverend Dr Francis Hare* (1720); Daniel Neal, *A letter from a dissenter to the author of the Craftsman* (1733).

[68] E.g. Daniel Neal, *The history of the puritans or Protestant non-conformists* (4 vols., 1732–8), I:28–9.

[69] Ibid., I:66. [70] Ibid., I:108. [71] See above, p. 81.

lengthy and detailed coverage, foreign divines were fiercely opposed to the sartorial remnants of popery, and were only just prepared to put up with them as a very temporary expedient. They might have been wary of dividing English Protestantism in its infancy, but 'it was the unanimous Opinion of all the foreign Divines, that the *Habits* ought to be laid aside by Authority; and that in the mean Time they should not be urged on those that scrupled them'.[72]

By concentrating on such foreign disappointment with the English church, Neal cast the mid-Tudor establishment from the body of the European reformation in which Burnet had so carefully installed it. What drove the historians yet further apart was Neal's assessment of the Elizabethan church. Whilst Burnet had seen the late Tudor settlement as prudent (the reason he thought foreign divines had praised it), Neal saw it as a betrayal. When Elizabeth had come to the throne, the dissenter insisted, European Protestants had hoped the English would purge out the last remnants of popery, but instead they had lost courage in the face of the stubborn and conservative queen. The result was an unsatisfactory reform, and constant tension as foreign clerics and their domestic allies had worked to correct the mistake. In this worldview, it was not the puritans who had damaged the church. Rather, the conformists had been out of step with the broad reformation, and it was they who had split and weakened the godly cause. What made this betrayal particularly perfidious was its timing. In the 1560s and 1570s European Protestantism had faced a crisis. French Huguenots were losing their struggle with a bigoted Catholic faction at the Parisian court, and Philip II of Spain was persecuting the Protestant Dutch as he tried to end their rebellion. In response, Elizabeth did little except divide the church in her care. She refused to act against Philip until he threatened her politically, and she badgered her own Protestant subjects if they would not submit to her will. Consequently England, the leading reformed power, was hesitant and internally distracted through the continental turmoil. Even when thousands of Huguenots were butchered in the 1572 St Bartholomew's Day massacre, the English queen refused to respond and 'made no Concession for uniting her Protestant Subjects among themselves'.[73] Worse was to come. Towards the end of the reign, the church of England actually began to trail back towards Rome. At first, the queen's insistence on bishops in England had not questioned the validity of the non-episcopal churches abroad, but by 1580s the worth of these churches was openly 'disputed and denied'. The English thus broke the unity of the international reformation, and 'removed by Degrees to a greater distance from the foreign Protestants'.[74]

[72] Neal, *History of the puritans*, I:201. [73] Ibid., I:303. [74] Ibid., I:594.

Neal's interpretation received significant support in the early eighteenth century. Dissenters cited it as they continued to criticise the contemporary church, and it got backing from one of the most prolific and influential historians of the day. In 1724, John Oldmixon had published a history of England which had praised Burnet, though it had covered the sixteenth century relatively quickly.[75] In 1739 (after Neal's volumes had appeared) Oldmixon produced a much more detailed account of the Tudor age which still quoted Burnet, but transcribed even longer passages of Neal, and agreed that Romish elements among churchmen had betrayed a European movement. Tudor clerics, Oldmixon complained, had not gone so far 'in the Work as the Reformers had gone in other parts of *Christendom*'. More damningly, they had mistaken patriotism for piety.[76] Accusing some of the founders of the Tudor church of rejecting advanced Protestant forms simply because they were foreign, Oldmixon charged that they had replaced scripture with national sentiment and said he could not see how England's church could 'become more Orthodox only by being *English*'.[77] There could hardly be a pithier summary of the dissenting position. England's duty was to follow a righteous model of worship embodied in the wider European reformation. Any national religious identity, or claims to spiritual autonomy, had to be subsumed in a pan-continental truth embodied in a more radical Protestant international.

Of course, Neal's and Oldmixon's arguments were controversial. They denigrated the church of England, and besmirched the reputation of Elizabeth, its heroic founder. Very soon, establishment historians leapt to defend the Tudor settlement, in particular accusing Neal of editing out the intolerant fanaticism of the puritans and quoting Burnet extensively to prove their point.[78] Yet within the dispute, shared commitment to the Protestant international as the standard of religious value set a pattern of argument. As each round of debate unfolded, protagonists appealed more fervently to the foreign churches, and progressively widened their vision of continental Protestantism. Thus Neal's critics cited Burnet's examples of foreigners who had praised the church. Yet rather than concentrating on these particular souls, they also lambasted the dissenters' pinched view of the European reformation. Zachery Grey, for instance, accused Neal of using only Calvin and his direct followers when setting the European context for English reform.[79]

[75] John Oldmixon, *The critical history of England* (1724).

[76] John Oldmixon, *The history of England during the reigns of Henry VIII, Edward VI . . .* (1739), p. 172.

[77] Ibid., p. 273.

[78] E.g. *An expostulatory letter to Mr Daniel Neal* (1732); and Zachery Grey's systematic attacks on Neal's volumes as they appeared.

[79] Zachery Grey, *A review of Mr Daniel Neal's history* (Cambridge, 1744), pp. 51–2.

He reminded him that there were other strands of continental Protestantism feeding into the Tudor church, and that many of these had been far less critical. Isaac Maddox also appealed for the broadest view of the reformation. In 1733, Maddox, who was to become bishop of Worcester, wrote a *Vindication* of his church against Neal and charged dissenters of having a very restrictive view of the European Protestant movement. For Maddox, Neal had confused the reformation with the critical churches of France and Switzerland. He had quite forgotten the Lutheran churches of Scandinavia and Northern Germany, which had retained a form of hierarchy in church government, and had gone even less far in reforming ceremony or doctrine than Elizabeth's conformists.[80] Once the Lutherans entered the picture, it was clear the England's settlement was at the *centre* of the Protestant spectrum, not outside it. If any doubted this, Maddox cited the numbers of Lutheran and Calvinist Christians who had joined the English church. The two groups found it a short step from their own position to that prevailing on the northern shore of the Channel, notwithstanding the 'irreconcileableness' of the confessions to one another.[81] By such careful positioning at the moderate Protestant centre, Elizabeth had become far more useful to the European movement than Calvin or his puritan followers could ever be. She was not so 'bigoted to a single Branch' of the reformation as to alienate others, and to denounce her stance was to hobble England's unifying role. 'When finished', Maddox claimed, the English church 'was held in great Esteem abroad. It was look'd on by the *most temperate* Protestants as a happy *Medium* between Calvinists and Lutherans, and as such, most proper for that *Princess*, who resolved to support the whole reformed Interest.'[82]

The pattern of debate thus involved a steadily broadening vision of the reformation. Burnet, defending his church against nonconformists who claimed it had ignored the continental movement, quoted the support it received from certain foreign divines. Neal, hostile to Burnet's establishment, had brought in more critical voices from France and Switzerland, and implied Burnet had quoted his foreign sources selectively. Maddox, slating Neal, had called on the Lutheran church to balance the Calvinist, and reminded him that England had to lead the whole, varied, reformation. At some level, this steady polemical expansion suggests a unity behind the disagreements. Whilst not concurring in their interpretations, the battling historians felt obliged to explain English reform within the Protestant international movement, and were convinced victory lay in taking the broadest possible view of this.

80 Isaac Maddox, *A vindication of the government, doctrine and worship of the church of England* (1733), pp. 34, 55.
81 Ibid., p. 84. 82 Ibid., p. 105.

It is possible some of these writers would have been happy to leave things there. They bickered, but shared assumptions contained disputes between people who in fact had much in common. Moderate churchmen agreed with dissenters that Protestants faced their greatest threat from popery rather than from a diversity of opinion within the movement. They also agreed that persecuting those whose honest (if perhaps misled) consciences would not allow them to join an official church would weaken the joint Protestant cause. By discussing the past in the framework described above, moderate churchmen and nonconformists constructed a mode of discussion which kept their reformation together. All accepted continental influence on the English church. All stressed debts and obligations to a wide reformation composed of groups who had made several different arrangements for worship and government. All struggled to welcome more and more people under their movement's umbrella, and so fostered a diverse and inclusive vision of the true church which went beyond any individual institution. In a later chapter we will see how the immediate political dispute between churchmen and nonconformists cooled in the last decades of the Stuart era. We will also see that a common ideology, based on a broad and flexible reading of the European reformation, paved the way.[83] For all the disputes over details of foreign Protestant involvement in the sixteenth century, the notion that this had been an enriching contribution from a legitimately varied movement provided the historical underpinnings for an English Protestant consensus in the eighteenth century.

Yet unfortunately this valuable – if not always cosy – agreement was haunted by a very different reading of the sixteenth century. In 1661, Peter Heylyn had published his *Ecclesia restaurata*. When supplemented by its author's many other writings, this account of the Tudor establishment denied and denounced continental influence on the new body, and constituted a standing challenge to the international Protestantism of other histories. In fact, many of the interpretations we have been describing were responses to Heylyn's analysis of the past. Burnet had certainly wanted to answer him directly. Although formally citing Nicholas Saunders' sixteenth-century Catholic history of England as its target, the preface to the first volume of the *History of the reformation* also said it must correct Heylyn's mistakes.[84] This author, more than any other, had to be refuted. His vision of the past threatened the entire Burnetine universe.

Peter Heylyn had good personal reason to blacken 'broad Protestant' readings of the reformation. In the 1630s he had been chaplain to Archbishop

[83] See below, pp. 313–40.

[84] Burnet's formal target was Nicholas Saunders, *De origine ac progressu schismatis Anglicani liber* (1586), recently translated as *Histoire du schisme d'Angleterre* (Paris, 1676).

William Laud. He had therefore been at the centre of the 'Laudian' drive to emphasise the medieval Catholic heritage of the church, and he had written in support of the insistence on ceremony, and the high view of episcopal authority, which this had entailed. In the civil war, he had suffered with all of Laud's followers. A prime cause of the revolt against Charles I had been disgust at Laudianism (seen as a return to popery), and as parliamentary forces had gained ground, the archbishop's policies and adherents were anathematised. In the 1640s, ceremonial innovations were reversed, episcopacy was abolished, and the primate himself was executed. His followers fared only somewhat better. Hounded out of their positions, they were banned from using their beloved liturgy and constantly investigated as potential royalist sympathisers. Heylyn himself lost his livings in Hampshire and at Westminster Abbey and paid fines to keep his other estates. Given all this, it was understandable if an embittered Laudian party was ready for revenge when monarchy was restored in 1660. It was also understandable if Heylyn, as the Laudians' chief propagandist, wanted to play his part. He accordingly wrote a stream of works which identified and denounced the corrupting influences which he thought had led to the 1640s revolt.[85]

At the heart of these heresies was foreign Protestant influence over the English church. In his pre-war writings, Heylyn had tried to reposition the English establishment between the Roman Catholics and European Protestantism. While most earlier writers had seen England's church as part of a broad international reformation united in opposition to Rome, Heylyn had 'ignored a century of Protestant reasoning' to place it closer to the old enemy.[86] He had denied that the pope was antichrist; he had argued that the Roman communion was a true – if corrupted – church; and he had suggested the church of England was a part of this true communion which had purged itself of vices. In his restoration writings Heylyn developed this vision further. He condemned the idea that England was part of a radical European reform, and denounced the links with foreigners which this error had sponsored. The first, and milder, part of the case was made through the account of the Edwardian reform. While 'Protestant' readings of this process placed much emphasis on English receptions of Luther, and on the advice and example of Calvin and Bucer, Heylyn presented a more 'English' reformation. He might admit in the preface that the commissions who had designed the Edwardian church had looked to 'such Foreign Churches, as seemed to have most consonancy to the ancient Forms', but this was only one source of inspiration. It was listed after 'the Word of God' (scripture);

[85] See Anthony Milton, 'Heylyn, Peter', *ODNB*, XXVI:954–8.

[86] Anthony Milton, *Catholic and reformed: the Roman and Protestant churches in English Protestant thought, 1600–1640* (Cambridge, 1995), p. 117.

'the Practice of the Primitive Times' (that is, the example of the churches in the first centuries after Christ); and 'the general current and consent of the old Catholick Doctours' (or the early Christian thinkers who were acknowledged as authorities by all Christians).[87] Following these lights, the English had done a better job of reform than people in Germany, France or Switzerland. Their church had come closer to the ideal pattern of doctrine, government and worship than any other, and was in fact of a piece with the practices of the apostles.[88] In the main bulk of the text, the position was clearer still. By this point, Heylyn was determined to eliminate *any* foreign influences in English reform. The historian admitted that Martin Bucer and Peter Martyr had come over, and that they had offered advice to the commission which had composed Edward's first prayer book in 1548, but he insisted they had arrived too late to have an impact. Calvin had pitched in too, but Cranmer – alive to Genevan bullying – had rebuffed his contribution. Wisely, therefore, the commissioners worked without outside help. They were resolved, Heylyn claimed, 'that none but *English* Heads or Hands should be used . . . lest otherwise it might be thought, or perhaps Objected, that they rather followed the Example of all other Churches, or were swayed by the Authority of those Foreign Assistants; then by the Word of God.'[89]

Such a version of Edwardian history obviously disrupted the close links between England and the continent seen in other writers. What utterly severed them was Heylyn's account of challenges to the settlement reached. He, like those who came after him, recognised that the example of more reformed churches abroad had inspired a party in England to ask for more thoroughgoing change; but unlike other writers he could not see this as a useful, if occasionally troublesome, contribution. For Heylyn, attacks on ceremony and liturgy were simple heresy, which overturned pillars of Christianity built on scripture and centuries of tradition. The trouble had started in Edward's reign. As the regime tried to implement its first reforms, it suffered a barrage of criticism from foreign zealots who wished doctrine to move beyond accommodating formulae, and wanted to purge worship of all traditional ornament. In this context, Bucer's and Martyr's encouragements to further reform were presented as interfering rather than helpful, and Calvin's letters were motivated by a personal pride which led to endless meddling 'in such Matters, as belonged not to him'.[90] Worse still were the exiled churches granted sanctuary in London by the Edwardian regime. Even Burnet would complain that a party of Poles led by John à Lasco had abused those who had offered them refuge by criticising their church, but Heylyn was more forthright. He roundly attacked the regime for allowing these

[87] Peter Heylyn, *Ecclesia restaurata* (1661), preface. [88] Ibid., epistle dedicatory.
[89] Ibid., p. 65. [90] Ibid., p. 80.

people to worship according to their own extreme notions and to encourage natives to condemn official practice.[91] Soon, Heylyn complained that a disruptive '*Zuinglian*' party (labelled after the Swiss reformer) had become entrenched among the English themselves. Bishop Hooper's refusal to wear vestments was the result of 'the desire of the Zwinglian Faction to reduce this Church unto the Nakedness and Simplicity, of the Transmarine Churches'; whilst the damaging controversies which had forced the regime to revise the prayer book in 1552 were the result of Calvin's plotting with his English followers.[92] If foreign influence under Edward was bad, real disaster came during the exile of the next reign. English Protestants fled Mary's persecution, but this brought them into contact with radical churches in Frankfurt, Strasbourg and Geneva. Although some honoured the Edwardian settlement whilst abroad, others such as John Knox fell under Calvin's influence and demanded that the refugee communities adopt his style of worship, church government and discipline. When Mary died, this corrupted group would return to England and form the core of the seditious puritan party. Wanting England reduced to Genevan Protestantism, this faction plagued Elizabeth's ecclesiastical government, and would be joined by French exiles who provided the same sort of bad example as Lasco's group under Edward.[93] The *Ecclesia restaurata* ran out of steam in the mid-1560s, but by then its message was clear. As Heylyn insisted in his closing paragraphs, the dangerous rebels of the mid-seventeenth century were simply the heirs of those perverted by foreigners a hundred years before.

At first sight, Heylyn's version of the reformation looks like a separatist chronology. In huge contrast to Burnet and the dissenting histories, it isolated England from Protestants abroad, suggesting that the country had founded its church by itself, and had learnt nothing but error from the continent. Throughout, Heylyn trumpeted the unique holiness of the English church. He insisted she alone had purged popery without abandoning the models of scripture or first Christians, whilst foreigners had been misled by their own overheated wills. Heylyn was sure those abroad had broken the continuity of the church by pretending to found it anew, and had swept away many of the marks of a true communion so carefully retained on his side of the Channel. Yet for all this apparent English chauvinism, Heylyn's history actually had as rich a European dimension as the 'Protestant' alternatives. Although his case against the puritans demanded he paint England's church as an isolated paragon, other imperatives drove him back towards the continent. His very pathology of nonconformity depended on close European commentary, whilst his explanation of the sixteenth century ultimately provided one of the most embracing international contexts for English religion. In fact,

[91] Ibid., pp. 89–90. [92] Ibid., pp. 95, 107. [93] Ibid., p. 133 (second pagination).

Heylyn was probably the least parochial historian in our sample. He provided some of the most extensive coverage of foreign Christians, and some of the deepest (if most controversial) thinking about their true status.

First and most obviously, the author's analysis of an international threat drove him to close consideration of Europe. He provided detailed descriptions of events on the continent to explain where attacks on his church had originated, so that his international dimension was actually rather richer than Burnet's. In the *Ecclesia restaurata*, for example, he would provide close and extended narratives of John à Lasco's disruptions, of Hooper's 'foreign' position on vestments (he had picked this up from Bullinger in Zurich during an exile after 1540), and of the disputes between the Marian exiles in Frankfurt.[94] More dramatically, Heylyn would expound a sweeping history of European Protestantism in his 1670 (and posthumous) *Aerius redivivus*. In this – frankly deranged – work, the author traced the errors of English puritans from origins in Switzerland through a series of intermediate countries. For Heylyn, the presbyterian heresy had seeped from Geneva 'into *France*, from *France* into the *Netherlands*, from the *Netherlands* to *Scotland*, and from then to *England*', and he hounded it all the way.[95] Accordingly the reader was treated to extensive coverage of the Genevan reformation; and then to close consideration of the birth of the Huguenot church in France and the progress of Dutch and Scots Protestantism. There was also an account of a wider Genevan mission which also affected Bohemia, Germany, Poland and Sweden, and which came close to establishing Calvin as a Protestant pope. 'International Calvinism' is a modern historians' phrase, used to express the network of contacts between reformed churches which tied England to Europe.[96] Ironically, though, it was the great enemy of this phenomenon who first identified it. Convinced his church had been assaulted by a multiheaded and pan-continental hydra, Heylyn anatomised the beast. As he did so, the sweep of his prose over the Alps, down the Rhine and Seine, and across the Baltic and North Seas, matched any other international vision.

More positively, Heylyn found he could not leave the church of England alone in Europe. Although he wanted to distance the English from Calvin, and so insisted they had reformed without outside influence, this position left him with the difficulty of identifying Christians abroad. He had approved England's destruction of popery and so had confirmed the Roman communion was not godly. Yet by presenting most foreign Protestants as unholy as well, he came close to limiting the true church to one country. Theologically, this was untenable. God would not have left the world outside England with

94 Ibid., pp. 89–90, 59–64 (second pagination).
95 Peter Heylyn, *Aerius redivivus* (1670), preface.
96 Embodied in Menna Prestwich, ed., *International Calvinism, 1541–1715* (Oxford, 1985).

no valid ecclesiastical body and, as we shall see, those involved in the religious debates of Charles II's reign charged this absurdity upon one another as a favoured rhetorical move.[97] Heylyn skirted the trap by reaching out to one particular branch of the European reformation. Observing that the Lutherans had been more moderate than the Calvinists in their reform, and fixing on Luther's associate Philip Melancthon as the most moderate even of these, Heylyn suggested this theologian had outlined an ecclesiology virtually identical to that of the English.

Heylyn's enthusiasm for Melancthonian Lutheranism was evident in the preface to *Ecclesia restaurata*. There, we will recall, he did admit some foreign influence on the English church. He had spoken with respect of those institutions abroad with most 'consonancy to the ancient forms'. In the rest of his works, it became clear he had been referring to the moderate Lutherans. As he explained, they had had been guided by scripture and primitive example rather than their own immoderate zeal, and so had provided partners for England by retaining the useful ceremony, doctrine and episcopacy of the medieval church.[98] Of course, there had been differences and tensions between Lutherans and the English. In particular, the northern Germans had not offered refuge to those fleeing Mary's persecution in the 1550s, but in fact this rupture had ultimately illustrated deeper affinities between the two groups. The Lutherans, it turned out, had been alienated by John à Lasco. He had fled through Germany before any natives left London, and had spread false rumours that the English had converted to the full Calvinist position which Lutherans rejected.[99] Crucially, Philip Melancthon had denounced Lasco and tried to correct the breach he had caused; and this made him even more of a hero to Heylyn. With his tempered and scholarly approach to reform, Melancthon had been the greatest light of the sixteenth-century church, and Heylyn regretted he had not been able to come to England to advise on the Tudor settlement. He had, however, been present in his 'learned writings' on the commission restating doctrine; and had been – the historian extravagantly claimed – as influential as St Augustine.[100]

Melancthonism, then, proved an English-style reformation had not enlightened England alone. In some passages, Heylyn took this analysis even further. He suggested Melancthon might have reconciled other European churches, and so reintegrated England into a universal communion. By adopting a moderate position, and being willing to retain parts of the medieval heritage, Melancthon had positioned the Lutherans on ground the English had also tried to occupy, and was not so far from the Roman

[97] See below, pp. 284–313.
[98] See especially, Peter Heylyn, *Cyprianus anglicus* (1668), p. 3.
[99] Heylyn, *Ecclesia restaurata*, p. 80 (second pagination). [100] Ibid., p. 108.

Catholics that they would automatically reject his stance. This was particularly true in the theology of salvation. As Heylyn explained in his great apology for Archbishop Laud, moderate Lutherans came close to healing the reformation rupture. Although the original quarrel between Luther and the pope had centred on whether good works were necessary for salvation (Luther overthrew the medieval position by insisting faith alone was required), once tempers had cooled Melancthon had explored a middle way. He suggested faith was the saving agent, but that it only operated when attended by good works, and Heylyn argued that even many Romanists had come to the same conclusion. In fact, there was a growing consensus on salvation, which followed ancient models and which could include England in a new universal church. As Heylyn put it, 'The *Moderate* or *Melancthonian Lutherans*, together with the *Jesuits* and *Franciscans*, appeal unto the general current of the ancient Fathers . . . And to this . . . the church of *England* most enclines.'[101]

By presenting Melancthon in this way, Heylyn was making his most unusual move. Although his earlier interpretations had a very different political spin to other historians, their intellectual underpinnings had actually been quite similar. For example, Heylyn's insistence that the English themselves had led their reformation was not so far from Burnet's. The later historian would acknowledge the role of domestic study of scripture in the 1540s and merely supplemented this with a strong input from abroad. Similarly, Heylyn's denunciation of the Genevan faction was simply a harsh opinion of an influence all historians would emphasise; whilst even his identification with moderate Lutheranism was not fundamentally different from Burnet's analysis. Burnet had seen the English participating in a broad European reformation; Heylyn was simply choosier about which foreign Protestants he wanted as friends. By contrast, by proposing Melancthon as the man to unite Protestants and Romanists, Heylyn was advancing something truly radical. Building on his pre-war writings, he was suggesting that the true context of the English reformation was not simply continental Protestantism, but was rather the Christian church as a whole. For Heylyn, the English had not joined a breakaway movement in the sixteenth century but, like moderate Lutherans, had remained within the old international institution. Certainly they had purged the blemishes of the medieval European church, and denied the authority of the corrupted papacy. Yet they had nevertheless respected its basic unity, heritage and structures, and had tried to erect a standard around which it might re-form. In this vision, the English had followed Melancthon in trying to avoid a split in the traditional establishment. Preserving episcopacy, ceremony and a theology of salvation with a place for

[101] Heylyn, *Cyprianus*, p. 30.

good works, they had not moved so far from Rome, nor denounced her so completely, that separation must be final. This, of course, was a profoundly internationalist position. It was, however, very different from the *Protestant* international we have encountered this far. It was a universal, we might dare to say 'catholic', worldview which embraced Christians in southern Europe as much as the north.

This element in Heylyn's thought was further revealed in his account of the authority for the reformation. Historians of the church of England obviously needed to explain what had given it the right to break with Rome and alter its worship and doctrinal statements. To answer this puzzle, most scholars did what Burnet did. They appealed to royal power or the fundamental autonomy of the national church, often mixing this with a sense that popish corruptions were so gross that almost any process against them must be justified. For Heylyn, however, these principles did too much damage to his ideal of a still-united European church. He *did* grant the national church autonomy (though not the king – his civil war experience of what secular power might do to clerics led him to reject lay control), but this autonomy was not theoretically fundamental. Rather, it was allowed *in default* of action by the international communion. For Heylyn, the universal church had sovereignty over its constituent national parts; these parts only gained autonomy when the universal body could not perform its duties.

To make this clearer, we should examine the point in Heylyn's history when the issue of authority arose. It came when the Edwardian church commission issued its doctrinal statement. Approving this condemnation of aspects of medieval belief, Heylyn said he faced the wrath of those who tried to delegitimise the English reformation by demanding a general council of the whole church before such changes were approved. He had to answer those (mainly Roman Catholic detractors) who argued that the definition of heresy, and therefore a programme for its correction, could only come from a body representating all Christians.[102] Heylyn's answer was subtle. He first admitted that a general council would be 'the best and safeste Physick', and so upheld the idea that a universal assembly was the highest authority in the church.[103] He then, however, pointed out that such a council had been utterly impractical in the 1540s. Not only were Christians in the Eastern Mediterreanean prevented from travelling to the west by their Turkish masters, but those who were still free were sundered by disputes. If the pope called a meeting, no Protestant would go, yet Romanists would not attend anything summoned by anyone else. A true general council was thus 'an empty Dream'.[104] In this situation, Heylyn looked to early precedent to permit the English church to purify its doctrine and practices. The historian described the Tudor reformers

[102] Heylyn, *Ecclesia restaurata*, p. 123. [103] Ibid., p. 124. [104] Ibid.

following the example of the Christians of the first centuries who had found it dangerous to come together in times of persecution. These men had given authority to local assemblies if a universal meeting could not be convened, and for Heylyn it was *this* which had justified England's autonomous definition of doctrine. The English had not therefore enjoyed an essential autonomy as they had made changes under Edward. Instead they had reformed themselves using emergency powers. These were powers which were allowed to individual groups of the faithful in disordered times, and which had been approved by the very founders of the church.

Of course, there was considerable rhetorical stretching here. Heylyn asserted that power rested with the international communion, but provided grounds for the English to excuse themselves from this universal authority if there was the slightest doubt about its actual ability to meet. He performed the same trick when describing the English bishops' refusal of an invitation to the council of Trent in 1560s. This was the body first convened by the Roman Catholics to respond to the Protestant challenge, and which was now hoping to reunite all Christians under a reformed papacy, but as Heylyn had Bishop John Jewel explaining, no English official could attend because the meeting was not truly general. Protestants would not feel safe travelling to Catholic lands or speaking freely in them, and even if promises of safe passage were sincere (which Jewel doubted), large parts of the Christian world would be absent. No one from Denmark, Sweden, Scotland or north Germany was going and 'a great part of the World professing the name of *Christ*, (as *Greeks*, *Armenians*, *Aybssines*, &c with all the Eastern Church) were neither sent . . . nor summoned'.[105] Here Heylyn again asserted the right of the English church to stand aside from the Roman communion. Yet it is nevertheless important to note the argument rested on 'catholic' rather than national or Protestant grounds. Jewel had not refused to go to Trent because universal councils lacked authority over local churches, or even, technically, because it had been called by the pope. Rather he denounced this proposed meeting because it was not universal enough. If representatives of all Christians had been invited, if they had all been persuaded to come, and if the Romanists had not bullied or silenced dissent in any meeting, Heylyn implied England would have recognised the authority of the council.

Heylyn's European vision was challenging – but he was not a wholly isolated figure. In a later chapter, we will see many supporters of the established church using its supposed membership of a universal, 'catholic', communion to defend it against dissenting critics. Such rhetoric frequently cited events in the sixteenth century, and so upheld Heylyn's account of the

[105] Ibid., p. 147 (second pagination).

reformation.[106] Even among more systematic histories, the themes expounded in *Ecclesia restaurata* were frequently rehearsed. For example, only historians from a fully nonconformist background wholly excused the excesses of the puritans, and few failed to acknowledge that overzealous prompting from abroad could cause these. Again, many constructed the English church as a moderate mean between the extremes of Catholicism and Protestantism, and this implied praise for the institution's respect for the heritage of the medieval transnational communion. Perhaps most interestingly, historians took up Heylyn's vision in order to fence the church from the encroachment of secular power. Particularly among the large number of non-juring scholars (that is, those clerics who were thrown out of the church for refusing to swear loyalty to William III after the 1688 revolution), Heylyn's case that spiritual authority sat with universal church councils – rather than lay governments – was understandingly popular. This was the context in which to understand Heylyn's most influential follower, Jeremy Collier.

Today, Jeremy Collier is best known for his attack on the English stage.[107] His denunciation of the moral turpitude of late Stuart drama generated sharp replies from such luminaries as William Congreve and John Vanbrugh, but he was rather more than a scourge of playwrights.[108] Having lost his own church position in 1689, he became one of the main polemicists for the non-juring cause, defending the position with complaints both that William III's seizure of power had been illegal, and that even if it had not been, the king could not invade the church to eject those who did not transfer their loyalty.[109] From 1708, his polemic took the form of his *Ecclesiastical history of Great Britain*. Over two huge volumes (the second published in 1714), this asserted that the past demonstrated the essential independence of the clergy from secular power, and quoted Heylyn's account of the reformation extensively as it did so.[110] Collier's position on royal authority was obviously very different from Burnet's. The latter accepted the purge of non-jurors, and praised monarchical action in imposing Protestantism under the Tudors. This divergence generated heated controversy between the two men, but what interests us here is the closely related differences over England's place in the European church.[111] Rejecting Burnet's

106 See below, pp. 293–6, 332–4.
107 Jeremy Collier, *A short view of the immorality and profaneness of the English stage* (1698); this is the focus of Eric Salmon, 'Collier, Jeremy', *ODNB*, XII:640–5.
108 William Congreve, *Amendments to M. Collier's false and imperfect citations* (1698); John Vanbrugh, *A short vindication* (1698).
109 E.g. Jeremy Collier, *The desertion discussed* (1689); Jeremy Collier, *Doctor Sherlock's 'Case of allegiance' considered* (1691); Jeremy Collier, *A brief essay of the independency of church power* (1692).
110 Jeremy Collier, *An ecclesiastical history of Great Britain* (2 vols., 1708–14).
111 For the tensions, Starkie, 'Contested histories'.

international Protestantism as a Genevan plot, Collier followed Heylyn in basing clerical independence on an even broader communion of Christians.[112] Such internationalism transcended both the reformation and the power of any particular king, and Collier celebrated it as a barrier against William's national Protestant monarchy. The writer was therefore as concerned as Heylyn to show the English had not departed from the old continental establishment in the sixteenth century, and as keen as his predecessor on signs that England's moderate settlement might bring the whole Christian community back together.

Thus Collier extended Heylyn's suggestion that the early reformation in England might have provided a standard around which all Christians could muster. He praised the doctrinal moderation of Henry VIII's church as a foundation for ecumenism, and set English reform in the context of several attempts to heal the breaches between Protestants and Catholics across the continent.[113] For example, Collier stressed papal attempts at reform of the Roman communion, believing that if Protestants had taken them as seriously as they deserved, they might have led to reconciliation. He similarly denounced the factionalism which had overcome European Christians in the sixteenth century and even suggested that Luther himself had come to regret his readiness to break away from Rome.[114] Perhaps most importantly, Collier showed Heylyn's interest in at least the principle of general councils. He expanded on the earlier scholar's coverage of the English response to Trent (they had been right not to go to a meeting 'packed and prejudiced against them', but Jewel's carefully considered arguments showed they would still consider the idea of a genuine meeting of the universal church); and he laid out a similar reaction to an invitation to an assembly at Mantua in 1536.[115]

Collier, then, joined Heylyn in telling the story of the English reformation in a very wide continental context. Accepting this, it seems we were wrong to suggest these men challenged the ever broader appeal to Europe in ecclesiological dispute between English Protestants. Rather, we could see them as a radical, transforming extension of it. Attempting to overturn the old Tudor tradition which saw the church of England as part of a family of reformed churches, Heylyn expanded the international dimension beyond Protestantism itself. Right at the start of our period he played the ultimate trump card. He reminded Englishmen that they were Christians as well as Protestants; that they were members of a universal church as well as activists of its purified branch. Burnet and the other 'broad Protestants' therefore had to spend the next century coping with this daring move. Reasserting the Protestant international, and insisting on the utter degeneracy of popery,

[112] For Genevan plotting see Collier, *Ecclesiastical history*, II:476. [113] Ibid., II:128.
[114] Ibid., II:170–2. [115] Ibid., II:476–7, 139.

they scrabbled back from the ecumenical precipice to which Heylyn had led them. Yet they were never entirely successful. Given the tendency to draw the reformation wider in their own disputes, given the vigour of Heylyn's rival interpretation, and given the difficulty of relating events before the sixteenth century without recognising a universal church (the subject of our next section), history was quite literally on their opponents' side. English confessional chronology would contain at least as strong a sense of Heylyn's Catholic church as of Burnet's international Protestant alternative.

THE MIDDLE AGES: WHERE WAS YOUR CHURCH BEYOND ENGLAND?

English accounts of the sixteenth century had become embroiled in disputes between Protestants about the nature of their church. Their narratives of the medieval period would also bear the marks of these battles, but in addition they would have to answer a major challenge from Roman Catholics. The shorthand for this challenge was 'where was your church before Luther?' Since the reformatioin, Romanists had been trying to discredit Protestantism by asking where the true community of the faithful had been in the hundreds of years before reformed Christians said they had rediscovered it. Papal polemicists had pointed out that Rome had been all that had been on offer before Luther protested against it; they had insisted that God would not have left his followers without a true church on earth through the long medieval centuries; and so had concluded that the body Protestants had left must have been Christ's faithful communion. The reformers were thus revealed as sinners. Breaking with a godly institution, Luther and his colleagues had fallen into schism and their followers had inherited that same guilt. Of course, Protestants had faced this challenge for long enough to counter it. Unfortunately, however, the English branch of the reformation had come up with two pretty incompatible responses. We must explore these in some depth since they continued to influence interpretation in the late Stuart and Georgian periods, and came to represent poles between which historians oscillated.

The first answer was that popularised by John Foxe.[116] Much of his 'Book of martyrs' (first published 1563) was devoted to the sufferings of those Protestants persecuted under Mary Tudor, yet by extending the story back to chronicle medieval persecutions, Foxe reminded Catholics that the old church had not quite monopolised English Christianity. There had been

116 John Bale, *The image of both churches* [1548?], envisaged the church as a succession of persecuted dissenters, but it was Foxe who popularised this. Stephen Reed Cattley, ed., *The acts and monuments of John Foxe* (12 vols., 1837) has been superseded by the Foxe Project's edition (www.hironline.ac.uk/foxe/index.html), but is sometimes easier to use.

those – for example, the thirteenth-century 'heretic' John Wyclif and his Lollard followers – who had spoken against the church's perversion of doctrine and had been cruelly punished for it.[117] If a continuous tradition of dissent could be established, its adherents might be shown to be the true church; although they had been an isolated minority, these people had kept faith alive by brave and constant protest against the evil around them. This 'Foxean' answer to the challenge of the medieval church was deeply cosmopolitan. Although Foxe was once seen as a proto-nationalist because his parade of English martyrs suggested England was a unique and special home of godliness, most scholars would now accept this was a misreading of his text.[118] Foxe concentrated on English martyrs simply because he wanted to tell the story of the church *in England*. Faithful Christians had certainly protested against popery in other lands and where their stories expanded or illustrated Foxe's tale, he was happy to include them. There was, therefore, coverage of the medieval French dissidents, especially the Albigensians of the thirteenth century, and a massive discussion of Jan Hus' protests against clerical corruption in fourteenth-century Bohemia.[119] In fact, Foxe's account gelled well with the international protestantism we have been exploring. He saw the true church in the middle ages as groups of true believers scattered across Europe, but united in their disgust at the perversions of the entrenched clergy, and so he provided perfect ancestors for a pan-continental Protestantism. In the sixteenth century, the English reformation had been part of a geographically broad recovery of true Christianity. Following the providential inspiration of Luther's protests in Germany, isolated groups elsewhere had made contact with each other; they had suddenly found an audience beyond their tiny communities, and had mustered the strength to topple popery in great areas of Europe.[120]

The second answer to the Catholic challenge was also international, but it was very different. First fully adumbrated by the Elizabethan theologian Richard Hooker, and taken further by the Laudian clerics under the early Stuarts, this pulled the rug from under the Romanists' feet by accepting that the Rome-centred communion had been the true church in the middle ages.[121] According to this view, the medieval church had fallen into error, but it had never invalidated itself, so there was no need to identify

117 Cattley, *Acts*, II:790–1: Wyclif's story unfolds over this second volume and the next.

118 See William Haller, *Foxe's 'Book of martyrs' and the elect nation* (1963), for the 'nationalist' reading; and Patrick Collinson, *The birthpangs of Protestand England* (Basingstoke, 1988), ch. 1, for recent doubts about this.

119 Cattley, *Acts*, II:376–83; III:309–11, 405–16, 425–511.

120 Coverage of Luther begins at Cattley, *Acts*, IV:260. Foxe drew the scattered European heretics together when he claimed signs prepared them for Luther's coming: ibid., IV:253–60.

121 For Hooker, see Peter Lake, *Anglicans and puritans* (1988), ch. 4.

pockets of godly people outside the institution. Of course, the medieval church had introduced ridiculous superstition. It has also added unscriptural elements to doctrine, and, damningly, it had extended the pope's spiritual and temporal power far beyond warrant. Nevertheless, it had remained the true community of Christians on earth, and occasionally it had remembered its proper structure and function. It had continued to teach the core truths of scripture, genuinely pious people had lived and died in its communion, and from time to time its members had protested that the pontiff had usurped powers. Very closely linked to Heylyn's reading of the reformation (indeed Heylyn did much to advance it), this second answer to the Romanists' challenge drew attention away from international Protestantism and towards a broader vision of Christianity. For Laudian interpreters, the Tudor establishment had not *become* part of the true church by reform. It had always *been* part of Christ's universal communion, even before Henry VIII took it out of Rome's orbit, and had merely polished its godliness by purging the corruptions of the medieval body in the sixteenth century. In this vision, England's godly brethren abroad had not been isolated groups of protestors before Luther, but had simply been members of other branches of the institutional Catholic church. Some of these other branches would reform themselves in the sixteenth century, but even those which remained under the pope were integral (if imperfect) limbs of the same tree.[122]

Obviously these two readings of the middle ages would support very different interpretations of our historians' contemporary world. In a later chapter we will see how they affected arguments over dissent in the restoration era, about the health of the church under Queen Anne, and about the independence of the clergy from lay control throughout the whole period.[123] For now, however, we must concentrate on the impact of the clash of traditions on English understandings of the distant past. The Foxean and Laudian traditions survived beyond 1660 and stirred debate over the nation's early history. Their competing internationalisms produced contrasting English chronologies, and offered very different identities for their English audiences.

The first contest was over England's initial conversion to the Christian faith. The broad pattern of events was pretty much agreed, but analysis of the details, and the weight put on individual parts of the narrative, varied wildly. Almost all accepted that the faith had first come to their islands in the first centuries after Christ's death. Christians had evangelised the Roman and native British inhabitants, so by the time Emperor Constantine (who, significantly, had begun his bid for power from Britain) converted his whole imperial realm, Christianity already had a substantial presence. Of course,

122 For this interpretation in the early Stuart period, see Milton, *Catholic and reformed*, ch. 3.
123 See below, pp. 284–340.

this early progress suffered a devastating setback in the fifth century. Rome's power had declined; she had abandoned her island provinces; and although a collection of Romano-British kingdoms kept the faith for a while, they would be swept out of the area which would become England by the pagan Anglo-Saxons. As a result, Christianity soon survived only in the remote lands of Cornwall and Wales, as well as in Ireland and Scotland (places which had been beyond Roman political control, but not her religious influence). Recovery from this disaster had been slow, but steady. Missionaries from the Celtic lands worked on the Angles, whilst in the year 597 Pope Gregory had sent St Augustine as his apostle to the kingdom of Kent. Securing good relations with its ruler Ethelbert, Augustine converted the royal court and then used Ethelbert's dominance over other monarchs of the island to push for their conversion.

This broad narrative was agreed, but there was one huge problem with it. Augustine's mission had been sent from papal Rome – and whatever role the Romano-British churches may have played in establishing Christianity, this popish effort had clearly done most to set up the new faith *among the English*. English people, after all, were the descendants of the pagan Anglo-Saxons. The earlier history of Christianity in Roman Britain was therefore irrelevant to them, and although the Scots and Irish had played some part in their conversion, this Celtic mission had made little headway until Augustine arrived from Rome. Once the saint had come, progress accelerated dramatically. Kingdoms fell to the new faith like ninepins and Augustine, the first archbishop of Canterbury, carried out vigorous organisational work setting up bishoprics and insisting on Roman rites and Roman doctrine. As he did this, Augustine had swept aside the rival traditions of the Scots and Irish churches and had ensured the medieval English establishment would owe its structures, practices and institutional continuity to him. This pattern of events gave Catholics powerful arguments against Protestants. Augustine's loyalty and obedience to Gregory incorporated England into the Roman communion: by implication the sixteenth-century reformation had been a monstrously ungrateful betrayal.[124]

Both Laudian and Foxean traditions had answers to this Catholic polemic – but, as we would expect, their different visions of the international church ensured these responses would diverge. For those attached to Foxean readings, Augustine's mission was so embarrassing that they had to dethrone it. Seeing the true church as scattered protestors against Rome, they had to discredit Gregory as the founder of English Christianity, and this involved stressing the corruption which had entered with his emissary.

[124] The standard modern account remains Henry Mayr-Harting, *The coming of Christianity to Anglo-Saxon England* (1972).

John Oldmixon, for example (whose sympathy for radical Protestantism put him in the Foxean camp), thought Augustine had brought little but perversion. Denouncing those who had lionised the 'saint', Oldmixon refused to recognise Christianity in 'so much of the Romish Superstition as *Austin* [i.e. Augustine] the *Monk* brought hither with him', and to illustrate his doubts, made much of an incident originally recounted in Bede's seventh-century *Ecclesiastical history of the English people*.[125] When Augustine had first arrived, Bede had reported, the surviving British churches in Wales had not known how to react. Was this mission, they wondered, a godsend; or was it some kind of threat? Unsure, the clergy had consulted an old and respected abbot of Bangor in Wales, who had advised them that any true Christian would behave as Christ had done. If a real man of God, he would be charitable, poor, humble and meek; but if he surrounded himself with worldly authority and splendour, he would be a false prophet. On going back to meet Augustine, the British priests found him matching the abbot's darkest description. He arrived, according to Oldmixon (who at this point hugely elaborated on Bede's narrative), 'with his *Banner and Cross with singing, Procession, and great Pomp*', and proceeded to assume superiority to his hosts because of his commission from the pope. The British priests left shocked and saddened, but for Oldmixon even greater damage had been done.[126] Augustine had proved an invalidating vainglory had already infected the Roman communion, and that with the success of his mission, the English passed straight from '*Paganism* to *Popery*' without any intervening period of piety.[127]

Having rejected an Augustinian conversion, historians of the Foxean tradition obviously needed an alternative. They found it in communities outside the church the saint had established: an interpretation exemplified by William Gearing, who published his ecclesiastical history of Britain in 1674. Although Gearing acknowledged that Augustine had done some valuable work, he concentrated at least as much on the saint's unholy pride, and praised instead the old British churches in Wales as the true Christianity in the islands. For Gearing, these old churches had maintained the uncorrupted truth of the gospel, and had suffered at the hands of the Romanists for this. To illustrate their struggle, Gearing recounted another old tradition, this time the story of Augustine's revenge on Bangor. When the archbishop had failed to secure authority over the Welsh, he had retaliated by provoking an attack upon them by rival secular powers, and nearly 1,200 Bangorian monks had been slaughtered.[128] With such actions Rome unchurched

[125] Bede, *A history of the English church and people*, trans. Leo Shirley-Pine (Harmondsworth, 1955), bk II, ch. 2.

[126] Oldmixon, *Critical history*, pp. 75–8.

[127] Ibid., p. 73.

[128] [William Gearing], *The history of the church of Great Britain* (1674), pp. 9–13.

its establishment in the territory which would become England, and instead handed the torch of faith to those who protested at papal hegemony. It was not entirely clear how Celts passed the flame back to the Anglo-Saxons, but Christ ensured there would always be some true followers in the nation, and Gearing implied Welsh example inspired later Englishmen who objected to Roman perversion. Importantly, this vision of conversion tied England into an international movement. Gearing called the tiny groups of true Christians a 'forlorn Hope', but he said the movement consisted not only of persecuted Englishmen but also 'the like of other Nations', and made it clear it would culminate in the German heroics of Martin Luther.[129] Some decades later, Oldmixon confirmed this interpretation. He saw the true early church in the 'praying, fasting, persecuted' groups who had survived from imperial times 'without Power or Revenues', but he was aware the clash between these people and the papal church had been played out 'in other parts of Christendom' as well as the British isles.[130]

In contrast to all this, the Laudian version of England's conversion was happy to accept Augustine as the founder of the English Christianity. It insisted the Europe-wide institutional church had been the true communion in England in the middle ages, so it was relatively untroubled that Pope Gregory might have founded this body. In this view, Rome's corruption was real, but it could be dated to a later period. Other influences on England's faith could therefore be played down (especially as there was relatively little evidence the Celts had actually inspired Englishmen); and both Gregory and Augustine could be lauded as pious heroes. As we might expect from his 'catholic' reading of the reformation, Jeremy Collier was one historian shaped by this reading in the late Stuart era. His *Ecclesiastical history* suggested nobody had been meeting the Anglo-Saxons' evident thirst for the gospel until the 'holy pope' Gregory sent Augustine; and he then argued that Rome had initiated the succession of English bishops and determined most of the other central features of their church.[131] Collier did recognise the first signs of papal pretension in Augustine's arrogance, but otherwise praised Gregory's communion as a primitive ideal.[132] The early church's doctrine and liturgy were uncorrupted, and even its attachment to monasticism and images in church were innocent since these had not yet degenerated into exploitation and superstition.[133] Vitally, Gregory also had a true vision of authority within the international communion. The pope led the church, but flatly rejected a commanding judicial supremacy.[134] Instead, his authority stemmed from the respect earned by his holy life and by the charity he

[129] Ibid., epistle. [130] Oldmixon, *Critical history*, pp. 66–8, 36.
[131] Collier, *Ecclesiastical history*, I:64–6. [132] Ibid., I:79. [133] Ibid., I:65.
[134] Ibid., I:66.

had shown in wanting to rescue the English from pagan darkness. Collier lamented that this model for the European church had not been continued. If it had, later disputes could have been avoided and England might still be part of a universal ecclesia, inspired, but not dictated to, by Rome. As Collier put it, if Gregory's successors had 'kept close to his Doctrine' it was 'probable the Church would have continued in its Primitive good Correspondence, and the Divisions of *Christendom* been prevented'.[135]

Foxean and Laudian accounts of England's conversion thus tied the nation to two very different international entities. Whilst the latter was broadly happy with the visible European church (at least because it was relatively uncorrupted in the sixth century), the former saw English Christians bound to pockets of men who resisted the rapidly growing hydra of Rome. Surprisingly, given the distance between the two readings, they found more consensus in recounting the next period of history, through into the high middle ages. Those celebrating opposition to the papacy delighted in its worsening abominations in the centuries after Augustine's mission, but those who saw England as an integral part of the papally led church were also happy to chart its growing corruption. Laudians thought the Roman communion had remained a true church, but their support for the establishment which emerged from the English reformation demanded an account of that medieval communion losing its way. According, nearly all historians detailed how unsound new doctrines (such as purgatory, or transubstantiation) had been introduced; how the clergy had encouraged popular superstition; and especially how the papacy had grossly expanded its claims beyond moral leadership. For nearly everybody, England had suffered as aggressive popes had insisted they had binding judicial authority over all clergy, and gone on to demand supremacy over lay powers.[136] If there were differences in attitude, they centred on the English crown's periodic attempts to control the church. Some scholars made heroes of King John (who had defied Pope Innocent III) or Henry II (who had disciplined Archbishop Thomas Becket), but for others, lay attacks on the church were troubling.[137] The church may have been corrupt, but it was still Christ's representative on earth, and it must correct its own errors. For Collier, this was the main point of his history. Writing less laudatory accounts of royal action, Collier found folly in King John and merits in Becket's position, and insisted that rejecting papal interference did not mean surrendering to royal power.[138] There was a 'third seat' for the privilege of spiritual authority, and that was the autonomous 'bishops of the country'.[139]

[135] Ibid., I:79.
[136] E.g. Oldmixon, *Critical history*, pp. 37–41; Collier, *Ecclesiastical history*, I:259.
[137] The pro-monarchical tradition went back at least to John Bale, *King John* (1538).
[138] Collier, *Ecclesiastical history*, I:375, 421–2. [139] Ibid., II:257.

For the later middle ages, readings of English church history again diverged. The central event of this era was the protest of John Wyclif. An Oxford scholar, Wyclif's biblical study led to him to conclude that the Roman communion, and most of its teachings, were irredeemably degenerate, and he was soon in full intellectual rebellion. He denied the doctrine of transubstantiation; he cast doubt on the church's doctrine of salvation; and insisted that the bible – and not ecclesiastical tradition or papal diktat – contained all necessary truth. Perhaps most controversially, he denounced the institutional church itself. For him, the pope and the entire clerical hierarchy were an anti-Christian perversion, revelling in worldly power rather than spiritual truth. With this iconoclastic message, Wyclif gained support. He inspired clerical disciples, attracted a popular audience through their preaching and even won over sections of the English elite. By his death in 1384 he had been condemned by the church authorities, but had also founded a movement (later known as the Lollards) which was vigorous enough to survive as an underground culture.[140]

For followers of the Foxean tradition, Wyclif was a hero. He was compelling evidence of the tradition of dissent which had been the true church before Luther, and he was slotted into the international movement which would eventually destroy the papacy's power. Gearing and Oldmixon again exemplify this reading. In the mid-eighteenth century, Oldmixon would laud Wyclif and the 'morning star of the reformation', who nearly performed Luther's role two centuries before that reformer made his name. Like Luther, Wyclif bravely challenged papal power and doctrine, and again like the later German, he gained popular support both in his own country and across Europe. 'From the *Wiclivists*', Oldmixon explained, 'sprang the *Hussites*.' These were followers of Jan Hus, who established a church purged of popish superstition in Bohemia, and were able to exclude Rome's power among the Czechs until the seventeenth century. From this base around Prague, Oldmixon further claimed, anti-papal ideas had found a foothold in Austria and Germany, and only vigorous persecution had delayed a general religious revolt until Luther's time.[141] In the 1670s, Gearing's hostility to Rome had created a similar reading of Wyclif. In fact, Gearing was so keen to incorporate the theologian into his international church of the protesting godly that he wrote errant nonsense about his subject. With no accurate evidence to back the incident, Gearing had Wyclif exiled by the English court, fleeing to Bohemia, and starting the Hussite movement personally. The Oxford schoolman 'had diverse Conversations' with Hus in Prague and encouraged

[140] K. B. McFarlane, *Wycliffe and English non-conformity* (Harmondsworth, 1972); though Richard Rex, *The Lollards* (Houndmills, 2002), summarises recent scholarship to claim Lollardy's importance has been overestimated.

[141] Oldmixon, *History of England*, p. ii.

him in his defiance of the clergy before (for reasons Gearing was unable to provide) he was recalled to England to continue his career there.[142]

For Laudians, all this would have been heresy even without the historical fantasy. Though Wyclif may have identified some of the doctrinal errors of popery, his rabid anti-clericalism had been a great sin. By denouncing the institutional church as antichrist, he had put himself outside it, and cut himself off from the international community of Christians. Thus Collier took a cool view of the Lollards. They had played to the crowds, whipping up popular hostility to the clergy and flattering nobles who wanted to despoil the church. He took an even cooler view of historians who praised Wyclif. For some, he observed, *any* protest against the medieval establishment must be welcomed and this was ridiculous logic. 'By this Standard,' he protested, 'we may reform to the *Alcoran*, and, which is worse, even as far as Atheism itself.'[143] Paul de Rapin Thoyras would celebrate Wyclif, so pitched against Collier, but he did put his finger neatly on the difference between the two interpretations. The Oxford scholar had prefigured most of the articles of modern English faith, Rapin explained, but many members of the church of England did not honour him because he had attacked clerical institutions. Many writers, especially those who were clergymen, had 'very little Esteem for that *Doctor*, because he has combated the *Hierarchy* which she has thought fit to retain'.[144]

To this point we have presented the Foxean and Laudian readings of the medieval church as if they were defined schools which carved historical interpretation between them. This has brought clarity, and it is appropriate for writers like Collier and Oldmixon who rarely diverged from one of the lines. For many historians, however, such pigeonholing would be misleading. For those who wished to defend their contemporary church of England, neither of the interpretations we have been exploring was wholly satisfactory or could be endorsed wholeheartedly. Laudian celebration of the institutional church as founded by Augustine could let in Rome's claims. On the other hand, Foxean concentration on dissidents appeared to praise the psychology of contemporary nonconformists, and cast doubt on the medieval heritage of the modern establishment. Whilst the English church had been reformed in the sixteenth century, crucial features such as the succession of diocesan bishops, or the basic pattern of daily ritual, had come down to it through the middle ages, so it would be as uncomfortable to identify too closely with the old church's critics as to admit its entanglement with Rome. In this difficult situation, many historians wavered. As we shall see, they clouded a coherent reading of the past as they attempted to celebrate both Augustine and

142 [Gearing], *History of the church*, p. 113.

143 Collier, *Ecclesiastical history*, I:564.

144 Rapin, *History*, VI:483.

the British churches, both Wyclif and the virtue of England's ecclesiastical institutions in the middle ages.

One way out of this dilemma was to try to isolate the English church from both Foxean and Laudian internationalism. One might suggest that England's institutional communion had survived from an autonomous and pre-Augustinian establishment on the island which had been remarkably unaffected by movements elsewhere. If a true church had been founded in Britain before Rome muscled in, and if it had survived as the local ecclesiastical body in the middle ages, then this indigenous institution could be the ancestor of the modern English communion. Such a church would be free of the continental corruptions of popery, but it need not be equated with scattered protestors across Europe, and so could convey its episcopal government and its daily ritual to the contemporary ecclesiastical body. In our period, the most influential attempt to establish the pre-Augustinian purity and autonomy of the English church was that by Edward Stillingfleet and John Inett. Between them, these scholars provided a chronology which might allow Protestants to trace their ancestry through the medieval establishment, for all its error, superstition and attachment to the pope.

Stillingfleet was a London clergyman, and an associate of Burnet's, who made his name as a controversialist in the restoration period and who broadly shared his ally's position in ecclesiastical debate. He admitted that dissenters had a case against the English church, but argued that the duty to preserve Christian union should have overridden minor quarrels with a godly institution, and that nonconformists were therefore in the wrong. In 1685, Stillingfleet published his *Origenes britannicae*. This was an account of the Christian religion in Britain before Augustine which served as a further vindication of his church, and rapidly became the most influential work on this dark era of ecclesiastical history. In 1704, the volume was supplemented by the first instalment of Inett's *Origine*s *anglicanae*. Inett was another church of England minister who attempted to defend his institution by continuing Stillingfleet's history through the middle ages, and indeed hoped his volume would fill the gap between the *Origines britannicae* and Burnet's coverage of the sixteenth century. Given all this, it is reasonable to see evocations of a surviving pre-Augustinian church as the characteristic medieval vision of moderate churchmen. A strand of opinion whose interpretation of the reformation came from Burnet used this narrative of preserved local purity to provide its account of earlier centuries.

The main point of the two *Origines* was to prove the early and pure conversion of the territories England would come to occupy, and the transmission of this true, domestic Christianity to the medieval English church. Stillingfleet began the story with the claim that the Romano-British had come to the true faith in its very first, and thus unsullied, years. As if terrified that any transmission through continental Europe would taint religion with popery, the historian had the apostles themselves evangelise Britain. Though one could dismiss the legend that St Peter had arrived almost immediately after the crucifixion (and anyway conversion by St Peter, the first pope, might land one back under Roman Catholic authority), Stillingfleet argued that St Paul had come a few years later. With formidable erudition, the historian proved Paul had had time to make the trip; he cited early sources which talked of a Pauline mission to islands on the western edge of Europe; and he argued this journey was likely, since many Romans were coming and settling in Britain at the time and Paul would simply have followed a general flow. If Paul had not come, there was still overwhelming evidence of an early plantation of Christianity in apostolic times.[145] Stillingfleet thus argued British faith had flowed more or less directly from its pristine fountainhead in Palestine, and went on to suggest that it was rapidly organised as an autonomous institutional church. It had had its own succession of bishops from its earliest foundation, and its adherents had followed a pure, non-Roman liturgy (surprisingly similar to that used by the modern establishment). Of course, this church had been challenged by the Saxon invasions. Yet it had survived in the Celtic kingdoms of the north and west, and had had the self-confidence to stand up to Pope Gregory's mission. Stillingfleet repeated Bede's story of Augustine's condemnation by the abbot of Bangor, and defended the British churches in their defiance of Rome's writ.[146]

The *Origines britannicae*, therefore, outlined an autonomous island faith, owing nothing to the Roman communion, which had an institutional heritage to transmit to the later middle ages. There was still the problem that this was a Celtic, rather than English, religion; but Inett thought he could answer this objection. In his continuation of the story, he stressed that the original British churches had contributed much to their English counterpart, and especially that they had given it the courage to resist papal encroachments. Thus Inett complained that Augustine had been given too much credit in the conversion of England. He argued that 'long before the coming of Austin' the Anglo-Saxons had had contact with the Picts and Scots 'who were Christians; and it is reasonable to think that their Neighbourhood and Friendship with those Peoples could not but give them some knowledge of the Christian Religion'.[147] Even if Augustine had done some of the initial evangelism, he had not reached all parts, and many of his churches had to be refounded later by the Celts. In the large realm of Northumbria, for example, a Roman monk, Paulinus, had converted the ruler, but his regime had

145 Edward Stillingfleet, *Origines britannicae* (1685), pp. 37–45.

146 Ibid., pp. 74–83, 216–37, 357–64.

147 Inett, *Origines anglicanea: or a history of the English church beginning where Bishop Stillingfleet ended* (2 vols., 1704–10), I:14.

soon been overthrown by civil conflict. Northumbrian Christianity was only secure when King Oswald, who had been in exile in Ireland and had converted there, fought his way to the throne. Oswald appointed a Scot as his first archbishop of York, perhaps revealing he was happier with Celtic forms of worship. The central realm of Mercia, too, owed nothing to Augustine, having been won to the true faith by the Christian Welsh.[148]

It was true that Rome had gradually extended its influence over the Celtic-style churches established in large parts of England at these conversions, but Inett claimed their spirit of independence had survived even as this process took hold. Before Augustine arrived, the British churches had been outside the pope's command, and English Christians – occupying the same island – assumed they were autonomous too. England, for example, failed to follow Pope Gregory's instructions for internal organisation. He had wanted the metropolitan established in London, and the archbishop of York to be subordinate to that office, but the English had never moved the primacy from Canterbury, and York was not demoted to a lower status until centuries later. Similarly, early councils of England's bishops made bold statements of liberty. As they handled doctrinal disputes, they asserted that these debates must be settled in the branch of the church in which they arose, with no appeal to wider jurisdiction.[149] In fact, for Inett, the Anglo-Saxons had maintained ecclesiastical independence at least until the Norman invasion of 1066. Only when their bishops had been replaced by Frenchmen in the wake of William I's conquest did the English begin to slip under papal servitude. The second volume of Inett's work, published in 1710, charted this sad process. William was in debt to the pope for Roman sanction of his invasion, and in consequence his new realm lost her freedoms. Even at this point, though, old English stubbornness rubbed off. William's foreign appointees, especially Lanfranc at Canterbury, began to assert the autonomy of their island sees once they were in place.[150]

Between Stillingfleet and Inett, the English were provided with a potentially usable vision of ecclesiastical autonomy. It built on the Tudor scholarship which had tried to justify the church of England in a similar manner, and was supported by numerous other histories which boasted of the apostolic preciousness, purity and self-sufficiency of British faith.[151] Yet in the end, the vision had serious intellectual shortcomings, and ultimately did not succeed. This left audiences to choose between Foxean and Laudian understandings of the medieval past, and ultimately strengthened the latter vision.

[148] Ibid., I:47–8, 72–4. [149] Ibid., I:2, 128. [150] Inett, *Origines*, II:47.

[151] For Tudor scholarship: Felicity Heal, 'Appropriating history: Catholic and Protestant polemics and the national past', *HLQ*, 68 (2005), 109–32. For an example of sixteenth-century scholarship being recycled: [Matthew Parker, trans.], *A testimony of antiquity* (1675).

The first problem with Stillingfleet's interpretation was an extreme thinness of evidence. Records of the Romano-British Christians were very patchy, and historians had to supplement them with much inference and interpolation. In 1685, the careful constitutional historian Robert Brady would call accounts of the early church 'lame and incoherent', and Stillingfleet himself understood he was on shaky ground.[152] There was, for instance, no direct evidence for his contention that Britain had been converted by St Paul. Stillingfleet responded by creating a persona as an exact and critical judge of evidence whom the reader could trust where sources were few, but even as he did this, he highlighted how much speculation, myth and legend must accompany histories of his period. The historian therefore demolished the tale that Joseph of Arimathea, the man who had lent his tomb for Jesus, had evangelised Britain. It was 'an *Invention* of the *Monks* of *Glastonbury*' which served their interests once they had claimed Joseph was buried in the grounds of their monastery.[153] More widely, Stillingfleet ridiculed the notion that anyone who had known Christ personally had come to Britain, pointing out the island had been too remote from the Levantine regions where scripture insisted the earliest evangelical efforts had been concentrated.[154] All this, of course, polished Stillingfleet's credentials as a historian, but rather than convincing his audience of his assertions about St Paul, it may as easily have undermined any argument about the early church. The scholar left readers with a powerful sense of the uncertainty and speculation of all Dark Age history (including his own), and suspicion was not allayed as both Stillingfleet and Inett used the tiniest fragments of evidence to establish the coherence, continuity and influence of the British churches.[155]

A second and important problem was that the argument for an indigenous English establishment isolated national history. In essence, Stillingfleet and Inett were suggesting that England was a peculiar case. She, unlike most nations, had received the purest form of Christianity from the apostles via the British, and had then protected it for some centuries from the perversions of a pan-continental church. This implied England had had an extraordinary experience of the faith, and perhaps a unique relationship with God. In the wrong hands, this could easily topple over into absurdity, and in fact the years before Stillingfleet published had seen a number of less than scholarly accounts of England's early past which suggested *only* this country had a fully Christian history. For example, Daniel Langhorne's 1676 *Introduction to the history of England* had biblical figures falling over themselves to convert Britain. St Paul had come, but so had St Peter, St James, James'

[152] Robert Brady, *A compleat history of England* (1685), p. 109.
[153] Stillingfleet, *Origines*, p. 6. [154] Ibid., pp. 1–5.
[155] Oldmixon would criticise Stillingfleet for these sorts of sins: see his *Critical history*, p. 56.

parents Salome and Zebedee, St Barnabus, Joseph of Arimathea, and Simon Zelotes.[156] With all these people so busy in the island in the first century, readers might have wondered who converted the rest of the world. Similarly, Sir Winston Churchill – the father of the first duke of Marlborough and a popular amateur historian – published notes on British rulers through the ages which had England's church alone escaping popery; whilst many writers made much of King Lucius, whom they claimed had been a second-century, but Christian, monarch of Britiain.[157] If this hoary old legend had been true, Lucius' realm would have been the earliest converted kingdom in the world, despite its distance from Jesus' place of birth and the impossibility of dating his dominion since Romans had ruled his island through the period he would have reigned.[158] As writers seized on the British origins of the Emperor Constantine, they even displaced Palestine as the homeland of Christianity. Jesus may have lived in the Levant, they conceded, but the imperial ruler who converted all Europe had gained his faith in Britain.[159]

Of course, it was technically possible that providence had marked out a unique place for the Romano-British and their English successors. Perhaps England had been prepared for her reformation role as the champion of God's religion from the very beginnings of Christian time; but most scholars accepted the theological difficulty, and the historical absurdity, of following this line. Nobody could sensibly claim only England had enjoyed true godliness. Scripture made it clear Jesus' message was for all mankind; the English creeds themselves expressed belief in a universal church; and records of early conversion were far stronger for other parts of Europe than Britain.[160] Inevitably, such doubts damaged even Stillingfleet's careful constructions of an autonomous and indigenous Christianity. In the mid-eighteenth century, the historian Thomas Carte would ridicule people who 'took up any pretence' to claim the priority of their nation's faith, but Stillingfleet himself had signalled discomfort at exaggerated accounts of England's specialness.[161] He prefaced his attack on the legend of Joseph of Arimathea by observing that all men (even Laplanders) had such a love of their country that they were prepared to believe impossible things about it, and then went on to destroy

[156] Daniel Langhorne, *An introduction to the history of England* (1676), pp. 103–5.

[157] Winston Churchill, *Divi britannici* (1676), p. 26.

[158] Stillingfleet wrestled with this story, concluding if Lucius had existed, he must have been merely a client ruler for the Romans: Stillingfleet, *Origines*, pp. 58–69.

[159] Langhorne, *Introduction*, pp. 118–21, 144; George Meriton, *Anglorum gesta* (1675), pp. 22–3, 32; H. C., *The plain Englishman's historian* (1678), p. 3.

[160] Acts 10 insisted gentiles as well as Jews must be baptised; the Nicene and Apostles' creeds spoke of the 'catholic' nature of God's church; Acts and Eusebius' *Ecclesiastical history* provided evidence for the early spread of Christianity in the Levant.

[161] Thomas Carte, *A general history of England* (4 vols., 1747), I:139.

the narratives which made his land the first fully Christian society.[162] In Stillingfleet's embarrassment, we are close to the crucial dilemma facing moderate ecclesiastical historians. They tried to answer the question, 'Where was your church before Luther?' But as they avoided Laudian and Foxean internationals, their stress on the autonomy of a pristine national church raised another difficulty. Put crudely, this was, 'Where was your church beyond England?' Whilst the scholars had found a response to this when writing about the Tudor period (the English communion was one member of a family of reformed churches), things became much more difficult examining the era before the reformation provided this option. Medieval Catholicsm had been pan-European but grossly corrupt; its critics had been too few to look much like Christ's true church, and had attacked the institution from which the modern English establishment was descended; but an autonomous indigenous institution risked denying a Christian community outside England.

Stillingfleet and Inett would answer the question of the church beyond England. Significantly, however, their response took them much closer to the position of Laudian scholars than they may have wished. These historians would chronicle the English battle to retain liberty from papal encroachment both during and after Augustine's mission, yet to avoid total disconnection from the rest of the continent they would stress that other people's institutional churches had struggled to do the same at the same time. England was thus presented as the local branch of a universal communion composed of the original establishments of each Christian nation, and – in so far as these establishments were shown aiding each other in the battle against popish corruption – a sort of federation was implied between them. This explanation provided the English with brethren abroad. Significantly, however, it flirted with a Laudian vision. As moderate churchmen charted a European dimension for their pre-Augustinain communion and its survival beyond the sixth century, they accepted it was part of a continent-wide structure embodied in the institutional churches of other European countries. These, of course, were the very organisations which became the Catholic churches of the high middle ages, and which Heylyn and Collier insisted remained valid for all their corruptions.

So Stillingfleet's coverage of the Romano-British churches set them in a 'catholic' context. Arguing that they had had bishops, the scholar admitted the direct documentary sources were fragmentary, but then asserted they must have had episcopal government because every communion across the Roman world had had this feature. Evidence was particularly strong for the churches along the southern shore of the Mediterranean, but there were

[162] Stillingfleet, *Origines*, preface.

no cases of Christians ruling themselves in another way.[163] Britain's ecclesiastical arrangements were thus confirmed by institutional establishments elsewhere, and if anyone doubted the existence of bishops, Stillingfleet had another argument which also relied on the broader church. He pointed out that in the year 314 the ecclesiastical council of Arles had included episcopal representatives from the British provinces. He therefore presented the communion in England participating in consultations to co-ordinate policy across Europe, and came even closer to a Laudian vision when explaining the relationship between this council and the pope. Stillingfleet admitted that the assembled clergy had sent their resolutions to Rome, but insisted their resolutions had been binding without papal blessing.[164] This meant that the British churches were part of a far-flung yet co-ordinated European communion in which authority rested with representatives who governed in consultation with their brethren from other lands. When supplemented by Stillingfleet's belief in the authority of general councils, this vision produced a usable – but Heylynesque – reading of early ecclesiastical history.[165] The British church was free of Rome's tyranny, but had enjoyed an institutional heritage which it could pass to its English successors, and was part of a family of such bodies which could serve as its foreign arms.

Inett's narrative of the English conversion and its aftermath was similarly 'catholic'. Earlier, we saw him transfer the honour of evangelising the Anglo-Saxons from Rome to the British churches. He had done this to establish the autonomy of the island faith, but we must now admit his account was more complex, and more continental, than this. First, Inett thought the pagan English had become familiar with Christianity, not only in Wales, Ireland and Scotland, but also in France, Brittany and Spain. Such contacts were safe, because these other churches were still asserting their own independence of Rome, but in a second and more surprising concession, Inett thought the papacy itself had played a useful role.[166] Although there were some worrying signs of its later perversion, the Roman curia had not been utterly corrupted by the end of the sixth century, and Pope Gregory in particular had upheld the principle of equality between branches of the universal church. It was disappointing (and out of character) that Gregory betrayed his own ideals by granting Augustine authority over the indigenous British church, but his claims had been far more moderate than those made by outlandish successors, so he had merited the 'veneration of succeeding Ages' for converting Kent.[167] In this way, Rome was still presented as a valid member of an ecclesiastical federation which had not yet succumbed to full-blown

163 Ibid., p. 77. 164 Ibid., pp. 74–5, 83–4.
165 Stillingfleet cited the general council of Nice on local autonomy: ibid., pp. 100–1.
166 Inett, *Origines*, I:8–11, 34. 167 Ibid., I:16, 27–8.

popery, and the pope was acknowledged as the potential moral leader of the whole co-ordinated alliance. Similarly, Inett's passionate case for the juridical independence of the English church after its foundation did not rest wholly on an inheritance from autonomous British forebears. English ecclesiastical synods – such as those of Hatfield in 679 or Calcuith in 816 – declared their freedom from papal diktat, but did so citing the principles of the universal European church. Those assembled at Hatfield endorsed the decisions of the earliest general councils because these confirmed that individual provinces should settle controversies without appeal to supposedly higher powers, but also because they expressed the opinion of united Christian churches.[168] At Calcuith, the clerics resolved that Christianity was held together by faith, hope and charity, not submission to Rome; but they nevertheless noted this principle had been accepted by foreign authorities and bodies representing all nations. For the English clergy of 816, a union of love (not formal obedience) had been the language of 'St *Cyprian* and other Archbishops of *Carthage*, and Primates of *Africa*; of the Churches of *Cyprus* and *Constance*'; and it had been formally endorsed at the general council of Ephesus.[169]

Such a 'catholic' reading of the medieval church became standard for historians from the moderate tradition. Scholars such as William Lloyd (a collaborator with, and episcopal colleague of, Stillingfleet and Burnet from the 1690s) supported the preceding account of the earliest Christians in Britain, whilst others followed Inett's analysis of the later medieval period as one in which Rome tried to subdue a family of European churches.[170] One who took the story forward was Ferdinando Warner. In 1756–7, this London clergyman published the two volumes of his *Ecclesiastical history of England* which covered the story of the church from its origins to the eighteenth century and explicitly hoped to supply gaps in the accounts by Stillingfleet, Inett and Burnet. Although space meant Warner concentrated tightly on English affairs, and asked readers to 'look into other histories' for events abroad, his medieval sections nevertheless held an implicit international vision.[171] The history demonstrated 'the rise, the progress, and declension' of the power of the popes in the English church, but throughout it was clear this was just a local manifestation of a universal problem. National institutional churches all across Europe had tried to remain pure and in communion with one another, but this had become harder as popes had invaded their rights and subverted their faith. Thus England had accepted help from Rome in its early days, and had been reluctant to resist her Italian sister until she 'introduced customs and authority unknown in earlier ages'.[172] Similarly, as the

168 Ibid., I:107, 128. 169 Ibid., I:253.

170 William Lloyd, *An historical account of church government* (1684). The preface to Inett's 1710 second volume condemned Pope Gregory VII in exactly these terms.

171 Warner, *Ecclesiastical history*, I:537. 172 Ibid., I: preface.

English held out against pontifical encroachment they had initially been supported by others in Gaul and Milan.[173] Again, England's medieval tussles with the papacy (detailed by Warner in the reigns of William I, Henry II, King John and Edward III) were part of a wider struggle in which Rome strove to lord it over all the national churches of Europe.[174] It was true that Warner swung back to a Foxean reading when dealing with late medieval heresy. He praised Wyclif as forerunner of later reform, spreading an underground faith which would ultimately bear fruit in Luther's protest.[175] Yet when he tackled the first stages of the English reformation, Warner again stressed a 'catholic' framework. England's right to purify ritual and doctrine came not from Wyclif's inspiration, but from the ancient structures of the universal institutional church, which had asserted in scripture, general council and early precedent that bishops were autonomous within their provinces.[176]

If Warner plugged gaps in medieval ecclesiastical history, the writer who informed most people about this period was Paul de Rapin Thoyras. At first, it might not be clear what role this author could play in a survey of English attitudes to their past. Savoyard by birth, Provençal by upbringing, and writing his history in French while living in Cleves in northern Germany, Rapin appears more qualified as a foreign commentator on England than an English author himself. Yet Rapin's career, sympathies and reception made him English enough to be included in the Victorian *Dictionary of national biography* and establish him as a major influence on English attitudes. Although the author had grown up in the French Alps, he was a Protestant and was hounded from France by the intolerance of Louis XIV's Catholic regime. Joining William III on his expedition to England in 1688, and serving in the English army in Ireland, he lived in London in the 1690s as governor to the earl of Portland's son, before moving via Holland to Germany, where he wrote his huge *History of England* as a retirement hobby. Rapin thus knew England well, and was grateful for its refuge. The huge popularity of his work once it was translated (it became the standard reference for three decades after it began to appear in 1725) cemented his place at the core of English culture.

To a very large extent, Rapin's history followed the Foxean tradition. As a persecuted French Protestant, the author had affinities with isolated dissident groups, and entertained an understandable disgust at the entrenched institutional churches which tended to oppress them. The section of his work which covered ecclesiastical history, therefore, exhibited an intense anti-clericalism which drew stinging rebuke from other commentators, and lionised almost

[173] Ibid., I:52. [174] For example, ibid., I:262, 426.
[175] Ibid., I:506–11; II:23. [176] Ibid., II:128.

any rebel (whether English or not) who had battled the inherent, inevitable corruption of the priesthood.[177] Yet for all this, Rapin had 'great Respect' for the established church of England, even though he was convinced its clergy had shared in the general degeneration of Christianity. It was the official Protestant faith of the country which had given him shelter, and which had fought so steadfastly against his enemy, Louis XIV. As his translator explained, Rapin felt these obligations, and had always taken anglican communion when in the country.[178] The historian therefore faced the same problem as moderate English churchmen: how could he defend his loyalty to a church which owed so many features to the papally led establishment of the middle ages? His solution rested heavily on theirs. Like Stillingfleet, Inett, Warner and others, he posited a family of European national churches, which once had affection for Rome as one of their number, and which – whilst struggling against the pope's later usurpations – must be identified with the established Catholic institutions of the medieval period.

Thus Rapin accepted Augustine's role in the conversion of England. Because Pope Gregory had abdicated formal authority over other bishops, there was still some virtue left in his church, and it could claim genuine credit (though not the monopoly of achievement it was usually awarded) for the spread of the faith.[179] At this stage, England had been integrated into a valid European federation of institutional establishments, inspired, but not dictated to, by the papacy. Afterwards, of course, Rome had lost its holiness, but the English were not alone in their fight against this. Rapin's descriptions of England's battles were peppered with references to the rest of Europe, which made it clear there was a pan-continental battle going on. For example, England was praised for standing against papal claims to ban clerical marriage without a general council, but her stance was unique only as it lasted so late. 'The *Italians*, *French*, *Spaniards*, and *Germans* had submitted' but only 'at length, after long Struggles' of their own.[180] At other points the English had actually been *less* heroic that other nations. They, for instance, had not participated the questioning of papal doctrine which had occurred in the German, Italian and French establishments early in the second millennium (though their distraction by the recent turmoil of the Norman conquest provided some excuse); and they had got off lightly during Pope Gregory VII's eleventh-century campaign to monopolise control of the church north of the Alps.[181] Later, Rome was shown usurping *all* local autonomies as it ruled 'National *Synods* . . . out of Doors'; whilst English resentment by the fifteenth century was much more widely felt: 'all *Europe*

[177] For criticism, see *A defence of English history against the misrepresentations of M. de Rapin Thoyras* (1734).

[178] Rapin, *History*, translator's preface. [179] Ibid., I:223–92, esp. 238.

[180] Ibid., II:438–9. [181] Ibid., II:429, 453–8.

passionately wished that the *Church* might be reformed'.[182] Throughout, therefore, Rapin could stress he was telling only the English episodes of a continental drama. He stated he could easily add to England's experience many instances that were 'acted on the same score, in the other Christian kingdoms'.[183]

Rapin's interpretation of the middle ages was as emblematic of moderate English thought as it was popular with its audience. Foxean celebrations of international dissent were attractive to Protestants, but they were not entirely appropriate for members of an institutional church with a medieval heritage. Attempts to construct a uniquely pristine English establishment, descended directly from the apostles, had some appeal – but failed to identify a godly communion overseas. It therefore flunked a basic theological test, as well as leaving a man like Rapin – who spent the majority of his life in France, Ireland, the Netherlands and Germany – cold. This left only the more Laudian vision of federated national churches. Rapin and other moderate commentators might have hated Heylyn's or Collier's defence of the clergy, but the logic of history pushed them close to their basic description of ecclesiastical structures. Rapin – originally a member of the thoroughly Protestant French Huguenot church, and a man with a deep sympathy for medieval heretics – spoke of national clerical synods and general councils with an almost Laudian ease. Similarly, Stillingfleet, Inett and Warner could see the danger of admitting Rome's claims to have converted the English, but they nevertheless found ways to give credit to St Augustine and accordingly integrated their establishment into a pan-continental body headed (in a least some sense) by the pope.

PROTESTANTISM AND CHRISTENDOM IN THE ENGLISH HISTORICAL IMAGINATION

In this survey of historical writing, there has been one great silence. We have not covered accounts of the early seventeenth century, that period of turmoil in whose shadow the authors wrote. Obviously, interpretations of the civil war and its origins would dominate English self-conception in our era. Several of our historians, and much of their audience, had lived through the breakdown, and even those too young to remember it were challenged by the issues it raised. As modern scholars of the century after the restoration have begun to stress, recollection of the conflict, and disputes unresolved in 1660, were the stuff of contemporary culture. One commentator, Jonathan Scott, has gone as far as to claim that the fifty years after Charles II regained his throne were a close replay of the half-century before it, and that events

[182] Ibid., VI:454, 458. [183] Ibid., III:499.

only took a different turn as people became worryingly aware they had come this way before.[184]

Yet, for all the importance of the early Stuart decades, we cannot spend much time now considering how they were written up as history. Even though classics such as Clarendon's *History of the rebellion* dealt with the period, and were central to the development of English perceptions of the past, there are good reasons to move on quickly. Most importantly, we would actually learn little new by reviewing the early Stuart decades. In the particular aspect of history we are concerned with – confessional chronology – writers about the reigns of James I and his son Charles used tools very familiar from our consideration of the reformation.[185] Those who told the story with sympathy for the rebels saw the kings betraying the Protestant indentity of England. The rulers' Laudian church policies, with their high view of ceremony and episcopal status, tore the English church from its proper moorings in the international reformation and drove it headlong towards the evils of Rome. To set things straight, good Protestant Englishmen, still appealing to the examples of Switzerland, Holland and elsewhere, would have to take drastic action to save their church.[186] By contrast, those who justified the royal cause saw the rebellion as the simple extension of Heylyn's Genevan plot. Wild puritans, in treasonous correspondence with continentals, had tried to destroy a perfectly valid branch of the universal church.[187] There was a moderate position, well painted by Clarendon, but his insistence that the civil war was an accident caused by an unfortunate conjunction of personal failings (albeit mixed with rising fanaticism on the parliamentary side), and his refusal to trace the conflict much before Charles I's reign, found rather few takers.[188] At least before Hume's efforts, most people described the early Stuart period in the terms they had used for the Tudor.

And even without close consideration of James I's or Charles I's reign, we have enough material to trace the main lineaments of English confessional

[184] Jonathan Scott, *Algernon Sidney and the English republic, 1623–1677*, (Cambridge, 1991), pp. 26–49; Jonathan Scott, *England's troubles* (Cambridge, 2000), pp. 161–204.

[185] Though the story was also told with reference to England's constitution and liberties: Richardson, *Debate on the English revolution*, chs. 2–3.

[186] E.g. Neal, *History of the puritans*, II; Oldmixon, *History of England*, II – esp. the preface's declaration of intent; Rapin, *History*, IX–XI.

[187] Apart from Collier's continuation into the early Stuart era – Collier, *Ecclesiastical history*, II, bk II, chs. 8–9, and the attack on anti-Laudian Genevans in Heylyn's *Cyprianus* – see William Dugdale, *A short view of the late troubles in England* (1681), preface and chs. 1–2; John Nalson, *An impartial collection of the great affairs of state* (1682), pp. xxxvii–xliii; William Nicholls, *A defence of the doctrine and discipline of the church of England* (1715), introduction. All these writers traced Stuart rebellion to continental influence during the Marian exile.

[188] Edward Hyde, earl of Clarendon, *The history of the rebellion and civil wars in England*, ed. W. Dunn Macray (Oxford, 6 vols., 1888), I:3–4.

chronology. To a large extent, England's consideration of her past led to the same conclusion as her treatment of contemporary neighbours. Many historians recognised, as most argued, that the English were closely bound to a Protestant international. Certainly they had designed an autonomous, and pretty much unique, church in the sixteenth century, but through the process they had been intimately involved in a continental movement. As the English church emerged under the Tudors, reformed Christians from all over Europe had designed, advised, encouraged, praised, joined, berated, sheltered, corresponded with, appealed to and sought refuge among it. As this story unfolded, there could be no doubt the English establishment was part of a much wider brotherhood, or that its welfare depended on the success of the whole continental reformation.

Yet, as we have seen, simple identification with the Protestant international would not do. Those peculiar features of the English church attracted loyal followers, who saw links to foreign reformed Christians as potential threats to the rituals and hierarchy they admired. They therefore retold the reformation as an exercise in renewal by a national branch of the universal church. An establishment which had been, and which throughout remained, part of the European 'catholic' community took up its rights to return to the pristine principles of that international body when it found general reform blocked by papal intransigence. Moreover, even many writers who celebrated England's participation in the Protestant international took a far more 'catholic' position when describing the middle ages. Stumped for a church before Luther – or a church beyond England – if they were to accept any heritage from the medieval establishment, they reached towards Heylyn's vision of the universal, institutional faith. This account of the past thus became rather more than the factional weapon which Anthony Milton has found in early Stuart ecclesiastical debates. In the period Milton studied, catholicity was a Laudian weapon against puritans within the church of England.[189] By the Restoration era, however, it became vital to a more comprehensive ecclesiastical apologetic. With the 1662 settlement, it finally became clear that ritual liturgy and an elevated episcopacy were essential to the official faith of the nation, and not what the puritans had hoped they would be – transitional features to be left behind as the church moved towards continental models. Consequently, there was a problem for all who stayed within the national church (and this was estimated at 96 per cent of the population in 1676).[190] The vast majority of Englishmen had to explain how and why their communion had retained

[189] Milton, *Catholic and reformed.*
[190] The figure suggested by contemporary survey: Anne Whiteman, ed., *The Compton census of 1676* (Oxford, 1987).

characteristics of the medieval body – and catholicity was the only coherent way to do this.[191]

Of course, there were confusions and contradictions here. Laudian churchmen might have triumphed in descriptions of the middle ages, but for the sixteenth century they had to accept the reality of the Protestant international. When their branch of the universal church had reformed itself, it could not ignore the Protestants who had separated from the medieval institution on the continent, and whose ideas fed into the English process. Even Heylyn, therefore, had embraced Melancthon. Similarly, historians such as Oldmixon or Neal, who had sympathies with dissenters and with the Foxean tradition, could not ignore the protests the English establishment had made against Rome in both the medieval and reformation periods. They therefore praised the institution their fundamental stance set them against. In particular, our moderate anglicans, led by Burnet, were equivocal. They were serious about their own Protestant heritage, and denounced persecution of dissenters who were inspired by this identity. They therefore stressed the English reformation as an international movement of protest against an old institutional church, even as they cherished their inheritance from that body and described it in 'catholic' terms. These conclusions are not neat, but such contradictions must stand as the point of this chapter. Confessional chronology reveals the English had multiple, complex and contradictory identities. Beyond their Englishness, even beyond their Protestantism, they felt the pull of a universal Christian heritage.

The rest of this book will explore these levels of identity. It will show them interacting in the political and cultural debates of the century after the civil war, and shaping the development of England in that period. We will see Englishness flourishing despite the cosmopolitanism we will stress. Our subjects will appeal to English national interests when discussing foreign policy; they will take stands on the English constitution and an Englishman's rights when debating the structure of government, and will underline the uniqueness and autonomy of the English church as they wrestle with their faith. At the same time we will note the huge influence of the Protestant international. Time and again, the English were asked to support their Protestant brethren abroad; to provide them with refuge or military leadership; to consider their interests when making domestic settlements; and – most peculiar to modern eyes – to imagine a European Protestant audience for every argument they made.

Cutting across both these obligations were duties to a universal Christianity. As we explore this identity, it will expand and deepen well beyond

[191] John Spurr, *The restoration church of England* (New Haven, 1991), ch. 3, charts the advance of 'catholic' ecclesiology.

ecclesiological technicalities. Belonging to this body meant far more than acknowledging institutional churches elsewhere. It meant helping to defend the territories of these churches against non-Christian attack. It meant behaving in a Christian manner towards members of those churches, and punishing those who did not. It meant working for peace and harmony between Christians, and modelling England domestically so she could best take on these duties. In short, the universal church to which the English felt they belonged was a moral, political, military and cultural body as well as an ecclesiastical one. Given this, it probably needs a more encompassing label, and here we are unlikely to do better than contemporaries who talked of 'Christendom'. Although historians have assumed this concept was drained of meaning at the reformation, the people we will be studying used the word all the time; and when they did, it had real purchase. Christendom was not simply a rhetorical alternative to Europe, but described an identity, a set of obligations and values, which demanded action to defend and fulfil. In its way, therefore, 'Christendom' was as real and pressing a concern as England or Protestantism. It is impossible to understand restoration, late Stuart or early Georgian people without understanding this.

3

England in Europe: the rise of a great power

A FAMOUS VICTORY: ENGLAND'S EMERGENCE AS A WORLD POWER

On the morning of 2 August 1704, the duke of Marlborough launched an attack on the French army on the Danube at Blenheim. For two years, his English forces had been allied with most of the other powers of Europe in a war to prevent the Bourbon house of France inheriting the Spanish throne. In the summer of 1704, the French king had sent his soldiers through the territories of his Bavarian ally to attack Austria, and Marlborough had been dispatched from the Low Countries to prevent the disastrous loss of Vienna. The move was daring – involving difficult river crossings and long marches though the heat of July – but the general persevered and caught up with French and Bavarians by the end of the month. With the enemy unaware he was so close, he was able to surprise them completely. Within hours, the English soldiers secured one of the most dramatic victories in their nation's history. Nearly two-thirds of the opposition's 50,000 troops were killed or captured; the threat to the Austrians was eliminated; Bavarian resistance collapsed; and French forces fled back to their own country.[1]

When accounts reached England, elation was unrestrained. The *London Gazette* printed a dispatch detailing the battle, and the good news was repeated in newspapers, broadsides, poetry and narratives.[2] A public thanksgiving was ordered so the nation could celebrate with prayers, bonfires and a tediously large number of sermons, and even politicians who had been

[1] J. R. Jones, *Marlborough* (Cambridge, 1993), ch. 2.

[2] *London Gazette*, 4044 (10 August 1704). For other reports: *The Post Man*, 1307 (12 August 1704); *The Flying Post or Post Master*, 1447 (12 August 1704). Broadsides included *This afternoon arrived an express with a letter from his grace* (1704). Narratives included *An exact journal of the campaign in Germany for the year 1704* (1704); *England's triumph, or the glorious campaign* (1704). Poetry included *The English hero* (1704); *A congratulatory poem to his grace the duke of Marlborough* (1704); John Dennis, *Britannia triumphans* (1704).

carping about war strategy were pacified.[3] According to one wag, Marlborough's success was 'far more for their 4s in the pound' (the rate of land tax) than MPs had ever yet seen.[4] Soon the country would grant its victorious general the funds for a magnificent palace to be constructed in Oxfordshire, and named after the battlesite.[5] They thereby commissioned one of the most extraordinary buildings in England, and initiated decades of bickering between the architects and Marlborough's redoubtable wife.[6]

This hysterical gratitude was fed by the contrast with a century of English military failure. With the exception of the republican regimes of the mid-seventeenth century, the English had not had any great success in European warfare since the defeat of Spain's Armada in 1588. Even that victory had owed as much to luck, the Dutch and the weather, as native gallantry; and after it, Elizabeth's war with Spain had gone badly. Attempts to cripple the enemy's navy had been almost as disastrous as its attempt to invade England, and by the late 1590s the economic strains of the conflict were leading to widespread discontent.[7] In 1603, Elizabeth's successor, James, had been wise to make peace. Given the country's lack of military competence, he had been just as sensible to try to preserve it thereafter: when his hot-headed son, Charles, led England into war against the Catholic powers, the results were as bad as James had feared. In 1625, Count Mansfeld's expedition to Germany dissolved before leaving the ports of the Netherlands, and in 1627 the duke of Buckingham's attempt to relieve French rebels were repulsed – unfortunately after pamphlets had trumpeted its success.[8] In the light of these debacles, Charles recoiled from his own war policy. In 1629 he settled with the continental powers, and spent the 1630s rebuilding the navy and reforming the militia. Sadly, however, his autocratic methods alienated his subjects, so that when he provoked Scotland to revolt in 1637, he was unable to respond. Units of his militia refused to march to meet the invading Scots, and civilians denied the king funds to do anything but capitulate.[9]

[3] Using 'sermon' and 'thanksgiving' as search terms on Eighteenth Century Collections Online (www.gale.com/eighteenthcentury) yields fifteen Blenheim sermons. There would have been unpublished preaching in most parish churches and dissenting meetings.

[4] Geoffrey Holmes, *British politics in the age of Anne* (1967), p. 68.

[5] *An act for the better enabling her majesty to grant the honour and manor of Woodstock* (1704).

[6] Frances Harris, *A passion for government: the life of Sarah Churchill* (Oxford, 1991), pp. 112–14.

[7] For Elizabeth's reign: John Guy, ed., *The reign of Elizabeth I: court and culture in the last decade* (Cambridge, 1995).

[8] For Buckingham and the press: Thomas Cogswell, 'The people's love: the duke of Buckingham and popularity', in Thomas Cogswell, Richard Cust and Peter Lake, eds., *Politics, religion and popularity in early Stuart Britain* (Cambridge, 2002), pp. 211–34.

[9] Conrad Russell, *The fall of the British monarchies, 1637–1642* (Oxford, 1991).

Between 1642 and 1648, English military activity was more competent. Large armies were raised, and they were effectively trained, deployed and financed. Ironically, though, these forces did little for England's international prestige, since they were attacking each other in the nation's civil wars.[10] The 1650s brought advances against the Dutch and Spanish, but the peculiar circumstances of the era meant these offered no lasting solution to military weakness. Success on the battlefield resulted from the political domination of the parliamentary army which had won the struggle of the preceding decade. This, however, disgusted the majority of the political classes, and nurtured such nostalgia for the old monarchy that Charles II was restored to the throne in 1660. Predictably, the restoration returned England's fighting abilities to their embarrassing norm. Two wars with the Dutch (1665–7 and 1672–4) were humiliating, with the nadir coming in 1667. Then Holland's mariners sailed up the Medway and broke the boom protecting the Stuart navy in its port. Once through the defences, Admiral de Ruyter sunk most of his enemy's fleet and towed off its flagship as a trophy. The second conflict lacked any such individual disaster, but a frustrating failure to land any convincing blow soon led to a waning of public enthusiasm and urgent suits for peace.[11] William III's wars against France in the 1690s were more impressive (how could they be less?), but he had come to power because James II's English army had melted in the face of his foreign troops; and the subsequent battles covered native battalions in little additional glory. The stunning Irish campaigns of 1690 and 1691 were conducted mostly by Dutch, German and Danish troops, whilst the painfully slow advances through the Low Countries in the mid-decade came only after seasons of retreats. The only real progress since Charles II's reign was the sustainability of the war. The grinding reverses of 1689 to 1694 had not forced England out of the conflict: financial arrangements, political will and public support for the battle just about held.[12]

The victory at Blenheim, therefore, represented a real break with the established pattern of English enterprise. It was in fact so surprising that one poet asked plaintively why the goddess victory had abandoned England for so many decades before the battle, whilst the bishop of Gloucester, who had been a day's ride from London when he heard about the triumph, was so

[10] For aspects: Ronald Hutton, *The royalist war effort, 1642–1646* (2nd edn, 1999); I. J. Gentiles, *The new model army* (Oxford, 1992).

[11] For succinct coverage: J. R. Jones, *The Anglo-Dutch wars of the seventeenth century* (1996).

[12] For the logistical and economic strains of the war: John Childs, *The British army of William III, 1689–1702* (Manchester, 1987); D. L. Jones, *War and economy in the age of William III and Marlborough* (Oxford, 1988).

astonished that he had thought the news a sham.[13] Moreover, it soon became clear that Blenheim was a turning point. After this battle, the nation enjoyed a string of successes almost as unbroken as her earlier defeats. Queen Anne's war saw Marlborough successful at Ramillies (1706) and Oudenarde (1708); and he made an incursion into the Iberian peninsula, winning at Malplaquet in 1709. Although performances in the last years of the conflict were lacklustre, so that Spain had to be abandoned to the Bourbons, England was still strong enough at the 1713 treaty of Utrecht to gain overseas territories in Gibralta, Minorca and maritime Canada, and to cow the French so much that war with them was unnecessary for three decades.[14] When England did return to the battlefield, her military superiority was rapidly established. The war of Austrian succession (1740–8) was an overall draw; but it saw important naval victories in the Atlantic; the stunning land success at Dettingen; and an outpouring of boastful music including *Rule Britannia, God save the king* and Handel's *Dettingen Te Deum*.[15] By the end of the Seven Years War (1756–63), England had emerged as the prime contender for global supremacy. Having captured Lower Canada, and seen off French threats to her colonies on the Atlantic seaboard, she was now the unchallenged master of North America, whilst gains in India and the Caribbean ensured her primacy elsewhere.[16]

What accounted for this sudden and remarkable turn of fortune? Whilst nothing should detract from Marlborough's personal achievement, it is clear that profound structural changes had allowed England to emerge from her military incompetence. The duke had been successful because the state he fought for had overcome its earlier problems of recruiting, organising and financing its armed forces. It went on being successful because these structural advances outlived Marlborough himself. The chief reason for the advance had been greater military experience. Although many of wars of the later seventeenth century had been civil, inglorious or unpopular, they *had* kept the nation in a higher state of bellicose readiness than she had been used to, and this had slowly forced military solutions.

The truth was that England had been pretty passive before her civil conflict. For all the celebrations of Armada heroism, both Elizabeth and James had resisted conflict for decades, and Charles had quickly learned that peace was his only real option. As a result, the nation had barely participated in the great European conflicts of the era, and the advances of the contemporary

[13] *A hymn to victory* (1704); Edward Fowler, *A sermon preached at the chappel at Guild-Hall, upon Thursday 7th September, 1704* (1704), p. 12.

[14] See below, pp. 208–9.

[15] For the war, see below, pp. 208–9, 211–12. For music: William Forbes Gray, 'Who wrote *Rule Britannia*?', *Scots Magazine*, 1 (1924), 449–57; Donald Burrows, *Handel* (Oxford, 1994), pp. 272, 291.

[16] A triumph conveyed by Frank McLynn, *1759: the year Britain became master of the world* (2004).

'military revolution' had passed her by.[17] As late as the 1630s, England was reliant on laughably unsophisticated forces. Although she had a navy, her only established land force was an occasionally mustered and ill-supplied militia. No native Englishman had much experience of commanding armies, and antiquated systems of taxation and credit broke down each time the nation was mobilised. After 1642, by contrast, England's passivity ended, and the nation faced its military failings. For the first time, the civil wars involved mass recruitment for prolonged campaigns, and systems had to be devised to support this. Especially on the parliamentary side, commanders learnt from repeated battles; rank and file discipline was improved; and logistical infrastructure was perfected. Perhaps most importantly, heavy and systematic taxation (including a new levy, the excise) paid for the whole machine. These advances were taken forward by the republican regimes which emerged from the conflagration, and they help explain their victories, first against the Irish and Scots, and then against the Dutch and Spain.[18] On his restoration, Charles II was supposed to reverse interregnum militarism; but in the event he used loopholes in the law, and kept England in a state of constant international tension, to preserve much of what his republican predecessors had achieved. Thus the court fomented wars with the Dutch in hopes of boosting its military machine. Campaigns to quell the Barbary pirates, and occasional alliances with the Netherlands against France, served similar purposes. Meanwhile, the navy lay outside constitutional controls, and was generally well maintained; whilst the core of a professional army was concealed in Scotland and Ireland, in the king's personal guard and in the garrison of the English base at Tangier.[19] Infrastructure also benefited from this high state of preparedness. Civil servants such as Samuel Pepys at the admiralty, or William Blathwayt in the army office, worked hard to build reliable systems of supply, whilst Treasury hard man George Downing preserved the republic's excise, rationalised financial administration and reorganised public credit.[20] By the late 1680s, these improvements meant James II could refit a substantial navy and maintain a 30,000 strong army,

[17] The military revolution has been debated since Geoffrey Parker, *The military revolution* (Cambridge, 1988). See Jeremy Black, *A military revolution?* (1991); Geoffrey Parker, 'Afterword', in his *The military revolution* (Cambridge, 2nd edn, 1996). There is, however, little doubt that military techniques became more expensive and infrastructurally complex 1500–1700.

[18] The role of mid-century war is stressed by M. J. Braddick, *The nerves of state* (Manchester, 1996); James Scott Wheeler, *The making of a world power: war and the military revolution* (Stroud, 1999).

[19] For the forces: John Childs, *The army of Charles II* (1976); J. D. Davies, *Gentlemen and tarpaulins: the officers and men of the restoration navy* (Oxford, 1991).

[20] G. A. Jacobson, *William Blathwayt: a late seventeenth century administrator* (1932). Of all the work on Pepys, C. S. Knighton, 'Pepys, Samuel', *ODNB*, XLIII:644–52, has good focus on the navy, and useful sources. Jonathan Scott, 'Downing, Sir George', *ODNB*, XVI:807–10, assesses his contribution.

and although there were strains, these came from the political controversy of their Catholic officers, not logistical difficulties.[21]

Final transformation came with William III's war against Louis XIV. In this titanic struggle, England drafted nearly two per cent of her entire population into the army or navy, and was forced to find ways to support them. As the war dragged on, supply systems were regularised, a new generation of commanders finalised their battlefield education and military administration was improved by rigorous parliamentary scrutiny. Most importantly, the problem of financing warfare was solved. In the 1690s, the military was paid for by extending the excise, by implementing a fair and efficient land tax and by reconceptualising government borrowing. From this point on, the English state began requesting long-term loans, and backing them with receipts from future taxation. It was therefore able to reduce the interest on its debts by guaranteeing constant payment over many years, and it transferred some of its liabilities to the newly created Bank of England. Marlborough therefore inherited over fifty years of growing strategic, logistic and financial know-how.[22]

If it was this continuous military preparation which finally taught England how to fight wars, the search for an ultimate explanation of her power must shift to ideology. After all, conflict between states does not just happen. It is almost always conceived, explained and promoted with reference to ideological imperatives. Although some wars may appear cynical – and, below, Charles II's attacks on the Dutch may appear very cynical indeed – their proponents usually believe them to be principled affairs, and even if they do not, they must justify conflict to the wider population to secure the consent needed to mobilise society. Arguably this is true at all times and everywhere. Warfare demands so much of people that even authoritarian regimes must convince folk they are fighting for a broadly justifiable cause. In early modern England, though, the need to persuade was absolute. Before the bureaucratic expansion of the Victorian era, the English system of government depended so heavily on active consent that warfare was inconceivable without it. Most obviously, extraordinary taxes could only be granted by a representative parliament. Without gaining the trust of the House of Commons, money to fight would not be forthcoming. More generally, the whole administration depended on the propertied classes volunteering to take public roles. The English state had only very few professional servants, so government relied on groups of unpaid laymen such as justices of the peace and members of

[21] John Childs, *The army, James II, and the Glorious Revolution* (Manchester, 1980); Davies, *Gentlemen*, ch. 11.

[22] For stress on the 1690s (somewhat at odds with Braddick and Wheeler above), Tony Claydon, *William III: profiles in power* (2002), ch. 5; John Brewer, *The sinews of power: war, money and the English state* (1989), ch. 5; Craig Rose, *England in the 1690s* (Oxford, 1991), ch. 4.

borough corporations, and if these people were not squared before war was launched, the whole system could come apart. Charles I found this when he tried to mobilise against the Scots in 1640. Charles II was to discover it during his second Dutch war. James II saw it demonstrated in 1688 when he tried to use his army to fend off the prince of Orange's forces.[23] On all these occasions, English opinion turned against the struggle, and kings found their military tools disintegrating in their hands. By contrast, most of Charles II's mobilisations, and – more dramatically – the warfare of William III, were sustained by public support. Commanders, administrators and financiers learnt their trade in the 1690s only because parliament was persuaded to vote for regular sums for the conflict, and the public they represented was prepared to co-operate in the wartime administration.

English regimes themselves understood the importance of polemic. Every war of the era was accompanied by a massive outpouring of official, and semi-official, rhetoric. The monarchs themselves led the way by publishing their declarations of war; by producing accounts of the diplomacy which had made battle necessary; and by printing their speeches to the parliaments called to finance the conflict. Their ministers joined in. By tradition, the lord chancellor expanded on the king or queen's words to the legislature after his prince had finished speaking, and when published this oratory further bolstered the call to arms.[24] Other royal servants made their own speeches, reproduced their own justifications, or organised print campaigns, and a leading figure usually emerged as a head propagandist. Men such as Lord Arlington under Charles II, or Robert Harley under Queen Anne, ran stables of pamphleteers who cheer-led the military, and answered critics with devastating speed and ridicule.[25] The church also played a role. In all conflicts, fasts were called to secure God's blessing on the army in return for national atonement, whilst thanksgivings demonstrated gratitude to heaven for any victories. These occasions suspended work for a day, and herded the people into church to hear special preaching and prayers. The proclamations which called these events, the liturgy which shaped them and the sermons which explained their message constituted the most systematic war propaganda of the age.[26] Surrounding all this official activity were the efforts of the regime's wider supporters. Independently produced broadsides, ballads, heroic odes, pamphlets, plays and even patriotic painting and pottery attempted to sway

[23] Russell, *Fall*; Jones, *Anglo-Dutch wars*; Childs, *William III*, *James II*. For the strike in local government under James II: Paul Halliday, *Dismembering the body politic: partisan politics in England's towns, 1650–1730* (Cambridge, 1998), ch. 7.

[24] Examples scattered through this chapter.

[25] For Arlington, James R. Jacob, *Henry Stubbe* (Cambridge, 1983), ch. 6; for Harley, J. A. Downie, *Robert Harley and the press* (Cambridge, 1979).

[26] For the 1690s fasts, Tony Claydon, *William III and the godly revolution* (Cambridge, 1996), pp. 100–10.

public opinion. All realised that monarchs must be as much persuaders, as commanders, in chief.

If ideology was so vital to maintaining the war machine, we need to examine the huge swathes of polemic to discover how international tensions were understood and legitimated in the key decades after 1660. It was under Charles II and William III that constant preparation for war taught England to mobilise successfully, so we need to see how their monarchical, but consent-based, governments persuaded subjects to arm. In the past, concepts of national interest have been thought key to this persuasion. Whilst fervour against popery might have driven the English against Spain before 1660, such religious ideology was thought to have faded thereafter, and conflict in the later Stuart period has been explained largely on economic or strategic grounds. The English, we have been told, waged war because they thought they were a trading nation, who must keep markets open and must prevent a one-power domination of Europe which might block commercial expansion.[27] Such concepts certainly played a role in the anti-Dutch and anti-French wars of the late Stuart era. As we shall see, there was acute concern about trade and about continental hegemony, usually couched as fear of a 'universal monarch' who might crush all other kingdoms, or love of a 'balance of power' which would prevent such a monster emerging.[28] Yet for all the currency of these languages, it would be a mistake to grant them sole agency. As we shall also soon see, public discussion of foreign affairs involved a wide variety of different arguments, among which commercial self-interest and geopolitical balance were only two. Of the other discourses, views of England's duties as a Protestant, and as a Christian, power were central. Admittedly, these religious ideals often grated against each other. They also had to adapt extensively to respond changing circumstances and they constantly interacted with other lines of thought. For all this, however, the Protestant international and Christendom remained at the heart of England's beliefs about her place in the world. Despite the disagreements and contradictions within English foreign policy, deeply ingrained religious identities led to the battlefield at Blenheim.

WHO CAN STYLE THEM CHRISTIANS? ENGLAND AND THE DUTCH, 1660–1674

Perhaps the main reason religion was thought to have faded as a guide to foreign policy after 1660 was that England spent the early restoration era fighting the Dutch. Instead of continuing Elizabeth I's or Cromwell's crusade against popish Spain, Charles II's regime fell back on the policy of the

[27] See below, pp. 134–6, 155–6. [28] See below, pp. 139–40, 156–60, 194–6.

Lord Protector's predecessors, the statesmen of the 1649–53 commonwealth. Those republicans had picked quarrels with the *Protestant* United Provinces of the Netherlands, and once back in power, Charles' ministers did the same.

Despite attempts to resolve disputes left from the 1650s conflict, tensions between England and Holland grew in the early years of the restored regime. The nations argued about commercial policy, they fell out over points of international etiquette and their merchants competed (sometimes violently) in markets as distant as the East Indies and Africa. By 1664 many close to Charles II were calling for war. They persuaded the House of Commons to pass a resolution critical of the Netherlands, and in 1665 fighting began in earnest. Dutch and English fleets clashed off Lowestoft, and conflict was to continue for a further two years. Early naval encounters were indecisive, but in 1666 the French tipped the balance by engaging on the Netherlands' side. The next year, the catastrophe on the Medway forced Charles to negotiate, and he was lucky that Dutch fears about France persuaded them to accept the *status quo ante bellum*. Unfortunately, the settlement caused its own problems. It left tensions unresolved and it soured English politicians who became determined to reverse the national humiliation. Soon, war loomed again. Although England entered into a formal alliance with the Dutch in 1668, this proved duplicitious. In 1670 Charles sealed a secret treaty with the French at Dover, which promised collaboration in a new attack on the Netherlands. Two years later, the treaty was put into effect. Whilst the English raided the Dutch merchant fleet, the French poured troops into the United Provinces from the lands of their ally, the bishop of Münster. Being one of Charles' wars, the enterprise was shambolic. Although France initially overran the Netherlands, Charles' fleet could neither defeat its enemy, nor land forces on the European coast, and by 1674 money and popular enthusiasm had waned. The French continued their war until 1678, but England abandoned her ally and made peace in a new, and rather more honest, treaty of Dover.[29]

In these conflicts, of course, international solidarity against Catholicism was broken. The two strongest Protesant countries had been at war, and each in turn had sought help from the papists of France. In this situation, historians have found it difficult to see faith as a motor of policy. It was not that wars with Holland could never be religious. The commonwealth's conflict in the early 1650s had in fact had a strong spiritual element, despite the shared reformation of the combatants. The English republicans had endorsed such a rigorous version of Protestantism that many of them felt Holland had not matched its perfection, and had denounced Netherlanders as half-popish.[30]

29 Jones, *Anglo-Dutch wars*. Jonathan Israel, *The Dutch republic* (Oxford, 1995), ch. 31, charts the impact in Holland.

30 Steven C. A. Pincus, *Protestantism and patriotism: ideology and the making of English foreign policy, 1650–1668* (Cambridge, 1996) pt 2.

Yet Charles II's attacks could not easily be cast in such moulds. The broad, and probably insincere, Protestantism of his regime was unlikely to quarrel with anyone for lack of reformation zeal, and this has robbed modern commentators of any obvious religious ideology. In response, they have fallen into some confusion. Historians have disagreed about the meaning of the early restoration conflicts; they have suggested different groups may have been fighting for different reasons; and they have advanced a mishmash of economic, strategic and political arguments about contemporary understanding of the war. Unfortunately, therefore, an extensive survey is necessary to summarise their varied positions.

For some historians (and not a few contemporary critics), the wars were cynical power-plays by factions at court. J. R. Jones and Ronald Hutton, for example, have suggested that the first conflict was promoted by a group around the king's brother: James, duke of York. An alliance of courtiers planned to seize power from Lord Chancellor Clarendon by promoting a war in which James – as lord high admiral – would play a crucial role. When this ended in the disasters of 1667, the faction remained frustrated and fomented the 1672–4 conflict as a second chance to promote themselves.[31] Closely linked to this interpretation was Jones' view of the wars as an absolutist scheme. Men such as Thomas Clifford, James and even Charles himself may have hoped that conflict would neutralise a House of Commons which had become increasingly critical of the monarchy. In the national emergency of warfare, the king might claim the right to raise taxes without MPs' approval and build an armed force to overawe parliament. In this interpretation, the war of the early 1670s was also the price of French support. Backed by pensions from Louis XIV, Charles might end his dependence on the troublesome Commons. Alternatively, according to Paul Seaward, the 1665 war may have been a factional miscalculation. Those pressing for it hoped to gain prestige by threatening the Dutch, but then found that Clarendon's warnings that this would end in real fighting were well founded.[32] In all these scenarios, the main ideological element was national honour. The aggressive faction at court had to generate anger to provoke the public to demand war, so they magnified Dutch insults to England and insisted it was Charles' duty to avenge such disrespectful behaviour.

Other commentators have stressed more concrete interests and have interpreted the wars as commercial struggles. The background here was the longstanding trade rivalry between the two countries. Since the Dutch emerged

[31] Jones, *Anglo-Dutch wars*, pp. 88–92. Ronald Hutton, *The restoration* (Oxford, 1985), pt 4, identified the same faction.

[32] Paul Seaward, *The cavalier parliament and the reconstruction of the old regime, 1661–1667* (Cambridge, 1988), pp. 233–5; Paul Seaward, 'The House of Commons' committee of trade and the origins of the second Anglo-Dutch war', *HJ*, 30 (1987), 437–52.

as an independent mercantile power in the late sixteenth century, they had competed vigorously with the English. They had muscled in on North Sea fisheries, wrested control of the Baltic and Mediterranean trades, set up Amsterdam as a rival entrepôt to London, and sought commercial bases in America and West Africa to establish an Atlantic business. Most dramatically, the Dutch East India Company attempted to monopolise dealings with the Orient. Such trade rivalry had led to clashes of arms. Conflict rumbled around the world as the two sides captured shipping, islands, forts and trading bases from each other, and in 1651 the English commonwealth had provoked full-scale war with a navigation act which prevented Netherlanders' ships importing anything but Dutch goods to England.[33] Given this history, it was tempting to see the restoration battles as a simple continuation of established trading conflict. Charles Wilson's classic study from 1957 took this line, and it has been joined by more recent writings which described the wars as signs of unresolved economic tensions. In this view, the commonwealth's war with the Provinces settled little. The restoration parliament confirmed the navigation act; arguments over compensation for earlier losses proved impossible to resolve; and the English continued to fear Dutch monopolisation of intercontinental trade. Disagreement escalated, and England finally went to war to preserve her economy. Ideologically, the 1665–7 conflict was defended on mercantile grounds. The Dutch were accused of unfair trading practices (especially of using violence to exclude others from markets); and the importance of maintaining English commerce (as a source of wealth, tax revenue, and vessels to support the royal navy) were stressed. When Charles' first war ended in failure, it was natural for the regime to try again to secure its commercial advantages. The 1672–4 conflict was thus a repeat performance: war was justified by the need to humble a dangerous and cheating economic rival.[34]

In the final years of the twentieth century, still further takes on Charles' foreign policy were advanced by Steven Pincus. In a brilliant series of works, Pincus accepted some economic dimension to the wars, but insisted this was a relatively minor part of contemporary thinking. For him, the conflicts could not be essentially commercial. Fighting would disrupt England's trade without certain long-term benefit, and a remarkably small section of the nation's merchant community backed either outbreak. Instead, war

[33] Jonathan Israel, *Dutch primacy in world trade, 1585–1740* (Oxford, 1989).

[34] Charles Wilson, *Profit and power: a study of England and the Dutch wars* (1957); Jeremy Black, *A system of ambition? British foreign policy 1660–1793* (1991), pp. 123–5; Israel, *Dutch primacy*, suggest economic causes. N. H. Keeble, *The restoration: England in the 1660s* (Oxford, 2002), p. 102, stresses African trading disputes. Michael Mckeon, *Poetry and politics in restoration England* (Cambridge, MA, 1975), ch. 3, blames court connections to one commercial interest.

was promoted by two somewhat different arguments. First, Stuart loyalists painted the Dutch government as a threat to the restored regime. They feared that the republican 'states' party (which had dominated the Netherlands since the 1650s) were trying to punish Charles for his support of his nephew the prince of Orange (their rival in Dutch politics), and in response they portrayed the Dutch as ungovernable rebels. Hollanders, these loyalists insisted, could not bear any monarchy anywhere, and must be defeated before they linked up with Charles' republican enemies in England. Alongside this analysis ran a second, more widely endorsed argument which centred on universal monarchy. According to this rhetoric, the greatest threat to the nation was that an expansionist rival (a universal monarch) would overawe all other states. In the sixteenth century, Spain had been the most obvious candidate, but her glory had faltered and the Dutch were now contenders for the evil crown. As European society had developed, power no longer came from the massed armies the Spanish commanded but instead flowed to whoever could engross the world's commerce. Holland was therefore on her way to universal dominance and must be stopped; not simply on economic grounds, but because her hegemony threatened all other powers.[35]

Choosing between these varying accounts of the wars is extremely difficult, as there is evidence to back all of them. As tension built, and during conflict itself, the court gave a variety of excuses for its action. When joined by allies among preachers, poets and pamphleteers, the propaganda effort became bewilderingly diverse, and in fact it is hard to avoid the impression of a regime unsure why it actually was fighting. Official polemic floundered around, searching desperately for a theme which would give the propaganda some sort of coherence, and grasping at any issue which seemed to excuse the repeated attacks upon the Dutch. So trade was sometimes presented as crucial. As early as 1662, Lord Chancellor Clarendon had complained to both houses of parliament about Holland's economic usurpations, and – following this lead – some politicians stage-managed the succeeding years as an escalating commercial dispute.[36] One key moment was the 1664 Commons resolution against the Dutch. This had originated in a committee investigating a trade slump, but as the group met, those embittered against the Netherlands had subverted it into a wholesale condemnation of Holland's merchants. In particular, the leading minister Thomas Clifford arranged for the Royal Company of Merchant Adventurers to give evidence. Although

[35] Pincus, *Protestantism*, later sections; Steven Pincus, 'Popery, trade and universal monarchy: the ideological context of the outbreak of the second Anglo-Dutch war', *EHR*, 107 (1992), 1–29; Steven Pincus, 'From butterboxes to wooden shoes: the shift in English popular sentiment from anti-Dutch to anti-French in the 1670s', *HJ*, 38 (1995), 37–62.

[36] *His majesties most gracious speech . . . Monday the nineteenth of May, 1662* (1662), p. 12.

other traders had complained little about the Provinces, the Adventurers presented such a grim litany of Dutch attacks on their interests that MPs issued a blood-curdling declaration against the Netherlands. On the back of this resolution, both Charles' wars would be accompanied by commercial propaganda. In the first conflict, the king used the Commons' complaints to remind MPs they had called for war, and this bent royal ideology in a mercantile direction.[37] Thus Sir George Downing published an account of his early 1660s mission to The Hague, in which Dutch commercial transgression loomed large. He accused the Provinces of refusing to discuss outstanding trade disputes, of illegally excluding the English from markets and of building trading posts in English spheres of influence.[38] Similarly, the court produced a formal catalogue of the injuries suffered by English merchants around the world, whilst sermons, ballads, royal speeches and pamphlets all complained about Dutch theft of markets.[39] In the 1672–4 contest, the regime's pamphleteering supporters covered much the same ground.[40] Downing's *Discourse* was republished, and the king's declaration of war asserted that as soon as peace had been settled in 1667, the enemy had returned to their old bad habits of 'supplanting our Trade'.[41]

Yet if commerce was important, it certainly did not monopolise the field. National honour was also crucial to the propaganda: the Dutch, polemicists insisted, had gone out of their way to besmirch the glory of the Stuart monarchy.[42] The key dispute here was over the 'narrow seas'. This was a pretty technical matter – but we need to understand it to illustrate how obsessed by national dignity pro-war propagandists could become. Traditionally, the English crown had claimed that the English Channel and the southern North Sea were part of its sovereign territory. This had few concrete consequences, but it created an issue of honour, since foreign vessels were supposed to acknowledge their trespass on the king's possessions by saluting English ships when they met them on this part of the ocean. Generally, the Dutch had performed this politeness as it cost them little. They did not,

37 *His majesties most gracious speech . . . October 10, 1665* (1665).

38 George Downing, *A discourse written by Sir George Downing* (1664), p. 15.

39 *A catalogue of the damages for which the English demand reparation* (1664). Also Edward Adams, *A brief relation of the surprising several English merchants goods* (1664); Simon Ford, *The lord's wonders in the deep, being a sermon preached at Allhallows Northampton, July 4, 1665* (1665). Later, Thomas Price, *A short and true account of the material passages in the late war* (1671), preface, assumed the cause lay in 'niceties about Trade'.

40 E.g. [William de Britaine], *The interest of England in the present war with Holland* (1672); Henry Stubbe, *A justification of the present war against the United Netherlands* (1672), esp. epistle; *A discourse between George, a true hearted Englishman, and Hans, a Dutch merchant* (1672).

41 Downing, *Discourse*; *His majesties declaration against the states general* (1672), p. 4.

42 Sometimes in vague terms: *A proclamation for a generall fast* (1664); John Dolben, *A sermon preached before the king, August 14, 1666* (1666), p. 30.

however, accept the territorial claim which lay behind the salute because they questioned the idea of legal sovereignty over open seas, and bridled at a doctrine which meant they could not leave their home ports without sailing into foreign waters.[43] Thus when Anglo-Dutch relations were poor, some Dutch ships refused to lower their topsail on seeing an English ship, as English readings of maritime etiquette demanded. In both Charles' wars, such incidents were magnified into major insults, and were put at the heart of wounded Stuart pride. So on the 1665 outbreak of hostilities, English dominion over the seas was stressed in a number of publications. The pamphleteer Robert Codrington urged war to avenge Dutch challenges to the notion; and the royal chaplain Simon Ford, preaching in Northampton, stressed that even such inland towns should care about England's maritime dignity.[44] In 1672, the issue was even more prominent. Perhaps because the Dutch had actually provided few real provocations since the 1667 peace, official justifications for conflict rested heavily on rather shallow points of honour. Although the king's declaration of war opened with disputes in the Indies, he went on to complain that the salute had been denied to his majesty's ships in the Channel, and that the Provinces had been arguing against England's sovereignty of the seas in foreign courts.[45] The Dutch (and some brave English writers) pointed out that this was a pretty flimsy basis on which to attack a neighbour – but royal dignity must be preserved.[46] Charles' maritime rights remained central to English polemic, and some even insisted his honour was the very soul of monarchy. If the Dutch undermined royal dignity at sea, they warned, the crown might fall into general contempt.[47]

Beyond trade and honour, the ideological themes suggested by Steven Pincus were also prominent in the polemic. As has just been hinted, an important strand of propaganda stressed Dutch hostility to kingship, and emphasised the threat that the 'states' party posed to the Stuart house. There were

[43] Thomas W. Fulton, *The sovereignty of the seas* (1911).

[44] Robert Codrington, *His majesties propriety and dominion on the British seas asserted* (1665); Ford, *Lord's wonders*, pp. 9–12.

[45] *His majesties declaration against the states general*, pp. 4–6.

[46] For complaints: *A letter sent by the states general of the United Provinces* (1673); *The answer of the states general of the United Provinces* (The Hague, 1674); [Robert McWard], *The English ballance, weighing the reasons of England's present conjuncture with France* (1672); *Considerations upon the present state of the United Netherlands* (1672). One pamphlet – *Two letters, one from the states-general to his most Christian majesty* (1672) – was supposed to bolster Charles' alliance with Louis, but also aired Dutch protests at the slight pretences for enmity.

[47] Henry Stubbe, *A justification of the present war against the United Netherlands* (1672), pp. 1–2. In a related argument, Benjamin Laney, *A sermon preached before the king at Whitehall, March 18, 1665/6* (1666), suggested monarchy must uphold national honour.

accusations that the Dutch hated royalty, and had made contact with English malcontents to overthrow the crown.[48] At least until the summer of 1672, there were also complaints that the Netherlanders had excluded the prince of Orange from government. This was seen as monstrous ingratitude, since the house of Orange had led the liberation of the Dutch from Spain, and also as a subversion of the principle that all societies should be led by a monarchical figure.[49] The rhetoric relating specifically to the Dutch dynasty collapsed in 1672 when the French invasion brought William of Orange to power, and he proved as determined to resist the English as the displaced 'states' party, but despite this, more general monarchical propaganda characterised both periods of war. Polemicists insisted the Dutch were natural rebels; that they were too proud to submit to royal rule; and that they must be defeated before their dangerously democratic principles spread. Thus in 1666 Sir John Birkenhead compared the Dutch leaders to the Rump parliament which had commanded England after Charles I's execution. He implied they spread a similar anti-royalist poison, but promised the Stuarts would eventually triumph over them as they had vanquished their own rebellious subjects.[50] Around the same time, balladeers managed surprisingly hummable analysis of upstart republics in their bar-room jingles: 'When slaves are turn'd princes, no tyrants so evil,' they harmonised, 'When beggars are mounted, they ride to the Devil.'[51] Finally, the Netherlands were accused of universal monarchy. Since the Provinces' route to global hegemony would lie through economic power, it can be difficult to disentangle this rhetoric from more general commercial concerns, but Pincus is absolutely right to find fears of Dutch global dominance in English propaganda. In 1665, for example, the author of *Europae modernae speculum* said the Dutch had been stealing trade, and that if they were not stopped they would 'gain all the Wealth in the World in their Hands'.[52] In 1672, William de Britaine claimed that in the East Indies the Dutch were styling themselves 'Commanders of all the Seas of the World; Protectors of all the Kings and Princes of *Europe*; and Supreme Moderators of all the affairs of Christendom', and implied they might soon make these boasts a reality back home.[53] In 1673, the rhetoric of

[48] E.g. *His majesties most gracious speech . . . October 10, 1665*, pp. 11–12; Charles Molloy, *Holland's ingratitude: or a serious expostulation with the Dutch* (1666), pp. 3–6; *His majesties most gracious speech . . . Tuesday February 4, 1672/3* (1673), pp. 7–8.

[49] [Edward Cliffe], *An abbreviate of Hollands deliverance by and ingratitude to the crown of England* (1665); Stubbe, *Justification*, pp. 11–28; [William de Britaine], *The Dutch usurpation* (1672), p. 35.

[50] [Sir John Birkenhead], *A new ballad of a famous German prince* (1666).

[51] *Holland turn'd to tinder* [1666]. Also: *England's valour, and Holland's terror* [1665?]; *The English seaman's resolution* [1665?].

[52] *Europae modernae speculum* (1665), p. 62.

[53] [De Britaine], *Dutch usurpation*, p. 20.

universal monarchy entered even official statements, when the lord chancellor told parliament that only England stood in the way of a Dutch '*Universal Empire*, as great as *Rome*'.[54]

From this survey, the impression is of a war propaganda so diverse it verged on confusion. Not only were a variety of arguments being run, many propagandists amalgamated them into shapeless composite performances. For example, the poet Edmund Waller cited two arguments in rapid succession as he claimed the 1665 battles were for our 'Nation's Glory / and our Trades increase'.[55] Similarly, the lord chancellor's 1673 warning against a universal Dutch imperium included accusations that the Provinces were enemies to all monarchies, and that they were dangerous competitors for trade, within that very same sentence.[56] Of course, one could view this rhetoric as a brave attempt at synthesis, but at least one contemporary commentator complained such flailing discourse smacked of desperation and was probably hiding some disreputable motives for the conflict. In 1667, a poet – who was almost certainly Andrew Marvell, and who wisely published from the Netherlands – satirised Waller by running through a gamut of unconvincing justifications for war. 'Having fought,' the poet complained, 'we know not why.' If the war had been launched to control the world's seas, this had failed, as other powers had united against England's attempt at naval dominance. If it had been fought for economic gain, the prizes had not been won. If military action had aimed at helping the prince of Orange, he was now in a worse position than he had been before. If it had been intended to set up a standing army and undermine parliament, then this was so disgraceful as to warrant this single-word response, 'alas'. Only the suggestion that the conflict had been to benefit cronies and mistresses of the king ran true.[57] Certainly this writer repined loudest at military incompetence, but his widely cast fishing for possible reasons for the war seems to mirror the investigations of modern historians.

There is a way to bring greater clarity to the propaganda of the Anglo-Dutch wars, but it starts by adding to the discursive cacophony. Simply put, it suggests that most commentators have ignored additional rhetoric which was as important as the various alternatives we have been exploring. Although appearing somewhat banal at first (probably one reason why it has been played down), this discourse provided the emotional heart of the case against the Dutch, and (another reason why it has not been emphasised) it reintroduced religious language to a conflict where it seemed unemployable.

[54] *His majesties most gracious speech . . . February 4, 1672/3*, p. 8.

[55] [Edmund Waller], *Instructions to a painter for the drawing of a picture of the posture and progress of his majesties forces* (1666), p. 17.

[56] *His majesties most gracious speech . . . February 4, 1672/3*, pp. 7–8.

[57] *The second and third advice . . . in answer to Mr Waller* (Breda, 1667), p. 15.

Historians have passed over an ideology which looked simply like vulgar abuse, and have ignored Christian polemic as they have assumed faith could play no role. In fact, if we take another look at anti-Dutch polemic between 1660 and 1674, we find the overwhelming theme was the simple immorality of Netherlanders. Whilst they were certainly ambitious traders, crazed republicans, and potential universal monarchs, they were even more frequently sunk in general vice. They were, therefore, ungodly; and could be attacked on religious grounds.

Some accusations stemmed from stock images of Dutchmen. For decades, the English had made jokes about the Netherlanders' drunkenness, pride and avarice, and in wartime these accusations were pushed hard.[58] Beyond this, however, three further charges received deeper analysis and created a clear pathology of the Dutch. Hollanders, it was claimed, exceeded all others in ingratitude, in cruelty and in treachery. These faults had revealed the Dutch as profoundly sinful; they must be fought, both to punish such iniquity, and to prevent them becoming a disastrous example to the rest of mankind. Ingratitude was the clearest indictment. It was so central that it featured in many of the titles of works condemning the Dutch enemy: witness here *Ingratitude revenged: or a poem on the happy victory of his majesties forces* (1665), Edward Cliffe's *An abbreviate of Holland's deliverance by and ingratitude to the crown of England* (1665), Charles Molloy's *Holland's ingratitude: or a serious expostulation with the Dutch* (1666), or John Beaumont's *The emblem of ingratitude* (1672). The key charge of these productions was that the Dutch had attacked England even though they owed her their very existence. Readers were reminded that Elizabeth I had sent aid when Holland's first revolt against Spain had nearly been crushed, and that if she had not, the Spaniards would have overrun the country and massacred its inhabitants. The Stuarts too had helped. They had offered trade and fishing privileges to get the fledgling republic on its feet, and had led the crowned heads of Europe in recognising the new and potentially illegitimate republic. Yet, polemicists went on to ask, how had the Dutch repaid all this kindness? They had ruthlessly exploited English benevolence to steal English markets. They had harassed English merchants around the globe. Now they allied with England's enemies, fired at her navy, and threatened her coast. Such men, it was clear, did not understand the first rules of obligation. In a common image, they were 'vipers'.[59] In popular mythology, this breed of snakes ate the bowels of their parents, and the Dutch did likewise, destroying those who had first succoured them.

[58] E.g. *A form of common prayer to be used on Wednesday the 5th April, being the day of the general fast appointed* (1665), accused the Dutch of pride and malice.

[59] E.g. *The Dutch boare dissected* (1665); Codrington, *His majesties propriety*, p. 121.

Cruelty was the second prominent charge against the Dutch. The intense trading rivalries of the two nations provided the background for this accusation. As Holland and England had struggled for commercial mastery in this sphere, rivalry had spilled over into bloodshed, and the two sides began to compile lists of outrages against each other. At the heart of the dispute were the events of 1623 at Amboyna in the Spice Islands. In February of that year, the governor of this Dutch settlement, which had become vital to control of the whole Indonesian archipelago, had convinced himself there was an English plot to storm his castle. Although there were fewer than twenty Englishmen in the vicinity, he had come to believe the preposterous story of a captured Japanese mercenary who claimed these alien merchants were planning to ally with locals to overpower the Netherlanders. The ensuing overreaction was the most notorious incident in the long struggle for the Indies. Arresting the entire English population, the governor had them tortured to extract information about the nonexistent conspiracy. They were burnt with fire, subjected to repeated near-drownings, and irons were riveted to their legs. Faced with intolerable pain, virtually all confessed. Since what they had admitted to was treason under Dutch law, and since the punishment for this was death, ten men were executed. Of those accused, only two were spared, and – astonishingly – their names had been drawn by lot: the Hollanders had wanted to avoid having to wind up the English factory in the town, and picked two prisoners at random to do this for them.[60] Of course one could set the governor's actions in the context of his precarious position in a vital outpost far from home. It was also true that Dutch observers had themselves been horrified by what had happened, and that the governor was recalled to Amsterdam to explain himself (though he died before he could face any inquisition). Nevertheless, Dutch treatment of the Englishmen had been brutal, and back in London, no excuse would cut ice. Published accounts of the suffering – some in verse and accompanied by lurid illustrations – turned Amboyna into a *cause célèbre*.[61] Soon, it was labelled a 'massacre' and embellished into a pornographic series of tortures, to be rehearsed every time tensions between England and Holland rose. During Charles' two wars, the story had numerous new airings. It was cited in almost every ballad or pamphlet, turned into a play by Dryden, and listed as a continued grievance in official complaints against the enemy.[62] When linked with

[60] Giles Milton, *Nathaniel's nutmeg: how one man's courage changed the course of history* (1999), tells ripping yarns, but conveys the horror well.

[61] Sir John Skinner, *A true relation of the unjust, cruell and barbarous proceedings against the English at Amboyna* (1624); *News out of London* (1624).

[62] John Dryden, *Amboyna: a tragedy* (1673). For other uses of Amboyna: *The English and Dutch affairs displayed to the life* (1664), epistle; *The royal victory* [1665]; *Ingratitude reveng'd: or a poem on the happy victory* (1665); John Darrell, *A true and compendious narration of sundry notorious or remarkable injuries* (1665); *A letter to Sir Thomas Osbourne, one of his majesties privy council* (1672), p. 7.

other tales of coercion, imprisonment and torture, Amboyna established a wrathful inhumanity at the core of Dutch character. In one particularly pithy phrase, Hollanders were styled 'the *bloody Patrons of Cruelty*'.[63]

Treachery was the final vice for which the Dutch were castigated. It was implied in the other failings, since ingratitude was a form of perfidy, and those who had been cruelly used by the Netherlanders had sometimes put themselves in their power after false promises of fair treatment. The martyrs of Amboyna, for instance, had been frequent social guests at the castle and had walked to their imprisonment after being asked to come to discuss business. Yet more alarming than individual betrayal was the treachery of the state itself. The United Provinces, propagandists explained, would break a treaty the moment it suited their material interests.[64] Ever ambitious and avaricious, they put a far higher value on personal gain than on the minor business of keeping one's word, so were happy to sign trade deals but to recommence encroachments on the rivals' interests as soon as the ink was dry. Several publications claimed they had behaved like this after their 1619 treaty with James I. Works detailing Amboyna usually explained it fitted a pattern of attacks on English merchants, all in direct contravention of the agreement sealed just before.[65] Dutch sincerity in recent settlements was also denied. They had not negotiated grievances as they were required to do under the treaty of 1654, and they had instantly broken the commercial terms of the 1667 peace.[66] In fact, the official justification for both Charles' conflicts focused on such supposed betrayals. Explaining the need for war in 1665, the lord chancellor characterised the Dutch as 'pretending one thing, and intending another; . . . promising with all solemnity, and never resolving to perform; . . . swearing this day not to do a thing, when they had served their turn by having done it yesterday'.[67] In 1672, the king's declaration against the United Provinces charged that after the last conflict, 'Peace was no sooner made, but they returned to their usual custom of breaking Articles.'[68]

Of course, much of this propaganda was simply vulgar abuse. Nations always accuse each other of the most terrible vices in the heat of war, so such charges might be thought the small change of rhetoric – bandied about in support of other arguments but not amounting to a coherent ideology on their own. In some cases, this was true. Dutch immorality was used to dramatise their republicanism, their trading ambitions or their impending universal monarchy. In particular, the charge of ingratitude was linked with

63 Codrington, *His majesties propriety*, p. 133.
64 Ballads stressed Dutch treachery: *England's royal conquest* [1666]; *England's valour*. See also the rambling history in *Some remarkable passages concerning the Hollanders* (1673).
65 E.g. John Beaumont, *The emblem of ingratitude* (1672), epistle.
66 For recent bad faith: Codrington, *His majesties propriety*, p. 170; Molloy, *Holland's ingratitude*, p. 7; [de Britaine], *Dutch usurpation*, p. 27.
67 *His majesties most gracious speech . . . October 10, 1665*, p. 8.
68 *His majesties declaration against the states general*, p. 4

anti-Orangeism. Dutch failure to return favours explained why they denigrated the house which had led them to freedom in the war of independence, and why they refused to grant the present prince his proper dignity.[69] Yet despite this, accusations of vice had a harder centre. They did support an independent ideology, being advanced to bolster *religious* interpretations of the war. Through an analysis of the Provinces' sins, the English were urged to fight to save their faith.

Surprisingly, some accusations of vice pointed towards a Protestant defence of conflict. Although this was made complex by the enemy's own Protestantism, and although this language was neither very common nor fully worked out, there were hints that the Dutch had betrayed the reformation through their wickedness. Having failed to be good Protestants, they had forfeited the right to English loyalty, and must now be violently purged from the community of godly nations. Such a suggestion lurked behind many of the narratives of English help to the Dutch in the sixteenth century. Elizabeth, they implied, had been propagating the true religion when helping the rebels against Spain, but Dutch ingratitude had broken the community of reformed Christians, and perhaps the reformation could only advance if this disloyalty were chastened.[70] Beyond this, the pamphleteer Henry Stubbe made explicitly Protestant defences of conflict. Amongst his extremely diverse arguments, this author suggested that the Netherlanders' immorality demanded that England wrest away leadership of the reformation, and he even argued that war would be good for its adherents in Holland, since smiting might purge them of iniquity and return them to a godly faith.[71] Admittedly, these were isolated attempts to revive the rhetoric of the 1652–4 war, but they showed revival was still possible. Accusations of sin could open the door to confessional justifications of war.

Rather more importantly, the Provinces' immorality permitted a defence of the conflict on broader Christian grounds. By highlighting Dutch iniquity, propagandists could cast the enemy out of Christendom, and justify the wars as crusades to save the faith. In an earlier chapter, we have seen how a notion of a united Christendom survived in the era after the civil war. Writers explained English history in the context of a community of faith which extended beyond narrow confessional bounds to embrace a universal church. In the anti-Dutch polemic of the restoration era, this vision was extended as propagandists gave Christendom a *moral* as well as an ecclesiological dimension. In their view, belonging to Christendom set rules for

[69] There was sustained treatment in Cliffe, *Abbreviate*, pp. 3–31.

[70] E.g. *A discourse between George, a true hearted English gentleman, and Hans* (1672), esp. p. 15. *The Belgick lyon discover'd* (1665) accused the Dutch of forgetting 'what great ELIZA did' for them.

[71] Henry Stubbe, *A further justification of the present war* (1672), pp. 25–6.

ethical behaviour and if these were broken, transgressors would exclude themselves from the community of faith. No explicit list of rules was supplied, but their general nature was clear from the charges laid against the Dutch and they were, in any case, obvious to anyone who reflected on Christ's injunctions to his followers. The Messiah had taught that the faithful must live in charity with one another. Later theologians had argued that bonds of love and reciprocity were essential to the community of believers which was Christ's mystical body on earth. Obviously, to behave as the Dutch were accused of behaving was to tear this body: ingratitude, cruelty and treachery were about as far from the ties of charity as one could get. There could be no meaningful Christendom if people showed no thankful appreciation for help provided, if they showed no mercy in their cruel assaults on others, and if they broke all promises. Thus by acting as they did, the Dutch endangered the faith. War might be justified to punish the errant nation lest its example corrode the entire religion and decompose Christendom into a mass of selfish individuals.

Here, of course, it would be useful to be able to illustrate these rhetorical trends in specific propaganda. Unfortunately, however, the best starting point is the eccentric Henry Stubbe. Stubbe provided the richest justification of war as a defence of Christianity, but he was also one of the most exasperating polemicists a historian could imagine. On one hand he was as close as we get to an official government spokesman. His 1672 pamphlets were paid for by royal ministers to counter Dutch writings, and the government provided material to help support his position. Yet on the other hand, Stubbe was one of the most atypical minds of the seventeenth century. The man who put the regime's case was also a man of huge ideological originality and complexity, who advanced a variety of quite startling arguments. It is therefore unclear which of his lines of rhetoric he really took seriously; and hard to know how many other (if any) contemporaries thought as he did.[72]

Even a brief survey of his personal history reveals what an odd propagandist Stubbe was. In the 1650s, he had been a passionate supporter of the republic. However, as James Jacob has discovered, this support came from a very different source than the committed Protestantism of many of its adherents. By Cromwell's era, Stubbe had conceived an unorthodox set of beliefs which held that religion was intended to maintain civil peace and unity. At base, he thought, true faith taught only patriotism, civil concord and co-operation for prosperity; any more elaborate theories about ceremony, church government or even the nature of God were dangerous speculations. In fact, most doctrines were the selfish and divisive inventions of priests, who had created mysteries to suggest they were the privileged guardians of the

[72] For the fullest coverage of Stubbe's career: Jacob, *Henry Stubbe*.

cult. To erase their influence, Stubbe advocated radical reform. He wanted to strip religion back to a 'primitive' Christianity, which he maintained had been held by the faith's earliest followers, and which stressed little more than God's existence and what Stubbe thought was a divine duty to collaborate for the good of one's country. Such a purge of extraneous doctrine would remove the false embellishments and also reduce religious strife. For Stubbe, faith should be so basic that all Christians could agree on its tenets, and in his more radical moments, he suggested his ideals could support an even wider ecumenism. His ideas, he claimed, were the true core of Judaism, and were embodied in Mahomet's reworking of the biblical faith.[73] Stubbe's support for the commonwealth therefore had nothing to do with Protestant enthusiasm. Rather, he had warmed to the republic's religious toleration (which at least avoided priestly fanatics imposing their religious inventions on others), and its stress on public service.

It might be thought such a writer was too outlandish, and too far from the ideals of the restored monarchical regime, to serve as a polemicist for Charles' wars. However, after 1660, Stubbe swung remarkably closely behind the returning government and even entered its service. Once Charles was back in power, the king became the guarantor of the civil peace which Stubbe craved. The writer also approved of the king's personal religious tolerance, and saw Charles' enemies as threats to his own ideals. Radical Protestants (in league with the Dutch) were endangering political concord with their plotting against the crown, and they seemed bent on a set of rigid beliefs which were as contrived – and as far from primitive faith – as those of the church Charles supported. Stubbe therefore defended the king's rule, and when Arlington began to consider propaganda for the 1672 war he recruited the unorthodox writer as an able polemicist. In two wide-ranging *Justifications* of Charles' policy, Stubbe answered the Provinces' propaganda and appealed to all varieties of Englishmen to rally to the cause.

The problem with this biography, of course, is that it makes it hard to judge the cogency and sincerity of Stubbe's pamphlets. Some of the lines of argument in the *Justifications* were as idiosyncratic as the core beliefs they sprang from. For example, in one sustained section the author dismissed Protestant objections to attacks on another reformed nation on the grounds that wars should be about state interest, not religion.[74] This was clearly rooted in his belief that the main point of faith was civil concord, rather than religious truth, and, pursuing this line to its logical conclusion, Stubbe even excused alliances Christians had made with the Turks. Such

[73] Henry Stubbe, *An account of the rise and progress of Mahometanism* (first published 1911), had existed in manuscript since being written in the early 1670s. See Jacob, *Henry Stubbe*, ch. 4.

[74] *Further justification*, pp. 20–6.

pacts were perfectly reasonable given his view of the nature of religion, and they also satisfied his interest in Islam as a fundamentally sound faith.[75] The problem with this argument, of course, was that it sprang from a very unusual set of assumptions. Given that most contemporaries thought religion was about truth rather than convenience, Stubbe's polemic could easily have been rejected; and his decision to tuck away this part of the case in his second publication may suggest he knew this. Much of the pamphleteer's other effort, by contrast, *did* suggest religious justifications for war. Stubbe's war propaganda revived Protestant arguments from the 1650s (as we saw him do above), and analysed the Christian values of the combatants, even though he discounted such rhetoric elsewhere. This is why citing Stubbe is so frustrating. The 1672 works were rooted in a personal commitment to the regime and the war, but those roots grew in such strange soil that the writer had to depart from his core beliefs to make an acceptable case. The result was writing of innovation and passion; but of equal incoherence and insincerity.

All of this serves as a prominent health warning on the crucial passage in Stubbe. Although it seems unlikely he was personally committed to it, the emotional heart of his case was an attack on Dutchmen's faith. Very soon after the start of the first pamphlet, Stubbe began a sustained argument that the enemy were simply not Christians. Citing instances of their perfidiousness in breaking treaties, their cruelty in the Far East, and their ingratitude to benefactors, Stubbe maintained that these sins proved the Dutch did not share the common beliefs of Europeans. Instead, he suggested, they were infidels at the heart of the continent. Stubbe's attack was most stark when showing how Dutch cruelty had destroyed Christians around the globe. At Amboyna, of course, they had demonstrated 'their little regard to *Christian blood*', but this was but one of 'a thousand actions no less cruel'.[76] In Japan the Dutch had behaved particularly badly. They had gained trading advantages by abjuring their faith when the Japanese emperor objected to it, but had then added barbarity to apostasy by urging the ruler to deal with those Europeans who refused to 'put away their bibles'. The result was the massacre of many non-Dutchmen, and a free hand for Hollanders in Japan's commerce.[77] Dutch treachery and ingratitude also proved their infidelity. The Turks were better at adhering to treaties than Hollanders (another comment inspired by Stubbe's admiration for Islam); whilst Dutch refusal to laud the house of Orange broke all Christian injunctions to thankfulness. If anyone had missed the drift of these opening passages, Stubbe drove the message home. 'I should injure *Christendom* to make the *United Netherlands* a part thereof,' he claimed.[78] After hearing of the Japanese horror, he challenged:

[75] Ibid., p. 23. [76] *Justification*, pp. 31–2. [77] Ibid., pp. 2–4. [78] Ibid., p. 2.

'Let who can style them *Christians*.'[79] Whilst some might believe they were one of the most purely reformed parts of the Christian world, Stubbe would have none of it. 'Whilst others behold the *Dutch* as *Protestants* and *Christians*, I cannot but rank them amongst the worst of *mankind*, not to be parallel'd by any known race of *Pagans* and *Savages*.'[80]

As has been suggested, it is hard to know what to make of this polemic. Attacks on Dutch Christianity jar when coming from a man who was barely Christian himself. Also, this line of argument – though prominently placed in the first pamphlet – was merely one of many which Stubbe hurled at the enemy. Other parts of his writings stressed Dutch threats to English trade, to monarchy, to control of the narrow seas or to the European balance of power, so in truth the two *Justifications* were a microcosm of the confusion of the whole propaganda campaign. Despite this, however, Stubbe's rant against the Lowlanders' infidelity demonstrates how standard accusations of Dutch vice could be bound together into something more signficant than mere abuse. In an officially sponsored pamphlet, which gained wide circulation and was much discussed, the Provinces' treachery, cruelty and ingratitude were used to de-Christianise them and to transform the war into a holy crusade.

And fortunately, we have more than Stubbe to suggest a defence of Christendom behind the English military effort. Whilst other polemicists may not have analysed Dutch paganism with as much passion as the *Justifications*, many of them made vigorous use of the concept. Often, this was simply a matter of remarking on the un-Christian nature of the Hollanders' besetting sins. Treachery, ingratitude and cruelty were explicitly denounced as ungodly by numerous writers besides Stubbe, and even when this did not happen, tendencies in the language suggested the assumption was there. In this context, it is significant that the Hollanders' shabby treatment of benefactors, and their failure to keep to alliances, could be described as breaches of *faith*.[81] This implied the enemy had actually rejected Christianity as they failed in their Christian duties. Again, Dutch cruelty was almost always labelled 'barbarous'.[82] This term associated Hollanders with oriental infidels or the heathen natives of Africa, and again cast them outside the common religion of Europeans. Beyond all this, two particular strands of rhetoric were used to cast the Dutch from Christendom. These people, it was claimed, cared so little about godliness that they were in league with Mahometans; and they had behaved so disgracefully in their American, African and Asian enterprises that they had brought God's faith into disrepute.

[79] Ibid., p. 4. [80] Ibid., p. 28.

[81] E.g. *The letter sent by the states-general of the United Provinces* (1673), p. 20.

[82] E.g. Downing, *Discourse*, p. 13; *Ingratitude reveng'd*, p. 12; Seth Ward, *A sermon preached before the peers, in the abby church at Westminster, October 10th, 1666* (1666), p. 27.

Equation of the Dutch with an Islamist threat was partly a rhetorical flourish. Once Hollanders had been de-Christianised, it was easy to compare their threat with the danger Muslims had long posed to western Europe. Just as the Turk had invaded Christian nations in past ages, the Dutch did now, and it did not require Stubbe's unorthodox sympathy for Islam to suggest the Dutch might actually be the worse peril. Often, their cruelties had exceeded those of any oriental power. Even if they had not, the Netherlands' position at heart of Christendom meant they posed more of a problem. The Turks, as William de Britaine explained, were 'at a great distance, and [had] only Land-forces'. By alarming contrast, the Dutch were 'in the Centre of Europe, and being so Potent at Sea, and rich in Treasure, may cast an Army, and with that, blood and confusion into any Princes Dominion'.[83] Such rhetorical juxtapositions were bolstered by accusations of real, material help. Sometimes this simply meant Dutch aggression divided Christendom and gave the Turk opportunities in the Balkans, but there was a more specific charge stemming from the Charles II's earlier wars with the Mediterranean pirates.[84]

For many decades, merchantmen off the coast of North Africa had been harried by ships from Algiers, Tunis and Tripoli. These Muslim cities made their living capturing Christian (including English) vessels, and in the early 1660s the restored Stuart regime decided to do something about the menace. From this point, English propaganda complained that Christian efforts had been scuppered by the Dutch. Charles had invited the United Provinces to join him in schemes to rid the seas of pirates, but whilst promising help, the Hollanders had actually exploited the situation to their own ends. The Dutch Admiral de Ruyter had gone to the Straits of Gibraltar, dissembling support for the Royal Navy, but had then diverted to attack English interests in Africa whilst Charles' fleet was otherwise engaged. This betrayal of a united Christian enterprise formed an important part of English justifications of war, especially in the 1660s. For example, Sir George Downing's account of his failed diplomacy put de Ruyter's behaviour at the centre of its complaint. Whilst Charles was engaging his fleet against 'the *Common Enemies* of the very *Name* of *CHRISTIAN*', Downing asserted that the Dutch had 'call'd off' their efforts, and 'turn'd against' those who were leading God's forces.[85] In 1665, the lord chancellor also highlighted the incident in his report to parliament. The worst of the betrayals of which we have already heard him complain were the diversion of de Ruyter, and a more general

83 [de Britaine], *Dutch usurpation*, pp. 33–4.
84 John Tabor, *Seasonable thoughts in sad times* (1667), urged Christians to unite against the Turk, but blamed the Dutch for the war.
85 Downing, *Discourse*, p. 20.

Dutch willingness to grab what they could whilst the English were involved in the Straits.[86]

Alongside the indictments about aiding Islam ran the charge of bringing Christianity into disrepute beyond Europe. English polemic at this time had an ambiguous attitude to the native peoples of Africa, America and the East Indies. Certainly, they were savages; but at the same time they were potential converts to Christianity, who should be won over to the true faith by the charitable behaviour of its adherents.[87] Which aspect was expressed depended on rhetorical context. When propagandists reached for metaphors for Dutch cruelty to Englishmen, they denounced the barbarism their oppressors shared with primitives. Yet when writers denigrated the Dutch colonial record as a whole, they showed some sympathy for natives, suggesting Hollanders treated them even worse than everyone else. English writers therefore claimed that the Dutch always settled areas by force and fraud. They usually tricked the local inhabitants into treaties which granted the Provinces' trading privileges, but then reneged on these and violated the natives' rights. Frequently, Netherlanders herded people into slavery, and massacred them to boot. All this was in stark contrast to the English. His majesty's subjects had always been honest in their imperial dealings, and had always settled peacefully with the undeceived consent of local rulers.[88] Much of this language, of course, was simple boasting of England's greater civilisation. Some, however, turned the Dutch into enemies of Christianity by claiming it harmed conversion. Not being Christians themselves, Hollanders made no effort to spread the faith, and Stubbe's story of their behaviour in Japan was commonly retold.[89] Worse, by acting so badly, the Dutch gave such a poor impression of the Christian faith that unconverted peoples were hardened against it. William de Britaine claimed that when the persecuted Molucca islanders asked who these men were who had used them so ill, the Dutch told them they were Christians, and as a result, the very name of the faith became 'abominable to the Natives'.[90] Other writers thought the Dutch example might be corrupting local inhabitants so completely that they could no longer be converted. The poet John Crouch, writing in 1665, accused Hollanders of having souls blacker than the natives' faces, and of having 'Reform'd [them] more Heathen by your Christian sins'.[91]

86 *His majesties most gracious speech . . . October 10, 1665*, pp. 7–8. Also: *His majesties declaration touching his proceedings for reparation* (1664).

87 These views of native peoples survived into the eighteenth century: see Kathleen Wilson, 'The island race: Captain Cook, Protestant evangelism and the construction of English national identity, 1760–1800', in Tony Claydon and Ian McBride, eds., *Protestantism and national identity: Britain and Ireland, 1660–1850* (Cambridge, 1998), pp. 265–90.

88 E.g. Codrington, *His majesties propriety*, epistle.

89 E.g. [Beaumont], *Emblem of ingratitude*, pp. 88–9.

90 [de Britaine], *Interest of England*, p. 3.

91 John Crouch, *The Dutch embargo on their state fleet* (1665).

There were other strands to English attacks on Dutch faith, which show just how vigorous this polemic was during Charles II's wars. Hollanders, it was frequently claimed, had replaced Christianity by the grossest material gain as the official religion of their state.[92] Those who objected to the Provinces' wide toleration said so many confessions were indulged because the Dutch took none of them seriously.[93] The king's diplomatic efforts before each conflict were presented as Christian peacemaking (highly ironic given their own insincerity); and the Provinces' rejection of them was seen as a Satanic rejection of godly charity.[94] Among all this, however, it was the comparison with Islam, and worries about Christianity's reputation outside Europe, which were at the heart of the discourse. The Dutch were not simply un-Christian in their behaviour, they were enemies to Christendom itself. Facing such monsters, crusade was the only option. As John Dolben preached before the king in 1665, Christians should never go to war lightly and conflict would be unnecessary if the commands of Christ were universally obeyed. Yet when other nations shattered God's injunctions, people had a duty to punish them, just as they must punish criminals who breached the moral law within their own realm.[95]

Taking all this material together, we find strong defences of England's wars with the Netherlands on religious grounds. Certainly, these rhetorics could appear banal, especially when they rested on the sort of accusations of vice which nations make almost every time they fall out. Certainly too, these rhetorics shared the field with many other discourses and often combined with them, so we might suspect they were acting as ornaments, rather than cores of philosophy. Nevertheless, at a time and in wars in which commentators have claimed religious argument was fading, these strands of argument thrived. There were some attempts to see the conflicts as defences of true Protestantism, and many more to present them as crusades for true Christianity. Reading the propaganda in the round, one is even left with the impression that religion packed the real punch. Writers might construct forensic indictments of Dutch trading practices, their encroachments on English rights, or their threat to a balance of power; but when they tried to whip up a real indignation, they charged the Netherlands with being infidels. Historians

[92] E.g. Molloy, *Holland's ingratitude*; *Hogan-morganides: or the Dutch Hudibras* (1674), pp. 97–8.

[93] E.g. [Arise Evans], *A light to the Jews* (1664), postscript; *Hogan-morganides*, p. 97; *The Dutch drawn to life* (1664), p. 49.

[94] E.g. the injured tone in the *Catalogue of the damages*; Charles' claim that he had worked 'for the peace of Christendom' – *His majesties declaration against the states general*; his insistence that war continued because the Dutch rejected his peace proposals – *His majesties most gracious speech . . . October 27, 1673* (1673).

[95] John Dolben, *Sermon preached before the king on Tuesday June 20th 1665* (1665), pp. 13–14. The same point was made in prophecy – *The Dutch Nebuchadnezzar* (1666); and was implied by official prayer: *A form of common prayer with thanksgiving for the late victory* (1665), service to be used at sea.

might dismiss this as rhetorical hyperbole – or imagine such attacks were becoming outdated – but the effort put into de-Christianising the Dutch tells against them.

The importance of religious polemic is reinforced as we turn to consider the next stage of England's foreign policy. From the mid-1670s, most of the English came to see France, rather than the Netherlands, as the greatest threat to the nation. There were military scares from the end of the decade, and full-scale conflict began in 1689. If the Dutch wars had truly broken religious propaganda, we would expect to see tensions with the French explained on secular grounds. Yet although France was seen as a commercial rival, and as a geopolitical hegemonist, we also see her condemned as a popish, and above all as an anti-Christian, power. Charles II's attacks on Protestants had therefore not crippled religious languages. In fact, they may have strengthened them. Faced with a war between reformed Christians yet still wishing to recruit God to their cause, writers had explained that promoting the reformation was only a part of heaven's work. They had developed the concept of Christendom as a moral entity which England must uphold; and they had consequently given religious polemic a range, robustness and flexibility which it would exploit in the decades ahead.

GREAT TURK, UNIVERSAL MONARCH AND ANTICHRIST: ENGLAND AND FRANCE, 1660–1702

Among the English, suspicion of France became so ingrained in the eighteenth and nineteenth centuries that the two nations have seemed natural and inevitable enemies. Yet before 1660, this had not been the case. Although rivalries had survived from medieval wars, relations with Paris had been fairly good from the start of Elizabeth's reign, largely because the French posed little threat. In the Tudor era France had collapsed into civil war between her Protestant and Catholic factions, and when she began to recover she had seemed a useful counterweight to the Spanish and Austrian Habsburgs. Whilst there could still be conflict (as briefly 1625–9), French willingness to support the Protestants of Germany in the Thirty Years War (1618–48) was appreciated over the Channel in a country horrified by the advances of the counter-reformation. Perhaps, therefore, it was not surprising that James I allied with the Bourbon dynasty and forced his son to marry one of them, nor that even the English republic swallowed France's popery for the diplomatic recognition she offered.[96]

These good relations, however, soured in the later seventeenth century. The great reason was Louis XIV. From the moment this French king declared his

[96] Richard Cust, *Charles I: a political life* (Harlow, 2005), pp. 42–3; Timothy Venning, *Cromwellian foreign policy* (1995).

majority in 1661, it was clear he aimed for the domination of Europe, and that he would start with expansion over his eastern borders. First, Louis claimed that many of the micro-territories along the Rhine had originally been French and used this fiction to bully and absorb the statelets of this region. Second, Louis made a play for the Spanish Netherlands. This area, roughly coterminous with modern Belgium, had not revolted against the Habsburgs in the sixteenth century and had thus allowed Spain to squeeze France between two blocks of her territory. Louis dealt with this threat by arguing that his marriage to the Spanish infanta (part of a peace deal of 1659) had given him rightful claims on the area, and by sending armies to enforce his claims. Supporting both these polices was a growing hostility to the Dutch. Recognising that the Provinces would oppose his absorption of Flanders (which served as a buffer between France and the Dutch homeland) and that they would be nervous about any further gains along the Rhine, Louis tried to crush them. He invaded them in 1672; he continued his attacks on them until 1678; and he then put pressure on fortresses near their borders until full-scale conflict returned in 1688. To the English, this behaviour was unacceptable. As Spain's decline made her threat less credible, Louis' tight control over his country, his efficient raising of taxes and armies and his external aggression became ever more frightening. Here was a king who overawed all other states, and was gaining an increasingly secure grip on the continent.[97]

As might be expected, Anglo-French relations deteriorated steadily. During the 1665–7 war with the Dutch, some Englishmen complained that their country had chosen the wrong enemy. In 1666, there was widespread shock and considerable anger as Louis entered the war against them. When that conflict ended, many were left fretting about French hegemony, and the country joined with the United Provinces and Sweden to threaten Louis out of recent gains in the Spanish Netherlands.[98] By the time Charles allied with Louis in 1670, the public mood was so francophobe that much of the deal had to be kept secret.[99] In 1672, the king's thin excuses for his French-backed attack on the United Provinces left many unconvinced; and Dutch propaganda – which emphasised the folly of aiding Louis – soon turned opinion against the war.[100] Tension rapidly grew further. War nearly broke out in 1677–8 as Louis made alarmingly swift advances in his continuing war with Holland, and although the Stuart kings (who were receiving pensions from France) managed to avoid conflict for most of the 1680s, the majority

[97] Geoffrey Treasure, *Louis XIV* (2001), chs. 6, 8. *The characters and pourtraits of the present court of France* (1668) gave early warning of Louis' ambition.

[98] This policy was publicised: *A perpetual league of mutual defence and alliance between his majesty and the estates general* (1668).

[99] For Dover and the 1688 triple alliance: John Miller, *Charles II* (1991), ch. 7, esp. pp. 146–7.

[100] K. H. D. Haley, *William of Orange and the English opposition, 1672–1674* (Oxford, 1953).

of their subjects became convinced the Bourbons must be humbled. As a result, James II lost support by failing to stand up to Louis.[101] In 1688 – when James fell – the English welcomed William III even though most knew they would be recruited to his lifelong crusade against France.[102] England fought Louis for nearly all of the next quarter-century: the brief years of calm (1697–1702) were marred by an escalating crisis over the future of Spain, and a military build-up which began almost as soon as forces had been disbanded from the preceding war.[103]

Looking past the hostility to its ideological support, we might expect clearer confessional arguments than were possible in the Dutch wars. Louis, after all, was a Catholic. His eastward expansion threatened Protestant states in the Netherlands and in Germany, and he used his faith to play on the Romanist sympathies of Charles and James to neutralise England. Consequently, opposing Louis should not present the polemical problems of blackening the Protestant Dutch. The anti-papist rhetoric of earlier wars against Spain, we might think, could simply be dusted off and applied to this new scourge of the reformation. To some extent this happened. When the French joined in the attack on England in 1666, there was an almost audible sigh of relief among propagandists. They could now abandon their complex examination of Dutch motives to concentrate on Louis' Catholic evil, and within weeks the French were attacked for their ridiculous superstition; reports from the Netherlands suggested local Protestants were so disgusted by the ungodliness of Louis' forces that they were regretting their alliance with them; and even Charles' declaration against France found a loyalty to 'those of the Reformed Religion', which had not surfaced hitherto.[104] The war of 1672–4 also saw Protestant francophobia. Although much of the opposition to conflict with the Dutch stressed France's simple geopolitical threat, some remembered the common faith of England and the Netherlands, and asked why one branch of the reformation must betray another.[105] Yet whilst such basic anti-popery was important on occasion, there was still a

[101] Steven Pincus, '"To protect English liberties": the English nationalist revolution of 1688–1689', in Claydon and McBride, *Protestantism*, pp. 75–104, sect. ii.

[102] Colin Brooks, 'The country persuasion and political responsibility in England in the the 1690s', *Parliaments, Estates and Representations*, 4 (1984), 135–46, and Robert D. McJimsey, 'A country divided? English politics and the Nine Years War', *Albion*, 23 (1991), 61–74, stress broad commitment to William's war.

[103] See below, p. 184.

[104] *Propositions for peace and a declaration of the Dutch against the French* (1666); *Poor Robin's character of France* (1666); *His majesties declaration against the French king* (1666), p. 5.

[105] [McWard], *English ballance*, pp. 5–6; [Slingsby Bethel], *Observations on the letter written to Sir Thomas Osbourne* (1673), p. 3; [Pierre de Moulin], *England's appeal from the private cabal at Whitehall* (1673), p. 1 – this was a propaganda masterpiece, credited with ending English involvement in the war; Haley, *William of Orange*.

difficulty in deploying it. Although the English turned to face a Catholic enemy after 1674, political realities meant she could not launch a simple Protestant crusade.

The complicating factor was the position of the Habsburg powers. Although Louis' expansion was a danger to Protestant Europeans, it was even more alarming to Spain and to Austria, the champions of the counter-reformation. Not only had Louis revived France – their oldest and bitterest rival – but his encroachments had also stolen their territory and undermined alliances on which their security depended. Most directly, French advance in the Netherlands confiscated Spain's provinces. More generally, expansion along the Rhine threatened to encircle Madrid's lands in Flanders, and caused problems for the Austrians as well. As Holy Roman Emperors, the rulers in Vienna were expected to protect all German states and they relied on their leadership of Germany to defend their territorial core. French interference challenged ties of loyalty between the Habsburgs and the Germans, and it distracted the emperor from the Turkish threat in the east. England therefore had natural allies in Spain and Austria in opposing France. She exploited this sympathy, supporting the Habsburgs' cause in the late 1660s and late 1670s and fighting alongside them from 1689. This was useful and necessary co-operation, but of course it meant the clean religious lines of the Anglo-French dispute were lost.

In the face of the Habsburg alliances, understanding of England's opposition to Louis could not be starkly confessional. If spiritual zeal were to continue, it would need to be supplemented with explanations of (or at least excuses for) its embarrassing Catholic friends. For some historians, the language simply did not survive the shock. Instead, English rivalry with France was portrayed in secular terms. It was the result of national interest, which justified hostility to a threatening rival without reference to faith. In this view, France was not opposed because she was Catholic. Rather, she must be stopped because England could never allow one power to dominate the European continent – especially if that power had vigorous commercial ambitions and a powerful navy, and might gain control of the whole Channel coast.[106] Once again, Steven Pincus has translated this interpretation into a cogent ideological analysis. For him, the discourse of universal monarchy, which had been deployed to attack the Dutch in the early restoration era, was simply transferred to savage the French in the 1670s. The Provinces' near collapse when attacked by Louis in 1672 ended fears of Holland, but France now became the candidate for global domination, and it became

[106] Much writing has assumed nations ceased to follow a religious foreign policy after the Thirty Years War. For dissenting comment: Andrew Thompson, *Britain, Hanover, and the Protestant interest, 1688–1757* (Woodbridge, 2006), ch. 1.

England's most pressing task to build an alliance, of whatever confessional stripe, against her.[107]

Support for this view comes from the earliest full statements of the anti-French position to become popular in England. These emerged in 1667, as the English were forced to end their war with the Netherlands. The disaster of the Medway had snuffed out any lingering hopes of military victory; the scale of the catastrophe crystallised unease that the wrong war had been fought; and English opinion seemed to turn from hatred of the Provinces to a horror of France. In particular, there was a widespread feeling that the French had deceived England. Captured letters proved Louis had intended to join the Dutch in their destruction of the royal navy, and this caused outrage as France had seemed to promise Charles an alliance whilst actually plotting to come in on the Netherlands' side.[108] Obviously the events of 1667 shattered confidence in recent foreign policy. Yet instead of reigniting a sense of Protestant solidarity with the Dutch (which we might expect from the undermining of the policy of friendship with France), something rather different happened. The new mood was actually captured by a *Catholic* polemicist. Piling into the ideological breach caused by the collapse of the war with the Netherlands, François, baron de Lisola, published his wildly successful *Buckler of state and justice*. This provided a set of non-confessional principles for foreign policy and provided a compelling guide to English action in a disorientating new situation.

De Lisola was the Austrian emperor's ambassador to the United Provinces. For some time, his government had been concerned about French expansion, and was working to build a league against it. By the mid-1660s, de Lisola was arguing his case in the Netherlands, and making contact with the English envoy, Sir William Temple, who was coming to agree with him.[109] As part of his diplomacy, he penned the *Buckler*. This was an extended analysis of the French danger, which was soon exploited in London by new ministers who used the Medway fiasco to destroy Clarendon and were looking for radical critiques of his record to complete the humiliation. De Lisola's prose fitted the bill so perfectly that Lord Arlington – at the core of the new ministry – had *The Buckler* translated and printed.[110] It was an instant success, and it burned an image of French universal monarchy onto the public mind. As might be expected from a Catholic author, this pamphlet did not call for Protestant crusade. Rather, it demanded that Europe do something about a king who desired 'absolute empire' over all his neighbours. France, de Lisola pointed out, had already posited legal claims to the Spanish Netherlands and

[107] Pincus, 'From butterboxes'. [108] Pincus, *Protestantism*, pp. 410–12.
[109] Ibid., pp. 433–44.
[110] Arlington's approval of the work appeared opposite its title page.

large parts of the Rhineland, but these were just the first step in a design to rule Germany, and then subdue the rest of the world. Acting to stop others uniting against him, Louis had fomented the Anglo-Dutch war and was trying to trick Protestants into believing the Habsburgs still posed a threat to them. The only way to block this design was to overcome confessional suspicions. England and the Netherlands should recognise Spain and Austria were too tightly bound by the French to bid for hegemony, and should unite with these Catholic powers in a grand front against Louis.[111]

De Lisola's analysis was cemented in place by the events of the next few years. Once peace with the Netherlands had been settled, the most pressing problem to face England was France's encroachment in the Low Countries. When marrying a Spanish princess in 1659, Louis had renounced all claims on Flanders which he might make through his wife, but he now argued this agreement had been nullified by Spain's failure to deliver the whole dowry, and by the refusal of the *parlement* of Paris to ratify the treaty. Louis therefore sent troops into Flanders, and left England with the unsettling prospect of his controlling the whole Channel coast from Zeeland to Brittany. In this situation, England joined the Triple Alliance (1668) with the Netherlands and Sweden. Superficially, this alliance might look like a Protestant front to face down the papist Louis – but in fact its objective was to secure Flanders for Catholic Spain. Protestant arguments for the league would not, therefore, do, and the rhetoric of universal monarchy seemed far more appropriate. If the greatest danger facing England was France's ambition in the near continent, placing a Habsburg fence in her way was sound policy, and the strategy must not be spoilt by spiritual scruples.

Again, it was Arlington who pressed the polemic. Emboldened by the success of de Lisola's *Buckler*, he sponsored a new pamphlet to popularise his policy: *A free conference touching the present state of England*. Somewhat bizarrely, this purported to be an account of a conversation between the king's ministers which had been overheard while the author was hiding under a bedcover in their conference room. What he was doing there was somewhat unclear (even to those who ploughed through the turgid first few pages of the work), but once readers got past the preposterous framing device they were rewarded with a reasonably intelligent debate on England's international interest. A few of the ministers urged joining the winning side and hoping for reward for helping France. Ostend, the chief port of the Spanish Netherlands, was mentioned as a possible prize. The majority, by contrast, thought this was folly. France, it was explained, was an emerging universal monarchy, and such a power could never be trusted. Those aiming for complete dominion did not share their spoils, and once France controlled Flanders she would be

[111] [François de Lisola], *The buckler of state and justice* (1667), quote p. 4.

too powerful to be in anyone's debt. Rather, England must defend Spanish interests. Spain was no longer a candidate for world empire; France was growing ever stronger; and England must support the Habsburgs for fear that Louis would be unstoppable if he were victorious. England had long been the 'counter-balance' on the continent. She must now play this role again, and Madrid's Catholicism seemed to worry the conversation little.[112]

Once put in play by the circumstances of 1667–8, fear of a French universal monarchy remained prominent in English discourse. It may have been swept to one side in the early excitements of the last Anglo-Dutch struggle, but it played a part in the considerable opposition to that war, and re-emerged strongly as the conflict went badly for the English. As the people suffered the losses of battle, and as Dutch defences dissolved before Louis' invasion, many wondered if they had again been duped into aiding French hegemony.[113] Over the next decade, opinion remained resolutely hostile to Louis as a potential world tyrant. From the end of the1670s, writers rehearsed their horror of his boundless ambition, and some of their works became minor classics to be reproduced later whenever tension rose. For example, Marchamont Needham's *Christianissimus Christianandus* was written in 1678 as France made worrying advances against the Dutch in Flanders. It warned its readers that French ministers aimed at '*Universal Empire* abroad', and it was republished in 1692 when English troops fought the French on exactly the same battlefields.[114] Similarly in 1681, Jean-Paul de Cerdan's pamphlet *Europe a slave unless England break her chains* was translated into English. It told Charles II's subjects they must act swiftly or Louis would 'jump into the Universal Monarchy' – and it reappeared in 1706, when English troops were once again in action.[115] This continuity of concern extended through James II's reign. As Steven Pincus has shown, popular expectation fixed on this king to contain Versailles: but when he did little, disappointment fuelled the popular opposition which destroyed him. By the time he fell, the English public was determined to resist a French imperium they feared would engulf all other peoples.[116]

And it was in the war of 1689–97 that the rhetoric of universal monarchy reached its apogee. This was unsurprising, as the instigator of the conflict, William III, had been fighting French hegemony all his life. He had come to power in the Netherlands in 1672 when France's troops had nearly

112 *A free conference touching the present state of England* (1668), esp. pp. 8–10, 60.
113 Pincus, 'From butterboxes'.
114 [Marchamont Needham], *Christianissimus Christianandus: or reasons for the reduction of France* (1678), p. 3; Marchamont Needham, *Christianissimus Christianandus . . . by Marchamont Needham* (1692).
115 [Jean-Paul de Cerdan], *Europe a slave unless England break her chains* (1681), p. 13; 1706 reissue by Richard Baldwin.
116 Pincus, 'To protect', sects. ii–iii.

overrun his country, and he had survived by rallying his nation against the invader and building a trans-confessional league to check Versailles.[117] He had persuaded popish Austria and the 'most Catholic' king of Spain that they could not afford to lose a Dutch counterweight to France, and he was soon co-ordinating military campaigns with them. By 1673, Habsburg troops were helping to fight French armies in Flanders and were harrying Louis' strongholds in western Germany. In this way, the Provinces were saved, and the experience taught William a strategy he never abandoned. Until he died, he was convinced France was a threat to all other powers and that the only way for still-independent nations to protect themselves was to lay aside religious difference in common cause.[118] Accordingly, he remained in alliance with the Habsburgs. He fought alongside them until the 1678 peace of Nijmegen; he spent most of the 1680s trying to persuade the Dutch states-general (with whom he shared power in the Netherlands) to defend Habsburg interests in Flanders and Germany; and he was careful to square Madrid and Vienna before embarking on his 1688 expedition to England.[119]

Once on the throne in London, William continued along his chosen path. In the spring of 1689, his new realm joined a 'Grand Alliance' to reverse Louis' gains which included the Calvinist Dutch, the Lutheran Brandenburgers, and the Catholic Habsburgs. Given this religious variety, a secular propaganda denouncing the French as universal monarchs was convenient, and it was cranked up instantly. The king himself described the war in this way. In speeches to parliament he emphasised that France was eroding liberties of all Europeans, and boasted of the diverse league of princes and states ranged against her.[120] Pamphleteers agreed. Almost all feared Louis would crush every other nation, and warned of 'the project of *France* concerning the Universal Monarchy of Christendom', of her ambition for the 'Universal Monarchy of *Europe*', or that she set up for 'an *Universal Commerce* as well as for an *Universal Monarchy*'.[121] Some went further and attacked alternative interpretations of the war. Louis was a Catholic, but no one should think of the conflict as a confessional crusade. France, everyone must be reminded, was a threat to *all* nations. Unless they united without regard for religion, she would be handed victory, and with Louis presenting himself as a Catholic

117 For the importance of this in William's career: Tony Claydon, *William III: profiles in power* (Harlow, 2002), ch. 1.

118 William, though, had a personal commitment to Protestantism: Tony Claydon, 'William III and II', *ODNB*, LIX:91–2.

119 Wout Troost, *William III: the stadholder-king* (Aldershot, 2005), chs. 7–8, takes the latest scholarship into account.

120 E.g. *LJ*, XIV:128; XV:102–3, 599.

121 *A view of the true interest of the several states of Europe* (1689), p. 45; *Nero Gallicanus: or the true portraiture of Lewis XIV* (1690), p. 2; *A short discourse of the present war against France* (1688) – this claimed to be based on a lost 1677 work.

crusader, it was actually dangerous to suggest this was a fight for the reformation. If the Habsburgs came to see William's struggle as a war of religion, they would worry they were aiding Protestants against good popish soldiers, so the English must deny that this was a confessional war. One journalist warned that to believe this conflict was religious would be a 'silly . . . trap' given that Austria, Spain and the pope were also against France.[122] Another author spelt out the message in the very title of his pamphlet: *The present king of France demonstrated an enemy to Catholick as well as Protestant religion* (1689).

Overall, therefore, it was abundantly clear that England's hostility to France could not be explained in simple Protestant terms. She was part of a very diverse alliance against Louis, and many found this easiest to justify by pointing to the danger of universal monarchy. As Steven Pincus has pointed out, this was a secular, even nationalist, vision. Within the rhetoric of universal monarchy, the highest ideal was not confessional truth, but rather the independence of nations. It assumed that all realms had the right to pursue their interests, to decide their laws and to protect their cultures without outside coercion – and whilst the argument might include an appeal to protect English Protestantism, this did not elevate religious reformation as a universal goal. Rather, any religious element of the language was merely the nationalist claim that the English people had chosen their faith for themselves. They had enshrined reformed Christianity in their laws, and had a right to defend this action against bullying foreigners. The ultimate loyalty of all Europeans must be to the independence of their nation, and – by extension – to the autonomy of all nations. Given geopolitical realities, it could not be to an all-encompassing faith.[123]

Yet for all the nationalistic secularism of some brands of this rhetoric, it was not in fact as dominant as the foregoing survey has supposed. Even as Louis emerged as a credible universal monarch, the nation continued to consider foreign policy in spiritual terms. Of course, given the Habsburg alliances, simple Protestantism was impossible. But a simple polemic of confessional crusade was never offered. Rather, English understanding of their duties to people abroad evolved to meet new circumstances. Alongside the rhetoric of universal monarchy, polemics retained a strong sense of religious obligation. First, defences of Protestantism developed from simple calls for crusades against Rome until they could comprehend Habsburg alliances. Second, that notion of a defence of Christendom – which had been so useful when the enemy had been the Protestant Dutch – was also adapted to denounce the French.

[122] *Monthly Account*, 2:4 (1689), 124 – cited in Pincus, 'To protect', p. 101.
[123] Pincus, 'To protect', sect. iv.

Obviously, the stories of these linguistic changes, which involve simultaneous adaptations of interlocking rhetorics, were complex. Making them clearer requires abandoning strict chronological narrative, since relating the events in exact order would involve dizzying switches between arguments (often when describing the content of a single speech, pamphlet or sermon; or even – indeed – when analysing the structure of individual sentences). Instead, therefore, we will concentrate in turn on three particular developments which kept religious discourses in play. First, the French king's persecution of Protestants allowed him to be portrayed as a particular type of popish antichrist, and provided excuses for alliances with more moderate Catholics to stop him. Second, the re-emergence of a Turkish threat in the east revivified the concept of Christendom, and made it easier to paint Louis as an enemy of that spiritual union. Finally, Louis' growing record of treaty-breaking suggested he was incapable of keeping faith, and branded him as the betrayer of all Christian values.

To start, then, with Louis' image as a persecutor. To understand this fully, it is important to delve back through French history to the sixteenth century. In that era, France had not withstood the tide of the Protestant reformation as firmly as Spain or Italy. Instead, a sizeable proportion of the population had been converted to a Calvinist faith, and this community – labelled Huguenots – had become so powerful that it had contended violently for the French crown. By the late 1590s, their candidate for the throne, Henri, king of Navarre, was close to success. Yet recognising that his rule would be insecure unless he found a religious settlement, he compromised. Reassuring Catholics by converting to their faith, he calmed Protestants – once he had been crowned as Henri IV – with the 1598 edict of Nantes. This granted Huguenots the right to worship at a large number of designated 'temples'; it allowed them to organise local church structures; it conceded them separate courts to judge religious issues; and it awarded them predominant power in towns where they were a majority. Also permitting Protestants considerable military privileges, the edict came close to creating a Protestant state-within-a-state.[124]

As a short-term solution to conflict, Henri's provisions worked well. However, they rapidly got into trouble. The Nantes settlement was resented by Catholics, it worried succeeding kings who objected to the semi-autonomy of some of their subjects, and it was tested by a still ambitious Huguenot faction which rebelled in 1626. Accordingly, campaigns to scale back the concessions had begun almost as soon as they were awarded. With the defeat of the Huguenot rebellion in 1629, military privileges were forfeited, Protestant nobles were largely disarmed, and the walls of Protestant cities demolished.

[124] Mack P. Holt, *The French wars of religion, 1562–1629* (Cambridge, 1995).

Legal judgements also began to limit their freedom, as royal courts and councils interpreted the 1598 edict as narrowly as possible. Although harassment was often suspended during negotiations with Protestant powers, or when the court looked for Huguenot support during the 1640s Fronde revolt, it was clear that the Nantes settlement was being eroded by the time Louis came to power.[125]

The new king accelerated the process. It is true he was no theologian. He showed little interest in the detailed doctrinal case for Catholicism, and pragmatic considerations (such as his need to organise his almost constant warfare) could push religious policy to one side for extended periods. Nevertheless, Louis had inherited a simple Catholic faith from his mother, and he distrusted Protestants as potential rebels. So in the 1660s, the legal campaign against Huguenot privileges intensified. These were steadily withdrawn, and although war with the Dutch held back a wholesale pogrom for some time, Louis was freer to pursue his religious aims after the peace of Nijmegen. From 1678, Protestants were progressively excluded from the government of many of their towns; the special courts protecting their interests were abolished; taxes were imposed more heavily on them than on Catholic neighbours; and their churches were demolished if they attracted fewer than ten worshippers. Soon, this legal bullying was joined by more direct coercion. Soldiers were billeted on Huguenot households, and their unwilling hosts found themselves facing substantial costs. Stories also circulated that troops were over-enthusiastic in their master's cause. Exaggerated – but not wholly unfounded – tales had soldiers dragging their landlords to Catholic churches or threatening them at sword point until they renounced their religion.[126]

In 1685, Louis' persecution culminated in the revocation of the edict of Nantes. Quite why this dramatic step was taken has been debated. Probably, Louis had been misled by reports that his earlier harassment had been efficient and that most Huguenots had now given up their faith. The king may therefore have felt the revocation was affecting rather few people. Perhaps Louis also felt his bullying had stoked resentment, and that urgent action must be taken to crush any Huguenot rebellion. Whatever the reason, the revocation outlawed Protestantism, abolished privileges and sanctioned aggressive steps to stamp out the reformed faith. Thus all Protestant temples were demolished; ministers were ordered to leave France if they did not convert to Catholicism; and Protestant children were to be baptised and educated in the Roman faith. In what many saw as a particularly heartless measure, Huguenot laymen were forbidden to leave the country. This meant

[125] Holt, *French wars*, ch. 7; Treasure, *Louis XIV*, pp. 212–17.

[126] Stories were gleefully reported in England: *A brief relation of the persecution and sufferings of the reformed churches in France* (1668); *The present state of the Protestants in France* (1681).

they were denied even the miserable option of exile – and it proved counter-productive as people left with nothing to lose found courage to resist their oppressors. Instead of the limited mopping-up Louis had envisaged, therefore, he faced a sizeable and stubborn population which he was committed to convert by force. Over the months after revocation, Protestants were bullied and maltreated, they were dragooned to church under threat of death, they had their houses destroyed and they were forced into destitution as their posts and trades were taken from them.[127]

The revocation of the edict of Nantes became the defining moment in Louis' image abroad. Whatever its value in eliminating a potentially troublesome minority, the policy was a public relations disaster. All over Europe, it allowed Louis' enemies to portray him as an arch-persecutor, and in England especially each stage of the attack on Protestants was reported in the goriest detail. As early as the 1660s, English audiences were hearing of Huguenots 'hanged, . . . burnt, . . . scourg'd, . . . banished', whilst further disturbing reports escaped in the next decade.[128] By the 1680s, such martyr narratives were in full flood, and they exploded in number after the revocation itself. Taken together, the corpus established a stock of violent images. In the pamphlets, no story was complete until Protestants had been set on fire, boiled alive, dragged to papist churches behind horses, or had had their children forcibly abducted for miseducation by cruel clergy.[129] Some publications raised special horror by retelling the 1572 St Bartholomew's day massacre. On that infamous occasion, huge numbers of Huguenots had been slaughtered by Catholic plotters who had invited them to celebrate Henri of Navarre's wedding into the royal family, and writers now implied parallel inhumanities were unfolding.[130] If any doubted the printed reports of the modern atrocities, first-hand accounts were available. Throughout Louis' reign many Protestants fled France, and many came to London, an accessible Protestant capital whose rulers said they welcomed the unfortunates. As the exiles arrived they brought tales of the barbarism back home, and in fact they peddled their sufferings vigorously to defuse local resentment at their arrival. The Huguenots were an alien community whose artisan skills

[127] For summaries: Treasure, *Louis XIV*, ch. 9; Paul Sonnino, ed., *The reign of Louis XIV* (1990), ch. 10.

[128] *Brief relation of the persecution*, p. 14

[129] E.g. [Edmond Everard], *The great pressures and grievances of the Protestants in France* (1681); *The horrible persecution of the French Protestants, in the province of Poitou* (1681); *A true and perfect relation of the new invented way of persecuting the Protestants* (1682); *A full account of the barbarous and unhumane usage of the Protestants* (1686); Jean Claude, *An account of the persecutions and oppressions of the Protestants in France* (1686); *The French king's decree against Protestants* (1689).

[130] *A relation of the barbarous and bloody massacre of about an hundred thousand Protestants* (1678).

might undercut English workers. Reminding their hosts and new neighbours of what they had been through, they tried to blunt any backlash against them.[131]

As a result of such propaganda, Louis became fixed in the English mind as a merciless bigot who had destroyed one of the great communities of reformed Europe. He was the author of 'innumerable Desolations', of 'all sorts of afflictions', and of 'Superlative Excesses of Cruelty'.[132] Yet even though this picture was black, it is not instantly clear that it would influence discussion of England's foreign policy. There might be sympathy for the oppressed, but there were very good reasons for avoiding intervention to prevent persecutions abroad. Quite apart from the endless warfare a general protection of Protestants might cause, there was widespread acceptance that monarchs had the right to impose religious uniformity on their realms, and (at least until the very end of the seventeenth century) there no was great enthusiasm for the general principle of religious toleration.[133] Nevertheless, Louis' image as a persecutor *did* inject religious elements into the conceptions of foreign policy and – paradoxically – even offered ways to explain those alliances with Catholics which seemed to demand secular justifications.

The most obvious reason for this was the apparent link between Louis' domestic policy and his continental ambitions. As the French king's career unfolded, it became clear that his anti-Protestantism was not just aimed at his own population. Worryingly, it seemed to threaten the reformation everywhere. As Louis' troops conquered, they recaptured territory for a Catholic ruler, and set about reconverting the areas they now controlled. In some cases, this counter-reformation was mild. In Strasbourg, for instance, the cathedral and other major churches were handed back to the Romanists when the French annexed the city in 1681, but the previously dominant Lutherans retained freedom of worship and were granted impressive city-centre buildings. Elsewhere, by frightening contrast, Protestants fared very badly. In Orange, Louis' absorption of the city exposed its reformed population to the full rigours of state policy. Back in England the cruelties were

131 E.g. *Present state of the Protestants*, pp. 30–1.

132 *Brief relation of the persecution*, p. 1; *Present state of the Protestants*, p. 29; *French king's decree*, p. 15.

133 John Coffey, *Persecution and toleration in Protestant England* (Harlow, 2000), stressed toleration made progress in the seventeenth century, but also emphasised its slow and partial success. Gordon Schochet, 'The act of toleration and the failure of comprehension', in Dale Hoak and Mordechai Feingold, eds., *The world of William and Mary* (Stanford, 1996), pp. 165–87, argues even the 1689 toleration act aimed to preserve discrimination. Alexandra Walsham, *Charitable hatred: tolerance and intolerance in England, 1500–1700* (Manchester, 2006), also stressed the slow progress of tolerationist ideas.

reported as some of the worst excesses of the French king's troops.[134] When Louis invaded the United Provinces in 1672, priests poured back into cities such as Utrecht and staged triumphant celebrations in the cathedrals: this was also reported in the English press. In Savoy, Louis' bullying of the duke led to persecution of the Vaudois of the Alpine valleys. This touched a particularly raw nerve in England, as the Vaudois, who were supposed to be descended from medieval heretics, had long been portrayed as the last remnant of a pure, pre-popish church.[135] When Louis used religious propaganda to discourage Habsburg action against him (most of his wars were justified as crusades to spread the Roman faith), it was hard to avoid the conclusion that the revocation of the Nantes edict was not a local matter. It was part of a wholesale campaign to eliminate European Protestantism.

Such a pattern made Louis' expansion a general crisis for the continental reformation as well as the first stage in his campaign for universal monarchy. Anti-French polemicists could therefore suggest the king was a papist antichrist, and could argue that all adherents of the true faith must unite against him. Cast in these terms, Louis' persecution imposed obligations on England. As the strongest Protestant power, she must bring all reformed states together, and lead efforts to save the true gospel. At first sight, this response would rule out collaboration with the Habsburgs. Yet in fact, the very scale of the crisis could excuse such co-operation. Writers who wanted England to save the reformation were aware she might have to ally with Spain and Austria, but this did not discourage them, since they argued these were quite extraordinary times in which Protestantism faced such danger that God would accept whatever preservative action was necessary. Indeed, some used the need for Catholic support to stress the starkness of the situation. European Protestants had been so weakened by their French nemesis that their own actions were no longer enough. As Edmund Everard (the admittedly unprincipled pamphleteer) explained in the late 1670s, God understood how precarious his cause was and had arranged a split in the Catholic front to rescue it. Heaven had enfeebled the Habsburgs so they were looking for help in resisting the French: Protestants would be impious if they missed this providential opportunity to co-operate with Vienna and Madrid.[136]

Soon, we will explore in more detail how the notion of a universal Protestant crisis interacted with the fact of Habsburg alliance and the apparently

134 See *A general and true memorial of what has been done in the city and principality of Orange* (1687); Jacques Pineton de Chambrun, *The history of the persecutions of the Protestants by the French king in the principality of Orange* (translated 1689).

135 This tradition lasted into the nineteenth century: Hugh Dyke Acland, *A brief sketch of the history and present situations of the Valdenses* (1825).

136 [Edmund Everard], *Discourses on the present state of the Protestant princes of Europe* (1679), pp. 15–19. For the career of this turncoat: Alan Marshall, 'Everard, Edmund', *ODNB*, XVIII:779–80.

secular talk of universal monarchy. Before we do, however, we should note another, more subtle, way in which Louis' persecutions eased collaboration with Catholics. To understand this we need to revisit the sixteenth century, this time to analyse English images of the popish antichrist from their origins. Under the Tudors, Protestants in England had developed two rather different ways of recognising the evil of the false church. In the late Stuart age, Louis' persecution ensured he fitted one of these templates of inquity far better than the other – and this would prove significant, since the one he matched did not demand confessional purity in the struggle against him.

We have already met the first English analysis of antichrist when discussing the assumptions which underlay travellers' descriptions of popish Europe. Following the insights of Luther, who had identified Rome as Babylon, early English Protestants had objected to the *teachings* of the medieval church. They had claimed it distorted Christ's words to the advantage of the clergy, and so rejected transubstantiation, purgatory and papal supremacy as deceptions to boost the church's power. In this worldview, the popish antichrist was the fount of wicked error: he was identified primarily by his formulation of corrupt doctrine. Alongside this understanding, however, another description of antichrist also became established. As the early Protestant movement suffered oppression – particularly during periods under Henry VIII, and dramatically under the Catholic Queen Mary – an alternative image of evil emerged, this time centring on *persecution* rather than precise teaching. In this mental universe, the popish antichrist was identified by his cruelty and bloodlust. He had pursued a centuries-long campaign to extirpate the true faith by massacre, torture and slow fire, and this was more horrifying and characteristic than his doctrine. The works of John Bale and John Foxe illustrate this alternative vision clearly. These early Protestant propagandists had suffered cruel setbacks at the hands of religious conservatives and so tended to mark the papal church at least as much by its tyrannical misuse of coercive force as by its false theology.[137]

Of course, there was no pressing contradiction between the two antichrists in the English imagination. One who perverted doctrine would persecute those who did not believe his lies; and since the papal church had both deceived and oppressed, the two images could serve as alternative confirmations that Rome was the great Satan. Nevertheless, there was a logical distinction between the two analyses, which might lead to different perceptions of the antichrist's true threat. The difference concerned the degree of doctrinal purity required of the true church. According to the first view, any departure from a particular reading of God was suspect, and put all but the impeccably

[137] For Foxe and Bale, see above, pp. 101–2.

faithful in league with the antichrist. The second view, by contrast, put much less emphasis on doctrinal orthodoxy, instead identifying true Christians as those who had experienced or resisted persecution. The consequences can be seen in the chief manifesto for English Protestantism. Foxe's book of martyrs provided a history of the true church through the centuries, yet because it concentrated on the cruelties of Rome and the heroic sufferings of Christians at its hands, it swept a doctrinally diverse crew onto the godly side. Although Foxe no doubt believed all his martyrs held something like Protestant beliefs, his horror of anti-Christian barbarism blunted his scholarship, and he recruited almost any victim of the papacy as a hero of the story. Thus the Protestants who had died under Mary were seen as ornaments of the true church; but so (as we have seen) were medieval 'heretics' such Lollards, Hussites and Waldensians. These folk were some way from the doctrine of Luther or Calvin; whilst the Albigensians of thirteenth-century Provence were even more unorthodox. These unfortunate people had certainly been slaughtered by popish crusades, and were included by Foxe among the godly, but their radically dualist beliefs meant they could not really be counted as Christians at all.[138]

The doctrinal flabbiness of the persecuting antichrist served English Protestantism well as its story unfolded. As it concentrated on the behaviour of its papal enemy, rather than on complex doctrine, it was easier to convey to a population beyond the universities where the reformed faith had first flourished. Similarly, as it promoted tales of lurid cruelty, it provided a more visceral argument against popery than subtle theological debates. The image of a persecuting antichrist therefore stood at the heart of much Tudor Protestant propaganda: sermons recounted tales of popish bloodlust, whilst engravings (most famously in editions of Foxe) portrayed burning faggots piled around the godly. In the seventeenth century, too, a stress on persecution proved useful when Protestants themselves divided. From the mid-Tudor era, they had disagreed on ceremony and forms of church government.[139] Under the Stuarts they split over the precise mechanism of salvation, and the need for a national church.[140] In these circumstances, the image of antichrist as persecutor was a focus for unity, or at least suggested a way for people of different views to live together. Throughout the period, the need to oppose a heartless,

[138] Cattley, *Acts*, II:76–83. For Albigensian beliefs: Malcolm Barber, *The Cathars* (Harlow, 2000), pp. 81–93.

[139] See above, p. 78, and below, pp. 284–6.

[140] The literature on these divisions is vast, but see Nicholas Tyacke, *Anti-Calvinists: the rise of English Arminianism, 1590–1640* (Oxford, 1987); Anthony Milton, *Catholic and reformed: The Roman and Protestant churches in English Protestant thought, 1600–1640* (Cambridge, 1995); Michael R. Watts, *The dissenters: from the reformation to the French revolution* (Oxford, 1978); John Spurr, *The restoration church of England* (New Haven, 1991).

torturing popery blunted the internal conflicts of reformed Christians.[141] By the restoration era, clerics such as Gilbert Burnet were implying that people with quite a spectrum of beliefs could be part of the godly community, since the true signs of antichrist were bigotry and intolerance, rather than deviation from an exact set of beliefs.[142]

The point of this history has been to demonstrate that English Protestants often identified their religious foes, not with a precise theological position, but simply by their violence towards other Christians. In this set of assumptions, Louis' persecution of Protestants cast him as the cruel, rather than as the lying, antichrist and so veiled the importance of confessional differences when discussing how to deal with him. Within the worldview called to mind by French cruelty, the key distinction between good and evil was that between charity and bloodlust; whether someone believed in purgatory, transubstantiation or papal supremacy was relatively unimportant. Unwittingly, therefore, Louis had created an ideological field in England which distracted attention from her Catholic allies. He had fallen into a conceptual gap in the English psyche between anti-Christian popery (defined as persecution of the reformed), and merely erroneous Roman Catholic belief. Faced with Louis' barbarism, the English might excuse allying with those foreign rulers whose only crime was to uphold Roman doctrine (as they had begun to excuse those English Catholics whose only crime was to believe the clergy's ridiculous tales), so long as those alliances were aimed against a persecutor of Protestants.[143] Indeed, if the French monarch's cruelty could be stressed hard enough, there was every chance audiences would forget how hybrid the league against him was.

In the 1690s, when England finally engaged in all-out war with Louis, the possibilities discussed above were exploited. The promoters of the war combined a strong insistence on Louis' barbarism, with the notion of a general crisis for the European reformation, to produce *Protestant* polemics which survived the shock of William's co-operation with Habsburgs. Examining the propaganda of the 1689–97 war again, it is clear that although a nationalist and secular rhetoric of universal monarchy was prominent, it shared space with calls for solidarity with the Protestant international.

This was most evident in the series of fasts for the war staged by William's government. I have written about these extensively elsewhere, but the

[141] For examples: W. M. Lamont, *Godly rule: politics and religion, 1603–1659* (1969), ch. 1; David Cressy, *Bonfires and bells: national memory and the Protestant calendar* (1989).

[142] For Burnet's capacious view of Protestantism by 1689, see below, p. 317. Gilbert Burnet, *A sermon preach'd in the chappel of St James, before his highness the prince of Orange* (1689), pp. 28–9, heralded the tolerance of the post-revolutionary regime by opposing any pogrom against Catholics. See also: Simon Patrick, *A sermon preached in the chappel of St James . . . 20 January, 1688/9* (1689).

[143] For local tolerance: Walsham, *Charitable hatred*, esp. ch. 5.

material bears repeating because the fasts were perhaps the most sustained and co-ordinated propaganda campaign launched by a regime to this point.[144] Each spring during the conflict, the king would issue a proclamation ordering his subjects to observe a day's solemn fasting and humiliation to implore God's blessing on English troops. They were expected to avoid unnecessary work for the day, and instead were asked to attend church services where they would hear sermons and a specially composed liturgy calling on them to repent their sins. Once the services were over, the population was expected to return home quietly, and spend the rest of the day in prayer and sober reflection. In the early 1690s, these regular events were made still more systematic by orders that they should be repeated every month through the summer, and each stage of these solemnities was attended by pro-war polemic. The proclamations which called them, the liturgies which structured worship and the sermons (which were frequently printed afterwards) were heavy with explanations of the struggle against Louis. And the main themes of the fast propaganda were Louis' cruelty to Protestants. Although the initial proclamations boasted of the wide range of powers opposed to France (and so might seem to suggest a non-confessional struggle), and although some of the sermons presented Louis as a universal monarch, the main message was that the European reformation faced crisis and that a time of penance would steel its adherents for its defence.[145] In fact, in England the very idea of fasting in response to political developments carried this idea. From the Tudor period this form of humiliation had been the traditional Protestant response to threats to that faith. It had become popular under Elizabeth as England defined herself as a reformed nation and fended off Philip II's armada; it had been a propaganda tool in the 1620s as the English battled the Catholic Spanish and French; and it had been used again in the 1640s as parliamentarian forces mobilised against what they thought was a popishly affected court.[146] More recently, it had been the first reaction of Charles II's parliaments to the heir to the throne's conversion to Catholicism in 1673, and of the supposed popish plot to assassinate Charles II in 1678.[147] On

[144] For my earlier account: Claydon, *William III . . . revolution*, pp. 100–10, chs. 4–6 passim.

[145] For deeper discussion: Tony Claydon, 'Protestantism, universal monarchy and Christendom in William's war propaganda, 1689–1697', in Esther Mijers and David Onnekink, *Redefining William III* (Aldershot, 2007).

[146] Roland Bartel, 'The story of public fast days in England', *Anglican Theological Review*, 37 (1955), 190–220; W. S. Hudson, 'Fast days and civil religion', in W. S. Hudson and L. J. Trinterud, eds., *Theology in sixteenth and seventeenth century England* (Los Angeles, 1971). For 1620s fasting: *A forme of common prayer, together with an order of fasting* (1625); *A forme of prayers, necessary to be used in these dangerous times of warre: wherein we are appointed to fast* (1628). For the 1640s: John F. Wilkins, *Pulpit in parliament* (Princeton, 1969).

[147] In both cases, the legislature had called for a fast as its first action against popery: *LJ*, XII:603–4; XIII:266–7.

all these occasions, fasting had been promoted to restore the nation's godly zeal in the face of Rome's anti-Christian challenge; this established meaning ensured William's wartime fasts would be understood as part of a crusade to rescue the reformed faith.

Beyond the message coded into the very nature of the fasts, the rhetoric which accompanied them confirmed the confessional credentials of the war. Many sermons set the solemnities in the context of a general reformation crisis. They asked for repentance, both to thank God for his gift of a truly Protestant monarch, and to fashion the nation into an appropriate and divinely favoured saviour of Protestants abroad. The preaching therefore portrayed Louis as the arch-persecutor, and outlined his barbarism in horrific detail. For example, Gilbert Burnet surveyed the state of Europe when preaching to the royal court on the new regime's very first fast day. He expressed relief at the arrival of William and Mary in England, emphasising that this providence had saved the country from the horrors Louis had unleashed on Germany and Savoy and which he insisted were still menacing the Netherlands and Ireland.[148] The next year, Simon Patrick reminded his congregation of the 'Whips, and Gibbets, and Racks' which Louis had used against his Protestant population in France; while another year on, William Talbot preached that Louis had breathed 'nothing but Blood, Fire and Devastation' over the continent.[149] Within such polemic, the inconvenience of Catholic alliances might be forgotten. In 1689 Thomas Tenison, a future archbishop of Canterbury, described Louis' persecutions, expulsion and cruelties to a fasting House of Commons, and assured them they were 'engaged in the *Evangelical Cause* against *Popish Superstition*'.[150] In 1690, the incumbent archbishop, John Tillotson, told the Corporation of London that England was the best hope for all reformed Christians. She was the nation 'upon whom the eyes of all *Protestants* abroad are fixed, as the Glory of the *Reformation*, and the great bulwark and support of it'.[151]

If anyone missed the sermon's implication that William's struggle was a war of liberation for European Protestants, the liturgies drove it home. Each fast day was accompanied by a specially written form of prayers, which would structure worship in anglican churches. These followed the standard patterns for morning, communion and evening services laid down in the common prayer, but they altered particular passages to suit the occasion. Among a number of changes which had been designed to stress William's

148 Gilbert Burnet, *Some sermons preached on several occasions* (1713), pp. 39–40.

149 Simon Patrick, *A sermon preached before the king and queen at Whitehall, April 16, 1690* (1690), p. 28; William Talbot, *A sermon preached at the cathedral church of Worcester . . . September 16, 1691* (1691), p. 8.

150 Thomas Tenison, *A sermon against self love . . . 5 June, 1689* (1689), p. 23.

151 John Tillotson, *A sermon preached at St Mary le Bow . . . Wed 18th June* (1690), p. 33.

providential role, the most significant was the inclusion of a collect 'for all reformed churches'. A version of this prayer had been used back in the 1620s, when England was fighting all the leading Catholic powers of the continent.[152] Now it was revived, and it again suggested that the country must act to succour the international reformation. The prayer therefore stressed that the foreign churches were in a 'sad and mournful estate', suffering under 'superstitious and merciless men'. It emphasised that the English were united with these unfortunates in the 'holy Church, the mystical body of Christ', and so implied something must be done to help these brethren.[153] The version of the prayer used in 1689 was particularly pressing. As William launched his war, it placed the struggle in a near apocalyptic context, suggesting that the cruelties experienced by Protestants abroad were so severe because they were nearly over. 'How long', the liturgy asked God, 'wilt thou forget thy People that prayeth!' Implying that William would soon relieve the suffering, the prayer continued: 'Oh let the Blood of the Saints, and the sighing of the Prisons come before thee! . . . Deliver thou those that are Sheep appointed to the Slaughter!'[154]

Given the ideological heritage of fasting, we might have expected a rich strand of Protestant solidarity in its argument. We might even suspect that this confessional bias was not typical of Williamite propaganda as a whole. Yet it remains significant that the regime put so much effort into this particular form of communication. We must remember that the 1690s fasts were the most intense series of humiliations the English were ever asked to perform, and so may represent the apogee of the anti-popish ideology they enshrined. Besides, plenty of evidence from outside these solemnities confirms that defence of the continental reformation was a stated war aim: even in performances which deployed the rhetoric of universal monarchy, the propagandists left space for confessional discourse. For example, William's speeches to parliament would often remind legislators that almost all Europe was united against France, but would then adopt a less inclusive tone, telling them that the war was 'for the support of the Protestant interest both here and abroad' or asking them to remember the state of the French godly who were suffering for their faith.[155] Similarly, many of the pamphlets which described Louis as a universal monarch also spent time narrating his butchery of the Huguenots, implying that the English must mobilise as

152 E.g. 'Prayer for all the reformed churches', in *A forme of prayers, necessary to be used in these dangerous times*.

153 'A prayer for all the reformed churches', in *A form of prayer to be used on Wednesday the twelfth day of March* (1690) – most later fast liturgies included a version.

154 'A prayer for all the reformed churches', in *A form of prayer to be used the fifth day of June* (1689).

155 *LJ*, XIV:126; XV:599.

Protestants as well as to defend national liberties.[156] Of course these works can be accused of ideological incoherence. Yet in the passages portraying Louis as a popish persecutor, the obvious question about William's Catholic alliances was suppressed. Faced with tales of inhuman cruelty, audiences would almost certainly have forgotten geopolitical realities in their Protestant outrage. If reminded that England was fighting alongside Habsburgs, they would either reflect that the reformation must seek any help in this storm, or that ecclesiastical differences between Catholics and Protestants were far less important than the gulf between the charitable godly and their cruel oppressor.

By now the reader will be realising that many different defences of the war with France emerged in the years after 1689. We will come to discuss how successfully these were combined later, but now we have to add even more discourses to the mix. As well as the rhetorics of universal monarchy and Protestantism which we have been examining, Louis' detractors reached for broader Christian arguments, and so further extended the flexibility and the spiritual resonance of their case. The first of these 'Christian' polemics was depiction of the French king as a 'Great Turk'. This became possible because the last substantial Ottoman incursion into Europe coincided with Louis' aggression. The sudden re-emergence of an Islamic threat encouraged a new concern for the security of Christendom which William's polemicists found they could turn against France.

For over three hundred years the Ottoman Turks had been the principal threat to Christian Europe. Although medieval rulers had pushed Arab Muslims from the Iberian and Italian peninsulas, an aggressive new force had advanced through Asia Minor and Greece in the fifteenth century. By 1483 the non-Arabic Turks had captured the whole Byzantine empire, including its capital Constantinople, and – after a brief pause to conquer Syria, Arabia and Egypt – had resumed westward expansion in the 1500s. Under Sultan Suleiman the Magnificent (1520–66) the Ottomans had gained naval domination of the eastern Mediterranean and advanced to the borders of Germany, so when Philip II of Spain defeated the Turks at the naval battle of Lepanto (1571) it was seen as a providential rescue for the whole Christian faith.[157] By the middle of the seventeenth century, however, the Turks were once again on the move. From 1645 they began a struggle with Venice which expunged her influence beyond the Adriatic, and then turned to defeat the Poles and Russians along the Black Sea. Next in the firing line was Austria. By the mid-1660s, the Ottomans had wrested much of Hungary from the

[156] For amalgamated discourses, see below, pp. 187–92.

[157] For the Ottomans: *The Cambridge history of Islam*, vol. 1 (Cambridge, 1970). For Lepanto: Henry Kamen, *Philip of Spain* (New Haven, 1997), pp. 138–40.

Habsburg empire, and extracted tribute from the rulers in Vienna. Most alarming, they launched a full-scale invasion in 1683. In March, a huge Turkish army poured from its base near Constantinople and batted away the imperial troops sent to block its path into Europe. As the Muslim armies advanced across the Hungarian plain, the imperial court retreated to Passau, and left its capital defended by just 12,000 men. By the middle of July Vienna was besieged: the garrison held out for two heroic months.[158]

The response to these events was Europe-wide. Pope Innocent IX called on all Christian rulers to aid Austria in its defence of their religion, and his words inspired a crusade which engulfed remarkably wide swathes of the continent.[159] By the late summer, the Catholic rulers of Poland and Bavaria had raised troops to aid the emperor, and Lutheran Saxony and other German Protestants had done the same. As a result, it was a diverse Christian force which poured down on Vienna in September and swept the Turks from the city. All of this, naturally, fostered feelings of Christian solidarity. If Vienna had fallen (and the enemy had already breached its walls when it was rescued), all Europe could see the Turks would have had an open path into the heart of Germany and there would have oppressed the reformed as much as the Romanists. The Habsburgs themselves recognised they had only defeated the Turks with outside help, and appreciated the Protestant role in the victory.[160]

England may have been far from the conflict on the Danube, but she too became aware of the unity and vulnerability of Christendom as it unfolded. In the decades after the restoration the English were informed about the Turkish advance, and it lurked as a nagging concern in public discourse. We have already encountered this unease. When Hollanders were accused of betraying Christianity in the Anglo-Dutch wars, part of the case rested on their dividing nations who should be working together against the infidel.[161] More generally, authors warned that Christian Europe was not concentrating sufficiently on the Turkish threat – and of course this concern became acute in 1683.[162] Numerous publications reported the advance of the Turks that year, and presented it as a crisis for the whole Christian faith. In this material, Vienna was called the 'bulwark' of Christendom and it was made

158 For Ottoman recovery: Jean Berenger, *A history of the Habsburg empire, 1273–1700* (Harlow, 1994), ch. 24. For Vienna: John Stoye, *The siege of Vienna* (New York, 1964).

159 For Innocent: J. N. D. Kelly, *The Oxford dictionary of popes* (Oxford, 1996), p. 288.

160 *A memorial which his excellency the count de Thunn, envoy extraordinary from his imperial majesty, presented to the king of Great Britain* (1683) publicised the Habsburgs' stance. *A defiance and indiction of war sent by Sultan Mohomet IV to Leopold* (1683) was a fabricated declaration against all Christians.

161 See above, pp. 148–50.

162 For early concern: Henry Marsh, *A new survey of the Turkish empire* (1663); *Europae modernae speculum*.

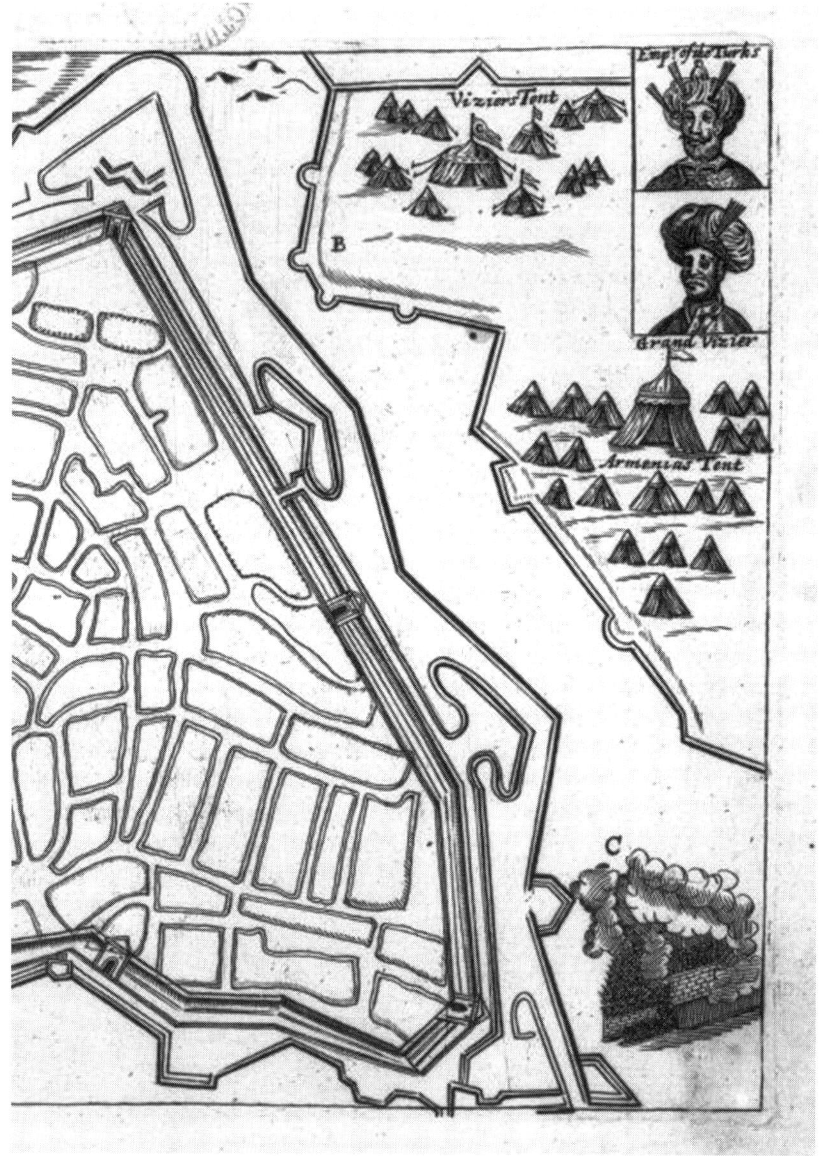

Fig. 2. Detail of *An exact description of Vienna* (1683)

clear that more than Austria would fall if the city were taken.[163] Several pieces included pictorial representations of the siege to dramatise the clash of civilisations. Prospects of Vienna were darkened by the huge Muslim force camped outside its walls: by showing a turbaned horde literally at the gates of western Europe, illustrators emphasised the strangeness of the Turks' dress, manner and physiognomy.[164]

As the emperor began to recover, the sense of a united Christendom strengthened further. The English pamphlets made no adverse reflection on the pope's role in co-ordinating resistance, nor did they comment that it was a Roman Catholic capital that had been saved. Instead they celebrated the broad alliance of forces which had repulsed the Turk: in the pamphlets, the emperor's troops were always referred to as the 'Christian army', whilst one asserted that the victory had preserved the 'whole Christian Commonwealth'.[165] Over the next years, as the Turks were driven back across the Hungarian plain, there were continued calls for Christian co-operation. The author of the mystically prophetic *Predictions of the sudden and total collapse of the Turkish empire* (1684) observed that it would be a happy day if 'there were no other Emulation among Christians than a Vying who should do the bravest Act against the Common Enemy'.[166] In 1685, John Shirley's history of the war claimed Christian divisions had been the very 'foundation of the *Ottoman* empire' and called for a unanimous prosecution of the conflict.[167] In 1686, the Austrian capture of Buda was greeted by descriptions lauding the victorious armies 'of so many Christian Princes' and the (admittedly limited) English participation.[168] The deliverance also provoked a specially composed thanksgiving liturgy, performed in the royal chapels at Whitehall and Windsor, which asked God to maintain all 'Christian Kings, Princes and Governours, in Peace, Amity and Concord'.[169]

163 The word 'bulwark' appeared in *A particular account of the sudden and unexpected siege of Vienna* (1683); published before the city's relief, this was a major source for later pamphlets.

164 E.g. *A true and exact description of the city of Vienna, together with the encampment of the Turks* (1683); *A description of Vienna in its ancient and present state* (1683), detail in fig. 2.

165 W. B., *A true copy of a letter sent from Vienna* (1683); *A true and exact relation of the raising of the siege of Vienna* (1683); N. N., *An account of the defeat of Count Teckely ...* [1683]; *A full and true account of the great battle ... before the city of Presburg* (1683), p. 12.

166 *Predictions of the sudden and total collapse of the Turkish empire* (1684), p. 4.

167 John Shirley, *The history of the wars of Hungary* (1685), preface.

168 *A historical description of the glorious conquest of the city of Buda* (1686), p. 68; Jacob Richards, *A journal of the siege and taking of Buda* (1687); *A historical description of the glorious conquest of the city of Buda* (1686).

169 *A form of prayer and thanksgiving ... for the prosperity of Christian arms* (1686).

The Turkish incursion thus reinforced the notion of Christendom in England. In fact, it could be argued that this entity, which we have already met as an ecclesiological and as a moral body, was strengthened by the revival of a medieval conception of the Christian realm. In the middle ages, Christians had faced the first onslaughts of Islam, and had been acutely aware that their territorial borders were vulnerable. They had therefore viewed Christendom as a military entity: a fortress whose defenders must secure by uniting in crusade. It is easy to assume that this vision faded as Europe divided in the reformation, and as Muslim powers lost their early drive. However, with the Turks at the gates of Vienna, this militarised vision of Christian unity reawakened. At least until the 1699 treaty of Karlowitz secured Austria's eastern frontier, the English saw Europe's faith as a precarious bastion. They were prepared to accept the traditional leadership of the Holy Roman (now Austrian) emperors in its armed defence, and were told that shared effort against the infidel on the battlefield was every Christian's highest duty.

Unfortunately for Louis, it was hard to include him in this consolidated Christian enterprise – and this began his transformation into the 'Great Turk'. The problem was his diplomatic position. Although the French king had not positively encouraged the Turkish incursion, it had gelled with several trends in his foreign policy, and this made him a sitting target for English denigration. First, Louis had been trying to keep good relations with the Turks. France had long viewed the Ottomans as a useful balance against the Habsburgs, and she had also soothed the sultan to discourage him from aiding the Barbary pirates who might harry French shipping. When the Turks invaded Austria, therefore, Louis did not heed the entreaties of the French clergy to send help to Vienna; in fact, he protested little about it. Second, Louis found the Ottoman action useful in his own expansion along the Rhine. In the early 1680s, France was actively absorbing territory along her eastern frontier, and she welcomed the Turks' distraction of the Habsburg. With Vienna endangered, it was unlikely the Austrians would lead any united German protest against French incursion, and Louis benefited very directly in 1684 when the emperor recognised all of his recent annexations in order to free his hands in the east. Finally, the Turkish invasion became entangled with France's policy in Hungary. For some decades the (largely Protestant) Hungarian nobility had been struggling to free themselves from Habsburg rule. France had financed the nobles as a way of weakening the rival empire, but in the early 1680s the Hungarians had tried to exert more leverage in Vienna by offering troops to the Turks. This brought the French into a proxy (if not officially authorised) alliance with the Ottomans, and naturally set Louis up for considerable embarrassment. When the Turks invaded the Austrian lands in 1683, Hungarian forces joined the horde, and since these had been bankrolled by France, Louis appeared rather closer to the Muslim than the Christian cause.[170]

As might be expected, English polemicists jumped on this French failure to defend Christendom. As the Turkish danger became clear, and as evidence mounted that Louis was not exerting all his efforts against it, writers began to accuse him of collaboration with the Muslims – though complaint was not initially very specific. The pamphlets which first put the case for an anti-French foreign policy centred on Louis' growing hegemony, and introduced a (rather generalised) Turkish element only in passing. Some were, nevertheless, outraged by French policy in the east. De Lisola's *Buckler of state* once again led the way: whilst this thought the French king was chiefly dangerous for upsetting the balance of power *within* Europe, it also suggested his expansion distracted Christians from the external danger. De Lisola argued that Turkish advances had been helped by an understanding with the French, and that France had staged a series of 'diversions' to frustrate 'those who have desired to undertake something against the Common Enemy'.[171] Other early pamphleteers joined accusations against Louis' un-Christian collaboration, particularly arguing his campaign against the Habsburgs weakened Europe's best bulwark against Islam. Thus the author of the 1677 *Present state of Christendom* used a language of universal monarchy, but also claimed Louis' hostility to Austria did the Turk's work. By 'breaking down the only Fence that has preserv'd us all this while from the Incursions of the Ottoman Power', the writer raged, France had risked the bondage of Christendom and an 'effusion of more Christian blood'.[172] Similarly, William Temple worried that France would use the Turks to advance in the Low Countries, whilst Marchamont Needham plagiarised de Lisola in his 1678 analysis of France's threat, and a burst of pamphlets during the exclusion crisis suggested the Turks had been drawn into French plans for world domination.[173]

After 1683 this passionate, but somewhat generalised, disgust at French behaviour was replaced by more precise charges. Observing France's reluctance to act when the Austrian capital was besieged, English pamphleteers became convinced the whole Ottoman incursion had been a French plot. Admittedly, publishing such views was difficult during the reigns of

[170] John B.Wolf, *Louis XIV* (New York, 1968), damns Louis' policy, but others – e.g. John A. Lynn, *The wars of Louis XIV* (Harlow, 1999), pp. 165–6 – are not as convinced Louis directly helped the Ottomans.

[171] [De Lisola], *Buckler*, p. 291.

[172] *The present state of Christendom and the interest of England* (1677), p. 26.

[173] [William Temple], *Miscellanea*, pt 1 (1680), p. 6; [Needham], *Christianissimus*, p. 53; *The politicks of France* (1680), pp. 195–6; *The French politician found out* (1680), pp. 19–21; [de Cerdan], *Europe a slave*; *The French intrigues discovered with methods and arts to retrench the potency of France* (1681), pp. 11–12.

Charles II and James II because these kings needed good relations with Versailles and censored the press. Although some 1683 descriptions of Vienna claimed Turkish gunners were being helped by French artillery, and that many of the dead Ottoman soldiers were found with French coins in their pockets, most contemporary commentators limited themselves to leaving Louis out of the roll of Christian heroes.[174] Restraint, however, was removed in 1689. William's regime was looking for justifications for its war on France, and rumours that Louis had helped the Turks earlier in the 1680s met its demands perfectly. Consequently, the years after the Glorious Revolution were filled with a torrent of material retelling the Vienna campaign which presented Louis as involved in a dastardly design against Christendom. He had nearly sacrificed the security of all the faithful for his boundless ambition and invited the Turk into the heart of Europe.

The best way into this propaganda is *The intreigues of the French king at Constantinople* (1689). In the finest traditions of investigative journalism, this pamphlet used leaked documents to present a web of conspiracy, and in particular cited letters from Louis, allegedly found among the papers of the Hungarian rebel Count Teckely. Large passages of these epistles were blotted out, and they lacked the oral instructions the French king would have sent with his emissaries, but this simply allowed the author to reconstruct Louis' full intentions by inference. At the root of the plot was the Bourbon monarch's desire to usurp the Habsburgs. Ever since marrying the Spanish infanta, he had longed to control Spain's territories, and he had always envied the Austrians their imperial title.[175]

In the early 1680s he saw a way to accomplish his ends by encouraging the Turks to attack Austria. In the chaos which would follow, Vienna would be too preoccupied to help the Spaniards if France moved against them, and the German princes might become so terrified of the Ottomans that they would ask the French king to replace the emperor. Accordingly, Louis stirred the Turk. He wrote to the sultan, pointing out that Austria was facing rebellion from her Hungarian subjects, so now was the moment to break the treaty with the empire. If an attack were launched, France promised an alliance and a diversionary assault on the Rhine.[176] At the same time, Louis wrote to the Hungarians. In these letters the king sympathised with their oppression and offered friendship, money and possibly men (this part of the letter was inconveniently erased), if they would time a revolt to coincide with the Turkish attack.[177] As the author of the *Intreigues* lamented, this plot had

174 *True and exact relation of the raising of the siege*, p. 6. Also: *The history of the late war with the Turk . . . with an account of the underhand dealings of France* (1684).

175 *The intreigues of the French king at Constantinople to embroil Christendom* (1689), pp. 2–7.

176 Ibid., pp. 7–8.

177 Ibid., pp. 14–15.

come to fruition in 1683. The Turks had invaded; the Hungarians had risen; and only the resolve of the united Christian armies had saved the day. Louis' conspiracy, however, was not over. In the months after Vienna's rescue, the French king schemed furiously to save his plans. More money flowed to Teckely, and the French besieged Luxembourg to divert the Austrian troops. Louis also convinced the Ottomans not to sign a peace with the emperor. Faced with defeat, the sultan had been tempted to do this, but promises of a massive French attack on Germany (realised in Louis' 1689 descent on Philipsburg) dissuaded him. Most imaginatively, Louis activated his agent in Warsaw to neutralise Poland's effort against the Turk. His sleeper there was the French mistress of the Polish king: using her considerable wiles, she had pulled the Poles out of the Christian alliance by enticing their leader away from the battlefield and back to her arms.[178]

The *Intreigues of the French king* was an exaggerated and sensationalist exposé, but its themes were standard in Williamite polemic. The charge that Louis had allied with the Turk, and had endangered Christendom by undermining its Austrian bulwark, was repeated *ad nauseam* in the waves of pamphlets which backed war in the 1690s. Very many authors claimed that Louis' attacks on the Rhine were timed to divert the Habsburgs from their struggle on the Danube.[179] Many also reported Louis' links with the Austrian rebels, and expressed shock that a Christian king could endanger his faith by allying with the infidel.[180] Most specifically, some shared the *Intreigues*' horror at Louis' reaction to the lifting of the Vienna siege. The original work had complained the French king had been so dismayed by the Christian victory that he had shut himself up in his chamber for two days and had fallen into a fever of wrath and disappointment.[181] Other writers confirmed the picture, noting, for example, that the French clergy had been forbidden to sing *Te Deums* for relief from the Turk.[182] Pamphlets can, of course, betray the idiosyncrasies of their authors, but Louis' friendship with Islam became an official indictment in the 1689 Commons address on the war. When William came to the throne, he sought a request from parliament

[178] Ibid., p. 17.

[179] E.g. *The emperor's letter to James II* (1689); *A new declaration of the confederate princes and states against Lewis the fourteenth* (1689), p. 3; *A brief display of the French counsels representing the wiles and artifices of France* (1694), pp. 128–9.

[180] E.g. *The spirit of France and the politick maxims of Lewis XIV* (1689); *Tyrconnel's letter to the French king* (1690), p. 2; *Monsieur in a mouse trap* (1691); *The consequences of tolerating gold and silver to be exported* [1692?]; *A true and authentick copy of the most horrid and stupendous oath, whereby the French king confirmed his alliance with the Turks* (1694); *A dialogue between the French king and the late King James* (1697), p. 19.

[181] *Intreigues of the French*, pp. 16–17.

[182] *Spirit of France*, p. 20. See also: *Reflexions on the conditions of peace offer'd by France* (1694), pp. 4–5; *Letters written by a French gentleman giving a faithful and particular account of the transactions at the court of France* (1695), p. 36.

for action against France, calculating that this would bind the legislature more tightly into the war effort than a royal declaration of hostility. When parliament's address came, on 19 April, it indicted Louis on many counts, but his policy in the near east was prominent. The French king, the Commons complained, had boasted zeal for the Catholic religion, but this was belied by his encouraging Protestant Hungarians to rise against the emperor, and by his promises of assistance as they fought 'in Conjunction with the Turk'.[183] Further, Louis had invaded Philipsburg 'at the same time that his Imperial Majesty was imploying all his Forces against the Common Enemy of the Christian Faith'; and 'to facilitate his Conquests upon Neighbour Princes, he ingaged the Turks in a War against Christendom'.[184]

By asserting that Louis was in alliance with the Ottomans, English polemicists made a serious charge against him. At a time when Christendom had been threatened, and when anxiety about its future was at its height in English public discourse, the French king had imperilled the whole Christian faith, aiding 'the sworn Enemies of the Holy Cross' in their 'War against *Jesus Christ*'.[185] What allowed writers to move beyond this, and suggest Louis had actually *become* the Great Turk, was their deeper analysis of his diplomatic motives. According to Williamite pamphleteers, Louis found it easy to co-operate with Islam because he shared its methods and aims. In dealing with other Europeans, Louis showed the same barbarity which the Turks were thought to have exercised on their Christian enemies, and this cruelty was rooted in a Turk-like indifference to Christian believers.

The starting point for this argument was the destruction Louis' wars had caused. As the French had invaded Flanders in the 1660s, the Netherlands in the 1670s and the Rhineland in 1689, they had naturally caused damage and bloodshed, but for English polemicists this was more than the usual cost of conflict. Instead, it had to be seen in the context of Louis' alliance with Constantinople. A man who could betray the faith so completely must have as little concern for its adherents as his infidel friends, and this was why his wars were conducted with such inhumanity. Louis was therefore described as being 'as fierce as a Turk'. The blood he spilt – like that the Muslims wasted – was invariable 'Christian'. In his incursions into the Low Countries the king had burnt and pillaged 'after the Turkish manner', whilst his troops had been guilty of greater barbarities than the Ottomans has yet managed.[186]

This cruelty to Christians was made possible by indifference to them, but it went further than this. For English writers, Louis' horrific policies actually stemmed from an aversion to the central tenets of Christ's faith. Pamphleteers

[183] *An address agreed at the committee for the French war* (1689), p. 2. [184] Ibid., p. 3.
[185] *Emperor's letter*; *The detestable designs of France expos'd* (1689), p. 23.
[186] *Spirit of France*, p. 19; *New declaration*, p. 8.

were more concerned to abuse the French king than offer a full psychological profile of him, so one has to distil the explanations of this hatred from their prose. Nevertheless, it is clear writers thought Louis loathed the true faith because it jarred with his vaulting ambition. As he tried to conquer the world, Christians would accuse him of breaking Jesus' injunctions to humility and peace, so he had resolved to extirpate their faith. Thus the French targeted the symbols and infrastructure of Christianity. In Louis' wars churches were robbed; religious institutions were despoiled; towns were attacked on the holiest festival days; and the bells, clocks and roofs of ecclesiastical buildings were melted into armaments.[187] Such violence to the faith deepened the Turkish alliance beyond diplomatic convenience. Louis did not just see the Turks as a useful counter-balance to the Habsburgs; he actually shared their aim of eliminating Christ's teachings, and writers even claimed to detect promotion of Islam in his actions. According to one author, the Turks would be grateful to the French for their counter-evangelism. When news of their invasions reached the Porte, 'the Divan will lift up their hands to Heaven, and give God thanks for revenging themselves upon the Christians by the Christians themselves'.[188] In the words of others, Louis must be a Muslim, for only this could explain his perfidy to Christ's followers; he thought military setbacks were the result of Allah's anger that he had hidden Islam and promised to march under the crescent in future; whilst the king was said to prefer the Koran to the bible, for Islam's holy book did not condemn his acts (or at least he had not sworn not to abjure them on it).[189] Perhaps most graphically, authors accused Louis of replacing churches with mosques. His troops in the east had demolished Christian temples whilst helping local Muslims to rebuild theirs, and this had been possible since this king was indifferent to the truth of religion. He didn't mind whether 'the *Turks* . . . set up the Standard of *Mahomet* above the Cross of Christ, provided [he] satisfie his Ambition', and bringing the threat much closer to home, one writer thought Louis put even England's Christian heritage in danger.[190] He was willing to ally with Barbary pirates as well as the Turk, so if he gained control of the Channel he might settle the corsairs along the south coast, and minarets would sprout in English seaports.[191]

[187] *Emperor's letter*; *Detestable designs*, p. 26; *Spirit of France*, p. 19; *New declaration*, pp. 7, 14.
[188] *Detestable designs*, p. 28.
[189] *The present French king demonstrated an enemy to the Catholick as well as Protestant religion* (1691), preface; *New declaration*, p. 8; *A letter from the French king to the Great Turk* (1692), p. 1; *The French king proved a bastard* (1691), preface.
[190] *The means to free Europe from French usurpation* (1689), p. 160; *A brief display of the French counsels* (1694), p. 129.
[191] *Means to free Europe*, p. 160.

Combining Louis' alliance with the Ottomans and his hostility to Christianity, pamphleteers found it a short step to the final and most heinous charge. The French king had now actually displaced the eastern power as the most pressing and destructive threat to Christendom, and so had become the Great Turk himself. This accusation lay behind much of the popular polemic written against the French in the 1690s, emerging in warnings that Christians were failing to mobilise against Louis (just as they had failed to take the Turkish threat seriously), or in frequent charges that life under the French would be even worse than under the Ottomans.[192] Some pamphleteers were still more explicit, with the most eloquent passage coming from the author of *A view of the true interests of the several states of Europe* (1689). Opening his work, this polemicist argued that the continent had been worrying about the wrong danger:

> The Christian princes have two great and potent Enemies, that have united and entered into mutual Leagues, to ruin and depopulate Christendom, and to make all the Potentates and Republics of *Europe* their Subjects . . . One is the King of France, and the other is the Emperor of the *Turks*. The former is the interior Enemy, whose Dominions lie in the midst of *Christendom*, whereas the latter is an exterior one, of whom we may easily be aware, and consequently is less to be feared.[193]

Another writer made this point as much in the magnificent title as in the relentless content of his pamphlet. Satirising Louis' official title as the 'most Christian' king of France, one tract promised *The most Christian Turk: or a view of the life and bloody reign of Lewis XIV*. It delivered on this promise, consisting of a litany of Louis' crimes against Christendom in league with the Porte.[194]

The image of Louis as a Great Turk thus added to his role as a persecuting antichrist: and, of course, provided another excuse for William's alliance with Catholic powers. This rhetoric stressed the unity of Christendom in the face of an infidel threat, and so urged all denominations to collaborate to face the danger. As one pamphlet put it, the great division of Europe was between the faithful and Christ's enemies, and anyone who did not sign up to William's confederacy should be 'set in the number of the Turks and the French'.[195] Moreover, the rhetoric provided a special excuse for

[192] For warnings against delay: *The present state of Europe briefly examined* (1689), p. 2; *Means to free Europe*, pp. 3–7. For Turks as preferable: *The secret intreagues of the French king's ministers* (1690), p. 57; *The true interests of the princes of Europe in the present state of affairs* (1689), p. 34.

[193] *View of the true interest*, preface.

[194] *The most Christian Turk: or a view of the life and bloody reign of Lewis XIV* (1690). One pamphlet warned against attacking the actual Turk, when the French were the real threat: *The management of the present war against France* (1690).

[195] *Means to free Europe*, p. 145.

England's co-operation with the Habsburgs. Obviously the rulers in Madrid and Vienna were Romanists, and the English had clashed with them on this count. Despite this, however, all had recognised and had been grateful for their role in holding back the Turk. The Spaniards had won at Lepanto; whilst the Austrians had repulsed the infidel in 1683 and as technical successors to the medieval Roman emperors had met the traditional duty to co-ordinate Christian crusades. Now that a new and greater Turk had emerged in France, this rhetoric tapped into the English sympathies for the Habsburgs created by their defence against Islam, and so may have rendered William's diplomacy far more acceptable.

So far, quite a number of derogatory descriptions of Louis have been recovered from late Stuart polemic. Eventually we will examine how these diverse views were combined, but there is one final strand of discourse to be explored before we do. Like the rhetoric of the great Turk, this depended on the notion of Christendom; but unlike it, it was not primarily concerned with the medieval vision of that body as an externally endangered fortress. Rather, it took up the conception we began to explore when considering the Dutch wars, namely Christendom as a moral entity. Louis attacked Christianity physically through his eastern alliance; but he also undermined its ethical fabric, setting examples which could make Christian society unviable.

In anti-French polemic, Louis' vices were legion. Like the Dutch before him, he was ambitious, avaricious and – as his treatment of the Huguenots and conquered people demonstrated – unbelievably cruel. Adding particular failings of his own, he was proud and vainglorious (pamphleteers had endless fun with the fulsome odes, and blasphemously idolatrous inscriptions, produced for the king in France) and led a court whose sexual incontinence was notorious.[196] Tales surrounding the French king's birth were repeated to back these points. Louis could be proved a bastard, and it was said he had been born with teeth so sharp they made his wet-nurse bleed (this, pamphleteers assured their readers, was a certain sign of the insatiable greed which would direct his career).[197] Among this blizzard of abuse, however, one charge stood out. Again and again, Louis was accused of perfidy. This was a man who could not keep his word. He might enter into leagues and treaties, and he might promise future actions with the solemnest oaths, but he would always be insincere. Louis kept agreements only as long as they

[196] E.g. *The cabinet open'd or the secret history of the amours of Madam de Maintenon* (1690); *Most Christian Turk*, pp. 67–71; *The English spy* (1691), pp. 115–35; *A faithful account of the renewed persecution of the churches of Lower Aquitaine* (1692), pp. 3–8; *The royal mistresses of France* (1695).

[197] E.g. *The great bastard, protector of the little one* (1689); *Most Christian Turk*, pp. 1–4; *French king proved a bastard*; *The royal cuckold or great bastard* (1693). Stories survived into Anne's reign: *The French king vindicated* (1712), pp. 5–7.

suited his purposes, and his diplomacy was nothing but a snare for those foolish enough to trust it.

This indictment was built upon Louis' political record. From the very start, he had broken agreements. In 1659, when marrying the daughter of the Spanish king, he had renounced all claims on Spain's territory which this match might bring. Despite this, however, he invaded the Spanish Netherlands in 1667, asserting that his wife's heritage gave him legitimate interests there. The pattern extended to his dealings with the English and Dutch. In 1666 Charles II had thought he was close to an alliance with the French king against the Provinces, but then watched in horror as Louis entered the war on his enemy's side. In 1672 France attacked the Netherlands without warning, and this treachery continued into the 1680s. Both the 1678 treaty of Nijmegen and the truce of 1684 had promised ends to French expansion, but the 1689 descent on the Palatinate was merely a culmination of unbroken pressure on the Rhine. Over the preceding decade almost every city in Louis' way had been annexed, besieged, interfered with or otherwise bullied.[198] The greatest betrayal came in 1700. After the 1697 peace of Ryswick, the French king and William III had agreed to resolve the great remaining threat to international relations. Realising that the death of Carlos II, the heirless king of Spain, would destroy the balance of Europe if his whole empire were to fall into either Austrian or French hands, the monarchs had agreed 'partition' treaties which divided Spain's Italian lands between Austria and France, but kept Spain, Flanders and the New World out of the direct control of Versailles or Vienna.[199] However, when Carlos II finally passed away at the end of 1700, he left all of his territories to a younger grandson of Louis. Despite the fact that this abrogated the principle of dividing Italy, and that it put a cadet Bourbon in charge in Spain instead of the cadet Habsburg envisaged in the treaty, Louis accepted Carlos' will. He vowed to fight to secure the whole Spanish realm for his grandson, in direct contradiction of his promises to William.[200]

Of course, Louis had defences for his actions. Changes in circumstances can make almost any treaty invalid; there were questions over the legality of the 1659 renunciation of claims on Spain; and there were even factors which mitigated the shock of 1700. Louis could point out that Austria and Spain had rejected the partition treaties so he would have to fight for what they had awarded him, and he could argue that his acceptance of Carlos' will could be reconciled with the balance of power. Even with his grandson in Madrid, the English, the Dutch and the Austrians remained powerful counter-weights

[198] Lynn, *Wars of Louis XIV*, ch. 56.
[199] David Ogg, *England in the reigns of James II and William III* (Oxford, 1955), ch. 15, provides a clear guide to dizzying diplomacy.
[200] Francois Bluche, *Louis XIV* (Oxford, 1996), pp. 513–20, covers French calculations.

to France, whilst the new Bourbon dynasty in Spain would remain separate from the French royal line and might soon go native. As we shall see, *some* Englishmen accepted these arguments. In 1700–1, Tory authors suggested England acquiesce in Louis' actions to avoid war – though the ground was cut from them by Louis' inept recognition of James II's son as the legitimate Stuart king.[201] For the anti-French party, however, 1700 was merely the latest in a long line of outrageous betrayals, and it was their rhetoric which persuaded the nation back to war in 1702. Ratting over partition confirmed the character flaw in Louis which English polemicists had been analysing for forty years.

Accusations of French perfidy were so ubiquitous in the late Stuart era that there is almost no point providing examples. The charge that Louis broke treaties was made in almost every work attacking France from de Lisola's first call to arms, through the warnings of universal monarchy in the 1680s and 1690s, to the outraged analysis of the discarded partition treaties. Many writers built long sections – or even the whole – of their works on dense narratives of treachery. By 1680, the author of *The French politician found out* could recite what had become a canonical catalogue of trampled treaties. Louis had broken the peaces of Westphalia (1648), the Pyrenees (1659), Breda (1667) and Nijmegen (1678).[202] By 1683, the author of *An exact survey of the grand affairs of France* could bring the story right up to date with tales of Louis' most recent duplicities along the Rhine.[203] Such rehearsals of untrustworthiness continued through William III's war, and reached a crescendo when Louis reneged on partition. By the start of the war of Spanish succession in 1702, English poets were blackening a monarch who 'broke all . . . Leagues', and was 'to promises ne'er true'; whilst prose polemicists talked of their nation's 'indisputable Ground to resent the Perfidiousness' of the French monarch, and of her 'just Abhorence for a Breach of a Treaty . . . so solemnly Sign'd and Swore to in the Name of God'.[204]

What is important about this complaint is that it was not simply political. As suggested by the last cited pamphlet's horror at the breach of a treaty sworn to God, English censure was Christian as well as national. Writers were certainly upset that England's interests had been damaged by trusting Louis, but this hurt was usually translated into the allegation that France had threatened their faith. In the anti-French literature of the late seventeenth century, Christendom was a moral entity. It was a community whose members had duties to live in peace and protect their weakest brethren, and as part of

201 E.g. *An argument against war* (1701).
202 *French politician*, p. 23.
203 *An exact survey of the grand affairs of France* (1683).
204 *The French tyrant or the royal slave* (1702), p. 11; *Two letters to a friend concerning the partition treaty* (1702), p. 13; *Reasons prov'd to be unreasonable* (1702), p. 23.

this, Christians had to keep their promises. Pacts kept societies in harmony, and ensured that the weak were sheltered from the arbitrary actions of the powerful. In international affairs, this principle of agreement was enshrined in public treaties. Such agreements between nations kept peace and protected communities with smaller armies, so by breaching treaties Louis was abrogating the central purposes of Christianity. Just as his alliance with the Ottomans cast him out of Christendom, Louis' constant perfidy made him the common enemy of all Christians (and the two discourses were mentally close – Sir Paul Rycaut had made the Turks' lack of respect for promises the defining mark of their Muslim religion).[205] Given all this, Catholics and Protestants had a shared spiritual duty to oppose and punish the French. Indeed, since Spain and Austria were most directly wronged by Louis' betrayals, the English had particular cause to stand by the Romanist Habsburgs.

This case was made from the very start of anti-French polemic. De Lisola, a pioneer here as in so many other strands of rhetoric, charged that by ignoring his earlier renunciation of claims in the Netherlands, Louis had broken an agreement 'solemnly decided by a publick Treatie, upon the Faith whereof all Christendome did solely found their Quiet'.[206] He urged that other 'Christian princes' punish this breach, or human society would be reduced to the level of tameless beasts, and he argued that Europe must 'remove out of the sight of Christendom a scandalous example, which by its lamentable consequences would expose the weakest to the discretion of the most powerfull'.[207] This argument was rapidly taken up by English writers, who were equally convinced that Louis transgressed religious principles. As with the Dutch, it is important that French crimes were almost always described as breaches of *faith*: whilst this meant untrustworthiness, the choice of word implied a deeper and more worrying failing. Beyond this, many writers were more explicitly analytical. Like de Lisola, they posited a collapse of Christian society if Louis' example became general, and suggested that only rapid punishment of the transgression could remove the danger. In 1668, *A free conference touching the present state of England* (the work Arlington sponsored to underline de Lisola) shared the Austrian's outrage, and accused France of being bound by nothing but her own interest. The reckless violation of a peace 'so solemnly and piously established' spoke to 'the Root of our Consciences'. It called the English to do their duty to 'Justice, Pity, good Neighbourhood, the Publick Cause of Christendom, and our Selves'.[208] To pick other instances scattered across the period: in 1678 Marchamont Needham asserted that peace was the subject of Christ's last sermon, but

[205] Paul Rycaut, *The present state of the Ottoman empire* (1668), pp. 95–7.
[206] [De Lisola], *Buckler of state*, preface. [207] Ibid., pp. 274–5.
[208] *A free conference touching*, pp. 60–1.

that the actions of Louis 'whom no Treaties or Intreaties can reduce to a more *Christian State*' had ensured there had been no peace in Europe since he came to power.[209] In 1684, an author (wisely claiming to publish from Cologne) complained that the French monarch's 'infidelity' broke all principles of peace and justice, and gave the lie to his title of the most Christian king.[210] In 1689, William III, declaring war on Louis, listed the damage he had done to England's national interests, but then said he was joining his diverse allies to oppose 'the Common Enemy of the Christian World', whose worst crimes included 'manifest Violation of Treaties'.[211] In 1690, the author of a furious ad hominem attack on Louis listed all his breaches of leagues, and called them 'the Violation of all the Laws of God and Nature'. With the French king, oaths were but flimsy barriers 'to defend the common Bulwark of Christendom' from his vast design of conquest, and the shared interest of all Christian princes must be to 'prevent the introducing of *Maxims* into this World which will destroy all commerce among Men, and will certainly render humane Society no less dangerous and insupportable than that of *Lions* and *Tygers*'.[212]

With the vision of Louis as a betraying threat to all Christian values, our summary of the main images of France in late Stuart polemic is complete. The English went to war with the French king because he was a potential universal monarch: but also because he was an anti-Christian persecutor of the reformed religion; a Great Turk who had allied with and then displaced the Ottomans as the main military threat to Christendom; and a supremely vicious man whose perfidy contradicted the Christian faith. These three latter discourses were religious, but by stressing cruelty over doctrine, or suggesting the whole faith was in danger rather than just its reformed version, they avoided the trap of a narrow confessional argument. Notions of the Protestant international and of Christendom could cope with the Habsburg alliances, and at least shared the field with concern about naked French power. Indeed, they probably did more than this. If we move beyond the mere survival of religious discourses, and examine how they interrelated with universal monarchy, we may question whether even this rhetoric was a secular as has been claimed.

One of the remarkable features of the arguments we have been examining is their easy coexistence in late Stuart polemic. Although proceeding from rather different premises, and very occasionally attacking one another's

209 [Needham], *Christianissimus*, p. 60.
210 *Monsieur Colbert's ghost: or France without bounds* (Cologne, 1684).
211 *Their majesties declaration against the French king, 7 May, 1689* (1689).
212 *Nero Gallicanus: or a true portraiture of Lewis XIV* (1690), pp. 63–5. For other attacks on Louis' trustworthiness: *The bounds set to France by the Pyrenean treaty* (1694); *An answer to a paper written by Count d'Avaux* (1694), p. 3.

axioms, the different discourses were usually jumbled together. In fact, it is hard to find many speeches, poems, pamphlets or sermons which did not combine at least two of them. Often, spokesmen moved between different images of Louis in a single passage, or even a single sentence, without pausing to consider the contradictions this might involve. For instance, the author of *The most Christian Turk*, whilst promoting one depiction in his title, actually deployed all the others in his prose. Louis was accused of seeking universal monarchy, of breaking all treaties, and of attempting to extirpate the Protestant religion. Similarly we have already seen royal speeches deploying a confused plethora of arguments through the 1690s: Louis had trampled on the liberties of all European nations – but the war was also being fought to preserve the international reformation.[213]

What probably saved these performances from ideological collapse (and it is surprising how little comment there was on their incoherence) was the lack of close contemporary scrutiny. Most people are a welter of inconsistent assumptions and prejudices: if we accept this is true of ourselves, we should not be surprised that late Stuart polemicists mixed their metaphors of evil or that their audiences, swept up in the various lurid descriptions of the national enemy, failed to reflect closely on their compatibility. Significantly, however, the propaganda was also rescued by the close affinities between the images of Louis it deployed. Despite their different ideological origins, the actual descriptions of a universal monarch, of a persecuting antichrist, of a Great Turk or of a perfidious betrayer of Christian values shared key elements. Cruelty, for example, was an obvious trait shared by all the images. Persecutors and Turks were cruel by definition – but universal monarchs could not expand their territories without launching bloody wars, and monsters who broke treaties released their troops to butcher those they had gulled. Vainglorious pride was another common characteristic. It was the essence of an aspiring universal monarch; it was part of the traditional description of antichrist; it was an attribute of the Turk Louis had now displaced; and it was a prime motive for treaty-breaking. Such merging of imagery eased the shifts between rhetorics in late Stuart francophobia. Within a description of cruelty or pride, it could be unclear which analysis was actually being deployed, and this allowed considerable polemic flexibility. To take our example, *The most Christian Turk*. Its author smoothed changes of discourse by concentrating on the barbarity of Louis' rule. He kept returning to the slaughters and bloodlust of Louis' troops as he successively denounced the revocation of Nantes, the alliance with the Ottomans, the breaking of treaties, and the destruction of the European balance of power. This hybrid discourse was even given pictorial form in the frontispiece to the pamphlet. Behind the

213 See above, p. 171.

main figures of this, French troops sack an anonymous city, and butcher its inhabitants outside its walls. Yet whether these folk are Protestants, Christians or people defending their national liberties against a rampaging hegemonist is not made clear. In the foreground the rearing horseback figure of Louis XIV triumphs. His steed balances on a globe, which might be taken as a simple depiction of universal monarchy – were not the beast framed by a black-robed Jesuit priest (to remind us of Louis' anti-Christian persecution of Protestants), and a turbaned Sultan (to remind us he is the new Great Turk).[214]

Affinities of image thus allowed different discourses to be used together, but they also suggest the languages were not far apart in the first place. In particular, the rhetoric of universal monarchy – introduced above as a *secular* solution to the problem of Catholic alliances – might have had more in common with the religious languages than we have supposed. It was smoothly compatible with Christian denunciations of cruelty and pride; and through these shared descriptions of evil, it could be combined with attacks on treaty-breaking, Turkish alliances, and even the persecution of Protestants. As deployed by the late Stuart propagandists, it breathed the same spirit as the other polemics, raising the same nightmares and employing the same tropes. Perhaps we should not be too surprised by this. After all, the discourse of universal monarchy had not simply sprung into existence in the mid-seventeenth century to cope with attacks on the Protestant Dutch or with Habsburg alliances. Rather, it had been adapted to these purposes from an older language: reformation-era warnings about the hegemony of Spain. In this earlier, sixteenth-century manifestation, universal monarchy had *not* been secular. It had alerted Protestants that a Catholic power was on the verge of world domination, and that their religion would be crushed if this were realised.[215] Under the Stuarts these older associations had been disrupted by transfer of the rhetoric to attack the Protestant Dutch, and then to denounce Louis (whose relations with the papacy were notoriously bad), but they had not been destroyed.[216] Quite apart from borrowing the anti-Christian imagery of a proud and cruel tyrant in the descriptions of universal monarchs, some who used this language still gave it a Protestant spin. Preachers of fast sermons, for instance, were adept at deploying the rhetoric of universal monarchy in combination with confessional discourse, as I have shown elsewhere.[217] Similarly, many pamphleteers stressed that

[214] See fig. 3.
[215] Thompson, *Britain, Hanover*, pp. 36–9, explains the English associated universal monarchy with clerical oppression and religious persecution – and so popery.
[216] Kelly, *Oxford dictionary of popes*, pp. 285–6.
[217] Claydon, 'Protestantism, universal monarchy'.

Fig. 3. Frontispiece of *The most Christian Turk: the life and bloody reign of Lewis XIV* (1690)

Louis' universal domination of the continent would be even more disastrous for Protestants than for others.[218]

Yet perhaps more significant than the survival of Protestantism within concerns about global hegemony was the seventeenth-century development

[218] E.g. *An account of the reasons which induced Charles II, king of England, to declare war* (1689), esp. p. 2; *Means to free Europe*, dedication; *The safety of France to Monsieur the Dauphin* (1690); *Most Christian Turk*.

of more generally Christian elements in the discourse. As pamphleteers analysed Louis' growing dominance, they became increasingly convinced that a monopolistic ruler would not, and in fact *could* not, govern in a Christian manner. For them, the very goal of world domination insulted Christ's injunctions to humility, and the methods a universal monarch would use to achieve his goal were inevitably un-Christian too. There would be cruelty as his armies advanced; there would be greed as he seized other people's lands and properties; and there would be wholesale dishonesty as he duped, bribed and blackmailed other powers. Here again, the choice of a word is important. In warning of universal monarchy, it was almost invariably 'Christendom' which was said to be under threat. Although this was partly because Louis only endangered Christian nations at present (he was in his outrageous alliance with the Turk), it was used instead of the available alternative 'Europe', and it indicated that France's expansion threatened a set of values and a faith-based community as well as a geographical area.[219]

This spiritual and ethical dimension to universal monarchy was strongly implied in almost every piece of propaganda which employed it, but in 1702 a couple of works made the point in a more explicit and sustained way. *Anguis in herba*, a pamphlet warning that the English could not avoid war with France over the Spanish succession, built its case on the inherent anti-Christianism of an aspiring hegemonist. A man trying to expand his empire could have no faith, for he must deceive in order to prosper; he could have no regard for justice, because he was working for 'universal Robbery'; and he could have no 'Tenderness or Compassion for the Miseries of Mankind', because his methods would inevitably be 'the most barbarous, inhuman and cruel that are possible to be acted'.[220] According to this writer, therefore, a universal monarch could bring only 'Treasons, Rebellions, Wars, Blood, general Desolations and Oppressions', and he could not '*bona fide* be of any Religion, because both the End proposed and the necessary Means of obtaining that End, are most unjust, violent, cruel and directly repugnant to the Principles of all Religion'.[221]

Charles Davenant, a Tory pamphleteer, underlined this. Davenant was sceptical about renewed war with France at the start of Queen Anne's reign, but he nevertheless agreed with the analysis of world domination contained in *Anguis in herba*. In his *Essay on universal monarchy* he raised a question surprisingly rarely asked in the anti-French literature. He wanted to discuss what was actually wrong with a single authority for the whole globe, when one could easily think of benefits it might bring if it ended strife between

219 For widespread use of 'Christendom' against Louis: Claydon, 'Protestantism, universal monarchy'.

220 *Anguis in herba: or the fatal consequences of a treaty with France* (1702), p. 4.

221 Ibid., pp. 4–5.

nations. Answering this, Davenant admitted global hegemony might police international tensions, and had seemed to bring cultural, economic and technological advance under the Romans, but in the end he rejected it as morally repugnant. For him, universal monarchy was founded in an original sin of ambition. It was therefore corrupted from its roots, and its methods could only be 'Battels, Sieges, Sackings, and those other Effects of War, that involve Humanekind in various sorts of Misery'.[222] Global hegemony was no better once it had been achieved. Universal monarchs did not bring peace and virtue, but as the properly analysed history of the Romans showed, they merely ran to seed. Lust, civil discord and luxury abounded; trade was distorted to enrich the centre at the expense of the provinces; and order was only maintained by oppression. Moving back to origins of the idea of universal monarchy in Protestant thought, Davenant even warned that spiritual persecution was inevitable. World rulers would always be terrified that religious diversity would undermine their tyranny. They would therefore try to stamp it out, and this had been terribly illustrated by the close alliance an ambitious Spain, and then a still more dangerous France, had built with bloodthirsty Jesuits.[223]

In summary, then, detailed analysis of English polemic reveals a more complex, and certainly more spiritualised, understanding of foreign policy in the late Stuart era than emphasis on universal monarchy would allow. Yes, the English fought Louis because they feared he would dominate the world. But they also hated him as an anti-Christian persecutor of the Protestant international; and their strong sense of participation in Christendom painted him as a Great Turk, and as a perfidious betrayer of Christian principles. These images were used blunderbuss fashion – propagandists firing them off indiscriminately – but they could work together because they had much in common, and particularly because universal monarchy was an ethical and religious evil, as well as a political and nationalist one. This fundamental compatibility between Protestant, Christian and power rhetorics was to be essential in the next stage of English foreign policy as the practical limitations of religious crusade became apparent.

THE PROTESTANT INTEREST: ENGLAND AND FRANCE, 1697–1756

William's war with Louis was both the triumph and the nemesis of the anti-French polemics we have been studying. On one hand, Protestant and Christian rhetoric painted the French king as an incorrigible evil and persuaded

222 [Charles Davenant], *Essays* (1701), p. 281.
223 Ibid., after 292 (book mispaginated beyond here).

the nation to fight. Despite the growing hardship, the English battled for nine years and then recommenced struggle when Louis refused to reverse his Spanish policy. Yet at the same time, the realities of conflict forced some reconsideration. Louis had been portrayed as an ungodly enemy and some might have hoped that heaven would help England to a rapid victory. In fact, however, the war had not gone well. The conquest of Ireland took three years; William was retreating in Flanders until 1695; and the peace of 1697 was one of exhaustion, which left Louis holding most of his recent gains. The English, therefore, had to come to terms with their inability to crush their un-Christian foe. For the more providentially minded, the lesson was clear. God was denying victory because of England's own vices. Heaven *would* destroy Louis, but only once his foes had reformed their own lives to make them worthy instruments of its will.[224] For others, however, there were doubts about such language. If England were ever to enjoy peace, she might have to learn to live with a powerful France. Polarised images of antichrists, Great Turks and irreligious betrayers might not help a necessary settlement with the Bourbon crown.

Over the half-century following 1688, there were several periods when harsher views of France might have to be laid aside because the English were negotiating with that country. As early as 1692, William realised he was unlikely to defeat Louis completely, and began to discuss terms for peace. Rancour prevented much progress, but informal diplomatic contacts were maintained until they bore fruit in the 1697 treaty of Ryswick.[225] In the late 1690s, of course, William and Louis were trying to resolve Spain's succession without conflict, and this produced the second period of diplomacy. The partition treaties emerged from close contacts between the agents of the two monarchs, and these contacts proved prolonged since the electoral prince of Bavaria, around whom a first agreement had been built, promptly died and the whole deal had to be renegotiated.[226] After 1709 too, France and England talked peace once they had accepted they would not gain all they wanted through war. Whilst Marlborough's stunning victories initially allowed the English to hope for triumph, the general's magic began to run out after the battle of Malplaquet, and his political masters took a more pragmatic view. Talks took years because the French overplayed their hand, and the English were divided over whether they might still winkle the Bourbons from Madrid, but peace eventually came in 1713.[227] Under the treaty of Utrecht, Louis' grandson Philip was allowed to remain king of Spain, so long as he

224 This common 1690s theme returned when Anne's wars went badly: e.g. George Stanhope, *A sermon preach'd . . . November 7th 1710* (1710).
225 Mark A. Thomson, 'William III and Louis XIV, 1689–97', in Ragnhild Hatton and J. S. Bromley, eds., *William III and Louis XIV* (Liverpool, 1968), pp. 24–48.
226 See n. 199 above. 227 See below, pp. 195–6, 204–8.

surrendered his other European holdings. More stable relations with France also seemed sensible after the succession of the Hanoverians to the English throne in 1714 and the death of Louis XIV a year later. The 1715 Jacobite rising against George I, and political uncertainty in Paris, brought a desire for international calm and led to an alliance with the French which lasted from 1716 to 1731.[228] This prevented challenges to Utrecht and gave both incoming regimes time to bed down, but – along with the other periods of negotiation – it proved a challenge to the bellicose languages which we have been outlining.

There *was* a discourse which could justify deals with the French, but it required a change in emphasis within the English rhetorical universe. The language in question had been an element of the polemic of universal monarchy, but unlike that rhetoric it concentrated less on describing the *evils* of hegemony than on analysing how to stop it. Its central concept was the balance of power. It suggested that global domination could be prevented if contenders for that position were kept broadly equal – and that if alliances and treaty settlements were calculated to ensure this equality, aggressors would be dissuaded by the powerful forces lining up with their potential victims. This argument had had airings in the seventeenth century, but from the mid-1690s the 'balance of power' became the key discourse in discussion of England's foreign relations.[229] Because it drew attention away from the wrongdoings of France and towards the simple question of how to contain her, it allowed more sober analysis of the enemy. Because it admitted Louis might retain considerable strength to form one side of the balance, it allowed dealings with him not predicated on unrealistic calls for the total destruction of a devilish foe.

Balance of power language first came to the fore in defence of the partition treaties. These were controversial, not, in the event, because England had dealt with the Satanic French king, but because opposition Tories found they could use the pacts against a Whig ministry. The treaties had been concluded without consulting parliament; they might commit England to a war to enforce them; and they seemed to grant France too much territory in Italy – so Tories savaged an unsound foreign entanglement, entered without proper consent. Obviously the Whigs (whom William had actually consulted as little as any one else) had to defend agreements made on their watch, but the

[228] Jeremy Black, *Natural and necessary enemies: Anglo-French relations in the eighteenth century* (1986), suggests the two nations were closer than a standard picture of tension implies.

[229] Henri de Rohan, *A treatise of the interest of the princes and states of Christendome* (1641, new edn 1663), popularised the notion; and was republished: *The true interest of Christian princes* (1686). For the relationship between universal monarchy and balance of power: Thompson, *Britain, Hanover*, ch. 1.

nature of the treaties forced them away from established polemic. Because partition tried to maintain peace with Louis, and actually granted him more territory to try to achieve this, ministers could hardly deploy the old rhetoric of French sin. Instead, they developed the notion of the balance of power. It was true Louis had been appeased by satisfying some of his demands, but this was less significant than the careful hedging of Versailles by the countervailing forces of Austria and a still-independent Spain. As an early anonymous work by Daniel Defoe put it, '*a just Ballance of Power is the Life of Peace*', and the partition negotiations were aimed at maintaining the balance of power in Europe.[230] Other writers made the same argument and ensured that when the war of Spanish succession came, it would be promoted in similar terms.[231] Once partition had been constructed as essential to the balance of power, Louis' breaking of the deal must be interpreted as a threat to this balance, so even official justifications of conflict took this line. Queen Anne's declaration of war in 1702 spoke of 'preserving the Liberty and Balance of *Europe*, and . . . reducing the exorbitant power of *France*',[232] whilst later royal speeches warned that the 'balance of power in Europe is utterly destroyed' if Louis held Spain, and said Anne hoped to 'see such a balance of power established in Europe, that it shall no longer be at the pleasure of one prince, to disturb the repose . . . of this part of the world'.[233]

If the Spanish war began with discussion of the balance of power, changing circumstances guaranteed that it would end with it. As the conflict wore on, it became clear that France would not be quickly defeated and many in England began to worry that the strain of battle was harming the country more than any possible advantage. More importantly, the death of Emperor Joseph in 1711 made Archduke Charles heir to Austria as well as the English candidate for the Spanish crown; this threatened to unite Spain with another great power and so facilitated the sort of continental hegemony the partition treaties had hoped to avoid. In this new situation, some Englishmen (particularly Tories) began to argue for a swift end to the war. They urged a quick peace even if it meant leaving Louis' grandson in charge in Madrid, and found they could do this by appealing to the balance of power. France, Tories argued, may not have collapsed but she had been considerably weakened since 1702. She might therefore be contained by rival nations without Britain fighting to sap her further. Tories added that Louis might accept a peace which separated parts of the Spanish heritage if it meant his relative could rule Spain itself, and suggested the detached territories might be given

230 [Daniel Defoe], *The two great questions considered* (1700), p. 15.

231 E.g. *A letter to a friend concerning the partition treaty* [1700]; *The partition examined* (1701).

232 *Her majesties declaration of war against France and Spain* (1702).

233 Cobbett, VI:451, 543.

to France's rivals to check her power. By contrast, if the confederacy continued to fight for the Habsburg control in Madrid, disaster might ensue. This struggle risked uniting Spain, America, Italy, the Netherlands *and* Austria, and founding an empire more terrifying than France. Accordingly, balance of power polemic spewed from Tory presses, and after the party's election victory in 1710 it shaped negotiations for peace.[234]

In response to all this, Whiggish opponents of a deal were themselves forced to analyse the balance of power. They did so by insisting it was still Louis who threatened equilibrium, and that anything but comprehensive victory would leave him still able to expand unchecked through Europe. Thus Whigs passed a 1708 Commons address which demanded there be 'no peace without Spain' (that is, that Habsburg possession of Spain must remain a non-negotiable war aim), and insisted that 'nothing could restore a just balance of power in Europe, but the reducing of the whole Spanish monarchy to the obedience of the House of Austria'.[235] In swathes of subsequent propaganda they reminded the English of the threat Louis posed to safe equality between empires, and one pamphleteer even entitled his piece *The ballance of power*. He argued that France was stronger now than when she had held her own against the Habsburgs in the sixteenth century, and that she benefited from her national unity whilst the counter-weight was a confederacy which might weaken itself by division.[236]

From 1697, then, the balance of power became the most common discourse through which the English discussed foreign relations. This dominance lasted into the high eighteenth century. It dictated England's diplomatic dance through the 1720s and 1730s (she manoeuvred to prevent a hegemonic threat emerging), and then urged her eventual return to war in the 1740s when it appeared France could not be contained by peaceful means.[237] Rather than follow the rhetoric in detail into these decades, however, we should consider its impact on the Protestant and Christian languages we have been following. In particular, we should ask if this shift to the balance of power signalled that secularisation of debate which we failed to find during the Anglo-Dutch wars, or the anti-French conjuction with the Habsburgs.

At first glance, the answer seems to be yes. The emerging rhetoric, after all, called for a cold-blooded calculation of the strengths of European states,

[234] Holmes, *British politics*, pp. 75–81. [235] Cobbett, VI:609.

[236] *The ballance of power, or a comparison of the strength of the emperor and the French king* (1711). See also: *A few words upon the Examiner's scandalous peace* (1711); *A full answer to the conduct of the allies* (1712); and most Whig pamphlets below. *The thoughts of a member of the October club* (1711) reprinted Tory warnings against Louis from 1701 to mock their current policy.

[237] See below, pp. 208–9.

with little apparent room for confessional, or even broader Christian, considerations. Within this set of assumptions, England's interests were to be maintained by international rivalries, not religious injunctions, and in fact spiritual demands might get in the way of establishing the balance if (for example) a group of nations allied on grounds of faith, and then proved too powerful for others to contain.[238] Talk in 'balance of power' polemic therefore concentrated on the concrete and very worldly advantages of holding certain provinces, or entering particular leagues: by the 1730s and 1740s many analysts discussed Europe in these terms.[239] Yet despite the secular tone of much eighteenth-century writing, it would once again be a mistake to dismiss the concepts of Christendom or the Protestant international. In several important respects, these religious identities continued to influence discussion of foreign policy, and to fuel England's transforming wars with France.

To start, there were periods when negotiation with the French was off the agenda. In the early years of the war of Spanish succession, for example, Marlborough's victories brought real hopes that Louis might be utterly crushed. In this period, there was no perceived need for a saving settlement with the French, and highly polarised religious ideals could cheer-lead for the war. Memories of 1683 might have faded, so the rhetoric of the Great Turk might be less prominent, and discussion of the balance of power in 1702 might have popularised talk of military equilibrium – but otherwise the polemic looked very like that of the 1690s. Louis was condemned as an ungodly ruler: he aimed at an un-Christian universal monarchy; he persecuted righteous Protestants; and he flouted Christian principles by breaking his word over Spain.[240] Pamphlets continued to take these lines, but as might be expected, sermons on the war's fasts and thanksgivings were their chief showcase. Edward Fowler, that bishop of Gloucester who had been so surprised by Blenheim, preached on the victory in apocalyptic tones. Concentrating on Louis' sins, and especially his persecution of Protestants, he

238 English commentators worried European Catholics might unite and overwhelm Protestants, see below, pp. 205–8, 210–11.

239 See below, pp. 205–19.

240 E.g. *The dangers of Europe from the growing power of France* (1702), pp. 1–7; *Division our destruction: or a short history of the French faction in England* (1702); *The French tyrant or the royal slave* (1702), pp. 11–14; John Harris, *A sermon preach'd in the parish church of St Mary Magdelen, Old Fish Street* (1703); *A copy of a letter concerning the siege of Landaw* (1704), p. 8; *A memorial dispersed in Holland, by an emissary of France* (1706); *The alcoran of Lewis XIV* (1707), prologue; *A compleat history of the affairs of Spain* (1708); [Joseph Addison], *The state of the war and the necessity of an augmentation* (1708), pp. 1–2; Daniel Pead, *Parturiunt montes: or Lewis and Clement taken in their own snare* (1709); *The life and history of Lewis XIV* (1709). For the continuing prominence of Protestant language: Pasi Ihalainen, *Protestant nations redefined: changing perceptions of national identity, 1685–1772* (Leiden, 2005), pp. 246–7.

interpreted the battle as the fall of Babylon.[241] Fowler had become somewhat eccentric in his old age, but plenty of his clerical colleagues went nearly as far. John Grant, John Evans, Joseph Stennett and Andrew Archer saw Blenheim as a deliverance for Protestantism; Richard Chapman, Nathaniel Hough and John Piggot saw it as punishment for perfidy; whilst Richard Norris mixed both themes with attacks on France's supposed alliance with Islam.[242] Two years later, Gilbert Burnet welcomed further victories over Louis in similar terms. He preached that 'to the Perfidy of Injust and Cruel Wars' the French king had 'added a Series of new and unheard of Persecutions', and charged that he had 'become Drunk with the Blood of the Saints'.[243]

There was another burst of crusading spirit in the aftermath of George II's triumph at Dettingen in 1743, but even beyond such moments of military optimism, spiritual languages were not wholly eclipsed by the balance of power.[244] Initially, this was due to that rhetorical mixing which we have already noted in contemporary polemic. Just as the language of universal monarchy failed to monopolise performances before 1697, writers and speakers went on deploying propaganda in blunderbuss fashion after Ryswick, so the secular-sounding balance of power was rarely unalloyed with more 'religious' discourse. A good case here is the debate about peace without Spain in the later years of Anne's reign. In this, Tories argued that Habsburg preponderance had become a real menace, and Whigs countered that France was still the unbalanced weight in Europe, but neither side relied on these arguments alone. Whigs, for instance, insisted that an unchastened Louis would continue his persecutions of Protestants or mocked their opponents' confidence in Louis' faith.[245] If Tories were to have the peace they wanted, Whigs pointed out, then Britain would have to seal a treaty with France – but there was no point making a treaty because Louis was ungodly and would simply break it.[246] Numerous pamphlets said this, and some went further to suggest Britain herself would sin if she betrayed her promises to

241 Edward Fowler, *A sermon preached . . . Thursday the 7th September, 1704* (1704), p. 23.

242 John Grant, *Deborah and Barak* (1704); John Evans, *The being and benefits of divine providence* (1704); Joseph Stennett, *A sermon preach'd on Thursday 7 September, 1704* (1704); Andrew Archer, *A sermon preached in the chappel at Tunbridge Wells, September 7* (1704); Richard Chapman, *The lawfulness of war in general* (1704); Nathaniel Hough, *Success, when the signs of divine favour* (1704); John Piggot, *A sermon preach'd on the 7th of September 1704* (1704); Richard Norris, *A sermon preach'd on September 7, 1704* (1704).

243 Gilbert Burnet, *A sermon preach'd . . . the xxviith day of June MDCCVI* (1706), p. 3.

244 E.g. John Owen, *The song of Deborah applied to the battle of Dettingen* (1743).

245 E.g. *Semper eadem: or Great Britian's assistance of an honourable peace* (1709).

246 E.g. *A generall collection of treatys* (1710), introduction; *A caveat to the treaties* (1711); [Francis Hare], *The management of the war* (1711), esp. p. 42; *A clear view of the French king's bona fide* (1711); *The allies and the last ministry defended against France* (1711), p. 9; *The French king's promise to the pretender* (1712), esp. p. 21; *The friendship of King Lewis always fatal* (1712).

recover Spain. One 1711 work observed that a premature settlement would have no regard to 'Justice, to Obligations and to Treaties' and might unravel the whole moral fibre of Europe. 'Nobody knows where it may end,' the author groaned, 'what secret Bargains may be made for other Kingdoms.'[247] Tories, similarly, did not rest satisfied with their warnings about a Habsburg threat to the balance of power. Rather, the heart of their case rested in the sort of denunciations of confederates which Jonathan Swift popularised in his *The conduct of the allies* (1711) – and while these attacked the Dutch and Austrians for using the war to waste English money and troops, they also reinvigorated older tropes. In particular, criticism of the Dutch revived the Christian language of the early restoration. Swift and his supporters accused Holland of bottomless ingratitude, avarice and ambition; and several accused the Dutch of betraying allies, or revived accounts of their denial of Christianity in the orient.[248] Again, after decades of suppressed memory, pro-peace writers recalled that the Habsburgs were Catholic bigots. They had never 'laid aside the Thirst after Protestant Blood, so inherent in that Family', and England owed nothing to these persecuting monsters.[249] In all these writings, the balance of power might have provided the intellectual structure – but, once again, religious languages were drafted in to pack the emotional punch.

To understand a second, and more significant, way in which spiritual discourses survived into the balance of power age, it is important to recall the origins of this rhetoric. Above we noted that the balance of power had been part of the earlier analysis of universal monarchy. Some time before that, however, we noted that this earlier polemic had not been entirely secular. It had first been aired as a Protestant warning about the most Catholic kings of Spain; and as deployed against Louis XIV, it had cautioned that the rule of a universal monarch must transgress the principles of Christianity.[250] Although talk of the balance of power was often couched as an objective calculation of national capabilities, it frequently betrayed these theological roots as the balance was conceived as the base of European moral order. The balance preserved a space in which the principles of Christianity could

[247] *Remarks on the present negotiations of peace* (1711), pp. 9–10. Also: *A vindication of the present M_y* (1711), pp. 8–9, 15–18; *Armageddon: or the necessity of carrying on the war* [1711], pp. 13, 19.

[248] Jacobites used such rhetoric in 1690s: e.g. [Nathaniel Johnston], *The dear bargain* (1690); [James Montgomery], *The people of England's grievances* (1693). For comment under Queen Anne: *The queen, the present ministry, Lewis XIV and Philip V unanswerably vindicated* (2nd edn, 1712), pp. 10–11; *A letter to the Examiner, concerning the barrier treaty* (1713), p. 13.

[249] [Daniel Defoe], *A review of the state of the British nation*, vol. VIII, no. 115, p. 462 (11 December 1711). See also *The ballance of Europe* (1711), pp. 17–18.

[250] See above, pp. 189–92.

be upheld, and in which Protestants could be protected from the ravages of their popish enemies.

The 'Christian' dimension of the discourse was a little vague, but was nevertheless real. Like condemnations of universal monarchy, it insisted that 'Christendom' as much as 'Europe' was in danger if its conclusions were not followed; and many writers who deployed the idiom of balance claimed its arguments promoted religious goals. A just balance of power was said to restrain sinful ambition; it would ensure rulers kept their word; and it would avoid the effusions of Christian blood which accompanied war. In fact for some, the balance of power became the highest moral principle. It could overturn a monarch's rights over his realm (what Whigs said after 1700 to nullify Carlos' will); or it could negate earlier diplomacy (as Tories argued after 1711 when denying Spain to the Habsburgs). The balance of power maintained the 'peace of Christendom', so almost any other consideration must bow before it.[251] There was a superb flavour of this Christian equilibrium in White Kennett's thanksgiving sermon for Blenheim. This denounced Louis for breaking faith and inflicting endless 'wounds on the rest of *Europe*', and it went to on claim the French king was suffering divine punishment for these manifold sins. Fascinatingly, though, Kennett had heaven imposing its writ in a thoroughly eighteenth-century manner. The deity, who was 'a God of Peace', was also a 'God whose *ways are equal*' (that is, he would ensure the different powers of Europe would be of roughly equal strength). His providence was therefore checking Louis to 'keep the Government of the World in an *even Balance*', and would establish that 'foundation of all Publick Tranquillity and Happiness, *i.e.* . . . the Balance of *Europe*'.[252]

The 'Protestant' element of the balance of power was stronger and clearer, and perhaps represents the most important development in discussions of foreign policy after 1688. It emerged in the concept of 'the Protestant interest'. This phrase had been used throughout the restoration period with a variety of meanings, from an umbrella term for dissenters and churchmen in England, to leagues of Protestant powers, to the whole community of the reformation in Europe. None of these meanings had been very precise, however, and there were plenty of alternative labels for the same concepts, such as 'the Protestant states and princes' or 'the reformed churches'. Yet once

251 *Two letters to a friend concerning the partition treaty* (1702), p. 10. Also: William Sherlock, *A sermon preach'd before the queen at the cathedral church of St Paul, London* (1704), p. 26, said Anne would 'hold the Balance, and give peace to Europe', p. 26; *A memorial dispersed in Holland* (1706) – France must be balanced by Holland and England to save Christendom; John Adams, *A sermon preach'd at the cathedral church of St Paul . . . on Tuesday, Novemb. 22, 1709* (1709), p. 11 – the balance of power preserved peace and Christianity; Samuel Harris, *A blow to France, or a sermon preach'd . . . Nov. 22 1709* (1709), p. 16 – a God of peace preserved the balance of power.

252 White Kennett, *A sermon preached . . . on September VII 1704* (1704), pp. 19–21.

balance of power language became dominant, talk of a 'Protestant interest' became more prominent and far more focused. In the words of the polemicists, the 'interest' was a confessional entity – the body of Protestants in Europe – but, specifically, it was this entity considered as part of a *power* analysis. The interest encompassed the military and diplomatic clout the Protestants could deploy, along with their 'great-power-like' objectives (the survival, security and prosperity of their number). By developing this concept, analysts preserved the idea of a Protestant international in an idiom which had not appeared conducive to it. They presented Protestantism as if it were itself a great power, and so could discuss its welfare whilst promoting the balance between states.

Much credit for developing the Protestant interest belongs to Daniel Defoe. In the decades before 1713, this great publicist was launching his literary career. He was using his extensive contacts among booksellers to pick up work as a hack writer, and hoping to earn enough from this (along with his other enterprises manufacturing bricks and organising lotteries) to rescue him from constant financial troubles. Defoe therefore penned a barrage of poetry and prose. These included early masterpieces such as *The trueborn Englishman* (1701); his thrice-weekly *Review*; and his 1702 satire on Tories, *The shortest way with dissenters*, which led to the pillory and prison as penalties for sedition. Some of these works he composed freelance. Others he wrote as a paid author, producing material which printers thought would sell or writing for politicians who rewarded him with money or offers of posts in the public service.[253] Given this career, it was not surprising that Defoe was drawn into the intense debates about foreign policy in Queen Anne's reign. He wrote his own pamphlets on European affairs, and worked for ministers who wanted a propagandist with a reputation for speed, effectiveness and style.

Mastering Defoe's views in these works can be bewildering, since they expressed a wide variety of positions within very short spaces of time. In 1700–1, for instance, he wrote to support the partition treaties, but warned against the war with France that would certainly be needed to enforce them.[254] From 1711, he urged a settlement that would leave Spain to the Bourbons, but also deplored the anti-Dutch prejudice which was the Tories' main argument for an early peace.[255] Much of this inconsistency came from his role as a hired pen. Though Whiggish by inclination, he wrote copiously

[253] Paula Backscheider, *Daniel Defoe, his life* (Baltimore, 1989), pts 1–2.

[254] E.g. [Defoe], *Two great questions*; [Daniel Defoe], *Reasons against a war with France* (1701).

[255] Contrast [Daniel Defoe], *Reasons why this nation ought to put a speedy end to this expensive war* (1711), or [Daniel Defoe], *An essay at a plain exposition of the difficult phrase a good peace* (1711), with [Daniel Defoe], *A defence of the allies* (1712).

for Tory ministers – especially his longtime patron, Robert Harley – and this could mean writing against his deeper convictions. It certainly involved rapid shifts of position to match changing politics and adopting various personae to reach the audiences his paymasters wished to persuade.[256] Ambiguity is compounded by the tendency of later scholars to attribute many anonymous works to Defoe. As he was the most prolific – and subsequently the most famous – pamphleteer of his day, historians have assumed he penned almost anything unsigned.[257] As a result, Defoe has become a confusing figure, whose true position (assuming he had one on every topic he tackled) can be unclear. What remained constant in his shifts and contradictions, however, was a deep commitment to the survival of Protestantism in Europe. His works constantly returned to this goal, and were characterised by an innovative pragmatism about how it might be achieved.[258]

An early work which demonstrated these features was the 1701 *Danger of the Protestant religion*. This appears to have been one of the author's freelance efforts, and it expresses many of his most repeated concerns, so we may be close to his true thoughts with this production. In its opening passages, Defoe bucked the contemporary trend of foreign analysis. Rather than calculate the balance of power, he instead urged readers to think about the future of reformed Christianity in Europe and even complained this concern had been lost in secular fears of French might. Once focused on Protestantism, Defoe concluded its prospects were dim. He pointed out that reformed Christians in France and Bohemia had been persecuted out of existence; he worried that the rulers of Saxony and the Palatinate had converted to Catholicism; and he sighed that there were fewer and fewer Protestant nations to withstand papists. In short, God's true religion was being snuffed out, and England could not expect to preserve it long.[259]

Yet whilst Defoe's warning read like an outdated spiritual jeremiad for the reformation, his remedy for the situation swung back to a 'modern' consideration of the balance of power. To start, he demanded that Protestants stand together. Adding up the forces of Catholic and Protestant Europe, Defoe pointed out the former were stronger, and argued that all the reformed must cohere if they were to be any sort of counter-weight to popery. 'In the cause of Religion,' he stated, 'if the Swede, or Dane, or the most remote Nation be Attackt . . . we ought to help and relieve them.'[260] Defoe thus argued

[256] Downie, *Robert Harley*, p. 147; Backscheider, *Daniel Defoe*, chs. 11–13.

[257] P. N. Furbank and W. R. Owens, *The canonisation of Daniel Defoe* (New Haven, 1988). For works erroneously attributed: P. N. Furbank and W. R. Owens, eds., *Defoe de-attributions* (1994); for what remains of Defoe's canon: P. N. Furbank and W. R. Owens, eds., *A critical bibliography of Daniel Defoe* (1998).

[258] For religious analysis of Defoe: Manuel Schonhorn, *Defoe's politics: parliament, power, kingship and Robinson Crusoe* (Cambridge, 1991).

[259] [Daniel Defoe], *The danger of the Protestant religion* (1701), pp. 1–14.

[260] Ibid., pp. 18–19.

that Protestants must pool their strength, but he did far more than this. He pointed out that even if this united Protestant power were created, it would still be unlikely to survive a united Catholic attack. It would therefore have to work for a broader balance across Europe and ensure its potential enemies checked each other. Observing that most Protestants had fought against Louis after 1689, but had still only survived with Habsburg help, Defoe suggested the reformed cause must continue William's division of Catholic states, and that in current circumstances, this meant supporting Austrian claims to Spain.[261] Backing the Habsburgs would ensure they fought popish France, not Protestants; and would stop Louis becoming so powerful that he could crush the reformation. In fact, Defoe claimed Protestants must become as wily as the city of Hamburg. This German town had preserved its independence over centuries by playing off more powerful neighbours in Denmark and Brandenburg: Protestants must master a similarly sly game.[262]

In this analysis, Defoe married confessional and balance of power discourses in a startling manner. His concern had been that a religious war would end in the total defeat of Protestants, but his solution was to preserve a balance which would prevent that war occurring. Reformed nations must come together into an entity Defoe labelled the 'Protestant interest', but rather than launching any confessional crusade, this body would actually use force, guile and offers of alliance to keep its opponents divided. This view of the world was apparent in some of Defoe's other early pamphlets, but it came into its own in the debates over peace after 1709.[263] It helped the writer resolve a tension between his own commitment to the European reformation, and his work for a Tory minister determined to reach a settlement with the persecuting Louis.

Defoe's relations with Robert Harley shaped his entire output during Queen Anne's reign. The two had been close since 1703 when Harley had rescued Defoe from the disgrace of his libel conviction. The minister (the chief Tory in the mixed administration which managed the war until 1708) had been looking for someone to put the government's arguments, and in Defoe he recognised a suitable talent. He therefore arranged for the writer to be released from prison, and began employing him as his personal propagandist and spy. Over the next years, Defoe toured England reporting on political dissent; he was sent to Scotland before 1707 to drum up support for the union; and he bent the *Review* to reflect the administration's opinion.[264]

[261] Ibid., pp. 20–1. [262] Ibid., p. 26.

[263] For an earlier pamphlet: [Defoe], *Two great questions*.

[264] Defoe wrote in favour of union for both English and Scots audiences: [Daniel Defoe], *An essay at removing national prejudices against a union* (1706); [Daniel Defoe], *A reply to the Scots answer* (Edinburgh, 1706); [Daniel Defoe], *The trade of Britain stated* (Edinburgh, 1707).

After 1708, relations soured for a while since Defoe continued working for the ministry even when Harley lost an internal battle in the administration and resigned his post. With the Tory triumph in the general election of 1710, however, Harley swept back to power. He became Defoe's chief patron once again, and the stage was set for the writer's vigourous development of the 'Protestant interest'.[265]

The interest became crucial to Defoe at this point because of his role in Harley's propaganda machine. After 1710 Harley wished to appeal to two distinct audiences. First, there were the hardline Tories who had become convinced the whole war had been a plot to enrich Whigs. They demanded peace with France at almost any price; and they were encouraged by polemic such as Jonathan Swift's which denounced the displaced ministry and their foreign allies as leeches on the English nation. Second, Harley had to pitch for any middle ground. The minister knew he would have difficulty persuading the House of Lords to vote for peace without moderate support; he knew he needed broad backing to convince the enemy England would go on fighting if peace offers were insufficient; and – as a moderate Tory himself – he also wished to avoid dependence on the fanatical wing of his party led by his rival Henry St John. To reach out to middling opinion, Harley turned to Defoe. While scrupulously loyal to Harley, the writer's dissenting background gave him Whiggish sympathies, so it was natural for the minister to use Defoe in his pitch to moderates. In this scheme, the writer's *Review* and pamphlets were to argue for peace, but would do so whilst refuting Tory logic. They would therefore defend the Whigs' honesty; they would confirm it had originally been right to fight France and that it was only now safe to make peace; and they would reject Swift's attacks on the Dutch and other Protestant allies.[266] Defoe would also address religious concerns. Whig and moderate mistrust of Louis was strongly rooted in disgust at his persecution of reformed Christians. Defoe would catch this mood by openly sharing concern for Protestantism whilst arguing that that faith would be better secured by a peace settlement than by continuing the war. Within this carefully constructed position, the concept of a Protestant interest became Defoe's main rhetorical tool. The interest put Whig concerns at the centre of the debate, and probably allowed Defoe himself to square his own anxiety about the reformation with the case for a deal with the French.

The full emergence of the discourse can be traced over a few short weeks in the autumn of 1711. Until early October, Harley's official policy was still to pursue the war to force France to offer reasonable terms. Accordingly, Defoe's *Review* dismissed fears that England was exhausted, and as late as 1 September snorted that if Spain were surrendered to the Bourbons

[265] Backscheider, *Daniel Defoe*, pt 2. [266] Ibid., pp. 270, 314–18.

(a surrender being contemplated by those who wanted a early peace) the French might as well have Ireland too.[267] Yet even as Defoe blew battlefield trumpets, English diplomats were talking in Paris. Around the end of the month the pamphleteer was told preliminary articles for peace would soon be published, and since these *did* leave Spain in Bourbon hands, the *Review* would have to reverse its stance. It began by arguing the government could be trusted to negotiate a 'Safe' and 'Honourable' settlement if any treaty were to emerge, and then, on 11 October, it came out in favour of a peace to end England's suffering.[268]

The problem for Defoe, of course, was to reconcile this new position with his prior statements. Over the mid-October issues, he attempted to do this, wrestling with Whig pamphleteers whom he admitted had reminded him of his comparison of Spain and Ireland. At first, the *Review* adopted simple balance of power rhetoric. It argued the death of Emperor Joseph had changed everything, and that if Spain were still to go to the Austrian candidate, this would create an imperium more frightening than Louis'. According to the journal, the war had been 'to preserve the Ballance of Power', and that simply adhering to the allies' original strategy would set up a greater threat to that balance and would be jumping from the frying pan into the fire.[269] To meet objections based on Defoe's recent denial of Spain to the Bourbons, the author boldly asked, 'What do you mean by SPAIN?'[270] He claimed when he had written in September he had meant the entire Spanish empire, but the suggestion now was that Louis' grandson would gain only Iberia and America. France would not therefore be getting 'Spain' as defined: her Italian and Flemish provinces would go to others to preserve equity between powers.

As a justification for his shift, Defoe's appeals to changing circumstances and to the balance of power were logical enough. However, as October wore on, the writer developed his rhetoric further. Probably feeling the need for a spiritual case to flesh out his rational one, and perhaps himself uncomfortable with his rapid turnaround, Defoe built a defence of the Protestant interest into his discussion. The process began with the 16 October issue of the *Review*. In this, Defoe recalled the earlier consequences of Habsburg hegemony and reminded readers that when this dynasty had been powerful – under Charles V, Philip II or Ferdinand II – it had used its might against Protestants. In fact, even though the Austrian and Spanish branches had been separated since 1555, the Habsburgs had remained a real menace to the true faith. They had collaborated against the reformation, and over the decades had come close to extirpating 'the Interest of the Protestant

[267] [Defoe], *Review*, vol. VIII, no. 69. [268] Ibid., vol. VIII, no. 85, p. 343; vol. VIII, no. 86.
[269] Ibid., vol. VIII, no. 89, p. 357; vol. VIII, no. 87, p. 350.
[270] Ibid., vol. VIII, no. 87, p. 349.

Religion'.[271] Later issues enlarged on the theme. The *Review* cited persecutions of Protestants in Holland, Germany and Hungary to illustrate the danger; and used betrayals of reformed Christians under Habsburg rule to prove no powerful state could be trusted.[272] Such language allowed Defoe to present his balance of power as a security for the godly. After mid-October, those who opposed peace were not just unrealistic warmongers. By insisting that Spain go to Austria, they risked establishing an anti-Protestant powerhouse, and this was something 'no honest Man who has the Protestant Interest of *Europe* at his Heart' – nor any whose 'wishes for the Protestant Interest . . . are sincere' – could want to do.[273]

The full flowering of this discourse came in the 13 November number of the *Review*. After a calm start, referring the reader to the analysis of Habsburg history in the preceding issues, this swelled into a millenarian hymn to the Protestant interest. A couple of paragraphs in, Defoe raised the possibility that France and Austria might join for a religious war against Protestants, and from then on he insisted the current peace must be used to prevent this. The key was to use the partition of Spain to divide and balance the 'popish' states. Austria, therefore, should take the Italian and Flemish provinces. This would make her more threatening to France (thereby scotching any Bourbon–Habsburg entente); and would prevent Spain allying with the French to defend these territories. Iberia and America, on the other hand, could safely go to a cadet Bourbon since Spain's new world interests clashed with those of France and would spawn useful tensions across the Pyrenees. Meanwhile the Dutch and the English should take such strategic parts of the Spanish imperium as would allow them to defend themselves and correct the balance between Catholics. Here, Defoe was advocating a peace which tore Spain's popish realm into 'as many pieces as we can'.[274] The division should be calculated to set papist powers at each other's throats; and would allow Protestants to control their enemies by playing them against each other. To us, this may sound Machiavellian. To the *Review*, however, the end made it holy. This was an 'occasion God has offer'd you, of making the Protestant Power Superior to the Popish'. 'You may break the Popish Bands of Europe, and put the Balance in Protestant Hands.' Those who still wanted to give all of Spain to the Habsburgs were 'blindly laying the Foundation, of the Ruin and Destruction of the Protestant Interest in *Europe* . . . They are rejecting the most glorious Opportunity, of raising the *Protestant* Powers . . . into an Established Superiority over the *Popish*, so that they . . . shall never be able to carry on a Religious War'.[275]

[271] Ibid., vol. VIII, no. 88, p. 355. [272] Ibid., vol. VIII, nos. 95–9.
[273] Ibid., vol. VIII, no. 89, p. 357; vol. VIII, no. 97, p. 390.
[274] Ibid., vol. VIII, no. 100, p. 402. [275] Ibid., vol. VIII, no. 100, pp. 402–3.

Defoe continued to lay out his vision through the rest of 1711, and on into the next year. In a number of pamphlets, as well as further issues of the *Review*, he promoted a peace based on the partition of Spain, and argued that the Protestant cause was best guaranteed by balancing the power of Catholic states.[276] As he did so, he promoted a strong Anglo-Dutch alliance as the core of a Protestant interest. By offering alliances and joining with the weaker party, this interest could keep papists divided and prevent any one Catholic realm approaching hegemony.[277] Defoe also painted Austria as an ever blacker persecutor of the reformation. She could not be trusted with the influence the whole Spanish heritage would give her, and the writer warned constantly that one should not pull down France to set up this new monster. In a clear exposition of his new mode of thought, Defoe reminded Protestants that they had been glad of French power in the Thirty Years War when France had worked against the vicious Habsburgs and saved the reformation in Germany.[278] In order to survive, Protestants must learn this lesson, and be willing to switch partners rapidly to maintain the balance between their enemies.

Defoe cannot take sole credit for developing this analysis of the Protestant situation. As early as the 1700–2 debate on the partition treaties, the need to discuss reformed Christianity in a situation where the balance of power was at issue led some writers to use the term in much the way Defoe used it.[279] In fact, one 1700 work anticipated many of Defoe's 1711 arguments with an extraordinarily hard-bitten analysis of confessional welfare. The author of *A second letter to a friend concerning the partition treaty* had argued that war over the Spanish succession could be avoided if Louis' grandson received Spain's Italian provinces to compensate him for the loss of the Iberian throne itself. This would balance the extra influence Vienna would gain from controlling Madrid, and – more pertinently – would annoy the Austrians so much that they would plot against France instead of suppressing Protestants. As such a result would ensure there was no 'settled peace among Popish Powers', and would see conflict only in the far-off lands on the Mediterranean, it would be 'the highest Security to the Protestant Interest'.[280] Yet despite such other writings, Defoe should still be seen as the chief

276 See [Defoe], *Reasons why this nation* – published about 6 October 1711; [Defoe], *Essay at a plain exposition* – published around 9 October.

277 [Daniel Defoe], *The felonious treaty* (1711); [Defoe], *Review*, vol. VIII, no. 105.

278 Ibid., vol. VIII, no. 104.

279 E.g. *A letter to a member of parliament in the country concerning the present posture of affairs* (1700), p. 21; *Some reply to a letter pretended to be writ to a member of parliament* (1701), p. 3; *The present disposition of England consider'd* (1701), p. 1; *The partition examin'd and its rejection by the French king fully stated* (1701), p. 2; *Directions to the electors of the ensuing parliament* (1702), pp. 19–20.

280 *A second letter to a friend concerning the partition treaty* (1700), p. 4.

herald of this new take on the balance of power. His *Review* and his numerous pamphlets were widely read in the late years of Queen Anne's reign, and his call to divide Catholic powers struck a chord in a nation worried about international reformation but forced to be pragmatic in its diplomacy with France. As a result, Defoe's analysis provided the key concept in the closing stages of discussion of the war. As Tories used it to explain why one should not go on fighting for Austrian ambitions, Whigs seized on Defoe's calls for a co-ordinated Protestant interest to attack their enemies' more extreme prejudices. Responding to Swift's denigration of the Dutch, pamphleteers insisted union between London and The Hague was the vital core of a confessional alliance. The Dutch, wrote one, are 'next to *Great-Britain* . . . the strongest Bulwark and most zealous Supporters of the *Protestant* Interest'.[281] They had helped England rescue 'the Protestant Interest from the Oppression of France', opined another, and the only way to secure a safe peace was for the two powers 'to come to a good Understanding, and preserve a perfect Friendship with one another'.[282] Thus by the last years of Queen Anne's reign, circumstances and Defoe's journalism had made the Protestant interest a near universal tool of analysis. People might disagree how it could or should be promoted, but the idea that the reformed Christians of Europe should stick together to influence the balance of power had an extremely firm hold.

With the 1713 peace of Utrecht, a period of remarkable rhetorical adaptation appears to have ended. Since England began its battle with France, old analyses of universal monarchy, continental Protestantism and Christendom had been remodelled to attack Louis XIV. When it became clear that deals might have to be struck with Versailles, the British had advanced pragmatic (but Christianised) analyses of the balance of power, and had developed the notion of a Protestant interest to understand how faith fitted into this worldview. Over the decades following Utrecht, by contrast, few new languages emerged. The creativity of the late Stuart period seemed to have furnished all the defences needed for diplomacy through the years of almost uninterrupted peace until 1739, and even the return of war with France in the 1740s changed little. The balance of power and the Protestant interest shaped most defences of the conflict, with an old crusading spirit against popish universal monarchy revived at moments of particular martial excitement.

At Utrecht, Europe seemed to follow Defoe's suggestions for its future. Although Britain's allies, especially Austria, had wanted to fight on for Spain, Harley gave the kingdom up in preliminary talks with the French, and other states had to accept this once it was clear Britain was not willing to continue

[281] *The barrier treaty vindicated* (1712), pp. 12–13.
[282] *The treaty between her majesty and the states-general* (1712), p. 3.

war. To balance the new Bourbon regime in Iberia and the new world, Spain's Italian and Flemish possessions were given to the Austrians, whilst the maritime powers strengthened themselves with trading privileges and strategic bases (Britain took Gibraltar, the Netherlands a series of 'barrier' fortresses in Flanders).[283] Once this equilibrium was established, Britain looked for partners who would help maintain it. Surprisingly, for the first twenty years after the treaty, she chose France. The old enemies might still mistrust one another, but they were both keen to avoid another conflict, and believed that collaboration could warn off any destabilising aggression by others. Britain and France thus allied from 1716 to 1731; they joined in a brief war to stop Spain regaining Italian territory between 1718 and 1720; and they used their diplomatic muscle to face down the threat of an Austro-Spanish alliance in 1725.[284] In the 1730s, by contrast, the situation in Europe began to look different. First, there were worrying signs that France was becoming ambitious again now that her new king, Louis XV, had reached maturity. Second, Austria began to weaken visibly. She was surrounded by expansionist neighbours in Russia and Prussia, and since the heir to her throne was a woman, Maria Theresa, who technically could not rule under the Austrian constitution, there seemed ample opportunity for outside powers to interfere in her affairs. In this situation, British ministers began to shore up the German Habsburgs against Versailles. In 1739, imperial rivalries sparked a war between Britain and France's ally, Spain.[285] The next year, when Maria Theresa was attacked by the Prussians with support from the French, Britain began a staged mobilisation which eventually led to full-scale conflict.[286]

Throughout these manoeuvres, balance of power rhetoric controlled public discussion. Britain was visibly shifting between continental powers to ensure one did not dominate, and it was easy to describe and defend policy in these terms. Of course, this did not mean that polemic had been secularised. Those who appealed to the balance of power often presented it as part of that moral order which maintained the peace of Christendom, and they described it as a barrier to un-Christian universal monarchy. Moreover, as Defoe had shown, talk of balance was quite compatible with notions of a Protestant interest which must trim between Catholics to preserve its independence. Such an interest was frequently cited in contemporary rhetoric;

283 There has been little specific study of Utrecht since James W. Gerard, *The peace of Utrecht* (New York, 1885) – but see Linda and Marsh Frey, eds., *The treaties of the war of Spanish succession* (1995). Dr David Onnekink's planned tercentenary conference in Utrecht may supply the deficiency.

284 Black, *System of ambition?* pp. 150–6.

285 Philip Woodfine, *Britannia's glories: the Walpole ministry and the 1739 war with Spain* (1998).

286 For Maria Theresa's vulnerable position: Edward Crankshaw, *Maria Theresa* (1969), pt 1.

and it appears to have shaped many diplomatic initiatives.[287] The British maintained that broad co-operation with the Dutch which was central to Defoe's vision, and of course had special regard for Lutheran Hanover, that north German electorate which shared a ruler with Great Britain after the accession of George I in 1714.[288] Similarly, as Andrew Thompson has shown, both polemicists and policy makers calculated the Protestant interest in a series of foreign crises between 1719 and the 1730s. The first two Georges were presented – and presented themselves – as leaders of the European reformation as they battled to uphold Protestants' privileges in the complex politics of Germany in these decades.[289]

One example from this broad period will show how our familiar spiritual anxieties could affect even the most worldly understanding of diplomacy. In 1735 the author of *A series of wisdom and policy* sat down to defend Sir Robert Walpole's record. By this stage, this long-serving chief minister was under attack for his friendship with France, which some felt had weakened the Habsburg counter-weight and encouraged Louis XV to resume his predecessor's expansion.[290] In response, the *Series of wisdom* stated the Habsburgs themselves had been the danger in the 1720s. The Austrians had been intent on stealing English trade by building up their commerce through Ostend; the Spanish had plotted to take back Gibraltar; and only Britain's alliance with France had bullied them to the negotiating table. The author admitted that France could not be trusted. However, he explained that Walpole had relied on France's interest in the alliance rather than her word. At the particular juncture in question, Versailles had been as wary of the Habsburgs as London, and could be depended on to co-operate with the British.[291] Yet despite such pragmatic analysis, the pamphleteer made strong appeals to religion. He explained that the Austrians and Spanish had had to be restrained because their ambition 'foreboded no Good to *Christendom*', hinting at the spiritual order behind geopolitical calculation.[292] At rather greater length he argued that the Protestant interest would have been in horrible danger if Britain had not allied with France. First, Austrian commercial expansion

[287] E.g. *Some observations on the present state of affairs, in a letter to a member of the House of Commons* (1731); *A defence of the measures of the present administration* (1731).

[288] There has been little work here. Relations with Hanover are better explored: Jeremy Black, *British foreign policy in the age of Walpole* (Aldershot, 1985), ch. 2; Thompson, *Britain, Hanover*; and for cultural perceptions, Joseph Canning and Hermann Wellenreuther, *Britain and Germany Compared* (Göttingen, 2001).

[289] Thompson, *Britain, Hanover*, chs. 3–6.

[290] J. H. Plumb, *Sir Robert Walpole: the king's minister* (1960), ch. 6. For an influential pamphlet against Walpole's foreign policy: [William Pulteney], *The politicks on both sides, with regard to foreign affairs* (1734).

[291] *A series of wisdom and policy, manifested in a review of our foreign negotiations* (1735), esp. pp. 29–31.

[292] Ibid., p. 10.

at Ostend would have ruined the Dutch as well as damaging the British. This would have destroyed the two premier reformed states, whose ability to trim between Catholic powers kept those powers divided. Second, if Walpole had not secured French support, the Habsburgs might have wooed Louis. This, of course, would have created a terrifying Catholic bloc, which the reformed nations of Europe could not have withstood. Third, the Spanish and Austrians were supporting the exiled Stuarts. If the French alliance had not frightened them out of their plans, they might have supported an invasion to restore its old Catholic dynasty, and dealt a fatal blow to the whole reformation.[293] Considering all this, it was clear Walpole's critics did not care about international Protestantism. Although they claimed France was now threatening the reformation, and that this was Walpole's fault, their denunciations of his French alliance recklessly endangered the faith. Their policies, if pursued, would 'wrest the Balance of Power our of the Hands of the *Protestant* Maritime Interest, and transfer it to the *Popish* one'.[294]

The relative peace of 1713–39, then, did little to alter the pattern of British polemic. Defences of dealing with France in the 1730s read like proposals to deal with France in the last Stuart decade. Even the war with Spain and the war of Austrian succession which followed made only a limited difference. Despite the passage of over a quarter of a century since Britain had last engaged in prolonged conflict, many of the rhetorics used to discuss the battle were familiar.[295] Unfortunately, demonstrating this continuity in any detail is complex because the military situation on the continent was intricate and the domestic political scene very fluid. The period from 1739 to the peace of 1748 was marked by an elaborate quadrille of changing alliances among the European powers and an equally elaborate dance of British political factions which swept Walpole from power and led to a series of short-lived administrations.[296] To add to the confusion, there were stages before 1742 and after 1746 when parliamentary oppositions accused governments of half-heartedness, and at these points the ministry ceased to be chief cheerleader for the war it was supposed to be organising. Despite all this, however, some sense can be made of propaganda in the period. There was a basic shape to the conflict and a fundamental set of concepts used to explain it; reviewing these briefly should make clear how little the polemic had changed.

England first declared war on Spain in 1739. This was primarily a commercial conflict over trading rights and settlements in the new world, but it had

[293] Ibid., pp. 15–17, 23–7, 31. [294] Ibid., p. 17.

[295] Indeed Queen Anne era pamphlets were reprinted as publishers felt they were still relevant: Robert Harris, *A patriot press: national politics and the London press in the 1740s* (Oxford, 1993), pp. 93–4.

[296] For domestic politics: Paul Langford, *A polite and commercial people: England 1727–1783* (Oxford, 1989), pp. 49–57, 183–214.

an important European dimension as Spain and France had been in alliance since the early 1730s and the British were increasingly worried about a new threat from Versailles. In 1740, this French danger became very much more pressing when the Austrian emperor died and left his realm to the extremely vulnerable Maria Theresa. She was soon attacked by Saxony and Bavaria (whose rulers made claims to the Austrian throne now that it was held by a woman); by Prussia (who wished to annex the prize province of Silesia); and by Spain (who wished to pick up Austria's territories in Italy). France aided the aggressive powers and, in consequence, England became involved in a Europe-wide struggle. She continued her war with Spain, but also defended Maria Theresa as an essential counter-weight to Louis XV. England therefore sent the Austrians money and troops; begged Prussia to settle with the Habsburg power; bought off other hostile forces; and constructed anti-French alliances with the Dutch, the electorate of Hanover and Savoy. By 1744, British policy had led to open declarations of war with France, and to considerable deployment of British forces. Fleets and armies saw action in Europe to help the Austrians, Dutch, Hanoverians and Savoyards; around the world to attack French and Spanish trading interests; and finally even on the British mainland to subdue a French-backed rebellion by the supporters of the exiled Stuart royal family in 1745–6.[297]

As with all other conflicts, such effort required propaganda. Yet the need was particularly pressing for this war, as contemporaries found many reasons to question it. The struggle was costly – as such things always are – but this time there was very little compensation in military success. Apart from the 1743 victory at Dettingen, the destruction of the Stuarts' forces at Culloden in 1746 and some progress in America, there were few triumphs – and these were easily balanced by disasters. Britain squandered the advantage gained at Dettingen, and thereafter could not find enthusiastic allies. Despite being ruled by George II in his capacity of elector, Hanover declared neutrality for the early 1740s as it feared being swept aside by the French and Prussians. The Dutch were equally reluctant to commit, being similarly fearful of becoming a French target, and also convinced that British policy was calculated to support Hanover rather than themselves. Attempts to detach Prussia from the anti-Austrian coalition proved temporary. A British-brokered peace in 1742 broke down in 1744, and had to be renegotiated from scratch. Such setbacks weakened the war effort, and in 1745 humilation at the battle of Fountenoy opened Flanders to French troops. By 1747 things were going so badly that the ministry (now led by Henry Pelham) concluded peace was the only solution. In talks concluded at Aix-la-Chapelle in 1748 they were

[297] For clear coverage: Reed Browning, *The war of Austrian succession* (Stroud, 1994); M. S. Anderson, *The war of Austrian succession, 1740–48* (Harlow, 1995).

forced to bribe France to give up European advantages with the return of captured American territories.[298]

Given all this, it was hardly surprising that critics in parliament and the press lambasted war strategy. Some argued the government was putting too little effort into the struggle (particularly the friends of the bellicose John Carteret, second Earl Granville, who was out of office before 1742 and after 1744).[299] Others, by contrast, thought the whole affair fundamentally misconceived. Particularly in the years around 1743, many voices complained that Britain's war effort was being run in the interests of Hanover, which – they charged – explained the failure to drive home the advantage after Dettingen and the outrageous transfer of the costs of Hanoverian troops to the British Treasury.[300] Another line was that Britain should have little to do with the logistical difficulties and unreliable allies of continental Europe. Instead of sending armies across the Channel, she should use her navy to attack French and Spanish trading interests around the globe. This 'blue water policy' would be of obvious and instant advantage to the British, and (if French advance in Europe was really so worrying) it would bring the enemy to its knees as crucial sources of wealth were severed.[301]

Defence against such doubt continued to centre on the balance of power. Royal declarations and speeches to parliament which explained why Britain was investing so much in continental action repeatedly stressed that Louis XV was (like his predecessor) a potential hegemonist. The war might not be going well, and armchair strategists might suggest other ways of fighting it, but its official apologists stuck rigidly to the need to stop France overwhelming all other powers. Thus George II repeatedly told his legislature he must act to maintain 'the liberties and balance of Europe', and that he was engaged in the 'common cause' against a France which had 'long aspired to universal monarchy'.[302] Declaring war in 1744, the king accused Louis of trying to 'overturn the balance of power in Europe' and extend his 'dangerous influence', whilst preachers who performed on the fast day he called to ask God's blessing on this declaration agreed that French 'ambition' for 'nothing less than universal monarchy' was the evil all must face.[303] Pamphlets too stuck to this well-worn theme. They used, it, for instance, as they argued against a blue water policy: attacking France round the globe might gain trading advantages, but it would do too little to recover the lost balance

298 For British exhaustion: Langford, *Polite and commercial*, pp. 209–14.

299 John Cannon, 'Carteret, John', *ODNB*, X:381–6.

300 *The case of the Hanover forces* (1743) was supplemented by extensive parliamentary debate.

301 Harris, *Patriot press*, p. 145.

302 Cobbett, XII:116, 147–8, 186; XIII: 691–5.

303 Ibid., XIII:688–91; John Denne, *A sermon preached at the parish church of St Mary Lambeth, upon April 11th, 1744* (1744), p. 2; John Sloss, *A sermon preached on occasion of the fast April 11th 1744* (1744), p. 9; Bernard Wilson, *A sermon preached at Newark, Nottingham on Wednesday April 11, 1744* (1744), p. 9.

on the continent.[304] Polemicists also fell back on the balance as they denied British policy was being directed to Hanover's advantage. Britain's aim was to stop Europe falling under French domination – the electorate only benefited in so far as this would preserve its independence along with that of many other states.[305] To prove all this, authors presented the current war as a direct continuation of William's and Anne's struggles to maintain a balance of power.[306] These, of course, had pre-dated Britain's link with Hanover, and had required massive commitment of European land troops. As the essential continuity was established, writers told the story of the French threat to the balance since the 1660s, and so effectively summarised much of the contents of this present chapter.[307]

Of course, it was possible to worry about the balance of power without having a spiritual vision of a continental Christian community. By this stage, people may simply have worried about British independence in a world dominated by another power – and in fact, the word 'Christendom' was rarer in the 1740s than it had been under the Stuarts. Yet even if the rhetoric of balance had begun to loosen the religious moorings which had once secured it, it was certainly not yet untethered. When writers described the consequences of French ambitions they often reverted to a moral, and sometimes explicitly Christian, language which was recognisable from the seventeenth century and which hinted at the Christendom they no longer named. Thus in 1740, a writer who urged that the war with Spain must be extended to France in order to 'preserve the balance of power' implied Louis was abrogating a moral order. Recent European history was a scene of broken treaties, of countries 'ravaged and destroyed' and of 'many Millions slaughtered' as the Bourbons had pursued their 'Scheme of Universal Monarchy'.[308] Predictably, the fast preachers of 1744 agreed, and so did an author of the same year who spoke of the 'Desolation and Ruin' and the 'wantonly spilt Blood' which had followed in the French wake.[309] Perhaps most remarkably, some writers accused Louis XV of the same collaboration with the Turk which had marred Louis XIV's reputation. The author of *The French king's catechism*

[304] E.g. *The important question discussed: or a serious and impartial enquiry* (1746).

[305] E.g. *The interest of Great Britain steadily pursued* (1743); *Popular prejudice concerning partiality to the interests of Hanover* (1743); *An address to the people of Great Britain* (1744); *A letter to a friend concerning the electorate of Hanover* (1747); *The present measures the only means of securing the balance of power* (1744), p. 10.

[306] *Popular prejudice*, pp. 50–1, observed the Dutch once bore accusations now levelled at Hanover. *An apology for the conduct of the present administration* (1744), pp. 29, 50–3, saw Louis XV following Louis XIV, and compared George II with William III and Marlborough. See also *The plain reasoner* (1745), pp. 8, 30–2.

[307] E.g. *The criterion of the reason and necessity of the present war* (1745).

[308] *Reasons for an immediate war against France* (Dublin, 1740), p. 4.

[309] Sloss, *Sermon*, p. 9; Obadiah Hughes, *Obedience to God the best security* (1744), p. 49; *Present measures*, p. 19.

accused him of engaging in unjust wars and keeping no oath longer than it served his interest, but also of inciting the Ottomans against Maria Theresa to end the success she was having in Italy.[310] Two years later, the writer of the *Memoirs of the most Christian-brute* repeated much of the rhetoric of the 1690s (along with the style of pamphlet title) and so again cast the French out of Christendom. Louis was a 'Monster', a 'Rapacious, Bloody, Insatiable Tyrant' who was striving for universal dominion and so had urged the infidel Turks to attack his defenceless Austrian enemy. He therefore covered the French in 'Shame and Scandal, as both Men and Christians', and ignored the reproof of 'Fellow Christians' as he had long since ceased to be one.[311]

If an at least broadly Christian balance of power survived in the rhetoric of the 1740s war, so did the notion of the Protestant interest. At first this may seem surprising. Frederick of Prussia's decision to attack Austria to gain Silesia shattered any notion of a united Protestant front in Europe (most other reformation powers were sympathetic to Maria Theresa), and Andrew Thompson has argued the concept of a confessional interest suffered as a direct result.[312] Yet although Protestantism was divided, and the language of a Protestant interest was undoubtedly harder to deploy than in Queen Anne's time, it was not dealt an absolutely fatal blow. For a start, the opposition could use it. Before 1742, Carteret and his allies tried to displace Walpole by accusing him of a lack of vigour in the war, and of bringing about the situation in which such bitter bloodshed had become necessary. Press and parliamentarians claimed the first minister had failed to organise Europe against the growing threat from Louis in the 1730s, and a major part of this was permitting the shattering of the Protestant interest. Thus pamphlets supporting the campaign against Walpole accused him of incompetence, and especially of bungling his dealings with Frederick. The Austrians might, for example, have been persuaded to grant the Prussians Silesia, and thus to have kept the Northern Germans within the front facing France.[313] Instead, Berlin was now set against London, so (as one writer put it) 'the *Protestant Interest* is broke to pieces, and the *Grand Alliance* [i.e. the constellation of powers which had faced Versailles in Anne's reign] seems not to be in a Possibility of being restored'.[314] Another popular author, recounting the *Groans of Germany*, lamented that the British had fallen out with the Prussians, and that 'nothing could have been more fatal to . . . the *Protestant* Interest'.[315]

[310] *The French king's catechism, in a letter from Cardinal Tencin* [1745?].
[311] *Memoirs of the most Christian-brute* (1747), pp. 1, 2, 13.
[312] Thompson, *Britain, Hanover*, ch. 6.
[313] *A letter from a member of the last parliament, to a new member* (1742).
[314] *A review of the late motion for an address to his majesty against a certain great minister* (1741), p. 7.
[315] *The groans of Germany* (3rd edn, 1741), pp. 14, 27. Also: *The affecting case of the queen of Hungary* (1742), complaining France could 'disjoint' the Protestant interest.

Once Walpole had fallen, his critics came into the ministry, so their brand of polemic became an official support of the war. Accordingly, pamphlets praising the new administration boasted it was at last taking the future of the reformed faith seriously, and this explained the vigorous deployment of resources over the Channel which was the incoming regime's trademark. Such claims were strengthened by Carteret's success in persuading Frederick to settle with Maria Theresa at the 1742 peace of Breslau. This ended the embarrassing rift between the major Protestant powers and led to an Anglo-Prussian entente. Given these developments, the *Observations on the conduct of Great-Britain* could congratulate the ministry on its dealings with Prussia as it applauded the renewed commitment to a balance of power against France, and it noted that the country was now back in its proper position as 'the head of the Protestant and Independent Interest in *Europe*'.[316] Carteret's period of office also saw George II making open reference to the Protestant interest in addressing parliament, whilst legislators cited the Dutch faith as the basis of a 'natural' alliance across the North Sea and preachers presented the war as a struggle for the security of the reformation.[317] Similarly, the author of the *Considerations on the politics of France* could state that that country was dangerous both because she was an aspiring hegemonist and because she might lead a confessional war. She was, he assured his readers, pretending to be zealous for Rome in hopes that Catholic powers would unite against Britain – and this meant he was trying to lead a popish interest to counter an England esteemed across Europe as head of the Protestant one.[318]

Of course Carteret's fall and Prussia's renewed aggression against Austria in 1744 might again have complicated use of such language, but immediate fears of invasion from France and then the Jacobite rebellion (1745–6) distracted attention from the complex rifts within European Protestantism. In these years, the British faced imminent Catholic encroachment, and were swept along in a tide of anti-popery which spilled over into renewed desire to protect the reformation abroad.[319] In fact, the rising produced what has been called 'the highest point of international Protestantism within the genre of eighteenth-century state sermons'.[320] When Thomas Rutherforth preached to the House of Commons on the 30 January fast day, 1746, he challenged his audience to make themselves 'the glory and strength of the reformation', to 'take the lead in the Protestant cause' and 'protect our Protestant

[316] *Observations on the conduct of Great-Britain in respect of foreign affairs* (1742), p. 47.
[317] Cobbett, XIII:101, 695–6; Sloss, *Sermon*, p. 37; Wilson, *Sermon*, p. 10.
[318] *Considerations on the politics of France with regard to the present critical situation* (1744), p. 4.
[319] Ihalainen, *Protestant nations*, pp. 258–9; Colin Haydon, *Anti-Catholicism in eighteenth-century England, 1714–80* (Manchester, 1993), ch. 4.
[320] Ihalainen, *Protestant nations*, p. 258.

brethren from the cruelties and oppression of others'.[321] He even asked them to stand in the breach and be first to fall in the struggle for the survival of the reformed, though he may have been thinking of the recent battles in the British isles here, rather than expecting any overseas crusades. By the time attention swung back from domestic Jacobitism to the battlefield of Europe, war-weariness was demanding peace, but some writers still requested help for the continent lest the Protestant interest be destroyed. One 1747 commentator, for instance, asked for strong aid for Hanover, since her loss would tip the balance against the reformed faith in Germany, and (for all their desperation to end the draining conflict) British peace negotiators demanded security for Holland and the Protestant German princes.[322]

On this evidence, Britain's state-building wars were sold in the same way in the 1740s as they had been under the late Stuarts. Great armed forces had to be built and administered to preserve a balance of power which guaranteed a moral order in Christendom, and to serve as the backbone of a Protestant interest within that balance. Having said this, it is important to pause. Stating the case so boldly is probably misleading: new discourses did begin to emerge in this war and pointed to new, and perhaps non-religious, beliefs about Britain's place in the world. For example, Pasi Ihalainen has argued for a gradual change in the rhetoric used to denounce European hegemonists as the eighteenth century wore on. He suggests a commitment to a general human liberty from tyrants evolved from earlier fears about the fate of Protestants under popish universal monarchs, and cites state sermons of the 1740s as an important stage in the process.[323] Similarly, Robert Harris (backed by Ihalainen again) has pointed out that more and more commentators came to see the promotion of Britain's commercial empire as the chief point of the battle. Starting with George Barrington's 1744 collection of *Seasonable considerations*, and coming to fruition in a series of works sponsored by the ejected Carteret in the last years of the war, an important strand of argument advocated capturing strategic and trading bases across the oceans as a foundation of future national prosperity.[324] Again, some critics of the 1740s war became so disgusted at the waste of lives and money as success failed to materialise that they raised troubling questions about the

321 Thomas Rutherforth, *A sermon preached before the honourable House of Commons . . . January 30th, 1745–6* (1746), pp. 15–16.

322 *A letter to a friend concerning the electorate of Hanover* (1747), p. 24.

323 Ihalainen, *Protestant nations*, chs. 4, 9.

324 Harris, *Patriot press*, p. 145 and conclusion; Ihalainen, *Protestant nations*, ch. 10. For the pamphlets: George Barrington, *Seasonable considerations on the expediency of a war with France* (1744); *The state of the nation consider'd in a letter to a member of parliament* (1747); *The state of the nation for the year 1747 and respecting 1748* (1747); *The state of the nation with a general balance of the publick accounts* (1748); *A supplement to the state of the nation* (1748).

assumptions behind the military effort. Some bluntly accused governments of bleating about the balance of power to hide war profiteering, but a more analytic series of editorials in the *Daily Post* wondered if the whole idea of a balance had become outdated.[325] As the newspaper pointed out, the rise of new forces such as Russia and Prussia meant it was hard to tell who was gaining the upper hand in great power rivalry. It was therefore unlikely one country would emerge to dominate all its rivals, so Britain might be able to leave the continent to regulate itself. The paper observed that 'the system of Europe is so vastly altered from King William and Queen Anne's reign' that one did not know whom to ally with to promote the common cause of free polities.[326]

These works revealed a real willingness to break with traditions of thinking about Britain's place in the world, and were perhaps the first harbingers of a dramatic shift in rhetoric. In the next conflict, the Seven Years War of 1756–63, overtly religious language seems to have played a surprisingly small role; especially in light of the 'diplomatic revolution' which placed the great Catholic powers of Austria and France against a 'Protestant' alliance of Britain and Prussia.[327] This war – which finally established the British as the dominant nation in the world – appears to have been heavily promoted as a chance to expand commerce, to demonstrate the superiority of Britain's free constitution, and to uphold a universal concept of freedom against invading tyrants.[328] Yet whilst things were changing by the mid-eighteenth century, it is important not to exaggerate either the scale or the speed of this. In the 1740s, new ideas were only starting to emerge among the more traditional messages we have been exploring, and we must be careful before suggesting they were opposed to them. As we saw way back in the Anglo-Dutch wars, economic power could be seen as crucial in the fight against popery or anti-Christian hegemonists, and some of Carteret's authors discussed expanding Britain's trading empire in these terms.[329] Similarly, we have constantly seen how the apparently secular point that nations must be free from one-power hegemony actually expressed faith in a Christian moral order of relations between states: Ihalainen's analysis of the rhetoric of freedom assumed it evolved by gradual stages from traditional Protestant discourse and that this process was still ongoing during the war of Austrian succession.[330]

[325] *Case of the Hanover forces*, pp. 22–4; *A letter from Flanders, giving an account of the present state of the war* (1744), p. 29.

[326] *The Daily Post*, Friday, 3 May 1745. See also issues for 8 March 1745 and 16 August 1745.

[327] For the diplomatic revolution: Jeremy Black, *From Louis XIV to Napoleon* (1999), pp. 103–7.

[328] Ihalainen, *Protestant nations*, pp. 507–13, 535–46; Thompson, *Britain, Hanover*, ch. 6 and conclusion.

[329] *State of the nation . . . 1747*, pp. 15, 28–9 praised William III's (now betrayed) policies.

[330] Ihalianen's book argued new concepts emerged within Protestant discourse.

Even after that conflict, old ideas did not die. The treaty of Aix-la-Chapelle was criticised, and for reasons the Whigs of the Utrecht era would have recognised. It left France a dangerous threat to the balance of power, and left Protestant nations such as the United Provinces vulnerable.[331] These concerns certainly fed the tensions which led back to battle in 1756, and the rhetoric of the Seven Years War was not wholly unrecognisable. Although George II concentrated on trading disputes in the new world in his actual declaration of war against the French, his messages to parliament implied that an aggressive France was determined to destroy all independent powers, and noted the union of popish Vienna and Versailles which threatened 'oppression to the Protestant Interest'.[332] Meanwhile pamphlets recounted French policy since 1650 to prove this was the same struggle England had fought for a century against 'universal monarchy'; and fast sermons denounced a power which extirpated Protestants, broke through 'the most solemn Treaties' and would stop at nothing to gain its ambitious dream of 'Universal Empire'.[333] Such talk in the late 1750s had been standard since the English first began to worry about Louis XIV ninety years before. Certainly commercial rhetoric was more prominent, as was concern for human freedom, but in many senses Britain's enemies were still the same. She had built the military machine which would see her triumph as a defence against those who threatened reformed Christians across the continent, and who threatened the ideal of a Christian continent itself.

[331] The key attack: *Supplement to the state*. This was answered by *Consideration on the definitive treaty, signed at Aix-la-Chapelle, Oct. 7/18 1748* (1748) – arguing the treaty had done what it could to stop the Bourbons conquering in difficult circumstances.

[332] *His majesties declaration of war against the French king* (1756); *LJ*, XXIX:4, 197–8.

[333] E.g. *The progress of the French in their view of universal monarchy* (1756); Issac Smithson, *A sermon occasioned by the declaration of war against France* (1756), pp. 5–6.

4

Europe in England: the opening of politics

THE RISE OF PARTY IN ENGLAND

If regular warfare was one defining characteristic of English society in the century after 1660, the extraordinary openness of its political system was another. In these decades policy was publicly debated, and power explicitly contested, to an extent quite unknown before. The distance from earlier politics was dramatic. Before the civil wars, significant discussion had been concentrated on the royal court, and attempts to widen politics beyond had been greeted with censorship or shock. When, for example, open argument about James I's foreign policy had begun in the 1620s, the king had ripped records of parliamentary debate from the Commons journals, and ordered preachers to stick to bland topics.[1] Similarly, the burst of mass petitions and mob demonstrations in 1641 had so worried observers that many rallied to the previously friendless king to suppress it.[2] After the restoration, by contrast, public affairs were conducted through visible discussion and appeals to a mass audience. The exclusion crisis (1678–83); the revolution of 1688–9; the 1690s attack on the ministerial 'junto'; the political disagreements under Queen Anne; the battle for influence under the Hanoverians: all involved competing propaganda campaigns, and each dispute tumbled over the last in a constant frenzy of popular controversy.

The claim may sound Whiggish, but this new energy was a major stride towards representative politics. The 1640s and 1650s had seen public debate, but the instability of these decades and the spoiling role of Cromwell's army had not allowed any clear direction in the relationship between rulers and ruled. From 1660, however, a series of open breaches wrote the rules of a new political game. In the emerging world, divisions in the elite ensured that information, opinion and power were not corralled at court, but escaped into popular arenas. Policy was contested in the press, coffeehouses, clubs, elections and street demonstrations (forums Jürgen Habermas categorised as the

[1] See Roger Lockyer, *The early Stuarts* (4th edn, Harlow, 1993), pp. 140–1.
[2] See Anthony Fletcher, *The outbreak of the English civil war* (1981).

'public sphere'), and attempts to influence decision makers channelled these discussions back to government as expressions of a popular will.[3] Certainly these developments were not without precedent.[4] Nor were they triumphant by the Georgian era, and they did not progress smoothly (open politics was partly smothered in periods such as the mid-1680s).[5] Overall, however, it is fair to claim significant democratisation after 1660. A divided elite appealed to a wider population; this encouraged expressions of public opinion; and then fear of popular unrest, an administrative system demanding voluntary participation by the political nation and the rise of parliament guaranteed such opinion was taken seriously.[6]

Central to these processes was the emergence of party. Exactly what this phrase describes – and indeed whether it is exactly what happened – have been intensively analysed by historians. Some have doubted the coherence, organisation and even existence (beyond rhetoric) of the political groupings which others have claimed coalesced.[7] Mercifully there is no space for the frequently nit-picking arguments here; but we can narrate a story which should satisfy most scholars. This would start with the clear division of views. From the 1660s, there was intense debate in England along two spectra of opinion. The first was about the prerogatives and divinity of monarchy. The second was about the established church and the rights of those who objected to it. We will cover these disputes in much more detail later, but now we note the passion of argument and its organisation into a contest between Whig and Tory late in Charles II's reign. While opinions favouring royal sanctity and defending the church came to be labelled 'Tory', those putting limits on crown status or criticising the spiritual establishment were badged 'Whig'. How far these tags applied to real and opposed bands of people has been questioned, but there is at least some evidence that they did. By the early 1680s, individuals were being called Whigs and Tories (if only initially by their enemies), and identifiable networks of activists had emerged to organise pamphlet campaigns, election drives, petitioning, street protests

3 Jürgen Habermas, *The structural transformation of the public sphere*, trans. Thomas Burger and Frederick Lawrence (Cambridge, MA, 1989).

4 E.g. the campaign to persuade James I to go to war in the mid-1620s: Thomas Cogswell, *The blessed revolution* (Cambridge, 1985).

5 See below, p. 241.

6 For (qualified) arguments for a new representative society: Mark Knights, *Representation and misrepresentation in later Stuart Britain* (Oxford, 2005); Geoffrey Holmes, *The electorate and the national will in the first age of party* (Lancaster, 1976).

7 J. R. Jones, *The first Whigs* (1961), argued for party – but warned readers against overestimating its early coherence. There have been radical attacks on 'party': Jonathan Scott, 'Radicalism and restoration', *HJ*, 31(1988), pp. 453–67; and Jonathan Scott, *Algernon Sidney and the English republic, 1623–1677* (Cambridge, 1991); and see *Albion*, 25.4 (1992), devoted to the debate.

and parliamentary votes.[8] By the mid-decade, the two groups were sufficiently delineated to purge each other from power when they gained the ear of the monarch; and from William III's reign, most commentators described English politics as a struggle between them.[9] Certainly, these were not fully modern parties. They had no formal membership, programme or leaders; many individual people crossed between them; and some issues – such as 'country' complaints about court corruption – fell outside their purview. Unquestionably, however, they existed in a looser sense. They described the poles of belief on the central questions of the day; they swept many into close political collaboration; and they became the foundation of political identity as people came to think of themselves *as* Whigs or Tories. In these ways parties came to express, but also to exacerbate, the divisions which kept English politics open. By providing a structured rivalry between two political identities, they clarified and deepened differences. They then supplied the means (clubs, gossips, pamphleteers, electioneers, letter writers, preachers and rabble rousers) through which division was transmitted to the public; and provided the structures (votes, boycotts, petitions, tracts, lobbies and riots) by which popular opinion was brought to bear on governing elites.

If party was so central to the unique English system, we need to investigate what fuelled the phenomenon. At one level, of course, partisan politics was a simple contest for power between ambitious or grudge-bearing men. Above this, however, tension was sustained by real policy disputes. Our analysis will focus on the two main breaches, but we should note other controversies: those over public finance, immigration, military strategy, trade; and the (already covered) disagreements over foreign policy.[10] Yet for all these disagreements, Whigs and Tories were most fundamentally divided on the old restoration issues. Precise arguments changed over time, but Tories remained broad supporters of monarchy and church, Whigs retained their scepticism about these institutions.

As these were the main fissures in late Stuart and early Hanoverian society, they have received close attention. Historians of political thought have elucidated the ideology behind the disputes, and high political narratives have chronicled their manifestation in parliamentary campaigns. At the same time, social historians have investigated how they played out in particular localities, impinged on ordinary experience and shaped popular identities.[11]

[8] Tim Harris, *Restoration: Charles II and his kingdoms, 1660–1685* (2005), chs. 3–5.

[9] Henry Horwitz, 'The structure of parliamentary politics', in Geoffrey Holmes, ed., *Britain after the glorious revolution* (1969), pp. 96–115; Geoffrey Holmes, *British politics in the age of Anne* (1967), dismissed earlier non-party histories.

[10] Holmes, *British politics*, chs. 2–3, for Queen Anne's reign.

[11] E.g. Geoffrey Holmes, *The trial of Dr Sacheverell* (1973); H. T. Dickinson, *Liberty and property: political ideology in eighteenth-century Britain* (1977); J. P. Kenyon, *Revolution*

What has been missing, however, is specific and sustained coverage of the role played by concepts of Christendom and the Protestant international. Just as these entities influenced England's role in Europe, they introduced Europe to England's domestic affairs. Disputes about the crown and the church were certainly about how the English organised themselves, but they were also fired by duties to reformed Christians abroad, and to all Christians everywhere. To an under-recognised extent, English politics was riven by party, and so kept open, because people disagreed about exactly what these duties were, or which should take priority when they clashed.

PROTESTANTISM AND CHRISTENDOM IN THE EXCLUSION CRISIS

Party first coalesced in a great constitutional struggle, so it makes sense to consider division over the prerogatives of the crown before turning to ecclesiastical issues. By 1673, it had become clear that Charles II's brother, James, duke of York, had converted to Catholicism. This obviously caused disquiet in a fervently Protestant realm but it was not until 1678 that the situation reached a head. In that year, the charlatan Titus Oates claimed a group of Catholic conspirators were planning to kill the king and place James on the throne. His story was fantastic, but an almost equally incredible series of coincidences soon appeared to confirm it. The magistrate he approached was found murdered (historians still do not know why or by whom), and then privy council investigation of Oates' claims uncovered an unrelated, but this time real, plot among the duke of York's servants. The nation now became hypersensitive to popery. Some argued that the only way to make England safe was to exclude James from the succession by statute, so a parliamentary bill was introduced in March 1679 and the issue became whether the legislature could overrule Charles' reluctance to abrogate his brother's rights. Over the next two years, the king would call three parliaments, but each of these had a Commons majority for exclusion, so the king was repeatedly forced to dissolve his legislature. Each time this occurred, those worried about James questioned the royal right to behave in this way, but others were concerned pressure on the court threatened civil war. Divergence of opinion magnified as the divided elite appealed to the wider public. Demonstrations

principles: the politics of party, 1689–1720 (Cambridge, 1977); Brian W. Hill, *The growth of parliamentary parties, 1689–1742* (1976); Linda Colley, *In defiance of oligarchy: the Tory party, 1714–60* (Cambridge, 1982); Gary de Krey, *A fractured society: the politics of London in the first age of party* (Oxford, 1985); Nicholas Rogers, *Whigs and cities: popular politics in the age of Walpole and Pitt* (Oxford, 1990); Tim Harris, *Politics under the later Stuarts* (Harlow, 1993); Paul Halliday, *Dismembering the body politic: partisan politics in England's towns, 1650–1730* (Cambridge, 1998); Knights, *Representation.*

and petitions were organised; three general elections were contested; and a lapse in press censorship released a torrent of print. As this 'exclusion crisis' unfolded, party was born. Those who took a high view of the legislature's power were labelled 'Whigs'; those who insisted hereditary succession was essential for stable government, came to be called 'Tories'.[12]

As with the emergence of party more widely, exclusion has received great historical attention. The traditional, and in many ways most obvious, way to read the crisis was as a standard seventeenth-century tussle about the prerogatives of the crown. A king of absolutist tendencies, who believed that monarchy was divine and had a duty to rule without disturbance from the baying populace, faced parliamentarians who believed they must prevail, at least where public safety was paramount.[13] The crisis certainly centred on this, and much material debated exactly these constitutional issues. A myriad of parliamentary speeches, pamphlets, petitions and some of the earliest periodicals scoured English history for precedents, and more considered English legal principle, citing common law, coronation oaths and statute to determine what the king's powers were.[14] Some even ventured into abstract political philosophy. John Locke's famous *Second treatise of government* may not have been published until William III's reign, but it was written in the exclusion crisis and was one of the first English tracts to consider the inherent rights of men under government without recourse to specific national regimes.[15]

On this evidence, the first breach between the parties was about the nature of the English crown. Yet scholars who have examined the crisis more closely have suggested there were many other things going on. Some have proved there was no simple split between exclusionists and non-exclusionists. There was a range of constitutional opinion, and some took quite subtle positions. Many, for example, thought James should succeed, but were open to the idea of 'limitations' or restrictions on royal power to render rule by a Catholic safe.[16] Other historians have stressed issues went far wider than the duke of York's position. The second half of this chapter will examine the argument

[12] Harris, *Restoration*, chs. 3–5, for clear coverage.

[13] E.g. Dickinson, *Liberty and property*, sect. 1; C. C. Weston and J. R. Greenburg, *Subjects and sovereigns: the grand controversy over legal sovereignty in Stuart England* (1981).

[14] For historical approaches: e.g. *A short historical collection touching the succession to the crown* (1680); *A true history of the succession to the crown of England* (1680); [John Somers], *A brief history of the succession* [1681?]. Discussion of the law runs through many pieces.

[15] John Locke, *Two treatises of government*, ed. Peter Laslett (Cambridge, 1988), introduction. Other pamphlets also mused on the fundamental origins of power: e.g. J. D., *A word without doors concerning the bill for succession* [1679]; *Reasons for his majesty passing the bill of exclusion* (1681).

[16] Mark Knights, *Politics and opinion in crisis, 1678–81* (Cambridge, 1994), pp. 4–5, rejects the term 'exclusion crisis' since disputes ranged wider than one issue.

over the religious establishment which also polarised Whigs and Tories, and we will return to the foreign policy dimensions of debate even sooner.[17] Most interesting for our current purposes, however, have been attempts to widen the focus beyond England. Tim Harris has analysed a 'British' dimension to the crisis, showing how political instability in Scotland and Ireland fed the problems in the Stuarts' largest realm, emphasising that royal policies in Edinburgh and Dublin fuelled Whig fears, and proving that Charles' political recovery (which eventually defeated exclusion) began in those cities.[18] This British context is important but, as Jonathan Scott has argued, the crisis had an even grander stage. For him, concerns about crown power and Catholic succession were just aspects of fears for the future of Europe. By the late 1670s, the English were terrified that the counter-reformation and Louis XIV's absolutism were sweeping inexorably onwards. The exclusion crisis was therefore sparked by fears that England was at immediate risk from continental dangers, and that James' accession would destroy the country's last bulwarks against these.[19] This insight is important, but needs to be taken further than Scott could in his broad surveys of the seventeenth century. The European dimension provided fuel for the crisis, but it was more multifaceted and controlling than Scott's Whiggish dread of international popery which later faded in fears of domestic unrest. In fact, awareness of the continent subsumed much of the constitutional discussion of the era (which came to focus on means to prevent a European disaster); it included a powerful sense of Christendom as well as of the continental reformation; and it shaped the ideology of both emerging parties.

The first and most obvious point to make is that discussion of exclusion in England occurred at a very dark moment for European Protestantism. As Scott points out, the reformed faith was retreating on the continent in the late Stuart age, with the years of the crisis marking a particularly sharp decline. As the English debated their future, Europeans saw accelerating pressure on the Huguenots, Catholic absorption of Strasbourg and Orange, threats to the United Provinces, and growing Habsburg intolerance of their Protestants. The active discussion of foreign policy in the 1670s would have made many Englishmen aware of this situation, and those who missed this

17 See below, pp. 228–40. For stress on religion in the crisis: Tim Harris, *London crowds in the reign of Charles II* (Cambridge, 1987), pp. 91–4, 118–29; Tim Harris, Paul Seaward and Mark Goldie, eds., *The politics of religion in Restoration England* (Oxford, 1990).

18 Tim Harris, 'The British dimension, religion and the shaping of political identities during the reign of Charles II', in Tony Claydon and Ian McBride, eds., *Protestantism and national identity: Britain and Ireland, 1660–1850* (Cambridge, 1998), pp. 131–56; Harris, *Restoration* – esp. chs. 2, 6 and 7.

19 Scott, *Algernon Sidney*, pp. 38–44; Jonathan Scott, *England's troubles* (Cambridge, 2000), pp. 27–38.

would be informed by the flood of print once censorship lapsed.[20] Scholars of the exclusion crisis have always stressed how the press distributed news and views of the constitutional struggle, but we also need to note the extensive coverage given to Europe. Whilst numerous pamphlets and broadsheets lamented particular blows to Protestant communities abroad, much of the emerging newspaper market concentrated on continental information and provided a steady drip-feed of ill tidings about the reformed cause.[21] For example, the Whig publisher Ben Harris began producing his *Domestick Intelligence* in July 1679. Although its regular numbers carried what looked liked factual reporting rather than emotional comment, its news was frequently European (despite the paper's title), and just as frequently bad. The first ten issues alone spoke of Louis' military threat to the Protestant cities of Holland and Switzerland; of German fears that French Catholic armies were coming to burn them out; and of growing persecution of France's Calvinist population which was making everyday life intolerable.[22]

This sense of an international confessional struggle was essential in creating and sustaining the domestic constitutional crisis. Without it, domestic politics would have been unlikely to create a panic. After all, the English had known that the heir to their throne was a Romanist since 1673. This had caused tensions, but there had been no head of steam behind a stability-rupturing exclusion until Titus Oates' revelations. Before 1678, the duke of York had shown no animus against Protestantism beyond withdrawing from its worship; there was comfort in the overwhelming fidelity of the people to the faith; and proposals to protect the church of England should James become its supreme governor held promises of pragmatic settlement.[23] Of course this calm was destroyed by the dastardly nature of the plot Oates invented. Just as important, however, was the foreign element of his fantasy. Oates asserted, and press rumour confirmed, that Charles' assassination would be followed by an Irish Catholic rising and a French invasion.[24] The plot was thus incorporated into that wider collapse of Protestantism of which the English were so aware: and it was this which made it so pressing. With French and Irish involvement, James' accession was no longer a future domestic event which might be eased by political accommodation, but

[20] See above, ch. 3.

[21] E.g. *The True Protestant Mercury or Occurences Forrein and Domestick* (December 1680–October 1682); *Mercurius Anglicus* (November 1679–May 1680).

[22] *The Domestick Intelligence* was re-titled *The Protestant (Domestick) Intelligence* in 1680 and survived to April 1681.

[23] For these proposals see Mark Goldie, 'Danby, the bishops and the Whigs', in Harris, Seaward and Goldie, *Politics of religion*, pp. 75–105.

[24] Alan Marshall, 'Oates, Titus', *ODNB*, XLI:335–40, quote at 336. For pamphlets stressing the plot's international dimension: *The cabal of several notorious priests and Jesuits discovered* (1679); *The depositions and examinations of Mr Edward Everard* (1679).

was integrated into the immediate and international march of the counter-reformation.

The importance of this was most obvious in the Whig movement. Throughout the crisis, Whigs insisted exclusion was a barrier against a *European* terror. For them, James was unacceptable because he furthered a pan-continental scheme against true religion, so Whig polemicists stressed the overseas origin of the danger facing England. In their rhetoric, alien popish plotters were planning to take advantage of a Romanist ruler and were already active at court introducing un-English doctrines. Sometimes, the design involved a comic-book assortment of international villains. In pamphlets which confirmed Oates' wild stories, the evil plan was said to have been hatched at the papal curia in 1677; it was supposed to have involved 'the most Eminent of the Popish Clergy in *Europe*' (including leading Italians, Spaniards and Frenchmen); and to have incorporated both the Habsburgs and Bourbons (who had made peace to join in the attempt).[25] More often, Whigs saw a more focused (and to be honest, a not wholly mythical) conspiracy directed from Versailles.[26] Following the lead in Andrew Marvell's influential 1678 pamphlet *An account of the growth of popery and arbitrary power*, writers detected a French design to subvert English Protestantism by corrupting key statesmen, and they urged exclusion to frustrate its local agents.[27] Thus many Whig performances assumed Louis XIV was behind the crisis. His money and spies were already operating at the heart of Stuart government, and if James came to the throne, he would be Louis' puppet.[28]

In fact, insistence on foreign subversion became such an exclusionist trademark that Tories used it to blacken the cause. This was a key tactic in 1681, when the highly dodgy conspirator, Edward Fitzharris, penned a deliberately seditious pamphlet which he planned to plant in the earl of Shaftesbury's chamber to discredit this Whig leader. The tract went beyond demanding James' removal from the succession to insist Charles himself be deposed, but also alleged alien skulduggery. It claimed the royal brothers had been in the pocket of Louis XIV since their exile in Paris in the 1650s and that France's influence explained recent mis-steps in English policy.[29] Fitzharris therefore exploited the foreign obsession in exclusionist ideology as he tried to subvert it. He gave his tract plausibility by aping a prevailing Whig paranoia about Louis, and implied wild talk of alien threat was driving many to treason. In the event, Fitzharris was betrayed and arrested. Even then, though, his

25 *The popish plot taken out of several descriptions* [1680], p. 1; J. P., *A letter to a friend in the country: being a vindication of parliament's whole proceedings* (1679), p. 1.

26 E.g. S. M. Wynne, 'Keroualle, Louise', *ODNB*, XXXI:404–8, stresses the role of the king's mistress in communications between Louis and Charles.

27 Marvell's pamphlet pre-dated Oates' revelations but set the pattern of Whig analysis.

28 See Harris, *Restoration*, pp. 163–7.

29 For its text: *Treason in graine* (1682).

attempts to save himself by turning informer underlined the importance of continental bogeymen to the Whigs. Under interrogation, he delighted the exclusionist sheriffs of London by confirming he was part of a decade-long plot fomented in popish Paris, Portugal and elsewhere. This spurred Whigs to broadcast his claims, and ultimately led to a wrangle between Charles and the Commons which preoccupied the third crisis parliament. Whilst the king wanted the miscreant hung quickly to silence his destabilising nonsense, MPs tried to impeach him, hoping that an open trial would further air his tales.[30] Losing all friends and credibility, Fitzharris was finally executed. His sad career, however, illustrated how essential horror of continental popery was to exclusionist ideology.

Whigs thus presented an England assailed from abroad. Yet their use of Europe was more than narrow xenophobia. For them, the English were involved in a pan-European struggle, in which they must support all Protestants against the Roman church. One of the most influential agents expanding exclusionist horizons was Henry Care's *Weekly Pacquet of Advice from Rome*. Published every seven days from December 1678 to July 1683, this popular periodical has been recognised as a backbone of the Whig movement, but there has been remarkably little analysis of its nature. Compared to other Whiggish newspapers with which it has been bracketed, it devoted relatively little space to contemporary events.[31] Instead, it serialised a version of Catholic history which explained how the faith had been corrupted into an anti-Christian creed, and to this appended a satirical 'Popish Courant', which was initially styled like a newspaper (but in fact carried invented stories of Roman conspiracy) and later came to consist of dialogues between an honest 'Trueman' and a cast of vicious Tories and Jesuits. Both elements internationalised the Whig cause. The history chronicled popery's corruption of the whole continent and was thoroughly Foxean in creating a pan-European gallery of heroes. Like the book of martyrs (which Care admitted copying), it lauded Albigensians, Waldensians, Hussites and sixteenth-century Germans alongside Wyclif and the Tudor reformers, and it interpreted English faith as essentially the same as that of Luther, Bucer, Calvin and many others abroad.[32] The 'Popish Courant', meanwhile, spoke of a conspiracy against the entire Protestant world. Whilst the satire certainly concentrated on English events (in particular firing on Tory actions), there were plenty of asides to remind its audience that popery threatened the godly everywhere. Papists gloated at the misfortunes of French Huguenots and Spanish

[30] Relating parliamentary proceedings let Whigs repeat Fitzharris' claims: e.g. *The examination of Mr Edward Fitzharris* (1681).

[31] For such bracketing: Harris, *Restoration*, p. 142.

[32] [Henry Care], *Weekly Pacquet of Advice from Rome*, II:21; III:60; IV:9, 35. For the admission of plagiarism: IV:14.

'heretics'; they revelled in the forced conversions of Protestants in the German Palatinate; and one conspirator insisted that despite Oates' revelation of the English branch of the great design, 'in other Parts our *grand Plot* goes on amain'. He proved this, and comforted himself, with evidence of Protestant setbacks in Hungary, Danzig, the Netherlands and France.[33]

If one of the Whigs' main press organs stressed that this was a pan-continental crisis, so did the way they constructed one of their chief arguments. As one might expect, much of the exclusionist effort painted lurid pictures of what would happen if James ever came to the English throne. Publications such as *The prospect of a popish successor displayed by hell-bred cruelty* (1681) or *The character of a popish successor and what England may expect of such a one* (1681) delivered on these titles and depicted the horror of life after Charles. Yet even as exclusionists stressed effects in England, they encouraged audiences to think beyond to the fate of the European reformation. Warning of papist persecution, for example, Whigs deployed English evidence from the reign of Mary Tudor, or Guy Fawkes' treason, but they supplemented this with continental material. Thus the MP Hugh Boscowen, introducing the exclusion bill to the second crisis parliament, reminded his colleagues of massacres in Piedmont, Paris and Ireland over the previous century, and so added his voice to a barrage of such warnings in the press.[34] As a 1679 pamphleteer put it, the English should have sufficient warning from 'the cruel Murders and Massacres of some Hundred Thousand *Protestants* . . . in the *Netherlands, Ireland, Piedmont*, and the *Albigenses*', whilst another recommended reading that catalogue of cruelty – *The antichristian principle discovered* – to remember the 'bloudy Persecutions . . . exercised by the Papists throughout *Europe*'.[35] Two years later, a writer advertising the *Certain way to save England*, repeated a list of dangers which had become standard in Whig polemic, adding Dutch, French, Savoyard and Irish massacres to memories of bloody Mary and the gunpowder plot.[36] The situation was similar with warning of superstitious ignorance. Whigs might reach back to England's medieval past for examples, but these were less immediate than those from the contemporary continent, so the sort of material we encountered in travel guides was put to political purpose. Pamphlets gleefully recounted preposterous Catholic rituals or priestly greed from many different lands; newspapers reported the latest excesses and miracles from around the Catholic world (no matter how patently

33 Ibid., III:4, 16, 28, 60. 34 Cobbett, IV:1188.

35 *Sober and seasonable queries humbly offered to all good Protestants* [1679], p. 2; *A letter from St Omars in the farther confirmation of the truth of the papist plot* (1679), p. 3. Also: *An account of the several plots, conspiracies and hellish attempts* (1679). *The antichristian principle discovered* (1679) chronicled papist persecutions across the world in all ages.

36 *The certain way to save England* (1681), p. 16.

fraudulent or absurd); and the story of Jetzer and the Berne friars was reproduced as a separate pamphlet with the express purpose of dismissing doubts about Oates' claims.[37]

Moving beyond this sense that England was caught up in a universal confessional battle, Whigs insisted the outcome of her domestic dispute would be vital to its outcome. Of course, barring James would save an important Protestant country and block an advance for popery, but for the exclusionists, their measure was even more important than this. It was the only way to halt a deep-laid project to divide and destroy the continent's Protestants. Some of the clearest expressions of this came in parliamentary speeches. On 26 October 1680, the MP Henry Capel gave a magisterial oration in the Commons, explaining how clandestine Catholic influence had been making itself felt in England. Some of its effects had been domestic (illegal uses of the royal prerogative, state bankruptcy, even the Great Fire of London), but the most worrying had been the frustration of England's role as protector of Protestant Europe. In the 1660s and early 1670s, evil men at court had sent the country to war with the Dutch. This had weakened the reformed cause 'in order to the general destruction of it', and allowed the French (who had been behind the scheme) to look on 'while we poor protestants with great fury destroyed one another'. In the mid-1670s things had become even more troubling as papists had acted through James to secure secret support for France's 'war for Religion' in the Low Countries. Convinced that the plot was still active, Capel concluded that the interests of the French, the papists and the duke of York were all one, and so tied calls for exclusion to the entire survival of the reformation. Colleagues agreed. Back in 1679, Shaftesbury had warned the Lords that England's role in the 'Protection of the Protestants abroad' was being neglected as conspiracy advanced, whilst Hugh Boscowen had told the Commons that 'the whole protestant religion in Europe is aimed at, in a Popish Succession in England'.[38] Similarly, in November 1680 Goodwin Wharton accused James of fatally endangering the Dutch and the French Huguenots by his past actions; while in October, Ralph Montagu claimed England's whole foreign policy had been captured by a corrupt party. This, he was sure was 'to the great danger of . . . the Protestant religion both at home and abroad': if popery were established by James' accession, the true faith might be rooted from 'the face of the earth'.[39]

[37] E.g. *A character of popery and arbitrary government* (1679); *The character of a popish successor, and what England may expect* (1681), esp. p. 12; *Domestick Intelligence*, 2 (10 July 1679); William Waller, *The tragical history of Jetzer* (1679).

[38] *An impartial account of divers remarkable proceedings in the last session of parliament* (1679), pp. 22–4; Cobbett, IV:1135.

[39] Cobbett, IV:1206, 1170.

Parliamentarians, then, assumed the fate of Europe hung in the balance in their debates, but this conviction spread beyond Westminster, or the colleges of Oxford where Charles convened the third crisis legislature to avoid pressure from the capital's crowds. Across the country, advocates of exclusion repeated England's importance to the entire Protestant cause, and insisted the reformed elsewhere were watching her affairs with close attention. In November 1680, the Whig-dominated city of London petitioned Charles to listen to the exclusionist majority in his parliament as the best way to safeguard the peace of his kingdom, but went on to claim such an accommodation would build the 'Comfort and Encouragement of all your Protestant Neighbours abroad'.[40] Similarly, pamphlets recommending how men should vote when choosing MPs stressed that their duties ran far beyond their own nation. One addressing electors to the Oxford parliament said their choice would determine not only 'the happiness of his Majesties Dominions, but of the whole Protestant Religion, and of all the Reformed Churches'. A 'good' parliament could protect the English from their enemies, but this was listed after its work preserving Holland from Louis XIV, terrifying that king into treating his own Calvinist population better, and saving the Protestants of Ireland from papist rebellion.[41] Perhaps most remarkably, the Dutch themselves were recruited as passionate Whigs. In 1680, the views of the Netherlands' states general were published, and these were full of terror that Charles' resistance to exclusion had broken England as a counter-weight to popery. In what was claimed was a position paper given to the English ambassador in The Hague, the Dutch governing assembly begged the king not to stick on a disputed constitutional point lest 'the *Interests of Europe*, principally of all Protestant Princes, and of this *State* [i.e. the Netherlands], should be sacrificed'.[42]

Such close discussion of the continental reformation between 1679 and 1682 confirms Jonathan Scott's suggestion that a Protestant European context was crucial to the Whig worldview. However, even our fairly rapid survey of such material suggests we have not quite exhausted the exclusionists' international vision. Very frequently, the perceived threat from continental popery was entangled with the threat from Louis XIV's France. This was understandable since the French seemed to be the shock troops of counter-reformation, but of course it raised the question whether Louis was feared as a popish antichrist, or as a universal monarch. We have seen this polyvalence in foreign policy debate, and noted that it depended on a Christian

40 *To the king's most excellent majesty: the humble petition and address . . . of the city of London* (1680).

41 C. B., *An address to the honourable city of London and all other cities, shires and corporations* (1681), epistle.

42 *An intimation of the deputies of the states general* [1680], p. 3.

continental identity wider even than international Protestantism.[43] Inevitably, this broader discourse infected Whig polemic as it magnified the French threat. Athough the exclusionists often spoke as if all Catholic Europe were the enemy (Spanish and Italian papists had been involved in the plot against England, and some thought Charles' 1680 alliance with Spain might allow her to help suppress Protestant protest in London), those who concentrated on Louis were sometimes forced to admit Habsburgs and other Romanists might become necessary allies against Versailles, and this gave some Whigs at least the rudiments of a second European identity.[44]

Amid the hue and cry against popery, this additional dimension was relatively muted. Fully worked-out analysis of Louis' threat to a united Christendom was rare among Whigs, who stressed the evils of popery to explain why James could not be trusted. Nevertheless, there were hints. Quite apart from complaints that Charles' stubbornness was stopping England defeat Islam in the Mediterranean as well as the French nearer home, and a bizarre series of pamphlets which allegorised the whole crisis as a plot on a Christian ship endangered by Muslim pirates, several Whig commentators recognised that England might have to make common cause with the Habsburgs.[45] Despite its title, Andrew Marvell's *Account of the growth of popery* had seen the threat in primarily French rather than purely Romanist terms, and this allowed him to urge help for the Catholic Spaniards in holding Flanders.[46] Again taking his cue from Marvell, Henry Capel could mix his warnings about the fate of the reformation with denunciations of Louis as a universal monarch. He too worried as much about Catholic Flanders as the Protestant United Provinces, and such unconfessional thinking bled into Whig analysis.[47] So the party sometimes presented Spain as a necessary, if not wholly palatable, friend. They published the articles of the 1680 treaty with Madrid (concluded when the king was under pressure to assuage Whig opinion) and printed appeals by the Spanish ambassador to Charles to accept exclusion.[48] Pedro Ronquillo was presented begging Charles to settle with parliament so he could concentrate on the continental situation: the envoy stressed France had been restrained from even further expansion in the Low Countries by fears that England would come in against her, but that if the crisis in London continued she would be encouraged in his 'vast design'. In response, all the

[43] See above, pp. 152–92.

[44] For the wider conspiracy: e.g. *A just and modest vindication of the last two parliaments* [1681], p. 12.

[45] *The humble petition and address of . . . the City of London . . . 31 May, 1681* (1681). *A letter from Leghorn, December 1, 1679* [1680]; *An answer to another letter from Leghorn* (1680); *The answers to the letter from Leghorn answered* (1680).

[46] Andrew Marvell, *An account of the growth of popery and arbitrary power* (1678), p. 23.

[47] Cobbett, IV:1282 – debate on exclusion bill, 11 November 1680.

[48] *The articles of alliance between England and Spain, signed the 10th day of June, 1680* (1680).

'Princes and Powers of *Europe*' were looking to Charles to make concessions.[49] In this appeal, Spain joined the Netherlands in a grand front against the English king's policies. The Whigs, the Habsburgs and the Dutch asked Charles to accept exclusion to save both the reformation, and the liberties of all Christian states, from France.

So far, then, we have seen Whiggery shaped by transnational spiritual identities. In truth, however, we have probably rounded out, rather than revolutionised, understanding of the movement. Jonathan Scott has already insisted exclusion was rooted in fear of the counter-reformation, and some earlier historians at least mentioned the Whigs' sensitivity to the fate of foreign Protestants.[50] Where our stress on Christendom and the Protestant international may really pay dividends, however, is with the Tories. Analysing their rhetoric, we see people far from their standard image as a 'little England' grouping.[51] They were neither ignorant of, nor ignored, Europe: and in fact they constructed a case for rallying round Charles which depended on the fate of Protestants and Christians overseas. Initially this allowed them to respond effectively to Whig polemic, but ultimately it tied them close to the Whig worldview and qualified their support for royal power.

In existing accounts of Tory philosophy, there is little concern with abroad. This party was traditionally presented as a faction of Stuart loyalists, convinced of unstoppable royal power; or at least as the party of order convinced that Whig radicalism presented more of a danger to the existing settlement than a Catholic court.[52] In recent work there has been stress on the Tories' religious ideals, but these were again largely local. They were the party of the church of England, and they embraced a real but subtle version of anti-popery in which James' open Catholicism was less dangerous than a Roman plot which used Whig subversion to divide a Protestant nation.[53] None of these visions of the Tories is wrong. Each describes the domestic viewpoint of at least some within the Tory fold, but they do miss vital continental dimensions. Tories were concerned with the political and religious order in England, but the very fact that their rivals set out such a strong foreign agenda would have forced them to discuss Europe, even if they had not had a powerful continental sense of their own.

Admittedly, one of the most prominent continental perspectives in Tory propaganda involved defending England against foreign threat, rather than

[49] [Pedro Ronquillo], *The last memorial of the Spanish ambassador* (1681).
[50] Scott, *Algernon Sydney*, pp. 38–44; Harris, *London crowds*, p. 110.
[51] E.g. Holmes, *British politics*, p. 64, saw Tories uninterested in foreign affairs in the 1680s, and 'isolationist' and 'xenophobic' after 1688.
[52] E.g. Thomas Babington Macaulay, *The history of England to the death of William III* (2 vols., 1848), II: ch. 2; J. R. Western, *Monarchy and revolution: the English state in the* 1680s (1972), ch. 2; Dickinson, *Liberty and property*, ch. 1.
[53] Harris, *London crowds*, ch. 6

building transnational identities. Explaining Whig subversion of the Stuart monarchy, many polemicists seized on Peter Heylyn's notion of a pan-continental conspiracy of radical Protestants, and saw their rivals undermining domestic order to impose alien perversions. A chief promoter of this notion was Roger L'Estrange. L'Estrange had been Charles II's censor of the press, but when the lapse of print restrictions cost him his job in 1679, he started to pen an extraordinary flood of pamphlets which questioned the reality of the popish plot, defended the duke of York's rights, and assassinated the Whigs' character.[54] Perhaps most influentially, he produced *The Observator*. Published every few days from April 1681 to January 1684, this became the standard-bearer of the Tory periodicals and maintained a barrage of anti-exclusionist comment. Scattered through the material were denunciations of European Protestantism. The very first issue of the *Observator* warned that England's godly society was constantly imperilled by radicalised versions of the faith, and that if one needed to know how dangerous this was, one should look overseas. In sixteenth-century Germany, the paper noted, the ungovernable Tomas Münzer had first taught people to revolt against secular authority in order to fulfil his spiritual vision. This had cost 150,000 lives, and Whig willingness to follow his path proved they were his heirs.[55] Other Tory works bobbed in L'Estrange's wake. Periodicals such as *The Weekly Discovery of the Mystery of Inquity*, or Benjamin Tooke's *Heraclitus Ridens*, countered Henry Care's histories with their own account of plots. They listed bloody risings by European Protestants alongside Catholic massacres, and traced the immediate menace to England back to Geneva.[56] Pamphlets and ballads, meanwhile, agreed that Calvin (or his followers in Switzerland, the Netherlands or Scotland) was the root of all evil, and eventually provoked a bitter riposte from Care himself.[57] Responding to *A postscript of advice from Geneva* (a tract which painted as corrupt a picture of European reformers as Care did of Rome), the Whig denounced the whole gamut of Tory writers.[58] They, Care said, had set out to '*scandalise* all the learned pious instruments, which God hath made use of for the first Reformation: As not only *Calvin, Zwinglius* and *Beza* . . . but *Luther, Melancthon, Bucer* &c'.[59] This not

[54] Donald Wing, ed., *Short title catalogue of books printed in England . . . 1641–1700* (2nd edn revised, 3 vols., New York, 1982), II:418–21, lists over forty works by L'Estrange 1679–83.
[55] [Roger L'Estrange], *The Observator in Question and Answer*, 1 (13 April 1681)
[56] E.g. *The Weekly Discovery of the Mystery of Iniquity*, 1, 2 (5, 12 February 1681); and *Heraclitus Ridens*, 8:5, 8 (1, 22 March 1681).
[57] E.g. *Geneva and Rome: or the zeal of both boiling over* (1679); *The ripping up of Sir John Presbyter's garment* [1679]; *Fiat justitia, & ruat coelum* [1679], p. 1; *Advice to the men of Shaftesbury* (1681), p. 1; [Thomas Ashenden], *The presbyterians' pater noster* [1681]; *A litany from Geneva* (1682).
[58] *A postscript of advice from Geneva, to be added to each of Mr Care's several volumes* [1681].
[59] [Care], *Weekly Pacquet*, 4:1 (23 December 1681).

only besmirched God's chosen, but would have horrified Elizabethans such as Thomas Hooker and John Jewel, whom Tories lionised for establishing their English church, but who had in fact worked closely with the vilified continentals.

In exchanges like this, the exclusion crisis can seem a mere political rehearsal of historical dispute over the reformation. Whigs followed Burnet and integrated England into his glorious international movement: Tories filed behind Heylyn in seeing nothing but horror abroad.[60] Yet just as Heylyn's initially insular vision turned out to have powerful continental dimensions, so the Tories found comrades beyond the seas. Beyond blackening the Whigs' foreign friends as factious rebels, they genuinely engaged with their rivals' concerns, recognising England's duty to support wider forms of Christianity, but producing a very different reading of them. The first hint of this came early in the crisis. Above, we saw Andrew Marvell's *Account of the growth of popery* providing key themes of Whig polemic, even though it was published before the popish plot. Yet L'Estrange's rapid response was similarly precocious. His *Account of the growth of knavery* defended Charles' court from the accusation that it had been infiltrated by French conspirators, but although it spent most of its time denigrating Marvell, at one point it addressed his fears for Europe. The French, L'Estrange admitted, were dangerous. If they absorbed the Spanish Netherlands, as they nearly had, England would suffer horribly. L'Estrange thus began from the same point as Marvell, and it was only as he worked out the implications that he turned Whig logic on its head. At this 'critical juncture', L'Estrange complained, his target had not rallied round a king who might save Flanders. Instead he had chosen this moment for 'blasting both the Government and the Administration of it', and this led L'Estrange to ask who was most probably in Louis' pay. Were these evil men likely to be courtiers accused of conspiracy without any solid evidence, or were they more probably 'the *Calumniators themselves* . . . who are doing all that is possible towards the Facilitating of the Work of *France*, and the Putting of *England* out of Condition to defend it self'?[61] In this short passage, L'Estrange advertised a major theme of Tory polemic in the coming crisis. Far from dismissing threats to the European reformation, or the welfare of Christendom, Tories suggested only unity around the king would give him the strength he needed to resist Louis, and that such resistance was the only hope for the international entities. Loyalty was therefore essential. Protestants abroad, and England's foreign allies, were looking to Charles' subjects to work with their monarch, but instead they had to watch as Whigs divided the nation, preached

[60] For the histories, see above, pp. 74–101.
[61] [Roger L'Estrange], *An account of the growth of knavery* (1678), pp. 37–8.

rebellion and endangered the very continental movements they claimed to defend.

As we shall see, this argument was widely deployed. However, it was perhaps most effective in the hands of the monarch himself. Charles II has received considerable – if sometimes grudging – admiration for his handling of the crisis. Historians have recognised he rode the tiger well: he at first seemed to join Whiggish anxiety (he temporarily exiled his brother, punished supposed popish plotters and appointed Whigs to the privy council), but actually bought time until fears of political unrest swung opinion his way.[62] What has been less noticed is the way he used Europe within this strategy. Throughout, his public pronouncements emphasised danger to the international reformation and to Christendom (and thus presented him as sharing Whig concerns), but Charles constantly pleaded he could do nothing to avert this whilst exclusionists turned his country upon itself. Take, for example, the royal speech opening the first exclusion parliament in March 1679. Charles had already called for unity in the face of the popish plot by referring to the worrying European situation, but now his oration (expanded upon, as was traditional, by the lord chancellor) set domestic politics in a firm continental context.[63] The king himself outlined measures the court had taken to contain popery and urged a curbing of 'unruly Spirits', since differences among Englishmen would disrupt a union which he hoped 'could be extended to Protestants abroad', and were likely to be 'fatal there as well as at home'.[64] Moments later, the chancellor elaborated on what his master meant. The nation was facing a foreign Catholic plot based in France, government action had thwarted the English branch of this design, but a wider threat remained. Spanish and Dutch forces were too exhausted to stand in Louis' way and 'when We consider the Afflicted Condition of the Protestants abroad, We may be sure every Calamity they suffer, is in some measure a Weakening of the Protestant Interest, and looks as if it were intended to make Way for a General Extirpation.'[65] Given this, rallying round the crown was vital. Parliamentarians must not engage in factious controversy, and must be generous in settling revenue so England could stand against the French popish menace. 'The Whole World is in Great Expectation of those Resolutions which shall be taken here', he said, echoing Whig insistence that Europe looked to Westminster.[66] Reversing their argument, however, he urged that this make-or-break moment demanded unity with the crown: 'Would you

[62] E.g. Ronald Hutton, *Charles II* (Oxford, 1989), chs. 14–15; John Miller, *Charles II* (1991), chs. 11–13.

[63] For king's earlier call: *His majesties most gracious speech . . . Monday, 21st October, 1678* (1678).

[64] *His majesties most gracious speech . . . Thursday 6th March 1678/9* (1679), pp. 4–5.

[65] Ibid., p. 15. [66] Ibid., p. 11.

Secure Religion at Home, and Strengthen it from abroad by uniting the Interests of all the Protestants in *Europe*? This is the Time. Would you let the Christian World see the King in a Condition able to protect those who shall Adhere to Him, or Depend upon Him? This is the Time.'[67]

These performances did not dissuade the Commons from introducing an exclusion bill, nor from denying finance as a lever to advance it. Yet 1679 was not wholly disastrous for Charles. He faced strong opposition, but could use this to prove Whig irresponsibility in pressing controversial measures in the face of international catastrophe. Opening the second exclusion parliament in October 1680, the king boasted he had used the period since the first to build an alliance against Louis. He had concluded a defensive treaty with the Habsburgs to match the one he had with the Netherlands, and now urged parliamentarians to back him. His policies were the best measures for the safety of England and for 'the repose of Christendom', and they could only fail 'if our Divisions at home . . . render Our Friendship less considerable abroad'.[68] Warning the Whigs that he would never abrogate his brother's rights to the throne (thus establishing that their ambitions must be disruptive), he suggested the parlous state of the English garrison at Tangiers in the face of local Muslims was another foreign reason for domestic harmony, and then again stated 'All Europe now have their Eyes upon this Assembly.'[69] Charles' speech was therefore almost wholly taken up with the fate of international Christian communities. This is some distance from the standard picture of a king emphasising his prerogatives under the English constitution, but it was crucial to his rhetoric as it allowed him to lambast the Whigs on their own territory. Speaking to parliament in December 1680, he referred back to his speech opening the body. He had called for action to contain France, yet those keenly observing foreigners must see how little parliamentarians had done for Europe. If England's' neighbours concluded she was too internally conflicted to 'make Our Alliance valuable', they might be forced to seek refuge with Louis, and meanwhile Christendom might suffer another blow since no reinforcements had gone to Tangier.[70] The next month, Charles again told the Commons to consider the 'Condition of Christendom' instead of pining after exclusion, and his strategy was repeated when the Oxford parliament met in March.[71] Opening this, Charles reported he had had to dissolve its predecessor because it had done so little against Louis

[67] Ibid., p. 17.
[68] *His majesties gracious speech . . . Thursday 21st October, 1680* (1680), pp. 3–4.
[69] Ibid., p. 6.
[70] *His majesties most gracious speech . . . Wednesday 15th December, 1680* (1680), p. 4.
[71] *His majesties gracious message to the Commons in parliament, January the fourth 1680/1* (1681).

or for Tangier.[72] Closing it when legislators still concentrated on the succession, he returned to the same themes. In the declaration explaining why he had dissolved this assembly (a document which became an iconic statement of the Tory position), the monarch complained that his repeated pleas for action against the French and the Moors had been met with nothing but illegal resolutions by the Commons.[73]

Where the king led, many Tory spokesmen followed. The periodical press, parliamentary speeches and popular literature rang to the threat to the reformation and Christendom, and insisted that Whig factiousness neutralised England at this vital stage in the struggle. To take representative instances: on 2 November 1680, William Garroway warned the Commons that a divisive campaign for exclusion would disappoint the eyes of Europe fixed on their meeting; the next summer Benjamin Tooke's *Heraclitus Ridens* wondered how denying Charles support could save Flanders from the French; and a tract engaged with the Whig writers who had allegorised the crisis as a mutiny on a Christian ship by accusing them of being an infidel fifth column themselves.[74] Further evidence of Tory concern for Europe comes from the printed reaction to Charles' declaration after the Oxford parliament. In the months after this was issued, floods of grateful 'loyal addresses' came from the Tory boroughs and counties of England. These were published in the *London Gazette*, as individual broadsides and as a collected *Vox angliae*. Whilst all of these thanked Charles for ending domestic unrest, several mentioned foreign affairs and implied the king now had the support he needed to act against Louis and the Moors. Thus the address from Salisbury spent a fifth of its length talking of the threat to Tangiers, 'a City of Christians among Mahumetans'; that from Hereford insisted England could now take its proper role abroad defending the 'True Protestant Religion'; whilst submissions from Hertford, Southampton and several other places either mentioned the situation in North Africa or spoke of the importance of England helping her foreign neighbours.[75]

The full flowering of this rhetoric came in a series of pamphlets from 1681 and 1682, which attacked the earl of Shaftesbury. As the Whigs' leader (in so far as the movement was organised to have such a thing), Shaftesbury became the prime target of Tory abuse, and their chief weapon was his

[72] *His majesties most gracious speech . . . Monday the 21st March, 1680/1* (1681).

[73] *His majesties declaration to all his loving subjects touching the causes and reasons that moved him to dissolve the last two parliaments* (1681).

[74] Cobbett, VI:1177; *Heraclitus Ridens* 6:29 (16 August 1681); *Another letter from Leghorn, to an eminent merchant in London* (1680), p. 1.

[75] *An address to his majesty from the common council of New Sarum, April 27 1681* (1681); *To the king's most excellent majesty the humble address . . . of the city of Hereford* (1681); *Vox angliae: or the voice of the kingdom* (1682), pp. 2–3, 15. For more on addressing: Knights, *Representation*, ch. 3; Harris, *Restoration*, pp. 266–81.

record in fulfilling England's duties abroad. Although the earl might currently lead exclusionist denunciation of France, Tories reminded their audiences he had been a courtier in the early 1670s and so had presided over that dangerous turn in English foreign policy which had caused current troubles. In 1668, writers recalled, Charles II had formed a Protestant alliance with Sweden and the Netherlands to restrain Louis. Soon, however, evil counsellors had undermined this, and persuaded the king to join France in the 1672 attack on the Dutch. This French escape from containment led directly to the peril Europe was now in, and Shaftesbury – the king's adviser – had been behind it. Thus L'Estrange asserted all the world knows who 'persuaded the breaking of the *Triple League* . . . [and] *nurst up the King of* France *to this height*'.[76] Another author thought people would have an 'ill memory' not to accuse the earl, and a third blamed him for a war which had 'weaken'd the Protestant Interest throughout the World, and strangely advanced the Growth and Power of *France*'.[77] This last pamphleteer went further, and saw exclusion as a simple extension of Shaftesbury's malice. Once found out and sacked by the king, the minister had turned to the mob, hoping to serve masters at Versailles by stirring England against its ruler. By 1678 his spurious complaints of corruption had so weakened the country that the Dutch despaired of help. The result was the disadvantageous treaty of Nijmegen, and continued French encroachments on '*Flanders, Alsace, Strasbourg* and *Cazel* (the Keys into *Germany*)'.[78] From 1679, things had got even worse. Shaftesbury inspired the exclusionist campaign which emasculated England in Europe, and allowed the collapse of the very foreign causes about which Whigs claimed to care. An England divided by rebellious extremism stood by as Louis extirpated the Huguenots, became a universal monarch, and 'totally destroyed the Protestant Religion abroad'.[79] In sum, Shaftesbury and his allies behaved like Thames watermen. Facing one way as they actually rowed another, they carried on 'the Popish Plot apace, which they so violently Decry'.[80]

Now, it has been known for some time that Tories reversed Whig rhetoric. Tim Harris has shown they hijacked exclusionist fears of popery, charging that it was their rivals who actually promoted Catholic power. Whigs weakened a Protestant monarchy; their theories of resistance had first been advanced by papists; and in probability they were Romanist in disguise.[81] Yet although this feature of the Tory case has been acknowledged, its crucial

76 [Roger L'Estrange], *A gentle reflection on a modest account and a vindication of the loyal abhorrers* (1682), p. 11.
77 *A seasonable address to both houses of parliament concerning the succession* (1681), p. 13; *Plain dealing is a jewel and honesty the best policy* (1682), p. 7.
78 *Plain dealing*, pp. 8–9. 79 Ibid., p. 11. 80 Ibid., p. 10.
81 Harris, *London crowds*, ch. 6; Harris, *Restoration*, ch. 4.

international dimension has not. This is important because without understanding Tory commitment to the reformation and to Christendom, we may mistake the true nature of the exclusion crisis. This was not a clash between diametrically opposed ideologies. Both sides began with concern that papists were attacking the European reformation and that France was subverting Christendom's moral order (though perhaps Tories placed more emphasis on the latter problem, finding some of the continent's more zealous Protestantism unpalatable). Given this consensus, the only real difference was how to respond to the commonly recognised danger. Whigs stressed parliament must contain a popish French plot which they thought had bedded down at court and prevented England playing its European spiritual role; Tories, by (not so much) contrast, believed a still basically sound court could fill that role if only it were not distracted by the Whig campaign. This suggests a polity less divided than many historians have assumed, and may help explain why the crisis avoided civil war. In particular it may explain the considerable shift from Whig to Tory which marked the early 1680s, and gave the king the strength to restore stability. A populace which voted for three exclusionist parliaments and turned up in thousands to Whig demonstrations before 1681 transmuted into one thanking Charles for his resolution in seeing off his challengers after the Oxford dissolution. This shift has engaged several scholars, but it may be easier to understand if we recognise it was not a Damascan conversion between widely separated positions.[82] Rather, people agreed with the Whigs that the English must help Christendom and the European reformation, but as the crisis deepened they began to worry this aid was endangered by the Whig agitation itself.

Recognising the exclusion crisis as a debate about how to save international spiritual entities also leads to reassessment of its longer-term outcome. Whig fortunes did not revive. In the last years of Charles' reign, the king denied exclusionists a parliamentary forum and gained considerable support as he eliminated them from public office and prosecuted them for past actions. Yet from what we have said, this 'tory reaction' was not quite as it can be portrayed. It was not a victory for monarchical absolutism (though Tory enthusiasm for the king may have threatened this). Neither was it simply a victory for domestic forces of order, or the resurgence of conservative sentiment which wished to protect the established settlement from revolutionary change (though it certainly was partly these).[83] To a significant degree the Tory reaction was the triumph of people who recognised England's duties to

[82] For reflections on the Whig–tory split: Scott, *Algernon Sidney*, pp. 44–9; Scott, *England's troubles*, pp. 434–53; Harris, *Restoration*, pp. 263–92; John Miller, *After the civil wars* (Harlow, 2000), ch. 13.

[83] Grant Tapsell, *The personal rule of Charles II, 1681–1685* (Woodbridge, 2007), supersedes other studies of the Tory reaction.

Protestants and Christians abroad, but who concluded the English must rally round the court if they were to fulfil these duties. From this it follows that the victors' attachment to the Stuarts was even more conditional than some scholars have argued. The monarchs could forfeit Tory support by themselves becoming a threat to established order (as James, of course, promptly did). Yet they could also get into trouble it they disappointed in the urgent task of facing European popery and the power of France. Understanding this, we can take the story of the struggle between the parties through to the Glorious Revolution.

EUROPE, RELIGION AND THE REVOLUTION OF 1688–1689

In the years from 1683 to 1688 there was little overt constitutional exchange between Whigs and Tories. Party tensions remained, but they were played out in other arenas, and circumstances forced such rapid shifts of position that clear distinctions between groups were lost. Initially, high constitutional debate was smothered by the scale of the Tory triumph. As the king and his allies gained strength, they denied Whigs platforms from which to spread their creed, and terrified them from expounding it at all. The refusal to meet parliament after the Oxford assembly was crucial. Not only did it mean the representative assembly could not lead calls to bar James, it also ended the rounds of elections which had generated Whig speeches, Whig advice sheets to voters and pamphlets urging the return of staunch exclusionists.[84] Action against the press was also vital. Censorship was reimposed in 1683, and as early as August 1681 the execution of the radical polemicist Stephen College warned how far the court would go to suppress unwelcome opinion.[85] Meanwhile prosecution cowed the Whig leadership. Shaftesbury was indicted for treason in 1681, and although discharged by a supportive grand jury, felt it best to flee into exile a year later.[86] In 1683, other exclusionist grandees were executed for their supposed part in a plot to kill the king. Finally, the Tory campaign drove so deep even into the Whigs' local strongholds that its targets' concern became basic political survival, rather than open campaigning. For the four years after the Oxford parliament, commissions of the peace were purged, and borough corporations were remodelled to favour Tories.[87]

If Charles calmed constitutional discussion by suppressing one side of the debate, his brother (ruling from 1685) hopelessly confused it by breaking

84 Though see Grant Tapsell, 'Parliament and politics in the last years of Charles II', *Parliamentary History*, 22 (2003), 243–62.

85 Gary S. de Krey, 'College, Stephen', *ODNB*, XII:616–19. Tory polemicists highlighted the case: e.g. [Roger L'Estrange], *Notes upon Stephen College* (1681).

86 K. H. D. Haley, *The first earl of Shaftesbury* (Oxford, 1968), chs. 28–30.

87 Harris, *Restoration*, pp. 293–300; Halliday, *Dismembering*, ch. 6.

with the Tories. Relations had started well. The Tories dominated the parliament called at the start of the reign, and as the king continued to appoint them to national and local office, they supported James against a rebellion by the duke of Monmouth (who, incidentally, followed the usual Whig line by appealing to 'the expectations of the *Protestant Nations* round about us' when justifying his incompetent bid for the crown).[88] Rupture, however, soon followed. Not only was James a pig-headed bigot who was capable of alienating the closest ally, but his actions to favour Roman Catholics endangered the established church: and this was the one institution closer to Tory hearts than the crown. Thus the Tory parliament objected to James' promotion of Romanists, and when it resisted his call for a repeal of the penal laws against Catholics, it was prorogued. From this point, James looked for other allies in his struggle to grant a religious liberty. He dismissed Tory ministers, and began to explore whether the Whigs (who were attracted to spiritual toleration despite their suspicion of James himself) might collaborate.[89] Royal purges of local government now flowed in the opposite direction, and the king tried to recruit what was left of the Whig political machine to secure a more pliant parliament.[90]

What confused constitutional argument here, of course, was James' use of crown power. Tories had supported Charles' right to face down anarchy, but now found the prerogatives they had espoused deployed against them. They thus protested as James ignored parliament, as he granted religious indulgence in contravention of statute, and as he went on to remodel borough charters to disenfranchise enemies, to erode the legal rights of the church and even to prosecute clerics who petitioned against his policies. Whig and Tory positions thus began to converge, and when the queen, Mary of Modena, gave birth to a son in the summer of 1688, the prospect of continuing authoritarianism drove them to similar despair. The only solution involved a remarkable break in Tory thinking.[91] When William of Orange indicated he was willing to support opposition to the king, both Tories and Whigs welcomed a check on court power, and key figures from both parties signed a secret invitation for him to intervene with force.[92] Once William had arrived, men of both sides rallied to his banner and agreed to the meeting of a special constitutional convention (to be constituted in the same way as a parliament), when James unexpectedly fled the country. In that

[88] *The declaration of James, duke of Monmouth* (1685), p. 3.
[89] John Miller, *James II* (1978), ch. 12.
[90] Western, *Monarchy and revolution*, chs. 3, 6–7; J. R. Jones, *The revolution of 1688 in England* (Oxford, 1972), chs. 3, 6; and Halliday, *Dismembering*, chs. 6–7.
[91] Tim Harris, *Revolution: the great crisis of the British monarchy, 1685–1720* (2006), chs. 6–7.
[92] Andrew Browning, ed., *English historical documents, 1660–1714* (1953), pp. 120–2.

convention, which first met in January 1689, some Tories tried to preserve the succession by having William declared a regent for the exiled monarch, or elevating Princess Mary (as James' daughter) to the throne. Yet when practical objections defeated these ideas, most acquiesced as William became joint monarch with his wife.[93] Old animosities seemed, therefore, to have been buried. Shared hostility to James masked tensions and allowed a settlement to emerge remarkably harmoniously. Not only was the immediate occupancy of the throne decided, but rules for the future succession were fixed (Catholics were henceforth barred from the throne), and all agreed to a 'declaration of right' clarifying the prerogatives of the crown.[94]

So, the period from 1683 to 1689 marked a hiatus in clear party debate, but included a profound shift in one group's constitutional position which is the key conundrum in the ensuing revolution. In 1688–9, most Tories supported foreign intervention against the very man whose rights they had coalesced to defend. Although many had not intended William to become monarch (the prince initially promised he was only seeking a free parliament to enquire into James' misgovernment), most accepted his elevation once it had happened, and all those in the convention joined its unanimous resolution that England should never again be ruled by a popish prince.[95] They therefore adopted exactly the tenets they had defeated in the exclusion crisis. Kings might be rejected for their faith, and the succession might bend to this principle. Of course, there were clear domestic reasons for this reversal. James' attack on Tories obviously strained their loyalty, and we should remember they had never been absolutely hostile to parliamentary checks on the court. Although they had objected to the overweening parliaments of 1679–81, they had themselves protested when James overrode the 1685 legislature, and rejected the prerogative right to suspend parliamentary acts. Perhaps most importantly, Tories were horrified by James' attacks on the church. The second half of this chapter will explore how central this body was to the party, and how its members were prepared to defend it whatever the constitutional consequences. William recognised these specifically English concerns in his 1688 manifesto: carefully appealing for Tory as well as Whig support, he protested at the turning out of loyal officials, he demanded a free parliament as a solution to the nation's ills, and he rehearsed recent illegalities by stressing instances where the church had suffered.[96]

93 For recent coverage: Edward Vallance, *The Glorious Revolution* (St Ives, 2006). W. A. Speck, *Reluctant revolutionaries: Englishmen and the revolution of 1688* (Oxford, 1988), has a clear constitutional focus.

94 For Tories' role in the declaration: Tony Claydon, 'William III's *Declaration of reasons* and the Glorious Revolution', *HJ*, 39 (1996), 87–108.

95 *CJ*, X:17–18.

96 *The declaration of his highness William Henry, prince of Orange, of the reasons inducing him to appear in arms* (The Hague, 1688).

Yet for all these local explanations of Tory revision, underlying concerns for European Protestantism, and for the salvation of Christians from universal monarchy, were also central. With the dizzying whirlwind of domestic politics under James II, it can be difficult to demonstrate its exact importance, but we do have some significant suggestions and clues. For example, the ever-stimulating Steven Pincus has argued that Tories shared a general disillusionment that James did not rally his country against France.[97] At the start of the reign there had been hopes this martial monarch (who had seen active service, and who wanted independence from other powers) might recognise the danger Louis posed to Europe, even if his Catholic faith would stop him leading an anti-popish crusade.[98] Loyal poets urged the king to humble France's pride, and the overwhelmingly Tory parliament of 1685 drew up an address calling on him to declare an 'actual war' upon Versailles.[99] In the face of this enthusiasm, however, James had done nothing. Instead of restraining Louis, his relatively passive attitude to France's expansion had fuelled rumours he was about to ally with him, and his subjects, including the Tories, had turned to William as the only man willing to act. It is true that Pincus played down any religious aspect of this reaction. He suggested it indicated an emerging English nationalism, determined to preserve the country's law and culture against alien influence. Yet if we see English francophobia rooted in loyalty to the reformation and Christendom (as the preceding chapter argued), we might read the disappointment differently. Tories, we could suggest, were coming to accept Whig doubts about James' ability to serve their European causes, and their commitment to international spiritual identities was weakening their constitutional argument for royal autonomy.

More concretely, we might learn why Tories swallowed William's elevation by examining what they said as it happened. We might, for instance, home in on the convention of 1689 to see how those who had opposed exclusion under Charles II explained their *volte face*. We have to look past difficulties with the historic record here, but again there may be hints as to what was going on. The problems of evidence are various. First we have no official account of debates in the convention. All that survives are the minutes of decisions taken, and the hurried notes of some of the participants which vary in details.[100] Second, the records tend to be of Whig contributions. There is

97 Steven Pincus, '"To protect English liberties": the English nationalist revolution of 1688–9', in Tony Claydon and Ian McBride, eds., *Protestantism and national identity: Britain and Ireland, 1660–1850* (Cambridge, 1998), pp. 75–104.

98 For James' desire for independence: Wout Troost, *William III: the stadholder-king* (Aldershot, 2005), ch. 8.

99 BL Add. MS 63773, fo. 25.

100 Apart from sources quoted below, we have *LJ*, *CJ*, Lord Clarendon's notes – Pepys Library MS 2179; Lord Danby's notes – BL MS 3345, bundle 3.

little mystery in these: they predictably upheld the rights of the people's representatives to alter monarchy to protect public safety, and defined this safety partly in terms of the wider Protestant and European entities in which England participated.[101] Third, the versions of Tory speeches we have belie how their authors' went on to behave. Most objected to Whiggish interpretations of what was happening, and so rejected the obvious arguments for advancing William, but the very people who did this accepted the prince's promotion. Men who would swear allegiance to the prince of Orange days later dismissed the notion that the throne was vacant (a position which might imply it was elective), or any idea that James had forfeited power by acting illegally. Despite these difficulties, however, there are shafts of light into Tory souls. Perhaps most importantly, it is clear they had given up on the old king by the time the convention met. On 28 January, those in the lower house (which had been constituted in the same way as a House of Commons) grumbled against the vacancy in a motion declaring James was no longer sovereign, but only three of them actually voted against it, and this fell to one when the framing committee reported back to the formal full body.[102] Those in the upper house (the peers of the realm) also rejected vacancy, but promised to do all they could to stop James coming back to England and capitulated on the points in the dispute after a free conference between the Lords and Commons.[103] Meanwhile Tories in both chambers accepted the resolution against future government by popish princes; some even explained that a monarch who turned Catholic must be treated at least as severely as one who had run mad.[104]

The general tone of debate in January and February 1689 may explain why Tories felt this way. Whilst members of the convention picked over fine legal points for much of their discussion, it was clear an international dimension lay in the background and was brought forward whenever people urged dispatch or reminded members of the importance of this moment. Participants in the debate stressed that a settlement must be found quickly – and moreover insisted it must be found without including James – because the European continent and its reformation faced acute danger from France. Thus one of the first speeches, by Henry Capel on 22 January, asked all to remember foreign Protestants before they delayed any decisions. It was the reformed Christians of Europe who had made William's expedition possible; they were waiting uneasily 'till they hear how we proceed'; and the prince's troops were

101 E.g. John Somers' speech, 28 January – Anchitell Grey, *Debates in the House of Commons from 1667 to 1694* (10 vols., 1769), IX:16–17; John Hampden's speech, 5 February – *The debate at large between the Lords and Commons* (2nd edn, 1689), pp. 256–7.

102 D. L. Jones, *A parliamentary history of the Glorious Revolution* (1988), pp. 21–2.

103 *CJ*, X:20.

104 See Heneage Finch's contribution, 28 January; Grey, *Debates*, IX:19; and the bishop of Ely's, 6 February, *Debate at large*, p. 15.

urgently needed back at home to protect Holland against Louis.[105] The next day, the prince of Orange stressed continental conditions as he pressed the convention to dispatch. In his first address to the body, he asked it to consider the 'condition of affairs abroad' and the 'safety of all Europe', rhetorically privileging these foreign factors over a local constitutional settlement.[106] The debate in the lower house on 28 January (which ended in the resolution that the throne was vacant) also took up these concerns. Several interventions handled the international context and used it to explain why James must be removed. Members were reminded that Ireland lay in the hands of Catholics; that the old regime could easily exploit hostile forces from outside the kingdom; and that there was 'no Popish prince in *Europe* but would destroy all Protestants: as in *Spain, France* and *Hungary*'.[107] Above all, the convention was reminded repeatedly that France (James' place of refuge) was a pressing threat.[108] Using her faith and influence she might come to lead an international popish alliance against England and her allies: as Sir James Oxenden put it, 'The King went away to raise France against us, & to raise Ireland against us, & indeed all Europe against us.' This awareness probably explains why the lower house broke from constitutional discussion on 29 January to impose economic sanctions on Louis.[109]

Though many of the statements above were by Whigs, the atmosphere they created almost certainly swayed Tory opinion. Old anti-exclusionists begged colleagues not to change England's government fundamentally, but in the prevailing European crisis, they accepted the situation should be settled quickly and that James must not come back. Thus on 28 January Christopher Musgrave admitted 'we are in great danger, should the King return again'.[110] He said this immediately after Thomas Wharton had spoken of the threats to all Protestants if this should happen, and in a context where James was sheltering with Louis it is hard not to conclude that the wider continental threat to the reformation had convinced him. At the end of the debate, Heneage Finch similarly denied the Tory position was leaving a 'loop-hole' for the King's return.[111] After discussions dominated by the state of Europe it seems likely it was this which made any restoration unthinkable, and the Whig Robert Howard exploited this mood by arguing France would find endless claimants to the English throne unless the old royal family was unequivocally displaced. Perhaps most explicitly, Sir Robert Sawyer departed from old Tory shibboleths in fear at the continental situation. Sawyer had been named as a possible chief justice at the height of the Tory reaction, but now was so appalled by James' actions that he was prepared to think he had abdicated,

105 Grey, *Debates*, IX:4–5. 106 For William's speech: *CJ*, X:10.
107 Grey, *Debates*, IX:6–25, esp. p. 12.
108 E.g. Sir Robert Howard and Sir John Knight: W. Strahan and T. Cadell, eds., *Miscellaneous state papers from 1501 to 1726* (2 vols., 1778), II:411.
109 *CJ*, X:14–15. 110 Grey, *Debates*, IX:11. 111 Ibid., IX:24.

and crucially, he got ready to accept William by excusing the Orange invasion as essential to the wider European reformation. 'The Protestant Religion here was interwoven with all the Protestant States of *Europe*,' Sawyer explained to the convention, 'and that principle justifies the Prince of *Orange*'s coming over.' The reformation in England and abroad must hold together, he went on, for if one branch were to fall, 'all falls with it'.[112] In the convention, therefore, those who had opposed exclusion acknowledged that conditions abroad ruled out James' government of England. This left them little room for constitutional manoeuvre, and perhaps explains why their resistance to Whig logic was half-hearted and short-lived.

Tories, then, abandoned James amid assertions of international calamity. Further evidence that this was *why* they accepted his exclusion may come from how they justified it retrospectively. Here Mark Goldie has provided magisterial surveys of Tory thought after the revolution, but although his explication has centred on various understandings of the English law, it is possible to show these positions were combined with a deep sense of duty to the faithful abroad.[113] At base, Goldie demonstrates that Tories tried to accept the change of monarch whilst denying subjects the right to resist rulers. The party had abandoned James, but it had been founded on fears of popular agitation in the early 1680s, and refused to accept arguments for such insubordination now. Thus some Tories believed William had conquered the nation and enjoyed power by that simple right.[114] Others suggested the extraordinary success of the Dutch expedition indicated it had been providentially managed by God.[115] Still others argued that whatever the rights and wrongs of William's coming to power, it was everyone's duty to obey a *de facto* monarch (even if a ruler was technically illegal, he protected the country from anarchy); whilst others again thought James' flight meant he had abandoned government (which might be thought a voluntary abdication).[116] Tories therefore insisted it was not the English people who had sacked their king, but William (conquest theories), or God (accounts

[112] Ibid., IX:23.

[113] Mark Goldie, 'Tory political thought, 1689–1714' (Cambridge Ph.D. thesis, 1977); Mark Goldie, 'The revolution of 1689 and the structure of political argument', *Bulletin of Research in the Humanities*, 83 (1980), 473–564.

[114] The classic statement, [Charles Blount], *King William and Queen Mary conquerors* (1693), was written by a Whig who argued conquest was only legitimate if it secured people's rights. Tories, however, used the notion widely, at least in combination with others: e.g. [Edward Fowler], *A vindication of the divines of the church of England* (1689); *An entire vindication of Dr Sherlock* (1691); *An enquiry into the nature and obligation of legal rights* (1693).

[115] Providence was used throughout Tory literature: G. M. Straka, 'The final phase of divine right theory in England, 1688–1702', *EHR*, 77 (1962), 638–58.

[116] E.g. [Edmund Bohun], *The history of the desertion* (1689) – the first history of the revolution – stressed abdication in its very title. William Sherlock convinced himself to support the revolution on *de facto* grounds: [William Sherlock], *The case of allegiance due to sovereign powers* (1690); [William Sherlock], *The case of allegiance due to sovereign powers, further consider'd* (1691).

of providence), or circumstance (arguments for a *de facto* regime), or James (who by abdicating had sacked himself).

These notions prevented Tories defending popular rebellion, but – and here we go beyond Goldie – they were of limited use because they lacked positive endorsement of William. Of course, some Tories never accepted the prince of Orange as their ruler. They passed into Jacobitism (active support of James' continuing claims), or at least retreated into a political sulk which involved refusing the oaths to the new monarchs and withdrawing from public administration.[117] Most Tories, however, were keen to keep the exiled Stuarts out. They had become thoroughly alienated from their displaced king, they wanted to continue their careers and they tried to bolster their party by persuading their more suspicious allies to remain politically engaged with the incoming ruler.[118] These 'Williamite' Tories found their technical explanations of 1688 inadequate to express any deeper satisfaction with the change of regime, so were left looking for a language in which to express their enthusiasm for their new Dutch master. Conquest and *de facto* theories could not do this, as they made no claim that the latest prince would be less tyrannical than the one he replaced. In both justifications for the revolution, men would have to obey William even if he did even greater damage to English faith or freedoms than James. The argument from abdication, meanwhile, did not explain why the prince of Orange should exercise power instead of other possible replacements (and in particular questioned why Mary or James' young son had not succeeded); whilst providence – as Gilbert Burnet lamented in a late 1688 sermon – ran the risk of equating simple success with right.[119] All the Tory positions therefore needed more than bare statement if they were to be positive celebrations of the change of government, and William's European destiny provided this. In the few years after the revolution, Tories backed constitutional argument with stress on the king's role as protector of the international reformation and leader of a Christian league against a universal monarch: this may well have been what attracted them to him in the first place.

I have presented part of the evidence for Tory internationalism under William elsewhere, and will not repeat the material at length. As I have shown, the new regime reached out to the old exclusionist party by playing down any detailed constitutionalism, and instead concentrated on

117 For general accounts: Paul Monod, *Jacobitism and the English people, 1688–1788* (Cambridge, 1989); Daniel Szechi, *The Jacobite movement* (Oxford, 2002).

118 E.g. [Henry Maurice], *The lawfulness of taking the new oaths asserted* (1689), pleaded with Tories not to forfeit their posts.

119 Gilbert Burnet, *A sermon preached in the chapel of St James' . . . 23 December 1688* (1689); for analysis: Tony Claydon, *William III and the godly revolution* (Cambridge, 1996), pp. 28–52.

providential polemic presenting the new king as an instrument of heaven. The prince of Orange, propaganda insisted, would reinvigorate the English reformation and renew the people's covenant with God, and an important part of this rhetoric was European. It stressed the new king's divine war against Louis XIV, a papist antichrist, which made him the saviour of all European Protestants.[120] In more recent works, I have glossed this, explaining the regime's account of its continental role included the defence of all Christians from the evils of Louis' universal monarchy, deploying much of the evidence we surveyed in the previous chapter.[121] Tories were happy to go along with this polemic. It allowed them to express loyalty to William without accepting a Whig interpretation of 1688; and indeed some of them promoted the line themselves. Here we can illustrate with an example from one of the most intransigent. Later in this chapter we will meet Francis Atterbury, a clergyman who would become the Tories' chief spokesmen on ecclesiastical affairs in the late 1690s.[122] In 1692, however, he preached before Queen Mary on the anniversary of the 1660 restoration. For the bulk of the performance, Atterbury merely outlined the good Christian's duty to give thanks to God for blessings. At the end of the sermon, however, he turned what could have been a simple Tory assertion of Stuart legitimacy into an endorsement of the 1689 revolution, using William's war against France to perform the trick. Atterbury said the English must be grateful for 1660, but their duty to give thanks for the return of monarchy had recently been overshadowed by the even greater obligation to celebrate the new rulers' victory over the French fleet at La Hogue. Borrowing the Williamite language of an international crusade, the preacher said God had blessed 'Their Majesties Forces with a great and signal Victory over the most haughty and insolent of Enemies'. He had given hopes of an end 'to the Destruction of the Destroyer', supported the king and queen's throne, and strengthened 'the Hands of Their Allies'.[123]

Tory endorsement of the court's polemic suggests how they came to accept 1689, but there is even stronger evidence from their own arguments to persuade sceptical sections of their party. As they tried to preventing a haemorrhage to Jacobitism, they produced a burst of pamphlets which formed part of the contemporary 'allegiance controversy' which debated the nature and rights of William's accession. Tory contributions to this debate attempted to prove that accepting a new ruler was consistent with their old principles,

120 Claydon, *William III . . . revolution*, esp. ch. 4; Tony Claydon, *William III: profiles in power* (Harlow, 2002), pp. 134–43.

121 Tony Claydon, 'Protestantism, universal monarchy, and Christendom in William's war propaganda, 1689–1697', in Esther Mijers and David Onnekink, eds., *Redefining William III* (Aldershot, 2007), pp. 125–42.

122 See below, p. 340.

123 Francis Atterbury, *A sermon before the queen at Whitehall, May 29, 1692* (1692), pp. 29–31.

and made extensive use of the foreign godly as they did so. One of the most active writers was Thomas Long. As we shall see, Long had been a Tory stalwart under Charles II, but he accepted William in 1689 and addressed a string of works at those who baulked.[124] In these, the author stressed the revolution had not granted subjects the right to oppose their rulers. The new king should be accepted because James had abdicated, because William had conquered the country and was now in *de facto* control, and because people should always accept a providential rescue from oppression.[125] Long also argued, however, that the principle of non-resistance – whilst nearly always holding good – had exceptions in extreme conditions, and particularly that it could not logically apply if rulers were bent on the utter destruction of his subjects. Non-resistance saved people from the horrors of anarchic rebellion, yet if a Satanic tyrant was attacking them, it no longer preserved them from a worse situation and it must be (very temporarily) modified. Of course, the difficulty with Long's position was that James had not been extirpating his people. He had, arguably, infringed their constitution; but there had been no massacre which might possibly be worse than anarchy. So to make his argument about 1688 stand, Long needed proof that James was more threatening than he appeared. He had to show the king was merely in the early stages of a campaign which would lead to destruction, or that he was already involved in a wider oppression which, for the moment, had its worst effects elsewhere. Of course, Long found this evidence in the plight of Protestants and Christians abroad. James had to be removed because he was allied with a French king who *was* currently crushing the godly on the continent, and planned to do so in England. The English could throw him off now because although they had so far suffered little, they were part of international spiritual communities which were being actively persecuted.

Thus Long stressed the plight of the international reformation. Reminding readers of previous Catholic oppressions in Holland, La Rochelle, Savoy, Paris, Ulster and Scotland, he argued that no sane person would have insisted on non-resistance to them, and the same surely applied today as the French king exercised 'barbarous Cruelties' upon Huguenots.[126] With Louis imposing 'Popery and Slavery' on 'the Protestant Nations throughout Europe' – and with 'the Protestant Cause . . . almost desperate' – the English had a right to defend themselves.[127] They could take action 'against such violent and

[124] See below, p. 291.

[125] [Thomas Long], *A resolution of certain quaeries concerning submission* (1689); [Thomas Long], *Reflections on a late book entitled the case of allegiance consider'd* (1689); [Thomas Long], *A full answer to all the popular objections that have yet appeared for not taking the oath* (1689); [Thomas Long], *The historian unmask'd* (1689).

[126] [Long], *Full answer*, p. 6. Long refered to cruelties abroad throughout his pamphlets.

[127] [Long], *Resolution*, pp. 55–61.

illegal attempts as were made, not only against our selves, but against the whole Protestant interest throughout all *Europe*, having such dreadful instances of Persecution in the neighbouring Nations of *France* and *Piedmont*'.[128] Nor should the English worry simply because they were Protestants. Louis' campaign for universal monarchy made them part of a wider Christendom which feared for its survival, so Long noted the struggle in which all non-French powers were involved. He reminded readers that 'almost all the Princes of *Christendom*, do joyn to prevent the ambitious design of *France*'; and that all '(except only France, who aspires to Universal Monarchy) have owned our King and Queen as rightful Soveraigns'.[129] Interestingly too, Long countered suggestions that one must bear tyrants as punishments from God by showing the doleful consequences such a doctrine would have for the Christian faith as a whole. On these grounds, he pointed out, 'it would not be lawful for Christians to fight against those *Turks* and *Tartars* which invade *Christendom*'.[130]

It is true that Long was an anomalous case in the Tory writings of the allegiance controversy. He had been prepared to modify absolute rejection of resistance in extreme circumstances, and this was further than many Tories could go.[131] Yet examining other contributors to the allegiance debate – ones who never wobbled over subjects' passivity – we find the international reformation and Christendom remained important in supporting legal arguments. A crucial example is William Sherlock. This cleric and polemicist spent months after the prince of Orange's invasion agonising over whether he could swear allegiance to this newcomer, and when he decided he could, explained himself in one of the most controversial pamphlets of the era. In *The case of allegiance due to sovereign powers* (1691), Sherlock squared his conscience on the strictly *de facto* grounds that scripture, prudence and reason ordered us to respect authorities once they were in settled possession of power; though he found this caused extended debate, with Jacobites blaming him for apostasy, and Whigs for implying James must be obeyed if he ever got back to the throne.[132] Ironically, however, *de facto* principles may not have been the most important consideration in Sherlock's conversion. In 1692, in a pamphlet arguing against those who might support a Jacobite invasion, the author suggested a different and more pressing reason for upholding the new regime. Arguing in the first section of the work that James' return would lead to French-style persecutions, Sherlock expanded his concern abroad,

128 Ibid., p. 47. 129 [Long], *Full answer*, p. 50; [Long], *Historian unmask'd*, p. 60.
130 [Long], *Full answer*, p. 52.
131 It can be hard to say if Long's pamphlets were Tory or Whig: Goldie, 'Revolution of 1689', described *Resolution* as 'very moderate tory', and *Historian unmask'd* as treading a 'via media', pp. 549–50.
132 Goldie, 'Revolution of 1689', p. 557, counted thirty-one Whig or Jacobite replies.

observing that 'what I have said hitherto concerns only *England*'. If one were to take a properly full view, he insisted, one must 'look a little further abroad, and consider, what a fatal Instance a French Conquest of *England* will have upon the Affairs of *Europe*'.[133] What followed was a series of stark warnings about the international reformation and about Christendom. William should be supported lest the French monarch become 'the sole and absolute *Monarch* of the *West*'. If Louis ever got to that position it was 'easie to read the Fate of *Protestants*'.[134] To fight for James was therefore to fight for 'Heresy and Idolatry against the true Faith', for '*Anti-christ*, and against Christ', and to bring 'a Persecution upon his faithful Disciples'.[135] In sum, the English must uphold the post-revolution regime because they had duties beyond their own country. Although 'Subjects of *England*', they had 'Obligations to Mankind, and to other Princes, as well as to our own'.[136]

Sherlock was not alone among solid Tories in bolstering *de facto* arguments with William's European role. The writer Thomas Bainbrigg countered Jacobite interpretations of non-resistance by stating one could accept a providential deliverance, and one had a duty to obey powers which established themselves. Yet he also celebrated the revolution's victory for the international reformation. William had ensured that 'the Northern Heresie' (the pope's name for Protestantism) had not been extirpated, and in accepting his protection the English had done no more than French Huguenots had when seeking refuge with foreign Protestants.[137] Similarly Edward Fowler (not yet the Whig of later ecclesiastical disputes) defended those clergy who had transferred allegiance to William. He did so on the grounds that the prince had conquered the country and was now the effective authority, but he also pointed out that supporting James would help Louis, a man who had the same plans for the English as for the distressed Huguenots and was 'the Greatest and most Formidable Enemy, his three Kingdoms, and all Protestant Nations, have in the World'.[138] Gilbert Burnet provided another example of internationalist Toryism. Burnet was not a Tory himself, but adopted a Tory persona as he tried to convince the clergy of his Salisbury diocese to fall in behind the new regime, and he recognised concern for the reformation and Christendom was a cogent part of his pose. Thus he told his colleagues William was legitimate because he was providential and was now in possession of the government. Yet it was also clear the prince had rescued England from Louis' designs against all Protestants and other Christian kingdoms, and that this was a further reason to accept him. The three great terrors

133 [William Sherlock], *A letter to a friend concerning a French invasion* (1692), p. 22.
134 Ibid., p. 23. 135 Ibid., pp. 24–5. 136 Ibid., p. 26.
137 [Thomas Bainbrigg], *Seasonable reflections on a late pamphlet entitled a history of passive obedience* (1690), pp. 27–8.
138 [Fowler], *Vindication*, p. 7

defeated by the revolution were 'Popish Tyranny, An Irish Conquest and Massacre, and French Barbarity and Cruelty', and these terms were printed in heavy Gothic type, as if their very listing were not scary enough.[139] In the light of such a cosmopolitan horror, William had had a right to intervene because a country in which he had an interest had been about to slip into the hands of a 'Foreign Jurisdiction'; though whether that meant falling under the pope's universal spiritual tyranny, or Louis' temporal one, was left fertilely obscure.[140]

By now, we have perhaps made a sufficiently solid case for the role of Europe in the Tory conversion at the revolution. If Steven Pincus is right, they cooled to James when he did nothing to contain Louis. If I am right, they finally abandoned him in an atmosphere where the pressing danger to the international reformation from popery, and the freedom of all Christian states from Versailles, was constantly being expressed. Although they had sound legal and constitutional arguments to explain their shift of position, many backed these with appeals to follow William in his pan-Protestant crusade against popery and his leadership of all Christendom against universal monarchy. If all this is correct, it explains why Whigs and Tories could work so closely together in 1689. Whigs had always believed the English could bend their succession to help the godly everywhere. Tories might still baulk at telling the English people they could do the bending, but if the constitution got bent anyway, they could celebrate if this helped those wider communities of Christians. Put like this, it is easier to understand the realignment. Tories adjusted their domestic political doctrines, but their underlying concern for Europe remained intact from the exclusion crisis. When accepting William, therefore, they were altering second-order principles, not fundamental ones. James mistook the Tories' loyalty to the Stuarts for their key philosophy: it is important that historians do not make the same error.

EUROPE AND CONSTITUTIONAL DISPUTES UNDER THE LATE STUARTS

Sadly for political harmony, the rapprochement between Whigs and Tories did not last long. Although the parties had worked together in the crisis of 1689, tensions between them survived – and constitutional cudgels were soon grasped again. Most of the blame lay with the Whigs. From the moment William began to govern, and made it clear he wanted to include both parties in his administration, the old exclusionists nursed resentment. Some had hoped the new king would be their man and allow them to punish their

139 Gilbert Burnet, *A pastoral letter writ by the . . . lord bishop of Sarum* (1689), p. 4
140 Ibid., p. 20.

enemies, so when William failed to join in their vendetta, they attempted to proscribe Tory understandings of the revolution. A polemical campaign suggested that conquest, providential and *de facto* theories denied the rights of Englishmen to depose tyranny; and that since they would technically demand support for the exiled Stuarts if they ever fought back to power, these notions proved the Tories were Jacobites in disguise.[141] Obviously this was an attack on opponents' loyalty and reputation. It was not, however, mere name-calling. It was linked to consistent Whig pressure to force all government servants to swear that William was the 'rightful' and 'lawful' king. This was something which Tories who accepted the revolution on *de facto* grounds could not do, and which had been dropped as a requirement in 1689 to broaden support for the new regime. The Whigs' campaign thus threatened to exclude Tories from office: establishing the precise constitutional basis for the change of monarch became a game of high stakes.[142]

Of course, given Whig strategy here, much of the debate would be about the English legal system, about English history and about Englishmen's rights. To attack the Tories, their opponents insisted the country's constitution was a contract in which royal power was conditional on respecting the liberties of subjects. To deny this, Whigs asserted, was to misrepresent the powers of parliament and the principles of common law, it was to negate past statements of monarchical duties such as Magna Carta or coronation oaths and it was to reduce free Englishmen to chattel slaves.[143] Yet whilst much Whig polemic had a domestic focus, not all did. Since Williamite Tories placed so much stress on defending the international reformation and Christendom, Whigs targeted them by demonstrating one could not uphold these entities whilst denying people the right to reject rulers. Supporting the godly abroad would mean acknowledging their revolts against popish antichrists and universal monarchs: Tories were therefore contradicting themselves if they pretended to be good Christians (and especially if they stressed they cared about the European reformation) whilst refusing to contemplate popular resistance.

In the years immediately after the Glorious Revolution, the Whigs deployed a number of arguments to prove that solidarity with foreign faithful meant accepting a right to rebellion. Most obviously, they suggested

141 Goldie, 'Revolution of 1689', is the best guide.

142 For campaigns to proscribe *de facto* understandings: Claydon, *William III: profiles*, pp. 95–6.

143 These arguments were at their most partisan in attacks on Sherlock, implying his *de facto* support for William meant he was only a fair weather friend: e.g. *Sherlock against Sherlock* (1690); *Sherlokianus delineatus* (1690); *A dialogue between Dr Sherlock, the king of France, the Great Turk, and Dr. Oates* (1691); *The trimming court divine, or reflexions on Dr Sherlock's book* (1690); *Some modest remarks on Dr Sherlock's new book about the case of allegiance* (1691).

the present condition of the European reformation meant Protestants must resist. Louis was bent on extirpating the true faith: if the English were not prepared to let this happen, they would have to support those who defied his authority, even if he were their ruler. Thus England must stand alongside the Huguenots and the other reformed Christians caught in the path of Bourbon expansion. France's Protestants were subjects of Louis, but nobody could expect them to stand meekly by as their lives were destroyed. Whigs also insisted that accepting 1688 as a legitimate popular rebellion was essential to the future of European Protestantism. The only hope of containing French popery was to put England in the scales against it, but one could only guarantee the country would stay on that side of the balance if the revolution were an irreversible forfeiture of the throne by the Stuarts. Risking a Jacobite restoration, as Tory ideology did, would crush ancient English liberties, but would also kill the hopes of the reformed abroad and condemn them to the horrors those in France had already suffered.[144]

Whigs therefore insisted the immediate fate of the reformation demanded acceptance of rights against rulers, but they tied their doctrine even more closely to the European entity by showing resistance was inherent in its history. As Protestantism had begun in revolt against the temporal power of the medieval church, and as it had involved defiance of Catholic rulers, Whigs insisted all its leading exponents had accepted that people might have to throw off the authority of ungodly magistrates. To object to this would mean breaking a longstanding Protestant consensus, and to show this several writers listed the early reformers who had endorsed popular rights. Prefiguring modern scholars of political thought, who have charted the origins of resistance theory to the arguments of the first Lutherans, they cited the European pantheon of heroes established by historians of the reformation and claimed these men denied magisterial absolutism as firmly as medieval theology.[145] Thus according to Timothy Wilson, Luther had inevitably alienated the powerful men of his world. Those who lost dominion denounced him as the 'Trumpeter of Rebellion', and this demonstrated that spreading God's truth and defying authority would often have to be the same thing. Similarly, the radical (and admittedly somewhat eccentric) Edward Stephens suggested

[144] E.g. *K. William or K. Lewis* (1689); *A defence of their majesties King William and Queen Mary* (1689) – set the transfer of allegiance in the context of France's European persecutions; *The new oath of allegiance justified* (1689), p. 4 – linked constitutional arguments to the interest of 'the Reformed Religion, throughout *Europe*'; *The fate of France* (1690), p. 3 and *passim* – excused English 'rebellion' on the same grounds as the Huguenots' resistance. Samuel Johnson, *An argument proving that the abrogation of King James* (1692) – five editions by 1693 – savaged conquest theories because they gave those invaded by Louis no rights against him, pp. 22–3, 30.

[145] E.g. Quentin Skinner, *The foundations of modern political thought*, vol. 2 (Cambridge, 1978), chs. 1–3.

'divers Reformed Churches' had rejected passive suffering under authority 'upon great deliberation in their own Case'.[146] Meanwhile an answer to Abednego Sellar's *History of passive obedience* (a Jacobite tract claiming the early reformers were united against resistance) listed the sixteenth-century rebellions by the Protestants of Germany, France and Holland; whilst other anonymous pamphleteers marvelled at rejections of a contractual view of monarchy in the face of arguments 'taken from the Example of . . . Reformed Religion throughout *Europe*', or given that 'Protestants in all Ages did Resist their Evil and Destructive Princes'.[147]

Perhaps most powerfully, the translator of Pierre Jurieu's *Judgement upon the question of defending our religion by arms* asked England to fall into line with continental Protestants. Jurieu was a leading spokesman for the exiled French Huguenots: introducing his defence of the right to use force against anti-Christian oppressors, his translator took him as a representative of all Europeans and attacked Englishmen who disagreed for forfeiting their place in the reformation. We should, the writer insisted, 'be glad to hear what foreign Churches say of those Doctrines which are disputed amongst us'. 'He is an enemy of the Church of *England*,' the author went on, 'who would set it up against the Reformed Churches of *France* and *Germany*, and of the *Northern* Crowns.' Truly getting into his stride, the translator presented the whole history of Protestantism as series of reciprocal aids by godly nations to those who had demoted papist rulers. In the sixteenth century, the English church had 'assisted the foreign Protestants, both with their Prayers and Purses'. Given this, Dutch help for England in 1688 was a 'happy day of Retribution, where we were to eat that Bread which was cast upon the Waters an hundred Years before'. England could now again return the favour, since they were ruled by the 'Head of the Protestant Interest' whose work spreading true religion through Europe would make him 'another British Constantine to the World'.[148]

The image of reciprocal help against oppressors brings us to another refinement of Whig arguments for resistance. Not only should the English defend popular rights because Protestants did so abroad, they should do so to uphold the original principles of their own church. As a good Protestant communion, the English establishment had originally accepted resistance to support the faith; the doctrine of passive obedience had been an intrusion

146 Timothy Wilson, *Conscience satisfied in a cardinal and loyal submitting to the present government* (1690), p. 20; [Edward Stephens], *Important questions of government* (1689), p. 7.

147 [Abednego Sellar], *The history of passive obedience since the reformation* (1689); *The history of self-defence* (1689); *The new oath of allegiance justified* (1689), p. 4; *Political aphorisms, or the true maxims of government display'd* (1690), title page.

148 *Monsieur Jurieu's judgement upon the question of defending our religion with arms* (1689), translator's preface.

of the mid-seventeenth century. It had come in with the Catholic-leaning Laudians, so Tories who upheld absolute authority had been seduced by a perverted worldview which had corrupted political as well as ecclesiological thought.[149] Whigs maintained true anglicanism welcomed godly rebellion in Europe, and built a canon of English approval from early examples. So, Elizabeth had opened her reign by helping the Calvinist Scots throw off the papist Queen Mary. Later she had sent help to the Dutch Protestants rebelling against Philip of Spain; she had lent her forces to French Huguenots battling against the Catholic court in Paris; and she had succoured the Genevans as they fended off the duke of Savoy. In several of these cases, the clergy of the English church had supported the monarch by collecting funds to send to those in revolt. In the early seventeenth century too, English Protestants had supported foreign rebels. James had recognised the United Provinces of the Netherlands even though the new state had been born in revolution, and (remarkably for a man who would soon fall under the spell of absolutistism) even Charles I had granted the Dutch trading privileges. Still more surprisingly, Charles had sent help to the Protestants of La Rochelle when they excluded the French king's armies from their city. Even a monarch who would be executed by rebels had not discountenanced rebellion if it served the godly cause.

Rehearsal of this canon was common in Whig contributions to the allegiance controversy. In an *Examination of the scruples of those who refuse to take the oath*, a writer who spent the first section of his work arguing that government was a reciprocal contract, moved on to attack Tory interpretations of the church's political doctrine. The establishment's Tudor founders had in fact 'taken the part of *Luther, Melancthon* and other Reformers' who had allowed resistance under certain circumstances; and had given this practical expression in their support for those suffering abroad. Under Elizabeth the clergy had voted subsidies to relieve 'the States of *Holland*, when they shook off the Yoke of *Philip* the Second, as well as the Protestants of *France*, who were oppressed and persecuted contrary to the Laws'.[150] Similarly, the author of the *Case of allegiance in our present circumstances* reported that the true opinion of the Tudor church could be discerned in the money it gave to 'the *Scotch, French* and *Dutch* in their defence of their *Liberties* and *Religion* against the unjust oppressions of their Princes', whilst the veteran Whig writer Samuel Johnson (who was only released from gaol in the spring of 1689, having been incarcerated for his exclusion era efforts) remembered the clergy's applause for Elizabeth as she assisted 'the Scots, Dutch and French

149 E.g. Timothy Wilson, *The vanity and falsity of the history of passive obedience detected* (1690).

150 *An examination of the scruples of those who refuse to take the oath* (1689), pp. 18–19.

in their several Defences of themselves against *Tyranny* and *Oppression*'.[151] In further instances, we have already seen Pierre Jurieu's translator refer to early English help to European Protestants, whilst a Dutch defence of 1688 – translated by Whigs for its assertion that kings were in a position of trust which they could abuse – thanked the English church for its earlier solidarity with reformed Holland.[152]

At this point it is worth repeating the Whigs did not base their whole case around the godly abroad. Their chief charge against the Tories remained their enemies' dangerous misunderstanding of the English constitution, which – if unchallenged – would leave subjects defenceless against tyranny. Nevertheless, the close association of international Protestantism and political resistance was a notable sub-theme of Whig polemic, and it was backed by another European discourse of exclusion vintage. As Whigs stressed that Tory objections to resistance encouraged Jacobites, they warned this promoted France's universal monarchy. Unless subjects were allowed to rise against masters, they argued, un-Christian hegemony threatened the whole continent. James' dependence on Versailles had turned him into Louis' chief lieutenant; if the English had not been allowed to remove him, the confederacy against France would have been fatally weakened, the liberties of the continent would be lost, and so would Christians' rights to live in peace and security.

One of the clearest illustrations of this line of thought was penned by the physician turned journalist, James Welwood. In 1689 King James went to Ireland to lead the forces which had remained loyal to him there. When he issued a declaration claiming his moderate conduct in the western kingdom showed how wrong his opponents in England had been about him, Welwood exploded in passionate refutation.[153] Much of this denied James' moderation. Welwood listed the sufferings of Irish subjects and implied such misrule justified England's action against the deposed ruler. Much of it also stressed international Protestant solidarity in the face of this popish threat. William, Welwood was sure, had been backed by the reformed churches of Europe: they had been clear James was an agent of a planned general extirpation of the reformation which had already started in France and Savoy. The threat, however, went wider than this, since behind James lay Louis. The French king's ambition endangered all Christendom, and Welwood deployed the standard anathemas of universal monarchy against him. So Louis' treatment of his own subjects was so barbarous it disgusted the faithful of whatever

[151] *The case of allegiance in our present circumstances considered* (1689), p. 33; [Samuel Johnson], *Reflections on the history of passive obedience* (1689), p. 3.

[152] *Monsiuer Jurieu's judgement*, translator's preface; *A defence of their majesties*, pp. 35–6.

[153] *A declaration of his most sacred majesty, King James II, to all his loving subjects* (Dublin, 1689).

confession. Louis had outdone the pagan emperors Nero and Julian in his persecution of the cross, and the pope had called him '*the Common Enemy of the Christian Part of Europe*'.[154] Consequently it had not only been Protestants who had cheered William in 1688. Moreover, everyone recognised Louis's bloody expansion was a threat to the continent's moral order. All the states of Europe were now allying to 'bridle *Louis le Grand* within his proper *Boundaries*'; the new king of England was the great supporter of their liberties; and 'in conjunction with his Allies' would be best able to contain 'that *insupportable Enemy of Christendom*'.[155] James, meanwhile, as a stooge of the French project, was described as an infidel challenge to the whole faith. His methods against his people were a 'strange Essay in *Mahometan Government*' and his demands to absolute power were 'beyond what the Great *Turk* claims'.[156]

Other Whigs were just as convinced that William's fight against Louis justified his accession in England. The lawyer Matthew Tindal, for instance, was a passionate advocate of the 1688 revolution who stressed consent as the basis of all authority, but nevertheless lionised the new king as France's enemy.[157] Similarly, the moderate Whig author of *Just principles of complying with the new oaths* rounded out a constitutional argument for a right of rebellion against a 'ruining prince' by stressing 1688 was a salvation from France. Just as Thomas Long had needed stronger evidence that James was destroying his subjects than the king's own actions provided, this pamphleteer emphasised that the monarch's dependence on Versailles ensured disaster was only a matter of time. The old Stuart's 'Combination with the common Enemy of Christendom, ruinous to the State of *Europe*, and the Protestant Party of *Europe*, may justly denominate Him a *ruining Prince* at a Superlative rate'.[158] We find a further example in the writing of Richard Claridge. This Quaker schoolmaster made an unlikely Whig (the Society of Friends had benefited from the indulgences granted by James, and some of its leaders lent towards Jacobitism), but Claridge published defences of William's government which mixed insistence that authority was a contractual trust with horror of France. James had been impeached for '*Arbitrariness, breach of Contract selling us for Slaves to a Foreign Prince*' [by which he meant Louis], and ultimately for participating in Versailles' 'great *Plot*' to dominate the continent.[159]

154 [James Welwood], *An answer to the late King James' declaration* (1689), p. 9.
155 Ibid., pp. 23–4. 156 Ibid., pp. 7, 29.
157 [Matthew Tindal], *An essay concerning obedience to the supreme powers* (1694), pp. 66–7.
158 *Just principles of complying with the new oath of allegiance* (1689), pp. 4, 14.
159 [Richard Claridge], *A defence of the present government under King William* (1689), pp. 6, 8.

Whig rhetorical strategy in the early 1690s thus demonstrated the continuing purchase of the international dimension in their constitutional polemic. But it also set the terms of their stance in the set-piece debates of Queen Anne's reign. Beyond the immediate allegiance controversy, Whigs continued to lambast Tories as closet Jacobites, and their accusations concentrated on the two great controversies of the early eighteenth century. The first was the trial of Dr Henry Sacheverell in 1710. Sacheverell was a church of England minister and Oxford don, who burst onto the political stage at the dawn of the eighteenth century. In Queen Anne's early years, he upheld her right to the throne, but as a good (if choleric) Tory he had refused to accept that that right was founded on popular resistance in 1688 and had become outrageously outspoken against the Whigs and their nonconformist allies.[160] Preaching at London's St Paul's cathedral on 5 November 1709, he went too far. Whilst most of his sermon denounced religious dissenters (of which more later), some also attacked resistance theorists as 'false brethren', including figures he came close to naming among the queen's ministers. These men, Sacheverell claimed, pretended to support the post-1688 monarchy but actually promoted a dangerous insubordination which would overthrow it.[161] Incensed, the Whig ministry moved straight to the party's tactic of labelling enemies Jacobites. Articles of impeachment were introduced in the House of Commons, and these – whilst condemning his incendiary attacks on nonconformists and his seditious blackening of the queen's servants – also accused him of delegitimating the 1688 revolution. To deny resistance, the articles implied, was to remove the only justification for William's accession, and so for the arrangements by which the current queen had come to the throne.[162] The stage was therefore set for a show trial before the House of Lords, and one of the most extraordinary bursts of party vitriol in our whole period. From the moment Sacheverell's sermon was published, political discussion was about little else.[163] A slew of pamphlets (so large the Victorians assembled a bibliography) debated the issues involved; London mobs rioted in support of the doctor; and popular interest in the trial proved so great that

[160] His most discussed works were Henry Sacheverell, *The political union* (1702); Henry Sacheverell, *The character of a low church man* (1702); Henry Sacheverell, *The nature, observation and measures of conscience* (1706); and Henry Sacheverell, *The communication of sin* (1709).

[161] Henry Sacheverell, *The perils of false brethren, both in church and state: set forth in sermon . . . 5th November, 1709* (1709). This received multiple editions and was probably the best circulated tract of the late Stuart period: Goldie, 'Tory political thought', pp. 36–42.

[162] The articles were widely publicised: e.g. *The articles of impeachment exhibited against Dr Henry Sacheverell* (1710), pp. 1–2 for the preamble and first article (which connected denying resistance with treason).

[163] *The mischief of prejudice, or some impartial thoughts on Dr Sacheverell's sermon* (1710), p. 3, noted 'all the talk here [in London] is about one Dr Sacheverell'.

Sir Christopher Wren was hired to design galleries of seating in Westminster Hall.[164]

Throughout the fandango, Whigs remained true to their allegiance controversy arguments. Numerous pamphlets insisted support for godly rebels abroad was essential to English Protestantism; one even consisted of letters from James I and Charles I justifying the earlier king's recognition of the rebellious Dutch, and his son's aid to the Huguenot rebels of La Rochelle.[165] The parliamentary case against Sacheverell was couched in similar terms. Speaking at the trial on the article accusing the preacher of denying legitimate resistance, Gilbert Burnet gave a lengthy and international history of Protestant insubordination, citing the precedents of James and Charles, adding Elizabeth's help to Holland and the Huguenots, and arguing that although the anglican homilies which Sacheverell had quoted seemed to oppose rebellion, they must be read in the context of their author's other writings. The homilies, Burnet reminded the House, had been composed by the Elizabethan theologian John Jewel. In themselves they might seem Tory, but Jewel's more famous *Apology for the church of England* had excused the Scots for rising against their popish queen and had praised Luther, Melancthon and French Protestant nobles for resisting oppression. In the light of this, Burnet explained, Jewel's homilies must be cited carefully. They only forbade resistance to pious monarchs who executed the law; they did not apply to ungodly tyrants.[166] Burnet's episcopal colleague, William Talbot of Oxford, backed his points. Yes, said Talbot, the bible usually ruled against resistance. Yet all general precepts had exceptions, and one could therefore rebel if conditions became unbearable. Applying this to the history of the last two centuries, Talbot insisted Catholic treatment of the reformed in many places in Europe had been intolerable, and that the help Elizabeth, James and Charles had given to Scots, French and Dutch proved they understood this. It is true the bishop's coverage of these stories was brief, but this actually underlined the importance of the Protestant international in Whig resistance theory. Talbot explained he had not expanded on cases of English help to godly rebels because they were very well known and he was sure someone would detail them the course of the debate, and – of course – Burnet's long

164 Holmes, *Trial of Dr Sacheverell*; Geoffrey Holmes, 'The Sacheverell riots', in Paul Slack, ed., *Rebellion, popular protest and the social order in early modern England* (Cambridge, 1984), pp. 232–62; Falconer Madan, *A bibliography of Dr Henry Sacheverell* (Oxford, 1884).

165 *The judgement of K. James the first, and King Charles the first against non-resistance* (1710). Also: *A speech without doors* (1710), p. 7; *A prelude to the trial of skill between Sacheverellism and the constitution* (1710), pp. 22–3.

166 *The bishop of Salisbury's and the bishop of Oxford's speeches in the House of Lords* (1710), pp. 5–10.

account justified his confidence.[167] Still adhering to well-worn themes, the anti-Sacheverell hysteria was also marked by concern about France's universal monarchy. Polemicists spoke of Louis' encroachments and cruelties, and then accused Sacheverell of belonging to a French fifth column. He was, they insisted, determined to undermine English faith in their governors by delegitimating the post-revolutionary regimes, and he was paving the path for French invasion.[168] William Bisset, Sacheverell's most vehement and popular detractor, made such accusations the meat of his polemic.[169]

The second great constitutional battle of the early eighteenth century was even more directly connected to the succession. In 1710, war-weariness and a backlash against Sacheverell's victimisation sank the Whig ministry. The preacher escaped with a laughably light penalty, his subsequent progress through England demonstrated a surge in support for the Tories, and this was confirmed in the general election the same year. This victory proved a mixed blessing, however, as it swept into the Commons some of the sections of the party which had had doubts about 1689. Opportunistically led by Henry St John, Viscount Bolingbroke, most of these men were loyal enough to Anne as a good Stuart – but they wondered whether her death might be an opportunity to restore the old royal line and avoid an unknown German dynasty. Although committed Jacobites may not have been a majority of the parliamentary party, these men represented a strand of Tory opinion, and had to be conciliated by Robert Harley, the premier minister who needed Tory support to manage the Commons.[170] This, of course, gave Whigs a further chance to denigrate their rivals. In a final spat over the constitution, they seized on signs of Jacobite sympathies amongst their opponents, and once again accused them of regretting the revolution of 1688–9. After George I was successfully installed on the throne, they continued the tactic, using instances of Tory support for the Stuarts' 1715 invasion, and a further series of plots into the 1720s, to label their enemies traitors.

In all this, Whig concern for the Protestant international and a Christendom safe from France again loomed large. Many of the works celebrating

[167] Ibid., pp. 6–7 – pagination restarts at beginning of Talbot's speech.
[168] See *The cherubim with a flaming sword that appeared on the fifth of November last* (1709); *The history of Dr Sacheverell faithfully translated from the Paris Gazette* (1711).
[169] William Bisset, *The modern fanatick* (1710), esp. pp. 32–7 – ran through eleven editions in 1710 alone. Also William Bisset, *Remarks on Dr Sach——'s sermon to the cathedral of St Paul* [1709].
[170] Judging Jacobite strength is hard, as there was a spectrum of commitment. Certainly clear anti-Hanoverian sentiment was evident in the Tory press – e.g. [Francis Atterbury], *English advice to the freeholders of England* (1714); and leading Tories such as Bolingbroke worked for the exiled Stuarts after 1714. Yet there were also Hanoverian Tories, and some merely flirted with the romance of Jacobitism. For an assessment: Holmes, *British politics*, pp. 279–84. For the difficulties caused to Harley: Brian W. Hill, *Robert Harley* (New Haven, CT, 1988), chs. 14–15.

such victories over Jacobitism as George's arrival in England, or the defeat of the 1715 rebellion, set the threat in a European context. Whig-leaning sermons, for example, presented the Hanoverian succession as a defence against the continent-wide dangers of popery and French hegemony, and they implied Tories were trying to undermine England as the only powerful bulwark against these.[171] Perhaps the most popular presentation of the case (it sold multiple editions in its first year) was John Toland's *State-anatomy of Great Britain* (1717). Savaging Tories as absolutists who had cheered on the recent Jacobite revolt, this also accused them of turning their back on distressed Protestants of the continent, of having a narrow view of the reformation which excluded many of its foreign branches, and of obstructing King's George's chief aims in external policy: '*to support the Protestant interest everywhere*' and '*to keep the balance of* Europe *equal*'.[172] Toland's work elicited responses but was not quite as controversial as Richard Steele's *Crisis*, published four years earlier.[173] This not only sold 40,000 copies, and sparked passionate press debate, but got its author expelled from the Commons.[174] Written at a time when Tory enthusiasm for a German dynasty was genuinely debatable, this tract listed the statutes enshrining the Hanoverian settlement, but then questioned whether such legal guarantees would be enough if Tories were in the ascendant. The resounding 'no' was thoroughly international. 'Our condition cannot be judged,' he insisted, 'but from the Circumstances of the Affairs of *Europe* in general, as well as of *Great Britain* in particular.'[175] What followed was a panicked description of the progress of Louis XIV and of Catholicism across the continent, together with reminders of their past enormities, and horror that Tory-led England was doing nothing to stop them. Thus peace had been made too quickly with France. The result was a weakened Protestant interest and a Bourbon house bidding 'fairer for an Universal Monarchy, and to engross the whole Trade of *Europe*, than it did before the War'.[176] Similarly, Englishmen were openly flirting with Catholic successors. They did this even though neighbouring popish rulers had recently tortured and banished Protestants, and 'hot and terrible' persecutions in France and Savoy proved popery would never change its spots.[177]

[171] E.g. William Talbot, *A sermon preach'd at the coronation of King George . . . October the 20th, 1714* (1714), esp. pp. 14–17; William Wake, *A sermon preached before the king in St James' chapel, upon the first of August, 1715* (1715), esp. pp. 22–3; White Kennett, *A thanksgiving sermon for the blessing of God, in suppressing the late unnatural rebellion . . . Thursday the 7th June, 1716* (1716), esp. pp. 18–22.

[172] [John Toland], *The state-anatomy of Great Britain* [1717], pp. 14–19, 53–5, 60–5.

[173] For responses to Toland: *A farther argument against enobling foreigners* (1717); William Somervile, *Reasons against repealing the test and corporation acts* (1717).

[174] Wittan Colhoun, 'Steele, Richard', *ODNB*, LII:358–64, esp. 362.

[175] Richard Steele, *The crisis* (1714), p. 29. [176] Ibid., pp. 29–31. [177] Ibid., pp. 34–5.

So, for thirty years after the Glorious Revolution, Whigs stuck to such a standard constitutional polemic that rehearsing it becomes tedious. Tories, they insisted, denied the possibility of political resistance, and this led straight to Jacobitism. Supporting the exiled Stuart dynasty, they posed a threat to local liberties, but their treachery spread wider to betray continental entities. By stressing absolute obedience, Tories broke an international Protestant consensus on the right to resist ungodly rulers; they left the faithful abroad with no legitimate hope in the face of blasphemous oppressors, and – by aiding the French who wished to restore the Stuarts to create a puppet regime in Britain – they abetted the common enemy of all Christians.

In responding to these arguments, some Tories flatly denied their logic. A section of the party was so disgusted at Whig rhetoric that it wrote England out of close involvement with the European reformation, or refused to accept that France was a threat to Christendom. This was essentially the reaction of the Jacobites themselves, who continued to paint the Protestant Dutch as the greatest threat to England, but it also affected the wings of the party which had accepted 1689. So some of Sacheverell's supporters disputed whether earlier help for foreign Protestants could be cited to support popular rights. For example, one pamphleteer who answered Burnet's speech on the first article of impeachment drew a distinction between subjects' duties to rulers, and relations between independent princes. Whilst subjects must always obey, other rulers had no obligation to uphold authority elsewhere, and it was on this principle of sovereign autonomy (not because Protestant solidarity excused rebellion) that Elizabeth, James and Charles had aided the Scots, French and Dutch.[178] Other writers went further. Criticising Talbot's speech on the impeachment, they simply suggested England's earlier support for resistance had been a mistake. For one, decisions to intervene abroad had been made without proper thought. The monarchs had not acted 'strictly by the view of the Lawfulness' of what they did, but had been swayed by political convenience.[179] Another used a familiar metaphor to put the point. The actions of Elizabeth, James and Charles had been so unprincipled they could create no precedents: princes, like Shaftesbury in the exclusion crisis, were too often watermen, looking one way as they rowed another.[180] Meanwhile, Luke Milbourne, whose intemperate pulpit attacks on rebellion got him entangled in the Sacheverell controversy, boldly asserted God punished foreign Protestants who rebelled against their masters. When the Bohemians had risen against the Habsburgs in 1618, they had lost 'their *Religion* and

[178] *Some considerations humbly offer'd to the right reverend bishop of Salisbury* (1710), pp. 27–30.
[179] *An answer to the arguments in the lord bishop of Oxford's speech* (1710), p. 18.
[180] *A serious answer to the lord bishop of Oxford's speech* (1710), p. 15

Liberty together'.[181] The same had happened to the Hungarians in recent decades, and the effects of revolt in France had been so terrible that leading Huguenot divines now declared against all taking up of arms.[182] As for denials that France threatened universal monarchy, we have already seen this in Tory thought at the end of Anne's reign.[183] Within their account of foreign policy, Swift and others reanalysed the balance of power to acquit Versailles of ambition, but they took this beyond geopolitics to attack Whig smears on their constitutional position. Ridiculing Steele's contention that Tories supported a Stuart succession as part of a French plot for dominance, they insisted Louis was so far from such hegemony that the charge was fatuous. Swift satirised Whig dependence on a French/Stuart bogey, and portrayed a Christendom in stable equilibrium between Britain, France, Holland, Spain and Austria.[184] Another pamphleteer savaged Steele by praising the peace of Utrecht and pointing out that even though the Bourbons now had Spain they posed no danger, having simultaneously lost Catalonia, Naples, the Balearics, Sardinia, Milan, Gibraltar, Flanders, Newfoundland, Nova Scotia and Hudson's Bay.[185]

Yet for all the vigour of such Tory attacks, they were not representative of the party's position as a whole. We have seen that the Tories of the 1680s shared concerns about the Protestant international and Christendom, and only diverged from their rivals on the best way to support these. Outright denial of Whig assumptions about the continent would therefore strain Tories' founding principles, and few spokesmen wanted or dared to take so radical a step. Instead, they concurred that the revolution must be welcomed because it freed England to protect the faithful abroad, and only disagreed by insisting one did not have to endorse popular resistance to embrace this opportunity. This was the predominant response in the 1690s allegiance controversy: Tories stressed that *de facto*, providential and conquest arguments justified loyalty to William, but also argued support was due to the leader of the European reformation and the convenor of the Christian alliance against Louis.[186]

There was a similar pattern to the constitutional battles of the next reign. Examining Sacheverell's response to his impeachment, for instance, loyalty to the European mission of the post-revolutionary regimes remained prominent. It is true that Simon Harcourt, the accused's attorney at the trial, largely

181 Luke Milbourne, *The impiety and folly of resisting lawful governors by force in a sermon . . . thirtieth of January, 1710/11* (1711), p. 20.
182 Ibid., p. 24; Luke Milbourne, *The measures of resistance to the higher powers . . . in a sermon preached on January 30th, 1709/10* (1710), p. 31.
183 See above, pp. 195–6.
184 [Jonathan Swift], *The publick spirit of the Whigs* (2nd edn, 1714).
185 *Remarks on Mr Steele's 'Crisis' &c. by one of the clergy* (1714), p. 19.
186 See above, pp. 248–53.

ignored the continent in his philosophically constructed defence speech. He claimed extreme circumstances allowed exceptions to the principle of non-resistance, and that Sacheverell had tacitly acknowledged 1688–9 as an example.[187] Yet the cleric himself put stress elsewhere. Probably because he did not in truth share his lawyer's belief in exceptions to obedience, his own contribution to his defence asserted his principles meant unwavering support for the post-revolutionary rulers and that their policies on the continent were grounds to celebrate this. Important here was Sacheverell's use of a sermon he had delivered in 1702 which justified Anne's war with Louis. The accused cited this work in his initial response to impeachment; he quoted it at length in his speech at the trial; and it was republished in 1710 because it was so important to his case.[188] Referring to this sermon, Sacheverell reminded everyone he had portrayed Anne standing for Christian and Protestant values across Europe. In the words of his decade-old preaching, she was the providential punisher of an 'Idolatrous' enemy (the French king), whose constant infidelity endangered '*Publick Faith*', and whose 'Boundless and Insatiable Lust' threatened universal hegemony.[189] Beyond this backlist sermon, Sacheverell ended his trial speech with further nods to Europe. For example, he hoped Anne would outshine Elizabeth's glory abroad. Since the old queen's reputation rested on defending international Protestantism, this placed the present monarch in the same role and silently rebuked Tory writers who criticised the Tudors' foreign policy. He also said he supported the Hanoverian succession. Technically this was because it was the will of a sovereign he must not oppose, but it also recognised international solidarities of faith. He was acknowledging that a good Protestant ruler, even if a foreigner, would be England's best security against popery.[190]

Sacheverell's endorsement of a German succession to fend off accusations of Jacobitism set the style for most of his party in the difficult years after his trial. As Whigs accused Tories of favouring a return of the Stuarts on Anne's death, their spokesmen vehemently denied this. They insisted they had taken every reasonable step to secure the Hanoverian succession and were fully awake to possible threats to Protestantism and the balance of Christendom. They also, however, accused their rivals of exaggerating and distorting the current threat of such dangers as a partisan weapon against an honest Tory ministry. Thus although Tories rejected Whig analysis of

[187] *The tryal of Dr Henry Sacheverell before the house of peers* (1710), pp. 179–96.

[188] Henry Sacheverell, *The answer of Henry Sacheverell D.D. to the articles of impeachment* (1710), p. 24; *Tryal of Dr Henry Sacheverell*, pp. 342–3 – Sacheverell's speech was reprinted in several editions as Henry Sacheverell, *The speech of Henry Sacheverell D.D. upon his impeachment* (1710).

[189] Henry Sacheverell, *A defence of her majesties title to the crown . . . a sermon preached before the University of Oxford, on the 10th day of June, 1702* (1702), pp. 6, 11, 23.

[190] *Tryal of Dr Henry Sacheverell*, pp. 345–6.

the present state of Europe, they generally acknowledged the same potential dangers. This included agreeing that England must not fall under the sway of France (particularly by accepting back the Stuarts) because this would stop her leading the continent against any future threats to the reformation and the Christian community. Reactions to Steele's *Crisis* illustrate this nicely. Although Tories denied they were placating a dangerous Louis, they accepted that France would be a danger were she not ringed by the opposing powers they had ranged against her, and most were staunch in their support for the Hanoverian dynasty as a guarantee of these necessary safeguards. Thus both the pamphlets we quoted earlier insisted one could disagree with Steele, whilst still worrying about the international spiritual entities he claimed to defend. Jonathan Swift complained that Steele had accused the Tories of plotting to 'enslave all Europe' to France and popery, even though this was against the '*Faith of Nations, and the Honour of God*', and that there was no evidence at all that Tory ministers had behaved so despicably.[191] Far from helping France, they had constructed a powerful balance of power to hedge her in (and had spotted an even greater danger from Austria which the Whigs had ignored); and as for Steele's charge of Jacobitism, Swift thought fewer than ten Tories in the whole country would do anything but 'abhor the Thoughts of the Pretender reigning over us'.[192] Similarly, the anonymous author of the *Remarks on Mr Steele's Crisis* insisted Tories had been careful to construct a balance of power and keep out the exiled Stuarts. Lopping off large parts of the Spanish empire before giving it to a Frenchman, they had secured the peace and security of Europe; understanding the importance of the Protestant succession, no group had been more loyal to it.[193]

What we are seeing in these Tory statements is more evidence of the limits to political polarisation provided by a common concern for Europe. Tories either genuinely shared fears about the international reformation and Christendom (which their stated position since the exclusion crisis would suggest), or they at least judged the public so concerned about these entities that they had to consider them in any argument. If this was so, ideological division was being contained by the continental context. Debates could not be about ends (all agreed the Protestant and Christian communities of Europe must be defended against their enemies), so were confined to means (how should one identify the most pressing danger and what was the most appropriate domestic response to this?). Certainly, discussion of means could be bitter. The controversies over allegiance to William III, Sacheverell's sermon and the Hanoverian succession were full-scale paper wars, which sometimes spilled over into actual violence. Yet ultimately agreement about continental ends

191 [Swift], *Publick spirit*, p. 11 192 Ibid., pp. 28, 10.
193 *Remarks on Mr Steele's 'Crisis'*, pp. 10, 20.

prevented complete alienation. Tories could not reject the 1688–9 revolution or a German succession without seeming to endanger European Protestants or the Christian balance of nations. These men, therefore, found their own ways of supporting 1689 and 1714. Their polemic savaged the Whigs, but only by disagreeing about the correct way to argue for the same thing. It is thus possible that the Protestant and Christian identities of these two parties help explain the strange 'stability despite fissure' on which political historians of the late Stuart age have long remarked. Although the gulf between Whig and Tory appeared deep, the threat of actual political rupture seemed to recede after William's reign, and party tensions were played out in peaceful arenas such as pamphleteering and electioneering. There was a ritualistic element to party battles which contained conflict, and which we may now believe was made possible by an underlying ideological agreement.[194] To underline this suggestion, we can examine the final stages of constitutional argument in our period, through to the radical reconfiguring of party in the 1750s.

EUROPE AND CONSTITUTIONAL DISPUTES UNDER THE HANOVERIANS

Once the immediate excitement of George I's accession was over, constitutional debate between the parties was transformed. In fact, so different did it appear, that some historians have claimed Whig and Tory ceased to be a significant divide in the period.[195] We will not go quite that far here (there were differences of emphasis in the two parties' languages which have been carefully anatomised by Linda Colley), but the change in scene was dramatic.[196] Suddenly our familiar debates about the power of parliament to regulate the succession, the rights of subjects to resist tyranny or the precise prerogatives of the crown were swept away by an alternative set of concerns. At the same time, arguments about the location and use of political power in England ceased to define a clear party fissure. Instead, many Whigs joined the Tories in a broadly united attack upon the remainder of the Whig party. Most historians have therefore picked up an alternative polarity, and talked

[194] For discussion of stability and its origins: J. H. Plumb, *The growth of political stability in England, 1675–1725* (1967); Linda Colley, *In defiance*, ch. 1; Geoffrey Holmes, 'The achievement of political stability', in Geoffrey Holmes, ed., *Politics, religion and society in England, 1679–1742* (1986), pp. 249–80; J. V. Beckett, 'Introduction', in Clyve Jones, ed., *Britain in the first age of party* (1987), pp. 1–18; Tony Claydon, *William III: profiles*, ch. 4; Knights, *Representation*, pp. 360–75.

[195] E.g. J. G. A. Pocock, *The Machiavellian moment* (Princeton, 1975); Dickinson, *Liberty and property*; and Isaac Kramnick, *Bolingbroke and his circle: the politics of nostalgia in the age of Walpole* (1968).

[196] Colley, *In defiance*, ch. 4.

of a battle between 'court' and 'country' instead of tensions between the classic exclusion-era alignments.

To start to understand this transformation we need to follow the parliamentary history of the first Georgian years. In this era, British politics was reshaped in ways which forged strange new alignments and promoted novel ideologies to match. Probably the most important change was the proscription of the Tory party. Although most Tories had supported the Hanoverian succession, they were weakened and divided by the Jacobite sympathies of some of their number, and this allowed the Whigs to strike. Presenting their rivals as unreliable supporters of the incoming regime, Whigs monopolised George I's favour and then used this to purge national and local government, to bend crown influence in the general election of 1715 and to blacken their enemies as Jacobites in the rising of the same year. Passing the septennial act in 1716 to extend the life of parliaments to seven years, they locked in their advantages, and condemned the Tories to decades of opposition.[197] As a result, the party which had always upheld crown power found itself excluded from court and facing a bewildering new position which demanded new languages to explain. Meanwhile 1717 saw a second significant development. The Whigs sundered into factions led by Earl Stanhope and Sir Robert Walpole, thus opening a saga of eighteenth-century schisms. As it turned out, the proscription of the Tories had proved a mixed blessing. As they secured themselves in power, the Whigs increased their tendency to split: they alienated sections of the party nervous about associating with the court and they eased divisions based on personality because such petty spats no longer risked a Tory revival. Consequently, a strong strand of opposition Whiggery emerged. Opposition Whigs worried that colleagues now in power (especially Walpole, the kings' leading minister from 1720 to 1742) had been seduced into compromise with the crown, and they were frequently joined by less principled politicians temporarily excluded from office by factional games in Walpole's ministry.[198] Anti-ministerial Whigs needed new languages to express anxiety about members of their own party. Doing the parliamentary arithmetic, they realised they needed the support of Tories, and developed a polemic to appeal to that group as it faced its own ideological flux.

The fallout from these manoeuvrings was a new 'country' rhetoric. Avoiding the old contentious issues, this united Tories with anti-executive Whigs, and shaped constitutional debate through into the 1750s. The country platform was expressed in a number of forums. Most directly, it was mouthed in

197 Ibid., pp. 177–95, for detailed narrative of Tory proscription.

198 The *New Oxford history of England* summarises Whig shenanigans: Julian Hoppit, *Land of liberty? England 1688–1727* (Oxford, 2000), ch. 12; Paul Langford, *A polite and commercial people: England 1727–1783* (Oxford, 1989), chs. 2, 5.

parliament. Anti-court Whigs such as William Pulteney joined Tories such as William Bromley in lambasting Walpole in the Commons.[199] Making a wider appeal, opposition writers produced a string of pamphlets from the 1720s through to the 1740s. These publicised particular mis-steps by the government, but – in tune with the parliamentary contributions – analysed these as manifestations of a deeper malaise. Perhaps most significantly, the new platform was encapsulated in two of the most famous serials England ever produced. From November 1720 to September 1722, the polemicists John Trenchard and Thomas Gordon published a series of *Cato's letters*. Addressing English freeholders, this warned the nation against Walpole's influence, and did much to develop and popularise a country ideology.[200] Similar in tone and purpose was *The craftsman*, published weekly from 1727. This included substantial contributions from Pulteney, yet its guiding light was Viscount Bolingbroke, the Jacobite-leaning Tory of the 1710–14 administration. Bolingbroke had fled to his Stuart heroes in exile on the accession of George I, but had become disillusioned with their cause and gained a pardon from the Hanoverians in 1723. He remained disqualified from parliament under the terms of this pardon, but was nevertheless determined to regain influence through the Tory party when he returned to England in 1725. Using the *Craftsman* to cement a Tory alliance with opposition Whigs, Bolingbroke turned it into the great stalwart of the country platform, relentlessly assaulting the ministry's policies, personnel and principles.[201]

As to its tenets, Hanoverian country politics shared much with the country platforms which had emerged at points throughout the seventeenth century.[202] Like them it was suspicious of the executive as a site of depravity and political ambition, but changing circumstances had forced some important adaptations to the analysis. Perhaps most importantly, the new polemic was not concerned that the crown might simply abolish the legislature's check on its power, as – for example – those who had gone to war with Charles I had feared. The 1689 settlement had placed clear limits on the royal prerogative which the monarch would now find hard to challenge, and the growth of public debt in the late Stuart wars would have made parliament indispensable to stable revenues even if the formal tenets of the revolution had not.

[199] The parliamentary session of 1734 saw the full range of country attacks: Cobbett, IX:251–3 (Pulteney arguing against the excise, 4 February); 267–9 (Pulteney attacking the land army, 6 February); 383–6 (Pulteney advancing a place bill on 15 February); 396–400 (Bromley proposing the repeal of the septenniel act, 13 March).

[200] Ronald Hamowy, ed., *Cato's letters: or essays on liberty* (2 vols., Indianapolis, 1995).

[201] H. T. Dickinson, *Bolingbroke* (1970), ch. 11, for summary of his thought in the 1720s and 1730s.

[202] Richard Cust and Anne Hughes, *Conflict in early Stuart England* (Harlow, 1989), pp. 19–21, 140–3; Harris, *Politics under the later Stuarts*, pp. 54–61; John Spurr, *England in the 1670s: this masquerading age* (Oxford, 2000), ch. 3.

Instead of these outdated concerns, therefore, the eighteenth-century country platform developed a more subtle account of executive vice. Observing changes in Britain since 1688, it argued that Walpole and his cronies nursed an insidious project to emasculate controls on their action but that, sneakily, these would leave the now-empty forms of balanced government in place. Ministers would therefore be able to claim they were upholding liberty even as they actually drained its lifeblood, and deceive the unwary with a mendacious defence of the revolution's parliamentary settlement.

The starting point for the analysis was the accusation that Walpole was corrupting the legislature. In eighteenth-century country polemic, the minister had no need to challenge the power of parliament because he had ensured it would always do his bidding. The septennial act was the main tool here. Because this statute saved MPs from facing election for seven years at a stretch, it altered the balance of influence between constituencies and the ministry. Walpole could bribe members into his interest with pensions or public offices, and the men concerned would have little fear of voter retribution since the next moment of selection would be so far off. When elections did eventually come round, corruption simply extended to voters. The ministry bought support with money in open constituencies, and used its influence in decayed boroughs to ensure the return of tame delegates. When combined with Walpole's iron grip on the representatives Scotland had sent to Westminster since the union of 1707, and his ability to sway the Lords by creating new peers, such techniques ended parliamentary independence. Formally, the ministry owed its position to support in the two houses. In fact, however, the legislature was dependent on it, and only campaigns to repeal the septennial act, to eject MPs who accepted ministerial largesse and to crack down on corrupt electoral practices could end this pernicious situation.[203]

Thus far, there was nothing absolutely new in Hanoverian arguments. There had been complaints about an overlong parliament, and bribery of MPs, in the years before the exclusion crisis. These had not, however, displaced older concerns about parliament's survival as they came to after 1714; and in one vital respect the Georgian opposition did break new ground. This was in its wider analysis of society. Going beyond the sporadic hints of earlier

[203] *Craftsman*, passim; but for a good example, no. 402 (16 March 1734), an ironic defence of the septennial act by Henry Fielding. Also Henry Fielding, *Don Quixote in England* (1734), satirising electoral bribery. [Henry St John, Viscount Bolingbroke], *The craftsman extraordinary, or the late dissertation on parties continued* (1734); [Henry St John, Viscount Bolingbroke], *The craftsman extraordinary, in which the right of the people to frequent elections . . . is fully considered* (1734), pressed for repeal of the septennial act and led to parliamentary debate: Cobbett, IX:396–472. The opposition also attempted bills against placemen ('almost annual', Dickinson, *Bolingbroke*, p. 242) and corrupt practices at elections (1729, 1733: both passed, but Walpole sabotaged their operation).

spokesmen, eighteenth-century critics claimed Walpole was attempting a systematic restructuring of the English nation so it would lose all interest in opposing him. Crucial here was the expansion of the state. As we have noted, government infrastructure grew from the late seventeenth century, but country opponents saw something more sinister than adaptation to the demands of modern war. For them, Walpole was increasing the numbers employed by the crown (especially in the bureaucracy of the revenue departments, and in an unnecessarily large standing army) as a selfish instrument of policy. He was not only providing himself with a rich source of patronage to bribe legislators, but was ensuring a very wide section of the general population depended on government pay and so would not support those who opposed his policy. Expanded government had other benefits. Armies might overawe the public, and nosey officials might spy on them, but – most importantly – a large state was expensive. It therefore had to be financed by heavy taxation and by heavy borrowing, and both swung the balance of power towards the ministry. Taxation was useful because it could be levied on the landed and trading parts of the nation. These were the people whose livings did not depend on the state, and who might therefore have the independence to question what its leaders did. If they could be taxed, they would be weakened economically and might be driven to a poverty precluding political action. Borrowing was good because it drew ever greater numbers into dependence on the administration. Once people had lent to the government, they would hold their wealth as public stock and would be terrified of any challenge to the ministry which might endanger interest payments.[204] Even more generally, Walpole was accused of undermining society's public spirit. By his example of selfishness and through his ministry's corruption of national culture and values, he encouraged people to put their own interests above that of the country as a whole. Immersed in dreams of private gain, the public lost the patriotism which might have made them care about misgovernment; in so far as they achieved that gain, they sank into a luxury which dulled any civic sense.[205]

This country analysis was put so energetically that it became the meat of constitutional debate. While opposition MPs, *Cato* and the *Craftsman*

[204] *Cato's letters* and *The craftsman* repeatedly stressed parts of the case, but for virtually complete statements: [Henry St John, Viscount Bolingbroke], *The freeholders political catechism* (1733); *The case of the opposition impartially stated* [1742]. One of the opposition's few successes was defeating Walpole's scheme to widen excise duties: Paul Langford, *The excise crisis: society and politics in the age of Walpole* (Oxford, 1975).

[205] Much of the canonical literature of the era was satire on Walpole's influence: e.g. [Jonathan Swift], *Travels into several remote nations of the world, by Capt. Lemuel Gulliver* (1727); Alexander Pope, *The Dunciad: a heroic poem* (1728); John Gay, *The beggar's opera* (1728). For summary of these: W. A. Speck, *Stability and strife: England 1714–1760* (1977), pp. 224–6.

built the case, Walpole's supporters in press and parliament accused them of endangering the revolution settlement. A great and patriotic chief minister, they insisted, owed his influence solely to parliamentary majorities, and his government worked tirelessly to uphold this free system established in 1689. Opposition critics were troublemakers who tried to undermine the best constitution in the world, and the only explanation for this behaviour was that they were tools of absolutist forces. Pointing to the Tories in the opposition, they saw Jacobitism and French money behind its complaints, and appealed to country Whigs to recognise they were being duped by men who only pretended to preserve liberties. This controversy dominated public discussion for decades after the 1710s, so we must ask what role the Protestant international and Christendom played within it. We have shown that earlier debates about succession, resistance and prerogative were substantially about English duties to the godly abroad; can this be said of Hanoverian discussion as well?

The main answer has to be no. The criticism of Walpolean corruption which drove debate was characterised by a remarkable absence of reference to European spiritual entities. There were vague concerns that England's Protestant faith might be in danger from men of such ambition and depravity, but apart from these, the polemic had no significant role for forms of Christianity. What was in danger was British political liberty, not true religion; and in two important respects the analysis turned decisively away from the concerns we have been exploring. The first was in its obsession with ancient Rome. As Bolingbroke and like-minded propagandists sought models for the sort of corruption they saw in contemporary England, they turned to the last days of the Roman republic. Here, for them, was a free system of government similarly losing its liberty to bribery, self-interest and an over-mighty state, so they analysed it exhaustively in tales of Caesar, Brutus, Cassius and Augustus. The very title of *Cato's letters* revealed the preoccupation (Cato had been the Roman tribune who denounced Caesar's early erosion of his countrymen's liberty), but it ran as a constant theme through the corpus.[206] For example, Bolingbroke's most succinct statement of his creed, the 1733 *Freeholder's political catechism*, used the Roman empire as an analogy for Walpole's subtle corruption. The empire, this suggested, was exactly like contemporary England, as it had retained the forms of a free polity (it still appointed the senate and consuls who had protected the people under the republic) whilst power had actually leached away to a tyrant.[207] The earl of Marchmont's influential exhortation to voters in the 1740 general

[206] For rich analysis of Roman history: Hamowy, *Cato's letters*, I:128–33, 164–74, 194–201, 288–94, 367–88.

[207] [Bolingbroke], *Freeholder's political catechism*, p. 10.

election made a very similar point.[208] What is important about this rhetoric, of course, was that there could be no reference to any species of Christian faith. The heroes and villains of late republican Rome had lived before the spread of the gospel, so defence of true religion could not have motivated them, and faith was redundant in an account of England built on the Roman analogy.

The second clear turn from religion was the socioeconomic bent of much country polemic. Because it relied heavily on a state perverting people's material interests through employment, taxation and credit, criticism of Walpole tended to see patterns of property-holding as crucial to political behaviour. Insisting that the merchants and landowners who did not owe their wealth to the government were the only people with an interest in liberty, country spokesmen pored over social structures, charting the gradual decline of these people relative to civil servants, brokers of public stock and the military. Solutions offered were similarly economic. The state must be rolled back to rebalance wealth in society; law must ensure a wide spread of property which would give as many people as possible a stake in a free political system; and luxury must be curbed to stem the dangerous self-interest which lulled so many into accepting tyranny.[209] Obviously, such materialistic analysis told against concern for spiritual entities abroad. Country spokesmen might talk about Europe, but when they did it was to illustrate a general decline in landed elites as nations had been debauched, and to demonstrate the consequent slide of so many into slavery.[210] What religious beliefs these foreign people held was irrelevant. As 'Cato' pointed out, men who had received the truth about God were just as likely to suffer socioeconomic decay as others – and whilst he believed popish states would inevitably decline, he thought this would be brought about by 'natural causes' (the misallocation of economic resources to idle clerics) rather than by providential smiting for adopting erroneous doctrine.[211]

It is clear, therefore, that the eighteenth-century country platform had little time for either the Protestant international or Christendom. It not only excluded them from the main thrust of its rhetoric, but its attachment to classical and socioeconomic discourses pretty much precluded them. This looks fatal to claims for the importance of the foreign faithful. The rhetoric which shaped constitutional discussion after 1714 ignored the European church almost entirely. Yet, though we must accept this, the pan-continental communities we have been following may still have been playing a role. One certainly has to look harder to see the discourses than during the late

208 [Hugh Hume, earl of Marchmont], *A serious exhortation to the electors of Great Britain* (1740), p. 11.

209 Attacks on the luxury caused by a bloated state were ubiquitous in country ideology. For law and property: Hamowy, *Cato's letters*, II:607–13 (no. 84, 7 July 1722).

210 E.g. ibid., I:124–8.

211 Ibid., II:797–802.

Stuart discussions, but there is at least the possibility that this was actually a sign of their triumph. Before we try to construct this paradox, however, it is worth noting that the country alignment's abandonment of international religious discourse was unilateral. Walpole's defenders argued his parliamentary regime was the embodiment, not the nemesis, of English liberty, but they also resorted to a vulgar scaremongering which still had important European dimensions.

We have already mentioned an important element here. Walpole accused opponents of Jacobitism, and of course delighted in 'proving' this from the prominence of Bolingbroke among his critics. This was the burden of the chief minister's major interventions in the Commons, it ran through most pro-court pamphlets and it was taken up energetically by such newspapers as the *Daily Courant*, the *London Journal* and the *Free Briton*.[212] All these insisted attacks on the ministry were simply part of a wider destabilisation of the Hanoverian regime, which must facilitate the return of a Stuart pretender. This summoning of a Jacobite bogey opened a door for the godly abroad. Court Whigs insisted Walpole's fall would be a disaster for domestic liberty, but they linked this to a victory for French popery which would damage continental Protestantism and promote an un-Christian universal monarchy. This drift in the polemic was particularly notable as Walpoleans brought up the politics of 1710–14. Reviving discourses of the Stuart era long after their critics had moved on, Walpoleans reminded everyone of the Tory ministry at the end of Anne's reign, which they suggested had been an organised betrayal of Protestants and Christians. Bolingbroke and his allies had led an administration which had flirted with the popish exiled dynasty; had sought a premature peace with a still over-mighty and persecuting France; and had signed a disastrous treaty at Utrecht which had secured neither the peace of Christendom nor the European reformation. This tactic was used repeatedly in the Walpolean press, but was perhaps most prominent in a pamphlet which helped drive Bolingbroke back into exile in 1735.[213] *The grand accuser the greatest of all criminals* (1734) was part of a campaign to expose the viscount's recent (and hopelessly imprudent) contacts with France; yet it spent much of its time recounting his career before 1713. The author claimed he had been driven to write as he had flicked through yellowing copies of the *Examiner* and realised that Swift's old attacks on

[212] E.g. *Sedition and defamation display'd, in a letter to the author of the Craftsman* (1731), esp. pp. 35–6; *Opposition no proof of patriotism* (1735), pp. 7, 17–20; 'The reasonableness and necessity of driving B——ke out of the kingdom', *Daily Courant*, 5868 (22 January 1735); Walpole's Commons attack on Bolingbroke – Cobbett, IX:471–2.

[213] For other examples: *An epistle to W. S. esq. containing some political remarks* (1728), pp. 14–15; *The conduct of the ministry compared with its consequences* (1733), pp. 25–7; 'The history of patriotism', *Free Briton*, 76–8, 82, 87 (nos. scattered between 13 May and 29 July 1731) – the last rebutted the *Craftsman*'s complaint that the Walpolean press had overplayed 1710–14.

Whig ministers served the same purpose as the contemporary *Craftsman*. Both Swift then, and Bolingbroke now, threatened the Protestant cause and all Europeans with a French universal monarchy and a Stuart pretender.[214] What followed was a detailed account of Bolingbroke's late Stuart career. Before 1713, Bolingbroke had promoted peace with the French because Versailles might help the exiled regime, and had not cared about the hegemony over Christendom this handed to Louis. As part of this campaign, he had vilified and betrayed the Dutch – and had even besmirched Protestant refugees from Louis' persecution – because such foreign Protestants would oppose a Jacobite succession.[215]

Walpole's attacks on Bolingbroke, then, harked back to the last era when the fate of Christendom and the international reformation had dominated domestic politics. They also, however, made what they could of these entities in the current age. The key here was to stress Walpole's care for the Protestant interest and the peace-preserving balance of power as cornerstones of his foreign policy. We have seen this promoted when discussing the geopolitical challenges of these years, but must now stress its role in wider claims that country opposition helped papists and un-Christian warmongers. Pamphlets and speeches insisted Walpole's government was doing its best for the Protestant interest and against universal monarchy in delicate diplomatic circumstances. Opponents might charge that this diplomatic subtlety eroded trust in the country, and was a symptom of the minister's underhand methods across politics, but this was simply a Jacobite effort to ruin a careful strategy.[216] So we have noted a 1735 pamphlet arguing that Walpole's alliance with France had done more to protect the Protestant interest than all the carping of its critics.[217] Four years earlier, a *Defence of the measures of the present administration* had set about its task in similar vein. Denouncing the opposition for raising every difficulty it could, the author stated the 1725 treaty between Austria and Spain had been a threat to 'the ballance of Europe', but that Walpole had coped admirably.[218] He had bound the Protestant princes of Germany to the Protestant Dutch, Scandinavians and English; he had duped popish France into protecting this confessional alliance and maintaining a peaceful equilibrium on the continent; and he had therefore secured 'the whole Protestant Interest Abroad, which is strictly speaking our own Safety'.[219] There were plenty more such defences. Walpole had tried

[214] *The grand accuser the greatest of all criminals* (1734), pp. 1–4.
[215] Ibid., passim, but esp. pp. 59–63.
[216] For attacks on Walpole's foreign policy, see n. 232 below: *The Craftsman*, 431 (5 October 1734), was a letter by Machiavelli from the underworld admiring Walpole's latest treaties.
[217] See above, pp. 210–11.
[218] *A defence of the measures of the present administration* (1731), p. 11.
[219] Ibid., p. 24.

to protect the faithful of the continent as jealous – or downright Jacobite – enemies swarmed around him at home.[220]

Government use of old languages in the high eighteenth century is interesting; but it only does a little to counter the secular drift of discourse. The agenda-setting constitutional position of the age remained the country one, and this was still remarkable for its lack of interest in European Christianity. Walpole might reply with the superannuated bogey of French popery, but even his supporters recognised they must respond to new arguments. They were therefore drawn away from foreign godliness as they advanced new models of the English constitution (insisting, for example, that a ministry must have influence in the legislature if government were not to end in obstreperous chaos), and as they deconstructed the opposition's social analysis (an expanded state was sanctioned by a parliament which could scrutinise and remedy its social ills; whilst the virtues required in a modern commercial community were very different from the lauded examples of ancient Rome).[221] Suggesting the continuing importance of our international concerns in constitutional debate must thus take another tack. In the promised paradox, it may have been the success of continental Protestantism and Christendom in shaping debate which resulted in their disappearance. Sternly policing the limits of argument, they may have found themselves redundant in the arena they had marked out.

The first step in this case is the simple observation that eighteenth-century constitutional disputes were not about the sort of fundamentals which had racked Stuart discussion. There was, for example, no debate about the succession. Both court and country Whigs were avid supporters of the Protestant Hanoverians; if any active Tories retained Jacobite sympathies, they kept silent as the price for collaborating with Walpole's Whig opponents; and as Linda Colley has shown, most of the party transferred its allegiance to the German kings, even translating its old support for monarchy into the argument that the Georges were the greatest prisoners of their corrupt chief minister.[222] Similarly, there was no question about the role of parliament in limiting the crown's prerogative or the subject's right to resist. Court Whigs

220 E.g. *A letter to a member of parliament concerning the present state of affairs* (1740); [James Whitehouse], *Seasonable expostulations with the worthy citizens of London* (1742); *Free Briton*, 285–8 (24 April–15 May 1735).

221 For court Whigs' constitutional thought: Reed Browning, *The political and constitutional ideas of the court whigs* (Baton Rouge, LA, 1982). For specific examples, see contributions by Newcastle, Argyll and Bangor in the Lords' debate on a pension bill, 20 February 1731: Cobbett, VIII:844–7. For the anachronism of judging by the standards of ancient Rome: Shelly G. Burtt, *Virtue transformed: political argument in England, 1688–1740* (Cambridge, 1992), ch. 6.

222 Colley, *In defiance*, pp. 25–52, 101–4. Loyalty to Hanoverian monarchs caused tensions in the country alliance because Whigs were thought to harbour republicanism: see *The loyal or revolutionary Tory* (1731).

insisted they upheld the primacy of the legislature confirmed at William's revolution; whilst the opposition demanded parliament be freed from ministerial bribery so it could perform its controlling function. On resistance, both pro- and anti-Walpolean Whigs used it to justify the exclusion of the Stuarts, and though Tories may have had theoretical doubts about a right to rebel, these did not divide them from the other party since obedience to authority now meant condemnation of Jacobite risings.[223] Thus for both sides the principles established in 1689 and 1714 were sacrosanct. The argument was simply whether these were being upheld; this explains both the stability of Hanoverian politics (there was never a hint of such a crippling constitutional crisis as had occurred in 1629, 1642, 1679 or 1688) and the blurring of party lines.

Moving on from this basic point, we can ask why the old fundamental fissures had disappeared. Here European faith may make a dramatic re-entry. If the argument of earlier sections of this chapter was correct, tension eased because seventeenth-century disputes were resolved through shared commitment to the reformation and Christendom. Whigs and Tories no longer debated the royal succession, or whether the king was absolute, because they had been forced to agree settlements which protected foreign Protestants and Christians. Taking this a step further, we can suggest the consensus – though created by concern for continental spiritual entities – may then have eliminated these entities from public discourse. First, agreement ended the deep polarity between parties which had generated such inflamed discussion of Europe. Tories had initially rejected the Whigs' account of the constitution. Yet they had done so out of an alternative reading of their duties to the faithful abroad, and when circumstances in the 1680s suggested their position would actually harm their European causes, they used these as a bridge to a more 'Whiggish' position. Tories accepted 1689 and 1714 in horror at the spread of European popery and France's designs on Christianity, and explained their shifts as necessary to counter these international threats.[224] Once this had happened, there was no real gulf between the parties over what duties to the foreign faithful implied about the structure of England's government, and passion faded. Second, the displacement of continent-focused rhetoric may have occurred as the new consensus destroyed a traditional focus for opposition. Before 1689, criticism of the court tended to centre on its failure to protect the Protestant international and Christendom. After the revolution, however, this opposition rhetoric was hard to mount since reconciliation between Whigs and Tories brought regimes to power which

[223] For this, and Charles I as an icon among Hanoverian Tories: Andrew Lacey, *The cult of King Charles the martyr* (2003), pp. 216–17.

[224] See above, pp. 241–53, 265–7.

appeared passionately committed to the Protestant interest and the defeat of un-Christian tyrants. In this situation, concern about executive mismanagement would not crystallise around belief that England's role in the world was being radically perverted, and instead focused on other fears.

This are pretty abstract suggestions, and hard to prove. Explanations of the *non*-appearance of rhetorics will, by their very nature, gather little positive evidence. Nevertheless, there is some circumstantial material. As far as the collapse of party polarity is concerned, it is interesting that the narrative given above matches Bolingbroke's own analysis. When Walpole attacked the country movement as a Jacobite stalking horse, its leader denied this by arguing that everyone, and especially Tories, had abandoned extreme positions. In a series of contributions to the *Craftsman* over 1733–4 Bolingbroke said all had rallied to the principles of 1689 and 1714, so there was little real difference between the factions, and their names had become empty labels.[225] It was true that much of the reconciliation concerned liberty rather than continental entities. Under James II, Bolingbroke argued, Tories had realised all Englishmen's freedom was in danger, and recanted their absolute support for Stuart power.[226] Yet in one crucial passage, the viscount hinted that consensus on the nation's proper role in Europe had also been vital. Outlining the origins of party in the exclusion crisis, he insisted the two groups had never actually been far apart, but had been driven asunder by the belief that their rivals were betraying the faithful abroad. On one side, Charles II's constant flirtation with France, and his pro-popish foreign policy, convinced Whigs there was a radical problem at court which only extreme action could remedy. On the other side, Tories reacted against this Whig hysteria, and fell under a French conspiracy to divide the English.[227] In this vision, harmony could be restored if only all saw they shared foreign goals. The two sides could have settled in the late 1670s if the European situation had allowed them to calm down; and according to some of Bolingbroke's other writings, rediscovery of shared foreign purpose did soon reunite them. When the viscount was forced into exile again in 1735, he spent some of his time writing remarks on the study and use of history. Although not generally published until the 1750s, these circulated around Bolingbroke's immediate circle much earlier, and they reveal the thick European context in which he understood the end of party bitterness.[228] In this narrative, the English had never divided over their basic duties to Europe. Charles II had boosted France till she threatened universal monarchy and – being popishly affected – had betrayed the

[225] The *Craftsman* contributions were later published as [Henry St John, Viscount Bolingbroke], *A dissertation on parties* (1735).

[226] E.g. *The works of Lord Bolingbroke* (4 vols., 1967), II:44.

[227] Ibid., II:45–7.

[228] Finally published as Henry St John, *Letters on the study and use of history* (1752) – but Alexander Pope circulated them privately from 1738.

Protestant Dutch: but, vitally, 'the crime was not national'.[229] The general population cried out against the king's evil even as it was committed, and on the fall of James II they joined enthusiastically with William to reverse it. Party distinctions were lost as the nation united in the new king's war, and participated 'with all imaginable zeal in the common cause of Europe, to reduce the exorbitant power of France'.[230] The agreement to accept the 1689 constitutional settlement was thus closely connected to a rediscovered unity in continental duty, and the revolution 'produced as great change in our foreign conduct, as in our domestic establishment'.[231]

Of course, that Bolingbroke argued constitutional division had ended in European consensus does not automatically mean it was so. Much of what he wrote was designed to paper over tensions in an alliance between the excluded Tories and the country Whigs, and its optimistic assessment of harmony must be read with this in mind. Nevertheless, the viscount was a keen observer of the political scene, who had played a major role in many of the events he described, and more importantly, his political strategy depended on his analysis being essentially correct. He was, after all, speaking for a coalition which included men of both parties. This would not have worked unless there was a reasonable common ground between these groups. Moreover, Bolingbroke was willing to lead his troops in attacks on Walpole's foreign policy. Particularly in the 1730s, country critics charged the corrupt minister with an overly subtle diplomacy and a neglect of the Bourbon's military threat which had allowed France to re-emerge as a menace to all Europe, and this suggests opposition consensus extended to the purpose and role of Britain on the continent.[232] Bolingbroke calculated he could campaign on foreign issues without his followers fragmenting: at least since the reconciliation under William III, all had acknowledged the prime importance of containing a popish and hegemonic Versailles.

If Bolingbroke's position suggests constitutional tensions were eased by shared concerns about Europe, and if this helps to explain the disappearance of international Protestantism and Christianity as a major feature of constitutional discussion, there may also have been a role for our second explanation. It is possible that the clear commitment by regimes to continental entities after 1689 disarmed a traditional form of opposition rhetoric. The

[229] *Works of Lord Bolingbroke*, II:265–6, 277.
[230] Ibid., II:277. [231] Ibid., II:280.
[232] For country attacks on foreign policy, see *Craftsman*, passim, but particularly nos. for September 1730–May 1731, later collected as [Henry St John, viscount Bolingbroke], *Remarks on the history of England* (1780). Also *Remarks in a pamphlet entitl'd a defence of the measures of the present administration* (1731); [Pulteney], *Politicks on both sides*. Bolingbroke led a campaign to accuse the ministry of doing nothing as France refortified Dunkirk, which culminated in parliamentary debates February 1730, in [Henry St John, viscount Bolingbroke], *The case of Dunkirk faithfully stated* (1730).

evidence here comes from timing. Cato and Bolingbroke's non-religious critique emerged almost immediately the Hanoverians were cemented in place. Once the first major challenge to the new dynasty had been defeated in 1715, it took only a few years for the new streams of country rhetoric to reach full flow. Although there are problems with arguing that abstract discontent searches for a language in which to express itself (language creates grievances as well as voicing them, so the causal direction is never clear), this chronology could suggest concerns about the dominant Whig executive were being forced into new channels by the security of a Protestant regime visibly committed to a continental balance of power. The court Whigs looked corrupt and authoritarian to those outside their circle, especially after the great financial scandal of the South Sea Bubble, and attacks on liberty such as suspensions of habeas corpus. Yet whilst there was concern about this, it could not adopt the master narrative of seventeenth-century oppositions, which had repeatedly argued that a popish and often French clique among courtiers was subverting English government. This had been the main fear expressed in the 1620s by parliamentary spokesmen opposed to James I and Charles I, by the followers of Pym in the run-up to the civil war and by the country critics of the 1670s who (in some ways) set the stage for the Whig movement.[233] Most importantly, Walpole's opponents could not argue – as these earlier people had – that failure to defend Protestants and Christians abroad was the clearest sign of the frightening conspiracy. The men of the early Stuart era had proved their plot from England's failure to become involved in the Thirty Years War, and we have seen the fears of those opposed to Charles II's and James II's co-operation with Louis XIV; but this sort of analysis was tricky after 1715.[234] The security of the Hanoverian regime meant an unimpeachably Protestant court, speaking a constant language of Protestant interest and international balance (not least because these protected its German territories from Austria and France). The old rhetoric of criticism was therefore difficult to deploy, and anxiety about the executive had to be expressed without concentrating on Christendom or the European reformation. The eighteenth-century discourse of opposition, with its secular, classical and sociological analysis of internal perversion, may have stepped into this breach.

Of course, this suggestion can be challenged from the decades immediately after 1689. William's and Anne's governments were as thoroughly Protestant as the Hanoverians, and fought long and draining wars to preserve Europe from French hegemony. If the logic above holds water, one might ask why a

[233] See the works cited in n. 202 above.

[234] For the foreign policy element of 1620s opposition: Cogswell, *Blessed revolution*. For opposition to Charles II and James II, see above, pp. 227–31, 244.

Bolingbrokian discourse did not dominate the 1690s and 1700s. There are several responses here. The first is that the older rhetoric centring on papist French plots at court could initially persevere by supposing the conspiracy had survived 1689. Especially in the early years of William's reign, spokesmen for a country position assumed misrule stemmed from ministers, civil servants or evil counsellors still in place from the days of Charles and James. Outcries against men such as the corrupt commissary John Shales in 1689, or the earl of Sunderland who became an advisor to William III after 1692, were fired by these people's earlier closeness to James.[235] Second, a break with the rhetorics of the past was prevented by the party rivalries we observed in a previous section. So long as Whigs could accuse Tory ministers of closet Jacobitism (as they could whilst Tories still made it into the administration, and before they had demonstrated the support for the Hanoverians which most of them did in 1714 and 1715), then court corruption could be blamed on men without a proper commitment to European faith. Tories, in turn, were drawn into defending their continental credentials and responding that it was the narrow factionalism of Whig ministers which actually put foreign Protestants and Christians in danger.[236]

Finally, and most importantly, one can point out that a rhetoric very similar to that of the eighteenth-century opposition *did* emerge soon after 1689. When pamphleteers such as John Trenchard, Walter Moyle and John Toland attacked William for trying to hold on to a large standing army after the peace of Ryswick, they analysed the world very much as Bolingbroke's men would. Standing armies had corrupted Rome; they were the result of social changes destroying the old feudal balance; and the oppression they brought was irrespective of religion. As the opening shot in the press controversy had it: 'putting an Epithet upon Tyranny is false Heraldry; for Protestant and Popish are both alike'.[237] Similarly, when the attack on the military was widened into wholesale condemnation of the wartime ministries by such writers as Charles Davenant, critics perceived a downright Walpolean corruption of England's economy, society and morals. In his 'Tom Double' pamphlets (1701–2) Davenant introduced his readers to a self-interested, luxurious and ambitious creature of the state, who encouraged vice, taxation, speculation, armed force and profitable office as means to his advance beyond honest traders and landholders.[238] In fact, as a school of scholars led by J. G. A. Pocock has established, Walpole's critics shared a heritage of ideas with the men of the 1690s which could be traced even further back to

[235] Claydon, *William III . . . revolution*, p. 200. [236] See above, pp. 266–7.

[237] [Walter Moyle and John Trenchard], *An argument shewing that a standing army is inconsistent with a free government* (1697), p. 18.

[238] [Charles Davenant], *The true picture of a modern Whig* (1701); [Charles Davenant], *Tom Double return'd out of the country* (1702).

the arguments of James Harrington in the 1650s.[239] Concentrating on the relationship between property holding and political power, and stressing the importance of civic virtue to maintain liberty, all these writers fretted that the erosion of an independent landed class was weakening the group whose stake in society gave them the motive and means to resist the excesses of central authority. The discourse had been adapted around the time of the exclusion crisis by men such as Henry Neville to become a 'neo-Harringtonianism', no longer committed to its founder's anti-monarchism, but its sociological concerns remained pretty constant through William's reign and into the Hanoverian age.[240]

Pocock established Bolingbroke's intellectual heritage, but we can now suggest something interesting about the periods when this tradition became prominent; and something which strengthens our argument about the disappearance of continental rhetoric after 1714. Examining the high Georgian era, the 1690s and Harrington's period, we notice these were all times when the English executive was cogently committed to European Protestantism and a Christian balance of power. This was true for Hanoverian and Williamite government, and it was true in the 1650s with Cromwell's aggressive interventions to block Spain (still perceived, at that stage, as the most likely popish hegemonist). In all these periods, therefore, it was hard to use the traditional opposition rhetoric which assumed a court conspiracy was undermining England's duties to the foreign godly. This even arguably applies to the mid-1670s, the formative moment for Pocock's neo-Harringtonianism. For all its other faults, the ministry of the day – Danby's – had appeared to share contemporary fears of popery and universal monarchy. It had broken Charles II's co-operation with Louis XIV, threatened the French king with war to control his expansion, and sought closer ties with the Protestant Dutch through the Princess Mary's marriage to the prince of Orange.[241] Given this pattern, we might argue the Harrington–Davenant–Bolingbroke critique had been a constantly available alternative to the traditional style of country rhetoric. Because it did not blame absolutist, foreign and Catholic plotters

239 See Pocock, *Machiavellian moment*; J. G. A. Pocock, 'Machiavelli, Harrington and English political ideologies in the eighteenth century', and 'Civic humanism and its role in Anglo-American thought', both in J. G. A. Pocock, *Politics, language and time: essays in political thought and history* (1971), pp. 80–147.

240 For Pocock, the key work of adaptation was Henry Neville, *Plato redivivus* (1681), which reconciled Harringtonian notions of public virtue with an attachment to England's ancient constitution: Pocock, *Politics, language and time*, p. 130.

241 For Danby's policies, see Andrew Browning, *Thomas Osbourne, earl of Danby and duke of Leeds, 1632–1712* (3 vols., Glasgow, 1951), chs. 9–12. In considering this we must remember that key works for Pocock, esp. Marvell's *Growth of popery*, also relied on the trope of French–popish corruption at court threatening the faithful of the continent. Pocock reads them selectively to produce manifestos of neo-Harringtonianism; I admit Danby's foreign policy did not utterly remove suspicion he was a French tool.

for the polity's ills, it became prominent when that more usual language of court conspiracy and betrayal of foreign Christians would not convince as an explanation of executive vice. If this is right, we have another way in which the Protestant international and Christendom faded from public discourse precisely because they had been triumphant. Securing a wide spectrum of support for regimes whose European zeal was hard to fault, they paradoxically weakened a type of anxiety about the court which had emphasised the need to worry about the faithful abroad.

In all this, we have underlined the chief message of our whole analysis of constitutional fissure between Whigs and Tories. This tension was fired by different conceptions of the Protestant international and Christendom, which must take a larger role in explanations of party battle than they have hitherto. Yet at the same time, dispute was limited by these entities. Because both sides were committed to the survival of the European reformation and the freedom of Christendom from a tyrannous hegemonist, they shared the same fundamental view of the world, and came to broad acceptance of the Georgian constitutional settlement. In the end, this meant a weakening of party alignments – allowing first the Whig–Tory coalitions in opposition to Walpole, and the eventual dissolution of the Tory party into different factions of Whigs in the 1750s. Our international spiritual entities thus both created and controlled party; we shall now see something very similar with regard to the other basic issue which divided Whigs and Tories – the nature, role and power of the church of England.

DEFENCES OF ANGLICANISM: RELIGION AND EUROPE UNDER CHARLES II

In 1662 the French clergyman Jean Durel published a defence of the church of England. Given that Durel had been born in Jersey and had spent much of his career there; given that he had long admired the English communion; and given that he had sought ordination by the exiled bishop of Galloway in Paris in 1651, his defence of the English establishment was not surprising. Its manner, however, was. At a time when dissenting ministers were protesting against the church's restoration of prayer-book ceremonies and hierarchical episcopacy, Durel berated them by convening a fantasy council. Just as modern soccer fans construct ideal teams from the stars of many different squads and believe their heroes would defeat all comers, the author gathered an imaginary assembly of the reformation's greatest international divines and dreamt they would humiliate puritan objectors. One by one, Martin Bucer, Peter Martyr, Pierre du Moulin, Theodore Beza, Heinrich Bullinger, Philip Melancthon and many other 'delegates of all Reformed Churches' addressed his phantasmal meeting. Each in turn quoted passages of their writing which expressed admiration for England's ecclesiastical arrangements, and then

John Calvin summed up as the council's fantasy president. By the end of the speeches, Durel supposed, English dissenters must recognise they were at odds with the entire Protestant movement. So complete was the agreement between anglicans and reformed communions abroad that local nonconformists had become a sect by themselves. They might flee to Europe, but once there they would quarrel with German, French or Swiss Protestants as much as with English churchmen, and would be shunned by the faithful abroad 'as well as here'.[242]

Of course, Durel's prose was a part of that effort to situate the church of England at the heart of the continental reformation which we observed in many ecclesiastical histories. It was, however, even more immediately political than these writings. Penned at the very moment that the restoration's religious settlement was being finalised, it was one of the very first polemical shots in a dispute which would be central to all debate and policy in our period, and which would eventually liberalise the kingdom as much as discussion of the constitution. While debate about crown power led directly to more open politics, disputes over the church would have more subtle, but just as powerful, effects. It is arguable, for example, that ecclesiastical struggle eased the path to religious toleration. If so, it weakened the spiritual monopoly which had bolstered royal influence, and permitted that plurality of belief and practice on which free societies depend. As profoundly, religious debate provided the poles around which organised political movements gathered. Soon after the restoration, groups formed to promote their respective sides of the argument, and fed that fissure between Englishmen which shaped their peculiarly open and critical polity. That one of the earliest protagonists in the great contest was a Frenchman, and that he called on all the reformed churches of Europe, indicates that spiritual internationalism had further roles to play in England's political development.

It is important to stress this dimension for two great reasons. First, ecclesiastical division fed straight into the rage of party which we have been examining. The more closely historians have examined the debates of the Restoration era, and especially the more closely they have looked at the emergence of Whigs and Tories in the exclusion crisis, the more convinced they are that polarisation over the church was crucial. Ideologically, it was as important as the constitution itself. When the 1662 religious settlement drove puritan ministers out of the English establishment and then persecuted them with a harsh series of discriminatory laws, there were many who felt this was an unnecessary sundering of Protestants and who pleaded for greater moderation. From 1662 onwards, both the ejected dissenters and their supporters within the establishment argued the church should

[242] Jean Durel, *A view of the government and publick worship of God* (1662), pp. 199–309, 313.

compromise over ritual and episcopacy to accommodate puritan objections, or should tolerate Protestants who worshipped outside it. By the 1670s this view was being clearly articulated by the group coalescing around the earl of Shaftesbury, so it was unsurprising that it was swept into the Whig movement at the end of the decade. Tories, by contrast, upheld the intransigent position of 1662. Their pamphlets, speeches and sermons insisted dissent was politically and spiritually dangerous: radical Protestants outside the true and official church threatened both the state, and the souls of those they seduced. Organisationally, too, religious division was crucial. From the restoration, dissenters had mobilised to oppose the harsh laws against them. They established networks of support and correspondence between local groups; they campaigned to secure the election of sympathetic MPs; and they wrote copious literature (evading press censorship whilst it was imposed, and exploiting the exclusion era when it was not) to put their point of view in print. When the Whigs emerged, they utilised the logistical experience of these key supporters, so that dissent acted as the midwife of party structures. In response, Tories employed the church to mobilise its activists. As bishops voted against exclusion in the House of Lords, clergy energised parishioners and pulpits became chief engines of anti-Whig propaganda.[243] Such religious division remained central to party belief and practice into the eighteenth century. It is therefore vital to understand its full, including its full international, nature.

The second great reason to stress the European dimension in ecclesiastical politics, is that the story of the divide is so often told without it. The 1662 settlement itself is usually narrated as a domestic revenge tragedy. Although some continental influence on the king is acknowledged (his exile in France and Brussels is thought to have converted him to a closet Catholicism, and made him willing to experiment with the forms of religious toleration), the reaction to his efforts is thought to have been shaped at home.[244] It was the settling of local scores, and popular revulsion at the excesses of Cromwell's godly commonwealth, which bullied puritan ministers out of their parishes.[245] Continental contexts have featured little more in coverage of the disputes which stemmed from 1662. Certainly, John Spurr has

[243] For party formation around religion: Douglas R. Lacey, *Dissent and parliamentary politics in England 1661–1689* (New Brunswick, NJ, 1969); Tim Harris, 'Revising the restoration', and Jonathan Barry, 'The politics of religion in restoration Bristol', both in Harris, Seaward and Goldie, *Politics of religion*, pp. 1–28, 163–98; Miller, *After the civil wars*, pp. 227–35, 254–61.

[244] I. M. Green, *The re-establishment of the church of England* (Oxford, 1978), pp. 28–30.

[245] There is scant consideration of European contexts in the standard accounts: Green, *Re-establishment*; John Spurr, *The restoration church of England, 1646–1689* (New Haven, 1991), pp. 29–42; Ronald Hutton, *The restoration* (Oxford, 1985), pp. 143–8, 171–80; N. H. Keeble, *The restoration: England in the 1660s* (Oxford, 2002) pp. 109–20. Any external analysis tends to relate to Scotland and Ireland: Green, *Re-establishment*, pp. 16–20; Jim Smyth, *The making of the United Kingdom, 1660–1800* (Harlow, 2001), pp. 19–34.

noted that the church's apology for the great expulsion was hampered by a reluctance to denounce beliefs still held by foreign Protestants.[246] Similarly, pressure for toleration in the later Stuart era is thought to have been strengthened by European thinkers and circumstances, including the need to allow all people of all opinions to contribute to national resources in an era of great power rivalry, or the desire not to offend foreign allies of differing religious stamp.[247] Yet overwhelmingly, the story continues to unfold within the narrow island. Objections to the restoration settlement centred on scriptural scholarship or analogy, or on a sense of duty to old parish flocks, rather than any participation in the European reformation.[248] The dissenters' psychological response to persecution was to internalise, not internationalise, their experience.[249] Meanwhile, conformists also kept their focus at home: defending their church for its national authority; as bulwark for England's monarchy; or as the guarantor of moral discipline in each community.[250] Arguments between churchmen and dissenters remained local as they were swept into the uniquely English tussle between Whigs and Tories, and when toleration came in 1689 it was largely a domestic political deal to secure wide support for William III.[251] Arguments after the revolution remain aspects of English politics. If issues such as the naturalisation of foreign Protestants occasionally injected a continental spirit into ecclesiastical debate, the great set-pieces – such as the trial of Sacheverell for his attack on toleration, or disputes over occasional conformity and the status of convocation – run without this fuel.[252]

[246] Spurr, *Restoration church*, ch. 3.

[247] John Coffey, *Persecution and toleration in Protestant England, 1558–1689* (2000), pp. 51–3, 71–2; Jonathan I. Israel, 'William III and toleration', in Ole Peter Grell, Jonathan Israel and Nicholas Tyacke, eds., *From persecution to toleration: the Glorious Revolution in England* (Oxford, 1991), pp. 129–70.

[248] E.g. Geoffrey Nuttall, 'The first non-conformists', in Geoffrey Nuttall and Owen Chadwick, eds., *From uniformity to unity, 1662–1962* (1962); Michael R. Watts, *The dissenters: from the reformation to the French revolution* (Oxford, 1978), ch. 3; John Spurr, 'From puritanism to dissent, 1660–1670', in Christopher Durston and Jacqueline Eales, eds., *The culture of English puritanism, 1560–1700* (Houndmills, 1996), pp. 234–65; Keeble, *Restoration*, ch. 6; Coffey, *Persecution*, pp. 58–68. Smyth, *Making*, ch. 3, provides a 'British', but not strongly European, dimension.

[249] N. H. Keeble, *The literary culture of non-conformity in later seventeenth-century England* (Athens, GA, 1987), ch. 6; Christopher Hill, *The experience of defeat: Milton and some contemporaries* (1984).

[250] E.g. Norman Sykes, *From Sheldon to Secker* (Cambridge, 1959), chs. 1–3. Spurr, *Restoration church*, has some sensitivity to the international context, but describes anglicanism largely in domestic terms.

[251] For religion in early party ideology: Harris, *London crowds*, chs. 4–6. Toleration had little positive support in 1689 – for explanation of the act: Henry Horwitz, *Parliament, policy and politics in the reign of William III* (Manchester, 1977), pp. 20–9.

[252] See Craig Rose, *England in the 1690s* (Oxford, 1999), pp. 171–8, 190–4; Holmes, *British politics*, esp. chs. 2, 3; W. A. Speck, *The birth of Britain* (Oxford, 1994), pp. 45–8, 76–80, 157–8, 163–74.

Yet, as Durel's intervention shows, and as our examination of English history writing has already made clear, the European arena was central to ecclesiastical discussion in the century after the civil war. To join in disputes between churchmen and dissenters was to take a position on the nature of the European reformation and England's place in Christendom. Though rarely noticed by modern commentators, contemporaries constantly appealed abroad as they considered the legitimacy of the dissenters' schism, the justice of imposing a ceremonial and episcopal establishment or the safety of allowing people to worship as they liked. It is, perhaps, too much to say that English religious disputes in the first age of party were *about* the country's relations with Christians elsewhere. Yet this often came close to being true, so if we are to understand this vital dimension in the battle between Whigs and Tories, we must explore how the two groups thought the English fitted into international spiritual entities.

To best place to start is with the apologia for the 1662 settlement. Defences of a monopolistic, episcopal and ceremonial church became a crucial plank of Tory ideology, but they also provided the key concepts which would be contested for the next several decades. There was a lot of such anglican polemic (with some risk of anachronism, we can use 'anglican' to denote those who remained in the official church under Charles II): those who had imposed bishops and rituals had to justify their intolerance of other Protestants, and the result was a steady rain of sermons, pamphlets and position papers which began at the restoration and continued unabated to the exclusion crisis and beyond. Examining this material we find a variety of arguments, but the key ones were visions of an international church. Anglicans sometimes justified themselves in a purely domestic context, but such attempts were not ultimately satisfactory and had to be bolstered by a keener European sense.

For instance, one purely domestic stance was to denounce dissenters as the heirs of the puritans who had led the Great Rebellion. In this view, objections to bishops and ceremony had led inexorably to political revolt, and a pre-war style church, with its stress on order and hierarchy, was a vital fence against such anarchy. This was the reasoning in the preamble of the act of uniformity, and many preachers linked anglican principles and obedience.[253] Yet though such arguments remained central to anglican apologetic throughout Charles II's reign, they could not serve on their own.[254] Although this polemic boasted that the English establishment secured Stuart power, it was not really a defence of the *church* at all. It made no claims for the spiritual

[253] 14 Car II, c. 4: *An act for the uniformity of public prayers* (1662). For an early sermon example: Thomas Pierce, *England's season for reformation of life* (1660).

[254] For later use: [Marchamont Needham], *A pacquet of advices and animadversions, sent from the men of London* (1676).

truth of anglicanism (just for its political convenience), and it ultimately collapsed with changes of circumstance. Under James II (1685–8) the monarch undermined the establishment and appealed for allies among disaffected dissenters. In this situation, clerical denunciations of nonconformity suddenly seemed unwise, and churchmen sought accommodation with people they had hitherto vilified as rebels.[255] With their political polemic so unsatisfactory and unstable, conformists would need more of a case than this.

Some sought justification in biblical or patristic scholarship. As the 1662 settlement took shape, anglicans scoured the earliest Christian literature for the purest patterns of the church, and claimed it supported the episcopal and ceremonial arrangements finally made.[256] According to this view, the act of uniformity imposed God's will and to dissent was to disobey the deity. This style of argument *did* provide a spiritual reason for conformity, but its problem was the international context. If the English establishment was close to the ideal church, its forms should be accepted everywhere. Yet in fact nothing abroad looked very much like it. Apart from the religious settlements of Scotland and Ireland (imposed by Stuart power to match English models), nobody had adopted England's peculiar mix of Protestant doctrine, episcopal government and moderately ceremonial worship, and this raised disturbing questions about all other Europeans. How could churches which did not match anglicanism's pure model be valid? It they were not, were their adherents in danger of damnation, and would God have made a world in which only one nation had the institutional means of salvation? Nervousness about such issues soon surfaced. Although claims for the biblical and patristic perfection of anglicanism persisted through Charles II's reign, conformists fretted they might deny non-Englishmen churches, and tried to limit discussion within their own island to avoid this. Witness here Henry Dodwell. In 1679, this Oxford academic attacked nonconformists for not submitting to the English bishops, but insisted he only had space to deal with these local sinners so could not discuss differences between communions across Europe.[257] Similarly in 1676, Robert Conold argued episcopacy was the ancient and valid form of government, but then had to defend himself from accusations that it had insulted non-episcopal Christians abroad. In a postscript to the second edition of his book, he said he doubted he would be read in Leiden, Geneva or the cantons of Switzerland, so there was little

255 See below, p. 313.

256 For such arguments: Henry Hammond, *A vindication of the ancient liturgie of the church of England* (1660); John Lloyd, *A treatise of the episcopacy, liturgies and ecclesiastical ceremonies of the primitive times* (1660).

257 Henry Dodwell, *Separation of churches from episcopal government* (1679), preface, p. iv – though this pamphlet was drawn into wider discussions: preface, p. xv, and below, p. 308.

'fear of provoking foreign animosities'.[258] Perhaps most embarrassed was William Sherlock. Denouncing dissenters in 1681, he too tried to limit discussion by saying he could not be expected to apply his domestic analysis 'to the various Communities of foreign Churches'.[259] Yet dissenting opponents charged Sherlock with condemning Europeans, and forced an admission in a second work that his principles might end up reducing the true 'church into a very narrow compass'.[260]

Thus far, then, anglicans had not found a convincing defence of their establishment. They had either veered into mere political reaction, or had raised doubts about foreign Christians which they had difficulty answering. To compensate for this, churchmen developed further apologias. Although divergent – indeed, as we shall see, incompatible – these arguments imposed the 1662 forms on England, whilst allowing churches abroad to differ from this style. They therefore attempted to condemn domestic dissent, but at the same time tried to excuse the various and dissimilar establishments in other countries. These discourses stood at the heart of the anglican apologetic and – to an extent which has been only dimly recognised – they set the terms of ecclesiastical debate through the late Stuart era.

The first argument was that pursued by Jean Durel. As we have seen, this enterprising Jerseyman tried to turn the tables on decades of Protestant dissent. Ever since Elizabeth had established her 'mixed' ecclesiastical settlement in the mid-sixteenth century, puritans had complained that the establishment must be further reformed to match the best Protestant churches abroad. By contrast, Durel (and the many who took his line) did what we have seen historians doing. He insisted the church of England stood in the main current of the international reformation, demonstrating both foreign Protestants' approval of the English establishment and parallels between its worship and theirs. In this way, Durel and his supporters suggested it was local dissenters who were out of line. The European reformation loved the English church and insisted on its authority over English Protestants: only domestic nonconformists carped. At one level, of course, this was a neat rhetorical manoeuvre to wrongfoot dissent. More profoundly, however, it suggested a solution to the lack of anglican-style churches abroad. In this vision, foreign Protestant churches might not be identical to England's establishment, but were still sufficiently valid to have their opinions and practices cited. The international reformation was thus a brotherhood of godly communities,

[258] Robert Conold, *The notion of schism stated* (2nd edn, 1677), p. 104. First edn 1676.
[259] [William Sherlock], *A discourse about church unity* (1681), p. 607.
[260] [William Sherlock], *A continuation and vindication of the defence of Dr Stillingfleet's unreasonableness* (1682), p. 240. Sherlock was attacked by Richard Baxter, *An answer to Mr Dodwell and Dr Sherlock* (1682); [John Humfrey and Stephen Lobb], *A reply to the defence of Dr Stillingfleet* (1681).

with the various Protestant groups across the continent constituting the true church in their own lands.

This Protestant apology for conformity became central to anglican identity at the restoration. It emerged very early: in fact at the very moment it became clear most churchmen would reject the king's early appeals for accommodation. In July 1660, a group of newly restored bishops issued a stinging riposte to a paper from the puritan Richard Baxter. This had made proposals for compromise on liturgy and episcopacy; yet although Baxter himself had not mentioned European forms, the bishops' rejection rested on them. They claimed, with some chutzpah, that their establishment could not be altered because it harmonised with European practice. The old common prayer was not 'dissonant from the Liturgies of the other Reformed Churches' and ceremonies had 'been retained by most of the Protestant Churches abroad'. It was true that there were some divergences between anglican and foreign worship, but where this was the case, the bishops were sure continentals were jealous. The English liturgy had been endorsed by 'sundry . . . Divines of the Reformed Churches abroad', and even in the churches where ritual had been purged most thoroughly, the English style was 'approved by the Judgement of the most Learned'.[261]

Having been launched at the restoration, this 'reformation' anglicanism thrived through Charles' reign. Clerics appealed to the varied communions of reformed Christians abroad (bodies whose very citation proved their validity in their own countries) to shame those who separated from the truly Protestant church of England: Thomas Long's 1673 work, *Calvinus redivivus*, providing a particularly fine example.[262] Those who could not find their own harmonies between the church of England and continental Protestantism could simply quote Durel. By 1662 he reinforced his fantasy council with an enthusiastic sermon, which provided further material to anchor the English church in the wider reformation.[263] One particularly powerful polemic suggested Europeans were appalled by nonconformists' disloyalty. Whatever the similarities between practice abroad and dissenting demands, conformists insisted that foreign Protestants were disgusted at

261 Matthew Sylvester, ed., *Reliquiae Baxterianae* (1696), pp. 242–7.

262 Thomas Long, *Calvinus redivivus* (1673). There was an early burst of works justifying liturgy and/or episcopacy because foreign Protestants had them: e.g. Hammond, *Vindication*, p. 5; John Gauden, *Considerations touching the liturgy* (1661); [Thomas Morton], *Confessions and proofs of the Protestant divines of reformed churches* (1662). Later, works arguing for anglicanism on other grounds also cited foreign approval: e.g. Timothy Puller, *The moderation of the church of England* (1679), p. 203; [John Cheney], *The conforming non-conformist* (1680), p. 48; William Saywell, *The original of all plots in Christendom* (1680), pp. 127–34; Edward Stillingfleet, *The unreasonableness of separation* (1681), pp. 186–91, 407; William Saywell, *Evangelical and catholic unity maintained in the church of England* (1682), epistle.

263 John Durel, *The liturgy of the church of England asserted* (1662).

puritan attacks on the valid English expression of their religion.[264] An early exponent of this argument was the London layman, Richard Lytler. Writing in 1662, he insisted foreigners had no real quarrel with English bishops or liturgy, and that the godly had a duty to work together to uphold their faith. Given this, Europeans would be far more upset that people were breaking from a fellow church than that they might adopt that church's forms above their own models. 'O Sirs,' cried Lytler as he appealed to dissenting ministers, 'be *perswaded* after all your Doubts.' 'Observe the *Act for Uniformity*; and take more care of giving offence to *Reformed Protestant Churches* abroad by your *Non-conformity*, then any offence they will take at you thereat.'[265]

The international reformation was central to anglican apologetic – but it did not exhaust clerical thought. Two further strands of argument explained why Englishmen must join one church, even though Europeans could worship in ones which looked different. The first was Erastianism. Following the thought of the sixteenth-century reformer, Thomas Erastus, some anglicans argued that the political authority in each state had the right to order religion as it saw fit. It was therefore perfectly logical that churches in each land would diverge: rulers had different personal preferences and political challenges to meet in their religious policy. Put this bluntly, the case did not sound particularly spritual. Yet as Edward Stillingfleet explained in his 1661 work, *Irenicum*, state control served Christian needs. The main reason was that Christ had left much about his worship undecided. Although fundamental doctrine was clear from the bible, Jesus had made no absolute decrees about the details of ecclesiastical ritual or government, so in these areas Christians were free to shape churches themselves. In this situation, something was needed to avoid chaos. Since Christ had not left complete instructions, there was a danger each person would run after their own fancies, and that this would disrupt the union of believers which the Messiah most definitely had enjoined. The answer to this problem was state coercion. If all in a nation were forced into an establishment by the civil power, and if that civil power ruled on the indifferent points of worship, this would serve God's desire for harmony.[266] Using this argument, Stillingfleet could condemn local dissent whilst allowing divergences across Europe. All Englishmen had civil and divine duties to submit to the anglican forms because they were the church instituted by their king and parliament. The people of other nations, however, were a different matter. They must obey their own rulers, so long as

264 Authors quoted disapproval of Tudor separatists by Bucer, Martyr, Calvin etc.: e.g. [Thomas Long], *No protestant but the dissenters plot discover'd* (1682), p. 83; John Norris, *A discourse concerning the pretended religious assembling in private conventicles* (1685).

265 Richard Lytler, *The reformed presbyterian* (1662), p. 155.

266 Edward Stillingfleet, *Irenicum: or a weapon-salve for the churches wounds* (1661).

these broke none of the fundamentals of faith when designing their particular church.[267]

Of course, Stillingfleet's careful explanation did not remove the initial shock of his position. Erastianism still struck many as making a Christian virtue out of naked political power, and – as we shall see – its opponents could point out some pretty uncomfortable consequences of the doctrine. Yet the discourse was surprisingly influential after 1660, not least because it gelled with the royal supremacy and the national organisation of the church. Since the Tudor era, the monarch had been 'supreme governor' of an establishment exactly coterminous with the realm. Generations of clerics had praised this arrangement (arguing that it gave the church a secular protector, made reform easier by giving the king the key role, and clarified ecclesiastical membership by equating it to political subjection), and in the restoration decades many churchmen flirted with Erastianism as they tried to defend these advantages.[268] As they did so, they presented the universal church as a federation of national, political, churches, and fitted anglicanism into a much wider whole.

The remaining argument was the newest of the church's defences. The idea that the English establishment was Protestant, and the notion that it was political, were both perfectly familiar to Tudor and early Stuart thinkers. In the mid-seventeenth century, however, a third interpretation had gained ground: namely, that the English church was still part of a universal ecclesia which extended far beyond the international reformation. According to this view (aspects of which we have already glimpsed in Peter Heylyn's and Jeremy Collier's histories), the earliest Christians had formed a single communion whose essential unity and authority had not been broken even as the faithful had multiplied, dispersed and diverged.[269] Although God's people had divided into particular ecclesiastical institutions as they had spread out from Palestine, a universal, or 'catholic', entity still bound them. This universal church legitimated communions that recognised its primitive forms and jurisdiction, but ejected those that denied its power or strayed too far from original ideals. Within this vision, the anglican church was valid because it had respected the universal authority, while true churches abroad were those which remained in conformity with its ideals. Dissenters, by contrast, had rebelled against this 'catholic' authority, and were damned.

267 *Irenicum* did not condemn dissent (written before the 1662 act), but Stillingfleet later did: *The mischief of separation: a sermon preached at the Guildhall Chappel May 11, 1680* (1680), esp. p. 16.

268 Erastianism, or at least affection for the royal supremacy, runs through Spurr, *Restoration church*, ch. 3.

269 For Heylyn, see above, pp. 90–9.

Put this way, the argument sounds somewhat abstract: and any reflection on it would raise disturbing questions about England's Tudor reformation, because this had occurred without consulting any universal church. In the hands of an exponent such as Herbert Thorndike, however, the discourse became much tighter.[270] Thorndike was a Cambridge scholar, who had been ejected from his college post by the parliamentarian authorities in the civil war for his anti-puritanism, and who had used his forced leisure over the next fifteen years to defend the old establishment.[271] The trick to grasping his thought is to understand the precise power his 'whole church' exercised over each particular branch. It did not lie in any contemporary international institution. If it had there might indeed be questions about England's sixteenth-century reformation. Rather, authority lay in the forms of church government and ceremony established at the birth of the faith, the most important of which was episcopacy. According to Thorndike, bishops had been instituted *jure divino* (by God's law), and then maintained by direct apostolic succession, to perform two vital roles. First, they ensured order within dioceses by exercising exclusive authority over other ministers. Second, they ensured harmony *between* dioceses. Because bishops controlled their local churches absolutely, they could speak for them collectively in dialogues with Christians elsewhere. They could hold the universal communion together by expressing concord with other prelates, or they could deal with threats to the cohesion of the faith by reproving other bishops whose dioceses lapsed into heresy, disunity or sin.[272] Given this, it becomes clearer what accepting the authority of the universal church meant. It meant reasonable closeness to the patterns of worship of the primitive Catholic church, but most essentially it required government by bishops. It also became clearer what rejecting that authority entailed. It might involve abolishing episcopacy (leaving the faithful with no way to settle local disputes, or of speaking with one voice to Christians elsewhere); or, as importantly, it might involve usurping authority over other dioceses.[273] Bishops should maintain Christian coherence by warning colleagues whose flocks fell into error, but to go beyond this to claim direct jurisdiction in other dioceses would confuse ecclesiastical discipline and break the mechanisms for ordering the church. In this way, the sin of the popes (who had wrongly claimed universal ecclesiastical

[270] For more detail: E. C. Miller, 'The doctrine of the church in the thought of Herbert Thorndike, 1598–1672' (Oxford D. Phil. thesis, 1990).

[271] See W. B. Patterson, 'Thorndike, Herbert', *ODNB*, LIV:595–8.

[272] The clearest summary was Herbert Thorndike, *Just weights and measures* (1662), ch. 6, esp. pp. 40–1.

[273] For presbyterians as schismatics: Herbert Thorndike, *The due way of composing the differences on foot* (1660), pp. 26–7; Herbert Thorndike, *A discourse of the forebearance, or the penalties that a due reformation requires* (1670), pp. 62–72.

authority) neatly balanced the errors of the English puritans (whose attack on episcopacy had swept away the ancient means of Christian unity).[274]

There were further subtleties in Thorndike's vision. For example, he sometimes implied that a general synod of *all* the world's bishops (were it ever to convene) would bind English dioceses, even if their own leaders objected; and sometimes included certain primitive ceremonies as well as episcopacy in his marks of a true church.[275] Similarly, Thorndike could be unclear what form episcopacy must take. So long as there was a bishop in each diocese, he seemed prepared to accept that these dioceses might be small, with their leaders working closely with ordinary ministers in their pastoral task.[276] This was a vision of 'reduced episcopacy' which had been advocated by Archbishop James Ussher of Armagh in the early Stuart period, and which some moderate dissenters such as Richard Baxter would have accepted.[277] Yet rather than be mired in these issues here, we should stress two things about Thorndike's line of argument. First, it identified a church beyond England. Within this ethos, local communions would be forgiven some variety of precise belief and practice so long as they kept to the rules for universal unity. The bishop-led churches of Europe (along, incidentally, with England's medieval institution) were therefore valid so long as they did not grossly transgress the example of the primitive church.[278] Second, as historians such as John Spurr and Jeff Collins have shown, Thorndike's vision became increasingly important as the later seventeenth century wore on.[279] Although writers differed in precise emphasis, the idea that episcopacy was the soul of the universal church advanced through the 1640s as the church was attacked by radical Protestants, and in the 1650s as it was assaulted by the civil power. Given such enemies, it was understandable if restoration clerics clung to episcopal legitimation. Recent experience told against a treacherous Erastianism which could excuse Cromwell's attacks on the church once he was in power,

274 For papal usurpation: Thorndike, *Discourse of the forebearance*, p. 76; Herbert Thorndike, *An epilogue to the tragedy of the church of England* (1659), bk III, p. 399. One later pamphleteer suggested papists' disregard of episcopal power made them presbyterians: *Animadversions on a late pamphlet entitled the naked truth* (1676), p. 63.

275 Critics accused Thorndike of surrendering England's ecclesiastical independence: e.g. Richard Baxter, *Against the revolt to foreign jurisdiction* (1691), pp. 119–27.

276 E.g. the suggested episcopal supervision of teams of presbyters in Herbert Thorndike, *Two discourses* (1650); or the colleges of presbyters in county towns suggested in Thorndike, *Due way*, pp. 38–44.

277 Reduced episcopacy involved bishops presiding over small dioceses and advised by synods of ordinary ministers. Ussher circulated his ideas in the 1640s but they were not published until he died: James Ussher, *The reduction of episcopacie* (1656).

278 Thorndike insisted the Roman church was true, if corrupted (e.g. *Just weights*, ch. 1), but also accepted the validity of Protestant episcopal churches: *Due way*, pp. 250–3; *Discourse of the forebearance*, pp. 75–7.

279 Spurr, *Restoration church*, 107–32; Jeffrey R. Collins, 'The restoration bishops and the royal supremacy', *Church History*, 68 (1999), 549–80.

and against a continental reformation whose thoroughgoing protestantism appeared to have inspired his puritan allies.

Taken together, the discourses we have been examining demonstrated how energetic the anglicans were in their defence of 1662. Faced with the need to suppress diversity at home, whilst allowing it across the continent, churchmen came up with not one apologetic, but three. In Europe, true communions were the people within an international brotherhood of local Protestant churches; they were political establishments instituted by civil governments; *and* they were the dioceses of bishops whose federation constituted the universal church and which respected primitive models of worship. Moreover, there is evidence that anglican arguments won over some of their intended audience. In 1660, the presbyterian minister John Humfrey briefly joined the re-established church. He did so on the Erastian grounds that episcopacy was not wholly evil, and that since the king had enjoined government by bishops, he would submit for the sake of Christian peace.[280] Similarly in 1661, the firebrand puritan Zachary Crofton was criticised for taking anglican communion whilst imprisoned in the Tower of London. He, however, defended himself by arguing that the official church was not wholly beyond hope, and proved this by citing foreign Protestant approval.[281]

Yet for all its vigour and occasional successes, anglican apologetic was badly flawed. In the years after 1662 the church faced continued challenge (from Roman Catholic kings who tried to use their prerogatives to break its monopoly, as much as from dissenters), but rather than help, its varied defences opened up internal divisions and handed polemical gifts to opponents. First, the defences cut across each other. Finding three different churches abroad, the discourses proved of varying attractiveness to different clergy, and so divided churchmen just as they needed unity. As we shall see, this aided the birth of party: some conformists were pulled to a Whiggish sympathy with dissent in reaction to anglican visions of the international communion they found distasteful. Second, each of the solutions to the European conundrum left anglicans vulnerable to attack from without. None ever quite policed diversity (allowing communions to differ across the continent always provided arguments for toleration within England itself); and each tucked the English in with strange foreign bedfellows. As a result, anglican propaganda probably did more to shape and encourage assaults on the church than defend it. It raised the issue of the universal communion, but found itself weak in this area. It thus ensured the debate about 1662 (which became so central to party division) would be lively and fought in exactly this arena.

[280] John Humfrey, *The question of re-ordination* (1661).
[281] Zachary Crofton, *Reformation not separation* (1662), esp. p. 43.

We can start with the incompatibilities in anglican propaganda. Even at an initial glance these were glaring. Anglicans had identified three quite different candidates for the true church abroad, and although many tried to combine the analyses (for example, allowing monarchs to set the boundaries of bishop-led dioceses; or citing foreign Protestant approval of an Erastian church), ultimately the strain told.[282] The problem was that contrasting emphases in the descriptions of the international church raised doubts about the harsh treatment of dissenters and compromised the united front against them. Whilst the vision of an episcopal catholic church condemned nonconformists absolutely, neither Erastianism nor Protestant brotherhood would go that far; and those attracted to these internationalisms might question whether English dissenters must be persecuted. Erastians, for example, could believe the civil power could have settled on a non-episcopal and non-ceremonial church, which would not have upset the English puritan tradition. They could also conceive a magistrate who sought civil peace by tolerating different denominations in the realm. Advocates of the international reformation, meanwhile, had to accept that parts of their Protestant brotherhood looked more like the churches English dissenters were demanding than their own establishment. This meant there could be no fundamental objection to reforming institutions to satisfy nonconformity (a Swiss, Dutch or Scots style church in England would remain a valid part of the European reformation), whilst the mutual respect shown by Protestants in different parts of Europe might be a model for an indulgent settlement at home. In the past, historians have noted such differences in attitude to nonconformity and have suggested some churchmen formed a 'latitudinarian' faction, hostile to prevailing 'high church' antipathy to dissent. This probably jumps the gun. There were clear ecclesiastical parties after 1689, but before then an almost universal condemnation of dissenters' schism (if not their religious preferences) blurred any factionalism.[283] Nevertheless, if we keep the focus on visions of the international church, there may be an argument for identifying latitudinarians (if that is what we must call them). Men who have been included in this group – Burnet, Stillingfleet, Edward Fowler, Simon Patrick or John Tillotson – were often more sympathetic to Erastian or Protestant

[282] Henry Hammond (who influenced Thorndike) grouped bishops into provinces with binding councils, but admitted princes also could call national councils: *Of schism: a defence of the church of England* (1654), pp. 59–60. Stillingfleet, *Unreasonableness*, quoted foreign Protestants to back his Erastianism, as did *Irenicum*, pp. 397–411. For the anglican's fudge on foreign Protestants: Spurr, *Restoration church*, ch. 3.

[283] For scepticism about early latitudinarianism: John Spurr, '"Latitudinarianism, and the restoration church', *HJ*, 31 (1988), 61–82; Richard Ashcraft, 'Latitudinarianism and toleration', in Richard Kroll, Richard Ashcraft and Perez Zagorin, eds., *Philosophy, science and religion in England, 1640–1700* (Cambridge, 1991), pp. 253–82.

positions than high episcopalian ones; this affected *how* they condemned dissent and may ultimately have undermined their willingness to do so.[284]

The problem of internal anglican tension is perhaps best illustrated in the restoration career of Edward Stillingfleet. We have met Stillingfleet repeatedly – but it is the response to his Erastianism we are interested in here. As we have seen, this writer provided a political defence of church establishments in his 1661 *Irenicum*. At that point the restoration settlement had not reached its final form, and Stillingfleet argued that the magistrate should opt for something rather less episcopal and ceremonial than the church which eventually emerged. When he lost this argument, however, the author's Erastian principles led him to be fiercely loyal to 1662, and he even became one of the most passionate critics of dissent. By the exclusion crisis, some had begun to countenance concessions to nonconformity to unite Protestants against the popish peril. Stillingfleet, however, denounced all departures from the establishment.[285] In a hugely controversial sermon, *The mischief of separation*, he exculpated nonconformists, charging that their disobedience to the law was a wilful destruction of Christian harmony.[286] Soon after, he answered his numerous critics with a weighty follow-up. His *Unreasonableness of separation* repeated his earlier attack, and included a blow-by-blow account of the political trouble puritans had caused since Tudor times.[287]

Reading Stillingfleet's work, one might imagine fellow clerics would be grateful for its robust defence of their position. A few were. Yet others, concerned about its implications for the international church, were decidedly cool. As John Marshall has pointed out, many restoration clerics accused Stillingfleet of 'Hobbism'. They charged that he had fallen under the spell of the reviled interregnum theorist Thomas Hobbes, and had simply equated true faith with the mere will of states.[288] As they did this, they echoed Thorndike and his appeal for a universally valid form of the church. In his restoration-era writings, Thorndike had objected to Erastian philosophy. He had suggested that the catholic communion of Christians (a body to which anglicans claimed they belonged when they recited the creeds) would mean nothing if the local will of rulers decided Christian practice, and so created huge variety from country to country.[289] Such fears were repeated by authors such as Henry Dodwell and Samuel Parker in the exclusion period. Whilst agreeing with Stillingfleet that dissenters were sinful, they warned their audiences off his arguments about the godly abroad. They complained that a party in the church was using dangerous Erastian principles to excuse

[284] See below, pp. 315–21, 326–9.
[285] Henry Horwitz, 'Protestant reconciliation in the exclusion crisis', *JEH*, 15 (1964), 201–17.
[286] Stillingfleet, *Mischief*. [287] Stillingfleet, *Unreasonableness*, pt 1.
[288] John Marshall, 'The ecclesiology of the latitude men, 1660–1689', *JEH*, 36 (1985), 407–27.
[289] Thorndike, *Due way*, pp. 228–9.

foreigners who diverged from proper episcopal government, and so were destroying the true basis of international unity.[290] William Sherlock followed suit, despite claiming to defend Stillingfleet. His pamphlets advertised support for the *Unreasonableness of separation* in their titles; but their contents belied this, again promoting episcopal, not state, establishments as the true church overseas.[291]

Such latent strains within anglicanism were bad enough, but in 1685 there was an open rupture. Curiously, it came as Stillingfleet attempted a retraction. From as early as 1662, the arch Erastian had been moderating his stance, coming to believe there were areas of church activity – such as excommunication – which should not be governed by the state.[292] He made further concessions at the end of Charles II's reign, admitting that he had been wrong about bishops. In a preface to a sermon delivered at an ordination (a core episcopal function) he defended his *Irenicum* as the well-meaning thoughts of a young scholar, but revealed he had altered his opinion on church government. Having originally thought bishops were human creations, which the state was free to either institute or not, Stillingfleet was now convinced these were very ancient offices, established by Christ through his apostles.[293] This might look like a gracious concession to the episcopalian position, but it riled the choleric vicar of St Dunstan's, Canterbury. Intransigent to his core, Simon Lowth protested in a *Letter to Edward Stillingfleet* that his correspondent had not utterly renounced his *Irenicum*, and concentrated fire on the international ramifications of this.[294] Since Stillingfleet had not clearly repented his belief that political establishment legitimated non-episcopal churches in Europe, he effectively backed rebels against the correct forms of ecclesiastical government. 'You,' cried Lowth, 'have sided all along with the foreign Divines, and used their Arguments against the *Divine Right of Episcopacy*.'[295] Worse, Stillingfleet was encouraging alien miscreants to infiltrate the realm. Lowth complained that presbyterians from abroad were arriving in England and claiming to be valid ministers here, but that instead of denouncing such subversive entryism, Stillingfleet comforted the men involved. He assured them that though they had to be ordained by a bishop before exercising ministry on the English side of the Channel, they should simply see this as conformity to the demands of the local civil magistrate. The ceremony cast no aspersions

290 Henry Dodwell, *Separation of churches from episcopal government* (1679), p. 35; Samuel Parker, *The case of the church of England* (1681), p. 4.

291 See above, n. 260.

292 Edward Stillingfleet, *A discourse concerning the power of excommunication* (1662).

293 Edward Stillingfleet, *A sermon preached at a publick ordination . . . March 15th, 1684/5* (1685).

294 Lowth had already denounced French Protestants for abolishing episcopacy: *Of the subject of church power* (1685), pp. 32–5.

295 Simon Lowth, *A letter to Edward Stillingfleet* (1687), p. 29.

on their earlier ministry in their own countries: this had been perfectly legitimate even though it had never been sanctioned by episcopacy.[296] The dispute came to involve Robert Grove, the future bishop of Chichester, and soon descended into nit-picking trivia, as late Stuart controversies would.[297] The damage, however, had been done. Stillingfleet, one of the strongest defenders of anglican monopoly, had been savaged by fellow churchmen who could not accept his account of the international communion.

The tensions between Stillingfleet and his detractors did not immediately leak out into party politics, as the writer had not adopted the Whig's pro-dissenting agenda. As we shall see, however, his different position on the international church eventually led him away from Tory colleagues, and other anglicans broke ranks earlier to feed partisan division from its origin. On several occasions under Charles II, and particularly in the exclusion era, churchmen asked if persecuting nonconformists was defensible and made it clear that thinking about Europe fed their doubts. In particular, several seemed concerned about the advance of Thorndikian arguments within anglican apologetic. Insistence on a universally binding episcopacy threatened the traditional English respect for Protestants elsewhere, and in reaction some embraced the continental reformation so enthusiastically they began to ask if domestic dissenters (who could be seen as another branch of that diverse movement) might be treated with more sympathy.

Herbert Croft, the bishop of Hereford, was an early example. In 1675, this always somewhat unorthodox cleric (as a young man he been a Jesuit for a brief while) raised a storm with his tract, *The naked truth*.[298] This appeal for moderation concentrated on patristic scholarship, but was also concerned about foreign Protestants. Croft noted that those who condemned nonconformists tended to insist on a binding primitive episcopacy, and complained that this would unchurch people on the continent. 'I humbly beseech you be not too positive in this point', Croft begged: those who were obsessed with the episcopal office both misunderstand scripture, and condemned 'all the Reformed Churches'.[299] Interestingly, some of those who replied to *The naked truth* realised what was goading its author, and tried to neutralise his concerns with the old 'reformation' anglicanism. The pamphleteer Philip Fell countered Croft's scholarship point by point, but also cited foreign Protestant approval of England's church to prove it was still a full member of the Protestant international. Croft was wrong, he said, to question the establishment because continentals – '*Germans, Hollanders, Danes, Swedes, French*

[296] Ibid., pp. 29–31.
[297] [Robert Grove], *An answer to Mr Lowth's letter to Dr Stillingfleet* (1687); [Simon Lowth], *A letter to a friend in answer to a letter written against Mr Lowth* (1688).
[298] William Marshall, 'Croft, Herbert', *ODNB*, XIV:239–41.
[299] [Herbert Croft], *The naked truth, or the true state of the primitive church* (1675), p. 42.

and *Swiss*' – had learned English and crossed the Channel to benefit from anglican worship.[300] Similarly Gilbert Burnet (who on this occasion allowed his hostility to dissenters to overcome his moderation) denied that conformist principles would condemn Protestants abroad. Bishops were the correct form of ecclesiastical government, but there was a difference between the English who had easy access to episcopacy and must therefore submit to it, and those Europeans who had lost their prelates in the turmoil of the sixteenth-century reformation and whose difficult circumstances excused aberration.[301]

Burnet and Fell tried to whip Croft back into conformity, but notions of a universal episcopal communion continued to gain ground, and in the exclusion crisis horror at this drove clerics clean out of the anglican consensus and into the arms of the Whigs. In fact, two of the most notorious clashes between Whig and Tory ecclesiology were fired by exactly this process. The first was the case of Samuel Bolde. In 1682, this vicar of Shapwick in Dorset preached a sermon appealing for funds to relieve the suffering Protestants of France. There was nothing controversial in this, but Bolde risked far more as he extended his sympathy beyond the Huguenots. He suggested English dissenters were the French Protestants' coreligionists, and that they should benefit from the sort of toleration people demanded for those foreign brethren.[302] Bolde predicted this stance would land him in hot water, and defended himself in a *Plea for moderation*. This called for Protestant unity against popery, and revealed the source of his concern was high episcopalianism. Ridiculing notions of a Catholic communion still binding from primitive times, Bolde pointed out this not only invalidated most Protestant communions, but effectively unchurched the whole earth, since no denomination could prove their bishops descended in an unbroken succession from the apostles. As for ceremony: if this was justified by ancient standards, why did anglicans not insist on exactly the same pattern of worship in all countries?[303] As might be expected at the height of the party tensions of the exclusion era, such words produced a vicious Tory backlash. Bolde's works were savaged in the Tory press, and the man himself was hauled before the diocesan courts for seditious libel. He was imprisoned for seven weeks until the fines imposed upon him were paid.[304]

Even more clearly partisan was the case of Daniel Whitby. In 1683, this prebend of Salisbury produced a *Protestant reconciler*, which – whilst

300 [Philip Fell], *Lex talionis, or the author of the naked truth stripped naked* (1676), p. 21.

301 Gilbert Burnet, *A modest survey of the most considerable things in a discourse lately published* (1676), pp. 26–8.

302 Samuel Bolde, *A sermon against persecution preached March 26 1682* (1682).

303 Samule Bolde, *A plea for moderation towards dissenters* (1682), pp. 15–18, 27–8.

304 Bolde was attacked in 'Remarks on Mr Bolde's plea for moderation', in J. B., *Catholic schismatology* (1685). For the other moves: Bryan W. Ball, 'Bold, Samuel', *ODNB*, VI:463–4.

arguing for moderation towards dissenters from patristic examples – made the European dimension the emotional core of his case. In a passionate, sixty-page preface, Whitby defended his position by asserting that compromise was the essence of the international reformation. Writers from across the continent were cited to prove that Protestants agreed to differ on unnecessary things (such as precise forms of worship) so that they could unite on fundamentals against Rome. A statement from the Transylvanians summed up: '*The Protestant Churches*, notwithstanding their differences, are to be moved to exercise *Moderation*, compassion and *Mutual Toleration* towards one another.'[305] Going further, Whitby subverted the usual anglican appeal to the reformation to argue for domestic indulgence. Of course, foreign Protestants from the whole spectrum of the reformation maintained communion with anglicans, and insisted England's official church was a true one. Yet exactly such tolerance for Protestant difference must be extended to English dissenters. The forbearance necessary to keep the anti-papal cause together meant the European reformation could not be an alliance of rigid territorial churches: unless it accepted variety it would lose its vital deeper unity. 'What Reason', Whitby asked, 'can be given why these [flexible] Conditions of Communion betwixt *Reformed Churches* should not obtain amongst Members of the same *Christian Church?*'[306] Importantly, this writer followed Bolde in revealing that concern at the spread of Thorndikean argument was a key motivation for speaking out. He mocked suggestions that anglicanism was set in stone by the authority of a universal communion: if that were so, why did churchmen not insist their forms be imposed abroad?[307] Whitby pushed this argument as he knew it caused real difficulties for Thorndike's disciples. It exposed their hostility to swathes of the European reformation (they had abandoned the church's old 'candor' to others); and it ran counter to their church's own official statements. Whitby gleefully quoted the preface to the 1662 prayer book which denied a universal authority for ceremony. '*We condemn no other Nations*,' the prayer book said, '*nor prescribe any thing but to our own People only*.'[308]

Whitby quoted the prayer book, and a plethora of earlier anglican scholars, to prove himself within the church's traditions. Unfortunately, however, he was caught in the same backlash which had overwhelmed Bolde. Nicknamed 'Whigby' (and he had in fact come close to advocating exclusion in another 1682 tract), he became the bête noire of the Tory press for a season – attacked by scholars such as William Sherlock for misrepresenting the early history of the English church, but also savaged in more popular works, including a bitterly ironical *Letters of thanks* from infamous rebels such as

[305] [Daniel Whitby], *The Protestant reconciler* (1683), preface, p. 41. [306] Ibid., p. 57.
[307] Ibid., p. 45 [308] Ibid., main text, p. 41.

the Münster anabaptists.[309] In fact, Whitby's views and fate escalated into a defining show of strength between the parties. The man himself followed his original work with a second part of the *Reconciler*.[310] This urged all to communion in the national church and so attempted to get the author out of trouble; but it craftily echoed the logic of the earlier section by insisting that dissenters had sinned against an international reformation which must show forbearance between its different parts. Unsurprisingly, Tories were not placated. 'Whigby' was brought before his bishop and forced to apologise for his publication. The Tory press gleefully reported this as a full recantation; the principles of the *Reconciler* were formally condemned by Oxford University in July 1683; and the book was publicly burned in the Schools Quadrangle immediately afterwards.[311]

The cases of Bolde and Whitby make it clear tensions between anglican accounts of the universal communion led to ruptures between churchmen, and fed the party tension of the exclusion era. Yet the European perspective was even more vivid in the truly key battle between Whigs and Tories: namely, the disputes between the establishment and the dissenters themselves. To a degree still to be acknowledged by historians, the nonconformists who fired the Whigs' case were encouraged by anglican Tory weakness on the international front. Dissenting spokesmen scented blood as their oppressors failed to agree a coherent vision of the continental church, and attacked at exactly this point. Of course, protest at coercing consciences and ejecting godly ministers was important within nonconformist polemic. But this was always joined with sustained mockery of anglican attempts to find a true church abroad. To start, dissenters questioned the foreign brethren which the established churchmen had chosen. They either denied that these foreigners wanted to associate with anglicans, or insisted anglicans should not want to associate with them. In addition, nonconformists asked whether churchmen had successfully policed diversity. If they admitted the true church might differ from country to country, could they really deny Christians the right to diverge within their own nation?

Interrogating the anglicans' foreign brethren took different forms according to the conformist discourse involved. In the case of the Durel-style

[309] William Sherlock, *A vindication of the rights of ecclesiastical authority* (1683); [David Jenner], *Beaufrons: or a new discovery of treason* (1683); Francis Fullwood, *The case of the times discussed* (1683); Laurence Womack, *Suffragium protestantium* (1683); S. T., *Remarks on the preface to the Protestant reconciler* (1683); *An awakening word in season to the grand-jury-men of the nation* (1684); *Three letters of thanks to the Protestant reconciler* (1683). For Whitby's exclusionism: Daniel Whitby, *Discourse concerning the laws ecclesiastical and civil* (1682). He wrote on the Whig side in allegiance controversy: [Daniel Whitby], *A letter from a city minister* (1689).

[310] Daniel Whitby, *The Protestant reconciler: part II* (1683).

[311] Jean-Louis Quantin, 'Whitby, Daniel', *ODNB*, LVIII:530–2.

association with an international reformation, there had been a long tradition of scepticism. For decades, puritans had complained that episcopacy and ceremony put the English church outside the international reformation, and they were not going to concede this point merely because Durel could cite a few cases where foreign Protestants seemed to approve of the Stuart establishment. Instead they accused churchmen of distorting the evidence from the continent, and found their opponents' arguments playing into their hands.[312] When nonconformists demanded the English move closer to European forms, churchmen had replied by pointing out the very wide variety of Protestant communions abroad. They had either used this to suggest reformation was essentially fractious and needed the discipline they were trying to impose, or that many foreign Protestants had retained high forms of episcopacy and ceremony, so the dissenters' appeal overseas might rebound on them.[313] Yet once anglicans themselves claimed foreigners approved their practices, the diversity of the continental reformation began to benefit dissent. Nonconformists could themselves ask where the general consensus to a set of forms was: in the rich profusion of the reformation, no particular church demonstrated many similarities with the English establishment, so any supposed endorsements were accidental and sporadic.

Exploiting these possibilities, Durel-baiting became a minor industry among restoration dissenters. The correspondence of Richard Baxter, perhaps the Restoration era's leading dissenter, shows his contacts were planning a definite answer to the Jerseyman in the late 1660s, and in 1672 the choleric Henry Hickman took aim with a lengthy assault on his position.[314] He accused Durel of editing out foreign criticisms of English forms, of quoting their approval out of context, and of wasting pages of print proving they supported features of anglican worship which dissenters had never rejected. Interestingly, too, he asked why churchmen had not followed the foreigners they admired more closely. Durel had quoted Lutherans who used rituals and had a form of episcopacy to legitimate the establishment. But Hickman pointed out these Germans also used Latin hymns, religious images and exorcism – things the anglicans had purged at the reformation. If Lutheran practice was to justify English bishops and ceremonies, he pondered, why was their example not equally binding in these other areas?[315] In 1679, an anonymous pamphleteer similarly accused Durel of cherry-picking. The writer agreed that his target had brutally edited the evidence from abroad (he claimed most of those at Durel's fantasy council had actually written

312 For early accusations: Sylvester, *Reliquiae*, p. 255.
313 E.g. [Henry Maurice], *A vindication of the primitive church* (1682), pp. 367–94.
314 N. H. Keeble and G. F. Nuttall, eds., *Calendar of the correspondence of Richard Baxter*, vol. 2, *1660–1696* (1991), pp. 78, 80, 85; [Henry Hickman], *Bonasus vapulans* (1672).
315 [Hickman], *Bonasus*, p. 30.

more in criticism of England than in praise); and suggested the vast range of European reform meant its occasional similarities to the English church proved very little. Instead of demonstrating that foreign communions systematically endorsed an anglican position, Durel had only shown that most anglican rites found some sort of parallel in one or other of the vast spectrum of continental churches. To argue, as Durel did, that these scattered parallels constituted harmony was like claiming languages were the same because they had a few words in common.[316]

If dissenters mocked anglican claims to participate in a continent-wide reformation, they raised darker fears about the church's other two defences. The problems with these, of course, were the communions identified by Erastians and by universal episcopalians overseas. Looking abroad, the churches supported by the civil magistrate and/or ruled by bishops were overwhelmingly Roman Catholic. Although Scandinavia and north Germany offered some comfort to anglicans (these regions had Protestant rulers and Protestant bishops), the official and episcopal establishments of France, Spain, Italy and large parts of Germany were irredeemably popish. Dissenters thus claimed (with considerable glee) that anglicans thought legitimated churches which generations of English theologians had taught were Satanic. Worse, it endorsed institutions which were actually persecuting Protestants – and, still more bizarrely, it justified bodies which had denounced the English establishment as heretical.

Nonconformist clamour was perhaps loudest against notions of a universal episcopal church. Dissenters repeatedly charged this analysis with legitimating popery, and in particular highlighted two disturbing developments in their oppressors' thought. First, they noted a growing tendency to admit Rome as a true church. After 1662, anglican advocates of a universal communion had continued a trend among certain early Stuart clerics, and insisted that, despite the errors and superstitions of papally led dioceses, they were in some sense valid. They still taught a basic core of Christian doctrine; they had retained bishops in a unbroken succession from the apostles; and they should therefore be considered true ecclesiastical bodies rather than limbs of antichrist.[317] Second, dissenters protested against a hardening of attitude towards the European reformation which had been palpable since the restoration. After 1662, anglican spokesmen became noticeably bolder in questioning the status of non-episcopal Protestants abroad. They were bolstered by the act of uniformity which insisted (for the first time) that clerics from lands without bishops must obtain episcopal ordination before they

[316] *The non-conformists vindicated from the abuses put upon them by Mr Durel* (1679), pp. 18–19.
[317] For this drift towards Rome: Spurr, *Restoration church*, ch. 3, esp. pp. 121–2.

were admitted to the English ministry, and so questioned whether Protestant Dutch, French, Swiss and southern German ministers were really ministers at all.[318]

The power of dissenting protest against such anglican positions was demonstrated from the earliest years of Charles II's reign. As the restoration church took shape, the great dilemma facing many puritan clergy was whether they could serve under bishops. Some felt they might, since they thought episcopacy could be legitimate if it did not surrender to its tendency to corruption, and because it initially seemed possible a 'reduced' version of the hierarchy might be offered. The problem, however, was re-ordination. Even before the uniformity act, some anglicans asserted that ministers had no valid orders until they went through a ceremony with a bishop. This stuck in gullets, not only because it suggested people had been leading parishes whilst unqualified to do so in the 1640s and 1650s, but also because it seemed to undermine so much of the European reformation. The career of John Humfrey illustrates the importance of this continental dimension. As has been mentioned, this Somerset puritan initially accepted a new ordination at the hands of his local bishop, William Piers. Publishing to explain himself, he said he was conforming for the sake of church unity, and because one could view episcopal ordination merely as civil confirmation of his earlier non-episcopal orders.[319] In response, however, less pliant puritans denounced him. Pamphlets accused him of casting doubt on his pre-restoration ministry and especially of delegitimating foreign Protestants. Re-ordination, thundered Zachary Crofton was a '*scandal* to the Reformed Churches'. It was a 'Ministry annulling, Reformation and Reformed-Churches-subverting' practice, which (since it determined 'the *non entity*' of Protestant communions in France, Holland and Scotland) must be a step on the path to Rome.[320] Similarly, although the author of *A peaceable enquiry into ... re-ordination* talked most about the logical impossibility of the practice named in his title, he also stressed he could not join 'Popish Idolatrous Prelates' in decrying 'the Reformed churches'. Accepting a new ceremony from bishops would cast reflections upon 'famous and numerous' communions abroad; it would therefore 'play the . . . Jesuits game' and might even provoke foreign Protestant princes against the country.[321]

318 Browning, *English historical documents, 1660–1714*, pp. 380–1. The act preserved recognition of ministry in 'foreign reformed churches', but this was longer valid in the establishment without episcopal ordination.

319 John Humfrey, *The question of re-ordination* (1661).

320 [Zachary Crofton], *A serious view of presbyters re-ordination* (1661), pp. 8, 24, 32.

321 I. R., *A peaceable enquiry into that novel controversie about re-ordination* (1661), epistle and pp. 37–8. Also, R[obert] A[lliene], *A letter to a friend, tending to prove that valid ordination ought not to be repeated* (1661), p. 2.

Under such pressure, Humfrey buckled. His first pamphlet apology had admitted he had suffered pangs of guilt about what he had done (rather poetically, he claimed he had worn his conscience as a thick coat in a hot summer), and revealed that the position of foreign churches had troubled him greatly. He had quoted their divines, and protested that the hierarchs were wrong to insist on re-ordination (even though he was prepared to submit to it) since it was 'manifestly scandalous to the Reformed Churches abroad'.[322] When faced with calls to consider foreign Protestants, Humfrey's doubts overcame him. He renounced the episcopal orders he had taken, and again explained himself in print. Whilst his *Second discourse* (1662) reaffirmed that re-ordination might work if words could be found to suggest it was merely a reconfirmation of already valid orders, Humfrey now explained he could not personally accept it. With hopes of ecclesiastical compromise gone by 1662, and with many bishops now insisting puritans recant their former ministry before they would re-ordain them, the cleric found he could not work in the establishment. In the final section of his work, Humfrey's grief at what had happened overflowed in a passionate attack on the bishops' disparagement of the European reformation. By rejecting a conciliatory form of words, they were not only hampering a union of English Christians, but passing over a ceremony which would have been of 'standing use' for 'those who came over to us from other Churches'. They were blackening themselves 'in the judgements of the Churches abroad', and rejecting the wisdom of 'the reformed Churches, who have had more light'.[323]

Given such early success in attacking anglican episcopalianism, the polemic remained central to dissenting assaults in the succeeding decades. Again and again churchmen were accused of betraying the international reformation with a principle which put them closer to foreign papists than Protestants. Bombardment became heavy in the 1670s, and reached a peak in the exclusion crisis. It was encouraged by press freedom and by the upsurge in universal episcopalianism, and it fed to the heart of the Whig campaign. An early indicator was Shaftesbury's 1676 *Letter to a person of quality*. Long recognised as Shaftsbury's first rallying cry against the French-inspired conspiracy he would imagine in the late decade crisis, this pamphlet has recently been reanalysed as part of a pro-dissenting attack on the high episcopalianism and so as an indication of the religious foundations of political parties.[324] What should interest us here is the role the foreign Protestant churches took. Although much of the work denounced anglican bishops for leading an absolutist faction at court, much also attacked their narrow

322 Humfrey, *Question*, p. 5.
323 John Humfrey, *A second discourse about ordination* (1662), pp. 129, 130, 132.
324 Mark Goldie, 'Danby, the bishops and the whigs', in Harris, Seaward and Goldie, *Politics of religion*, pp. 75–105, this at p. 83.

vision of true religion, and in particular their distance from non-episcopal churches in Europe. Echoing Humfrey almost word for word, Shaftesbury complained that clerics had unchurched whole swathes of the European reformation, and acted as catspaws for an international papist conspiracy. They had broken with the openness of England's first reformed Christians to the continent; they had shattered the alliance with 'the whole Protestant partie abroad'; and they had produced so dangerous a rupture within the reformed cause that the pope and his agent Louis XIV would have paid vast sums to achieve it.[325]

Once the exclusion crisis proper began, Whig polemic continued this line, and – as so often – Richard Baxter was in the thick of the brawl. Whilst co-ordinating dissenting polemic, this prolific pamphleteer mauled any who saw bishops as the essential mark of the true church, and his finest hour was his savaging of Henry Dodwell. Above, we saw Dodwell trying to protect himself from European arguments by saying he would only discuss the English implications for his episcopal doctrine.[326] Baxter, however, blasted apart this evasion, printing an exhaustive list of the logical consequences of his victim's position. Baxter insisted Dodwell believed Roman Catholicism was the true church in most of Europe, and took readers on a tour of the continent to show this. 'Those that live under Popish Bishops in *Italy*, [and] *Spain*,' the dissenter paraphrased, 'must live in their communion and under their command.' In France the poor persecuted Huguenots were in the wrong. They should rather 'joyn with the Papists, than . . . live as they do without [true] Sacraments or Church-communion'. Meanwhile in Switzerland, Holland and south Germany, the established Protestant churches had no episcopal ordination. They therefore had no true 'Ministers, Sacraments, Churches, nor Covenant-right to Salvation'. Protestants in north Germany and Scandinavia *did* had a form of episcopacy, but Baxter claimed even this wasn't good enough for Dodwell because the bishops in question had first been ordained by ordinary ministers in the sixteenth century. They thus had no direct succession from the apostles; their offices were invalid; and the Catholic clergy who claimed authority in these areas had a better case.[327]

Whilst dissenters could accuse high episcopalians of rank popery, they could level the same charges at Erastians. Roman Catholic churches on the continent were usually the official religion of the state – so those who had defended the civil magistrate's right to set spiritual forms in Europe were in the same trouble as those who supported bishops. John Tillotson found this in 1680. A close associate of Stillingfleet, he shared his colleague's views

[325] [Anthony Ashley Cooper, earl of Shaftesbury], *A letter from a person of quality* (1675), pp. 21–3.
[326] See above, p. 289. [327] Baxter, *Answer*, pp. 21–2.

on the secular ruler's right to set religion in each state, and expressed them in a startling manner when preaching to the king. Although most of his sermon condemned Rome's claims to be older and more widespread than anglicanism, one passage flattered the royal audience by insisting Christians had always bowed to the magistrate's will in religion (restricting protests to private piety) and that only a few recently emerged extremists questioned the principle of submission. 'No Protestant (that I know of),' Tillotson asserted, 'holds himself obliged to go and Preach up his Religion, and make Converts in *Spain* or *Italy*.'[328] Of course, this statement fitted the Erastian vision of a variety of churches supported by different rulers across Europe, but its stark implication that Protestants should not attempt to convert state-sponsored Catholics drew fire. John Humfrey (by now a committed dissenter) joined with Stephen Lobb in a sideswipe, protesting that Protestants avoided evangelising in Catholic Europe out of prudence, not principle, and because they knew there was little point casting pearls where they were sure to be trampled.[329] At greater length, the presbyterian John Collinges thanked Tillotson for rejecting Rome's claims on England, but could not accept that foreign popery must be left alone. The preacher's ideals, he pointed out, would condemn the heroes of the continental reformation. When Hus, Luther or Zwingli had first preached, popery was established by law, so Tillotson should think they had been wrong and by the same token was effectively demanding that Protestants must remain inactive now. Souls might be perishing in popish Italy and Spain, and heroic Protestants might be resisting the persecution of anti-Christian rulers in France, Savoy and elsewhere, yet Tillotson was insisting godly Englishmen should do nothing to disturb state religious policy in those places.[330]

If dissenters could protest at the true churches abroad generated by the strands of establishment polemic, they had a second rhetorical trump. They asked how anglicans proposed to police the diversity their apologetic had unleashed. To excuse the lack of anglican churches abroad, churchmen had admitted that Christians of different nations could worship in different ways, yet as part of this, they had had to construct excuses for variety between communities which did not simultaneously validate variety within one of them. Dissenters were unconvinced they ever managed such a feat. They asked repeatedly why they were barred from separating from the English establishment when it itself had separated from Rome; and they questioned why the political boundaries of the English state must define the smallest group of Christians who might choose how to worship. In an important respect,

328 John Tillotson, *The Protestant religion vindicated* (1680), p. 12.
329 [John Humfrey and Stephen Lobb], *An answer to Dr Stillingfleet's sermon* (1680), pp. 4–5.
330 [John Collinges], *Short animadversions upon a sermon lately preached* (1680), pp. 13, 14–16.

this was the most effective dissenting discourse of the era. It encapsulated an attractive appeal for Protestant freedom, and particularly sidestepped any counter-challenge from anglicans who might ask the nonconformists themselves to identify churches abroad. Dissenters were on shaky ground themselves here, since their various groups found it as hard as their persecutors to point to communions which shared many of their features in more than limited pockets of Europe. By suggesting that variety should not stop at national level, however, nonconformists shifted the terms of debate. No longer hamstrung by the difficulty of finding close foreign partners, they could discuss the freedom of individual congregations to worship as they pleased once variety was allowed.

We can see these pressures played out in the most sustained barrage of nonconformist polemic in the restoration era. As so often the fuse was lit by Edward Stillingfleet. Earlier, we noted that his 1680 *Mischief of separation* stressed that nonconformity broke Christian harmony and defied the godly power of the magistrate.[331] Yet in the middle of this sermon, Stillingfleet faced the problem of England's own break with Rome. The preacher solved this by stating that, whilst individuals must not leave churches, this did not prevent 'whole churches' diverging. Using his typical Erastianism, Stillingfleet defined 'whole churches' as those governed by secular powers. They were national, political communions; and more specifically they were the ecclesiastical institutions of 'such *Nations*, which upon the decay of the *Roman Empire* resumed their Right of Government to themselves, and – upon their owning Christianity – incorporated into one Christian Society under the same common ties and Rules of Order'.[332] This one sentence perhaps attracted more ridicule than any other uttered in Charles II's reign. A stream of dissenting pamphlets questioned how Stillingfleet had concluded that Christians could only divide along the borders of post-imperial states, and held up the logical absurdities of the position. Where, writers demanded, did any valid Christian text insist that the nations which succeeded the Romans were the fundamental units of Christ's church? Why were individual congregations, or the faithful of each city, not such autonomous bodies (at least these groups were mentioned in the bible, and had been addressed as churches by St Paul and St John)? If post-imperial states were the true building blocks of God's community, where did that leave the people who had worshipped in the Roman empire in their various localities before it broke up; or those such as Ethiopians or Armenians who still worshipped in places which Rome had never ruled? Was Stillingfleet suggesting these belonged to no church? Finally, if only national churches could separate from others, what should individuals do if they lived in country where

[331] See above, p. 298. [332] Stillingfleet, *Mischief*, p. 16.

they thought the established church was heretical? Stillingfleet demanded such people submit – but this condemned the reformation, and even Christianity, as both movements had begun in protest at corrupt political establishments.[333]

All these strands of dissenting polemic converged in their most robust challenge to the anglicans. Focusing their attacks on one particular point, key nonconformists asked what the English establishment thought was the true church in France. This was devastating, because churchmen had no cogent answer. If they plumped for the diocesan church there (as episcopalianism demanded, and as Erastianism would suggest, since this institution was supported by the French monarchy) then dissenters could simply accuse them of popery. Their enemies would have allied with a body which was a full part of Rome's communion, whatever its occasional complaints about the pontiff's interference in its internal affairs. If, on the other hand, anglicans picked the only available alternative and answered that the Huguenots were the true church in France, then nonconformists were as delighted. Suddenly their persecutors would have admitted that men might separate from an official church because they objected to its ceremony and episcopacy (dressed as the main reasons for the Huguenots' schism): why, English nonconformists could ask, did this logic not apply on their side of the Channel? The French situation thus encapsulated all the English establishment's embarrassments about the international church. They should not have been surprised that their critics returned to it several times as they made their case.[334]

Having surveyed the dissenting attack in the restoration era, it is useful to take stock of the whole debate over the church under Charles II. The basic lesson of our analysis has been the prominence of the European context. To an extent rarely recognised, the terms of controversy were set by the anglicans' search for sister churches abroad and by rejection of their varied solutions by nonconformists and even some churchmen themselves. If we observe that the justice of the 1662 settlement was at least as important in restoration history as the dispute over the power of the royal court, and if

333 For direct engagement with Stillingfleet's sentence: *Richard Baxter's answer to Dr Edward Stillingfleet's charge* (1680), pp. 30–41; John Owen, *A brief vindication of the non-conformists from the charge of schism* (1680), pp. 15–18; [John Howe], *An answer to Dr Stillingfleet's mischief of separation* (1680), pp. 24–6; [Vincent Alsop], *The mischief of impositions* (1680), pp. 22–3. For more general engagement with Stillingfleet: John Troughton, *An apology for the non-conformists* (1681); Richard Baxter, *An apology for the non-conformist ministry* (1681); Richard Baxter, *A second true defence of the meer nonconformists* (1681); John Owen, *An enquiry into the original . . . evangelical churches* (1681).

334 E.g. Baxter, *Answer*, pp. 20–1; [Alsop], *Mischief of impostions*, epistle dedicatory; [John Humfrey and Stephen Lobb], *Reply*, p. 12.

we remember that it drove the division between Whig and Tory, we could suggest the dispute over foreign Christianity was a crucial factor keeping Caroline politics so open and dynamic.

A second conclusion may be that the church's failure to find a cogent communion abroad paved the way for the more liberal religious settlement of 1689. This is a large claim, which must come with many caveats. As we shall soon see, it was the raw political pressure, rather than ecclesiological debate, which forced a reassessment after Charles II died. Moreover, even before 1685, there had been a number of encouragements to greater liberty which had little to do with finding a foreign faithful. For instance, in the Dutch wars of the 1660s and 1670s some commentators noted that Netherlanders allowed all their people to contribute to national resources by tolerating a variety of beliefs, and suggested England would only prevail if she followed that example.[335] Similarly, realisation that people would never be brought to agree the details of faith (perhaps fuelled by the mere survival of dissent) – and a growing conviction that Christianity was a charitable creed – told against persecution.[336] Yet despite all this, a good case can be made for the international context as the nemesis of 1662. As we have seen, it exposed the settlement to constant critique, and divided the anglican clergy who should have been its prime defenders. It also invigorated dissenters, helping to ensure they were so powerful they had to be conciliated when anglicans faced a more threatening foe after 1685. In addition, debate over foreign Christians swept people from the idea of a monopolistic church. We have seen John Humfrey, Daniel Whitby and Samuel Bolde caught in this tide as they found they could not reconcile any meaningful unity of faith in England with an acceptable account of the godly abroad. Richard Baxter is another particularly important example. He had always been from a moderate wing of dissent which had hoped for readmission to the establishment through accommodation, and had always been afraid of religious plurality. His attacks on Dodwell, however, led his logic away from the ideal of national church, to the principle that any sincere group of Christians must be allowed to break from others they found objectionable.[337] In fact, difficulties with the international context may do much more to explain the toleration act of 1689 than has ever been acknowledged. Finding a true communion overseas may have set a problem which could *only* be solved by abandoning a tight religious settlement. Restoration anglicans failed to marry uniformity and the foreign faithful; but after 1689 we shall see that many found they could explain their place in the world once they surrendered

[335] E.g. Henry Stubbe, *A further justification of the present war* (1672), pp. 27–75.
[336] Coffey, *Persecution*, ch. 3.
[337] One study of Baxter concludes he wobbled in support for a national church precisely when he was engaging Dodwell: William Lamont, *Richard Baxter and the millennium* (1979).

that uniformity. Church apologists squared the circle, but only by adopting a more flexible, diverse and tolerant anglicanism which *could* describe a church abroad.

CATHOLIC VERSUS REFORMED: THE FISSURE IN THE CHURCH, 1689–1720

Paradoxically, the arguments for anglican dominance collapsed just when that dominance seemed strongest. In the aftermath of the exclusion crisis, the victorious Tories took aim at their enemies, and this included persecuting dissent. During the 'Tory reaction' of 1682–5, the legislation against nonconformity was employed with full vigour, as was the argument that the church was the bulwark of obedience and order. Yet since this triumph was primarily political, it was horribly vulnerable to the political change, and this came in the second half of the decade. As soon as James II acceded to the throne, he began his campaign to promote his Catholic faith. Once he realised Tories would not aid him in this, he targeted the privileges of the church (its adherents were no longer to monopolise the universities, the army or public office); he claimed prerogative powers to grant religious liberty (there were declarations of indulgence in 1687 and 1688); and he recruited dissenters to displace the anglican governing elite.[338] This last aspect suddenly highlighted the dangers of persecuting nonconformity. Though wary dissenters refused to work with a papist monarch, bolder ones were tempted by James' offers and provided him with a grateful party in the country.[339] In response, the church began its own courtship of nonconformists. Denunciations of schism were replaced by friendly warnings that dissenters were being deceived by the king, and offers to look again at objections to 1662. As one sceptical observer put it, churchmen's anger was 'clear'd into a perfect *Calm*, and instead of *Force* and *Rigor*, we hear nothing now but of *Fair Invitations*'.[340] By the summer of 1688, the establishment was asking other denominations to join its protests when James prosecuted seven bishops for petitioning against his policies. The bishops' leader, William Sancroft of Canterbury, was ordering clerics to treat dissenters kindly, and hinting at revision of the restoration settlement to meet their aspirations.[341]

As we have seen, reaction against James' authoritarianism led to his removal in 1688. Yet prospects for anglican monopoly improved little. By

338 John Miller, *James II* (1978), chs. 9–12.

339 Mark Goldie, 'James II and the dissenter's revenge', *Historical Research*, 66 (1993), 53–88; Mark Goldie, 'John Locke's circle and James II', *HJ*, 35 (1992), 557–86; J. R. Jones, 'James II's Whig collaborators', *HJ*, 3 (1960), 65–73.

340 *Letter from a dissenter to the divines of the church of England* (1687), p. 1.

341 Browning, *English historical documents, 1660–1714*, p. 84.

now, even many churchmen were convinced refusal to accommodate dissent had created the crisis. If nonconformists had not been made bitter by their treatment, James would have seen less potential support for his attacks on the church, and would not have been tempted to promote Catholicism. Moreover, the replacement monarch was no enthusiast for the 1662 settlement. William was opposed to persecution on principle, and had been brought up in a Dutch church whose traditions were closer to many of England's dissenters than her establishment.[342] More importantly, his war forced change as it allied people of many different Christianities against Louis XIV, and required mobilisation by all Englishmen. Both these pressures demanded indulgence: the first so no ally would be offended by attacks on men of their own religious stripe, the second so no subject would be alienated from the military effort by religious prejudice.[343] To meet all these challenges, a group of London clergy close to the earl of Nottingham proposed an ecclesiastical settlement in the early spring of 1689. Their first proposal passed parliament rapidly. It was a measure to suspend penalties for breaches of uniformity (the so-called toleration act, though it applied only to orthodox Protestants, and on strict conditions). By contrast, the other element – a measure of comprehension – got into trouble. Designed to reduce the numbers worshipping outside the church, this offered concessions on ceremony and re-ordination to appease moderate dissenters, but it met opposition among the clergy and was abandoned by the start of 1690. The final arrangements, therefore, saw all nonconformists continuing in separation.[344]

In this collapse of church dominance, it might be thought the struggle over the international context would play little role. After all, the forces leading to the 1689 settlement had been political rather than ecclesiological. Moreover, the 1689 arrangements accepted religious diversity in England, so they removed the need for the restoration discourses which had tried to explain why a church which differed from all others in Europe should be allowed to impose its forms at home. Yet for all the power of these observations, visions of the international communion remained significant during and beyond the events of 1685–9. Far from withering into irrelevance, the old anglican languages adapted to the new circumstances, and remained central to party debate, even after the revolution. One of the discourses produced a variant which became the core of new acceptance of religious pluralism by an influential group of anglicans, and became vital to Whig ideology in the late Stuart era. Another, meanwhile, was affected by a reaction against the changes of 1689 and was refashioned into a Tory critique of its excesses. Unfortunately, the precise course of these changes can be difficult to

342 For William's religion: Claydon, *William III: profiles*, p. 99

343 Israel, 'William III and toleration', pp. 129–70.

344 Rose, *England*, pp. 161–71.

follow. Events moved quickly once James reached out to nonconformity, and many anglicans were busier with practical negotiation of new circumstances than ideological reformulation. The picture is doubly confusing, as what became the Whig position was initially endorsed by a wide spectrum of anglicans, and only narrowed to a party position in 1689. Nevertheless, the processes can be clarified if the story first concentrates on the emergence of this new discourse.

At first, James' religious policies caused little difficulty for established anglican apologias. All the polemics we have been exploring were designed to counter the challenge of Rome as much as dissent, so were actually invigorated in the church's campaign against royal Catholicism. From 1685 to at least 1687, clerics variously stressed that the pope had usurped the diocesan authority of other bishops within the universal primitive communion; that he threatened an international Protestant community of which the establishment was a full part; and that he interfered with the magistrate's proper authority (though the civil power in England might now have to be constructed as the 'king in parliament' which had passed anti-popish statutes, rather than by the Catholic monarch alone).[345] From 1686, however, anglicans had a problem. Once James reached out to non-conformists, they needed to remodel old discourses, or risk alienating dissenters whose support they had come to see as vital.

Their salvation was a variant of one of their restoration languages, which had adapted to accept religious diversity. This was a version of the international Protestant defence of anglicanism: one which Samuel Bolde and others had been hinted at during the exclusion crisis. We recall that in the early 1680s some anglicans had changed the stress within the church's traditional participation in the European reformation. Instead of seeing Protestant solidarity in the acknowledgement reformed churches gave to each other's local authority, they saw it in a willingness to differ on minor points in the face of the Roman threat.[346] In James' reign, as the popish danger became more pressing, these exclusionist hints were taken up and developed into a startlingly radical understanding of the anglicans' place in the reformation. Its starting point was, as ever, the recognition that Protestants in different parts of Europe diverged on the details of doctrine, church government and worship. In the new understanding, however, the solution was not to

[345] Anti-popish polemic was orchestrated (Spurr, *Restoration church*, pp. 90–1), and advertised itself: William Clagett, *The present state of the controversy between the church of England and the church of Rome* (1687); William Wake, *A continuation of the present state of the controversy* (1688). For continuities: Spurr, *Restoration church*, pp. 119–21. Edward Pelling, *The true mark of the beast, or the present degeneracy of the state of Rome* (1685), accused the papacy of undermining rulers (p. 15), usurping other bishops (pp. 16–21), and persecuting Protestants (pp. 29–30).

[346] See above, pp. 301–3.

divide into exclusive national establishments and respect each other's territorial monopoly – but rather to recognise the disputes were not fundamental, and to urge reformed Christians to live together in charity. In this looser vision of the international reformation, national churches must not be intolerant. Mutual forbearance and shared basic faith would ensure harmony between Protestants even if different species mixed in one place, and all should acknowledge that a minority in one location might hold very similar opinions to a church recognised as a legitimate establishment elsewhere. The logic of this, of course, was that anglicans abandon their persecution of dissent. Churchmen and their domestic rivals were both good Protestants; as parts of an endangered European movement, their duty was to seek accommodation instead of arguing each other into the ground. As an account of the international church this was less disciplined than anglicans were used to. It saw the reformation as a complex tapestry of overlapping denominations, of which English conformists, English nonconformists and the rival kinds of godly in many other countries were all full members. Despite this, however, the vision proved attractive to those who needed to conciliate dissent in the late 1680s. It provided a context in which an ideological shift could be made, solving the longstanding difficulty in finding a church abroad as it excused the abandonment of domestic monopoly.

As we said, tracing the exact process by which the new view found favour is difficult. Under James II, churchmen put most intellectual effort into their battle with Rome, and generally discussed approaches to dissent as a pragmatic alliance. Nevertheless, examining some of the key statements of this period, two factors appeared important in the transition. First, there was the general crisis of the continental reformation. Louis XIV's revocation of the edict of Nantes and his external expansion into Protestant areas put European Protestantism in real danger after 1685. The urgency of this situation transferred attention away from the internal organisation of the reformed continent (the question of authority over each territory which could be answered to favour anglican monopoly) and towards an overall defence of reformed Christianity which suggested disputes between Protestants must be suspended, at least until the whole edifice was secure. Second, William of Orange emerged as the most likely saviour of the English church. William's role as Protestant hope nudged opinion towards a less structured view of the international movement both because he was not an anglican (so was unlikely to uphold the church's existing monopoly) and because his preceding career had established him as the defender of the whole, diverse, reformation.[347] If William intervened, therefore, he might not preserve all anglican privileges,

[347] William's anti-French alliance included Calvinists and Lutherans: Troost, *William III*, chs. 6–8.

but churchmen could comfort themselves they would earn his protection as part of the overlapping alliance of denominations he was mobilising against Louis XIV.

Dutch propaganda in the last year of James' reign demonstrates how the new strand in anglican thought was encouraged. By 1687, William was trying to build up a party in England (even if it is unlikely he decided to invade until the spring of 1688), and his efforts involved circulating tracts written by close supporters.[348] The most famous was Gaspar Fagel's 1688 *Letter . . . to James Stewart*, but it was complemented by other works encouraging people to look to Holland for relief. At the heart of the message was Protestant reconciliation. Orange spokesmen asserted conformists and dissenters should unite against James' Catholic threat, and that William stood ready to broker and lead this alliance. Thus Fagel's letter told anglicans they should not persecute nonconformity. It also, however, warned dissenters to respect the church and ask for no more than bare freedom to worship. Similarly tracts by Gilbert Burnet (in exile in The Hague from 1686, and soon at the heart of Orange councils) tried to calm divisions between English Protestants and invited all to see William as their fair-minded patron.[349] The vital point about this propaganda was its broad view of the European reformation. Orange polemic stressed the whole movement had reached a moment of crisis, and that this demanded mutual forbearance and unity in the face of the Roman threat.[350] It also presented William as someone whose actions had proved he could lead *all* brands of reformed Englishmen. He had been the 'Head and Patron of all that profess the Reformed Religion'; he would 'embrace all Protestants with an equal tenderness'; and he came from a country whose domestic diversity and tolerance meant it could inspire all strands of that faith.[351]

This, of course, was only Orange propaganda, but it resonated with a surprisingly wide spectrum of anglicans, since its new vision of European Protestantism allowed English churchmen to approach rivals at home. For example, anglicans used it as they begged dissenters not to be seduced by James' offers of toleration. They stressed that it was not just the establishment that was in danger, 'nor any particular *Sect*', but the 'whole *Protestant* FAITH', so dissenters must support the official church to shore up the larger entity.[352] Similarly, polemic urged solidarity in England by citing French

[348] For the timing: Tony Claydon, 'William III and II (1650–1702)', *ODNB*, LIX:73–98.

[349] Gaspar Fagel, *A letter writ by Mijn Heer Fagel, pensioner of Holland* (1688).

[350] E.g. *Letter from several French ministers fled into Germany* (1688) – suffering foreign Protestants abroad demanding reconciliation in England. Fagel's *Letter* stressed Catholic persecution, p. 5.

[351] [Gilbert Burnet], *The ill effects of animosities among Protestants in England* (1688), p. 20.

[352] William Sherlock, *A sermon preached before the right honourable the Lord Mayor . . . Nov. 4, 1688* (1689), p. 20.

persecution, or the danger of a general war against all foreign and domestic Protestants.[353] Most explicitly, the closest we have to an official anglican olive branch used the language of a diverse Protestant international. When Archbishop Sancroft petitioned the king against a declaration of indulgence in 1688, he promised to consider an alternative relief for dissenters. In July, he backed this with a set of instructions to his clergy which told them to have 'tender regard to our *Brethren* the *Protestant Dissenters*', but which put this in a firm European setting. These injunctions portrayed a whole reformation in danger, and in need of 'godly love' between its parts, and the last article asked clergy to join dissenters in prayer for 'an Universal Blessed *Union* of all *Reformed Churches*, both at *Home and Abroad*, against our Common Enemies'. It is true that the prayer also asked for 'one Holy Communion' between all those who 'agreed in the Truth of [Christ's] Holy Word'.[354] It therefore urged reformed Christianity to cohere as a single entity and so clearly preferred the recreation of one communion in England above any general toleration. Nevertheless, the phrase 'Reformed Church*es*' (in the plural, and some of them at home) confirmed dissenters were true communions, and did so by acknowledging their place in the diverse European reformation.

By late 1688, then, an adapted version of anglican international Protestantism had received endorsement by the church's leadership, and widespread support in the establishment as a whole. It was leading people to accept approaches to dissent, and to acknowledge that nonconformists might have formed legitimate churches. Unfortunately, however, its fortunes dipped once William arrived. Although the discourse almost certainly helped the astonishingly easy passage of the toleration bill in the spring of 1689 (though the speed with which this happened has left later commentators grasping for a fully convincing explanation), it then retreated to the partisan position of a minority of the clergy. It was left stranded with one small (if influential) group as the bulk of churchmen defected back to more traditional arguments for anglican dominance. This process ensured debate about the position of the English church within Christendom would remain central to partisan politics. The majority of clergymen teamed up with the Tories to defend a church they thought was in danger; those still following the logic of 1688 sought support from the Whigs, and both sides drove their visions of the international communion to the heart of party programmes and polemic.

353 E.g. *The mystery of iniquity working in the dividing of Protestants* (1689), pp. 37–8; John Tillotson, *A sermon preached at Lincoln's Inn Chappel, on the 31st January, 1688* (1689). Both produced before William's authority was established.

354 William Sancroft, *The articles recommended by the arch-bishop of Canterbury to all the bishops* (1688), p. 4.

The first stage was the debate over comprehension in 1689. Although this measure was first promoted by the solidly anglican earl of Nottingham, it soon became controversial. Once the danger from James had passed, and once the toleration act had addressed the immediate problem of nonconformity, many clerics baulked at further compromise. In the first half of 1689 clerics bore repeated misfortune. They lost their legal monopoly of worship, seven bishops and many other clergy were suspended for not swearing loyalty to William, and the anglican-style episcopacy in Scotland collapsed, soon to be replaced by a presbyterian kirk. Unnerved by all this, most churchmen rejected further sops to dissenters. Allying with the parliamentary Tory party, they refused to consider more than bare indulgence for nonconformist worship. They first blocked the passage of comprehension in the Commons, then boycotted the special ecclesiastical commission convened to consider it in the autumn of 1689, and finally campaigned against the measure in a winter meeting of convocation (the representative assembly of the clergy, responsible for canon law).[355] As this rebellion unfolded, clear church parties emerged. We have seen tensions in the restoration establishment and how these have led some to identify 'high' and 'latitudinarian' factions under Charles II. As we said, however, this may be premature, for it was only with the debate on comprehension that there was an open rupture. In 1689, one group, whom we *can* now label the 'high church', rejected the measure. Meanwhile another faction (the 'low church', initially centred on Nottingham's clerical clients) continued to advocate compromise with nonconformity and entered a vigorous press debate with their rivals.[356]

The polemic of the comprehension controversy charts clearly how important European visions were to the arguments. If we look at the 'low' position, for instance, we see its spokesmen parading the new vision of the reformation as an overlapping and tolerant federation. In particular, they stressed their altered sense of the expectations foreign Protestants had of England. They no longer believed those abroad approved anglican persecution because the English establishment was a valid Protestant church; instead foreigners demanded reconciliation in England so the nation could lead the continental cause.

A key work here was Thomas Tenison's *Discourse concerning the ecclesiastical commission*. Written in October 1689 by a cleric of Nottingham's affinity, this answered William Jane's *Letter to a friend containing some quaeries*, which had questioned whether the special clerical meeting called to consider

355 For important context: John Spurr, 'The church of England, comprehension and the toleration act of 1689', *JEH*, 104 (1989), 927–46.

356 For dating church parties: Spurr, 'Latitudinarianism'.

comprehension was legal.[357] In his piece, Tenison paraded instances when the church had called commissions to consider its worship, but he soon turned from such dry precedent-hunting to more pressing reasons for change. Chief among these was the crisis of European Protestantism. Tenison alluded to the horrible danger the movement was facing – noting particularly the French and Irish Protestants who had been forced to flee to England – and suggested that in this grim situation 'the Eyes of the World are upon us'. The whole reformation was looking to the English to bury their differences so they could lead the cause: 'all the *Reformed Churches* are in expectation of something to be done which may make for Union and Peace'.[358] This tract was backed by other writers in a similar vein. Letters were published, supposedly from suffering ministers abroad, which insisted that English reconciliation was their only hope of salvation and that it would inspire similar unity elsewhere.[359] Other pamphlets agreed that union was needed because the whole European faith was in danger, and many suggested people across the continent were looking to England to lead accommodation as 'the *Centre of Protestant Unity*' or 'the greatest bulwark of the Protestant Religion in *Europe*'.[360] As importantly, sermons supporting comprehension breathed this cosmopolitan spirit. As they preached, Nottingham's men presented their measure as an appropriate response to William's salvation of international reform; whilst one performance, by our old friend Burnet, introduced a continent-wide theme which would become the leitmotif of the rest of his career.[361] Surveying the history of the entire reformed cause, Burnet lamented its rapid change of fortune. The initially rapid expansion of European Protestantism had recently come 'to a full stop'; and the preacher explained this was because 'those who embraced it, instead of carrying on their common Cause with an united Strength, have fallen a quarrelling among themselves over some Uncertain and Inconsiderable things'. Of course, English division was part of this picture, but Burnet was adamant this was only part of the problem. England shared the blame with Germans who had divided over the nature

357 [William Jane], *A letter to a friend, containing some quaeries about the new commission* [1689].

358 [Thomas Tenison], *A discourse concerning the ecclesiastical commission* (1689), p. 24.

359 *Some letters written by some French Protestants now refug'd in Germany* (1690).

360 N. N., *A letter to a member of parliament in favour of the bill* (1689), p. 6; *The interest of religion in England* [1690?], p. 7. Also: *The Protestant union* (1689); *A letter from a minister in the country to a member of the convocation* (1689), pp. 97–8; [Edward Stillingfleet], *Proposals tender'd to the consideration of both houses of parliament* (1689); *The vanity, mischief and danger of continuing ceremonies* (1690), pp. 36–8; *Vox regis and regni* (1690). *Vox populi, or the sense of the sober lay-men of the church of* England (1689) – p. 9 complained anti-comprehensionists were damaging relations with 'Reformed Churches abroad'.

361 E.g. Simon Patrick, *A sermon preached . . . before his highness, the prince of Orange, 20 January, 1688* (1689).

of the sacrament, and Dutchmen who had rowed over the precise process of salvation. Meanwhile, though the English had had a nasty scare under James, it was in the sufferings of French Protestants that the reversal was most keenly felt.[362] Viewed from this angle, the 'exhortation to peace and union' in the sermon's title was essentially international. English unity might strengthen their nation, but this was just one step in the general salvation of the Protestant cause.

In contrast to all this, opposition to comprehension returned to the older restoration discourses which had placed the establishment in the wider world. Before covering this, however, it is vital to note that the high church party rarely, if ever, called for the repeal of the toleration act. Although many clergy probably felt this measure was at the root of their troubles, their public spokesmen realised its removal was not practical politics. At the time of the comprehension dispute it had been passed very recently; once it had become settled law, monarchs opposed a move which would return their realm to religious turmoil and the dissenting community grew too visible to tackle head on. Moreover, accepting a bare liberty of worship paid polemical dividends. It allowed high churchmen to pose as moderates (they could deny they wanted a return to the dark days of persecution), and more particularly it allowed them to attack the low churchmen's European vision without sliding back into restoration difficulties.[363] In fact, swallowing toleration greatly aided the redeployment of old defences of anglicanism. The original, monopolistic purpose of these discourses might be jettisoned, but accepting a limited freedom to worship enabled them to be used against further compromise. Under Charles II, we remember, conformist argument fell into real difficulties because it had to admit the international church varied from place to place. It then had trouble squaring this with domestic persecution. If, however, clerics stopped demands for uniformity, their problems receded. They could now insist dissenters deserved no more than bare liberty because foreign endorsement, or the essential structure of the universal communion, proved anglicanism was the best church among those legally allowed in England. This could boost the establishment's claims without raising troubling questions about an illogical or inconsistent intolerance.

The comprehension campaign showed the advantages. As high churchmen rejected the measure, they could deploy all the old restoration defences of the establishment. Some, for instance, revived the old argument that the existing official church was admired by Protestants abroad. Thomas Long, who had

362 Gilbert Burnet, *An exhortation to peace and union in a sermon ... Thursday 26th November, 1689* (1689), pp. 13–14, 19–20.

363 [Thomas Wagstaff], *The case of moderation and occasional communion* (1705), advertisement, explained the author did not begrudge dissenters liberty of worship, so could not be branded 'an immoderate Man, and of a persecuting Spirit'.

written to establish foreign reformed approval of anglicanism back in the 1670s, now published a series of pamphlets re-emphasising that endorsement and arguing it blocked any rash alteration of the English settlement.[364] Others joined in. The anonymous author of a *Letter from a member of parliament* (1689) echoed Long's sentiments; whilst John Willes' *Judgement of the foreign reformed churches* (1690) was a Durelesque riposte to dissenting attempts to use foreign example against anglicanism. In such writing, low church insistence that European reform faced a crisis was turned on its head. All agreed that the movement was in peril; yet instead of insisting on comprehension as a response, high churchmen argued that this crisis was no time to mess with the reformation's most respected member. It would demoralise the continent's Protestants, and very probably divide them in their darkest hour. Thus both Willes and the *Letter* writer insisted anglicanism stood at the very heart of the reformation. Taking the middle way between Lutherans and Calvinists, it was respected by both branches of the reformed movement, and was 'the very Centre of Union and Harmony of all the Protestant Churches in the World'.[365] Given this, any change in England's establishment, even to conciliate dissent, would be dangerous. The Protestants of France, Holland and Geneva might be pleased at first because comprehension would move the English closer to their models. However, they would soon realise their mistake as they saw that pleasing English nonconformists would alienate the more hierarchical and ceremonial godly in Germany and Scandinavia, and so disrupt the international cause in its time of crisis.[366]

Some high churchmen were cheeky enough to include William in foreign Protestant admiration for the church. They therefore attempted to whistle their old Erastian tune along with their reformation one, even though this was a pretty hard sell. William, they knew, had been raised a presbyterian Calvinist. He had also shown a lifelong distaste for anglican rites and he actively supported comprehension in 1689.[367] Yet despite this, authors claimed William recognised the English church's superior virtues. They cited his participation in English worship whilst in London, and his series of flattering comments in his first year that anglicans had 'the best constituted

364 [Thomas Long], *The letter for toleration decipher'd* (1689), passim; [Thomas Long], *The case of persecution charg'd on the church of England* (1689), esp. p. 15; [Thomas Long], *The healing attempt examined* (1689), esp. p. 4; [Thomas Long], *Vox cleri: or the sense of the clergy* (1690), esp. p. 22. For Long's earlier writings, see above, p. 291.

365 [John Willes], *The judgment of the foreign reformed churches* (1690), p. 6; also *A letter from the member of parliament . . . concerning the bill for uniting Protestants* [1689], pp. 6–7.

366 [Willes], *Judgment*, epistle.

367 E.g. *His majesties gracious message to the convocation sent by the earl of Nottingham* (1689).

church in the world'.[368] In reality, of course, the king had been forced into this praise. He had not wanted to pick a fight with conformists on accepting the English throne, and he had soon found they were far more influential that he had been led to believe. In the spring of 1689 he had withdrawn a call to repeal the test acts when he faced overwhelming opposition in the Commons, and he began to suspect that the anti-church Whigs who had hitherto dominated his councils were a trouble-making minority.[369] None of this, though, stopped anti-comprehensionists claiming William was in fact a staunch anglican.[370] Like other foreign Protestants, he had accepted its authority when he arrived in England, and one author even drew an analogy with the Scots king, James VI and I. When this monarch had come from his Calvinist presbyterian realm, English puritans had imagined they had a ruler after their own hearts. However, they had been disappointed, as comprehensionists soon would be, that the imported monarch was actually more impressed with the church than their objections to it.[371]

A further strand of anti-comprehensionist rhetoric took up the themes Henry Thorndike had elaborated in the 1650s and 1660s. Several high churchmen insisted the current form of anglicanism must be preferred to any compromise with dissent because it remained within the parameters set by the primitive and universal communion of Christians. The most sustained performance of this position came from the rector of St Peter's Cornhill, William Beveridge. His sermon at the opening of the 1689 convocation accepted the English church might change its rites and features from time to time, and did not rule out alterations at this juncture for the peace of Christians. It nevertheless came from a lifelong opponent of comprehension, it insisted changes should only be made when absolutely necessary, and the core of its message was thoroughly Thorndikian.[372] Beveridge stressed that particular churches must consider all other assemblies of the faithful as they decided what their own worship should look like. If most churches in the world adopted or rejected a practice, this was a good sign the custom was of apostolic origin; and it would be schismatic for the English to change its arrangements if this would break the universal consensus. Beveridge avoided direct controversy by saying it would be up to convocation to decide if

368 Narcissus Luttrell, *A brief historical relation of state affairs* (6 vols., Oxford, 1857), I:606.
369 For changed attitudes: H. C. Foxcroft, *The life and letters of Sir George Savile* (2 vols., Oxford, 1898), II:203–7.
370 E.g. *Vox laici: or the layman's opinion* (1689), pp. 18, 23–4; [Long], *Case of persecution*, epistle; [Long], *Vox cleri*, p. 21; [Willes], *Judgement*, p. 11.
371 [Henry Maurice], *Remarks from the country: upon the two letters relating to the convocation* (1690), p. 18.
372 Once translated out of Latin it was quoted by [Long], *Vox cleri*, p. 12; and presented as a defence against sectarianism – William Beveridge, *A sermon preached before the convocation . . . Novemb. the 18th, 1689* (1689), preface.

proposed alterations would meet this test. Yet his hostility to nonconformists made it clear he thought the currently constituted establishment was closer to the catholic pattern than its rivals, and this weighed against conciliation. For Beveridge, dissenters were sectaries. Anglicanism, by contrast, was 'the most illustrious Image and Resemblence of the Catholick' communion, and England was 'buoy'd up by an omnipotent God, as a pure, and sound Member of his Universal Church'.[373] Other writers used similar language. Henry Maurice defended anglican ceremonies as 'the common badge of Christianity, and the practice of the Universal Church'. William Jane feared alterations would take England further from 'Conformity to the ancient Primitive and Apostolick Churches' and even John Willes thought leaving out apocryphal readings (as dissenters urged) would put the English at odds with 'the Primitive, the Eastern, Western, and *African* Churches' as well as most of his beloved foreign Protestants.[374]

Read in this light, the debate over comprehension in 1689 looks far more like a dispute over England's position in the international church than a domestic scrap about local dissenters. Men who had converted the European reformation into a loosely organised and tolerant league squared off against those whose old continental defences of the church had been reinvigorated by acceptance of toleration. The centrality of this tension became even clearer when convocation got down to business. In fact, dispute about Christians abroad displaced any actual discussion of concession; and it is useful to explore this since the convocation usually gets short shrift. The body met for only a few active days, and had achieved nothing concrete by the time William suspended it in despair of comprehension. Such failure has encouraged commentators to pass over the assembly in a few words, and has led them to ignore the one debate convocation *did* have before suspension. Bizarrely, this centred on the address of thanks to William, but its pedantic wrangling revealed the vital fissure in the body.

The row started on 4 December when the upper house of bishops proposed convocation express its gratitude for the king's zeal for 'the Protestant Religion in general, and the Church of *England* in particular'.[375] The lower house (composed of elected representatives of the ordinary clergy) objected to this suggestion because they insisted they had the honour of proposing addresses, but more importantly because they felt the wording had disturbing implications about the church's place in Europe. By the winter of 1689,

[373] Beveridge, *Sermon*, pp. 4, 27–8.
[374] [Maurice], *Remarks from the country*, p. 12; [Jane], *Letter to a friend*, p. 2; [Willes], *Judgment*, p. 21.
[375] Thomas Long's *Vox cleri* printed an account of the debates, this p. 59.

the suspension of bishops for refusing the oaths of loyalty meant comprehensionists were in a majority in the upper chamber, and ensured the address reflected their view of anglicanism as just one version of a broad reformation. The lower clergy refused to accept this, and instead insisted convocation speak only of the official English church.[376] They thus implied their communion was rather more special than a simple strand of Protestantism, and kept open 'catholic' as well as 'protestant' understandings of its nature. If this had been a trivial dispute about words, it might have ended here. The bishops might have thought one version of the thanks was as good as another, and simply dropped the first phrase of their draft. It was far more crucial than this, however, as shown by the energy of the upper house's reaction. They were adamant the reference to Protestantism stay, since without it the English church would not be anchored in a diverse and flexible reformation and their vision of its nature would be endangered. In messages to the lower house, they insisted William saw his actions as a defence of the whole Protestant movement. They also stressed that anglicanism was not distinguished 'from other Protestant Churches but by its [inessential] Hierarchy'; that the term 'Protestant' was important because it united all Christians of the west opposed to Rome; and that to leave the word out might question the establishment's commitment to the wider movement. It would have, they claimed, 'ill consequences, and be liable to strange constructions both at home and abroad'.[377]

From this point, mediation was attempted. Many members of convocation doubtless hoped they could get beyond squabbles over their opening address, but even as they looked for compromise, the international dispute remained and it took several iterations before an acceptable form of words was secured. On 9 December, the lower house came up with a new version. This thanked William for his actions for the church of Engand: 'whereby we doubt not, the Interest of all Protestant Churches, which is dear to us, will . . . be better secured'. This was a step towards the bishops' position since it mentioned non-anglican communions. However, it did not present the establishment simply as a member of a diverse and tolerant reformation, so could not satisfy the comprehensionists. To start, the lower house's draft suggested anglicanism led international Protestantism rather than simply being part of it. Worse, it could be interpreted as referring only to officially constituted Protestant communions in other countries, thus excluding domestic dissent from the cherished movement. In response, the upper house asked why this version talked of '*Protestant Churches*' instead of using the more inclusive '*Protestant Religion*'. When they replied, the lower clergy made it clear they

[376] [Long], *Vox cleri*, p. 62 [377] Ibid., pp. 63, 68.

had intended to exclude English nonconformity. They insisted they were 'representatives of a form'd established church' and had not thought to talk about a vague religion 'any further than it is the religion of some form'd established church'. The upper house could not accept this, as it implied the reformation was a highly structured federation of exclusive national communions. This would downplay the essential forbearance and flexibility of their vision, and do nothing for English dissent. According, they tried again. On 10 December, the bishops suggested the address talk of the interest of '*the Protestant Religion in this and all other Protestant Churches*', but for their opponents this still portrayed anglicanism as another run-of-the-mill denomination. The lower clergy therefore asked that the address drop the words 'this and' from their proposed phrase, and at last agreement was reached. On the 11 December, convocation thanked William for his salvation of the church of England adding that this had promoted 'the Protestant religion in all other Protestant churches'.[378]

Such laborious slogging over an address of thanks sounds absurd, and probably did nothing to endear the fractious assembly to William. Yet in fact it mapped the faultlines for decades of ecclesiastical and party politics (and was, incidentally, very nearly repeated the next time convocation tried to thank its monarch in 1701).[379] Dispute continued for many reasons, but the key ones were probably the promotion of low churchmen to leading positions in the establishment, and a continuing series of anglican misfortunes which bred further anger among ministers on the ground. The promotions occurred because William found vacancies on the episcopal bench (especially once men who refused the oaths had been deprived), and because Mary (who handled ecclesiastical patronage in the early 1690s) had always been close to the clerics of Nottingham's circle. Consequently, Burnet became bishop of Salisbury in 1689, whilst the early 1690s saw Stillingfleet advance to Worcester, Tillotson appointed archbishop of Canterbury – to be replaced by Tenison on his death in 1695; and allies of these men gaining preferment in a swathe of other dioceses.[380] By bitter contrast, the misfortunes of ordinary clergy persisted after 1689. Agricultural depression and wartime taxation hit their incomes; dissenters established meetings in direct competition with parish worship; nonconformists were often wealthy and sufficiently influential to undermine the remaining restrictions upon them; and in 1695 the lapse of

[378] Ibid., pp. 63–72.

[379] In 1701, the lower house demanded 'Protestant churches' replace 'Protestant religions' in the draft address: Thomas Lathbury, *A history of the convocation of the church of England* (1842), p. 286.

[380] For William's attachment to this group: Claydon, *William III . . . revolution*, pp. 64–71; G. V. Bennett, 'William III and the episcopacy', in G. V. Bennett and J. D. Walsh, eds., *Essays in modern church history* (1966), pp. 104–32.

press censorship seemed to permit a rash of publications questioning doctrinal orthodoxy.[381] These developments stoked tensions which were played out in continuing clashes of international vision. The newly promoted episcopate used its version of the European reformation to justify an innovative ecclesiastical strategy, whilst high church critics deployed their international polemic in a series of campaigns against this.

Historians have long argued that the men promoted by William brought a new approach to church leadership. Recognising the decisions of 1689, they abandoned coercion of dissent, and even put formal attempts at reunion on the back burner. Instead, they concentrated on improving the pastoral provision of the establishment (for instance by improving the quality of its ministers, educating the laity in Protestant principles and joining campaigns for the reformation of manners), and on cooling interdenominational disputes. These initiatives were worth pursuing for their own sake, and might – in the very long run – win over dissenters. Scholars have examined these activities, but few have stressed they were underpinned by a particular vision of Europe.[382] It is true that the bishops' new strategy was a practical response to decisions of 1689. Yet it was defended in the context of a broad and flexible reformation. The establishment could only fully understand its role after losing its local monopoly if it considered its participation in this movement. As one of the number of denominations which made up the European cause, the church's job was to benefit all: it should work for shared goals and reach out to other Protestants through evangelical endeavour.

It would be possible to illustrate the new attitude from the numerous sermons which William's episcopacy gave in the 1690s and beyond, especially as part of their thanksgiving and fast services for the anti-French wars. However, I have surveyed much of this material elsewhere, and we are lucky that this group supplemented their preaching with two works which outlined their philosophy even more systematically.[383] Both were written by Burnet, but it is clear he worked closely with his colleagues as he composed them – so they do represent more than the ravings of this one continent-obsessed cleric. In essence, the works – the *Discourse of the pastoral care* (1692), and the *Exposition of the thirty-nine articles* (1699) – set out an approach the

[381] For the church's misfortunes: Holmes, *Trial of Dr Sacheverell*, ch. 2. Clerics worried particularly about anti-trinitarianism in John Locke, *The reasonableness of Christianity* (1695) and John Toland, *Christianity not mysterious* (1696) – but Gilbert Burnet, *An exposition of the thirty-nine articles of the church of England* (1699), was also criticised for its inclusive theological approach: Martin Greig, 'Heresy hunt: Gilbert Burnet and the convocation controversy of 1701', *HJ*, 37 (1994), 569–92.

[382] G. V. Bennett, 'Archbishop Tenison and the reshaping of the church of England', *Friends of Lambeth Palace Library, Annual Report* (1981), pp. 10–17; Claydon, *William III . . . revolution*, pp. 173–5; Rose, *England*, pp. 182–90.

[383] Claydon, *William III . . . revolution*, passim, but esp. ch. 4.

church could adopt now it had lost authority over the whole population. The *Discourse* was a handbook for parish clergy in a post-toleration world. It urged churchmen to abandon harassment of dissent, and instead to try to win back nonconformists by peaceful persuasion and by impressing them with their diligence in their own ministry.[384] The *Exposition* was the church's first systematic attempt to explain and justify its doctrinal stance. In this, Burnet confirmed this was to be an age of forbearance: he acknowledged many points of Christian belief (particularly the argument over predestination) were difficult to resolve, but suggested that the church's articles of faith could be read thoughtfully and flexibly in order to accommodate a range of Protestant positions.

As we would expect, Europe was the context and reason for the suggested approaches. In passionate prefaces to the two works, the author rehearsed his account of reformation history, insisting that the progress of Protestantism had been halted by avoidable disputes among the reformed, and that the flexible attitudes he recommended for England offered a way out of this trap. Thus the introduction to the *Discourse* spoke of the crisis of European Protestantism. Its expansion had stalled: while 'Some Churches have been plucked up by the roots' others had 'fallen under terrible oppressions and shakings'.[385] There were several reasons for this (including the new energy among Catholics), but a key one was the diversion of effort from conversion to internal disputes. Losing the '*Power of Religion*', the godly across the continent had instead magnified the '*Form*' of it. They had been zealous only for their own 'Opinions and Customs', and had merely insisted theirs was the best version of the faith rather than working to ensure that it became so.[386] The preface to the *Exposition* was as explicit. Again Burnet lamented the divisions between European Protestants, and contrasted this starkly with the Roman ability to overlook internal disagreements. Even as popery advanced across the continent, German Lutherans were charging Calvinists with blasphemy, and Dutch and Swiss Protestants were answering that Lutherans were enemies of God.[387] Burnet insisted the two camps were not far apart, but noted that his attempts to point this out during his continental exile had met with a stinging, but just, rebuke. In 1686, he had talked to a German minister. This man had agreed his countrymen must bury disputes, but was resentful at being lectured to by someone from a land with an even worse record. At the time the conversation took place,

[384] The *Discourse of the pastoral care* has been debated: Mark Goldie, 'John Locke, Jonas Proast and religious toleration, 1689–1692', in John Walsh, Colin Haydon and Stephen Taylor, eds., *The church of England, c.1689–c.1833* (Cambridge, 1993), pp. 143–71; Claydon, *William III . . . revolution*, pp. 175–7; Rose, *England*, pp. 183–6.

[385] Gilbert Burnet, *The discourse of the pastoral care* (1692), preface, p. xvii.

[386] Ibid., pp. xix, xxxii. [387] Burnet, *Exposition*, preface, p.viii.

English Protestants had been in horrible danger from James II, yet had been wracked by even less excusable battles than those abroad. At least German arguments had been over crucial matters such as the attributes of God and the origins of sin; the disputes in England were over trivial forms of ecclesiastical government and worship. Ending his preface with this story, Burnet presented his moderate approach to doctrine as a service to the entire continental movement. If England could use thoughtfulness to move beyond her sterile disputes, then the German minister believed 'all the rest of the Reformed Churches will with great Respect admit of her Mediation to heal theirs'.[388]

Burnet and his allies thus presented their internationally inspired strategy as an encouraging new start for their establishment. High churchmen, however, could only see their communion losing influence under this leadership, and reacted with a series of campaigns which went to the heart of the Tory political platform. In the late 1690s they demanded that convocation be allowed to meet to counter the perceived upsurge in heresy (William had refused to meet the body again after 1689). From the start of Anne's reign they campaigned against 'occasional conformity' (the practice by which dissenters could take anglican communion once a year and so qualify for public office), and then voted for the 1714 'schism' act which banned dissenting academies (these were educational bodies established by nonconformists to compensate for their exclusion from the universities). They rallied behind Sacheverell in 1709–10 mainly because his attack on false brethren had included a savaging of non-anglicans, and throughout the period they insisted the church was 'in danger' – a phrase which became a semi-official Tory slogan.[389] In all these efforts, alternatives to the Burnetine vision of the international reformation were crucial. Providing the intellectual core, and frequently the emotional passion, of the campaigns, such concepts tied high church ideology to European visions. Often the international perspectives were simply the old restoration discourses, now freed from their embarrassments by acceptance of toleration. Yet rather than bore with endless demonstrations of continuity, we can let the evidence for constancy emerge as we also monitor changes over this period. Whilst high church conceptions of Europe remained *largely* familiar from Charles II's reign, there were developments which moved polemic on, and sharpened contrasts with the low church's vision.

First, and perhaps predictably, Erastianism ceased to be important in 'high' ecclesiology. The idea that each ruler should shape the church in his lands had

[388] Ibid., p. x.
[389] The classic account, with some international sensitivity, is George Every, *The high church party, 1688–1715* (1956).

had some attraction when kings upheld anglicanism, but once royal loyalty to this model was doubted, its allure faded. The problem was the attitude of post-revolutionary monarchs. Queen Mary and Queen Anne might have been raised in the English church, but William had not been, and after 1714 the succession of the Lutheran Hanoverians ensured there would be not be another king who was anglican by upbringing until George III in 1760. All of this naturally questioned whether the rulers really wanted to uphold the old conformist model, and suspicions were further provoked because monarchs presided over very different settlements in their other realms. William, notoriously, remained a member of the Dutch reformed church when in the Netherlands.[390] Later, the Georges remained good Lutherans in Hanover, whilst all the monarchs were heads of the presbyterian kirk in Scotland. If this had not been enough, royal policy was rarely as high churchmen would wish. As one might suspect from their origins in the diverse European reformation, William and the Georges were attracted to the low church view of the world, and overwhelmingly appointed its adherents to bishoprics.[391] They also opposed high church initiatives: William refused to let convocation meet until 1701; George I stopped it convening after 1717 and presided over the repeal of statutes passed under the Tory ministry of 1710–14 against occasional conformity and dissenting academies.[392] Anne was more sympathetic to Tory churchmen (she appointed several to the episcopal bench, and allowed anti-dissenting legislation in her last years), but even she joined the other monarchs in blocking total domination by high churchmen. As Edward Gregg has shown, she preferred a broad ecclesiastical balance, and feared anglican intransigence could divide her country.[393]

Given all this, Erastianism lost its appeal as a 'high' defence of the church. As we saw above, some clerics had always had reservations about the principle, but once England's magistrates refused to play ball it became impossible to use it against the establishment's rivals. In fact, Erastianism shaded into a low church doctrine. Stillingfleet and Tillotson, the leading restoration proponents of the ruler's ecclesiastical power, became low churchmen after the revolution and argued that mildness and toleration matched the new monarchs' wishes.[394] Meanwhile, high churchmen savaged the ideal. As Mark Goldie has pointed out, they took up non-juring arguments to

[390] For William's upbringing: Troost, *William III*, pp. 35–7; for summary of William's approach to religion: Tony Claydon, 'William III and II', *ODNB*, LIX:91–2.

[391] For William: Bennett, 'William III'. When it appears, the standard account for the later era will be Stephen Taylor, *The church and the Whigs* (Cambridge).

[392] Hoppit, *Land of liberty?*, p. 253.

[393] Edward Gregg, *Queen Anne* (1980), pp. 145–6.

[394] William Wake, *The authority of Christian princes over their ecclesiastical synods* (1697), and William Wake, *The state of the church and clergy of England* (1703), breathed trenchant low church Erastianism

curtail the magistrate, and so flirted with open denunciation of lay control.[395] When the non-jurors were ejected, some (especially that old opponent of Erastianism, Henry Dodwell) suggested the church was an autonomous spiritual authority.[396] This notion defended the conscience-struck clerics of 1689 against the king's discipline, but also proved attractive to those who took the oaths but became worried about the establishment after the revolution. If non-jurors were right about the church's independent spiritual authority, high clergymen reasoned, it might defend itself even if rulers were reluctance to help. The campaign for convocation in the late 1690s illustrated the new possibilities. Francis Atterbury's 1697 *Letter to a convocation man*, the clarion call for a clerical assembly, endorsed the autonomous power of the church. In a curious echo of Richard Baxter's attacks on restoration Erastianism, the *Letter* reminded its readers that Christ's church had existed for many years as an independent body before rulers converted to the faith, and that it still did so in places such as Greece and Turkey where local magistrates were infidels. The exercise of ecclesiastical jurisdiction was therefore 'not dependant on the Temporal Power' of each place, whilst the church was 'a Society instituted in order to a spiritual End; and, as such, must have an inherent Power of governing it self'.[397]

For reasons which will become clear later, we need to be rather more careful about the second major shift in high church polemic from the restoration era. This was the relative decline of 'protestant' defences of the church as part of an international movement against Rome, and the corresponding advance of 'catholic' notions of a primitive and still-binding communion. Caution is necessary because the development fits too neatly into a simple interpretation of late Stuart ecclesiastical history which would present it as the final divorce of incompatible internationalisms. Such a view might observe that the church of England had been in tension from its birth; that a 'puritan' wing had always looked to the continental reformation whilst 'conformists' had always felt part of a wider catholic entity; and that following the divisions Anthony Milton charted for the early Stuart era (and indeed those we surveyed under Charles II), the post-revolution establishment simply split into rival conceptions of its European position.[398] In this interpretation, England's 'protestant' identity became the low church ideology (once it had mutated to accept a more flexibly organised reformation

395 Mark Goldie, 'The non-jurors, episcopacy and the origins of the convocation controversy', in Eveline Cruickshanks, ed., *Ideology and conspiracy: aspects of Jacobitism 1689–1759* (Edinburgh, 1982), pp. 15–35.

396 [Henry Dodwell], *A vindication of the deprived bishops* (1692).

397 [Francis Atterbury], *A letter to a convocation man* (1697), pp. 18–19.

398 Anthony Milton, *Catholic and reformed: the Roman and Protestant churches in English Protestant thought, 1600–1640* (Cambridge, 1995).

and had swept up Erastianism to accommodate kings from foreign realms), whilst the 'catholic' identity proved useful to those wanting defences against the changes of 1689, and became the mark of the high church. This is a clear picture which fits many of the facts – but even before we rehearse it, we have to warn it does not tell the full story. As we will eventually see, the division was blurred by the persistence of mixed modes of arguing, and by the common heritage of both sides in familiar restoration discourses

For now, though, we must present the evidence for a 'catholic' high churchmanship after 1689, and for the party political tensions it caused. As low churchmen insisted the establishment was part of varied reformation, their opponents became more confident to fight this logic with the far less flexible rules of a universal episcopal church. They were even prepared to do this if it risked shattering the unity of the European reformation, or bringing England closer to Rome. One obvious sign of the shift was sourer objection to interference by foreign non-episcopal churches in English affairs. Whilst anglicans had always feared their institution might be subverted by more thoroughgoing Protestants from the continent, under Queen Anne such concern intensified into the conviction that there was a clear and present danger from this direction. Pamphleteers thought there was an active conspiracy and in 1705 wove it into Tory demands that parliament declare the church to be in peril. *The memorial of the church of England*, the central press weapon of this campaign, spoke of enemies who wished to impose 'the Sowre-Rules, and Saucy Encroachments' of Geneva; whilst Henry Sacheverell's contribution to this campaign accused dissenters of having collaborated with Dutch and French detractors for decades, and of now planning to use Hanoverian emissaries, and all manner of other imported strangers, to subvert the establishment.[399] Sacheverell in fact showed how such polemic could cut England off from the reformation cause. He acknowledged Queen Anne had an interest to 'Defend all Protestant Churches', but he insisted she was also bound by oath to defend her own, and that while she might have 'due Regard for all Protestants Abroad, yet we may hope she may be allow'd to make a Distinction of Favour' to her own establishment and counter the claims of dissenters.[400]

More disturbingly, high church polemic after 1689 became bolder in unchurching non-episcopal communions. Whilst restoration writers had tended to shy away from this (even though it was the logic of their position), by Queen Anne's reign there seemed more willingness to deny validity

[399] *The memorial of the church of England* (2nd edn, 1705), p. 20; [Henry Sacheverell], *The rights of the church of England asserted* (1705), pp. 6–7. Defoe satirised intolerance of foreign Protestants: [Daniel Defoe], *The high-church legion: or the memorial examined* (1705), pp. 8, 11.

[400] [Sacheverell], *Rights of the church*, pp. 10–11.

to large parts of the international reformation, to the point where opponents could accuse high churchmen of shading to Rome. A key factor here was the contribution of non-juring writers in high church campaigns. Men who had been deprived of clerical positions under William insisted the church was in danger under his successor, but as they wrote anonymously they could not be identified as defending an institution they had left, and could appear mainstream spokesmen of a concerned clergy. These non-jurors were important because they insisted episcopacy was essential for a true church. They did this because it countered the Erastianism which had sanctioned their deprivation, but as their works were incorporated into the high church canon, they moved Tory polemic in a decidedly 'catholic' direction.

A brace of pamphlets attacking James Owen illustrate the process. Owen was a nonconformist writer, who in 1703 published *Moderation a virtue*, his defence of occasional conformity. According to this tract, dissenters who went to take the sacrament in anglican churches were not cynically evading the prohibitions of the test act, but rather were showing their charity to another Protestant denomination. This argument was anathema to non-juring thinkers, who eagerly participated in the paper war Owen unleashed. First, Samuel Grascome claimed to pull off Owen's mask of moderation, and savaged 'foul-faced' dissent for pretending it could establish churches without an apostolic succession of bishops. Grascome knew his position questioned the status of many foreign churches and predicted a 'grievous Out-cry' against him – but claimed he did not care. Those who raised this point, he asserted, were trying to distract attention from their own sin by directing eyes to sufferings abroad. 'There is a sort of Men,' he suggested, 'who think to slip their own Necks out of the Collar, by seeming mightily concerned for others.'[401] The second non-juror, Charles Leslie, showed a similar intransigence towards ecclesiastical bodies in '*Schism* from *Episcopacy*, which is, from the *Catholick-Church* of all Ages'. Applying this to Europe, he divided the reformation into the Lutheran churches of Denmark and Sweden (which were excused because they had retained bishops), and the non-episcopal gatherings of southern Germans, Dutch, Scots and English dissenters, whom he heavily implied were plotting against Christ's universal communion.[402]

In Leslie's case such discourse led to hints of reconciliation with Rome, and set up an explicit battle over the church of England's true brethren abroad. In 1703, another of Leslie's contributions to the occasional conformity rumpus was a theological tract on the true notion of a Catholic church. This took the

401 [Samuel Grascome], *The mask of moderation pulled off* (1704), p. 45.

402 [Charles Leslie], *The wolf stript of his shepherd's cloathing* (1704), pp. 7, 36–7. Also: Henry Dodwell, *Occasional conformity fundamentally destructive* (1705).

Thorndikian line that bishops were the cement which bound the universal communion together and that to abolish them was sinful, but it initially protected itself against charges of popery with the standard argument that the Roman curia interfered in other episcopal jurisdictions and was therefore guilty of schismatic usurpation. From here, however, the pamphlet moved sharply back towards continental Catholicism. Downplaying liturgical and even doctrinal differences between anglicans and Catholics, it implied there was little to object to in continental popery but papal encroachments; and it openly stated that England might restore communion with France if her bishops (who had always railed at papal authority) would renounce Rome's supremacy.[403] For opponents of the high church, however, this was heresy. It presented anglicanism as a sort of independent Catholicism, closely allied with continental bishops (even against their Protestant populations), and ready and able to join with any part of the pope's European empire which restricted his authority. As Daniel Defoe put it in the *Review*, such views were leading the whole high church party into rank Catholicism: those who supported the *Memorial of the church of England* in 1705 would 'make out the Assertions of Mr *Lesly*, that the Church of *England*, and the Gallican Church of *Rome*, are nearer and may better Unite', than anglicans and other Protestant communions.[404]

By Queen Anne's reign, therefore, a high church 'catholicism' had emerged, in fairly stark contrast to a low church 'protestantism'. Whilst the first philosophy saw the international communion as a federation of episcopal churches challenged by an illegitimate Genevan conspiracy, the second evoked an overlapping set of reformed denominations threatened by both popery and those who raised unnecessary divisions between them. As church disputes fed into political disputes, this basic tension ensured that party battles came to be as much about the ecclesiological status of European Christians as anything else; and it becomes possible to describe much of the struggle between Whigs and Tories in these terms. For example, the touchstone issue of occasional conformity was played out with close reference to the faithful abroad. We have just seen how respondents to James Owen denounced him for rejecting episcopacy, but it is worth noting that his defence of dissenters was rooted in the Whigs' alternative continental vision – so the wider dispute he stimulated in the party press became a clear clash of Europeanisms. Owen saw occasional conformity as an act of charity by English dissenters towards the official church; but as importantly, he thought it one of the means by which

[403] Charles Leslie, *The true notion of the catholick church* (1703), pp. 258–80. For more enthusiasm for Gallicanism: [Charles Leslie], *The case of the regale and the pontificat* (1701), pp. 286–7. For denial that different forms of church government were valid: [Charles Leslie], *Querela temporum* (1694).

[404] [Daniel Defoe], *A review of the state of the British nation*, vol. II, no. 65 (2 August 1705).

the diverse, but fundamentally united, Protestant cause across Europe held together. Thus he explained that the strength of the church of England consisted in her 'Union with the *Refom'd Churches* abroad, and with all sound Protestants of what *Denomination soever* at home'. Rejecting nonconformist participation in the church would therefore sunder an international reformation whose members sympathised with England's dissenters, and would alienate foreigners who needed to come together to prevent 'the Extermination of all the Reformed Churches'.[405]

As such printed rhetoric translated into parliamentary debate, European ecclesiology remained prominent. When the Tories introduced their occasional conformity bill in 1703, discussion ranged over a variety of issues but many speeches and votes stressed familiar continental concerns. Opposing the measure, Whigs like Lord Haversham and Gilbert Burnet stressed that it would divide a cause which must unite against international popery.[406] Burnet published his House of Lords speech to advertise the bill's pernicious effects: he claimed it would destroy the traditional understanding between European Protestants which had allowed people from other countries to participate in local worship; it would be 'a Discouragement to all abroad, who expect Deliverance and Protection from hence'; and – most horrifyingly – it was sponsored by those who saw the popish church of France as closer to the anglicans than the reformed.[407] In very similar territory, one of the Tories' most controversial clauses tried to extend the bill to cover French and Dutch Protestants in England. Whigs in the House of Lords tried to strike this out, complaining that it revoked the longstanding toleration of foreign reformed churches in London, but the Tory majority in the Commons stood by their proposal. Concerned that the aliens were part of continent-wide conspiracy against anglicanism, they feared the French and Dutch might collaborate with the dissenters in exploiting a loophole in the legislation: the clause must stay, Tories insisted, or the foreign churches would 'open a door for evading this law'.[408]

The other great ecclesiastical clashes between Whigs and Tories in Queen Anne's reign had the same international dimensions. As we have seen, the Tories of 1705 insisted the church was in danger from a foreign Protestant conspiracy, but the leading Whig response, John Toland's *Memorial of the state of England*, charged that their accusers were heirs to a quite different plot. Since Laud's time, Toland argued, haughty clerics had subverted England's traditions of praying for the reformed churches abroad, of

405 [James Owen], *Moderation a virtue* (1703), pp. 35, 50.
406 For Haversham: Cobbett, VI:166.
407 Gilbert Burnet, *The bishop of Salisbury's speech in the House of Lords upon the bill against occasional conformity* (1704), p. 8.
408 Cobbett, VI:76.

acting to defend all branches of the reformation, and of accepting differences at home as a reflection of that diverse continental movement. To replace it, they had insisted anglicanism was the only true faith, so not only condemned dissenters to 'Penal Laws, Censures and Incapacities' but – in exulting *de jure* episcopacy – treated 'all *Protestants* abroad as if they were not *Christians*'.[409] Five years later, the ecclesiastical elements of Sacheverell's trial followed a similar pattern. As we noted, this Tory preacher thought dissenters were in league with alien extremists against the true church, but the Whigs who wanted him punished took a similarly international view.[410] They were as appalled at his lack of charity for the European godly as his intolerance at home, and were concerned that this high episcopalian saw the popish clergy of France as his natural brethren. Thus, one very popular pamphleteer was horrified that Sacheverell denounced foreign Protestants as 'miscreants', whilst John Toland complained that the cleric fell 'foul as furiously against GENEVA as ROME' and that his insistence on the apostolic succession of bishops unchurched most other Protestants.[411] Others writers agreed. The preacher clearly thought foreign churches could 'go to the Devil', and wanted a 'Union of the Churches of *England* and *France*'; and his most choleric critic – William Bisset – observed his enemy followed Charles Leslie's pro-Gallican ecclesiology and would 'condemn not only all that Dissent among us, but almost all other Reform'd Churches, as the *Dutch, North British, Swiss* &c'.[412] The same fundamental division occurred over the 1714 schism act. It is true that many Tory arguments against dissenting academies took a simple domestic position – suggesting that nonconformists had taken too much liberty, and that the 1689 toleration act did not grant them educational freedom – but some also took the Thorndikian line that those who rejected the universal authority of bishops deserved nothing.[413] Opposing this, Whigs protested that the schism measure threatened the flexible unity crucial for the whole reformation. They thus hinted the bill was inspired by a Catholic plot which had murdered thousands in neighbouring countries, and would have papists laughing up their sleeves as the reformed movement shattered.[414] The bill also discouraged foreign Protestants from seeking refuge

409 [John Toland], *The memorial of the state of England* (1705), esp. pp. 6–15, quote p. 12.
410 Sacheverell took another swipe at Genevans: *Perils of false brethren*, p. 19.
411 *A true answer to Dr Sacheverell's sermon before the Lord Mayor* (1709), p. 12 – had three editions. [John Toland], *Mr Toland's reflections on Mr Sacheverell's sermon* (1710), pp. 8–9, had an inbuilt European context, claiming to be a letter to a Hollander, published to let the English know how Sacheverell's case was playing abroad.
412 *An answer to Dr Sacheverell's sermon* (1710), p. 10; *A speech without doors* (1710), p. 16; Bisset, *Modern fanatick* (1710), p. 36; final quote from Bisset, *Remarks*, p. 4.
413 E.g. *Reasons for the law to prevent the further growth of schism* (1714), p. 26.
414 *Some thoughts on the bill to prevent the growth of schism* (1714), p. 21; *A letter to Mr Steele, occasioned by his letter to a member of parliament* (1714), pp. 38–40; *Reasons humbly offered to the right honourable peers of Great Britain* (1714), p. 8.

in England, and harassed those already here.[415] By withholding tolerance, it aped Louis XIV's treatment of the Huguenots, and it cast anglicanism out of a reformation built on free worship and unrestrained study.[416] Perhaps most importantly, accepting the bill would destroy Anne's claim to be the protector of the Protestant interest in Europe. Victimising dissenters, the monarch would betray true Christians, and annul her moral authority to denounce persecution of the godly in the Catholic continent.[417]

Two other issues can be fitted into this pattern of party battle shaped by rival visions of the international church. The first was the union with Scotland in 1707. This is a rich and complex subject with an increasingly sophisticated historiography, which we unfortunately have limited space to elaborate here.[418] Although issues of law, representation, commerce, cost and empire were extensively debated on both sides of the border, the core issue – the royal succession – was simple. By the early 1700s it was clear Queen Anne would have no children survive her. Under the English act of settlement (1701) she would be succeeded by the electoral house of Hanover, but this did not apply in the technically independent kingdom of Scotland, and Scots resentment at treatment by absentee monarchs threatened some other choice of ruler when Anne died. To prevent this, the English ministry resolved on full union. Led by Whigs, it launched a furious campaign of propaganda and bribery to persuade the Scots parliament to vote itself out of existence, and to incorporate their kingdom with its southern neighbour. Tories, however, were sceptical. Questioning the wisdom of union, they fired another party battle grounded in differing conceptions of the international church.

The relevant clash centred on the proposal that the Scots keep a separate and presbyterian kirk. Whigs were happy with this: it reduced the difficulty of persuading Scots to forgo autonomy and it gelled with their flexible vision of the European reformation. They saw the union expressing the fundamental harmony of Protestants, and as major strengthening of the European reformed cause. This attitude was clear in the writings of Daniel Defoe. He was was employed by the ministry as persuader-in-chief and prefigured his late wartime concern for the position of continental Protestants. Though much of his pamphleteering was aimed at a Scots audience and so

415 *Considerations on the bill now depending in parliament* (1714), p. 2; *The remedy worse than the disease* (1714), p. 5.

416 Richard Steele, *A letter to a member of parliament concerning the bill for preventing the growth of schism* (1714), pp. 11–12; *The sense of the church of England with respect to the schism* (1714), p. 5; *Considerations on the bill*, p. 2.

417 *A letter to a member of parliament relating to the bill for preventing the growth of schism* (1714), p. 4; 'The case of the Dutch and French Protestant churches in England', printed in *A collection of all the papers . . . in relation to the bill to prevent schism* (1714), p. 37.

418 For a guide to the literature: Tony Claydon, 'British history in the post-revolutionary world', in Glenn Burgess, ed., *The new British history*, pp. 118, 123–4, 128–9.

falls outside our study, some was intended for southerners and placed the union in the context of the threat to the whole reformation. Defoe warned only a united England and Scotland could stand up to the popish threat of France, and worried that without the merger, England might be distracted by her northern neighbour when 'the Protestant Cause in general' sought her help.[419] Such sentiments also ran through official encouragement to union from the court, and through a series of thanksgiving sermons published after the event.[420] Among these pulpit performances, dissenters were prominent (and they celebrated the 1707 deal as an encouragement to a broad reformation cause), but Whig-leaning anglicans also saw union as an alliance of '*Fellow-Protestants*' and a vital boost to the European cause.[421] None of this convinced Tories. They were horrified that a non-episcopal church was to be established within the new united kingdom, and – exhibiting their standard paranoia about presbyterian infiltrators from outside the realm – fretted this was the latest pan-Genevan plot against their holy faith. Thus one popular tract insisted only the conversion of the Scots to true episcopal government would render union safe. Without this, its author feared, the Scots would join a presbyterian faction which had already become too strong from the influx of French Huguenots, and boasted of its numbers in the Netherlands and Ireland as well as London.[422] Similarly Lord Haversham (in the process of converting to Toryism in the middle years of Queen Anne's reign) questioned those bishops who supported union in the upper house of parliament. Were they not, he asked, betraying episcopacy? The question provoked a lengthy disquisition on the validity of foreign Protestant churches from the Whiggish bishop of Oxford, William Talbot.[423]

The final dispute to fit our pattern was the argument over naturalisation. This rumbled through politics in the second half of Queen Anne's reign, and centred on what to do with the thousands of foreign Protestants who had come to England over recent decades. Most such people had formed settled communities, and it was clear many would be harshly treated if they went back to their native lands, so some argued their position should be regularised

[419] [Daniel Defoe], *A discourse on the union of the two kingdoms of England and Scotland* (1707), p. 21.

[420] *Her majesties gracious letter to the parliament of Scotland* (1706).

[421] John Ollyffe, *A sermon preached May the 4th 1707 at Uxbridge* (1707), p. 20. For dissenters: Daniel Williams, *A thanksgiving sermon, occasioned by the union of England and Scotland* (1707); Joseph Stennett, *A sermon preached on the first day of May, 1707* (1707). For another Whig celebration: William Talbot, *A sermon preach'd before the queen at the cathedral church of St Paul, on May the first, 1707* (1707), though this celebrated the union's role in preserving the balance of power.

[422] *The restoration of episcopacy to Scotland the only sure foundation for a lasting union* (1705) – 2nd edn titled *A letter to J. P. Barnet* (1706), see esp. pp. 4, 7.

[423] Cobbett, VI:571–6; William Talbot, *The bishop of Oxford's speech in the house of peers in answer to several speeches* (1707), pp. 4–7.

by naturalising them as English. The suggestion hung in the air for some time (Whigs advocated naturalisation to encourage useful immigration, Tories worried about burdensome foreigners), but two events around 1709 fanned it to white-hot controversy. First the Whig majority in parliament passed a naturalisation bill. This made subjects of anyone who was willing to take the oaths of loyalty and the sacrament in *any* Protestant church, but it outraged Tories who saw it as selling citizenship for the paltry administrative fee. Second, a great tide of economic migrants began arriving in England from the war-ravaged lands of the German Palatine. This created a refugee crisis involving as least 10,000 indigents, and Tories instantly blamed this on the lax entry policy implied by the preceding naturalisation.[424] The competing sides bolstered argument with their usual ecclesiological positions. Whigs defended both the 1709 act, and the welcome afforded the 'Poor Palatines', as debts due to a diverse reformation. Protestants must show solidarity, they stressed, so those from abroad must be protected even if they did not share their hosts' precise form of worship. Thus as Whigs raised funds to support the poor Germans, they insisted these people were the victims of religious persecution and that England's role as the head of the Protestant interest meant she must be a haven for them. Whig bishops appealing for money in their dioceses, and pamphleteers defending Whig policy, insisted England's place as the 'Bulwark of the Reformation' involved her being 'the common Refuge for those that are persecuted for it'; and both types of author reminded audiences of the nation's long history of offering shelter to 'Neighbouring Churches' in a storm.[425] Tories, however, were unmoved. They were concerned by the burden the refugees would place on English poor relief, but – predictably – they also rejected the Whig logic of Protestant solidarity. When the naturalisation bill had been passing through parliament, they had twice tried to restrict its terms to those who would take communion in their episcopal church.[426] When the Palatines turned up months later, they insisted they were economic – not religious – migrants and gleefully pointed out that many of the refugees were papists and that the rulers of their homelands had not restricted free worship. Perhaps more importantly, Palatines were not anglicans. Even the Protestants among them would be another community of schismatics from the true church, and welcoming them would

424 For coverage of party aspects, and reflection on attitude to Europe: H. T. Dickinson, 'The poor Palatines and the parties', *EHR*, 82 (1967), 464–85.

425 Official promotion of charity for Palatines was collected: *The piety and bounty of the queen of Great Britain* (1709) quotes from Thomas Tenison and William Talbot, pp. 12, 23. [Francis Hare], *The reception of the Palatines vindicated in a fifth letter to a Tory member* (1711), stressed England's record as Protestant refuge. *Some thoughts relating to the disposing of the poor Palatines* [1711] suggested English charity might protect foreign Protestants by threatening persecutors with an exodus of subjects.

426 Speck, *Birth*, pp. 157–8.

merely bolster the schismatic Whig party and could never 'Advantage ... the Establish'd Religion'.[427]

CATHOLIC AND REFORMED: CONSENSUS IN CHURCH POLITICS AFTER 1689

Given all these cases, it is tempting to conclude Whig–Tory contest under Queen Anne was determined by a fissure between conceptions of the international church. Over issue after issue, a flexible Whig reformation fought an episcopal Tory catholicism. Yet whilst this clash was an important and under-recognised dimension of conflict, we need to be cautious. As we hinted earlier, the separation of the two modes of argument was a tendency rather than an absolute divorce, and many continued to deploy the confused, mixed rhetoric of Charles II's reign. Looking closely at religious debate in the late Stuart era, it is clear that whilst the defences of the English church developed at the restoration were disparate, each exerted a powerful hold, and relatively few churchman abandoned any one completely. The result was rather less rhetorical polarity than we have been suggesting. Just as a common concern for European Christians inherited from the exclusion crisis prevented constitutional battles sundering politics in the decades after 1688, the common heritage of varied anglican internationalisms may have contained religious disputes. Tories and Whigs gravitated towards opposite ends of a polemical universe, but they nevertheless still inhabited the same one.

A prominent example of rhetorical survival was the continued high church appeal to the European reformation. We saw a clear instance of this in 1689 when anti-comprehensionists used the opinions of foreign Protestants to prevent a compromise with dissent, but they were not the last to use other reformed churches to defend anglican forms. It is, therefore, more accurate to see high episcopalianism as the predominant rather than the monopolistic mode of Tory thought under the late Stuarts. To make this point graphically, Francis Atterbury used Jean Durel's old discourse. His 1696 *Letter to a convocation man* is often presented as the spark for Tory campaigning in the last Stuart decades, but its rhetorical structure relied heavily on England's participation in the European reformation. Citing the spread of unorthodox doctrine as the main reason for the recall of convocation, Atterbury opened that case by explaining foreign Protestants were worried about this course. Both the synod of the Dutch reformed church and Pierre Jurieu, the leading Huguenot writer, were concerned that heretical beliefs were circulating on

[427] *A view of the queen and England's enemies in the case of the poor Palatines* [1711], p. 3. Also, [Atterbury], *English advice*, pp. 23–5.

the English side of the Channel and hoped the church of England was still uninfected. Wryly noting that low churchmen had pressed 'the Judgement and Example of the Reformed abroad' when it had suited their arguments, Atterbury exploited that sense of participation in a Protestant international to ask why the bishops did not take the action against unorthodoxy which their European brethren were demanding.[428]

The discourse similarly emerged in pamphlet debates over occasional conformity. Of course many Tory writers insisted dissenters were dangerous schismatics from episcopacy, but some also shamed them by citing foreign Protestant opinion of their practices. According to the Tory press, reformed Christians abroad deplored the nonconformists' needless separation from the church and none of them allowed people from outside established communions to qualify for public office by hypocritical practices. Moreover (and here there was an explicit rehearsal of Durel's position), many of the godly abroad were closer to anglicans than English dissenters.[429] Mary Astell – a high Tory polemicist as well as an early feminist philosopher – took up these themes as she countered James Owen's contention that to attack occasional conformity was to disrupt the English alliance with foreign churches. She thought it unlikely the reformed abroad would 'take Umbrage' if the anglican establishment disciplined nonconformists, since they understood, as Calvin had, that valid differences with churches in other countries were no excuse for schismatic separation in one's own.[430] Again, Tory organs such as Leslie's *Rehearsal* cited the Protestant continent in their general denigration of dissent, and provoked at least one pamphleteer to counter-cite the clear presbyterianism and ceremonial simplicity of most reformed foreigners against the contention that the English nonconformists were 'Schismaticks from all Churches'.[431]

Further evidence that some Tories were still thinking in broad reformation terms may come from a curious campaign in the middle of Queen Anne's reign. Around 1705, the Whigs' opponents suggested the Protestant succession would be in danger unless the designated claimant, the Electress Sophia, was immediately invited to England. Historians have puzzled about this, as

428 [Atterbury], *Letter*, pp. 3–6.

429 [William Higden], *Occasional conformity a most unjustifiable practice* (1704), p. 43; also Humphrey Mackworth, *Peace at home* (1703), p. 7; [Charles Leslie], *The new association of so called moderate churchmen* (1702), pp. 9, 14; [Sacheverell], *Rights of the church*, p. 46. For more on high church use of foreign Protestants: Eamon Duffy, 'Correspondence fraternelle: the SPCK, the SPG and the churches of Switzerland in the war of Spanish succession', in Derek Baker, ed., *Reform and reformation: England and the continent 1500–1750* (Oxford, 1979), pp. 251–80, esp. pp. 272–3.

430 [Mary Astell], *Moderation truly stated* (1704), pp. 39–40; Owen used the argument in *Moderation a virtue*.

431 *A fence for the English dissenters* (1708), title page.

concern to have a Hanoverian ready to take over the moment Anne died seemed to run counter to Tory doubts about this dynasty. Some have concluded the idea was simply to make trouble: a reversionary court in London might disrupt the cosy relations the existing queen had built with her Whig ministers in the middle years of her reign.[432] Yet there is another possible explanation. The Tories' clerical allies had always been interested in exploring union with the Lutheran church which was the official faith in Hanover. Preserving that sympathy for the moderate north German reformation which we saw in Heylyn's histories, they noted Lutherans had retained much ceremony, and that their ecclesiastical government through area 'supervisors' was not a world away from episcopal hierarchy. Some, including Francis Atterbury and George Smalridge, consequently wondered if Lutherans might accept English liturgy and ordination of their supervisors by English bishops as means to amalgamate the two communions; and Sophia may have entered the picture as a patron of this scheme. Personally eclectic in her religious views, she thought all the anti-Roman Christians of Europe (starting with those in her own Lutheran areas of Germany) might unite around an anglican-style church.[433] Certainly, this solution was 'catholic' in that it would extend episcopacy to new lands in Germany, and some low churchmen suspected such schemes might recruit the Germans as part of a federation of national establishments which would exclude English nonconformists.[434] Yet this Tory initiative (if that is what it was) also had 'protestant' elements. It approached a reformed church as a partner, and recognised its ministry as at least potentially valid.

Negotiations with the Lutherans never made any dramatic progress, yet the search for unity with Protestants abroad considerably softened Whig–Tory division. People of a wide spectrum of views looked for foreign partners after 1689; and if their exact reasoning may have differed, their attempts to place the church of England in an international reformed context led them to approach the same people. Thus the Whig churchman William Wake (archbishop of Canterbury from 1716) also became involved in lengthy talks with the Lutherans. In the years after 1714 he corresponded with Daniel Jablonski, the spiritual adviser to the elector of Brandenburg, in an effort to find a formula to unite the English and Prussian churches.[435] Elsewhere historians including George Every, Norman Sykes and Eamon Duffy have illustrated how various (though often intertwined) ecclesiastical visions drove all wings of the church to keep in close contact with Protestants in Europe, and William

432 E.g. Holmes, *British politics*, pp. 113–14.
433 Every, *High church*, p. 119. For Sophia's ecumenical protestantism: Andrew Thompson, *Britain, Hanover, and the Protestant interest, 1688–1757* (Woodbridge, 2006), p. 49.
434 For such tensions: Duffy, 'Correspondence'.
435 Norman Sykes, *William Wake* (2 vols., Cambridge, 1957), ch. 6.

Gibson has used this to back the idea that eighteenth-century clerics were far more unified than has been thought.[436] Meanwhile, Craig Rose has shown the huge spectrum of opinion involved in the Society for Promoting Christian Knowledge.[437] The SPCK was founded in 1699 to publish affordable religious tracts for the English, but it soon began to co-ordinate a network of correspondents across reformed Europe. As it did this, it became the clearing house of a vigorous Protestant international which exchanged news, theological enquiry and calls for assistance in the face of persecution.[438]

Importantly, however, the common interest in ecclesiastical union went further than exploring links with Protestants. It was built as much on continuing Whig sympathy for episcopal establishments abroad, as on surviving Tory sympathy for other reformed communions. Low churchmen were always interested in continental Christians as part of their vision of a flexible reformation, but some also found merit in the old 'catholic' notion that the bishop-led, but currently popish, churches of southern Europe were true communions. If only, they still believed, these churches would purge their superstition and throw off the pope's usurpation, they could be embraced by the English. So, for example, Burnet spoke warmly of signs of enlightenment and reform within the churches of France and even Italy.[439] More remarkably, Wake balanced his approaches to German Lutherans with talks with members of the French Catholic church. Sensing French resentment at papal interference in their internal affairs, the archbishop established contact with clerics at the Sorbonne, most notably Louis du Pin, and corresponded to discuss whether the 'Gallicans' (as the more independent clergy of France were known) might renounce the authority of Rome and join the anglicans in communion.[440] It is true that some of Wake's approaches got him into trouble. Many colleagues worried he was flirting with popery in his talks with Gallicans, and many Frenchmen themselves rejected any deal with a heretical Protestant establishment.[441] Yet his contacts warn us against any unbridgeable fissure between a 'catholic' and a 'protestant' anglicanism. In Wake we see the continuing purchase of both restoration visions of the church, but as we have seen, he was not alone in holding both in tension in his worldview.

[436] Duffy, 'Correspondence'; Sykes, *William Wake*; Every, *High church*, pp. 113–24; William Gibson, *The church of England, 1688–1832* (2001), ch. 6.
[437] Craig Rose, 'The origins and ideals of the SPCK, 1699–1716', in Walsh, Haydon and Taylor, *Church of England*, pp. 172–91.
[438] Sugiko Nishikawa, 'The SPCK and the defence of Protestant minorities in early eighteenth-century Europe', *JEH*, 56 (2005), 730–48.
[439] E.g. Gilbert Burnet, *Some letters containing an account* (1687), p. 175.
[440] Sykes, *William Wake*, ch. 4.
[441] Sykes, *William Wake*, I:300–2; Brian Young, 'A history of variations: the identity of the eighteenth century church of England', in Claydon and McBride, *Protestantism*, pp. 105–30, esp. pp. 108–13.

This still-shared interest in a variety of European contexts brings us to a broad parallel between constitutional and ecclesiastical debate. As Whigs and Tories argued over the correct location of power in the English political system, their common commitment to the Protestant interest and the community of Christian states on the continent limited their polarisation. In a similar way, the continuing attraction to each side of both a communion between reformed churches, and a federation of episcopal establishments, provided points of potential collaboration. At no time was this clearer than in the Bangorian controversy of 1717–20. This final burst of ecclesiological polemic in our period is sometimes presented as the last great clash of Whig and Tory churchmanship; but in fact it should be most famous for the rallying of parties against a radical vision from outside their spectrum of belief.

As its curious moniker suggests, the Bangorian was sparked by the bishop of Bangor, Benjamin Hoadly. Hoadly had been a London clergyman, who had emerged as a champion of Whig resistance theory in Queen Anne's reign, and received the reward of the north Welsh diocese soon after in the Whig triumph of 1714.[442] From this point on, however, a disturbing trend emerged in his rhetoric. Going beyond standard low church tolerance of dissent or attacks on the non-jurors' claim to be independent of lay power, he began to accuse the church of England of pretending to a Rome-like infallibility. The establishment, he claimed, included too many people with an overblown sense of clerical glory, who itched to persecute those outside, and who denied individuals the right to interpret scripture for themselves. Soon, two works took these ideas to a logical conclusion. The first, *A preservative against ... non-jurors* (1716), asserted that the essence of true religion was sincerity in what one believed.[443] In Hoadly's view, salvation could not depend on adherence to any particular creed or communion (however strident their claims to doctrinal purity), and the only reliable mark of a true church was a willingness to allow people to explore God's truth without coercive censure. The bishop's second work, *The nature of the kingdom ... of Christ* (a sermon delivered before the king in March 1717), argued the church should have no temporal power at all.[444] For Hoadly, Jesus was the sole legitimate authority over Christians; his rewards and punishments were reserved for the next life, and to anticipate these by placing spiritual jurisdiction in human

[442] Hoadly had preached conditional obedience: Benjamin Hoadly, *The happiness of the present establishment ... preach'd at the assizes at Hartford, March 22nd, 1707/8* (1708); Benjamin Hoadly, *St Paul's behaviour towards the civil magistrate* (1708). But he also pamphleteered: Benjamin Hoadly, *The measures of submission to the civil government considered* (1706).

[443] Benjamin Hoadly, *A preservative against the principles and practices of the non-jurors* (1716).

[444] Benjamin Hoadly, *The nature of the kingdom, or church, of Christ: a sermon preach'd before the king ... Sunday March 31, 1717* (1717).

hands would usurp his power. As might be imagined, such opinions sparked controversy. Hoadly exceeded normal Whig denunciation of persecution to question some of the core assumptions of English ecclesiastical provision. Making faith a matter purely of sincerity, and denying all forms of coercion to the institutional church, the bishop had undercut arguments for a legal establishment, and even threw doubt on its internal discipline. Could a state support a church with its worldly power? Could one defend a hierarchy of bishops and ministers if clerics could not exercise legitimate authority? Could a church even endorse codified statements of faith and impose them on its members? Hoadly pretty explicitly said no. Given such radicalism, a row was inevitable. The lower house of convocation condemned the bishop and he was rapidly answered in the press. When he found supporters, a full-scale paper war commenced. The two sides pursued each other over a wide range of issues; they generated over four hundred contributions; and the sallies only fizzled out in the 1720s.[445]

At first glance, it is easy to read the Bangorian controversy as a classic Whig–Tory battle. The committee of convocation which condemned Hoadly was dominated by high churchmen and many of his press detractors were Tories. By contrast, the bishop was supported by low church writers and by the Whig ministry of the day which dissolved the convocation as punishment for their attack upon his works (it did not meet again for substantive business until 1852). Furthermore, much of the dispute mapped the differences in understanding of the international church which we have seen at the heart of party conflict. Many of the bitterest attacks on Hoadly's ideas therefore took their stand on an episcopal catholic church. God, Tory writers argued, had placed spiritual authority in human hands when he instituted bishops, and to question this was to blaspheme against a divine power recognised by churches across the globe.[446] It is true that Hoadly's defence against these arguments was not immediately founded on a Protestant international. It analysed scripture to argue Christ denied his apostles worldly power and (continuing the bishop's earlier interest in the contractual origins of government) argued that temporal coercion must not stray beyond its founding function of protecting liberty and property.[447] In fact, we might see in Hoadly the start of serious efforts to discuss freedom to worship in terms of universal human rights, instead of assuring the protection of true

[445] For the structure of the controversy: Andrew Starkie, 'The Bangorian controversy, 1716–1721' (Cambridge Ph.D., 2002), appendix. The debate also catalogued itself: e.g. *All the advertisements and letters by the lord bishop of Bangor* (1717).

[446] E.g. Thomas Brett, *The independency of the church upon the state* (1717), esp. introduction and pp. 43–65; Thomas Brett, *The divine right of episcopacy* (1718); *A letter to the Reverend Dr Bradford* (1718), p. 7.

[447] For Hoadly's contractarianism: Benjamin Hoadly, *The original and institution of civil government discuss'd* (1710).

faith. Nevertheless, there is evidence that the bishop was concerned about the continent's reformed community, and that his appeal against temporal ecclesiastical authority was designed to protect them. Thus in broad terms, Hoadly's reluctance to enforce doctrine gelled with low church insistence that the reformation needed to accept variety if it was to co-operate against Rome. His use of language also suggested he saw tolerance as crucial in the battle for Europe's soul. Andrew Starkie has pointed out that he labelled all forms of persecution 'popish' and understood 'reformation' as the process of breaking its hold.[448]

More concretely, the bishop revealed concern for the foreign faithful as the controversy widened to engulf the test acts. In 1718, the clerical polemicist Thomas Sherlock accused Hoadly of wanting to dismantle sacramental qualifications for public office, but his target responded with worries about the godly abroad.[449] Sherlock, Hoadly argued, supported using a test to uphold the official Protestant church in his country, but allowing states to support particular religions would have dire consequences for the reformation elsewhere. The principle would be just 'as Good, as Just, and as Righteous in *France*, or *Spain*, or *Italy*', the bishop pointed out. It would 'defend with equal Justice the *Highest* Instances of *Persecution* and *Barbarity* of the Inquisition', it would allow the reformed to attack each other as much as papists to attack them, and it might ultimately, therefore, 'destroy the Whole *Protestant Cause*'.[450] By contrast, the bishop's latitude would benefit the suffering faithful. Instead of calling into question the 'foundation' of Protestant churches (as Sherlock did by denouncing any dissent from officially recognised faiths), it would relieve believers 'in any part of the World . . . differing from any Church established and supported by the *Civil Power*'.[451]

Given this, we could chalk up the whole Bangorian dispute as another battle fired by 'catholic' and 'reformed' perceptions of the continent. Yet in fact, this controversy did as much to blur as to confirm party battlelines. As historians have long noted, Hoadly did not get the support of the entire Whig movement. The ministry of the day promoted his ideas, but this was composed of only one Whig faction, a highly anti-clerical group led by the earls of Stanhope and Sunderland. As a result of party splits, a rival Whig phalanx around Sir Robert Walpole was in opposition in 1717, and was much cooler to Hoadly. Walpole's men played down hostility to the

448 Starkie, 'Bangorian controversy', pp. 115–47.

449 Thomas Sherlock, *A vindication of the corporation and test acts* (1718), preface. This sparked long exchanges: Benjamin Hoadly, *An answer to a calumny cast upon the bishop of Bangor* (1718); Thomas Sherlock, *The condition and example of our blessed saviour* (1718); Benjamin Hoadly, *An answer to a late book written by Dr Sherlock* (1718).

450 Benjamin Hoadly, *The common rights of subjects defended* (1719), pp. 210, 245–6, 267.

451 Ibid., p. 5.

clerical establishment; they calculated this would ease the path back to office and build bridges to the similarly excluded Tories, and so – for instance – they opposed the repeal of the occasional conformity bill when the ministry proposed this in 1719. More significantly, not all Whig churchmen rallied to the bishop of Bangor. Important figures such Francis Hare, John Potter and Edmund Gibson – who had been clients of Whig and low church bishops under William and Anne – became chief spokesmen against Hoadly.[452] Shocked that their earlier criticisms of a rigidly episcopal church could lead to questioning of worldly support for a particular faith, many recoiled and began to defend the church's earthly role and authorities.

Of course it is possible to explain this calming realignment after the Bangorian controversy by factional shifts in the Whig movement. As we explored when looking at constitutional issues, Tory impotence allowed room for splits among their enemies, and some of the resulting groups might be more sympathetic to the established church. It is important not to lose site of this most obvious reason for the different configuration of ecclesiastical politics in the Georgian era, nor to underestimate the simple shock of Hoadly's radical challenge to the idea of a national religious institution. Yet the rhetoric of the Bangorian controversy suggests another level of explanation. It shows the wings of the church united by shared visions of international communion. All types of anglicans could unite against Hoadly because his other-worldly understanding of Christ's body rendered *any* international context for anglicanism meaningless. For Hoadly, the church was an utterly mystical union of the sincere. It was therefore known only to God; it could not be identified by any earthly belief or membership; and so – as people across the spectrum lamented – it would be virtually impossible to spot or to offer practical support for one's spiritual brethren elsewhere. As importantly, zeal to defeat Hoadly drove people beyond their particular party's pet visions of European communion. Tories nodded to an otherwise suspected Protestant international, and Whigs to a wider – potentially Rome-endorsing – Christendom, so long as these stacked up witnesses against the bishop.

We can start the illustration on the Tory side. The opening, and in many ways definitive, statement of this case against Hoadly came from the committee of convocation which condemned him. Published as a pamphlet, this rapidly went through multiple editions, and sparked a considerable exchange

[452] Francis Hare, *The charge of God to Joshua* (1711), defended the Whig general Marlborough, of whose army he was chief chaplain. Hare also wrote against Tory peace plans, joining the campaign described above, pp. 198–9. Potter had been patronised by Marlborough and the Whig archbishop Thomas Tenison – though John Potter, *A discourse of church government* (1707) had a 'Tory' stress on clerical autonomy. Gibson had been Tenison's chaplain, and had taken over 'the main burden of developing the low church response' to Atterbury in the early years of Queen Anne: Stephen Taylor, 'Gibson, William', *ODNB*, XXII:68–75.

debating its case. In truth, the committee's report had little overt to say about foreign Christianity. It protested that Hoadly had abolished any clerical authority or discipline, and culminated in a long second section accusing the bishop of treasonously including the royal supremacy in that abolition. The first part, however, hinted at wider entities. It complained Hoadly made it impossible to identify the true godly anywhere, thundering that he put 'all Communions on an equal foot, without regard to any intrinsick Goodness, or whether they be Right or Wrong'.[453] As one might expect from its high church authors, this charge was used to defend a 'catholic' identity when complaining it undermined episcopacy, but it also stressed the threat to England's Protestant credentials. The bishop, the convocation men pointed out, had presented a very odd version of Tudor history. According to Hoadly, it had been merely Englishmen's sincere belief in Rome's corruption – not an actual corruption itself – which had justified their break with popery. Using language which hinted heavily this was to betray the European league of Protestant communions, the committee said this was a 'Point of tenderest Concern to the whole Reformation', which left no difference between Rome 'and our Reformed Church'.[454]

It is true that internationalism has to be somewhat distilled from the convocation's indictment, but audiences brought up on earlier ecclesiastical disputes would see the continent behind such phrases as the 'whole reformation' or defences of episcopal governance, and other high church writers were more explicit. Andrew Snape, for example, was one of Hoadly's first and most vehement Tory critics. His *Letter to the bishop of Bangor* went through no fewer than seventeen editions in 1717, and stimulated a string of responses which constituted a sub-genre within the whole Bangorian dispute.[455] The original work accused Hoadly of rejecting scriptural instructions that the church must be a disciplined body; but it also charged him with being indifferent between 'all Churches, and all Religions', and supported these points by suggesting he would delegitimate both 'catholic' and Protestant communities throughout the world.[456] Thus, since all communions had exercised worldly authority, Hoadly was effectively saying 'there never was any Part of the Catholick Church . . . in any Nation of the World, that has not . . . acted in direct Opposition to the Will of our Blessed Saviour'.[457] All acts of even the early general councils were void, and there could be no statements of faith to bind Christians together. At the same time, the

[453] *A report of the committee of the lower house of convocation appointed to draw up a representation* (1717), p. 11.
[454] Ibid., p. 12.
[455] Entering 'Snape' as a title search term in 'Eighteenth century collections online' (www.galegroup.com/EighteenthCentury) yields 113 hits.
[456] Andrew Snape, *A letter to the bishop of Bangor* (1717), p. 33.
[457] Ibid., p. 34.

narrower Protestant reformation was destroyed because it too had relied on temporal power. Reform had been completed by 'Earthly Rulers' in the sixteenth century, and had been protected by them ever since.[458] Other writers followed Snape's lead. Thomas Dawson ranted against dissenters in his contribution to the debate, but went on to argue that Protestantism as well as Christendom was in danger from Hoadly's extreme latitude. The bishop's creed put Christians on a level with '*Hereticks, Mahometans* and *Pagans*', but it was also a 'Reproach and Scandal to the *Reformation*' and it damaged the church of England 'which is acknowledg'd to be the great Bulwark of the *Protestant Interest*'.[459] William Law similarly balanced his warnings between two visions of international communion. His main argument was that scripture insisted on participation in Christ's universal church on earth as a condition of godliness. He asserted the church had worldly authority over believers, and that they should submit to the local branch of this international body. This vision was sufficiently 'catholic' that Law had to explain why it did not demand people take communion with papists in France, Spain and Italy; but as he did this, Law suggested solidarity with foreign Protestants. Because godliness was a matter of fact (and not simply of sincerity as Hoadly would have it), only communion in a 'sound' church actually constituted participation in the universal communion. This, of course, excused the nonconformity of Protestants in France, for instance, and so identified with the European reformation over any episcopal federation.[460] This balance in Law's arguments was carried over to the rhetorical climax of his 1719 *Reply to the bishop of Bangor*. Here Law exclaimed that Hoadly could not have come up with a better scheme had he 'meant ever so much harm to *Christianity* and the *Reformation*'. The bishop left no way to judge between creeds which made equal claims to their sincerity, and so set '*Christianity* and *Mahometanism*, the *Reformation* and *Quakerism*' on the same foot.[461] (The Quakers were singled out here for their supposed coolness to core Christian doctrine such as the atonement.)

Reference to international entities was even clearer on the Whig wing of the anti-Hoadly movement. Those low churchmen who could not follow the bishop of Bangor's logic were extremely bothered by his invalidation of the European reformation. They feared he undercut its claims to doctrinal superiority over popery, and that he would allow no earthly help to promote its wellbeing. A late intervention by Francis Hare expressed the latter concern particularly vividly. He pointed out that the counter-reformation was on the march – especially across Germany – and that the Protestants' only hope lay

458 Ibid., p. 38. 459 Thomas Dawson, *Suspira sacra* (1718), pp. 45, 83.
460 William Law, *A reply to the bishop of Bangor's answer to the representation* (1719), pp. 186–8.
461 Ibid., p. 227.

in vigour and unity. These could only be provided by authoritative churches, and the backing of temporal powers, so Hoadly was effectively condemning the whole movement to destruction as he refused these any role in the spiritual realm. 'What,' Hare asked in despair, 'does his Lordship think of the state of the *Protestant* Religion in the *Empire*? How long would it subsist, if the *Westphalian* Treaty [which gave legal recognition to Protestant princes] were abolished?'[462] Hare raised a different, but related, anxiety when accusing Hoadly of libelling the Protestant international. Every reformed church had declared its precise creed and policed this by condemning heretics; but Hoadly was now saying such coercive action was popish. He therefore cast '*odious Colours* upon the whole Body of *Protestant* Churches'; and John Potter agreed.[463] According to Potter, the bishop was 'displeas'd with the Doctrine and Practice both of the Church of *England*, and of the *Protestant* Churches abroad', thus revealing himself an enemy of the European reformation.[464]

Moderate Whigs therefore feared Hoadly had destroyed their favourite international context for faith, but like the Tories they also spoke of the alternative vision to prove how unacceptable Hoadly's ideas were. Potter therefore pointed out it was not only the reformed churches which had imposed creeds. They had done so because this had been the practice of '*the Catholick Church in all Ages*', and in fact Protestants tried to return to the doctrinal rigour of the first (and he might have added, bishop-led) general councils.[465] Francis Hare too had a strong sense of an authoritative universal communion. He saw this surviving from a primitive episcopal body which had spread across the globe, and opposed this to Hoadly's other-worldly church. So Hare became embroiled in his battle with the bishop after preaching that the New Testament had instituted a visible communion with the right to discipline its members.[466] His 1719 sermon had argued that this implied clear authority figures, and went on to show that the universal practice of the early church confirmed these figures should be ministers acting under the co-ordinating authority of episcopacy. As Hare's battle of words unfolded, he came ever closer to 'catholic' appeals to practice well beyond the reformation, stating at one point that to deny clerics power in this world

[462] Francis Hare, *Scripture vindicated from the misinterpretations of the lord bishop of Bangor* (1721), preface.

[463] [Francis Hare], *A new defence of the lord bishop of Bangor's sermon* (1720), p. 27.

[464] John Potter, *A defence of the late charge deliver'd to the clergy* (1720), p. 80.

[465] Potter, *Defence*, p. 4. This defended John Potter, *The bishop of Oxford's charge to the clergy of his diocese* (1720), which also insisted all churches believed temporal power should uphold doctrine, pp. 11–12.

[466] Francis Hare, *Church-authority vindicated in a sermon preached at Putney, May 5, 1719* (1719).

would reduce true communion to a disorganised mass of people and arraign the practice of 'all the Churches in the *Christian* World'.[467]

In this reading of the Bangorian controversy, shared commitment to visions of the international church united high and low wings against Hoadly. His arguments were shocking because they left no meaningful alliance with Christians across Europe, and so offended a set of identities which his opponents still held dear. If this conclusion bears weight, it is important, because the realignment in the first years of the Hanoverian period proved lasting and helped the remodelling of party politics which we have already begun to explore for the years after 1714. After strands of Whiggery had joined with Tories to defend a set of understandings of the church, religious tensions ceased to define and deepen the old partisan fissure. Although ecclesiastical controversy continued, it was pretty infrequent and it no longer sundered Whig clearly from Tory. So, on returning to power in 1720, Walpole continued his alliance with those clerics who thought a privileged church could discipline its members and should hold sway over the whole population. Gibson, firmly of this view, was promoted to the bishopric of London in 1723, and became the most influential adviser to the premier minister. Hare's and Potter's careers also accelerated under Walpole. The former was promoted to St Asaph, then Chichester, whilst the latter scaled the heights of Canterbury in 1737. Under the leadership of such men – who defended the legal establishment, opposed further concessions to dissent, and have come to be called 'high church Whigs' – tension between the wings of the English communion softened. Religion was much less of a political issue from the 1720s: historians such as Jeremy Gregory have noted men of very different attitudes working together on a range of pastoral initiatives throughout the Georgian era; and Geoffrey Chamberlain has seen high church clerics accommodated by a Whig-led episcopacy which had come to share many of their concerns.[468]

What controversy survived followed the pattern of the Bangorian dispute. At certain points, especially in the 1730s, dissenters and a few church allies agitated to repeal the test acts. Whilst their arguments appealed to universal rights to free worship and unfettered service to society, they also followed Hoadly in defending the European reformation. They quoted the bishop's works from the Bangorian controversy; they said foreign Protestants suffered when official churches were given privileges; they presented the test acts as the first step to the sort of full-scale persecution launched against the Protestants

467 Ibid., pp. 27–8; [Hare], *New defence*, p. 20 – also the defence of church councils, pp. 56–7.

468 Jeremy Gregory, 'The eighteenth-century reformation: the pastoral task of the anglican clergy after 1689', in Walsh, Haydon and Taylor, *Church of England*, pp. 67–85, esp. pp. 83–5; Jeffrey S. Chamberlain, *Accommodating high churchmen: the clergy of Sussex, 1700–1745* (Urbana, IL,1997).

of Salzburg in 1732; and they cited examples of Dutch and German states whose Protestant regimes benefited from employing different denominations of people.[469] In short they insisted that when one considered dissenters in England, one must also think of '*All Dissenters*', all over the world, and many of these were reformed Christians facing brutal popish regimes.[470] Yet whilst the style of anti-establishment argument was familiar from the Bangorian controversy, so was the political response. Tories were naturally hostile, but so were many (probably most) Whigs, and again the reaction was stoked by concern about the how the international church might defend itself if denied earthly weapons. Thus Walpole, speaking in the Commons in 1736, replied to Walter Plummer's bill to repeal the test acts by wondering what this would mean across all nations. No regime could or did allow those openly hostile to its religion to hold public office; on anti-test principles all the world's establishments would be guilty of persecution.[471] Pamphleteers backed him. In an influential work defending the acts, Gibson challenged his opponents to cite any country which did not favour adherents of its national religion, and sparked a debate about whether England's Protestant neighbours defended themselves by restricting access to state employment.[472] The rising Whig cleric Anthony Ellys joined this controversy. He argued that Holland, Prussia and the German states excluded religious dissidents *de facto*, even if they had no formal laws against them taking public office, and then tackled the argument that allowing discrimination could help popish regimes as much as reformed ones. Politically, he admitted, a state's right to defend its religion must apply to all governments. Morally, however, there was a distinction. Establishments were not '*equally rightful* in themselves': only pro-Protestant discrimination was justified in the eyes of God, so princes who upheld Islam or popery would be found wanting at their final judgement.[473] Examining this pattern of politics in the 1730s, it is tempting to see a situation turned full circle. As in the 1660s, both a 'reformed' and a 'catholic' vision of the international church defended the establishment against a small dissenting minority, and so prevented debate polarising into the evenly matched parties which had marked the intervening years. It may be worth recapping what

[469] E.g. *The nature and consequences of the sacramental test* (1731), p. 29; [Samuel Chandler], *The dispute better adjusted* (1732), pp. 23, 34–5; *The corporation and test acts shown to be of no importance* (1736); *The reasonableness of applying for the repeal or explanation of the corporation and test acts* (1736), pp. 44–50; *Short remarks upon the plea for the sacramental test* (1736), pp. 5–6, 19.

[470] *The objections against the repeal of the corporation and test acts considered* (1739), p. 46 (though this extended the principle to accept Catholics serving Protestant states).

[471] Cobbett, IX:1053.

[472] [Edmund Gibson], *The dispute adjusted* (1732), p. 15. Many pro-repeal works answered this.

[473] Anthony Ellys, *A plea for the sacramental test as a just security* (1736), pp. 9–10, 113–15.

happened over these decades, both to conclude this section, and because the story may further explain that creation and then cooling of Whig–Tory passion which we observed with constitutional issues.

Throughout this period, a 'catholic' vision of federated episcopacy legitimated the church of England and, over time, came to characterise a 'high church' or Tory position. This obviously alienated dissenters, who worried about the status of non-episcopal churches abroad, but it also came to concern those conformist churchmen who had conceived their communion as part of an international reformation. These people had initially used their European identity to defend the 1662 settlement, but as the popish threat had grown, their discourse was transformed into the Whig appeal for a flexible alliance of overlapping denominations. This alternative ideology appalled Tory episcopalians and fed party debates over the church into the late Stuart era. The polarisation was, however, softened by two factors. First, anglicans had always deployed a muddled barrage of arguments to justify their establishment, and they never cured themselves of this confusion. Even when they fissured into clear church parties after 1689, only some gravitated to an extreme end of the spectrum. Thus many Whig churchmen retained latent sympathies for an episcopal universal church; and many Tories retained a Protestant identity which kept them appealing to the European reformation. Second, the trajectory of the Whigs' vision did not stop with its appeal for forbearance between Protestants. In the hands of Hoadly and his followers, it collapsed any meaningful participation in an international church. Horror at popish use of temporal power in foreign countries, and fear that the principle of promoting one religion might harm Protestants abroad, resulted in a toleration so complete it forbade action to support reformed Christianity anywhere and a tendency to argue for a universal human freedom to worship, rather than loyalty to the international godly. In the face of this, many Whigs recoiled. They re-joined Tories in defence of a national religion which was seen as part of continental communions of the faithful. In this way they preserved their valued sense that they were part of something larger and more significant than their individual conscience, the establishment of their particular nation, or the abstract right of each person to believe anything without temporal coercion. In this way, 'catholic' and 'protestant' visions of the European church may ultimately have done more to contain party tensions than to create them. There were disputes about who an anglican's brethren abroad were, and these crucially shaped Whig and Tory philosophy. Yet both sides agreed such brethren could be identified, they concurred that these people must be supported in the face of godless enemies, and they even – in their confused and contradictory ways – felt the pull of their opponents' continental identities.

CONCLUSION: THE PARADOX OF PECULIARITY

When this book's introduction mused on the misfortunes of William Bromley, it advertised a number of lessons about English politics and culture. To keep the conclusion pithy, it could simply observe these have been more than learnt. Repeatedly, the studies presented here have shown the importance of religious entities wider than Englishness, or even Britishness, to England's inhabitants in the century after the civil war. A sense of belonging to a Protestant international with branches across the continent, and to a Christendom whose geographical range was even broader than this, shaped the English sense of space and time, influenced foreign policy and overseas military engagement and played a key role in dividing Whig from Tory. These loyalties have been shown to have broken any narrow insularity and to have provided flexible and constantly shifting identities. This was especially true as Protestantism and Christianity were imagined in a variety of ways, and shared the field with a still important national sense. We have seen, for example, different concepts of the reformation: some admitted almost any kind of Protestant, whilst others chose the truly godly much more carefully. Similarly there were different Christendoms on offer. These ranged through federations of episcopal churches, military alliances against the Turk and moral communities of people who must keep their word. Again, neither reformed nor Christian internationalism eliminated the English sense that they were English. Whilst caring about the faithful abroad, people still appealed to their own country's ancient constitution in the debates of the 1680s; or worried about their nation's commercial advantage in foreign wars from the 1660s to the 1750s; or expressed shock at the strangeness of even Protestant societies abroad. This would be more than enough material for a major reassessment of English history after 1660. The Protestant international and Christendom have not hitherto been given due weight: after the analysis just completed, they must be woven more deeply into our understanding of the country's development.

Moreover, the case has been made without reference to some of the strongest evidence for transnational spiritualities. Relatively little, for example, has been said about charitable relief for those suffering persecution abroad, yet this was one of the most notable features of English society in this period. Aiding unfortunates from France in the 1670s and 1680s, from the Palatine under Queen Anne and from central Europe in the 1720s and 1730s, the English demonstrated a continuing sympathy for their Protestant brethren which could lead them to considerable administrative, diplomatic and economic inconvenience.[1] Similarly, there has been almost no coverage of an accelerating missionary activity aimed at spreading Christianity (and especially reformed Christianity) to benighted lands. Always claimed as part of England's commercial and colonial expansion, efforts to convert natives were regularised – for the new world at least – by the Society for the Propagation of the Gospel from 1701.[2] Chartered by William III, this body collected funds for evangelism in the North American colonies, and issued promotional material which displayed the full range of English attitudes to others' faith. Urging the audience to be ashamed that England had converted fewer natives than the Jesuits sent from Spain (and so tacitly accepting Catholic efforts as an advance for Christ), preachers and pamphleteers nonetheless insisted Protestant messages and methods were more, perhaps uniquely, godly.[3] Another neglected aspect has been the overseas origin of many religious, social and cultural ideas. Throughout the period, England was influenced by contacts with the foreign faithful, and many of her key debates, concepts and movements were imported from them. For example, the ecclesiastical discussions of the 1660s were stoked by royalists who had been in France in the 1650s and had been unsure where to worship there; in 1707 a band of 'French Prophets' briefly stirred a mass millenarianism; whilst historians of Methodism have long recognised the role of Moravian

[1] For introductions to the Huguenots, see John M. Hintermaier, 'The first modern refugees?', *Albion*, 32 (2000), 429–49; Robin Gwynn, *Huguenot heritage* (2nd edn, Brighton, 2001). For efforts for the Palatines: H. T. Dickinson, 'The poor Palatines and the parties', *EHR*, 82 (1967), 464–85. For eighteenth-century efforts: Andrew Thompson, *Britain, Hanover and the Protestant interest, 1688–1757* (Woodbridge, 2006), chs. 3–6; and in particular the concerns for the Protestants of Salzburg expelled in 1732 – *An account of the sufferings of the persecuted Protestants in the archbishoprick of Salzburg* (1732), p. 99, appealed for funds to help.

[2] There has been no recent history of the SPG, but it chronicled its own early actions: *An account of the incorporated Society for the Propagation of the Gospel in Foreign Parts* (1706).

[3] For equivocal attitudes to the Roman mission: e.g. *An account of the propagation of the gospel in foreign parts* (1704), pp. 1–3; John Williams, *A sermon preached before the Society for the Propagation of the Gospel . . . Feb. 15 1705/5* (1706); John Moore, *Of the truth and excellency of the gospel: a sermon preach'd . . . 20th Feb. 1712/13* (1713), esp. pp. 32–3; Nicholas Clagget, *A sermon preached before the incorporated Society for the Propagation of the Gospel . . . February 17, 1736* (1737), pp. 33–5; Martin Benson, *A sermon preach'd before the incorporated Society for the Propagation of the Gospel* (1740), pp. 20–30.

thought on its founder, John Wesley.[4] Similarly, social historians have argued for the impact of Europeans on the organisation of work and welfare. In particular, some have pointed to the pietists of Halle, Saxony, who established structured social institutions as part of their scheme of religious revival, and may have provided models for mass institutions from factories to schools and workhouse in eighteenth-century England.[5]

The list could go on. For instance, the English of our period were touched by the European reformation and an ideal of Christendom as they were lobbied by the network of Huguenot writers which fanned across Europe after 1685, or as they participated in interwoven 'republics of letters' through which people across the continent spread news, opinion and learning.[6] I must also admit my decision to concentrate on the continental contexts of religious identity (over 'British', imperial or 'Atlantic' ones) has blinded this book to important aspects of religious internationalism. For example, the English constantly worried about the security of Irish Protestants in the face of the local Catholic majority, or about the radical reformation in Scotland which might serve as a threat or inspiration to breeds of England's faithful. These concerns have been mentioned sporadically, but are dimensions of the new 'British' history which could have been emphasised far more, and would have rounded out our picture of England's engagement with Christians beyond her borders.[7] Similarly, exploration of France's perceived

[4] For disputes among English exiles: Anthony Milton, 'Cosin, John', *ODNB*, XIII:531–8; Edward Martin, *Dr Martin, late dean of Ely, his opinion* (1662). For the prophets: Hillel Schwartz, *The French prophets* (Berkeley, 1980). For Methodism's European roots: Henry Rack, *Reasonable enthusiast: John Wesley and the rise of Methodism* (1989); Colin Podmore, 'The Moravians and the evangelical revival in England', *Transactions of the Moravian Historical Society*, 31 (2000); W. R. Ward, *The Protestant evangelical awakening* (Cambridge, 1992).

[5] See Tim Hitchcock, 'Paupers and preachers: the SPCK and the parochial workhouse movement', in Lee Davison, Tim Hitchcock, Tim Kiern and Robert Shoemaker, eds., *Stilling the grumbling hive: the response to social problems in England, 1689–1750* (Stroud, 1992), pp. 148–66 – this acknowledges its debts to W. R. Ward, 'The relation of enlightenment and religious revival in central Europe and the English speaking world', in Derek Beales, ed., *Reform and reformation: England and the continent, 1500–1750* (Oxford, 1979), pp. 281–305. See also D. L. Brunner, *Halle pietists in England* (Göttingen, 1993).

[6] For the Huguenots, see Laurence Huey Boles, *The Huguenots, the Protestant interest, and the war of Spanish succession, 1702–1714* (New York, 1997) and the huge number of writings by Pierre Jurieu. For different networks which exchanged ideas, see Sugiko Nishikawa, 'SPCK and the defence of Protestant minorities in early eighteenth-century Europe', *JEH*, 56 (2005), 730–48; Eamon Duffy, 'Correspondence fraternelle: the SPCK, the SPG and the churches of Switzerland in the war of Spanish succession', in Derek Baker, ed., *Reform and reformation: England and the continent 1500–1750* (Oxford, 1979); W. R. Ward, 'The eighteenth-century church: a European view', in John Walsh, Colin Haydon and Stephen Taylor, eds., *The Church of England c.1689–c.1833* (Cambridge, 1993), pp. 285–98; Anne Goldgar, *Impolite learning: conduct and community in the republic of letters, 1680–1750* (New Haven, CT, 1995), esp. pp. 202–18.

[7] For earlier mentions, see above, pp. 94, 320.

threats to godliness would have been enriched by considering her attempts to infiltrate the English dominion through Romanist Irishmen, Scots Jacobites, native Americans or French Canadians (none of whom shared England's dominant religion); whilst the thoughts of the Protestants of Ireland and North America (who continued to think of themselves as English at some level well into the eighteenth century) would have provided many fascinating sidelights on the metropolitan worldview.[8] Yet rather than lament how much more could be done to establish and elaborate our main conclusions, this last section will answer two obvious questions about the shape of the study. First, why stop around the accession of George III; and second, why concentrate on the particular aspects of foreign policy and Whig–Tory debate within England if there was clearly so much else to cover?

As for the first query, an end-date towards the end of the 1750s makes sense because there does seem to have been a shift in English discourse around this time. Certainly concern for foreign Protestants and Christians survived beyond this moment. Note, for example, the welcome afforded refugees from the atheistical terror of the French revolution; the continued use of fast days during foreign conflicts until the 1850s; or the sense of Protestant solidarity which has been perceived behind Anglo-American alliance into the twentieth century.[9] Nevertheless, whilst discourses could be familiar in the second century after the restoration, they no longer shaped public discussion as consistently as they once had. Some of the reasons for this were the triumphs of the rhetorics rather than their redundancy (as we saw when looking at constitutional disputes, people may have ceased to talk about faith overseas once the manner of England's participation in this was generally agreed), but towards the end of George II's life a series of new circumstances demoted the languages we have been studying and ushered in a somewhat different discursive universe.

[8] For a few works which have begun to discuss some of the areas: Jim Smyth, 'Like amphibious animals: Irish Protestants, ancient Britons, 1691–1707', *HJ*, 36 (1993), 785–97; Murray Pittock, *Inventing and resisting Britain: cultural identities in Britain and Ireland, 1685–1789* (Basingstoke, 1997); Thomas S. Kidd, 'Let hell and Rome do their worst: world news, anti-Catholicism and the Protestant interest in early eighteenth-century Boston', *New England Quarterly*, 76 (2003), 265–90; Thomas S. Kidd, *The Protestant interest: New England after puritanism* (New Haven, 2004).

[9] For refugees from the French revolution: Aiden Bellenger, 'Fearless resting place: the exiled French clergy in Great Britain, 1789–1815', in Kirsty Carpenter and Philip Mansel, eds., *The French émigrés in Europe* (Basingstoke, 1999). For later fasts, see Paul Langford, 'The English clergy and the American revolution', in Eckhard Hellmuth, ed., *The transformation of political culture* (Oxford, 1990), pp. 275–307; Roland Bartel, 'The story of public fast days in England', *Anglican Theological Review*, 37 (1955), 190–220. For transatlantic Protestant identities in the nineteenth century: John Wolffe, 'A transatlantic perspective: Protestantism and national identity in mid nineteenth-century Britain and the United States', in Tony Claydon and Ian McBride, eds., *Protestantism and national identity: Britain and Ireland, 1660–1850* (Cambridge, 1998), pp. 291–310.

In foreign affairs, to start, emerging factors militated against any simple conception of the forces of God and Satan. The rise of Prussia and Russia over the first half of the eighteenth century was perhaps the most significant. These were aggressive new powers, which did not easily fit into the previously prevailing pattern of international relations. Particularly they complicated that stand-off between Bourbon and Habsburg which the English had understood as a Christian balance of power preserving the welfare of a Protestant interest. Two new players upset basic European rivalries (as we have seen the *Daily Post* protesting in 1740s, they rendered old models of Europe obsolete), and neither behaved according to accepted scripts. Under the deistic Frederick the Great, Prussia became only nominally Lutheran, and put expansion above religious loyalty (for example, frustrating British aims with its invasion of Silesia in the 1740s). She therefore disrupted any sense of a united Protestant interest; and even when she was persuaded back into alliance with England in 1756, her self-interested strategy made any celebration of reformation unity problematic.[10] Russia's rise broke moulds too. It brought to prominence an empire which was neither Protestant nor Catholic, and tipped the balance of forces in the east further away from the Ottoman Turks. Constantinople had been a diminishing threat since the high-water mark in 1683 at Vienna, but by the 1750s they had lost the Serbian lands to Austria and had begun to suffer Russian expansion along the coasts of the Black Sea.[11] This Balkan activity blunted any sense of a united Christendom. There was far less need for Christ's people to unite against an Islamic threat once it was in retreat, and far less chance that anyone not throwing themselves into the cause could be accused of betraying the faith. By the 1760s, Habsburgs were allying with Ottomans to counter Russian expansion; this was accepted in England with very little comment.[12]

Another change in England's external relations was the steady growth of her extra-European interests. At Utrecht she had picked up strategic bases allowing her to expand around the globe; decades of commercial and colonial activity after this set her up for her triumphs in the Seven Years War. By 1760 it was fairly clear she would emerge with substantial interests not only in North America and the Caribbean, but throughout the Indian subcontinent and the Pacific basin as well. Although gratifying, these conquests diluted England's religious self-identity. First, they brought substantial numbers of non-Protestants under her direct rule. England had long had a Catholic

[10] For the *Daily Post*, and the impact of Prussia, see above, p. 218.

[11] For a basic introduction: Andrina Stiles, *Russia, Poland and the Ottoman Empire* (1991), ch. 9.

[12] There appear to have been no pamphlet attacks on this alliance – a stark contrast to the numerous denunciations of the far less formal collaboration between Louis XIV and the Ottomans a century earlier.

colony in Ireland; now she had to manage a populous one much further away in lower Canada, as well as cope with non-Christian subjects in Asia and beyond. This raised questions about whether vigorous assertion of Protestant or even Christian identity would be wise. Alienating populations by adopting a narrow religious policy might make them restive, and could cut imperialists off from human resources which might help them defend their gains. It is noticeable that not long into George III's rule, measures were being taken to placate Catholics in Quebec and Ireland as well as England (and especially to allow them to serve in the armed forces); and arguments were being advanced that lack of respect for local culture in India was the prime cause of England's difficulties there.[13] It seems people, of necessity, began to think of security above confession in their extended holdings, and this meant compromising with belief systems long blackened as 'the other'.

At home, too, political changes may have helped relegate international religious languages. Most pertinently, that split between Whigs and Tories, which was fuelled by different understandings of duty to the godly abroad, softened and blurred as the Georgian age wore on. For reasons explored above, the old animosities over the constitution and the church of England drained away. The two parties came to broad agreement that the constitutional settlements of 1689 and 1714, coupled with an ecclesiastical establishment which indulged dissent, were the only ways to secure stability at home and allow England to play her proper role defending the reformation and Christianity elsewhere.[14] What animus survived was weakened further by the failure of the Jacobite rebellion in 1745. With most Tories loyal to the Hanoverians in that revolt (and those who were not, no longer conceivably constructed as a threat after it fizzled out), the old Whig accusations that their enemies were a threat to international godliness became unusable. By the 1750s, tension had drained to the point that the old party structures collapsed. No longer divided from rivals by any profound ideological fissure, Tories lost their coherence, and were absorbed into various Whig factions.[15] Soon after the dissolution of the Tory party, the accession of George III removed another reason to discuss conditions abroad. One could accuse the new king of many things, but close attention to his German lands was not one of them. Brought up in England, and glorying in its identity, the monarch made it clear he put his British realm above Hanover, and so ended any need

[13] For key aspects: David Milobar, 'Quebec reform, the British constitution and the Atlantic empire', *Parliamentary History*, 14 (1995), 65–88; R. K. Donovan, 'The military origins of the Roman Catholic relief programme of 1778', *HJ*, 28 (1985), 79–102; Paul Langford, *The writings and speeches of Edmund Burke*, vol. 5, *India* (Oxford, 1981), introduction.

[14] See above, pp. 266–8.

[15] The exhaustively detailed study is J. C. D. Clark, *The dynamics of change: the crisis of the 1750s and the English party system* (Cambridge, 1982).

to set the sovereign's attitudes in the context of his European possession (a need which had been constant since 1689, with the brief exception of Anne's rule).[16]

A final set of changes around the middle of the eighteenth century might be put down to 'enlightenment'. This is a subject which one broaches only cautiously. There have been a series of debates about the precise nature, existence or relevance to England of a movement which may have led Europeans to view the world in a profoundly different way; and it is clear that the simplest account of an enlightenment – in which rational, secular analysis took over from Christianity as the dominant mode of thought – will not hold water.[17] In the work of many scholars, it is obvious the intellectual history of eighteenth-century Europe was very complex, that it varied greatly from country to country, that religion did not retreat uniformly in the face of a new rationalism and that many forms of Christian faith (notably those central to England's churches) adapted to any new intellectual climate and may even have been strengthened by it. Explaining that God was a reasonable ruler of the cosmos, and suggesting that his ways were comprehensible to people through ordered enquiry and reflection, many clerics and other people of faith led the English version of the key intellectual trends.[18] Given all this, I personally am profoundly agnostic about 'enlightenment'. The term tries to describe a movement which may be so diverse as to lack any really coherent meaning.

Nevertheless there was a change in intellectual fashion which appears to have affected England around 1750, which is usually seen as the sort of thing the enlightenment entailed, and which may have edged out international spiritual identities. It was that drift towards explaining human conditions in sociological or economic terms which we observed when looking at Bolingbroke. We noted that this intellectual current had its roots back in the seventeenth century, but we saw its triumph in political discourse waited until the 1720s, and can now add it made considerable headway in broader cultural analysis after this decade.[19] A series of thinkers (mostly from France and Scotland, but widely read in England) described phenomena such as

[16] John Cannon, 'George III', *ODNB*, XXI:833–53, opens with George's Britishness.

[17] For an exposition which put this as its central tenet, see Roy Porter, *Enlightenment: Britain and the making of the modern world* (2000): though the author also produced one of the clearest refutations of this idea – Roy Porter, 'Enlightenment in England', in Roy Porter and Mikulás Teich, *The enlightenment in national context* (Cambridge, 1981), pp. 1–18.

[18] For various aspects of this, see J. C. D. Clark, 'Providence, predestination and progress: or did the enlightenment fail?', *Albion*, 35 (2004), 559–89; Porter and Teich, *Enlightenment*; A. M. C. Waterman, *Revolution, economy and religion: Christian political economy* (Cambridge, 1991); David A. Pailin, 'Rational religion in England', in Sheridan Gilley and William J. Sheils, eds., *A history of religion in Britain* (Oxford, 1994), pp. 211–33.

[19] See above, p. 274.

government, culture or belief as rooted in material factors. The result was the popularity of, for instance, the baron de Montesquieu's work on the effect of climate on nations, or 'stadial' theories of development which suggested populations went through successive periods of different kinds of economic activity with particular sorts of society characteristic of each one.[20] This trend may have been important if it militated against religious movements as the key to understanding the universe: too mystical for sociological world-views, entities like international Protestantism or Christendom may have got into trouble as new fashions of thought spread. It can be suggested, for example, this development ended the traditions of writing analysed in this book's early chapters. By the 1750s, travel guides such as Thomas Nugent's were as careful as they could be to eliminate confessional bias in their objective observation of the political, cultural and economic factors influencing foreign societies, so solidarities of faith (whilst still present) become generally harder to distil from the text.[21] At the same time, Hume's *History of England* narrated its story as the result of human actions, not the playing out of God's plan for a faithful people. It thus raised questions far from the unfolding of England's reformation, or her ancient Christian heritage.[22]

For all these reasons, then, things were shifting by 1760, and it makes sense to stop around this time. But why concentrate upon debates over foreign policy, and between Whigs and Tories, when there were so many other aspects of England's interaction with Christian communities overseas? Partly, of course, this was simply because these were the central political discussions of the day. If one wanted to argue for the importance of European Protestantism and Christendom in England in this period, one would want to show their influence in these key areas. Yet there was another reason for exploring foreign relations and party tension in particular detail. These discussions help explain the most interesting features of England's development after the civil war; and the fact that continental entities played so prominent a part in these reveals a profound irony at their heart. There was a strange disjunction between the causes of change and its effects which might be labelled 'the paradox of peculiarity'.

The first element of the paradox is that the years after 1660 saw England diverging sharply from the nations round about her. From being an

[20] H. M. Höpfl, 'From savage to Scotsman: conjectural history in the Scottish enlightenment', *JBS*, 17 (1978), 19–40; Karen O'Brien, *Narratives of enlightenment: cosmopolitan history from Voltaire to Gibbon* (Cambridge, 1997), pp. 132–6; Karen O'Brien, 'Between enlightenment and stadial history: William Robertson on the history of Europe', *British Journal of Eighteenth Century Studies*, 16 (1993), 63–73.

[21] For comment on this, see above, p. 28.

[22] For analysis of Hume: O'Brien, *Narratives*, ch. 3; Nicholas Phillipson, *Hume* (1989); J. J. Burke, 'Hume's *History of England:* waking the English from dogmatic slumber', *Studies in Eighteenth Century Culture*, 7 (1978), 235–50.

idiosyncratic, but fairly unremarkable, society in the middle ages and sixteenth century, she rapidly emerged as a nation which the rest of the continent came to admire or to fear as a very unusual place indeed. There were two main aspects to this. First, as we have noted, she emerged as the premier world power.[23] This was surprising enough when compared to her relative impotence in previous centuries, but it was all the more remarkable given her very limited resources. Compared to France, for example, she had a very much smaller land mass, a very much less promising climate and a very much smaller population. She must, therefore, have come to use what she had with extraordinary efficiency: manpower, materials and money were directed to military might with unique determination and focus.[24] The second peculiarity, as we have again noted, was her open political system. Her constitutional settlements (particularly that in 1689) vested power in a representative parliament in which sharp exchanges of view were common, whilst a series of wider cultural changes (such as the emergence of a relatively free press, organised political movements and forums for public discussion) ensured these debates spread to a wider public.[25] England thus developed a genuinely participatory system, unusual in Europe outside small republics. In both her external power and her internal politics, therefore, England grew atypical of the continent, and for this she became the object of much examination, emulation and exasperation among her neighbours.[26]

Yet if the century after 1660 appears to show England separating from European norms, the reasons for this, which were explored in earlier chapters, construct the opposing part of the paradox. This nation became a great power because she was so constantly involved in warfare. Her political system was opened by the great ideological gulf between Whigs and Tories, but it was stabilised (rather than reverting to civil conflict) by underlying consensuses between these groups. There was also a productive feedback between these developments: the mobilisation of the resources needed for foreign adventures was extraordinarily efficient because adversarial politics encouraged criticism and investigation of government systems which uncovered and corrected their shortcomings (Commons auditing of military budgets is the clearest case in point).[27] Yet if constant warfare and divided but stable

[23] See above, pp. 125–32.

[24] For comment on this, see above, pp. 129–30, but also Michael Mann, *The sources of social power*, vol. 2, *The rise of classes and nation states* (Cambridge, 1993).

[25] See above, pp. 220–3.

[26] For external comment on the English in this period, see Paul Langford, *Englishness identified: manners and character, 1650–1850* (Oxford, 2000); Michael Maurer, 'Germany's image of England in the eighteenth century', in Joseph Canning and Hermann Wellenreuther, *Britain and Germany compared* (Göttingen, 2001), pp. 13–36.

[27] See Tony Claydon, *William III: profiles in power* (2002), ch. 5; John Brewer, *The sinews of power: war, money and the English state* (1989), ch. 5.

party politics explain why England became unlike Europe, both of these forces were shaped by intense engagement *with* Europe. Her military interventions were driven by determination to protect its Protestants, and to save all its people from un-Christian hegemony. She rose to dominance because she worried that popish, or persecuting, or perfidious, or Turkish tyrants might overrun the foreign faithful.[28] England became even more unlike her neighbours because her people divided over how to fulfil duties to the godly abroad, but then controlled that division in agreement that these duties were pressing. People split as they disagreed whether the royal succession must be altered to help the reformation and Christendom, and as they quarrelled about which version of the faith to recognise as the true church overseas. Politics were stabilised, however, as all recognised the Stuarts must be excluded for the sake of foreign Christians, and that the English must exercise flexibility in identifying the faithful in Europe or end in inconceivable ecclesiological isolation.[29] Although the English became powerful and peculiar enough to set themselves apart from believers elsewhere, they reached that position convinced that they shared, indeed were servants of, their cause.

This paradox of peculiarity will not explain everything. As has been constantly reiterated, there were purely domestic, and predominantly secular, considerations and discourses which influenced the English in this period. Not everyone spent all their time worrying about the Protestants and Christians of the continent: of course the Stuarts were excluded because they threatened England's own liberties and her own established church as much as for their incorrigible links with an anti-Christian France, and military interventions were certainly about commercial interest and geopolitical security as well as crusades for God's people. Yet to ignore the paradox – particularly to suggest the world after the civil war was very different, very much less religious or Europe-minded, than that before – also risks distortion. Alongside their identity as Englishmen, the people of England were Protestants and Christians too. Without recognising this, we will close our eyes to profound dimensions of their experience.

[28] See above, ch. 3. [29] See above, ch. 4.

INDEX

Titles in the series

The Common Peace: Participation and the Criminal Law in Seventeenth-Century England *
CYNTHIA B. HERRUP

Politics, Society and Civil War in Warwickshire, 1620–1660 *
ANN HUGHES

London Crowds in the Reign of Charles II: Propaganda and Politics from the Restoration to the Exclusion Crisis *
TIM HARRIS

Criticism and Compliment: The Politics of Literature in the England of Charles I *
KEVIN SHARPE

Central Government and the Localities: Hampshire, 1649–1689 *
ANDREW COLEBY

John Skelton and the Politics of the 1520s *
GREG WALKER

Algernon Sidney and the English Republic, 1623–1677 *
JONATHAN SCOTT

Thomas Starkey and the Commonweal: Humanist Politics and Religion in the Reign of Henry VIII *
THOMAS F. MAYER

The Blind Devotion of the People: Popular Religion and the English Reformation *
ROBERT WHITING

The Cavalier Parliament and the Reconstruction of the Old Regime, 1661–1667 *
PAUL SEAWARD

The Blessed Revolution: English Politics and the Coming of War, 1621–1624
THOMAS COGSWELL

Charles I and the Road to Personal Rule *
L. J. REEVE

George Lawson's 'Politica' and the English Revolution *
CONAL CONDREN

Puritans and Roundheads: The Harleys of Brampton Bryan and the Outbreak of the Civil War
JACQUELINE EALES

An Uncounselled King: Charles I and the Scottish Troubles, 1637–1641 *
PETER DONALD

Cheap Print and Popular Piety, 1550–1640 *
TESSA WATT

Protestantism and Patriotism: Ideologies and the Making of English Foreign Policy, 1650–1668 *
STEVEN C. A. PINCUS

*Gender in Mystical and Occult Thought: Behmenism and its Development in England**
B. J. GIBBONS

*William III and the Godly Revolution**
TONY CLAYDON

*Law-Making and Society in Late Elizabethan England: The Parliament of England, 1584–1601**
DAVID DEAN

Conversion, Politics and Religion in England, 1580–1625
MICHAEL C. QUESTIER

*Politics, Religion and the British Revolutions: The Mind of Samuel Rutherford**
JOHN COFFEY

*King James VI and I and the Reunion of Christendom**
W. B. PATTERSON

*The English Reformation and the Laity: Gloucestershire, 1540–1580**
CAROLINE LITZENBERGER

*Godly Clergy in Early Stuart England: The Caroline Puritan Movement, c.1620–1643**
TOM WEBSTER

*Prayer Book and People in Elizabethan and Early Stuart England**
JUDITH MALTBY

Sermons at Court, 1559–1629: Religion and Politics in Elizabethan and Jacobean Preaching
PETER E. MCCULLOUGH

*Dismembering the Body Politic: Partisan Politics in England's Towns, 1650–1730**
PAUL D. HALLIDAY

Women Waging Law in Elizabethan England
TIMOTHY STRETTON

*The Early Elizabethan Polity: William Cecil and the British Succession Crisis, 1558–1569**
STEPHEN ALFORD

*The Polarisation of Elizabethan Politics: The Political Career of Robert Devereux, 2nd Earl of Essex**
PAUL J. HAMMER

The Politics of Social Conflict: The Peak Country, 1520–1770
ANDY WOOD

*Crime and Mentalities in Early Modern England**
MALCOLM GASKILL

*The Pursuit of Stability: Social Relations in Elizabethan London**
IAN W. ARCHER

Prosecution and Punishment: Petty Crime and the Law in London and Rural Middlesex, c.1660–1725
ROBERT B. SHOEMAKER

Algernon Sidney and the Restoration Crisis, 1677–1683 *
JONATHAN SCOTT

Exile and Kingdom: History and Apocalypse in the Puritan Migration to America *
AVIHU ZAKAI

The Pillars of Priestcraft Shaken: The Church of England and its Enemies, 1660–1730
J. A. I. CHAMPION

Steward, Lords and People: The Estate Steward and his World in Later Stuart England
D. R. HAINSWORTH

Civil War and Restoration in the Three Stuart Kingdoms: The Career of Randal MacDonnell, Marquis of Antrim, 1609–1683
JANE H. OHLMEYER

The Family of Love in English Society, 1550–1630 *
CHRISTOPHER W. MARSH

The Bishops' Wars: Charles I's Campaigns against Scotland, 1638–1640 *
MARK FISSEL

John Locke: Resistance, Religion and Responsibility *
JOHN MARSHALL

Constitutional Royalism and the Search for Settlement, c.1640–1649 *
DAVID L. SMITH

Intelligence and Espionage in the Reign of Charles II, 1660–1685 *
ALAN MARSHALL

The Chief Governors: The Rise and Fall of Reform Government in Tudor Ireland, 1536–1588 *
CIARAN BRADY

Politics and Opinion in Crisis, 1678–1681
MARK KNIGHTS

Catholic and Reformed: The Roman and Protestant Churches in English Protestant Thought, 1600–1640 *
ANTHONY MILTON

Henry Parker and the English Civil War: The Political Thought of the Public's 'Privado' *
MICHAEL MENDLE

The Church in an Age of Danger: Parsons and Parishioners, 1660–1740
DONALD A. SPAETH

Reading History in Early Modern England
D. R. WOOLF

The Politics of Court Scandal in Early Modern England: News Culture and the Overbury Affair, 1603–1660
ALASTAIR BELLANY

The Politics of Religion in the Age of Mary, Queen of Scots: The Earl of Argyll and the Struggle for Britain and Ireland
JANE E. A. DAWSON

Treason and the State: Law, Politics and Ideology in the English Civil War
D. ALAN ORR

Preaching during the English Reformation
SUSAN WABUDA

Pamphlets and Pamphleteering in Early Modern Britain
JOAD RAYMOND

Patterns of Piety: Women, Gender and Religion in Late Medieval and Reformation England
CHRISTINE PETERS

*Popular Politics and the English Reformation**
ETHAN H. SHAGAN

Unquiet Lives: Marriage and Marriage Breakdown in England, 1660–1800
JOANNE BAILEY

The Gospel and Henry VIII: Evangelicals in the Early English Reformation
ALEC RYRIE

Mercy and Authority in the Tudor State
K. J. KESSELRING

Sir Matthew Hale, 1609–1676: Law, Religion and Natural Philosophy
ALAN CROMARTIE

Crime, Gender and Social Order in Early Modern England
GARTHINE WALKER

Images and Cultures of Law in Early Modern England: Justice and Political Power, 1558–1660
PAUL RAFFIELD

Print Culture and the Early Quakers
KATE PETERS

Ireland and the English Reformation: State Reform and Clerical Resistance in the Diocese of Dublin, 1534–1590
JAMES MURRAY

London and the Restoration, 1659–1683
GARY S. DE KREY

Defining the Jacobean Church: The Politics of Religious Controversy, 1603–1625
CHARLES W. A. PRIOR

Queenship and Political Discourse in the Elizabethan Realms
NATALIE MEARS

John Locke, Toleration and Early Enlightenment Culture
JOHN MARSHALL

The Devil in Early Modern England
NATHAN JOHNSTONE

Georgian Monarchy: Politics and Culture, 1714–1760
HANNAH SMITH

Catholicism and Community in Early Modern England: Politics, Aristocratic Patronage and Religion, c.1550–1640
MICHAEL C. QUESTIER

**Also published as a paperback*